Using BASIC
2nd Edition

PHIL FELDMAN
TOM RUGG

PROGRAMMING
S E R I E S

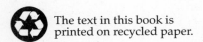

For Beans, the first master of the keyboard.

CREDITS

Publisher
Lloyd J. Short

Associate Publisher
Rick Ranucci

Operations Manager
Sheila Cunningham

Publishing Manager
Joseph Wikert

Acquisitions Editor
Sarah Browning

Product Development Specialist
Jay Munro

Production Editor
Bryan Gambrel

Figure Specialist
Wilfred Thebodeau

Editorial Assistant
Elizabeth D. Brown

Formatter
Jill L. Stanley

Production Manager
Corinne Walls

Proofreading/Indexing Coordinator
Joelynn Gifford

Production Analyst
Mary Beth Wakefield

Book Designer
Scott Cook

Cover Designer
Dan Armstrong

Graphic Image Specialists
Dennis Sheehan
Jerry Ellis
Susan VandeWalle

Indexers
Suzanne G. Snyder, Joy Dean Lee,
Johnna VanHoose

Production
Jeff Baker, Julie Brown, Brad Chinn, Jodie
Cantwell, Lisa Daugherty, Mark Enochs, Tim
Groeling, Bob LaRoche, Tom Loveman, Angela
Pozdol, Linda Seifert, Michelle Self, Sandra
Shay, Susan Shepard, Greg Simsic, Angie
Trzepacz, Kelli Widdifield, Phil Worthington

Composed in Cheltenham and MCPdigital by Prentice Hall Computer Publishing

Phil Feldman

Mr. Feldman received his B.A. degree in physics from the University of California in 1968 and did graduate work in computer science at U.C.L.A. For 15 years, he worked at TRW Systems, Inc., where he was a manager of software development on numerous aerospace engineering projects. He has contributed many articles to engineering journals and personal computer magazines. He has authored or coauthored with Tom Rugg more than 20 computer books, including several books on programming languages. Mr. Feldman is managing partner of 32 Plus, Inc., a software development and consulting firm.

Tom Rugg

Mr. Rugg received his B.S. degree in quantitative methods from California State University in 1969. His 20 years of experience in computer programming and systems analysis include positions with GTE Data Services, Inc., the U.S. Army (Pentagon), and Jet Propulsion Laboratory. He has written many articles for personal computer magazines. He has coauthored with Phil Feldman more than 20 computer books, including *Using QBasic* and *Using QuickBASIC 4*. Mr. Rugg is president of 32 Plus, Inc., a software development and consulting firm.

ACKNOWLEDGMENTS

We are most appreciative of the significant contributions made to this book by the first-rate staff at Que Corporation. Special thanks for the second edition to Joe Wikert, Jay Munro, and Bryan Gambrel for their project development and editing, and to Sarah Browning for her tactful prodding.

TABLE OF CONTENTS

24   Comparing the GW-BASIC (BASICA) Language to QBasic 703

25   Using QuickBASIC 717

Introduction

BASIC is a survivor. The BASIC programming language is indelibly linked with the growth of the microcomputer industry.

In the late 1970s, when microcomputers first became available, Microsoft Corporation supplied a version of BASIC with each new computer. With the onslaught of the IBM PC computer family throughout the 1980s, Microsoft continually provided newer, bigger, and better versions of BASIC.

On true IBM machines running PC DOS, the language became known as BASICA. On IBM-compatible (clone) computers running MS-DOS, the sister language was known as GW-BASIC. The first edition of this book, *Using BASIC,* explained how to program with GW-BASIC and BASICA.

However, with the release of MS-DOS 5 in 1991, Microsoft abandoned BASICA and GW-BASIC in favor of the deserved heir—QBasic.

QBasic represents a modernized, full-featured implementation of BASIC while still retaining the core components of the original language. So, this second edition of *Using BASIC* teaches you how to program with QBasic.

But that's not all. To provide you with a broader scope on BASIC programming, this book discusses other versions of BASIC which are popular today. Included in these discussions are the venerable "grandparents" of the modern BASIC languages, namely BASICA and GW-BASIC. QuickBASIC, which provides more advanced programming tools than QBasic, is covered. Finally, we introduce you to the state-of-the-art in graphic-oriented, event-driven BASIC programming: Visual Basic for Windows and Visual Basic for MS-DOS.

The popularity of BASIC remains strong. Just consider that more people program in BASIC than in any other computer language. That was true 20 years ago, and it is still true today (despite the arrival of "professional" languages such as Pascal and C).

Why Is BASIC So Popular?

There are three main reasons:

- BASIC is easy to learn. Commands are descriptive and English-like.
- BASIC is flexible. Most programming tasks can be accomplished with BASIC.
- BASIC is readily available. Most personal computers come with a version of BASIC.

BASIC remains popular with beginners and hobbyists. The language is ideal for those learning programming for the first time.

QBasic brings a modern version of BASIC to the masses, indeed to everybody with MS-DOS 5 or later. Fortunately, QBasic retains the distinctive flavor and appeal that has enabled the BASIC language to not only survive, but to flourish.

You probably have some questions about this book. Maybe we can anticipate your most likely questions...

Do I Need Any Prior Programming Experience?

None.

We wrote *Using Basic,* 2nd Edition with the needs of the novice programmer in mind. We don't expect you to know any programming terminology or have previous experience writing programs.

Perhaps you have had some exposure to BASIC or you dabbled with the language some time ago. That's fine. You can build on your prior experience as you work your way through the book. Those with a considerable BASIC background will find this book to be a QBasic reference resource.

Why Should I Learn Programming?

Everyone has their own reasons. Perhaps one (or more) of the following motives applies to you:

- You have a specific application (for home or business) for which you cannot find commercially available software. Programmers can write programs that do exactly what they need.

- You want to learn more about your computer. Programming puts you in control of your machine.

- You want to explore the possibility of a career in computers or programming. Many job opportunities exist for qualified programmers.

- Programming seems intriguing and you would like to dabble with a new skill. Programming is satisfying and provides a real sense of accomplishment.

- You *have* to learn programming, perhaps in school or at your job. Some people in this situation feel apprehensive. Relax. Programming is easier than you think and can be a lot of fun.

What Can I Get from This Book?

Whether you have had some experience or are taking your first programming plunge, you will be able to write sophisticated programs by the time you finish this book.

Exactly what this book offers you depends on your background.

If you have little or no programming experience:

- Your biggest concern is becoming productive and comfortable as soon as possible. QBasic can seem a little bewildering at first. Don't worry. Rest assured that QBasic is an excellent tool with which to learn programming. This book should make a trusted teacher and companion.

- In some ways you have an advantage over those with previous BASIC experience. After all, you don't have any bad programming habits to overcome. Throughout this book, we try to teach sound programming principles and present well-constructed program examples.

- Most importantly, use this book with your computer on. Nothing beats "learning by doing."

If you have some prior experience with QuickBASIC, the language from which QBasic descended:

■ You want to hone your skills and expand your knowledge. In the Index, the inside front and back covers, and the Table of Contents, you can quickly locate information about any problem or subject as the need arises. Cross-references in the text point to related material in the book.

■ Take time regularly to browse. In addition to increasing your QBasic knowledge, you will be in a better position to later use the book for reference.

If you are a BASICA or GW-BASIC programmer who has no prior QuickBASIC or QBasic experience:

■ You want to concentrate on two things: learning the QBasic environment and understanding the language enhancements available in QBasic.

■ Chapter 1, "An Overview of BASIC," and Chapter 2, "Up and Running with QBasic," provide an overview and a "hands-on" introduction to QBasic. Chapter 4, "Learning the QBasic Environment," and Chapter 5, "Using the QBasic Editor," provide and in-depth exploration of the QBasic programming environment.

■ During our examination of the QBasic language, which begins in Chapter 6, "Language Building Blocks," we frequently mention where QBasic differs from BASICA and GW-BASIC.

■ Pay special attention to Chapters 17, 18, and 19, titled "Modular Programming," "Interactive Debugging and Testing," and "Managing Memory." They describe QBasic's most significant departures from BASICA. Chapter 24, "Comparing the GW-BASIC (BASICA) Language to QBasic," shows how to convert GW-BASIC and BASICA programs to QBasic.

An Overview of the Contents

Chapter 1, "An Overview of BASIC," answers your most likely questions about the BASIC language in general and QBasic in particular.

Chapter 2, "Up and Running with QBasic," presents a short tutorial on installing QBasic, understanding the working environment, and editing and running a short program. You can quickly proceed from starting QBasic to writing a successfully executed program—even if you have never before seen a QBasic program.

In Chapter 3, "A Hands-On Introduction to Programming," you become a "real" programmer. We present many short programs that demonstrate the main features of QBasic. Our approach is action-oriented—lots of things to try, no long discourses. We want you to become familiar with entering and running programs, and to get a hands-on feeling for the diverse things that QBasic can do. This chapter is especially important for novice programmers and those whose previous programming experience is brief or in the distant past.

Chapter 4, "Learning the QBasic Environment," explains the QBasic programming environment with step-by-step practice in navigating the menu system, interacting with dialog boxes, and using QBasic windows. Also, you learn how to appropriately customize QBasic according to your preferences and to your hardware resources.

Chapter 5, "Using the QBasic Editor," describes the editor and emphasizes useful techniques for smooth program creation and editing. Also discussed are details about saving and loading programs to disk.

Chapters 6 through 16 introduce the QBasic language. Our approach remains experiential, but we now discuss each concept thoroughly. These chapters cover such subjects as program structure, logic flow, data types, text output, graphics, disk files, and using a printer. Many short program examples demonstrate the ideas.

Chapter 17, "Modular Programming," discusses one of QBasic's most important enhancements from earlier versions of BASIC: the user-defined procedure. The presentation includes several examples of parameter passing and localizing variables.

Chapter 18, "Interactive Debugging and Testing," is a survival guide for the times when things go wrong. We discuss many programming traps and errors, and show you how to recognize and correct common problems. The emphasis is on practical techniques for debugging, tracing, and setting breakpoints.

Chapter 19, "Managing Memory," contains an eclectic mix of several topics related to memory management in your programs.

Chapter 20, "Using Advanced Graphics," extends the coverage of graphics topics beyond the material provided in earlier chapters. Included are discussions of EGA and VGA programming, animation, and how to customize coordinate systems and pattern fills.

Chapter 21, "Trapping Errors and Events," shows you how to write programs that smoothly recover from errors. Also, this chapter explains how your programs can monitor external devices for certain events and branch to special routines if the events occur.

Chapter 22, "Understanding Advanced QBasic Topics," is an amalgam of advanced QBasic programming topics not covered in previous chapters. Subjects include chaining programs, shelling to DOS, using common blocks, and manipulating integers at the bit level. Here you can browse and supplement your QBasic knowledge.

Chapters 23 through 26 introduce various BASIC implementations other than QBasic. Chapters 23 and 24 cover GW-BASIC and BASICA, the BASIC programs supplied with MS-DOS and PC DOS in versions 4 and earlier. QuickBASIC, the parent language to QBasic, is the subject of Chapter 25. Visual Basic for Windows and Visual Basic for MS-DOS, the exciting new graphic-oriented, event-driven BASIC programs, are introduced in Chapter 26. The focus of these chapters is on how each implementation of BASIC differs from QBasic and what the language offers a QBasic programmer.

The "Keyword Reference" is a succinct survey of the QBasic language. This section presents each keyword along with a one-sentence description, the required syntax, and a single-line program example.

The six appendixes contain reference tables and supplementary information.

Finally, the book has an index that we have attempted to make detailed and thorough.

Getting Started with QBasic

PART

I

OUTLINE

Although QBasic is an ideal language for beginning programmers, it is a sophisticated software product. Before you can program successfully, you must feel comfortable with the programming environment. Our goal in Part I is to make you comfortable using QBasic.

To feel at ease, you must be confident and adept with the fundamentals. You must know which techniques are the most important, practice those techniques, and have a solid foundation in the general workings of the QBasic environment.

By the time you finish Part I, you will have experience in the following areas:

- Understanding the history, philosophy, and outstanding features of BASIC in general and QBasic in particular

- Gaining familiarity with the QBasic environment—the menu system, window displays, and dialog boxes

- Practicing simple programming and file manipulation

- Learning the rudiments of QBasic programming

- Becoming skilled in using the QBasic editor to create and manipulate programs

With this expertise, you will be suitably prepared to learn the details of the QBasic programming language, which follow in Parts II, III, and IV.

An Overview of BASIC

Programmers have power—the power to make a computer do exactly what they want.

This book gives you that power. By learning QBasic, the version of BASIC supplied with MS-DOS 5 and later, you can write programs that perform an endless variety of tasks, useful for business or in your home. Here are just a few programming ideas that you might tackle:

- Keep track of a hobby collection, such as a coin collection.

- Analyze sales for a business—and plot graphs showing the trends.

- Design and play a computer game. The game might include music and color graphics.

- Compute solutions to mathematical and scientific problems.

- Teach others a skill or subject that you know well.

Programming is creative, fun (most of the time), and challenging—a unique blend of art and skill. When your programs run properly, you enjoy a satisfying feeling of accomplishment. After all, you have successfully communicated with your computer *on the computer's own terms*.

This chapter is an overview of BASIC with special emphasis on QBasic. We discuss what a computer language is, provide a historical perspective on the BASIC language, find out where the QBasic rung fits on BASIC's evolutionary ladder, and talk a little about hardware and software. This material is for background—you can skim it if you want. In the next chapter, you will plunge right into using QBasic.

Here are answers to questions you might have.

Is QBasic Hard to Learn?

No, quite the contrary. BASIC is designed for novice programmers. In fact, the "B" in BASIC stands for "Beginners." BASIC is an acronym for *Beginners All-purpose Symbolic Instruction Code*. As a modern version of BASIC, QBasic retains the qualities that have always made BASIC an ideal first programming language.

Here are the three primary reasons why QBasic is so easy to learn:

■ QBasic instructions are descriptive and English-like. As a result, QBasic programs tend to be understandable and easy to read.

■ QBasic provides immediate feedback. When you run a program, the computer immediately executes your instructions and produces results.

■ QBasic is interactive. When an error occurs, QBasic immediately reports the error with an informative message. Built-in help is available. Often, you can quickly correct the problem and resume your program.

What Is a Computer Language?

At the heart of your computer is a hardware chip known as the *central processing unit (CPU)*. This chip controls everything going on inside your computer—from numerical calculations, to storing data in memory, to sending signals to your video screen.

To make a computer respond to your wishes, you must communicate with the central processor. You need a way to tell the central processor what you want the computer to do and a way to have the computer report the results.

Unfortunately, you can't just talk to the central processor in English. Imagine sitting down in front of your computer and saying, "Computer, add the outstanding checks in my account and display my bank balance on the screen. And please hurry, I'm late for lunch!"

Don't laugh too hard. This scenario is not farfetched. With the advances in computer technology, you *probably* will be able to do just that sometime during your lifetime.

But today, in the early 1990s, you must "talk" to the computer in a language the *computer* understands.

What Language *Does* the Computer Understand?

The central processor understands instructions in its native tongue, known as *machine language* (or *assembly language*). Machine language is primitive in that machine-level commands work only at the most fundamental levels of the computer. For example, a machine-level instruction might move a data bit from one internal machine register to another or store a data byte at a particular memory location.

But "primitive" does not mean ineffectual. With nothing but machine-level commands, you can get the computer to do anything of which it is capable. Furthermore, the computer executes machine-language instructions very quickly.

The problem is that something as simple as adding two numbers and displaying the result can require more than 25 machine-language instructions. A mistake in any one of these instructions could cause calamitous results.

Furthermore, machine language is not at all English-like. The instructions consist of many shorthand abbreviations and odd-looking terms.

You need a compromise. You *want* to communicate with the computer in English or at least a language close to English. But the computer accepts only commands in machine language.

Is a Compromise Available?

Yes. A *high-level computer language* is just such a compromise. Many high-level computer languages exist.

Is QBasic a High-Level Language?

Yes.

What Exactly Is a High-Level Language?

Using a high-level language, you write computer instructions expressed according to the rules and grammar of the high-level language. For many high-level languages, the instructions you write are English-like and easy to understand. The high-level language then turns your instructions into machine language instructions.

Essentially, a high-level computer language is a *translator*. You, the programmer, write instructions using the high-level language. The high-level language then *translates* your instructions into machine-level instructions that the computer understands. The computer can then execute these machine-level instructions. Figure 1.1 depicts the process of writing and running a QBasic program.

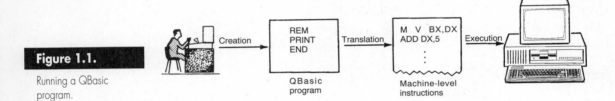

Figure 1.1.

Running a QBasic program.

Creation → REM PRINT END QBasic program → Translation → M V BX,DX ADD DX,5 ... Machine-level instructions → Execution

Are There Many High-Level Languages?

Yes. BASIC was designed as a high-level language. All the different versions of BASIC, including QBasic, are high-level languages.

Besides BASIC, some other high-level languages are Pascal, FORTRAN, COBOL, and C. Perhaps you've heard of one or more of these languages. Each language has its own strengths and weaknesses.

Just What Exactly Is a Program, Especially a BASIC Program?

A *program* is simply a series of instructions written according to the rules of the programming language. So a QBasic program is simply a series of instructions written in the QBasic language.

In some ways, a program is like a recipe for baking a cake. A recipe is a series of instructions, written for a person to perform. You execute the instructions and, if all goes okay, you end up with a delicious dessert.

A program is also a series of instructions, but written for a computer to perform. The computer executes the instructions and, if all goes okay, you end up with, well, a successful program.

How Do I Get a QBasic Program into My Computer?

You get a QBasic program into your computer in one of two principal ways:

1. Type the program directly into your computer. Anytime you create a brand-new program, you use this straightforward method.

2. Load a previously saved program from disk. As you work with QBasic, you probably will accumulate many programs on floppy disks (or on your hard disk). These programs can be programs you wrote originally, programs written by friends and coworkers, or perhaps programs you bought.

 Another Source for Programs

If you have a modem, you might have experience with a computer bulletin board or other online information services. (A modem lets your computer "call" other computers using regular phone lines.) Many online services, such as CompuServe, provide BASIC programs that you can download and save as disk files.

Throughout the country, there are numerous "electronic bulletin boards" operated by computer hobbyists. BASIC programmers often share their programs on such bulletin boards. You can download programs that you find interesting, and you can upload your programs so others can benefit from your best efforts. Everyone profits from this arrangement.

What Happens When I Run a QBasic Program?

You *run* a program when you command QBasic to execute the instructions of a program. To run your program, QBasic translates your program instructions into machine-language instructions. The computer then executes these result-ant machine-language instructions.

How Does the Computer Translate the QBasic Instructions?

You might be wondering, "If the computer only responds to machine language, how does the computer translate instructions written in QBasic?"

Simple. QBasic is itself a program *written in machine language*. This complex program, which contains thousands of machine-language instructions, enables you to write your programs using the rules of the QBasic language.

What Is the Origin of BASIC?

BASIC was developed in the mid-1960s at Dartmouth College by professors John Kemeny and Thomas Kurtz. Kemeny and Kurtz designed BASIC to be a vehicle with which to teach programming. BASIC, therefore, has English-like commands, is easy to use, and requires no specialized hardware knowledge.

Was BASIC Successful Immediately?

Yes. BASIC quickly caught on because several favorable circumstances coincided:

■ Computer literacy was in vogue. Faculty members were eager to teach programming, and students were eager to learn.

■ Time-sharing became available. On time-sharing systems, many program-mers use centralized computer facilities easily and economically. Such computing environments in a college setting were tailor-made for pro-gramming students to learn BASIC.

■ The BASIC design goals were achieved superbly. The new language was much easier to use and to teach than existing languages such as ALGOL and FORTRAN.

When and How Did Personal Computers Enter the Picture?

In 1975, in Boston, a young Honeywell employee named Paul Allen got wind of the first personal computer being developed. This computer, called the Altair, was being built by MITS Corporation of Albuquerque, New Mexico.

Paul relayed his excitement to Bill Gates, a student at Harvard University. Paul and Bill had known each other since their grade-school days together on the West Coast. They were drawn to each other by a common bond—a passionate interest in computers. Allen convinced Gates that they should develop a version of BASIC for the Altair.

Legend has it that the two men called MITS to see whether the company was interested in a BASIC implementation for their new computer. When the answer was "yes," Allen and Gates licensed their BASIC to MITS. Allen moved to Albuquerque, and became, in effect, the MITS software department.

Their first version of BASIC ran entirely in 4 kilobytes of memory, including the user's program and the variable storage. (Four kilobytes, or 4K, is 4,096 bytes of memory, a piddling sum by today's standards. In comparison, most IBM PCs or compatibles have *at least* 512K of main memory!) Gates, the primary developer, supposedly wrote this BASIC before he even saw the new computer. The program worked almost immediately.

Within a few years, Gates and Allen developed BASIC for other emerging microcomputers. They moved back to their hometown of Seattle, Washington, and Microsoft Corporation was born.

Today, Microsoft remains at the leading edge of software development. Gates is a billionaire. At a recent computer gathering, the venerable Microsoft chairman reminisced that "the 4K BASIC is the best program I ever wrote."

What about BASIC on the IBM Personal Computer?

By the late '70s, Microsoft was developing a version of BASIC for virtually every new personal computer, including offerings from Apple, Commodore, and Atari.

IBM was no exception. When "Big Blue" entered the fray in 1981 with the IBM PC, the computer came with a language called BASICA. This language, developed by Microsoft and leased to IBM, sold under the IBM nameplate. BASICA was a far cry from its 4K BASIC ancestor.

Featuring numerous enhancements, and improved over the years, BASICA has approximately 200 commands and requires more than 40K of memory.

What about BASIC for IBM-Compatible Computers?

As the IBM PC became a runaway success, several competing manufacturers entered the market by making IBM-compatibles (often called "clones"). As part of their agreement with IBM, Microsoft was free to distribute BASIC for these compatibles.

For compatibles, Microsoft developed a version of BASIC called GW-BASIC. Most compatible manufacturers license GW-BASIC from Microsoft and include the language with their computers. If you have a compatible but not BASIC, you can buy GW-BASIC as a stand-alone product.

Are BASICA and GW-BASIC Equivalent?

Almost. BASICA runs exclusively on IBM computers because part of the language is contained in IBM-proprietary ROM (read-only memory) chips. These chips are installed at the factory and only true IBM machines have them.

GW-BASIC, on the other hand, runs on any IBM computer or compatible. GW-BASIC requires only the regular RAM (random-access memory). No special hardware chips are necessary.

The features and functionality of BASICA and GW-BASIC are essentially identical. (There are a few trivial differences.) If you know one, you know the other. A program running successfully under BASICA runs successfully 99.9 percent of the time under GW-BASIC, and vice versa.

What Are the Limitations of BASICA and GW-BASIC?

BASICA and GW-BASIC work fine but are not suited for large programming tasks. Many professional programmers have migrated to more contemporary, structured programming languages such as C and Pascal.

Here are some of the limitations of BASICA and GW-BASIC:

- *Variables are global to the entire program.* As a result, inadvertent conflicts can readily develop in two parts of the same program. Moving a section of one program to another program requires careful avoidance of variable-naming clashes.

- *Block structures are inadequate.* IF-THEN, DEF FN, and other structures are limited to a single line. This situation severely cramps clarity.

- *Each line must have a line number.* To merge program components from different sources, you must resolve the amalgamated line numbers.

- *The editing environment is line by line.* You can only work with one screenful of a program at a time. Each line must be edited individually with limited editing commands.

- *You cannot define subprograms.* Except for the primitive DEF FN and GOSUB, you cannot create independent functions and subprograms that can be called from the main program.

- *A program cannot be larger than 64 kilobytes.*

- *You cannot create an executable file.* You cannot create a version of a program that you can run directly from DOS.

How Were BASICA and GW-BASIC's Limitations Addressed?

In the late 1980s, Microsoft introduced QuickBASIC. Sold as a separate product, QuickBASIC wasn't (and still isn't) bundled with any version of DOS. QuickBASIC is built from the core language of BASICA and GW-BASIC, but adds modern, structured language enhancements. Further, QuickBASIC contains a sleek user interface with full-screen editing and drop-down menus. QuickBASIC once again made BASIC a state-of-the-art language.

How Did QBasic Enter the Picture?

With the arrival of DOS 5 in mid-1991, Microsoft abandoned BASICA and GW-BASIC in favor of QBasic. QBasic is a slightly stripped down version of QuickBASIC. The "Q" in QBasic hints at the ancestral relationship to QuickBASIC.

How Does QBasic Compare to QuickBASIC?

The two products are quite similar, but not identical. The major difference is that QBasic cannot *compile* a program, whereas QuickBASIC can. This means that QBasic, like BASICA and GW-BASIC, cannot take a program and create a version that runs directly from DOS. To run a program using QBasic, you must load the program into the QBasic environment. For more about QuickBASIC and executable files, see Chapter 25, "Using QuickBASIC."

Does QBasic Correct the Shortcomings of BASICA and GW-BASIC?

Yes, and then some. QBasic—and QuickBASIC—makes BASIC a structured language in the same vein as C or Pascal.

What Are the Outstanding Features of QBasic?

QBasic provides a complete BASIC programming *environment*. Here are the major features of the QBasic environment:

- Compatibility with IBM BASICA and Microsoft's GW-BASIC
- A smoothly integrated environment that boasts a full-screen editor, file manager, and debugging tools, all accessible through pull-down menus

- Fast execution of programs

- Modern language enhancements, such as user-defined procedures, alphanumeric labels, local variables, and block structures, which bring structured programming to BASIC

- A "smart" editor that finds syntax errors as you type and reformats instructions into a standardized appearance

- Built-in help

- Support for most hardware peripherals including a mouse, math coprocessor, and color video adapter (CGA, EGA, and VGA)

What Is the QBasic Environment?

Like many of today's major software applications, QBasic runs from a central menu system. From various menus, you can access commands for editing, saving files, debugging, executing the program, and getting on-line help. The environment is reasonably intuitive.

What Is QBI?

QBasic is sometimes called QBI, an acronym for the *QuickBasic Interpreter*. The two terms are synonymous. When QBasic was in development, the product was often called the QuickBASIC Interpreter, in deference to its QuickBASIC ancestry. (Don't confuse QuickBASIC and the QuickBASIC Interpreter—these are two different products.) However, with the release of DOS 5, Microsoft has stuck with the new name, QBasic.

As if that isn't confusing enough, Microsoft *has* released a product called the QuickBASIC Interpreter. This version of BASIC is always bundled as part of another software package. For example, the Microsoft Gameshop package contains a collection of games programmed in QBasic; the package includes a version of BASIC called the QuickBASIC Interpreter. Essentially, QuickBASIC Interpreter and QBasic are two names for the same thing.

How Compatible Are QBasic and GW-BASIC (BASICA)?

For the most part, you can load your BASICA and GW-BASIC programs into QBasic and run them without modification. QBasic, however, does not support the BASICA and GW-BASIC commands that affect the program itself, such as AUTO, LIST, and RENUM.

Some BASICA and GW-BASIC instructions require modification. Throughout this book, we frequently mention differences between QBasic and GW-BASIC (BASICA) for the benefit of former BASICA programmers. Also, see Chapter 24, "Comparing the GW-BASIC (BASICA) Language to QBasic."

Does Learning QBasic Take a Long Time?

The time required depends on your programming experience.

If you do not have any programming experience, becoming an accomplished programmer will take some time and practice. But it's not drudgery. In fact, programming is fun, challenging, and rewarding.

We *expect* that many of our readers are programming novices with little or no BASIC experience. This book is designed to get you "up to speed from the ground up." Chapter 2, "Up and Running With QBasic," takes you step-by-step from installation to a running program in a matter of minutes. Chapter 3, "A Hands-On Introduction to Programming," is a tutorial that will have you creating substantive programs in a matter of hours. Later chapters build on this foundation.

If you have experience with BASICA, GW-BASIC or another version of BASIC, you won't have to spend much time learning QBasic. However, you *do* have to learn the QBasic environment: the fundamentals of entering, editing, and running a program with the menu system (see Chapter 4, "Learning the QBasic Environment," and Chapter 5, "Using the QBasic Editor"). After an hour or two, you should be able to write and run programs like an old hand. You should, of course, begin exploring the new language features that QBasic offers.

If you are familiar with QuickBASIC, you *already* know QBasic. Use this book for reference and to brush up on areas with which you are not familiar.

If you're anxious to get going, Chapter 2, "Up and Running With QBasic," helps you start running a program right away.

What Hardware Do I Need to Run QBasic?

You need an IBM computer (PC, XT, AT, PS/1, or PS/2) or an IBM-compatible computer running DOS 2.1 or later. Your computer should have the following equipment:

- *A monitor.* This is the video screen. Many different types of monitors exist. You can run QBasic with any type of monitor, but, as they say in the airline business, some restrictions apply. Your monitor (and video hardware) determines what graphics you can produce. You obviously need a color monitor to get color graphics. Furthermore, if you have a monochrome monitor, you cannot produce graphics at all. Monitors and QBasic graphics are discussed in Chapter 13, "Creating Graphics."

- *A disk drive or drives.* Your computer has one or more floppy disk drives (the devices into which you insert disks). If your system has one floppy drive, that drive is designated the A: drive. A second floppy drive is designated the B: drive. Your computer might also have one or more hard (fixed) disk drives built into the machine. Hard disk drives are designated with the letters C: and up. You don't need a hard disk drive to run QBasic. For more information about disk drives, see Chapter 14, "Using Sequential Disk Files."

- *A printer.* You don't need a printer to run QBasic, but having one is helpful. With a printer, you can list your programs and view the output at leisure. Most of the programs in this book are short and easily viewed on your monitor. A printer is nice, but not essential.

Do I Need To Know Much about DOS?

DOS is the operating system under which your computer runs. DOS, like QBasic, was developed by Microsoft Corporation. On IBM computers, DOS is called PC DOS. On compatibles, DOS is known as MS-DOS. In this book, we use the term DOS to refer to either PC DOS or MS-DOS.

We assume that you know how to do the simplest tasks in DOS such as formatting a new floppy disk and copying a file from one disk to another. Rudimentary knowledge of disk directories is desirable. However, you certainly don't need to be a whiz at DOS.

In this book, we try to provide detailed instructions whenever a DOS subject arises. For example, Chapter 14, "Using Sequential Disk Files," contains a brief tutorial on DOS directories and file naming. If you feel uncomfortable with even simple DOS commands, consult one of Que's excellent tutorial books, such as *Using MS-DOS 5*.

What about Running BASIC with Microsoft Windows?

QBasic, QuickBASIC, BASICA and GW-BASIC are all DOS products created to run under DOS. None of these versions of BASIC was designed to run under Windows as a full-fleged Windows application. However, you can start any of these versions of BASIC from Windows just as you can run any other DOS application from Windows. In addition, compiling a QuickBASIC program creates an executable DOS file which you can launch from Windows as a DOS application.

Is It Possible to Create Windows Programs Using BASIC?

Yes. In mid-1991, Microsoft introduced a landmark version of BASIC dubbed Visual Basic. Not only is the product itself a Windows application but, using Visual Basic, you can compile your programs into bona fide Windows applications. Visual BASIC is an innovative product which enables the BASIC programmer to create great-looking Windows applications with relative ease.

What Are the Outstanding Features of Visual Basic?

Visual Basic extends earlier versions of BASIC with numerous language enhancements geared for creating Windows applications. Two such features are prominent: the visual toolbox and event-driven procedures.

Because Windows has a graphical (visual) user interface, Visual Basic includes many built-in tools for incorporating graphical elements into your applications. By selecting objects from an on-screen toolbox, you can quickly design and create functional Windows-like interfaces in your programs. As well as a programmer, the Visual Basic user becomes something of an architect, designer, and builder.

Visual Basic is an event-driven language. As such, the programmer can associate programmed procedures with each graphical element of the designed interface. A procedure activates when an anticipated event (such as a mouse click or keypress) occurs.

For more about Visual BASIC, see Chapter 26, "Introducing Visual Basic."

Does This Book Explain Everything about QBasic?

Just about. Because our primary audience is beginners, we quickly treat a few of the advanced, complex features of QBasic that require detailed explanations (networking and multilanguage programming, for instance). When we do cursorily treat a subject or feature, we try to tell you what we've left out. That way, if the need ever arises, you can consult another reference.

We cover most of QBasic (maybe 98 percent) and certainly include every essential subject. Rest assured that when you finish this book you'll be able to tackle most any programming project and write quite sophisticated programs.

What Is Your Teaching Style?

We believe in learning by example. Programming is an *activity,* not an ivory-tower intellectual exercise. Like riding a bicycle, driving a car, or kissing your soul mate, you can fully learn only by doing—not just by reading a book.

We provide numerous short programs (and program fragments) that are to the point. (As a learning tool, long programs tend to be confusing and distracting.) We hope you will read this book with your computer on. Try the examples. Better yet, experiment on your own. The more you *do,* the faster you'll learn.

What Is Your Main Goal for This Book?

To make you a successful and confident QBasic programmer.

Up and Running

I t's time for action. You probably are eager to get going with QBasic, and that's exactly what you will do in this chapter.

Regardless of whether you have some experience with any form of BASIC, or no programming experience at all, this chapter will make you a QBasic programmer in a few short minutes.

Here is what you learn to do in this chapter:

- ■ Verify that QBasic is installed properly
- ■ Start QBasic
- ■ Type and edit a short QBasic program
- ■ Run the program and view output
- ■ Save the program as a disk file

The intent here is only to present the rudiments of these topics—enough to get you going. Later chapters treat these topics in greater detail (especially Chapters 4 and 5, which cover customized installation and editing particulars).

If you are new to QBasic or to programming in general, you will learn enough in this chapter to utilize the QBasic primer in Chapter 3, "A Hands-On Introduction to Programming."

Verifying Your Installation of QBasic

Before you can *use* QBasic, you must *install* it on your computer. The installation process is straightforward. In fact, most likely, you *already* have QBasic installed and ready for use.

For most readers, the following two provisions apply:

1. Your computer system has a hard (fixed) disk.

2. You have a normal installation of DOS 5 or later on your hard disk.

If these provisions apply to you, you're all set. MS-DOS 5 includes QBasic on a file named QBASIC.EXE. By installing DOS 5 on your computer system, you automatically install QBasic. You don't need to perform any extra installation procedure to have QBasic available. Skip ahead to the section titled "Starting QBasic." The following material applies to nonstandard QBasic installations.

Installing QBasic on Hard Disk Systems Not Running DOS 5

Although supplied with DOS 5, QBasic can run on earlier versions of DOS. You can run QBasic with any version of DOS from version 2.1 or higher.

If you prefer to install QBasic on a machine *not* running under DOS 5, the procedure is simple. First, create a directory to hold the QBasic program files. For example, the following DOS command creates a directory named \QBASIC directly off your root directory:

```
md \qbasic
```

Now copy the files QBASIC.EXE and QBASIC.HLP to this directory.

For convenience, you should probably include a path to this directory with a PATH command in your AUTOEXEC.BAT file. If you need information about how to use PATH commands, consult your DOS documentation.

T I P   **Installing the QBI Version of QBasic**

The QBI (QuickBASIC Interpreter) version of QBasic is an integral part of some Microsoft products such as Microsoft Gameshop. Each of these products contains directions that indicate how you gain access to the QBI interpreter when using that product.

For direct QBasic programming, you might want to access the QBI files independently from the product you are using. The trick is to identify which files correspond to QBasic's QBASIC.EXE and QBASIC.HLP files.

Search the disks supplied with your product for filenames beginning with QBI. (To do this search, you can use the DIR command from DOS or any file-searching utility you have available.) You should find a file with a .EXE extension that is approximately 250,000 bytes large. This file corresponds to the QBASIC.EXE file of QBasic. For example, with the Gameshop, the file is called QBI.EXE.

Also, find a file with a .HLP extension that is at least 130,000 bytes large (and possibly two or three times as large). This file corresponds to QBasic's QBASIC.HLP file. In Gameshop, this file is called QBIADVR.HLP.

You can then install the .EXE file and the .HLP file using any of the methods detailed in this section. Of course, you must substitute the actual names for your files where you see references to QBASIC.EXE and QBASIC.HLP. When starting QBasic from the command line, use the name of your .EXE file. For example, with Gameshop, start QBasic as follows:

```
C>qbi
```

Notice that the QBI files are similar, but not identical, to the QBasic files supplied with DOS 5. As you follow the examples in this book, you might find slight differences in the menu commands available or the way certain options operate. However, the emphasis is definitely on "slight." The text of the help messages, however, can vary considerably from product to product.

Installing QBasic on Floppy-Based Systems

QBasic does not require a hard disk and runs fine from a floppy disk. QBasic uses only two files: QBASIC.EXE and QBASIC.HLP. Only the QBASIC.EXE is actually required. QBASIC.HLP contains the text of various help messages. You can run QBasic without this help file but then you would not have the help text available.

To create a floppy-based QBasic capability, copy the QBASIC.EXE file to a floppy disk. QBASIC.EXE is approximately 250 kilobytes long, so the file easily fits on any size floppy disk, even on a 360 kilobyte, 5.25-inch floppy (double-sided, double-density).

The QBASIC.HLP file is approximately 140 kilobytes long. If your floppy has enough storage with QBASIC.EXE installed, you should copy QBASIC.HLP to the same floppy containing QBASIC.EXE.

NOTE You should have enough room for both QBASIC.EXE and QBASIC.HLP on one disk except with a 360 kilobyte, 5.25-inch floppy. That is, a high-density 5.25-inch floppy and any format 3.5-inch floppy has enough storage to hold both QBASIC.EXE and QBASIC.HLP.

You will place the QBASIC.EXE disk in your A: drive when you start QBasic. When reading the next section, start QBasic from the command line. Instead of a C> prompt, you will invoke from an A> prompt.

If your system has two floppy drives, you can save program files on a disk in your B: drive. If your system has only one floppy drive, you can store program files on the same disk containing QBASIC.EXE in your A: drive. Alternatively, you can store the programs in the B: drive and swap disks when prompted by DOS.

Starting QBasic

You can start QBasic in one of two ways:

1. If you are running the DOS Shell with DOS 5, select QBasic from the main menu as follows:

   a. Use the Tab key to move the highlight to the Main window at the bottom of the screen.

   b. Highlight MS-DOS QBasic by moving the cursor with the up- and down-arrow keys. Then press Enter.

   c. Press Enter again when the overlaying QBasic File window appears in the center of the screen. (For now, don't type a filename to retrieve or create.)

T I P   **Mouse Users**

With a mouse, you can start QBasic from the DOS Shell by simply double-clicking on the line which reads MS-DOS QBasic in the Main window. However, for simplicity, the directions in this chapter do not discuss manipulating the QBasic environment with a mouse.

For more about mouse techniques with QBasic, see chapter 4, "Learning the QBasic Environment" and Appendix D, "Hotkeys and Mouse Commands."

2. If you want to start QBasic from the command line, type qbasic at the DOS prompt.

    C>**qbasic**

    (The DOS prompt is typically c> on hard drive systems.) If you have DOS installed in a directory that is not included in a PATH statement of your AUTOEXEC.BAT file, you first need to make that directory the current directory. To do so, use a cd command like this:

    C>**cd \dos**

    If you have DOS installed in a directory with a name other than dos, use your directory name (and path) instead of dos as shown here.

    If you are running QBasic from a floppy disk, your prompt will be A> instead of c>.

Invoking QBasic on a Black and White Video System

If you run QBasic on a computer system with a color video adapter but a black-and-white monitor (many laptop computers have this configuration), there is a special way to invoke QBasic from the DOS command line. Use the /b parameter to get a readable display. At the DOS prompt, invoke QBasic as follows:

C>**qbasic /b**

Regardless of which method you choose, QBasic now initializes. A preliminary screen appears as shown in Figure 2.1.

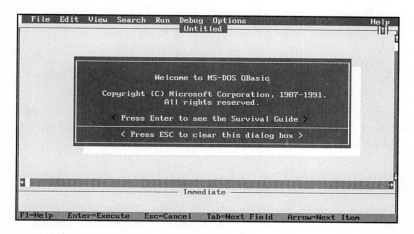

Figure 2.1.

The preliminary QBasic screen.

You now have two choices. You can press Enter or Esc.

- Pressing Enter invokes the QBasic Survival Guide. (The Survival Guide provides help about using QBasic. See the discussion of the help system in Chapter 5, "Using the QBasic Editor.")

- Pressing Esc clears the box in the center of the screen and prepares the editor for working on a QBasic program.

Press Esc. You now have a blank editor screen and can begin QBasic programming. Your screen should look like Figure 2.2.

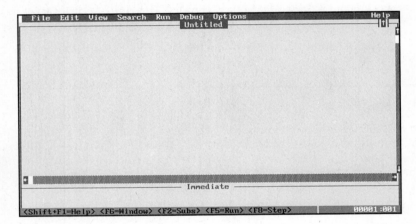

Figure 2.2.

The initial QBasic screen with a blank editing area.

Getting Acquainted with the QBasic Editor

QBasic operates in a full-screen editing environment. Full-screen editing means that you can move the cursor all around the screen to make changes. (Earlier forms of BASIC, including BASICA and GW-BASIC, required you to make changes line by line.)

The QBasic editor has many features available through drop-down menus. Take a moment to look at your screen (or at Figure 2.2). Table 2.1 explains the main items that you see.

| Table 2.1. Main items on the initial QBasic screen. ||
Item	Description
Menu bar	The line along the top of the screen that displays the available menus: File, Edit, View, and so on
Title bar	The short, centered bar just below the Menu bar that contains the name of the current program, which for now reads Untitled
Cursor	The flashing underscore character that indicates where the next text you type will be displayed
View window	The large boxed area below the Title bar in which the cursor currently resides

Notice that Table 2.1 does not mention the boxed area marked Immediate nor the bar at the bottom of the screen. This chapter discusses only a few of the major editing techniques and primary features of the QBasic environment.

Just wait! Chapters 4 and 5 explore the myriad features of the editor and the various menu options.

Entering Your First Program

With QBasic now initialized, the full-screen editor is at your command. This means you can now type a program. Using the editor, you enter and modify QBasic programs directly from the keyboard.

Try it. Notice the blinking cursor near the upper left corner of the View window. Type the following one-line program. Substitute your own name for John Doe. Don't forget the two quotation marks.

```
PRINT "This program was written by John Doe"
```

There's no need to press the Enter key at the end of this line, although if you do so, that's fine.

If you make any typing errors, use the cursor movement (arrow) keys to position the cursor at the location of the error. You can correct your mistake with one of the following techniques:

■ Insert a new character at the cursor location by typing the new character. Any text at or already to the right of the cursor moves over (one
space to the right) to accommodate the newly typed text.

■ Delete the character at the cursor by pressing the Del key. Any text already to the right of the cursor moves over one space to the left.

Running a Program
and Viewing Output

You have just typed a complete QBasic program, even though it is only one
line long. This short program consists entirely of a single PRINT instruction. A
PRINT instruction commands QBasic to display on-screen the message contained between the two quotation marks.

To run the program, you need to invoke the Run menu—one of the menu
options shown on the Menu bar (the screen's top line). Follow these steps:

1. To select a menu option, you hold down the Alt key and press the first
   letter of that option's name. In the present case, you want the Run menu,
   so press Alt-R to pop open the Run menu. Figure 2.3 shows what the
   screen looks like after opening the Run menu.

2. A pull-down submenu appears on the screen. The top bar on this
   submenu is highlighted. The highlighted bar reads (in part) Start. You
   can move the highlight up and down the menu with the arrow keys.
   Try it.

3. To execute a menu option, press Enter when the highlight is on the option you want. Move the highlight back to Start and press Enter.

4. The program now executes. The screen clears and then displays the output of your program. Your screen should look similar to the one shown in
   Figure 2.4 (except that your name is probably not John Doe!). When a program runs, QBasic clears the editor screen and switches the display to
   the output screen.

   Notice what happened. QBasic displayed the text message contained
   between the quotation marks of your PRINT instruction. You have successfully run a QBasic program!

5. Look along the bottom edge of your screen. After running a program to
   completion, QBasic displays the following message on the bottom of the
   output screen:

   ```
   Press any key to continue
   ```

   Press a key, and the QBasic editor screen is back in control.

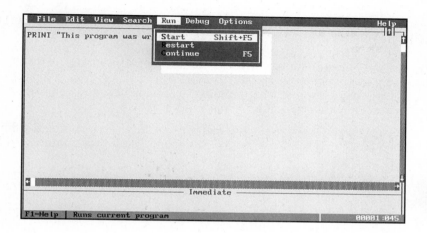

Figure 2.3.

The Run menu.

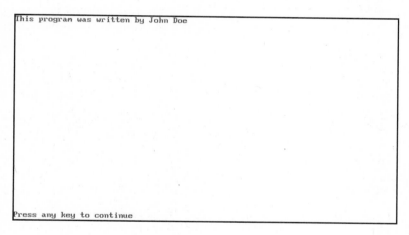

Figure 2.4.

Output from the one-line program.

Now, to learn a little more about the QBasic environment, try the following exercise:

1. Open the View menu by pressing Alt-V.

2. Move the highlight down to Output Screen and press Enter. The screen display switches back to the output screen. Anytime you are in the editor, you can view the output screen by selecting Output Screen from the View menu.

3. Press any key to return to the editor.

4. Press F4. Once again, the screen display switches to the output screen. This F4 keystroke is an example of a hotkey. A *hotkey* is an "express" keystroke that immediately invokes an option available from one of the pulldown menus. In this case, the F4 hotkey is equivalent to selecting Output Screen from the View menu.

5. Press Shift-F5. This hotkey is equivalent to selecting Start from the Run menu. By pressing Shift-F5, you run your program a second time. Notice that a second copy of the program's output message appears on the output window below the first copy. QBasic does not automatically blank the output screen between successive runs of a program. (Chapter 3, "A Hands-On Introduction to Programming," explains how you can blank the output screen with a CLS program instruction.)

   Whenever you run a program, you can choose between pressing the Shift-F5 hotkey or selecting Start from the Run menu. Most programmers find the hotkey simpler.

6. Press any key to return to the editor.

Saving a Program

Now save your program on disk. Follow these steps:

1. Invoke the File menu by pressing Alt-F.

2. Move the highlight down to Save As....

3. Press Enter. A dialog box opens for you to type the name of the file.

4. Type myname. You can type the filename in lowercase as shown (myname) or in uppercase (MYNAME) at your preference. See Figure 2.5. Notice that the dialog box indicates the path to the directory where the file will be saved. You can change this path by including a new path when you type the filename. You can specify a different disk drive as part of your newly specified path. (The window labeled Dirs/Drives shows subdirectories off of the current path and all disk drives on your system. The drives and subdirectories shown on your screen will likely differ from those shown in Figure 2.5.) See Chapter 5, "Using the QBasic Editor," for more about saving files and selecting paths.

5. Press Enter to save the program on disk.

Your screen should now look like Figure 2.6. Notice that the program name appears as MYNAME.BAS in the Title bar (near the upper center of the screen).

If you don't specify an extension by explicitly writing it, QBasic adds the .BAS extension to the filename. This default extension indicates that the file is a QBasic program. (You can optionally save the file with any other extension name that you specify by explicitly writing it.)

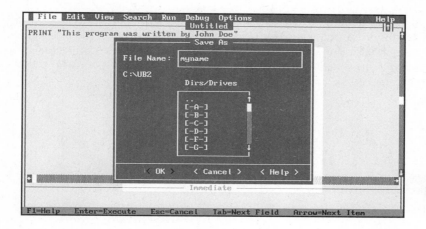

Figure 2.5.

The File Name dialog box.

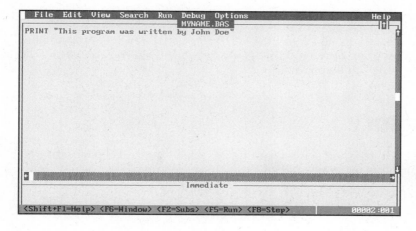

Figure 2.6.

The program is saved to disk.

Erasing an Old Program and Running a New Program

Suppose that you now want to type a new program. First you must erase MYNAME.BAS from the computer's memory and from the QBasic editing environment. Follow these steps:

1. Select the File menu (press Alt-F).

2. Notice the highlight is on New.

3. Press Enter.

The editor screen clears away the previous program. Notice that the View window no longer contains the text of MYNAME.BAS and the Title bar reads Untitled once again. You have erased MYNAME.BAS from the computer's memory (that is, from the QBasic editing environment). However, the program remains stored on disk for later use.

You can now type a new program and begin afresh.

Exiting from QBasic

To terminate a QBasic session, do the following:

1. Select the File menu (press Alt-F).
2. Move the highlight down to Exit.
3. Press Enter.

QBasic returns control back to the DOS Shell or to the DOS command line. If you have a program on-screen that is not yet saved, QBasic gives you a chance to save the program before exiting.

Summary

You have accomplished some major goals. You've started QBasic, entered a program, run the program, and saved the program on disk.

Congratulations! You're now a QBasic programmer.

A Hands-On Introduction to Programming

This chapter presents some simple programs that illustrate many important features and principles of QBasic programming. Our purpose is to give you an understanding of some commonly used programming techniques and to make you feel at ease typing programs. We want you to develop an intuitive feel for what QBasic programming is all about.

 Experienced BASIC Programmers, Take Note

This chapter is aimed especially at first-time programmers and those readers who might have had a brief exposure to BASIC, perhaps many years ago. This chapter provides a foundation for the more detailed QBasic material that follows. If you already possess a working knowledge of GW-BASIC, BASICA or another version of BASIC, you can skip ahead to Chapter 4, "Learning the QBasic Environment."

Please try the programs as they are presented. Even if the ideas seem simple and you are confident that you understand everything, you will gain the necessary experience only by doing. If you get the urge to deviate from our examples a little, by all means, go right ahead.

The programs introduce a smorgasbord of fundamental QBasic topics. We are brief in this chapter. Every topic covered in this chapter is discussed in depth later in the book.

So don't get bogged down. If you have trouble understanding something, just move ahead to the next topic. Wait till we cover your troublesome subject in a later chapter.

NOTE QBasic Is for Beginners

Some people are convinced that they will never understand how to program a computer—that they can't learn to write simple QBasic programs. If this is you, don't be afraid!

Remember that the *B* in BASIC stands for *Beginner's*. You will see that you don't need to be a technical genius, or even mathematically inclined, to use QBasic.

This chapter surveys several QBasic fundamentals. Here are some of the topics covered in this chapter:

- Typing with the "smart" editor
- Introducing variables and assigning values to them
- Using labels and line numbers
- Doing simple arithmetic
- Altering logic flow
- Manipulating strings
- Looping
- Drawing graphic shapes and figures

As you know by now, we are members of the "learn by doing" programming school. Instead of getting bogged down in a lot of programming philosophy and historical facts, let's plunge into the act of programming itself. The finer points of programming style can be covered later.

Some QBasic Fundamentals

Here is a program that's only a little more complicated than the simple one-line program you ran in the previous chapter:

```
100 PRINT "Hello"
200 PRINT "Goodbye"
300 END
```

Bet you can guess what this program does. Sure, the program displays the video message Hello followed by the message Goodbye. Then the program ends. Notice the following differences between this program and the similar one-line program you tried in the previous chapter:

■ Each line begins with a number.

■ An END instruction appears.

Understanding Line Numbers

Look at the first line of the program. The line looks very much like a PRINT instruction from the previous chapter. Now, however, the number 100 appears at the beginning of the line. The other lines of the program also begin with a number.

What do these numbers mean?

These are *line numbers*. Older versions of BASIC (such as GW-BASIC or BASICA) require a line number on every line.

With QBasic, line numbers are optional. You can omit line numbers entirely, number only those lines that need numbers, or for compatibility with older BASIC programs, include a line number on every line.

Introducing *END*

The program's third line ends the program. END does just what the name suggests—it ends the program. When QBasic encounters END, the program immediately terminates. More is said about END shortly.

Understanding Reserved Words (Keywords)

PRINT and END are two of QBasic's *reserved words*. The vocabulary of QBasic includes approximately 200 reserved words. Each reserved word has a special meaning that causes QBasic to take a particular action. You construct meaningful program instructions by using reserved words (along with other program components). A synonym for reserved word is *keyword*.

T I P **Why Doesn't *PRINT* Send Output to the Printer?**

You might be wondering why QBasic uses the word PRINT to display output on the video screen. Why doesn't PRINT send output to the printer?

The answer lies in a historical quirk. Early BASIC users had to use a printing terminal device. There were no screens like the ones used on today's personal computers. In the old days, PRINT *did* send output to the printer (which was the only output device). As video screens came into use, BASIC kept the keyword PRINT to mean "show the following output." Modern versions of BASIC retain the word PRINT even though some other word, such as DISPLAY, would be more appropriate.

Understanding the "Smart" Editor

To better acquaint yourself with the QBasic editor, try typing the preceding three-line program. Follow these steps:

1. If you have an old program in the editor, you must first erase the old program. To do so, use the New command on the File menu.

2. Type the first line of the program exactly as shown. Include the line number (100). Capitalize all the letters of PRINT but capitalize only the H in Hello. Don't forget the quotation marks before and after the word Hello. (Remember that, if you make any typing mistakes, move to the error with the arrow keys and retype. You can delete incorrect characters with the Del key.) After typing the line, press Enter. The cursor moves down a row and back to the leftmost column in anticipation of your next typed line.

3. Type the second line of the program as shown. Press Enter.

4. Type the third line. This time, type end with lowercase letters but don't press Enter just yet.

5. Now press Enter and watch what happens. The word END changes to an all uppercase END.

Surprised?

The QBasic editor is "smart." The editor reformats your typed program instructions according to a set style.

The editor capitalizes all keywords. You can type keywords such as END and PRINT in uppercase, lowercase, (or even mixed, like PRinT), and the editor converts them all into uppercase. Text between quotation marks, however, is preserved exactly the way you type it. This distinction means that you can display HELLO or Hello or hello or even HeLLO if you like. This book shows QBasic's reserved words in uppercase for compatibility with the editor's formatting.

Also, the editor manipulates each of your typed instructions into a standardized format: keywords in uppercase, one space between words and symbols, and so on. You will become more familiar with this formatting as you follow the exercises throughout the book. The editor is superbly adapted to the creation of QBasic programs.

Using *END*

You don't really *need* an END instruction as the final line of a program. (Recall that the one-line program from the previous chapter did not have an END instruction.)

QBasic realizes that your program ends after the final line. You could delete line 300 entirely and the program would still run fine.

END does *not* indicate the physical end of the program but rather the end of program execution. Whenever QBasic encounters an END instruction, your program immediately terminates.

You can have more than one END instruction in a program. (Later in the book, you will learn why some programs contain one or more imbedded END instructions.)

As an experiment, try adding an END instruction in the middle of your program. Follow these steps:

1. If you haven't done so already, run the current program by pressing Shift-F5. You can run the program several times if you want. Notice that you see both the Hello and Goodbye messages.

2. Press any key to return to the editor.

3. Move the cursor to the beginning of the second line (that is, to the 2 in 200).

4. Type the following line:

   ```
   150 END
   ```

5. Press Enter. You have inserted a new line in your program. Your new program looks like this:

   ```
   100 PRINT "Hello"
   150 END
   200 PRINT "Goodbye"
   300 END
   ```

6. Press Shift-F5 to run the program. You can repeat runs if you want.

When you run the program, Hello is displayed but not Goodbye. The new END instruction in line 150 terminates the program even though line 200 is still present.

Clearing the Screen with *CLS*

The output screen can become cluttered from successive program runs. As you have seen, QBasic does not automatically clear the output screen when you run a new program. Your output screen is probably full of Hello and Goodbye messages from running the previous programs. How can you get a fresh output slate?

A CLS instruction wipes the output screen clear. After a CLS instruction executes, a subsequent PRINT instruction displays output in the upper left corner of a blank screen. Like END, CLS is an example of a keyword that forms a valid QBasic instruction all by itself.

Look at this program:

```
CLS
PRINT "Hello"
PRINT "So long"
```

One thing that might strike you immediately about this program is that there are no line numbers. Remember, line numbers are optional in QBasic. In general, the programs in this book *don't* contain line numbers. When running a program, unless you specify otherwise, QBasic executes the lines of a program one after another in top-to-bottom sequence.

Type the new program. To get the program into the editor, you can do one of two things:

1. Edit the old program using the Del key to erase unwanted characters (including the line numbers).

2. Erase the previous program with the New command from the File menu. A dialog box opens to ask you if you want to save the old program. Press *N* for no and the editor screen clears. You can now type the new program from scratch.

Try running the program a few times. Notice that the screen clears at the beginning of each run. As a result, only one Hello message appears on the output screen with each run.

CLS stands for *CLear Screen*. A CLS instruction does not erase anything in the computer's memory, but wipes the output screen clear. Many programmers place CLS at the beginning of each program.

Understanding Fundamental Topics

Consider this program:

```
PRINT "Please enter your name"
INPUT YourName$
PRINT "Hello, "; YourName$
```

A new keyword in this program is NPUT. INPUT instructions request that the user provide some input while the program is running.

Who is the user? The user is the person running the program. If you run the program yourself, you are the user; if you give the program to someone else, that person is the user.

Introducing Variables

The INPUT instruction contains a *variable* named YourName$. A variable is actually nothing more than a name you give to a memory location or locations where data is stored. The value of the data can (and usually does) change while the program is running. By referencing a variable, you are telling the computer to use whatever value you currently have stored in the memory location reserved for that variable. Some QBasic instructions change the value of a variable; other instructions just retrieve and use the value.

A variable enables a program to do different things each time the program is run, depending on the value assigned to the variable. This program asks for the user's name, which can be almost anything.

Why does YourName$ end with a dollar sign? Why not just name the variable YourName and forget about that dollar sign?

Well, the dollar sign *is* important. QBasic categorizes data into two fundamentally different groups: *numeric* data and *string* (or text) data. Accordingly, QBasic variables fall into the following two fundamental categories (depending on which kind of data the variable can store):

- *Numeric variables:* These variables store numeric values, such as 14, 33.8, and so on. You can change the value stored in a numeric variable, but the value must always be a number.

- *String variables:* These variables store text information such as Hello, Indiana Jones, or 76 trombones. You can change the value stored in a string variable, but the value must always be text information.

Every variable is either a numeric variable or a string variable. A dollar sign at the end of a variable name indicates that the variable is a string variable.

String data is alphanumeric data (letters, digits, and other characters) that are "strung" together in any desired length. YourName$ is a string variable.

CAUTION

QBasic Ignores Case Distinctions in Variable Names

Variable names must follow certain rules, which have evolved over the years. Older versions of BASIC allowed only one- or two-character names, but QBasic allows much longer, descriptive names.

QBasic permits variable names of up to 40 characters. The first character of each variable name must be a letter. Subsequent characters (if any) can be letters, digits, and certain special characters.

Most versions of BASIC, including QBasic, treat upper- and lowercase letters in variable names as identical. For example, YOURNAME$, YourName$, and yourname$ are all treated as the same variable, not as three different variables.

Unlike keywords, which the editor converts to all uppercase, a variable name can have upper- or lowercase letters, depending on how you choose to type them.

For readability, we like to capitalize the first letter of each word in a compound variable name, as in YourName$.

A variable name that doesn't end with a dollar sign is a numeric variable. YourName is a numeric variable. Consequently, YourName would store a numeric quantity. YourName and YourName$ could coexist in the same program, but they would be two distinct variables, each storing different information. (In Chapter 6, "Language Building Blocks," you will see that there are actually four different types of numeric variables. For now, however, consider any variable with a name not ending with a dollar sign to be a generic numeric variable.)

In QBasic, a *literal* is any data value expressed explicitly. A *numeric literal* is a number written explicitly, such as 321 or 13.65. A *string literal* is text information written explicitly, such as Elvis or Hello out there.

Notice that in QBasic you place quotation marks around a string literal. The quotation marks signify that the enclosed text constitutes a string literal. You are already an old hand with string literals. You already used string literals in PRINT instructions to display messages on-screen.

Using *INPUT*

Again, here is the program under consideration.

```
PRINT "Please enter your name"
INPUT YourName$
PRINT "Hello, "; YourName$
```

What happens when you run this program? Try it.

The contents of the variable YourName$ depend on what you type when you are prompted by the INPUT instruction. When you run this program and type your name as a response, the output looks like this (at least if your name is Michael):

```
Please enter your name
? Michael
Hello, Michael
```

The first program line is no mystery. The PRINT instruction displays the following message on-screen: Please enter your name.

The computer then displays a question mark at the beginning of the next output line. This question mark is a prompt character produced by the INPUT instruction in the second line of the program. Here the program is prompting the user for input, much like a drama coach prompts an actor to speak lines. (By the way, you do not need to respond promptly to the prompt; computers are very patient.) INPUT, like PRINT, END, and CLS, is a QBasic keyword.

In this example, the user responded by typing **Michael** and pressing Enter. The INPUT instruction then stored the text string Michael into the string variable YourName$.

Displaying the Value of String Variables

The last line of the output comes from the PRINT instruction in the third line of the program. This instruction demonstrates more of the flexibility of PRINT. The instruction displays both the string literal ("Hello, ") *and* the value of the variable YourName$—namely, Michael.

Using Blank Spaces and Semicolon Separators

Look at the bottom line of the program. Did you notice the blank space after the comma that follows the word `Hello`? If you don't type that blank space, no blank space appears in the output between the comma and the user's name.

In this third program line, a semicolon separates the items to be displayed. A semicolon tells QBasic to juxtapose the two items (that is, don't add any additional spaces between the two items being displayed). Try changing the number of blank spaces after the comma to see how the output's spacing changes.

You might try rerunning the program and typing other names.

Assigning Values to Variables

QBasic provides many ways of assigning a value to a variable. The previous program demonstrates one way: an `INPUT` instruction that assigns a string value to a string variable. (In that program, `YourName$` is a string variable and the user types the string value to be assigned to `YourName$`.)

The most straightforward assignment method, however, uses the equal sign to assign a value to a variable. You place the variable name on the left of the equal sign and the value to be assigned on the right.

For example, try the following program:

```
MyName$ = "Phil Feldman"
MyAge = 39
PRINT MyName$
PRINT "is"
PRINT MyAge
```

Run this program and you get the following output:

```
Phil Feldman
is
 39
```

Notice how the first two lines assign values to the variables `MyName$` and `MyAge`, respectively. Instructions that directly assign values to variables are called, naturally enough, *assignment* instructions. As you can see, assignment instructions work equally well for both string and numeric variables.

However, you must be careful that you assign only numeric values to numeric variables, and only string values to string variables. The following two instructions are improper:

```
MyName$ = 25
```

```
MyAge = "Teenager"
```

Do you see why neither instruction is legal? The first instruction attempts to assign a numeric value to a string variable and the second line does the reverse.

Dealing with Programming Errors

T I P

What happens if you *do* run a program containing one of these illegal assignment instructions, or any illegal instruction for that matter? If you are curious, go ahead and find out. You will find that, when running the program, QBasic catches the error, returns to the editor, and displays an informative error message. Press Enter to remove the message box so that you can correct the erroneous instruction. Error correction is discussed in detail in Chapter 5, "Using the QBasic Editor" and Chapter 18, "Interactive Debugging and Testing."

Assignment instructions occur quite frequently in QBasic programs. The right side of assignment instructions can be simple (as in the present examples) or more complex. Sometimes the right side contains several terms.

Explaining Some Terminology

Before going on, we should clarify some terminology. We have been using terms like "instruction" and "reserved word" in proper context. Perhaps, however, some meanings are a bit unclear to you. If so, Table 3.1 should clear up any ambiguities.

Table 3.1. Definitions of some QBasic terms.

Term	Example	Meaning
Reserved word	END	A reserved word is a word with a special meaning to QBasic. Reserved words are integral parts of program instructions. Appendix A lists all of QBasic's reserved words.

continues

Table 3.1. Continued

Term	Example	Meaning
Keyword	`CLS`	Synonymous with *reserved word*.
Instruction	`PRINT A$`	A line of a program that commands QBasic to do something. Each instruction begins with a statement and usually contains other terms.
Statement	`PRINT`	Any keyword (or combination of keywords) that specifies the action that an instruction should perform. Not all keywords are statements. For example, `PRINT` and `INPUT` are keywords that also happen to be statements. `OFF` and `ON`, however, are keywords but not statements.
Command	Save	An action requested from one of the pull-down menus. This term does not refer to any component of a program, but rather to options available from the menu system.
Text literal	`"Hello"`	Any group of characters enclosed in quotation marks.
String literal	`"Me too"`	Synonymous with *text literal*.

Performing Simple Arithmetic

Let's try some simple calculations. Suppose you want a program that asks the user to supply two numbers and then calculates the sum and product of the two numbers.

An earlier program had a `PRINT` instruction that asks the user to enter certain information, followed by an `INPUT` instruction for the data entry. This next program uses another form of the `INPUT` instruction—a form that accomplishes both tasks.

```
PRINT "This program makes calculations using two numbers"
INPUT "First number"; Num1
INPUT "Second number"; Num2
PRINT "The sum is"; Num1 + Num2
PRINT "The product is"; Num1 * Num2
```

If you run this program and enter the numbers 7 and 5, the output looks like this:

```
This program makes calculations using two numbers
First number? 7
Second number? 5
The sum is 12
The product is 35
```

Notice that the variables in this program, Num1 and Num2, do not end with dollar signs. As you have seen, that makes Num1 and Num2 numeric variables. Within QBasic's rules, you could name the variables almost anything—Fred, TheFirstNumber, or XB47JQX35R, for example. However, choosing simple but descriptive variable names is an important part of writing understandable programs.

Also notice that QBasic uses the asterisk (*) to indicate multiplication. The plus and minus signs indicate addition and subtraction. The slash (/) denotes division.

Do you see how the two INPUT instructions work? Look again at the output and the INPUT instructions.

Each INPUT instruction contains a string literal separated from the variable name by a semicolon. When QBasic prompts the user on-screen, it displays the string literal (from the INPUT instruction) followed by a question mark. In this way, a single INPUT instruction replaces the PRINT and INPUT combination used previously.

Altering Logic Flow with *GOTO*

Suppose that you want to make the same calculations shown in the previous program for many pairs of numbers. Do you have to run the program from the beginning each time?

No. You can insert instructions that alter the logic flow. Instead of allowing this program to end after the bottom instruction, you can add a new instruction that tells QBasic to go back to the beginning of the program or to any other point in the program. By returning to earlier lines, you cause some instructions to repeat.

But a complication arises. How do you specify which line the program should jump to? You need a way to identify program lines.

This is where line numbers and the newer alternative, alphanumeric labels, come into play. Modify the program to look as follows:

```
PRINT "This program makes calculations using two numbers"
GetMoreNumbers:
    INPUT "First number"; Num1
    INPUT "Second number"; Num2
    PRINT "The sum is"; Num1 + Num2
    PRINT "The product is"; Num1 * Num2
GOTO GetMoreNumbers
```

In early versions of BASIC, every line began with a line number. (Because of the line numbers in earlier versions of BASIC, a GOTO instruction referenced only the line number, as in GOTO 20. You can still use this form in QBasic.)

An alphanumeric label, such as GetMoreNumbers, makes for more understandable programs than line numbers ever could. A colon is required after an alphanumeric label.

Look at the final program line. That GOTO instruction transfers program flow directly back to the line containing the label GetMoreNumbers. So after the last line executes, the program goes back and reexecutes the first INPUT instruction. From there, QBasic continues down the program reexecuting the second INPUT instruction and the subsequent PRINT instructions. When the last line comes up again, program control returns once more to the GetMoreNumbers label.

In a GOTO instruction, you do not use a colon after the name of the label. However, in the line containing the label itself, the colon must appear.

T I P   Using Indentation

The preceding program has four lines indented from the others. Indentation is entirely optional. You can put as many spaces as you want at the beginning of a line. Indentation provides a useful way to visually set off a block of related instructions.

Looping

The modified program has a problem. You might have detected the snag. How will the program ever end? The bottom line of the program always goes back to get two more numbers, creating an *endless loop* or *infinite loop*.

A *loop* is any group of instructions that executes repeatedly. Endless loops, as the name suggests, repeat endlessly. (At least until you take drastic action. If you are "stuck" in the program, press Ctrl-Break instead of entering a number, and you will interrupt the endless loop. Interrupting a program with Ctrl-Break is discussed later in this chapter.)

The indented lines of the program (the INPUT and PRINT instructions) constitute an endless loop because these lines repeat continuously.

The program needs a *conditional loop.* Such a loop repeats until a certain condition occurs. The following revised program solves the problem:

```
PRINT "This program makes calculations using two numbers"
GetMoreNumbers:
   INPUT "First number"; Num1
   INPUT "Second number"; Num2
   IF Num1 = 0 AND Num2 = 0 THEN PRINT "All Done": END
   PRINT "The sum is"; Num1 + Num2
   PRINT "The product is"; Num1 * Num2
GOTO GetMoreNumbers
```

An IF instruction now appears in the middle of the loop. This IF instruction causes the program to end when certain conditions are satisfied. The conditions are that both Num1 and Num2 must equal zero. (This occurs if you type 0 in response to both prompts.) When these conditions are met, the program displays the All Done message and ends. (IF is discussed in more detail later in this chapter.)

Looping is a powerful programming technique. Many kinds of loops exist. Most nontrivial programs contain one or more loops.

Placing Multiple Instructions on One Program Line

Notice the use of the colon (:) in the IF instruction. The colon is a way to combine two or more instructions on one program line. Don't confuse the colon with the semicolon; their uses are entirely different in spite of their similar appearance.

CAUTION

Punctuation Is Important

Punctuation characters are critical to QBasic programs. Simple (but hard to notice) typing errors involving punctuation can cause annoying error messages and incorrect program results.

Making Decisions with *IF*

In the last program, an IF instruction prevents an endless loop. IF is one of QBasic's most important statements because, with IF, you can program decisions.

Just as decision making is a significant and frequent part of your everyday life, decision making is a perpetual programming theme. Like a fork in the road, a "logic juncture" is a place in your program where the subsequent execution path can go different ways.

When you program a logic juncture, your thought process goes like this: "If such and such is True, I want this to happen. If not, then that should happen instead."

You choose the program path based on the evaluation of a test condition. Your foremost tool is the IF-THEN instruction, which tests whether a condition is True or False and then directs logic flow according to the result.

The following program demonstrates the basic form of the IF-THEN instruction:

```
INPUT "What is the temperature outside"; Temp
IF Temp > 100 THEN PRINT "It's hot"
PRINT "So long for now"
```

Here are two different runs of this program:

```
What is the temperature outside? 106
It's hot
So long for now
```

```
What is the temperature outside? 84
So long for now
```

The second line of the program is an IF-THEN instruction. If the value of the variable Temp is greater than 100, then the program displays the message It's hot. (The > character is a relational operator meaning "greater than." Relational operators are discussed in Chapter 7, "Program Flow and Decision Making.")

Look at the two sample runs. The first time the user gave the temperature as 106. Because 106 is greater than 100, the program dutifully displays the It's hot message.

But the second time the user input 84 for the temperature. What happened? Did the computer just ignore the part of the program line following THEN?

That's exactly what happened. When the test condition of an IF-THEN instruction is False, QBasic disregards the part of the instruction after THEN. The program moves immediately down to the next program line.

In the second run, the value of Temp is 84. The test condition is False because 84 is not greater than 100. As a result, QBasic ignores the part of the instruction after THEN (that is, the PRINT clause) and moves down to the next program line. In this case, the next line displays the So long for now message.

Beeping the Speaker

You can play sound effects or music through the computer's speaker. QBasic includes several keywords for constructing such instructions. The simplest of these keywords is BEEP, which forms a legal instruction all by itself.

BEEP creates a short (about a quarter second) tone. Use BEEP to get your user's attention. Typical occasions are when your program requests input and when it displays an error message.

For example, a checkbook balancing program might include the following two lines:

```
PRINT "Sorry, your checkbook is out of balance."
BEEP
```

To see (hear) the effect, try running the two lines as an entire program.

Interrupting a Program with Ctrl-Break

When testing a new program, you might discover that your program unfortunately goes into an endless loop. As you have seen, this happens when a section of your program executes over and over continuously. You might realize your programming error but, meanwhile, your program keeps running with no end in sight. Help!

The way out is Ctrl-Break. (While pressing the Ctrl key, you simultaneously press the Break key.) QBasic terminates your program and returns to the editor. You might think of Ctrl-Break as "Help, let me out of here!"

After interrupting a program with Ctrl-Break, you can resume execution with the Continue command from the Run menu. The F5 hotkey is equivalent to issuing the Continue command. F5 and Shift-F5 are not the same. Recall that Shift-F5 starts a program from the beginning. F5 resumes an interrupted program.

Try the following short program to acquaint yourself with Ctrl-Break:

```
StartLoop:
   BEEP
   GOTO StartLoop
```

This program creates an endless loop. The BEEP instruction executes continuously. The result is a constant drone from your speaker. (The individual beeps blend into one continuous sound.) The noise is pretty annoying, so you probably will press Ctrl-Break right away.

Introducing *FOR-NEXT* Loops

Earlier you saw some examples of loops. Recall that an endless loop executes forever (or at least until your electricity runs out, the computer breaks, or you press Ctrl-Break). Useful programming loops must have a predetermined way to end.

A loop that has an ending mechanism is called a conditional loop or *controlled loop*. A controlled loop executes until some predetermined condition is satisfied. Some form of controlled loop occurs in most nontrivial programs.

QBasic provides special structures and several keywords for programming controlled loops. The most common structure is the FOR-NEXT loop.

A FOR-NEXT loop uses a numeric variable to control the number of repetitions. This special variable is called a *counter variable* or *control variable.*

The easiest way to explain a FOR-NEXT loop is with an example. Here is a program that displays a table of the squares of the numbers from 0 to 6. (The *square* of a number is the number multiplied by itself.) This kind of task is perfect for a FOR-NEXT loop.

```
PRINT "Number", "Square"
FOR Number = 0 TO 6
   Square = Number * Number
   PRINT Number, Square
NEXT Number
PRINT "End of table"
```

Here's the output:

```
Number        Square
  0             0
  1             1
  2             4
  3             9
  4            16
```

```
5          25
6          36
End of table
```

Let's go over the *program*.

Understanding Print Zones

The first line displays the titles of the two columns of the table. But why are there so many spaces in the output between the words Number and Square?

If you separate two items in a PRINT instruction with a comma, QBasic displays each item at a predefined column position. These column positions, or print zones, are set automatically by QBasic. Using print zones, you can conveniently produce table-like output with PRINT instructions. See Chapter 12, "Writing Text on the Video Screen," for a detailed discussion of PRINT and print zones.

Executing a *FOR-NEXT* Loop

The loop starts with the FOR instruction in the second line. FOR signifies that a loop is beginning. In this example, the counter variable is Number. The value of Number changes each time through the loop. This FOR instruction specifies that the first value of Number should be 0 and the final value should be 6.

Three lines down, the NEXT instruction marks the end of the loop. FOR and NEXT are like a pair of bookends that surround a loop. In a FOR-NEXT loop, all the instructions between the FOR and NEXT keywords are called the *body* of the loop.

The body of a loop can contain any number of instructions. Occasionally, program loops have over 100 instructions. The body of our more modest loop consists of the two indented instructions between FOR and NEXT.

Do you see how the loop works? The body of the loop executes repetitively. In succession, Number takes on the values 0, 1, 2, 3, 4, 5, and 6. The PRINT instruction just above the NEXT instruction displays every one of the numeric lines in the table. (Again, the comma aligns the output into the predefined print zone columns.)

The first time through the loop, Number is zero. The assignment instruction (the instruction below FOR) computes the square of Number, so Square is also zero. The ensuing PRINT instruction then displays the first line of the table.

The NEXT instruction then effectively says, "We have now reached the bottom of the loop so it's time to increase the value of Number and go back through the loop."

By default, the value of a counter variable increases by 1 each time through a FOR-NEXT loop. So the new value of Number becomes 1 (0 + 1 equals 1).

The program now returns to the beginning of the loop, at the line just below the FOR instruction. Here the new value of Number (namely 1) is compared against the final value of the loop (6 in this case). Because the final value is not yet exceeded, the body of the loop executes again. Number is 1 and Square also becomes 1 (1 times 1 is 1). The next line then prints the second line of the table.

This looping process continues with Number continually increasing by 1. Eventually, Number reaches 6. The body of the loop still executes because Number has equalled—but not exceeded—the final value of the loop.

The NEXT instruction then increases the value of Number to 7. Now, when control returns to the FOR instruction at the top of the loop, the value of Number is finally greater than the maximum loop value of 6. This signals that the loop is over. The program then proceeds with the first line after the NEXT instruction. In our present case, control passes to the PRINT instruction at the end of the program, which prints the closing message.

Introducing Functions

A *function* operates on one or more arguments and produces ("returns" in programming lingo) a single value. Depending on the particular function, the arguments can be numeric or string. Also, the value returned can be numeric or string. QBasic provides a number of built-in functions, and each function is specified by a reserved keyword.

You just wrote a program that displays a table of the squares of the numbers from 0 to 6. Suppose now that you want to display the *square roots* of the numbers from 0 to 6. (The square root of a number is a new number that, when multiplied by itself, produces the value of the original number.)

QBasic provides the SQR function to calculate a square root. Here is the squares program modified to produce square roots:

```
PRINT "Number", "Square Root"
FOR Number = 0 TO 6
    PRINT Number, SQR(Number)
NEXT Number
PRINT "End of table"
```

The output is as follows:

```
Number          Square Root
  0               0
  1               1
  2               1.414214
  3               1.732051
  4               2
  5               2.236068
  6               2.44949
End of table
```

Consider the PRINT instruction inside the FOR-NEXT loop. SQR is a numeric function that determines the square root of whatever value is given in parentheses. In this program, the variable Number appears inside the parentheses. So each time the PRINT instruction executes, the SQR function returns the square root of the current value of Number.

Manipulating Strings

Many QBasic programs manipulate text data. You've seen several such programs in this chapter. Text data is stored in strings and QBasic has an entire group of string manipulation instructions that operate on text data. As you've seen, string variables are distinguished by the dollar sign at the end of the variable's name.

The Dollar Sign and Strings

T I P

Most programmers find that the dollar sign's resemblance to the letter *S* simplifies remembering how string variables are identified. In fact, many programmers consider the dollar sign to be equivalent to the word "string" when speaking about variable names. The variable YourName$, therefore, is pronounced "your name string" when two programmers discuss a program. Other programmers call the variable "your name dollar" with the understanding that "dollar" means a string variable.

Listing 3.1 is another program that does some string manipulation.

Listing 3.1.   The STRING1.BAS program.

```
REM - STRING1.BAS - This program manipulates strings
INPUT "What is your name"; YourName$
FOR Pointer = 1 TO LEN(YourName$)
   PRINT Pointer, MID$(YourName$, Pointer, 1)
NEXT Pointer
```

This program introduces several new QBasic keywords, but first take a look at what happens when John is supplied as the answer to What is your name?

```
What is your name? John
   1            J
   2            o
   3            h
   4            n
```

Commenting a Program

The first line in Listing 3.1 is something new—a REM instruction. REM stands for *REMark* and causes the remainder of the line to be treated as a programmer's comment rather than as an active program instruction. When REM occurs, QBasic ignores the remainder of the line and proceeds directly to the next line.

With REM instructions, programmers "self-document" their programs by inserting comments and explanations. When anyone looks at the program in the future, these remarks tell the person (who most likely is the original programmer) what the program is all about and how it works.

In this program, the REM instruction shows the program name (STRING1.BAS) along with a short description of what the program does. The hyphens around the program name are arbitrary; just a way to separate the program name from the description.

T I P   **A Comment on Comments**

Using numerous comments is a good idea. You will be amazed how much help a few comments can provide when you resume working with a program after a few months.

Look at the FOR-NEXT loop in the final three lines of Listing 3.1. How many times does this loop execute? Answering that question is a little tricky in this program, because the explanation depends on something not covered yet, the LEN function.

Using String Functions

LEN is a string function that calculates the length of whatever string is given in parentheses. In this program, the string in parentheses consists solely of the variable YourName$. The length does not refer to the length of the variable name, but rather to the length of the string data stored in that variable. If you type in the name John, then LEN(YourName$) is four. So in this particular case, the third program line is the same as saying

```
FOR Pointer = 1 TO 4
```

Well, then, why didn't the program just *say* that to begin with? Why complicate the program with this funny LEN function?

The answer is that the programmer didn't know how many characters would comprise the name that would be entered. LEN enables the program to do its job for any name, not just a four-character name.

Let's move on to the PRINT instruction in the fourth line. You already know that the comma causes the output to align into two printing zones. The first output on each line is the value of the counter variable, named Pointer in this case. In this loop, Pointer identifies or *points* to the character being processed in each repetition of the loop. But what is that MID$ expression that produces the second output on each line?

MID$ is another example of a QBasic string function. MID$ extracts a portion (that is, a *substring*) of a target string. MID$ can have two or three parameters. In the three-parameter form used here, the parameters specify the following, in order:

1. The string from which the substring is extracted

2. The character position where the extracted substring begins

3. The length of the extracted string

The first time the PRINT instruction executes, Pointer points at the first character, and MID$ extracts only that one character (the J in John). The second time, Pointer points to the second character (the o in John), and MID$ again extracts only that one character, and so on.

Try an experiment. Change the 1 in the PRINT instruction to 2 or even omit the third MID$ parameter (and the preceding comma) entirely. Watch closely what happens, and you should get an idea of how MID$ works. But if you are having trouble understanding MID$, don't worry. MID$ is a relatively fancy string function. Along with covering various string topics, we provide a detailed description of MID$ in Chapter 11, "Manipulating Strings."

QBasic contains many built-in functions, both string and numeric. Some examples of mathematical functions are trigonometric functions (SIN and COS), logarithmic functions (EXP and LOG), and arithmetic functions (ABS for absolute value and SQR for square roots).

Dealing with Run-Time Errors

Errors are a fact of programming life. All programmers make mistakes, so don't feel bad when the inevitable errors occur. Recognize that errors are bound to happen, learn from them, and forge ahead.

Errors that you don't discover until you run a program are called *run-time* errors. There are three fundamental types of run-time errors:

1. *Syntax errors.* A syntax error occurs when an instruction does not follow the rules of QBasic. For example, you might spell a keyword incorrectly, use improper punctuation, or combine keywords in an illegal way. In such a case, the instruction is meaningless. As a result, QBasic cannot even *attempt* to execute the instruction. See Chapter 5, "Using the QBasic Editor," for more information about dealing with syntax errors.

2. *Execution errors.* An execution error occurs when an instruction requests an action that QBasic cannot perform. For example, you might divide a number by zero. In such a case, no syntax error is present. (The instruction is legally constructed according to the rules of QBasic.) However, the instruction attempts something illegal in the context of the whole program. QBasic understands what the instruction means, but cannot perform the requested action. See Chapter 18, "Interactive Debugging and Testing," for a discussion of execution errors.

3. *Logic errors.* A logic error occurs when a program runs to completion but the results are incorrect. Somehow the program does not work correctly. In programming jargon, the program contains a *bug*. The programmer now must *debug* the program, which means finding and correcting the error. Chapter 18 shows many techniques for dealing with logic errors.

Programming Graphics

So far, our programs have worked with numbers and text. We now venture into the stimulating world of another kind of data—graphics.

The program in Listing 3.2 gives you a "sneak preview" of how QBasic can create many interesting visual pictures on the video screen. Be aware that graphics output is possible only if your video hardware supports graphics: The IBM Monochrome Display Adapter (MDA) does not support graphics, but the Color Graphics Adapter (CGA), Enhanced Graphics Adapter (EGA), and Video Graphics Array (VGA) do.

Listing 3.2. The GRTEST.BAS program.

```
REM Program: GRTEST.BAS (Draw circle and two overlapping boxes)
CLS
SCREEN 2
Xcent = 320: Ycent = 100
LINE (Xcent - 150, Ycent - 50)-(Xcent + 150, Ycent + 50), 3, B
LINE (Xcent - 100, Ycent - 70)-(Xcent + 100, Ycent + 70), 3, B
CIRCLE (Xcent, Ycent), 60
LOCATE 21, 35
PRINT "Graphics Test"
```

Run the program. You should see two rectangles and a circle as shown in Figure 3.1.

Be aware that, in general, graphics instructions provide many options. Rather than explaining all the options in detail, this section is intended to give you a general understanding of how the graphics work. Our explanations are brief. We hope this program whets your appetite for Chapter 13, "Creating Graphics," which explains graphics in detail.

The SCREEN instruction in the third line initializes one of QBasic's graphics modes. Depending on your hardware, you have many different screen modes available. SCREEN 2 is a graphics mode consisting of 640 dots horizontally and 200 dots vertically. See Chapter 13 for a complete discussion of the available SCREEN modes.

The fourth program line sets up the dot coordinates of the center of the screen, 320 dots horizontally and 100 dots vertically. With QBasic, the screen dots are referenced a bit differently from conventional x,y coordinates. In SCREEN MODE 2, the upper left corner is dot coordinate (0, 0) and the lower right corner is (639, 199).

Therefore the center of the screen is approximately 320 points to the right of the upper left corner and 100 points down from the top—(320, 100). The fourth program line doesn't actually *do* anything with this center point. All the line does is establish two variables (XCent and YCent) that the program uses to represent the x and y coordinates of the center.

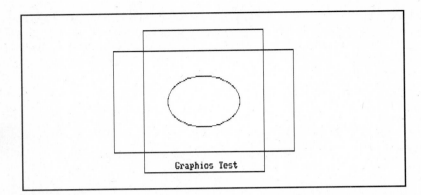

Figure 3.1.

Graphics output produced
by the GRTEST.BAS
program.

T I P   Putting Multiple Instructions on the Same Line

Notice that the fourth line of Listing 3.2 contains two assignment instructions separated by a colon. By using a colon to separate instructions, you can place two or more instructions on the same program line.

QBasic has a variety of graphics instructions that simplify drawing certain shapes. In particular, the LINE instruction draws either lines or rectangles (boxes), and the CIRCLE instruction draws circles.

In the process, the two LINE instructions draw the two rectangles. With LINE, you can draw a straight line between two specified points or draw a rectangle defined by two points on opposite corners.

The B parameter at the end of the LINE instruction indicates that, in this case, a rectangle is desired. (The B stands for *Box*.) If you omit the B, the instruction draws a straight diagonal line rather than a rectangle.

The 3 in each LINE instruction specifies the color of the rectangle, which in this case is white.

The two LINE instructions differ only in the constant numbers that are added or subtracted from the coordinates of the screen's center. This technique (adding or subtracting from the same starting position) centers the rectangles without forcing the programmer to do the arithmetic drudgery of calculating each set of coordinates. Let the computer do the work!

The first rectangle extends from 150 points left of center to 150 points right of center, and from 50 points above center to 50 points below center. This is the wider and shorter of the two rectangles. The second LINE instruction draws the taller rectangle.

After the two rectangles are drawn, a CIRCLE instruction draws a circle. This circle has a radius of 60 units, and its center matches the rectangles' center.

Notice that you can mix text with graphics. The program's last two lines combine to display a short text title on the same screen with the graphics output. The LOCATE instruction moves the invisible text cursor to the spot where subsequent text, such as that written by the upcoming PRINT instruction, will be displayed. In this case, the text will start on the 21st line (the top line is line 1, not 0), beginning in the 35th column position on that line.

If you feel adventurous, make a few modifications to the program. You cannot hurt your computer, even if you attempt to draw "outside" the normal screen boundaries. Change the value of the circle's radius (the 60 at the end of the CIRCLE instruction). Modify the LOCATE values to move the text to another part of the screen. Try altering the values of the X and Y center locations (in the third line of the program). Changes to the two LINE instructions will draw different rectangles. Play with the program to get a feel for everything it does.

Summary

A program collects a group of instructions together in a single unit. When you run a program, QBasic executes the program instructions one after another.

You took a whirlwind tour of several programming topics. You learned about variables, assignment, loops, strings, graphics, comments, and altering the logic flow.

All programmers make mistakes. Three kinds of programming errors are most common: syntax, execution, and logic. Logic errors are the most subtle because programs can run to completion even though the results are wrong.

QBasic has many keywords for use in constructing program instructions. You worked with programs that contained the following keywords: PRINT, END, CLS, INPUT, GOTO, IF, THEN, BEEP, FOR, NEXT, TO, SQR, REM, LEN, MID$, SCREEN, LINE, CIRCLE, and LOCATE.

Learning the QBasic Environment

This chapter is intended to make you feel comfortable with the QBasic programming environment. The previous chapters introduced you to the environment. This chapter fills in the gaps.

Like any sophisticated computer application, QBasic can seem bewildering at first. With a little experimentation, however, you soon can get the "feel." Everything is fairly intuitive.

If you are a GW-BASIC or BASICA programmer moving up to QBasic, and you feel a little intimidated, don't worry. Such anxiety is understandable; after all, you are migrating from a simple line-at-a-time environment to a world of menus, windows, and full-screen editors. Every QBasic user needs a little groundwork—a toehold for mastering a new environment. This chapter provides it.

Here are the major topics covered in this chapter:

- Learning the menu system
- Understanding QBasic windows
- Using dialog boxes
- Working with a mouse
- Customizing your screen display

An Overview of the Environment

This section provides a hands-on guide to the QBasic programming environment.

Understanding the Initial Screen

Follow these steps to make your screen look like the one in Figure 4.1:

1. Start QBasic with a blank editor screen.

2. Type the following one-line program:

   ```
   PRINT "Hello"
   ```

3. Press Enter about 9 or 10 times to move the cursor approximately half-way down the screen.

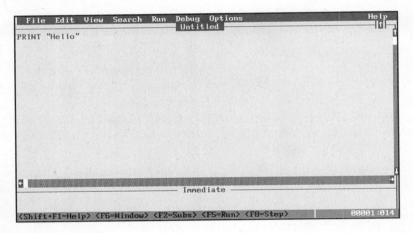

Figure 4.1.

The QBasic edit screen.

Table 4.1 briefly explains the major items on the screen.

Table 4.1. Components of the editor screen.	
Item	**Description**
Menu bar	The line along the top of the screen that displays the available menus: File, Edit, View, and so on.
Title bar	The short, centered bar just below the Menu bar that contains the name of the current program, which for now reads Untitled.

Item	Description
Reference bar	The line along the bottom of the screen that describes information about the process at hand and also shows certain hotkey options (this component is also known as the Information bar).
Scroll bars	The two matte strips—a vertical strip along the right edge and a horizontal strip just above the word Immediate—used with a mouse (this chapter later describes how to use scroll bars with a mouse).
View window	The large, boxed area in which the text of your program resides.
Immediate window	The boxed area bordered on the top by the word Immediate and on the bottom by the Reference bar; directly executes QBasic instructions, as explained later in this chapter.
Cursor	The flashing underscore character that indicates where the next text you type will be displayed.

Navigating the Menu System

The menu system is your control center, providing a number of commands at your fingertips. By selecting the proper menu command, you can load or save a program, run a program, set debugging options, print a listing, get on-line help, and perform many other tasks—all while your program remains in memory. After the command is executed, QBasic returns to the editor, and you can resume program editing.

Each main menu "pops open" with a pull-down submenu. The submenu lists the commands available under that main menu. The following guidelines apply to using the menu system:

- To activate a menu, press Alt and the first letter of the menu name. For example, press Alt-R to activate the Run menu, or Alt-S to activate the Search menu. You do not have to hold down the Alt key while you press the letter key. Instead, you can press and release Alt, and then press the letter key.

- After a main menu opens, you can move from one main menu to another by pressing the left- or right-arrow keys.

- Every time you open a main menu, the first command on the submenu is highlighted. You can move this highlight to the other submenu commands by pressing the up- or down-arrow keys. As you move the highlight, notice that the Reference bar displays a brief description of the highlighted command.

■ On a submenu command list, one letter of each command is emphasized. On color systems, the emphasized letter appears in high-intensity white.

■ Depending on your current editing context, some commands in a submenu list might not be available. In such a case, the submenu shows the command name in a dull color (usually gray) and no highlighted letter appears in the name. If you try to execute an unavailable command, the editor sounds a warning beep.

■ To execute a submenu command, either move the highlight to the desired command and press Enter, or press the key that corresponds to the emphasized letter.

■ The Escape key (Esc) is the "oops" key. Pressing Esc closes the menu system and returns you to the editor.

■ For convenience, many commonly used submenu commands have an associated hotkey. Pressing this hotkey while you are in the editor executes the command directly and bypasses the menu system. Several hotkeys are explained in this chapter, and others are explained later in this book. See Appendix D, "Hotkeys and Mouse Commands," for a complete list of hotkeys.

Try the following steps to enhance your "working feel" of the menu system:

1. Open the File menu by pressing Alt-F. A pull-down submenu appears on-screen (see Figure 4.2).

2. Press the left- and right-arrow keys to move among the main menus. Stop in any menu.

3. Press the up- and down-arrow keys. Notice that the Reference bar describes each command.

4. Press Esc to close the menu system and return to the editor.

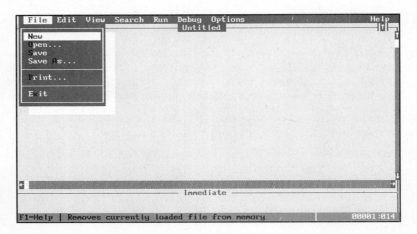

Figure 4.2.

Opening the File menu.

An Overview of the Menu Commands

Table 4.2 summarizes the menu commands. The table shows the major features available from each main menu and the chapter in which that topic is discussed.

Table 4.2. Overview of the main menu.

Menu	Major Features	Chapter
File	Loading and saving programs	5
	Printing text or a program listing	5
Edit	Cutting and pasting text	5
	Creating user-defined procedures	17
View	Viewing pieces of a program	4, 17
	Viewing the program output	4
Search	Finding and replacing specified text	5
Run	Executing your program	4, 19
Debug	Debugging your program	18
Options	Reconfiguring environment options	4, 5
Help	Displaying on-line help	5

Understanding Dialog Boxes

When you execute a command, depending on the command and the current context, either the command executes at once or a dialog box pops open. A dialog box popping open means that QBasic needs more information before your command can be completed. For example, if you invoke a command to save a new program, QBasic first needs to know what name to give the file. The dialog box prompts you for the needed name.

QBasic uses dialog boxes to get a variety of information. Sometimes you must type something, such as a filename or a search string. Other times you must choose from listed options. And still other times QBasic tries to protect you from yourself; for example, QBasic requires your confirmation if you try to exit QBasic without first saving a program that you have modified.

In the pull-down menus, three periods after a submenu command name indicate that a dialog box opens when you issue that command. Sometimes, depending on the circumstances, a command without three periods also will open a dialog box. When a dialog box opens, the following three keys have special significance:

■ Tab: Moves the input focus (the blinking cursor) from one area of the dialog box to the next area. After you specify information in one area, use Tab to move to the next area.

■ Esc: Press this "oops" key to abort the command in progress and return to the editor. Use Esc when you change your mind and want to cancel a command.

■ Enter: Press this "go ahead" key when you have all options in the dialog box specified and you are ready to execute the command. You press Enter only once while you are working inside a dialog box. Don't press Enter to move the input focus from one area of the dialog box to the next area; use Tab instead. This use of Tab and Enter sometimes frustrates new QBasic users. Most people have a natural tendency to press Enter after they type information such as a filename. Remember, when you need to specify additional information inside the dialog box, press Tab, not Enter.

Trying a Dialog Box Example

Dialog boxes are best illustrated with an example. Start with your screen looking like Figure 4.1. Through a menu command, you will replace the word Hello in your program with the word Goodbye.

The following example uses the Change... command available from the Search menu. When doing this example, don't dwell on the meaning of each option in the Change... dialog box. The complete meanings of the Change... dialog options are discussed in Chapter 5, "Using the QBasic Editor." The purpose here is only to examine the various techniques of manipulating the dialog box.

Follow these steps:

1. Invoke the Search menu by pressing Alt-S.

2. Move the highlight to Change... The three periods indicate that a dialog box opens.

3. Press Enter. A dialog box opens (see Figure 4.3).

4. Press Tab several times. Notice how the cursor moves around the screen. Return the cursor to the box labeled Find What:.

5. Type Hello, but don't press Enter. Remember that you press Enter only when you are ready to execute the command. In this case, you have more options to specify. By typing Hello, you have designated the word you want to change.

6. Press Tab. The cursor moves down to the box labeled Change To:.

7. Type Goodbye, but don't press Enter. Your screen should look like the one in Figure 4.4.

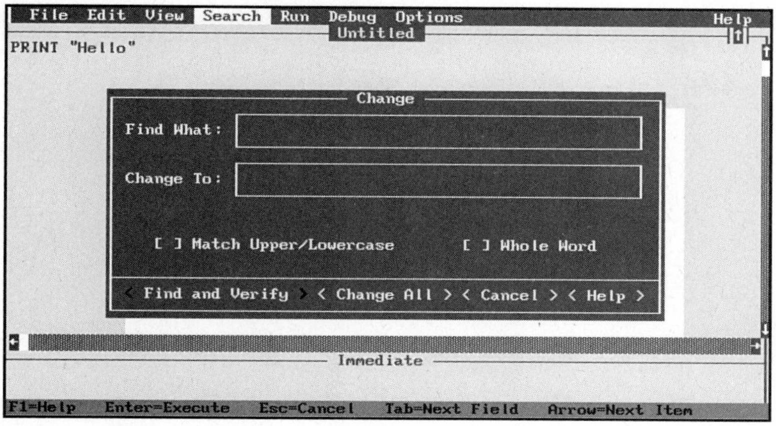

Figure 4.3.

The Change... command dialog box.

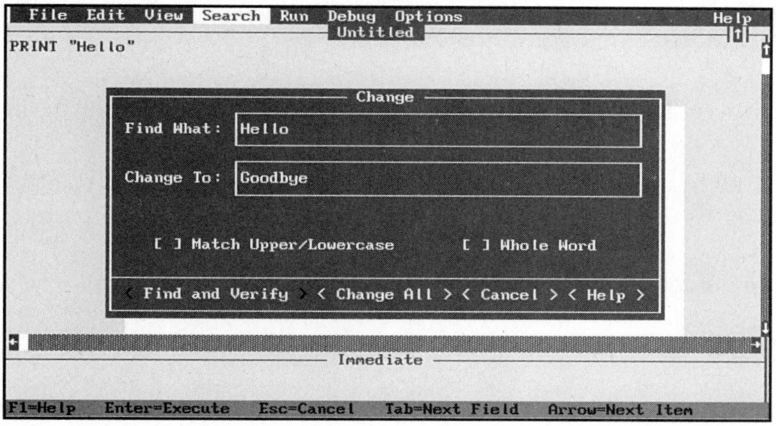

Figure 4.4.

Specifying the Find What and Change To options.

8. Press Tab to move the input focus to Match Upper/Lowercase. Repeatedly press the space bar or the highlighted letter—M in this case—to alternately turn the option on and off. (To see the highlighted letters, press Alt.)

   When the option is selected on, an X appears inside the brackets. When the option is selected off, no X appears inside the brackets. An option that can be turned on or off alternately with repeated keystrokes is called a *toggle*.

9. Toggle the option on by pressing the M key or the space bar. (The X should appear between the brackets.)

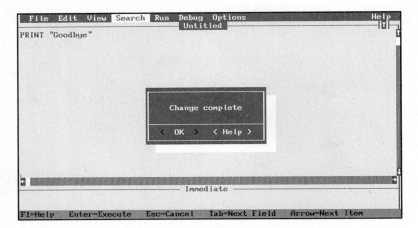

Figure 4.5.

The Change complete dialog box.

10. Press Tab to move the input focus to Whole Word. This option is another toggle, but leave this option switched off.

11. Press Tab to move the input focus to <Find and Verify>. Notice that this box is surrounded by highlighted angle brackets. The meaning of the highlights is explained in the next section.

12. Press Tab to move the input focus and the highlighted angle brackets to <Change All>.

13. Press Enter. The dialog box closes and a second dialog box labeled Change complete opens (see Figure 4.5). This new box informs you that the changes have been made and requests your confirmation before returning you to the editor.

14. Press Enter to select the <OK> option. The dialog box closes and you are back in the main editor.

    Your corrected one-line program should now look like the following:

    ```
    PRINT "Goodbye"
    ```

Understanding Highlights

Every dialog box contains one command alternative surrounded by highlighted angle brackets. This highlighted option identifies the action that takes place when you press Enter. Recall that you don't press Enter until you have *all* the dialog box options set the way you want.

If necessary, move the highlighted angle brackets to a desired option by repeatedly pressing Tab until the desired command is highlighted. Be sure not to press Enter until you have everything specified satisfactorily.

Using the Alt Key

Inside a dialog box, Alt is an "express" key. By pressing Alt and a highlighted letter, you activate an option even if the input focus is not in that respective area. Try the following exercise, which also demonstrates additional features of dialog boxes:

1. Reactivate the Change... command by pressing Alt-S (Search menu) and C. Your screen should look like Figure 4.6.

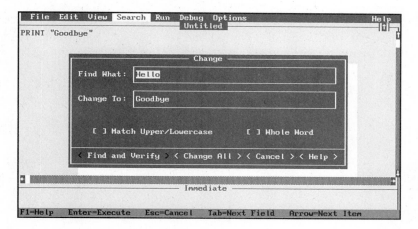

Figure 4.6.

Reactivating the Change... dialog box.

2. Compare Figures 4.3 and 4.6. This time, the dialog box opens with some options preset. The editor "remembers" what you typed earlier. This feature is a convenience because you often reissue a command such as Change... with the same or similar settings.

3. Hello is preset in the Find What: sub-box. Because the input focus is on this sub-box, you can start typing to change the value. Type something, but don't press Enter.

4. Press Alt. Notice how letters are highlighted in the various boxes. These highlighted letters work with the Alt key to select options.

5. Press Alt-W. This step toggles the Whole Word option and moves the input focus directly to Whole Word. You could set the Match Upper/Lowercase option similarly with Alt-M.

6. At this point, you could execute <Find and Verify> in one of the following two ways (but don't actually do it):

- ■ By pressing Enter. This step would work because the highlighted brackets are already on <Find and Verify>.

- ■ By pressing Alt-V. Notice that V is the highlighted letter in <Find and Verify>. Pressing the Alt key and a highlighted letter immediately executes the command.

7. Similarly, you could execute <Change All> in one of the following two ways (but, again, don't do it):

   - ■ By pressing Tab until the highlighted angle brackets move to <Change All>, and then pressing Enter.

   - ■ By pressing Alt-C. This step immediately executes <Change All>, even though the highlighted brackets are elsewhere. C is the highlighted letter.

8. Suppose that you decide against issuing the Change... command. You can close the dialog box and abort the command in one of the following two ways:

   - ■ By pressing Esc.

   - ■ By pressing Tab until the input focus is on Cancel, and then pressing Enter.

   Press Esc. The menu system closes and the program is ready for additional editing.

Exiting Without Saving

As you have seen, the Exit command on the File menu terminates a QBasic session. If you try to quit without saving a working program, the editor opens a dialog box to ask whether or not you want to save the program.

Running a Program and Viewing Output

After you have a program in the editor, you can run the program by following these steps:

1. Invoke the Run menu by pressing Alt-R.

2. Press Enter to select Start. The highlight bar is on Start when the Run menu opens.

As an alternative, you can use the Shift-F5 hotkey directly from the editor, which is equivalent to the two steps just mentioned.

You can interrupt a running program by pressing Ctrl-Break. You can then resume the program by using the Continue command on the Run menu or, equivalently, by pressing the F5 hotkey. Further, you can single-step through program execution. See Chapter 18, "Interactive Debugging and Testing," for a discussion of these topics and other debugging techniques.

For the time being, whenever you want to run a program that is already in the editor, press Shift-F5.

When you run a program, QBasic clears the editor screen and displays any existing output. When the program terminates, the message `Press any key to continue` appears at the bottom of the screen. When you press a key, the editor environment returns.

At this point, you should have the following one-line program in the editor:

```
PRINT "Goodbye"
```

Try running the program by following these steps:

1. Press Shift-F5.

2. The screen clears and QBasic displays your program's output, `Goodbye`. On the bottom of your screen, you see the message `Press any key to continue`.

3. Press a key. The editor is back in control.

When you are in the editor, you can view the output screen by selecting the Output Screen command from the View menu or alternatively by pressing the F4 hotkey. For example:

1. Press F4. The screen toggles to the previous output screen.

2. To return to the editor, press any key.

Understanding Windows

The QBasic screen is partitioned into windows. When you invoke QBasic, two windows are visible: the View window and the Immediate window. A third window, the Help window, opens when you request on-line help. Further, the View window can be split into two separate windows. Table 4.3 summarizes each QBasic window.

Table 4.3. QBasic windows.

Window	Brief Description
View	From here, the editor's nerve center, QBasic displays your programs and other text. All editing and text manipulation occurs in the View window. Editing techniques and splitting the View window are explained in Chapter 5, "Using the QBasic Editor."
Immediate	QBasic instructions typed in this window execute immediately. Using the Immediate window is discussed later in this chapter.
Help	The Help window opens at the top of the screen when you request on-line help from the Help menu. See Chapter 5.

Manipulating Windows

You can activate and resize windows using the following techniques:

- *To activate an alternate window:*

  Press F6 (or Shift-F6) to cycle the cursor from one window to another window. The window that contains the cursor is the *active* window. When a window is active, the Title bar for that window is highlighted.

- *To enlarge the active window one line:*

  Press Alt-*plus*, where *plus* is the gray + key near your numeric keypad.

- *To reduce the active window one line:*

  Press Alt-*minus*, where *minus* is the gray – key near your numeric keypad.

- *To make the active window fill the entire screen:*

  Press Ctrl-F10.

- *To return to a multiple-window screen after making the active window fill the entire screen:*

  Press Ctrl-F10. This keystroke is a toggle switch. Repeatedly pressing Ctrl-F10 alternates between a multiple-window view and a full-screen view of the active window.

Using the Immediate Window

The Immediate window executes QBasic instructions instantly. When you type a QBasic instruction in the Immediate window, the instruction runs as soon as you press Enter. Here are some of the things you can do with the Immediate window:

■ Calculate and display the value of any numeric or string expression

■ Display the value of a program variable after running or interrupting a program

■ Change the value of a variable and then resume execution of an interrupted program

■ Test a small group of QBasic instructions before adding the instructions to your program

If you have experience with GW-BASIC or BASICA, you will find the Immediate window similar to the direct mode of GW-BASIC and BASICA. With GW-BASIC or BASICA, any instruction you type without a line number executes immediately. With QBasic, any instruction you type in the Immediate window executes immediately.

Here is a short exercise to acquaint you with the Immediate window:

1. Activate the Immediate window by pressing F6 or Shift-F6 until the cursor moves inside the Immediate window. Notice that Immediate is highlighted.

2. Type **BEEP** and press Enter (see Figure 4.7). You should hear a beep from your speaker. BEEP is a QBasic instruction that sounds your speaker. (For more about BEEP, see Chapter 16, "Using Hardware Devices.")

3. Type the following instruction and press Enter:

   PRINT 25 / 16

   QBasic calculates the value of 25/16 and displays the result on the output screen.

4. Press any key to return to the Immediate window.

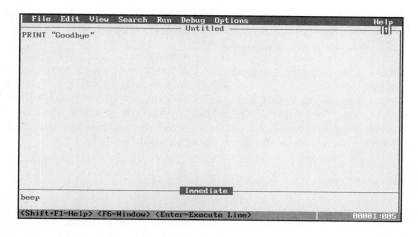

Figure 4.7.

Typing an instruction in the Immediate window.

5. Type the following instruction and press Enter:

   `A = 5`

   You just assigned the value 5 to a variable named A.

6. Type the following line and press Enter:

   `FOR Index = 1 TO A: PRINT "OK": NEXT Index`

   You should see OK displayed five times on your output screen. You placed a complete FOR-NEXT loop on one line by separating the individual instructions with a colon. Notice that QBasic "remembers" and uses the current value of A as the loop bound.

7. Press a key to return to the Immediate window.

8. Use the up- and down-arrow keys to scroll through the lines you have already typed.

9. Place the cursor back on the line that reads BEEP.

10. Press Enter. The speaker beeps. You can reexecute a line by placing the cursor on a previously typed line and then pressing Enter.

11. Expand the Immediate window to fill the entire screen by pressing Ctrl-F10. If you don't see all the lines you typed, press the up-arrow key until you do.

12. Shrink the Immediate window to its former size by pressing Ctrl-F10.

13. Press F6 to reactivate the View window.

The Immediate window can hold up to 10 lines at one time. Typing an additional line scrolls the first line off the screen. You can, however, type a new line over an existing line.

Splitting the View Window

You can split the View window horizontally. Doing so gives you a second copy of the current program in the new window. Both windows are visible simultaneously, but only one window is active at a time. You can perform any normal editing tasks in the active window. When you press Enter or move the cursor off a line, the text is updated in both windows. After you split a window, use the F6 key to move the focus from one window to another.

Splitting windows does not enable you to load a separate program independently in each window. You always work with two copies of the same program.

With split windows, you can do the following:

- View one section of the program in the dormant window while you edit a different section of the program in the active window.

- Cut and paste text from one window to the other.

- View user-defined procedures (subprograms and functions) in one window and the main program in the other window. See Chapter 17, "Modular Programming," for a discussion of user-defined procedures.

To split the View window, use the Split command on the View menu. Selecting Split a second time restores the single-window configuration.

Using a Mouse

A mouse is an excellent pointing device for graphics-based computer applications. However, for text-intensive applications such as programming, a mouse is less useful. The problem is that you continually move your hand back and forth between the keyboard and the mouse.

QBasic, nevertheless, supports a mouse. You can execute menu commands, many screen-manipulation tasks, and some text editing with a mouse. If you don't have a mouse, you can get along just fine. If you have a mouse, try it, and see what you think.

Installing a Mouse Driver

T I P

QBasic works with any Microsoft-compatible mouse and driver. If you have a mouse, you presumably know how to install and activate your mouse driver. If you are using MS-DOS 5, Microsoft supplies a mouse driver as part of your DOS package.

When the mouse is active, you see a special mouse cursor on-screen. The mouse cursor is a small rectangle about the size of one text character. As you move the mouse, the mouse cursor moves accordingly. Notice that the regular blinking cursor remains active. You can continue to use all the keyboard commands and features.

Here are some mouse pointers (pun intended):

- To open a menu and pop up the submenu, click on the menu name.

- To execute a submenu command, click on the command name in the submenu.

- To set an option in a dialog box, click on the desired option.

- To execute a dialog box action shown in angle brackets, click on the name between the brackets.

- To abort a menu, click on a location outside the menu.

- To activate a window, click anywhere inside the window.

- To move the cursor within the program, click on the desired location.

- To select text, drag the mouse over the text. That is, move the mouse pointer to one end of the text to be selected, then press and hold down the mouse button while you move the mouse across the text to be selected. Selecting text is explained in Chapter 5, "Using the QBasic Editor."

- To activate the editing window while a help screen is visible, click anywhere inside the editing window.

- To expand or shrink a window, drag the Title bar of the window up or down.

- To scroll the screen horizontally one character, click on the left- or right-arrow at either end of the horizontal scroll bar.

- To scroll the screen one character vertically, click on the up- or down-arrow at either end of the vertical scroll bar.

- To scroll text vertically to a desired position, move the mouse cursor to the scroll box, which is the inverted video rectangle inside the vertical scroll bar. Then drag the scroll box along the scroll bar to the desired position.

- To scroll text one page at a time, click on the vertical scroll bar anywhere between the scroll box and the top or bottom of the scroll bar.

- To scroll horizontally several positions at once, click on the horizontal scroll bar anywhere between the scroll box and the left or right end of the scroll bar.

- To execute a dialog box action shown in angle brackets, click on the name between the brackets.

- To execute any keystroke action shown in angle brackets in the Reference bar along the bottom of the screen, click on the name inside the angle brackets.

Appendix D, "Hotkeys and Mouse Commands," contains a comprehensive list of mouse techniques.

Customizing Your Screen's Appearance

The editor screen displays preset colors. You can customize most of these colors and other attributes with the Display... command from the Options menu.

If you have a color system, you might want different colors for the foreground and background text.

Also, if you do not use a mouse with the editor, you can remove the scroll bars.

Changing Colors and Removing Scroll Bars

To experiment with the options, try the following exercise:

1. Invoke the Options menu by pressing Alt-O.

2. Press Enter to select Display... (the highlight is already on Display...). A dialog box similar to Figure 4.8 opens. Depending on your hardware, the options shown in your dialog box might vary slightly from those shown in Figure 4.8.

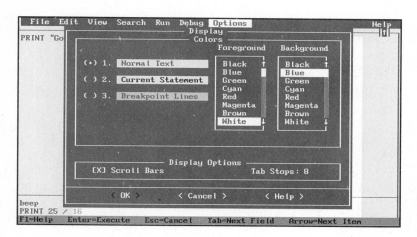

Figure 4.8.

The Display... dialog box.

3. The input focus is on Normal Text, which refers to the regular text displayed in the View and Immediate windows. A dot appears inside the parentheses adjacent to the term Normal Text. This dot, which indicates the currently selected option, is called a *button*. Press the up- or down-arrow keys to move the input focus to Current Statement and to Breakpoint Lines. (These options refer to lines displayed while you are debugging. See Chapter 18, "Interactive Debugging and Testing.") Notice how the button moves to indicate the option currently selected.

4. Press the up- or down-arrow key until the button is once again next to option 1, Normal Text.

5. Press Tab to move the input focus to the Foreground box. You can now select a new foreground text color (for normal text) by pressing the up- and down-arrow keys. The foreground box cycles through the colors available with your particular video hardware. Notice the text next to button 1, which reads Normal Text. As you press the arrow keys, the message in this box is displayed with the current foreground and background colors. Select a new foreground color by moving the highlight to your color choice. Don't press Enter yet because you have more selections to make before closing this dialog box.

6. Press Tab to move the input focus to the Background box.

7. Select a new background color in a manner similar to the way you selected a new foreground color.

8. Press Enter to return to the editor screen. You should see your new colors in use.

9. Repeat steps 1 and 2 to reopen the dialog box.

10. Press Tab several times to move the input focus to Scroll Bars. The X inside the brackets indicates that, currently, scroll bars are displayed.

11. Press the space bar or S to remove the X. This deselects the display of scroll bars.

12. Press Enter.

The scroll bars should be gone from your screen (see Figure 4.9).

If you don't use a mouse, you might consider removing the scroll bars. Many users think the screen has a less cluttered look with the scroll bars removed. Take your choice.

The Tab Stops option (in the Display... dialog box) is discussed in the next chapter.

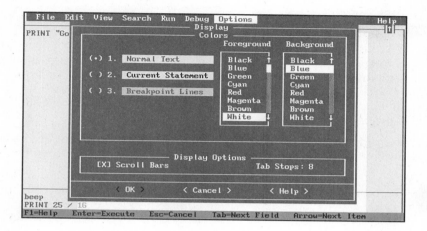

Figure 4.9.

Removing the scroll bars.

Saving Your Customized Settings

If you change one or more display options, QBasic automatically creates a file named QBASIC.INI that stores a record of your new screen configuration. QBasic saves QBASIC.INI in the directory containing your QBASIC.EXE file. (This directory is \DOS for most systems.)

When you restart at a later time, QBasic uses QBASIC.INI to restore the screen with your customized settings.

Every time you start QBasic, it looks for QBASIC.INI in the default directory or in the directory chain established by the PATH statements in your AUTOEXEC.BAT file. If you restart from a different directory, be sure that the editor has access to the QBASIC.INI file.

If you want to restore QBasic's original screen configuration, erase the QBASIC.INI file.

Terminating QBasic

Use the Exit command from the File menu to terminate a QBasic session. Before you quit, if you have an unsaved program in the environment, QBasic opens a dialog box to ask whether you want to save the program.

Summary

Like most of today's sophisticated computer applications, QBasic runs in a full-featured, menu-driven environment. Some of the features available from the menu system include managing files, searching and replacing text, running programs, and customizing your screen appearance. The environment supports a mouse and provides on-line help.

The main programming screen is partitioned into multiple windows. The large View window contains the text of the program currently in the environment. You can directly execute a QBasic instruction from the Immediate window.

With an understanding of the general working environment, you are ready for the next chapter, which discusses program editing in detail. Chapter 5, "Using the QBasic Editor," explains how the full-screen editor works and offers more detail about commands available from the menu system.

Using the QBasic Editor

Not only is the QBasic editor noteworthy as just a general text handler, it is also "smart." Every time you type a line, the editor checks for legal QBasic syntax. Minor errors are corrected automatically. Many other syntax errors elicit a diagnostic message when you press Enter. Some errors are not caught until you try to run the program.

Also, the editor manipulates each of your typed instructions into a standard-ized format: keywords in uppercase, one space between operators, and so on. You soon will become familiar with this formatting as you follow the examples throughout this chapter. The editor is adapted superbly to the creation of QBasic programs.

This chapter, a hands-on guide to the editor, is full of practical examples. To demonstrate editing techniques, we will build a simple program from scratch and use various editing techniques along the way. You will remember these techniques much better if you follow along on your own computer.

Here are some of the major subjects covered:

- Creating a program
- Editing existing lines
- Searching and replacing text
- Saving and loading files
- Using on-line help
- Making program listings on your printer

NOTE

You Might Already Be Familiar with the QBasic Editor!

If you are familiar with the MS-DOS editor supplied with MS-DOS 5, you will have no trouble learning the QBasic editor. Why? Because you *already* know how to use the QBasic editor!

The QBasic editor and the MS-DOS editor are closely related editors that share the same "look and feel." Both editors use the same operating environment: full-screen editing and similar drop-down menus. Editing techniques, mouse commands, and hotkeys are the same.

The major difference between the two editors is that the QBasic editor is adapted for working with programs whereas the MS-DOS editor is designed for text documents. The QBasic editor adds commands to run programs, view output, and debug errors. Also, the QBasic editor checks what you type for conformity with proper QBasic syntax.

MS-DOS furnishes QBasic in the file named QBASIC.EXE. This single file not only includes the QBasic programming language but the QBasic editor as well.

The MS-DOS editor is actually a stripped-down version of the QBasic editor. When you run the MS-DOS editor, the computer invokes the QBASIC.EXE file, extracts the editor from the file, and "discards" the part of the editor that specifically applies to QBasic programming.

The QBasic and MS-DOS editors share the same QBASIC.EXE file. That's why the editors are so similar.

Both the QBasic editor and the MS-DOS editor save files as pure text files in ASCII format. You can readily load files created with one editor into the other editor.

However, the two editors make different assumptions about the files that you create. In QBasic, the editor assumes that you are working on a QBasic program. The QBasic editor saves files with the .BAS extension if you don't specify an explicit extension.

In contrast, the MS-DOS editor makes no particular assumption about the type of text document being edited. By default, files are saved with the .TXT extension.

Typing a Program

When you start QBasic and begin to type, the editor assumes that you are creating a program. Every time you press Enter, QBasic examines the line you just typed for the following characteristics:

- *Syntax.* Many syntax errors cause a warning message to be displayed. Usually the message tells you exactly what kind of error was detected, such as a missing keyword or punctuation symbol. Some minor syntax errors are corrected automatically. Other syntax errors are diagnosed only when you run the program.

- *Format.* Each line of your program must conform to a standard format— keywords in uppercase, one space between operators, and so on. The editor automatically reformats each of your typed lines when you press Enter.

- *Consistency.* The editor checks for consistency and makes corrections. All occurrences of the same variable name, for example, are adjusted to consistent upper- and lowercase. Duplicate labels are not permitted.

Try the following exercise to familiarize yourself with the smart editor:

1. Start QBasic.

2. Type `print` in lowercase and press Enter. QBasic converts this keyword to uppercase: `PRINT`.

3. Type `print"Hello` and press Enter; leave no spaces on either side of the quotation mark, and don't type a trailing quotation mark. QBasic converts the line to `PRINT "Hello"`.

    Standard format requires a space after `PRINT`. A missing trailing quotation mark, which is a minor syntax error, was caught and corrected.

4. Type `print 0.3` and press Enter. QBasic converts the line to `PRINT .3`.

    QBasic has a standard format for displaying numbers. The editor automatically converts numbers you type to the standard format.

5. Type `MYAGE=32` and press Enter; do not leave a space on either side of the equal sign. QBasic adds a space before and after the equal sign. Standard format requires a space on both sides of an operator (such as the equal sign).

6. Type `PRINT MyAge` and press Enter. Notice the combination of upper- and lowercase. Nothing happens to this line, but look closely at the previous line. It now reads

    `MyAge = 32`

MyAge is a variable name. For consistency, when you type a variable name in a new line, QBasic adjusts all other occurrences of the same variable name to conform with the new upper- and lowercase form.

7. Type PRINT SQR(25(and press Enter. (Notice that both parentheses are left parentheses.) SQR is the square-root function. A dialog box opens (see Figure 5.1) with a message warning you about a syntax error. QBasic expects the second parenthesis to be a right parenthesis; instead, you typed an erroneous left parenthesis. Notice the highlight on the offending left parenthesis in your source program.

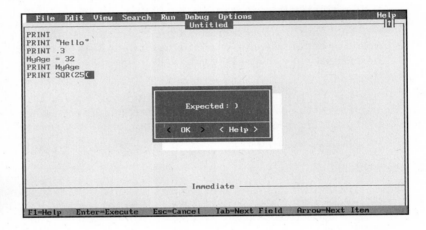

Figure 5.1.

A diagnostic dialog box.

8. Press Enter to close the dialog box. The cursor returns to your program at the location of the error.

9. To correct the error, press Del and then). Then press Enter. Your screen should look like Figure 5.2.

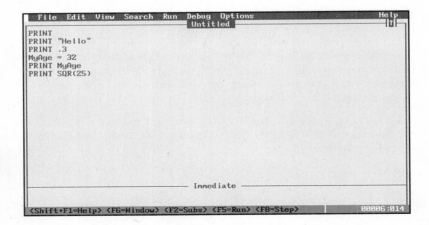

Figure 5.2.

A partially completed program with the detected error corrected.

When an error message dialog box opens, you do not have to correct the error. After you close the dialog box, you can move the cursor off of the offending line. Of course, if you don't correct the error, you get an error message when you try to run the program.

Fundamental Editing Techniques

Editing is a skill—almost a craft. Some editing techniques are simple and others are more complex. Many editing tasks can be performed in more than one way.

This section introduces the more fundamental skills, which include moving the cursor, scrolling, and inserting and deleting text.

Keypad Interface and WordStar-Style Interface

Editing commands require one or more keystroke sequences. People who have word-processing experience generally come from one of two camps, divided by the keystroke interface with which they feel most familiar:

- *Keypad interface:* the specialized IBM PC keys—the arrow keys, Ins, Del, and so on—govern most editing activities. To move the cursor up, for example, you use the up-arrow key.

- *WordStar-style interface:* Ctrl-key sequences govern most editing activities. To move the cursor up, for example, you press Ctrl-E.

For the most part, QBasic accommodates both camps. The majority of editing techniques are available with both keypad and WordStar-style key sequences. Some techniques require only one style and not the other one. In this chapter, we give preference to the keypad style. The WordStar-style key combination is not mentioned unless an editing technique requires it.

Appendix D, "Hotkeys and Mouse Commands," presents a complete list of editing keystrokes in both styles.

The Location Counter

Look at the right end of the Reference bar, in the lower right corner of your screen. You see two numbers, separated by a colon. The two numbers indicate the cursor's location within your file. The first number is the current row; the second number is the current column.

Use the arrow keys to move the cursor, and watch the numbers change. Press Num Lock; a capital N appears next to the location numbers to indicate that Num Lock is on. Press Num Lock a few more times to toggle the indicator on and off. Press Caps Lock; a capital C appears in the same area to indicate that the Caps Lock key is on.

Building a Sample Program

Your screen should look like the one in Figure 5.2. To demonstrate different editing techniques, follow these steps to expand the program you are creating:

1. If the cursor is not in column 1, repeatedly press the left arrow key until the cursor is at the leftmost column.

2. Press the down-arrow key repeatedly, or hold the key down until the cursor stops on the empty line just below the line that reads PRINT SQR(25). Notice that you cannot move the cursor below this line except, possibly, for a line or two.

3. Press Enter several times until the location counter reads 00015:001. Pressing Enter creates blank lines.

4. Type REM This is line 15 and press Enter. A REM instruction indicates a remark or comment in your program (see the previous chapter).

5. Press Enter until the location counter reads 00025:001.

6. Type REM This is line 25.

7. Press Enter until the location counter reads 00035:001.

8. Type REM followed by any long combination of letters and numbers. Keep typing until the cursor is at least to column 120. (Look at the location counter to verify the column location.) It doesn't matter what you type. Now press Enter. Notice how the screen scrolls horizontally as you type a long line. When you press Enter, QBasic returns to column 1.

9. Press Enter until the location reads 00050:001.

10. Type REM This is the end of the program.

11. Press Enter.

Moving the Cursor

After you have a program in the editor, you can move the cursor around the program in several ways. Experiment. Try the following techniques as you read them:

- To move to the beginning of the program, press Ctrl-Home.

- To move to the end of the program, press Ctrl-End.

- To move left or right one character, press Left or Right (the left- or right-arrow keys).

- To move up or down one line, press Up or Down (the up- or down-arrow keys).

- To move left one indentation level on the current line, press Home. This moves to column 1 if the line is not indented from the left margin.

- To move to column 1 in the current line, press the left arrow repeatedly (or press Ctrl-Q-S).

- To move to the last column in the current line, press End.

- To move left or right by one word, press Ctrl-Left or Ctrl-Right.

To get more familiar with these techniques, try the following exercise:

1. Press Ctrl-Home to move the cursor to the beginning of the file.

2. Use the four arrow keys to move the cursor around the first few lines. Notice that the up-and-down movement keeps the cursor in the same column.

3. Press Home and End alternately. Watch the cursor jump between the beginning and the end of the line.

4. Press Ctrl-Home.

5. Hold down the Ctrl key. Now press Right several times. Watch the cursor move a word at a time. What happens when you reach the end of a line? The cursor jumps down to the first word in the next line. Continue until you get to the REM instruction in line 25.

6. Press Ctrl-Left repeatedly. Notice the similar effect. When you reach the beginning of a line, the cursor jumps to the end of the line above.

Scrolling

Scrolling is the block movement of the text inside the View window. By scrolling, you adjust the visible portion of your program. Scrolling, which can be horizontal as well as vertical, keeps the cursor at the same row and column number.

- To scroll up one line, press Up when the cursor is in the uppermost row of the window.

- To scroll down one line, press Down when the cursor is in the bottom row of the window.

- To scroll up or down one line no matter where the cursor is positioned, press Ctrl-Up or Ctrl-Down.

- To scroll right one character, press Right when the cursor is at the rightmost boundary of the window.

- To scroll left one character, press Left when the cursor is at the leftmost boundary but not in column 1. Note: You cannot scroll left unless you have previously scrolled right.

- To scroll one page up or down, press PgUp or PgDn.

- To scroll one window left or right, press Ctrl-PgUp or Ctrl-PgDn.

The PgUp and PgDn keys make large-scale scrolling possible. Try these keys by themselves and in conjunction with the Ctrl key.

Inserting Text in a Line

Use these steps to insert text in an existing line:

1. Move the cursor to the position where you want to insert text.

2. Type the text that you want to insert.

3. Use a cursor-movement key, typically an arrow key, to move off the line.

As you type, text to the right of the cursor moves rightward to accommodate the inserted text. When you move from the line, QBasic checks the entire line for syntax, as though you typed the line for the first time. If the resulting line has a syntax error, a dialog box opens with a diagnostic message. Don't press Enter to move off the line. As explained later in this chapter, pressing Enter splits the line in two.

Try this example:

1. Move the cursor to the 3 in the program line that reads MyAge = 32. This line is the fourth program line.

2. Type 10+. Notice how the text moves to accommodate the insertion.

3. Press the down-arrow key. To conform with standard format, QBasic adds a space on either side of the plus sign.

```
PRINT MyAge = 10 + 32
```

Deleting Text in a Line

Use either one of the following two methods to delete a few characters inside a line:

■ Move the cursor under the character you want to delete. Press Del. To delete consecutive characters, continue pressing Del.

■ Move the cursor to the character just to the right of the character you want to delete. Press the Backspace key.

Most people find the first method more natural. Try both methods and make your own choice.

Splitting and Joining Lines

The following exercise demonstrates splitting and joining lines:

1. Move the cursor under the equal sign in the line that reads

   ```
   MyAge = 10 + 32
   ```

2. Press Enter. The line splits in two, and the second half moves down to form a new line. Succeeding lines are pushed down to accommodate the new line. The text in the vicinity of the split should look like the following lines:

   ```
   MyAge
   = 10 + 32
   PRINT MyAge
   ```

   The cursor is under the equal sign.

3. Press Backspace. The split fragment rejoins the line above. When you press Backspace with the cursor in column 1, the current line appends to the end of the line above it. Lines beneath the split line move up one line.

Inserting and Deleting an Entire Line

Use the techniques in this section to insert and delete an entire line.

To delete an entire line:

1. Place the cursor anywhere on the line.

2. Press Ctrl-Y.

To insert a blank line between two lines:

1. Move the cursor to column 1 in the lower of the two lines.

2. Press Ctrl-N. If you prefer, you can press Enter and then move the cursor up to the new blank line.

Overtyping

By default, the editor operates in *insert* mode. That means that, when you type text while the cursor is inside a line, the new text is inserted. Alternately, you can *overtype*. In overtype mode, the newly typed text replaces the former text.

To turn on overtype mode, press Ins. The cursor changes from a blinking line to a blinking box. The larger cursor signifies overtype mode, in which anything you type replaces the text being typed on. To return to standard insert mode, press Ins again. The Ins key acts as a toggle switch which alternates back and forth between insert mode and overtype mode.

Block Editing

You can edit blocks of text as a single unit. This section presents the following techniques:

- Selecting text for block operations
- Using the clipboard
- Cutting and pasting blocks of text

Selecting Text

A block of selected text is always a series of consecutive characters. The block might be one character, a few characters, a line, several lines, or even your whole program. A selected block appears in reverse video.

Follow these steps to select a block of text:

1. Move the cursor to one end of the block.

2. While you hold down the Shift key, use cursor-movement keys to select the block.

Appendix D, "Hotkeys and Mouse Commands," contains a table of the keys used for selecting text. In general, to select text you use the same keys you use to move the cursor.

After you have selected a block, you can deselect the block by pressing any arrow key (don't use Shift, however). The reverse video disappears, showing that the entire block is deselected.

Understanding the Clipboard

QBasic maintains a text storage area known as the *clipboard,* which acts like a halfway house for text. You can place a block of text into the clipboard and later retrieve the block. The clipboard is most commonly used either to delete an entire block of your program or to cut and paste (to move or copy a program block from one place to another).

The clipboard stores only one block of text at a time. You cannot add or subtract incrementally from the block. Whenever you place text in the clipboard, the new block of text completely replaces the previous contents. Similarly, retrieval is all or nothing. You cannot retrieve partial contents of the clipboard.

Working with Blocks

QBasic supports four block-oriented editing techniques (see Table 5.1). Each technique is available from the Edit menu by pressing Alt-E or by using the hotkey indicated in the table.

Table 5.1. Block-editing techniques.

Command	Hotkey	Description
Cut	Shift-Del	Deletes selected text from the program and places the selected text in the clipboard
Copy	Ctrl-Ins	Places a copy of the selected text in the clipboard. The text in the program remains selected.
Paste	Shift-Ins	Inserts clipboard text into the program at the cursor. A copy of the text remains in the clipboard. If the program currently has selected text, the clipboard text replaces the selected text.
Clear	Del	Deletes selected text from the program but leaves no effect on the clipboard.

To demonstrate some block-editing techniques, the following exercise copies program lines to a new location:

1. Press Ctrl-Home to return the cursor to the beginning of the program.

2. While you press the Shift key, press Down four times. You have selected the first four lines of the program, which are displayed in reverse video.

3. Invoke the Edit menu by pressing Alt-E.

4. Move the cursor down to Copy (see Figure 5.3).

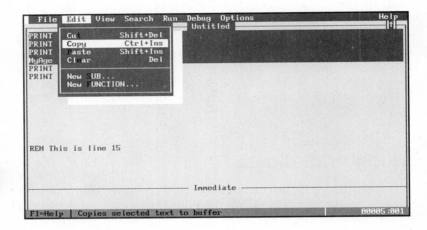

Figure 5.3.

Selecting Copy on the Edit menu.

5. Press Enter. A copy of the selected text moves to the clipboard.

6. Move the cursor to column 1 of line 10. Notice that the reverse video disappears. Pressing an arrow key deactivates any selected text.

7. Press Shift-Ins, which is the hotkey for Paste. A copy of the clipboard text is inserted at the cursor location. (The clipboard still retains a copy of the pasted text. You can insert additional copies of the clipboard text at new program locations.)

8. Move the cursor down to the next REM instruction.

9. Press Shift-Down five times. This step selects a block of text. Most of the lines are blank.

10. Press Shift-Ins. A copy of the clipboard text replaces the selected lines.

Searching and Replacing

The Search menu offers several options for finding, searching, and replacing text. These capabilities are most useful in long programs.

From the Search menu, you can do the following:

- Find one or more occurrences of a designated text string (which might be a variable name, label name, QBasic reserved word, string literal, or numeric literal)

- Replace one or more occurrences of a designated text string with a second text string

Finding or replacing text always involves a *search string,* which is the target of the search. A search string can be a single character or, more likely, a word or several consecutive characters. You cannot search for a string that spans two or more lines. The search string is confined to a group of characters that occupy a single line. As you see later, you can specify a search string in many different ways.

Searching begins at the cursor location and proceeds through your program. If the end of the program is reached, the search wraps around until the entire program is traversed. Table 5.2 summarizes the three commands available on the Search menu.

Table 5.2. Search menu commands.

Command	Hotkey	Description
Find...	None	Opens a dialog box in which you specify the search string. Finds the search string in your program.
Repeat Last Find	F3	Searches for the text specified in the last Find... command.
Change...	None	Replaces one text string with another, as explained later in this chapter.

Using Find...

To become familiar with the Find... command, try this exercise:

1. Press Ctrl-Home to return the cursor to the beginning of the program.

2. Invoke the Search menu by pressing Alt-S. Your screen should look like Figure 5.4.

3. Press Enter to select Find.... A dialog box opens with the input focus on the Find What: box. The word PRINT appears in the dialog box. When the dialog box opens, the Find What: box contains the word that appears at the current cursor location.

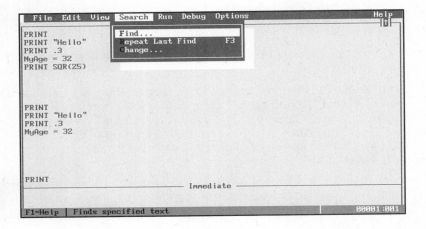

Figure 5.4.

The Search menu.

4. Type **Age** = but don't press Enter yet. Your screen should look like Figure 5.5.

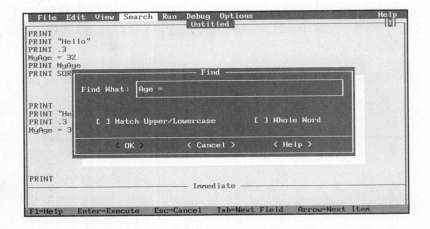

Figure 5.5.

The Find... dialog box.

5. Press Enter. QBasic locates the first occurrence of the search string in your file and selects (highlights) the found text.

6. Press F3, which is the hotkey for Repeat Last Find. QBasic moves to the next occurrence of the search string.

7. Press F3 several times to repeat the search.

Look again at Figure 5.5. The search is restricted by the following available options in the dialog box:

- Match Upper/Lowercase: If this option is not selected, upper- and lowercase letters are not differentiated. If the option is selected, upper- and lowercase letters must match exactly.

- Whole Word: If this option is selected, the search string must be an independent word—that is, not surrounded by letters, digits, or the characters %, &, !, #, or $. (The latter characters are data-type indicators that can be used as final characters of variable names.)

Using Change... on the Search Menu

The Change... command is demonstrated in Chapter 4, "Learning the QBasic Environment," in the section titled "Trying a Dialog Box Example." The purpose of that demonstration was to show the use of dialog boxes. You can review that demonstration to see how the Change... command works. Refer to Figures 4.3 through 4.6.

Notice that the Change... dialog box contains several options indicated with angle brackets. The following explains how these options affect the way Change... works:

<Find and Verify>   This option finds each occurrence of the target string (which you specify in the Find What: box) one at a time. When each occurrence of the target string is found, a second dialog box opens. This dialog box gives you the choice of making the substitution, skipping ahead to the next occurrence, or canceling the remaining search for more occurrences.

<Change All>   This option changes all occurrences of the target string to the string specified in the Change To: box. The changes occur all at once. A dialog box opens to inform you when the substitutions are complete.

<Cancel>   This option aborts the Change... command and closes the dialog box without making any substitutions. This option is equivalent to pressing Esc.

Indenting

When you type a line and press Enter, QBasic drops the cursor down one line but returns to the column where you began the previous line. In this way, you conveniently can type a series of indented lines. Indentation provides better readability in your programs, especially in structured sections of instructions such as FOR-NEXT loops.

Try these steps:

1. Move the cursor to column 1 of a blank line.

2. Type FOR Q = 1 TO 10 and press Enter.

3. Press the space bar three times to move the cursor to column 4.

4. Type PRINT and press Enter. Notice that the cursor remains indented on column 4.

5. Type PRINT Q and press Enter. The cursor remains indented.

6. Press Home to cancel the automatic indentation and return the cursor to column 1.

7. Type NEXT Q and press Enter.

The short program block should look like the following:

```
FOR Q = 1 TO 10
   PRINT
   PRINT Q
NEXT Q
```

You can nest indentation levels. Every time you press Enter, the cursor returns to the current level.

Tabbing

By default, tab stops are set every eight spaces. Anytime you press the Tab key, the cursor moves rightward to the beginning of the next tab zone. All text that started to the right of the cursor moves rightward when you press Tab.

Here are some additional tabbing techniques:

■ To indent an existing line a full tab position:

1. Move the cursor to the first (leftmost) column of the line.

2. Press Tab.

■ To remove leading spaces and move a line to the left:

1. Move the cursor anywhere on the line.

2. Press Shift-Tab.

■ To indent or "un-indent" an entire block of lines:

1. Select the target lines in the usual manner (while holding down the Shift key, press one of the cursor-movement keys).

2. Press Tab to indent the entire block, or Shift-Tab to "un-indent" the entire block.

■ To change the default tab stops from eight positions to something else:

1. Select Display... from the Options menu.

2. Press Tab several times to move the input focus to Tab stops:.

3. Type a new value for the number of characters per tab stop.

4. Press Enter to close the dialog box.

Turning Off Syntax Checking

Use the Syntax Checking command on the Options menu to alternately turn syntax checking on and off (see Figure 5.6). When you see a bullet alongside the name Syntax Checking, as shown in Figure 5.6, syntax checking is on.

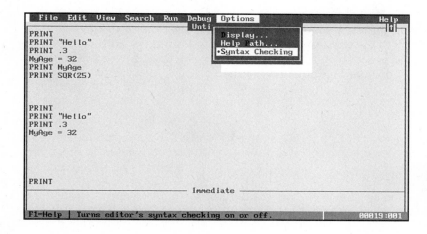

Figure 5.6.

Selecting Syntax Checking.

When syntax checking is turned off, QBasic still formats each line as you type. The following rules apply:

- If you type a line that contains illegal syntax, QBasic leaves the line alone. No error message is displayed, and no reformatting occurs. Of course, when you run the program, you get an error at this line.

- If you type a line that conforms to valid syntax, QBasic reformats the line to follow the editor's usual standards by capitalizing keywords, adding spaces, and so on.

Using Place Markers

A *place marker* designates a specific location—a row and column—in your text. You can set as many as four different place markers. After you set a place marker, you can instantly move the cursor from anywhere in your program to that marker's location. The markers are invisible. No character is displayed in the text to indicate a set marker.

To set a place marker, press Ctrl-K*n*, where *n* is a number from 0 to 3. This associates the current cursor position with the marker numbered *n*. To move the cursor to a previously set place marker, press Ctrl-Q*n*, where *n* is marker 0 to 3.

Splitting the View Window

You can split the View window horizontally in two. Doing so gives you a second copy of the current program in the new window. Both windows are visible simultaneously, but only one window at a time is active. You can perform any ordinary editing tasks in the active window. When you press Enter or move the cursor off a line, the text is updated in both windows. After you split a window, use the F6 key to move the focus from one window to another.

Splitting windows does not enable you to load a separate program independently in each window. You always work with two copies of the same program.

With split windows, you can do the following:

- View one section of the program in the dormant window while you edit a different section of the program in the active window.

- Cut and paste text from one window to the other.

- View user-defined procedures in one window and the main program in the other window.

To split a window, use the Split command on the View window. Selecting Split a second time restores the single-window configuration.

Managing Files

The QBasic editor closely oversees your disk files. Programs and other files can be saved and loaded. We assume that you are acquainted with the fundamentals of DOS disk files: names, paths, and directories. If you need a refresher, see Chapter 14, "Using Sequential Disk Files."

Overview of the File Menu

The File menu (see Figure 5.7) is your command center for loading and saving files. Here is a summary of the commands available on the File menu:

- The New command erases the file currently in the QBasic environment. The result is a clean slate, as though you just initialized QBasic. If the file previously was saved on disk, the disk copy is not erased; only the work copy in memory is erased.

- The Open... command loads a file from disk into the QBasic environment. You also can use this command to view a list of filenames in any directory.

- The Save command saves the current file to disk.

- The Save As... command saves the current file to disk after prompting you for the filename.

- The Print... command prints listings on a line printer.

- The Exit command terminates QBasic and returns to DOS.

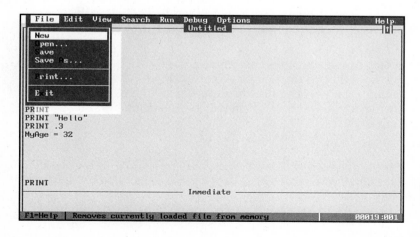

Figure 5.7.

The File menu.

Saving a File

When you save a file for the first time, you must specify the following two file attributes:

- The file path—the directory or disk on which to save the file
- The filename

QBasic stores programs as disk files in ASCII format. Such files are text files that most text editors and word processors can manipulate. QBasic does not support the compressed or tokenized file formats available with QuickBASIC or GW-BASIC/BASICA.

T I P   **Some File-Management Guidelines**

Here are a few file-management maxims:

- Until you give a file a name, QBasic displays the temporary name Untitled in the title bar.

- When you save a program, QBasic adds a .BAS extension to the filename if you do not specify another extension.

- If you try to leave QBasic without first saving a program in the editor, a dialog box opens to warn you. The same warning occurs if you try to open a new file without first saving a program in the editor.

Using the Save As... Command

Follow these steps to save the currently Untitled file:

1. Invoke the Save As... command from the File menu by pressing Alt-F and then A. A dialog box opens, as shown in Figure 5.8. Below the words File Name: you see the current path specification, which is C:\DOS in our example.

2. Type MYPROG (upper- or lowercase) in the File Name: box, but don't press Enter. QBasic will add the default file extension .BAS when you press Enter. If you want a different extension, specify the extension as part of the filename. If you want no extension, use a trailing period: MYPROG., for example.

3. Press Enter to save the file.

QBasic saves your file on disk. The filename appears in the Title bar as MYPROG.BAS. QBasic saves the file in the directory specified by the current path which, in the present example, is the root directory of the C: drive.

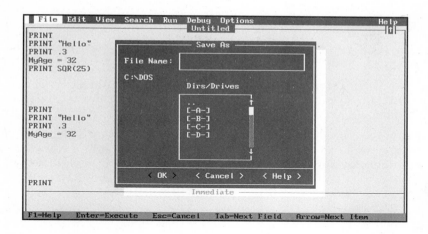

Figure 5.8.

The Save As... dialog box.

The Save As... command is commonly used for storing a second version of a file in a different directory or with a different name. Try the following steps:

1. Invoke the Save As... command from the File menu. The File Name: box contains the current filename.

2. Type **MEAGAIN**.

3. Press Enter.

QBasic stores the file on disk as MEAGAIN.BAS and changes the name accordingly in the Title bar. The file MYPROG remains stored on disk.

To store a file in a directory other than that specified by the current path, type the new directory path as part of the filename. For example, if you type the filename **PROGRAMS****MYWORK**, QBasic stores the file with the name MYWORK.BAS in the directory C:\PROGRAMS. After saving the file, the name MYWORK.BAS appears in the Title bar of the View window. When you subsequently invoke the Save As... dialog box, you will see the default directory path specified as C:\PROGRAMS. When you save a new file, if you specify the filename without including an explicit path, QBasic stores the file in the C:\PROGRAMS directory.

You can use this technique also to save files on different disk drives. For example, type the filename as **A:****MYPROG** to save the file in the root directory of the disk in the A: drive.

Using the Save Command

Use the Save command to store a program that you already have named. No dialog box appears. The file is stored on disk.

If you use the Save command when the file still remains untitled, QBasic opens the dialog box shown in Figure 5.8. The effect is the same as if you used the Save As... command instead.

The Save command provides an "express" save. When you edit a file, use the Save command periodically to update the current version of the file on disk. This precaution provides insurance against disasters such as power failures.

Using the Open... Command

After you have program files stored on disk, you can load a program into QBasic with the Open... command. Because this command lists files in any directory, you also can use Open... to search your directories for particular filenames. When you select Open..., a dialog box pops open. Figure 5.9 shows a representative example of this dialog box. Study this figure in conjunction with the following discussion.

The upper box is called the File Name: box. Below it is the current directory path (C:\ in Figure 5.9). The lower left box is the Files box, and the lower right box is the Dirs/Drives box. In the File Name: box, you can type an individual filename (with path), a directory path, or a name using the * and ? wildcard characters. By default, this box contains *.BAS, which is the wildcard designation for all files with a .BAS extension.

By specifying a path, you change the default directory path. If you don't specify a specific file or a group of files (using the wildcard characters), QBasic assumes the wildcard filename *.BAS. This name specifies all files in the current directory whose filename extension is .BAS.

The Files box contains the names of all files that satisfy the current directory path and filename specification. In Figure 5.9, the Files box shows all files that satisfy the path C:*.BAS.

The Dirs/Drives box lists any subdirectories that branch off the current directory path and all disk drives found in the environment. By pressing Tab a sufficient number of times, you can move the input focus to this box. Now, by pressing the up- and down-arrow keys, you can move the highlight to one of the directories or drives listed in this box. When you now press Enter, the default path changes accordingly.

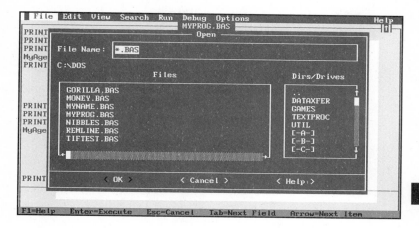

Figure 5.9.

The Open... dialog box.

Listing Directory Contents

To see a list of any directory's contents, just type the complete directory path in the File Name: box. You can group files by using wildcard characters. The Files box is updated appropriately to display all filenames that satisfy your directory path and wildcard designations. Table 5.3 shows some examples of file specifications that might be typed in the File Name: box.

Table 5.3. Sample file specifications.

Specification	Files Listed
.	All files in the current directory
MY*.*	All files (in the current directory) whose names begin with MY
MY?.*	All files (in the current directory) whose names begin with MY followed by a single character and that have any file extension.
B:*.*	All files in the root directory of drive B:
C:\ABC*.*	All files in the directory C:\ABC

Loading a Program

To load a specific program into the editor, use one of the following two techniques:

- Type the name of the specific file in the File Name: box. You can include a path or rely on the default path as shown below the box. QBasic assumes the extension .BAS if you do not specify an explicit extension. For example, with reference to Figure 5.9, type MYPROG to load the file specified by the complete path C:\MYPROG.BAS.

- Use the Files box if it contains the desired filename.

    1. Press Tab to move the input focus to the Files box.

    2. Use the arrow keys to highlight the desired filename. Alternatively, you can press the first letter of the filename to move the highlight.

    3. Press Enter.

    QBasic loads the desired program ready for you to edit or run.

CAUTION

Loading BASICA or GW-BASIC Programs

You can load a BASICA or GW-BASIC program into the QBasic environment only if the program is stored in ASCII format. QBasic cannot read the standard "tokenized" files saved with BASICA/GW-BASIC. To save a BASICA/GW-BASIC file in ASCII format, use the A parameter with the SAVE command in BASICA. For example:

```
SAVE "MYPROG.BAS", A
```

For more details, see Chapter 24, "Comparing the GW-BASIC (BASICA) Language to QBasic." You might also consult your BASICA or GW-BASIC documentation.

Loading a Program When Starting QBasic

You can load a previously saved program into the editor at the same time that you invoke QBasic. The technique depends on whether you are starting QBasic from the DOS Shell or from the command line:

- *Starting QBasic from the DOS 5 Shell*—After selecting MS-DOS QBasic from the MS-DOS 5 Shell menu, a box labeled QBASIC File pops open. The message QBasic File? prompts you to supply a filename. Type your desired filename. Include the path if the file is not located in the default directory. Now press Enter and you will invoke QBasic with your designated file loaded into the editor.

■ *Starting QBasic from the command line*—At the DOS prompt, type `qbasic` followed by the desired filename. Include the path if the file is not in the current directory. Type a blank space between `qbasic` and the filename. For example, type the following line to invoke QBasic with the file \SALES\MYPROG.BAS loaded into the editor:

```
C>qbasic \sales\myprog
```

Here are a few notes that apply when you load a program while starting QBasic (whether you start from the DOS Shell or from the command line):

■ QBasic assumes the extension .BAS if you don't specify an explicit extension as part of your filename.

■ QBasic initializes directly without taking the intermediate step of asking whether you want to see the help material in the on-screen Survival Guide.

■ If QBasic cannot find the specified file, it assumes that you want to create a new program with that name. Accordingly, QBasic initializes with a fresh editing slate that includes your designated filename in the Title bar. After typing the program, you can save the file directly with the Save command (that is, you don't need to use Save As... and specify the filename a second time).

Using the New Command

Use the New command when you want to stop work on one program and begin work on a brand new program. If you haven't saved the old program, QBasic opens a dialog box for confirmation. Otherwise the old program clears and the screen looks as though you just initiated QBasic. You see a blank View window showing Untitled in the Title bar.

Using the Help System

QBasic provides extensive on-line help through the Help menu (see Figure 5.10). Help screens include information on every QBasic keyword, editing hotkeys, programming topics, error handling, and even help on using the help system.

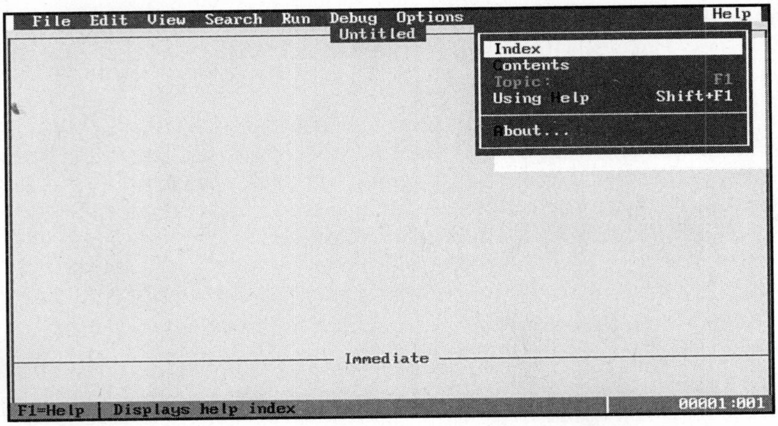

Figure 5.10.

The Help menu.

Five kinds of help are available from the Help menu:

- The Index command provides an alphabetical list of QBasic keywords about which you can request help.

- The Contents command has a functionally grouped collection of help information, including an orientation, a hotkey list, tips on using QBasic, and a quick reference.

- The Topic command provides context-sensitive help for the keyword at the current cursor location. Alternatively, while editing, you can place the cursor on any keyword and then press F1 to see help for that keyword.

- The Using Help command has information about how to use the help system.

- The About... command shows the QBasic version number and copyright information.

Here are some general notes on using the help system:

- Help screens open in a separate window. The Title bar of this window shows the help topic on display.

- To get help on a specific QBasic keyword, select the Index option from the Help menu. Now type the first letter of the keyword for which you want help. The screen shows a list of all keywords beginning with that letter. Now move the cursor onto the keyword for which you want help. Press Enter or F1.

- The F1 key provides "express" help about any keyword while you're programming. To get help on a keyword, first place the cursor on the keyword anywhere in your program. Then press F1 (or invoke the Topic command from the Help menu).

■ To get help about a general programming subject, select the Contents command on the Help menu. Press Tab to move the cursor to the topic for which you want help. Press Enter or F1.

■ To get help about an error when an error message occurs, move the cursor to the <Help> option in the error message box and press Enter.

■ To start the help system at any time, press Shift-F1. This hotkey provides help on using Help. Alternatively, you can select the Using Help command from the Help menu.

■ Sometime, at your leisure, consider browsing through all the help screens. To do so, press Shift-F1, then press Ctrl-F1 repeatedly.

■ To scroll any particular help screen, press PgUp or PgDn.

■ When Help is active, the help screens open in a separate window. You can move the cursor between the Help, View, and Immediate windows by pressing F6 (or Shift-F6).

■ Help screens for the individual keywords often include sample program fragments that demonstrate typical uses of each keyword. You can cut and paste these program lines directly from a help screen into your own program. To do so, use the standard editing keys (shifted arrow keys, and so on) to select the program lines on the help screen. Copy the selected lines to the clipboard. Now press F6 repeatedly until your program window becomes active. Then use the standard editing keys to paste the lines into your program. You can now reactivate the help screen by pressing F6 as many times as necessary.

■ When the help system is active, as in all QBasic contexts, the Reference bar on the bottom of the screen shows useful keystrokes. If a command on the Reference bar is surrounded by angle brackets, you can invoke that command by pressing the indicated keystroke or by clicking the mouse when the mouse cursor is on the command name in the Reference bar.

■ When you invoke QBasic, a dialog box opens that gives you the option of seeing the Survival Guide. Press Enter to see the guide. This activates the help system and displays a help screen with information about using QBasic and using the help system.

■ QBasic stores the help screen information on a file named QBASIC.HLP. To use the help system, QBasic must have access to this file. QBasic searches for this help file in the current directory or in directories specified by the PATH statements of your AUTOEXEC.BAT file. If the help file is located outside of your PATH specifications, you can supply QBasic with the path to the QBASIC.HLP file by selecting the Help Path... command on the Options menu.

■ To close the Help window and exit the help system, press Esc.

Printing a Program Listing

Your computer system probably includes a line printer—perhaps a dot-matrix, ink jet, or laser printer. Printed program listings provide a convenient way to study programs, mark changes, and discuss your programs with others.

Follow these steps to generate a printed listing while working with a program in the editor. You can print selected text or the complete program.

1. Invoke the File option from the Main menu (Alt-F).

2. Select the Print... command (use cursor keys or press P). This opens the Print... dialog box (see Figure 5.11).

3. Choose one of the three available options (use cursor keys or the hotkey highlighted on the screen and shown here in parentheses):

   ■ The Selected Text Only option (hotkey S) prints only the selected text in the active window. Selecting text is explained earlier in this chapter.

   ■ The Current Window option (hotkey C) prints the entire contents of the active window—not just what appears on the screen. The active window can be the main program, a help screen, or a SUB or FUNCTION procedure.

   ■ The Entire Program option (hotkey E) prints the entire program (the main program, subprograms and user-defined functions). This is the default option (when no text is selected in the active window).

4. Press Enter to begin printing.

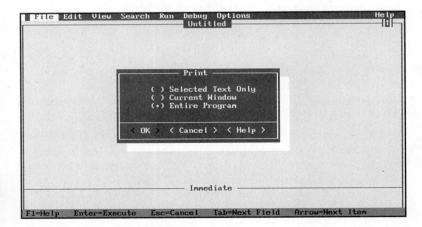

Using Other Editor Features

The QBasic editor includes some additional features that will be discussed in later chapters. These features provide assistance with the following two QBasic programming topics:

■ User-defined procedures. See Chapter 17, "Modular Programming."

■ Debugging tools. See Chapter 18, "Interactive Debugging and Testing."

Summary

On one hand, the QBasic editor is like any state-of-the-art text processor. Featuring pull-down menus, multiple windows, and full-screen editing, the QBasic editor is similar to the text editor supplied with MS-DOS. You can manipulate your programs as you would any text file. For example, you can insert and delete lines, move text in blocks, search and replace text characters, and save and locate files in DOS directories.

On the other hand, the QBasic editor is specially adapted to facilitate programming. The editor checks for correct QBasic syntax when you type instructions. Minor syntax errors are corrected automatically. Your typed program instructions are converted into a standardized format with keywords in uppercase and a single space between operators. A comprehensive help system provides context-sensitive explanations of the QBasic keywords, editing keys, and error processing.

Beginning Programming

PART

II

OUTLINE

QBasic is a flexible language suitable for both simple and complex programs. Our presentation of the language is from the ground up. We introduce the fundamentals, build a solid foundation, and then advance to the finer points.

Most of the example programs and program fragments are intentionally short. Simple examples provide succinct, uncluttered illustrations. As we move on to intermediate programming in Part III, we develop more detailed, full programs.

Please try most of the examples. Like any skill or craft, programming is something you must *do* to understand. Books are fine, but reading can take you only so far. Your experience is the ultimate teacher.

At times, you may wonder what would happen if you change an example slightly or if you use an alternative method. By all means, go ahead and find out. If this book inspires you to put QBasic through its paces, we have accomplished a major goal.

Language Building Blocks

As a child you might have played with a set of building blocks or some other construction kit to create a myriad of fancy structures. QBasic is also a kind of construction kit. With QBasic, just as with your childhood blocks, you have many pieces that you can rearrange to build finished products.

When you played with your blocks, you made all kinds of edifices. With QBasic, you make all kinds of programs. Using your QBasic "kit," you can construct programs ranging from simple "1-liners" to complex "20-pagers."

This chapter examines QBasic's fundamental building blocks—the various pieces that you join together to form a program—and just how the pieces fit together. The following key concepts are presented:

- Program structure
- Data types (numbers, strings, and constants)
- Data holders (variables and arrays)
- Expressions and operators
- Comments

An Overview of a Program

Suppose someone asks you: "What is a human being composed of?" You might say "two legs, two arms, a head," and so on. This is the large scale (macroscopic) view. A chemist, however, might say "carbon, hydrogen, oxygen, and other atoms." This is the small scale (microscopic) view. A doctor would probably adopt a middle position: "water, blood, muscle, and fat." Your answer depends on your point of view. The point is that you can look at something as complex as a person in many different ways.

Now consider this question: What is a program composed of?

Just as you analyze a human body, you can view the composition of QBasic programs in many different ways. Each view reveals different information. That's why it is useful to examine programs on both the larger and smaller scales.

The smallest, most fundamental components of a QBasic program are the individual characters that you type. These individual characters are QBasic's "atoms."

The characters combine to form QBasic's "molecules." Variable names, expressions, and reserved words such as PRINT and 14 + MyAge% are typical examples.

"Molecules" combine to form "compounds." At this level in QBasic are individual instructions such as the following:

```
PRINT "The total cost is"; SumTotal!
```

Finally, the instructions combine to form the finished product: a working program.

The Macroscopic View

Let's begin by stepping back and looking at a QBasic program from the large-scale, macroscopic view. When you look at a QBasic program, the first thing you might notice is that the program consists of a series of lines. Each line is one of the following:

■ A single instruction (or a group of instructions)

■ A label

■ A metacommand

A line is limited to 256 characters.

QBasic Instructions

An instruction is like a QBasic "sentence." Each instruction orders the computer to perform a particular task, such as calculating an arithmetic quantity, reading from or writing to a disk file, assigning a value to a variable, printing a result, or drawing graphics.

Here are two examples of QBasic instructions that you already understand:

```
PRINT "A stitch in time saves nine."

INPUT "What is your name"; YourName$
```

Every QBasic instruction begins with a *statement*. A statement is a reserved word (occasionally two or three reserved words) that specifies the particular action which that instruction performs. The statement in an instruction is like the verb in a sentence. The statements in the two sample instructions are PRINT and INPUT.

There are two exceptions to the rule that all instructions begin with a statement.

First, take a look at this typical assignment instruction (which assigns a value to the variable Score):

```
Score = 21
```

Isn't this a perfectly valid instruction that doesn't begin with a statement?

Yes and no. The same instruction could be written as follows with the *optional* statement LET:

```
LET Score = 21
```

Both instructions do exactly the same thing. The first form simply has an implied LET after the line number. So, if the LET is implied, this "exception" really conforms to the general rule after all.

Assignment and LET are discussed later in this chapter.

Second, the CALL statement is optional in instructions that invoke user-defined procedures and functions. As with LET, the keyword CALL is implied when not present. (See Chapter 17, "Modular Programming," for a discussion of CALL.)

Some statements, such as END and CLS, are instructions all by themselves. However, most instructions contain a statement *and* additional (required) information. The extra information might be expressions, parameters, or other keywords. The PRINT and INPUT instructions just given are examples of instructions that contain additional information.

Every QBasic instruction must follow the syntax rules associated with the relevant statement. If not, a syntax error occurs.

QBasic is a rich language that incorporates many different statements (over 125, in fact). All of them are covered in the course of this book.

Placing Multiple Instructions on a Line

You can place more than one instruction on a line. To do so, just place a colon between instructions. Here is an example of a multiple-instruction line:

```
Xvalue% = 18: Yvalue% = 31: Zvalue% = -5
```

This one line contains three individual instructions. Instead of typing this one line, you could write three individual lines with one instruction per line:

```
Xvalue% = 18
Yvalue% = 31
Zvalue% = -5
```

Line Numbers

If you have programmed with GW-BASIC or BASICA, or if you have had some exposure to older versions of BASIC, you might be wondering, "What about line numbers?" You're probably used to numbers beginning each line—something like this:

```
100 Xvalue% = 18
200 Yvalue% = 31
300 Zvalue% = -5
```

In QBasic, line numbers are optional. You can even mix lines with line numbers and lines without line numbers in the same program.

A *line number* must be a whole number from 0 to 65529 placed at the beginning of a line. In QBasic, line numbers serve as place names—that is, as a way to reference a particular line. See the "Some QBasic Fundamentals" section of Chapter 3, "A Hands-On Introduction to Programming," for an example of a program containing line numbers.

The line number is an outmoded technique. QBasic contains more flexible programming tools—notably alphanumeric labels and block structures—that make line numbers obsolete. Generally, the QBasic program examples in this book do not contain line numbers.

QBasic supports line numbers mainly so that you can run existing BASICA or GW-BASIC programs in QBasic without changing the old programs. (BASICA and GW-BASIC require each line to begin with a line number. For more about programming with BASICA and GW-BASIC, see Chapters 23 and 24.) However, as you write new programs, avoid line numbers.

See Chapter 7, "Program Flow and Decision Making," for more discussion about line numbers.

Labels

Like line numbers, labels identify lines. You can use a label at the beginning of a line containing one or more instructions. In such a case, a label is a kind of "alphanumeric line number." Alternatively, a label can stand alone as a complete line all by itself.

A *label* consists of a letter followed, optionally, by a combination of letters, digits, and periods. A colon terminates the label. A label can be from 1 to 40 characters long, not counting the terminating colon. Here are a few examples of valid labels:

```
SumRoutine:
```

```
A:
```

```
BobAndCarol:
```

```
modified09.18.90:
```

Labels are superior to line numbers because an alphanumeric name conveys more information than a simple line number. As you program, try to create meaningful label names such as `GraphRoutine` and `GetUserInput`. Your programs will be easier to read and understand.

See Chapter 7, "Program Flow and Decision Making," for a further discussion of labels.

Metacommands and Metastatements

The third type of QBasic line is the metacommand. For now, metacommands are discussed only briefly. They are advanced topics discussed in Chapter 19, "Managing Memory."

A *metacommand* is a special *language directive* that redirects the way QBasic interprets other instructions. As such, metacommands themselves are not executed like regular QBasic instructions.

A metacommand begins with a *metastatement*. There are two metastatements (see Table 6.1). Each of the two metastatements is a special keyword which begins with a dollar sign ($).

Table 6.1. QBasic metastatements.

Metastatement	Purpose
$DYNAMIC	Declares that arrays must be allocated dynamically
$STATIC	Declares that arrays must be allocated statically

If you are new to QBasic, you probably will write many programs before you
use your first metastatement.

Introduction to Data Types

Most programs manipulate data in one way or another. As you have seen, all
program data consists of the following two primary types:

■ Numbers—arithmetic data

■ Strings—text (character) data

The simplest way to specify a data value is to write the value explicitly. For
example, in the following PRINT instruction, the value 21 is written explicitly:

PRINT 21

Instead of writing data values explicitly, you can store and manipulate the
values with variables. For example, in the following instructions, the data value
for the PRINT instruction is stored in the variable MyAge%.

MyAge% = 21
PRINT MyAge%

When you write a data value explicitly, the data value is said to be specified by
a *literal*. In the instruction PRINT 21, the 21 is a literal. Why? Because the value
is specified with explicit numbers (that is, *literally*), not with a variable name
such as MyAge%.

(Some reference sources, such as your QBasic manual, use the term *constant*
rather than the term *literal*. However, throughout this book, the term *literal* is
used to refer to data values written explicitly.)

Numeric Literals

Numeric literals look quite natural—just the way most people write numbers.
You need a decimal point only if the number has a fractional part (that is, the
number is not a whole integer). Negative numbers must begin with a minus
sign. For positive numbers, the leading plus sign usually is omitted, but you
can include the plus sign if you want.

Consider the following program:

```
PRINT 458
PRINT -23.499
PRINT 0
PRINT .000012
```

The output echoes the values in the original instructions:

```
 458
-23.499
 0
 .000012
```

One thing you can't do is place commas inside large numbers. For example, the following is a no-no: MyNumber! = 25,128.14. Also, you cannot embed a blank space anywhere in a numeric literal.

String Literals

You worked with strings in Chapter 3, "A Hands-On Introduction to Programming." A *string* is a sequence of text characters treated as a single value. To express a string literal, place a double quotation mark (not an apostrophe, sometimes called the single quotation mark) at each end of the text. These paired double quotation marks are called *delimiters* because they mark the beginning and end of the string.

NOTE

Exponential Notation

When numbers become extremely large or extremely small, you need a specialized notation to express the numbers conveniently. To say the least, literals such as .0000000000000389 and 4589100000 are awkward.

To express such numbers, QBasic uses *exponential notation,* also called *scientific notation.* The literals 3.89E-14 and 4.5891E+09 specify the two numbers given in the previous paragraph. This notation is computer shorthand for the more common mathematical notations, 3.89×10^{-14} and 4.5891×10^{9}.

To interpret exponential notation, move the decimal point the number of places indicated by the exponent after the E. Move the decimal point to the right for positive exponents, left for negative exponents. (You might have to pad the number with zeroes to complete the alignment.)

For example, 2.89E+05 is 289,000; –1.67E–06 is –0.00000167.

Consider this one-line program which you already understand:

```
PRINT "Things are looking up"
```

The resulting output is an echo of the string literal with the quotation marks removed:

```
Things are looking up
```

Why do you need quotation marks around a string literal? Without the quotation marks, QBasic interprets the text as a sequence of variable names rather than as a string. To illustrate this, try running the following instruction (which is the last PRINT instruction without the quotation marks):

```
PRINT Things are looking up
```

The output is

```
 0  0  0  0
```

What are all these zeroes?

QBasic thinks the words Things, are, looking, and up are four variable names and not one long string literal. In this case, each variable has a value of zero. Because QBasic thinks that you want to display the values of the four variables, out come the four zeroes.

Remember, you need quotation marks to specify a string literal.

Data Holders: Variables, Constants, Arrays, and Records

Data holders store data for subsequent use. QBasic has four kinds of data holders: variables, constants, arrays, and records. Each is appropriate for specific sorts of tasks (see Table 6.2).

Table 6.2. Data holders.

Name	Type of Data Held
Variable	A single value that can change
Constant	A single value that remains fixed
Array	Multiple values of the same data type
Record	Multiple values of different data types

Variables and constants are *scalar* data holders, which means that they store only one data value at a time. Arrays and records are *structured* or *compound* data holders, which means they can store multiple values simultaneously.

Of the four types of data holders, variables and arrays are by far the most important. Almost any program you write will contain variables and many will use arrays. In practical programs, constants and records occur less often. This chapter discusses variables in depth and introduces the other three types of data holders. Substantial discussion of arrays, constants, and records is deferred to later chapters.

Understanding Variables

A *variable* is really just a name you give to an area of memory where a data value is stored. When you need to retrieve that data, or modify its value, you can refer to the memory location by the variable's name. For example, in a financial program, the variable BankBalance! might hold the value of the current balance in your checking account. As the program runs, the value stored in BankBalance! might change several times.

Picture a variable as a box. The box has a name, which you create, printed on the outside. The inside of the box has room for one data value (see Figure 6.1).

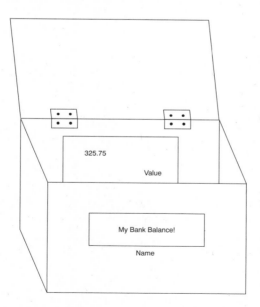

325.75

Value

My Bank Balance!

Name

Figure 6.1.

Picturing a variable as a box.

In a single program, you might use many such boxes, each box with a different name. To retrieve the data inside a box, or to change the value of the data, you refer to the name of the box.

You do not need any special instruction to create a variable. The first time your program uses a new variable name, you automatically create the variable.

Naming Variables

You are free to give variables meaningful, descriptive names. As you design your programs, think about what each variable represents, and choose an appropriately informative name.

QBasic does insist that you adhere to the following rules when choosing a variable name:

1. The first character must be a letter.

2. Succeeding characters can be letters, digits, or periods. (No other characters, including blank spaces, hyphens, or underscores, are allowed.)

3. The final character can be one of the type-declaration characters (%, &, !, #, and $).

4. The name is restricted to a 40-character maximum.

5. A variable name cannot be a reserved word, although embedded reserved words are allowed. (See Appendix A, "Reserved Words," for a list of such words.)

6. A variable name must not begin with the letters FN, which signals a call to a DEF FN function. (See Chapter 17, "Modular Programming.")

Remember that QBasic considers upper- and lowercase letters as equivalent in variable names. The names MyAge%, MYAGE%, and Myage% all refer to the same variable.

Table 6.3 shows some acceptable and unacceptable variable names.

Table 6.3. Example variable names.

Name	Status	Comment
MyAge	OK	No data type suffix.
MyAge%	OK	Uses data type suffix (see next section of this chapter).
X	OK	Single-letter variable names are acceptable.
123Graph	Error	Names must begin with a letter.
Figure 7.4	OK	Embedded periods are acceptable.

Name	Status	Comment
Bob&Ray	Error	An ampersand can only be at the end (as a data type suffix).
Color	Error	COLOR is a reserved word.
MyColor	OK	Color is okay if embedded.

Tips for Naming Variables

T I P

As you begin to write more and larger programs, you begin to appreciate how much well-chosen variable names enhance your programs. When variable names are meaningful, you have a much easier time understanding what's going on in a particular program. After all, the more understandable your programs are, the easier it will be for you to make modifications and track down any errors.

We suggest beginning each variable name with a capital letter. After that, use both upper- and lowercase letters to make it easier to readily identify your variable names. The QBasic editor displays reserved words in all uppercase letters. By using lowercase letters in variable names, you distinguish clearly between reserved words and variables.

Be creative with your variable naming. Some examples of good, clear variable names are Salary!, LastName$, and InvoiceNumber%.

All of us try shortcuts in our lives, and programming is no exception. Sometimes in the rush to get a program working or in the hope of saving some typing time, you might use short nondescriptive variable names such as X, A5, or JJ%. You can often rationalize using these names by thinking, "Hey, my memory is good; I'll remember what these variables mean." Six months later, you're apt to stare quizzically at your previous work and throw up your hands in disgust.

Avoid short (and shortsighted) nondescriptive names. Once you get in the habit of using descriptive, meaningful variable names, you actually can program faster with them than without them.

However, don't go overboard and make your variable names ridiculously long. Any good thing can be overdone. In your quest for meaningful variable names, you might get carried away with some multisyllabic tongue twisters. Such variable names are counterproductive. They make your programs cumbersome and awkward to read. You should never need such monstrosities as

NextCharacterInTheUsersInputString$

or

TeamScoreAtTheEndOfRegulation%

The Six Fundamental Data Types

Besides choosing a name, you must make another important decision for each variable: the type of data that the variable can store.

As mentioned earlier, the two primary data types are numbers and strings. But QBasic is even more specific. There are actually six fundamental data types—four different numeric types and two string (text) types (see Figure 6.2).

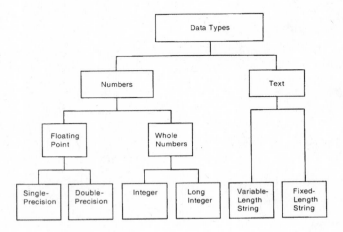

Figure 6.2.

The six fundamental data types.

Each variable you create will have one of these six data types. You will soon learn just how you assign your desired data type to each variable. The process of associating a data type with a variable is known as *variable typing* (assigning a data "type," not "typing" on the keyboard).

An individual variable can store only data of its assigned data type. An integer variable, for example, can store only an integer number, not a string or a single-precision number.

To stretch the box analogy, for each variable you have six different kinds of boxes from which to choose. Each kind of box stores only data of one particular type. You can change the value stored in the box, but only if the new value has the proper data type.

Numeric Data Types

Let's examine the four numeric data types a little closer:

1. *Integer* (also called *short integer* or *regular integer*). Integers are whole numbers—that is, numbers without fractional components. As such, integer values specify things that can be counted discretely. For example, an

integer variable can designate the number of runs scored in a baseball game, the number of times through a programming loop, or the number of orders processed by a shipping department. Integers can be negative, zero, or positive. The range of the integer data type is from –32,768 to +32,767.

2. *Long Integer.* Long integers extend the integer data type to a wider range of whole numbers. A long integer variable can store values from –2,147,483,648 to +2,147,483,647. The long integer data type does not exist in BASICA or GW-BASIC.

3. *Single-Precision.* Many numbers do not lend themselves to the integer or long integer data types. A number might, for example, have a fractional part, such as 89.22, or might be too large, such as 1.34E+15. The single-precision data type handles such numbers. The range of single precision is from (approximately) –3.4E+38 to +3.4E+38.

The price you pay for using single precision is that, in general, the computer cannot represent such numbers exactly, only approximately. For most purposes, the approximation is close enough. Single-precision numbers are accurate to the first seven digits. For example, the fraction one-third is actually .3333333333333 (with an endless string of threes). In QBasic however, the single-precision accuracy of one-third is .3333333 (exactly seven digits). In practice, you normally do not need to be concerned with possible inaccuracies resulting from single-precision calculations. Only the heaviest number-crunching programs are susceptible to significant errors.

4. *Double-Precision.* What do you do when you need more than single-precision accuracy? Double-precision comes to the rescue. Just as long integer extends the concept of integer, double-precision extends the concept of single-precision. Double-precision variables can store numbers ranging from approximately –1.8D+308 to +1.8D+308. Double-precision numbers are accurate to 15 or 16 digits. In QBasic, the fraction one-third is now accurate to .3333333333333333 (16 digits).

The exponential indicator for double-precision literals is D rather than E. The D indicates that the number should be interpreted as double-precision rather than single-precision.

String Data Types

There are two string data types:

1. *Variable-Length String.* Most string variables are variable-length string variables. As the name suggests, the key feature of a variable-length string variable is that the stored string can be any length. Well, almost

any length. The range is from a null (zero-length) string (`""`) to a medium-length string (such as `Zippety doo-dah`, `Zippety Aaay`) to a string of the maximum length of 32,767 characters.

Variable-length string variables can store only one data string at a time, but the length of this string can change frequently as the program runs. For example, the following program reassigns the value of the variable-length string variable `MyString$` from a short string to a much longer string:

```
MyString$ = "I'm not long"
PRINT MyString$
MyString$ = "Hey, you made me considerably l-o-n-g-e-r now"
PRINT MyString$
```

The output is

```
I'm not long
Hey, you made me considerably l-o-n-g-e-r now
```

All string variables in BASICA and GW-BASIC are variable-length strings.

2. *Fixed-Length String*. As the name implies, a fixed-length string variable can store only a string value of a predetermined length. For each such variable, you declare the fixed length to be from 0 to a maximum of 32,767 characters. The fixed-length string data type does not exist in BASICA or GW-BASIC.

Choosing Data Types

You might be wondering, "How do I know what data type to choose for each variable? What are the trade-offs? If double-precision variables are the most precise numeric variables, and variable-length strings are the most flexible strings, why not make all my numeric variables double-precision and all my strings variable-length?"

For numeric variables, the following three trade-offs come into play:

■ Use of computer memory

■ Speed of program execution

■ Accuracy of calculation

When storing numeric data in memory, QBasic converts numbers into a special binary representation. (Don't be concerned about how your numbers are converted. QBasic handles the details "behind the scenes.")

The amount of computer memory needed to store each variable depends only on the data type of the variable, not on the actual value stored. Even when the value of the variable changes, the amount of memory needed for the variable remains constant. Table 6.4 shows how much memory QBasic uses for each numeric variable type.

Table 6.4. Memory required to store numeric values.	
Data Type	**Memory Required**
Integer	2 bytes (16 bits)
Long integer	4 bytes (32 bits)
Single-precision	4 bytes (32 bits)
Double-precision	8 bytes (64 bits)

As Table 6.4 shows, you can save substantial memory if you use integer variables as much as possible.

Calculations are substantially faster with integer variables than with any other data type. Double-precision calculations consume the most time. The more you use integer variables rather than other data types, the faster your programs run.

As mentioned previously, integer and long integer variables also win in the accuracy contest. Double-precision, though still approximate, is more accurate than single-precision.

TIP

As a beginning programmer, you don't really need to concern yourself about speed considerations or memory usage. Your programs will tend to be small with relatively few variables and without large arrays. The computer will have plenty of memory and run your programs as fast as you could want. For beginners, single-precision variables will probably suffice for all your numeric variables.

However, as you gain programming skill and your programs start to get larger and more sophisticated, you will need to address memory conservation and speed considerations more and more. Then the choice of numeric data types becomes more critical. You'll find that experience is your best guide.

The conclusion is simple: Use the simplest data type capable of expressing the numbers involved. Use integer variables if possible.

As for strings, most of your string variables will be variable-length. The fixed-length string type is appropriate for special situations such as records (see Chapter 9, "Managing Large Amounts of Data") and data transfer to disk files (see Chapter 15, "Using Random and Binary Disk Files").

Giving Variables a Data Type

You have learned about the six different data types, but how do you tell QBasic which data type any particular variable should have?

You can assign a data type to a variable in four different ways:

1. Use a type-declaration suffix character.

   By appending one of the type-declaration suffixes to a variable name, you designate the data type for that variable. You are already familiar with this technique. Table 6.5 lists the available suffixes.

Table 6.5. Variable suffixes.

Suffix	Variable Type	Example Variable Name
%	Integer	Index%
&	Long integer	Population&
!	Single-precision	Area!
#	Double-precision	MyDebt#
$	Variable-length string	FullName$

2. Use a DEF*type* instruction.

   The statements DEFINT, DEFLNG, DEFSNG, DEFDBL, and DEFSTR (integer, long integer, single-precision, double-precision, and string) declare that variables beginning with particular letters have a specified data type. These instructions are explained in Chapter 22, "Understanding Advanced QBasic Topics."

3. Use an AS clause.

   The statements DIM, REDIM, COMMON, SHARED, and STATIC optionally can include a clause of the following form:

   varname AS *type*

   where *varname* is the name of a variable and *type* specifies the data type.

AS clause typing is discussed in conjunction with arrays in Chapter 9, "Managing Large Amounts of Data." See Chapter 17, "Modular Programming," and Chapter 19, "Managing Memory," for details on REDIM, COMMON, SHARED, and STATIC.

4. Do nothing!

When none of the three previous conditions apply, the variable type automatically becomes single-precision. The effect is as if the variable had a ! suffix. So if you name a variable Cost, for example, Cost is a numeric variable of type single-precision.

Variable Typing Conflicts

Variables with the same root name but different suffixes are distinct variables. For example, Price!, Price#, and Price$ are three independent variables that can coexist in the same program. Try this program for proof:

```
Price! = 349.62
Price# = 12345678.25
Price$ = "Too much"
PRINT Price!
PRINT Price#
PRINT Price$
```

The output is

```
 349.62
 12345678.25
Too much
```

Notice that all three variables (Price!, Price#, and Price$) retain individual identities. Each variable stores a different value, which the program displays with the three PRINT instructions.

Now suppose that you get cunning and introduce a variable named Price (with no suffix character). Add the following line as the new fourth line of your program:

```
Price = 2.95
```

Remember, QBasic treats any variable without a special suffix as a single-precision numeric variable. But our program already contains the variable Price!, which is single-precision and clearly has the same root name as the variable Price. What do you think happens? Let's find out. Here is the updated program:

```
Price! = 349.62
Price# = 12345678.25#
Price$ = "Too much"
Price = 2.95
PRINT Price!
PRINT Price#
PRINT Price$
```

And here is the new output:

```
 2.95
 12345678.25
Too much
```

The result is that the instruction PRINT Price! displays the value of Price! as 2.95, the value of the variable Price. Does the new fourth line reassign the value of the variable Price! as well as the value of the variable Price?

Yes. In fact, Price and Price! are the same variable. You can write single-precision variable names with or without the trailing exclamation point.

You might notice a subtle difference between the way you typed the second line and the way the line appears after you press Enter. QBasic adds a pound sign (#) to the numeric literal at the end of the line. This pound sign denotes that the literal is a double-precision number. Such literals are discussed in Chapter 10, "Manipulating Numbers."

T I P   We recommend that you use explicit data type suffixes on all your variable names. This avoids possible ambiguities and errors resulting from certain typos. Many programmers balk at this advice, complaining of the extra, cumbersome keystrokes needed for the suffix characters.

Our counter argument is that the extra keystrokes become easy and natural once you acquire the habit. And you can acquire the habit with just a few programs. Try it.

Introduction to Constants

Constants, or more formally *symbolic constants,* are similar to variables. Like a variable, a constant has a unique name and stores a data value. The difference is that the value stored in a constant can never change, but the value stored in a variable can.

Use a CONST instruction to define constants.

S
T
A
T
E
M
E
N
T

CONST *constname* = *expr*, *constname* = *expr* ...

where

    constname is the user-defined name for the constant,

and

    expr is an arithmetic or string expression defining the value for the constant.

A single CONST instruction can define one or more constants. If more than one *constname* is defined, use a comma between each definition.

For example, the following instruction defines the constant NormalTemp to have the value of 98.6:

```
CONST NormalTemp = 98.6
```

Each *constname* must conform to the same rules as a variable name. You can append a type-declaration suffix (%, &, !, #, or $) to a constant name; but unlike a suffix used with a variable name, this suffix is not actually part of the name. For example, suppose that you define a constant named PassingGrade% as follows:

```
CONST PassingGrade% = 65
```

In the body of your program, you don't need the % suffix to refer to PassingGrade%. The following instruction, for example, works fine:

```
IF Score% >= PassingGrade THEN PRINT "You passed!"
```

The data type of a constant is set by the type-declaration suffix used in *constname*. However, if you don't use such a suffix, *expr* determines the data type.

If *expr* is a string expression, a string constant results. When *expr* is numeric, the constant assumes the simplest numeric type that can represent the value of *expr* (integer is the simplest, followed by long integer, single-precision, and double-precision).

There are restrictions on the expressions that you can use to define the value of each constant. For a string constant, *expr* can only be a string literal surrounded by double quotation marks. For example:

```
CONST Salutation$ = "To Whom It May Concern"
```

For a numeric constant, *expr* can consist of the following elements:

- Literals, such as 438 or 53.44.
- Other constants previously defined.
- Arithmetic operators, such as + or /. However, the exponentiation operator (^) is not allowed. The arithmetic operators are discussed later in this chapter.
- Logical operators, such as AND or NOT. The logical operators are discussed in Chapter 7, "Program Flow and Decision Making."

expr cannot contain any variables or functions (such as the square root function SQR).

Here are some examples of typical CONST declarations:

```
CONST ConversionFactor = 454

CONST TRUE = -1, FALSE = 0

CONST MaxWeight = 538.5

CONST MinWeight = MaxWeight - 200
```

By assigning well-chosen, descriptive names to your constants, you make your programs much easier to understand. An appropriate constant name is much easier to read than a cryptic numeric literal. Compare these two instructions:

```
Profit! = Principal! * 8.5

Profit! = Principal! * InterestRate
```

When confronted by the first example, you might wonder where the number 8.5 comes from. The second example makes the meaning of the number clear. Near the beginning of the program, use a CONST instruction to set the actual value of InterestRate:

```
CONST InterestRate = 8.5
```

Use constants to make wholesale changes easy. In many programs, a particular literal might appear several times. By giving such a literal a declared constant name, you can later modify its value throughout the program simply by changing the value of the constant in the CONST instruction.

For example, a report-generating program might use the constant LinesPerPage several times to control the maximum number of lines printed on one report page. If you need to adjust this control number, the only modification required is one change to the definition of LinesPerPage in the CONST instruction.

Introduction to Arrays

Arrays are like "super variables." As you have seen, ordinary variables store only a single value. An ordinary variable can be of any data type, but can store only a single data value (of the appropriate type).

An array, by contrast, houses multiple data values. A single array is a collection of values, with each individual value having the same data type. An array is like a set of ordinary variables.

Like an ordinary variable, every array has a name you create. These names follow the same naming conventions as ordinary variable names, including an optional suffix that identifies the data type of all the values in the array.

We call each individual array value an *element* of the array. Distinct elements of the array are referenced by an *index number* (sometimes called a *subscript*).

To see how arrays work, consider this example. Suppose a company has 100 employees. The personnel department assigned each worker an employee number. Because there are 100 employees, these numbers range from 1 to 100. The salary of each employee is stored in an array called `Salary!`. To display the salary of employee number 73, for example, you use the following instruction:

```
PRINT Salary!(73)
```

Notice that you enclose the index number in parentheses after the array name. The parentheses tell QBasic that this is an array rather than an ordinary variable.

Arrays can contain string values also. For example, you might create an array called `WorkerName$` that contains the names of all the employees. Then you can store the name of good old employee number 73 with an instruction such as

```
WorkerName$(73) = "Joanna B. Nimble"
```

Arrays are a powerful tool for working with large groups of related data. Chapter 9, "Managing Large Amounts of Data," discusses the details of creating, managing, and utilizing arrays.

Another Look at Assignment Instructions

As mentioned previously, you directly assign a value to a variable using the equal sign. Here are two typical assignment instructions:

```
MyTemp! = 98.6

Title$ = "Night in Casablanca"
```

The Optional *LET*

You can optionally begin any assignment instruction with the keyword LET. For example, you can write the previous two instructions as follows:

```
LET MyTemp! = 98.6

LET Title$ = "Night in Casablanca"
```

Both forms (with or without LET) do exactly the same thing. (LET is a vestige from early versions of the BASIC language, which required LET in assignment instructions.)

Sometimes, programmers refer to assignment instructions as LET *instructions*. Today, QBasic programmers almost universally leave out the LET keyword in assignment instructions.

Right-Hand Sides of Assignment Instructions

The right-hand side of an assignment instruction can consist of a general expression as well as a data literal. Here is a closer look at how assignment instructions work:

S T A T E M E N T

```
LET varname = expr
```
or simply
```
varname = expr
```
where

  varname is a variable whose value is to be assigned,

and

  expr is an expression that provides the value to assign to *varname*.

Two things occur when an assignment instruction is executed:

1. The value of *expr* is calculated.

2. This value is assigned to the variable *varname*.

The proper way to interpret an assignment instruction is "assign the value of *expr* to the variable named *varname*."

Think of the equal sign in an assignment instruction as meaning "is now assigned the value of." Therefore, the instruction

```
NumItems% = 29
```

means "the variable NumItems% is now assigned the value of 29."

Here are some examples of right-hand sides containing general expressions:

```
Tax = COST * 0.06
```

```
YourAge% = 29 + 10
```

```
Volume = Depth * Height * Length / 9
```

Now take a look at this instruction:

```
X% = X% + 1
```

Does this instruction make sense? You might be thinking that no value of X% satisfies that equation.

However, when viewed as a reassignment of the variable X%, the instruction makes perfect sense. The instruction says "the new value of the variable X% shall become the old value of the variable X% plus 1."

In other words, first add 1 to the value of X%. Then store this updated value back into the variable named X%. The effect is that X% now contains a value 1 greater than its previous value. This kind of instruction occurs frequently in practical programs.

The general data type of *varname* and *expr* must correspond. That is, if the variable on the left-hand side is numeric, the expression on the right-hand side must also be numeric. Similarly, if the variable is a string, the expression also must be a string.

However, specific numeric data types do not have to correspond. If the variable is one of the four numeric data types (integer, long integer, single-precision, or double-precision), the expression on the right-hand side can be any of the four data types. For example, the following instruction is acceptable:

```
MyAge% = BigNum!
```

QBasic automatically converts the single-precision value in BigNum! to an integer value for MyAge%. See Chapter 10, "Manipulating Numbers," for a further discussion of numeric data type conversion.

Expressions and Operators

An *expression* specifies a single data value. Expressions occur frequently in QBasic instructions. You just saw that one place where expressions occur is on the right-hand side of assignment instructions. As you learn more about QBasic, you will see expressions in many other contexts.

An expression can be a single literal (such as 38.66 or "Hello out there"), a variable (MyValue%), an array element (Sales!(150)), a function (SQR(1.88)), or a combination of these elements formed with suitable operators (SQR(1.88 / MyValue%) + 38.66).

Every valid expression, whether simple or complex, evaluates to a single numeric or string value. For example, if the variable X has the value 2 and Y has the value 5, the expression X + Y has the value 7.

When an expression contains two or more parts, some sort of operator combines the parts to create the single value. An *operator* manipulates one or more *operands* to create a value. Each operand is itself a data value or expression. In the present example, X and Y are operands and the plus sign (+) is an operator. Most QBasic operators are special symbols (such as + and >), but some operators are keywords (such as NOT and MOD).

In general, wherever QBasic requires a single value, you can substitute an expression. Already you have used composite expressions on the right-hand side of some assignment instructions.

Types of Operators

QBasic has four categories of operators (see Table 6.6).

Table 6.6. Operator categories.

Category	Description
Arithmetic	Manipulates numbers
String	Manipulates strings
Relational	Compares numbers or strings
Logical	Manipulates Boolean (True or False) values

Arithmetic Operators

Table 6.7 shows the arithmetic operators. The operand abbreviations I, L, S, and D stand for the four arithmetic data types:

- I   Integer
- L   Long integer
- S   Single-precision
- D   Double-precision

Table 6.7. Arithmetic operators.

Symbol	Name	Operand Types	Example	Result
+	Addition	I, L, S, D	1.5 + 4.9	6.4
-	Subtraction	I, L, S, D	3.4 - 1.2	2.2
*	Multiplication	I, L, S, D	1.5 * 2.2	3.3
/	Division	I, L, S, D	4.5 / 2.5	1.8
^	Exponentiation	I, L, S, D	3 ^ 2	9
-	Negation	I, L, S, D	-21	-21
\	Integer division	I, L	6 \ 4	1
MOD	Remainder	I, L	6 MOD 4	2

You can freely mix numeric data types in an arithmetic expression. QBasic uses the simplest data type capable of expressing the result. For example, PRINT 2.5 * 0.4 produces 1, and PRINT 9 / 8 produces 1.125.

You're probably familiar with most of the arithmetic operations and the operators involved. Addition and subtraction use the plus (+) and minus (-) signs just as you would expect:

```
PRINT 25.6 + 14
PRINT 100 - 38
```

The result is

```
39.6
62
```

Multiplication and division use the asterisk (*) and "divide" sign (/) respectively:

```
PRINT 1.5 * 7
PRINT 9 / 2
```

Here is the result:

```
 10.5
 4.5
```

Exponentiation is the process of raising one number to a power. For example, the math expression 2^3 means 2 raised to the power of 3. In QBasic this operation is written 2 ^ 3. On most keyboards, the exponential operator (^) is Shift-6. By the way, what is 2 ^ 3? Let's find out.

```
PRINT 2 ^ 3
```

The answer is

```
 8
```

In an exponential expression, the operands don't have to be integers. For example,

```
PRINT 3.4 ^ 1.29
```

Here is the result:

```
 4.848505
```

Two arithmetic operations that might be new to you are integer division and remaindering. The integer division operator is the backslash (\ ), and the remaindering operator is the keyword MOD.

Integer division is the process of dividing one whole number by another. Only the whole number portion of the answer survives. Any remainder is discarded. If you attempt integer division with a single- or double-precision operand, the operand is first rounded to the nearest whole number.

The following program demonstrates the difference between regular division and integer division:

```
PRINT 14 / 5      'Regular division
PRINT 14 \ 5      'Integer division
```

The result is

```
 2.8
 2
```

Notice that the result of the integer division is to "throw away" the fractional part (0.8) of the regular division answer, not to round the answer to the nearest whole number. If rounded, the answer would be 3 rather than 2. When one or both operands are single- or double-precision numbers, the operands are first rounded to the nearest whole number before the integer division proceeds.

Remaindering is a close cousin to integer division. The MOD operator extracts the remainder after dividing by a modulus or divisor. Another way to look at remaindering is that the MOD operator returns the part "thrown away" during integer division. If you're unfamiliar with modular arithmetic, think of the schoolhouse mnemonic "goes into." For example, 4 "goes into" 11 twice with 3 remaining. Or more properly, 11 modulo 4 is 3. Here's how this looks in QBasic:

```
PRINT 11 \ 4          'Integer division quotient
PRINT 11 MOD 4        'Integer division remainder
```

Here's the outcome:

```
2
3
```

String Operators

The plus sign also works with string operands. Does this mean you can add two strings together? Well, sort of.

Instead of adding the strings in an arithmetic sense, the plus sign merges the text of two strings into one composite string. This process is known as *concatenation*. The text of one string is juxtaposed with the text of a second string to form one new string. The following program demonstrates the technique:

```
FirstPart$ = "Coca"
LastPart$ = "Cola"
FullName$ = FirstPart$ + LastPart$
PRINT FullName$
PRINT "Pepsi" + LastPart$
```

The output is

```
CocaCola
PepsiCola
```

The plus signs in the third and fifth lines perform concatenation. Look at the third line. This instruction concatenates the value of FirstPart$ (namely Coca) with the value of LastPart$ (namely Cola) to form the result (CocaCola) and then assigns the result to the variable FullName$.

Relational Operators

The relational operators compare two values to produce a "True" or "False" result. In this chapter, we'll only introduce the operators (see Table 6.8). We'll explore the use of the relational operators in Chapter 7, "Program Flow and Decision Making."

Table 6.8. Relational operators.

Symbol	Name	Operand Types	Example
=	Equals	All	4 = 4
<>	Not equal	All	"Dog" <> "Cat"
>	Greater than	All	8 > 5
<	Less than	All	3 < 6
>=	Greater than or equal to	All	9 >= 9
<=	Less than or equal to	All	"Hi" <= "Ho"

Each example in the last column of the table is True. Notice that relational operators work on strings as well as numbers.

The most common use of relational operators is to create testing expressions for decision instructions such as IF-THEN. Here is an example of an instruction:

```
IF OurScore% > TheirScore% THEN PRINT "We won."
```

IF-THEN and relational operators are discussed in depth when we explore conditional testing in Chapter 7, "Program Flow and Decision Making."

Logical Operators

The final set of QBasic operators are the logical operators. Logical operators manipulate Boolean operands to produce Boolean results. (The term "Boolean" comes from George Boole, a prominent 19th-century British mathematician.)

A Boolean operand is simply a True or False value.

Internally, QBasic represents True and False with arithmetic integers: 0 for False and –1 for True. You will see why when we examine logical operations in Chapter 10, "Manipulating Numbers."

For now, we simply present the six logical operators and their official-sounding names in Table 6.9. All the logical operators are keywords rather than symbols.

Table 6.9. Logical operators.

Operator	Meaning
NOT	Complement (logical negation)
AND	Conjunction
OR	Disjunction (inclusive or)
XOR	Exclusive or
EQV	Equivalence
IMP	Implication

Operator Precedence

So far our sample expressions have had two operands and one operator. What happens when an expression contains more than one operator? How does QBasic resolve the value of such expressions?

For example, consider this instruction:

```
PRINT 4 + 3 * 2
```

What is the result—14 or 10? Do you see the problem? The answer is 14 if you add 4 and 3 before multiplying by 2 (4 plus 3 is 7 and then 7 times 2 is 14). But the answer is 10 if you add 4 to the product of 3 times 2 (3 times 2 is 6 and then 4 plus 6 is 10). So what answer does QBasic produce?

QBasic returns 10. Why?

When multiple operators occur in an expression, certain operations are done before others. That is, some operators have *precedence* over others. Table 6.10 shows the hierarchy of operations. Each line in the table represents one level of precedence, from highest precedence at the top of the table to lowest precedence at the bottom.

When expressions contain two or more operators, higher precedence operations occur sooner. The expression 4 + 3 * 2 resolves to 10 because multiplication has higher precedence than addition (in Table 6.10, multiplication is at level 3 whereas addition is at level 6). In our expression, the multiplication is done before the addition. That is, 3 is first multiplied by 2 to yield 6. Then the 4 is added to 6 to finally produce 10.

When multiple operators occur at the same level of precedence, QBasic resolves the expression by proceeding from left to right. The expression 9 - 4 - 2 yields 3 because 4 is first subtracted from 9 to get 5 and then 2 is subtracted to produce the final answer of 3. (Notice that the result is 7 if the second subtraction is done first.)

Table 6.10. Operator precedence.

Level	Operator(s)	Name
1	^	Exponentiation
2	-	Negation
3	*, /	Multiplication and division
4	\	Integer division
5	MOD	Modulo arithmetic
6	+, -	Addition and subtraction
7	=, >, <, <>, >=, <=	Relational operators
8	NOT	Logical negation
9	AND	Conjunction
10	OR	Inclusive or
11	XOR	Exclusive or
12	EQV	Equivalence
13	IMP	Implication

Using Parentheses in Expressions

Let's take another look at this instruction:

```
PRINT 4 + 3 * 2
```

You saw that the result is 10. That's fine if you want the multiplication to occur first.

But suppose you want the addition to occur before the multiplication. Is there a way you can tell QBasic to do the addition first?

Yes. Use parentheses to override the standard operator precedence. When an expression contains parentheses, QBasic evaluates terms inside parentheses before terms outside parentheses. So here is how you tell QBasic to do the addition first:

```
PRINT (4 + 3) * 2
```

Now the result is

14

The parentheses force QBasic to evaluate 4 + 3 before multiplying this result by 2.

For more complicated expressions, parentheses can be nested inside each other. Deeper-nested parentheses evaluate first.

For example:

```
PRINT (24 - (3 * 5)) / 2
```

The result is

```
 4.5
```

In this example, QBasic first evaluates the expression in the deepest-nested parentheses. Therefore, the first calculation is 3 times 5 which is 15. Then this value of 15 is subtracted from 24 to get 9. Finally 9 is divided by 2 to yield the answer 4.5.

Complicated expressions often require parentheses. For example:

```
AtomicWeight! = Energy! / (3 * ((Size! + 1.9) / (Mass! ^ 3)))
```

Parentheses are not restricted to mathematical expressions. Relational, string, and logical expressions are also fair game.

```
IF (Cost! > 99.95) OR ((Form% = 39) AND (Status$ = "VIP")) ...
```

Even when operator precedence is not an issue, you should use parentheses liberally to clarify your expressions.

In a misguided effort to exhibit their programming sophistication, a few programmers go to great lengths to avoid parentheses. This often results in instructions that are hard to read and difficult to troubleshoot. Consider this instruction:

```
Profit! = 89.14 + 34.60 * 23.11 - 11.89 / 4.88 + 2.66
```

Here is a clearer rendition of the same instruction:

```
Profit! = (89.14) + (34.60 * 23.11) - (11.89 / 4.88) + (2.66)
```

We won't quibble if you prefer to leave out the first and last set of parentheses in this expression. Notice that the two preceding instructions are equivalent. Each instruction assigns exactly the same value to Profit!, but the second instruction is much easier to read and understand.

Program Comments

In general, QBasic programs are quite readable. Most keywords, such as IF, BEEP, and PRINT, are English words with natural meanings or easy-to-decipher abbreviations. Unlike other languages such as C or assembler, QBasic seldom requires obscure syntax.

However, as you begin to write substantial programs, you soon realize that many subtleties occur in the final code. The cumulative effect of several instructions cannot be easily grasped by someone scanning your program for the first time—that is, unless you place comments in your programs.

In QBasic, a *comment* is a remark added to a program. Such remarks usually supply factual data (such as when the program was written), clarify fine points, or just explain what's happening inside the program.

The sole purpose of a comment is to provide information for you or another person who might need to see or modify your program. When running a program, QBasic ignores all the comments.

You have two ways to place comments in your programs: the REM statement and the single quotation mark (apostrophe).

Using the *REM* Statement

The keyword REM identifies the rest of the line as a comment. (REM is short for REMark.)

S T A T E M E N T

```
REM remark
```

where

    remark is any sequence of characters.

For example, you might begin a loan amortization program like the one in Listing 6.1.

Listing 6.1. The LOAN program.

```
REM Program: LOAN
REM Get the principal and interest rate, calculate the payment.
PRINT "Loan Calculator"
```

You can place a REM instruction on a line with other instructions. However, everything following the REM is part of the comment. Be wary of this sort of trap:

```
Client$ = "ABC Plumbing": REM Get discount: Rate! = 23.14
```

This line *does* assign the string value "ABC Plumbing" to Client$. However, the REM instruction makes the *remainder* of the line a remark. The value of Rate! does not change.

Using the Apostrophe

The single quotation mark (or apostrophe) is a substitute for the REM keyword. An apostrophe signals that the remainder of the line is a comment. You can place an apostrophe at the beginning of a line (the whole line becomes a comment) or later in the line.

The apostrophe is often used to place a comment on the same line with other instructions. Unlike REM, you don't need a colon to separate the apostrophe from the other instructions on the same line. For example:

```
Deg.C! = ((Deg.F! - 32) * 5) / 9    'Fahrenheit to Centigrade
```

There are two exceptions to the apostrophe initiating a comment. First, an apostrophe inside a string literal is simply part of the literal. For example:

```
PRINT "Randy's Donut Shop"
```

This instruction displays Randy's Donut Shop. The apostrophe does not indicate a comment, but is, instead, part of the string literal.

Second, an apostrophe inside a DATA instruction is part of the data and does not initiate a comment. See Chapter 9, "Managing Large Amounts of Data," for information on the DATA instruction.

Tips on Using Comments

Use meaningful comments liberally.

Obviously, meaningful comments go a long way toward making any program more readable. By peppering your programs with comments, you enhance the self-documentation of your programs. This practice facilitates the later chores of troubleshooting or modifying the programs—whether by you or by someone else. Experienced programmers know that well-placed comments help you "get into" a program.

In a work environment, you might find yourself under time pressure. Sometimes you are tempted to forgo comments in the name of expediency. This is penny-wise and pound-foolish. Invariably, you will need that program (or part of it) later. You will spend some puzzling moments glaring at the enigmatic program that was so clear several months ago. You learn one of programming's most sobering lessons the first time you have to rewrite a program because you can't decipher what you did before.

In fact, the following maxim is worth highlighting:

> **Every minute spent writing comments will be saved at least tenfold later on.**

Consider the time you spend writing comments an investment. Your dividends come later in the forms of saved time and avoided frustration.

However, like ice cream and candy, any good thing can be overdone. In your zeal to provide comments, you can go overboard. Don't fall into the trap of commenting every line. Simple instructions with informative variable names require no comments.

```
NumChecks% = NumChecks% + 1     'increment NumChecks% by 1
PRINT NumChecks%                'display the number of checks
```

The comments on these two lines do nothing more than restate what's obvious from the instructions themselves. Such comments are frivolous and actually detract from the program's readability. Comments should add to the understanding. When each line is easily understood, you might write a comment every 10 or so lines to explain what the following group of lines accomplishes.

The Microscopic View— the QBasic Character Set

Now let's peer through the microscope and quickly examine QBasic at the "atomic" level. Table 6.11 presents all the individual characters recognized by QBasic. Notice that the third column, labeled **Primary Use**, lists only a single use for each character. In fact, many characters have multiple uses. For example, the uppercase letters are used to compose variable names as well as to compose keywords.

Table 6.11. QBasic character set.

Character(s)	Name	Primary Use
A-Z	Uppercase letters	Compose keywords
a-z	Lowercase letters	Compose identifiers
0-9	Digits	Compose numbers
	Blank space	Separator
!	Exclamation point	Single-precision suffix
#	Pound sign	Double-precision suffix
%	Percent sign	Integer suffix
&	Ampersand	Long integer suffix
$	Dollar sign	String suffix
"	Quotation mark	Delimit string literals
'	Apostrophe (single quote)	Initiate comments
.	Period	Compose numbers
,	Comma	Separate parameters
;	Semicolon	Separator
:	Colon	Separate instructions
+	Plus sign	Addition symbol
-	Minus sign	Subtraction symbol
*	Asterisk	Multiplication symbol
/	Slash	Division symbol
\	Backslash	Integer division symbol
^	Caret	Exponentiation symbol
=	Equal sign	Assignment symbol
<	Less than sign	Relational expressions
>	Greater than sign	Relational expressions
( )	Left and right parentheses	General delimiter
?	Question mark	Shorthand for PRINT
ENTER	Enter (carriage return)	Line terminator

Table 6.11 lists those characters that, in the appropriate contexts, have special meaning in QBasic. Other characters can be displayed in textual output. For example, curly braces, { }, can be placed inside a string literal:

```
PRINT "{ This works OK }"
```

The resulting output is

```
{ This works OK }
```

Programmers with BASICA or GW-BASIC experience might notice that Table 6.11 does not include the underscore character. In BASICA/GW-BASIC, but not in QBasic, the underscore character enables you to divide a long program line into two or more physical lines.

When the QBasic editor detects an underscore in an imported program, the underscore is removed and one long physical line results. However, you cannot use an underscore while creating a program in the QBasic editor.

Summary

This chapter examined the structure of QBasic programs and the building blocks (or components) that fit together to form programs. You saw that a program is a series of lines with each line being a single instruction, a group of instructions, a label, or a metacommand. All the characters in the QBasic character set were briefly introduced.

QBasic manipulates data of two fundamental types—numbers and text (strings). Numbers are further divided into the integer, long integer, single-precision, and double-precision data types. Strings can be variable-length or fixed-length strings.

Variables, which can have any data type, store a single data value. You can modify the value of a variable with an assignment instruction. Arrays are like composite variables, storing multiple data items.

QBasic has four different kinds of operators: arithmetic, string, relational, and logical. With the operators, you can form expressions to represent almost any quantity. In an expression, operands can consist of literals, variables, and parenthetical subexpressions. However, all expressions resolve to a single value.

Comments enhance any program's readability. Appropriate comments make a program easier to understand and help when tracking down errors.

Program Flow and Decision Making

P rogram flow refers to the order in which your program instructions execute. Generally, this flow proceeds line by line from the top of your program down to the bottom.

When you run a program, QBasic first executes the topmost line of the program. Line by line, the computer proceeds downward executing each program line in turn. Eventually (if no error or other termination occurs), QBasic executes the bottom (final) line of your program. With nothing more left to do, the computer ends your program, and you see the familiar Press any key to continue message at the bottom of your screen.

This sequential, "top-down" program order is straightforward and easy to understand. Many practical programs proceed entirely in this systematic sequence.

However, there is a limit to what you can accomplish with such simple, linear sequencing. Frequently, you need to redirect program flow. From one point in your program, you might want to transfer execution to a location a few lines away or perhaps several lines away. Usually, this redirection involves some sort of decision making, or testing.

Consider how many times you make decision tests in your everyday life. When you get in your car for a drive, for example, you probably look at the gas gauge. If necessary, you stop for gas. You "test" the value of the gas gauge and make a decision about where to go (or what to do) as a result.

Programs, like people, often need to test a condition and then make a decision depending on the result. For example, a program might add together the values of two variables and then transfer execution to one of several lines depending on the result.

This chapter examines the following ways that program flow can be altered from the normal sequential execution order:

- Unconditional branching (GOTO)
- Conditional branching (ON GOTO)
- Ending and restarting execution
- Conditional testing (IF-THEN)

Branching

Branching is the direct transfer from one line in your program to another line. In this chapter, you'll learn different ways you can make your program "jump" from one line to any other line.

Suppose one line of a program contains an instruction that causes QBasic to immediately jump down to another line. Then we say that the former line *branches* to the latter line.

Branching comes in two forms:

- *Unconditional branching* (program control transfers to a specific line in all cases)
- *Conditional branching* (program control transfers to one of several lines depending on the value of a testing expression)

Labels and Line Numbers

Labels and line numbers play a critical role in program branching. The reason is simple: If you want your program to branch somewhere, you need a way to indicate where that somewhere is! Just as highway signs and mileage markers designate locations along a highway, labels and line numbers designate locations in a QBasic program.

To divert execution to an explicit location, you must have a way to name (that is, specify) that location. QBasic provides two such ways—labels and line numbers.

As mentioned in the previous chapter, a label begins with a letter and ends with a colon. Here are some valid labels:

```
CalculateSum:
```

```
Call123:
```

```
Fred:
```

Within a given main program (or subprogram), each label must be unique. Upper- and lowercase letters are not distinguished in labels. Thus `MyLabel:`, `mylabel:`, and `MYLABEL:` are equivalent.

A label can appear at the beginning of a line containing one or more instructions. In this case, when execution is diverted to the label, the program immediately executes the instructions on that line.

Alternatively, a label can stand alone on a line. When you divert execution to such a label, the program next executes the instructions on the line immediately following the label.

You can place a line number at the beginning of any program line. The number must be an integer from 0 to 65529. Here are two examples of numbered lines:

```
100 PRINT "This line has a line number"
```

```
4001 A = 10: B = 6: C = 29
```

Line numbers do not specify the order in which QBasic should execute the program lines. Instead, a line number simply gives an identity to its line—a way to explicitly refer to that program line. If you want, you can place line number 500 between line number 1000 and line number 2000.

Of course, any specific line number can be used only once within a given program. Notice that line numbers are entirely optional; you can include them or omit them as you see fit. If you do use line numbers, you can number every line or only certain lines.

Modern programming practice favors labels over line numbers because an alphanumeric name conveys more information than a colorless line number. Create meaningful label names such as `GraphRoutine` or `GetUserInput`. Your programs will be easier to read and understand.

NOTE BASICA, GW-BASIC, and other BASIC interpreters require that each program line starts with a line number. In these interpreters, the numeric value of each line number indicates the proper sequence of the program lines. If necessary, BASICA and GW-BASIC realign program lines in ascending order from the smallest line number to the largest. (For more about line numbers in BASICA and GW-BASIC, see Chapters 23 and 24.)

QBasic does no such reordering. Line numbers can appear in any numerical order. Actually, QBasic supports line numbers simply for compatibility with BASICA/GW-BASIC. Most programs written in the QBasic environment do not use line numbers at all.

Unconditional Branching with *GOTO*

As mentioned in Chapter 3, "A Hands-On Introduction to Programming," you use GOTO for unconditional branches. The destination can be specified with either a label or a line number.

STATEMENT

GOTO *label*

or

GOTO *linenum*

where

 label is a label defined in the program,

and

 linenum is any line number in the program.

Of course, the destination must exist or a fatal error occurs (Label not defined). To get a feel for GOTO, try the following program:

```
    PRINT "I am"
    GOTO Message
    PRINT "not"
Message:
    PRINT "happy"
```

The result is

```
I am
happy
```

Notice that the PRINT "not" line never got a chance to do its thing. Do you see what happened? The GOTO instruction transferred control directly to the Message label. Therefore, the program continues with the final PRINT instruction, the next sequential instruction.

You might be thinking, "That's great, but what's the big deal? If we don't want the PRINT "not" line, why not just leave it out of the program entirely?" For the time being, the answer has to be "just wait and see." Later in this chapter, we'll discuss how GOTO combines with testing instructions such as IF-THEN to create powerful decision-making structures.

Notice that in a GOTO instruction, you don't include the trailing colon in the label name. However, in the line containing the label itself, the colon must appear after the label name.

You cannot use a variable for the *linenum* parameter. That is, if Target% is an integer variable, the following instruction is *not* legal:

```
GOTO Target%
```

This line results in a syntax error.

Using GOTO, you can branch anywhere in your program: to a previous line, to a subsequent line, even to the same line. However, you should branch only to another line at the same program level. That is, avoid branching into or out of a subprogram, multiline function definition, FOR loop, or similar structure. If you use GOTO inside such a structure, you should confine the branch within the structure. (If you are unfamiliar with these structures, don't worry. They are explained in upcoming chapters.)

As you might be aware, GOTO has a detestable reputation with many experienced programmers because haphazard GOTO statements create programs with logic flow branching in all directions. Such "spaghetti logic" is difficult to read and hard to debug.

Modern structured programming makes GOTO instructions obsolete. QBasic has the necessary language enhancements for writing any program without the need of a GOTO. See Chapter 17, "Modular Programming," for further discussion of this topic.

Conditional Branching with *ON-GOTO*

The ON-GOTO instruction extends the GOTO concept. With ON-GOTO, you branch to one of a specified set of lines according to the value of a numeric expression.

<table>
<tr><td>

STATEMENT

</td><td>

ON *numexpr* GOTO *labellist*

or

ON *numexpr* GOTO *linenumlist*

where

    numexpr is a general numeric expression,

    labellist is a list of one or more labels separated by commas,

and

    linenumlist is a list of one or more line numbers separated by commas.

</td></tr>
</table>

The value of the numeric expression determines which line in the label list or line number list executes next. Branching occurs to the corresponding line in the list; the first listed line if *numexpr* is one, the second listed line if *numexpr* is two, and so on.

If *numexpr* is zero or greater than the number of lines in the list, execution continues with the instruction immediately after the ON-GOTO. If *numexpr* is negative, your program terminates with the error Illegal function call.

The following example should make ON-GOTO clearer:

```
ON NumSingers% GOTO Solo, Duet, Trio, Quartet
```

The value of NumSingers% determines which line QBasic executes next. If NumSingers% equals 1, the program branches to the label Solo: and continues from there. If NumSingers% equals 2, the program goes to the label Duet:. If NumSingers% equals 3, the program branches to the label Trio:. If NumSingers% equals 4, the branch is to Quartet:.

If NumSingers% is 0 or greater than 4, the program continues with whatever line immediately follows the ON-GOTO instruction. If NumSingers% is negative, the Illegal function call error occurs.

The same destination can appear more than once in your line number list or label list. For example, the following instruction branches to line number 300 if MyValue% is 1, 3, or 5:

```
ON MyValue% GOTO 300, 200, 300, 400, 300, 500
```

As is shown in our examples so far, the numeric expression is simply a variable, but you can use any general expression. Here's an example of a more complicated expression:

```
ON ((MyScore% - 23) / Average%) GOTO First, Second, Third
```

The numeric expression should resolve to an integer number. A fractional value is rounded to the nearest whole integer, which determines the line branched to.

You *can* mix labels and line numbers in the same list.

Notice that once execution branches, there is no implied return to any common point. For example, consider this program fragment from a golf game:

```
ON Strokes% GOTO HoleInOne, Eagle, Birdie, Par
    PRINT "You got a bogie."
HoleInOne:
    PRINT "You got a hole in one!"
Eagle:
    PRINT "You got an eagle."
Birdie:
    PRINT "You got a birdie."
Par:
    PRINT "You got par."
```

Suppose that the value of Strokes% is 2. The program displays the following undesired result:

```
You got an eagle.
You got a birdie.
You got par.
```

For this type of ON-GOTO construction, additional branching instructions are necessary after each PRINT instruction. The following does the trick:

```
ON Strokes% GOTO HoleInOne, Eagle, Birdie, Par
    PRINT "You got a bogie.": GOTO Done
HoleInOne:
    PRINT "You got a hole in one!": GOTO Done
Eagle:
    PRINT "You got an eagle.": GOTO Done
Birdie:
    PRINT "You got a birdie.": GOTO Done
Par:
    PRINT "You got par."
Done:
    REM The program continues here
```

Later in this chapter, you will see another (more elegant) way to accomplish this same programming task.

In practice, ON-GOTO has limited use because the programming situation must be just right for ON-GOTO to be practical. It's not often that you have a program decision point where you want to branch to different line numbers depending on a numeric expression with possible values of 1, 2, 3, and so on.

Like GOTO, the ON-GOTO statement is outmoded and is provided mainly for compatibility with existing BASICA and GW-BASIC programs. QBasic's SELECT instruction and multiline IF statements (discussed later in this chapter) provide more flexible, modern tools for conditional branching.

Ending and Restarting Execution

The most abrupt way to alter program flow is simply to end execution. QBasic has three equivalent statements that terminate a program—END, STOP, and SYSTEM.

END

STOP

SYSTEM

Why do three instructions do the same thing? It's another quirk of QBasic providing compatibility with BASICA and GW-BASIC. (In BASICA and GW-BASIC, END, STOP, and SYSTEM produce slightly different effects.)

None of the statements accept any arguments. When an END or SYSTEM instruction occurs, all files are closed and control passes back to the QBasic environment.

A STOP instruction acts in a slightly different manner. STOP leaves files open, suspends execution, and returns to the program text with a highlight on the STOP instruction. From there, you can use the Immediate window and later resume execution (see Chapters 4, "Learning the QBasic Environment," and 18, "Interactive Debugging and Testing").

You can have more than one terminating instruction in a program, but no such instruction is required. If QBasic runs out of instructions to execute, the effect is as though an END instruction is at the end of the program.

However, it's a good idea to use END in each program, even if only one such instruction appears as the final line of the program. This shows, at least, that you expect the program to end at such a point.

You can restart execution from within a program. Use RUN to begin execution of a program—either the same program or a new program from disk.

RUN *linenumber*

or

RUN *filespec*

or just

RUN

where

    linenumber is the line number at which execution begins,

and

    filespec specifies a file on disk.

STATEMENT

With no arguments, RUN causes three things to happen:

1. All files are closed.

2. All variables (numeric and string) are cleared.

3. The program restarts execution from the beginning.

The effect is exactly like running the program for the first time.

With a *linenumber* argument, RUN begins execution at the specified line number. You cannot designate a label, only a line number.

Restarting a program is a graceful solution to certain errors. For example, suppose that your program prompts the user to supply some data. At a later point, the program detects inconsistencies in the provided input. The only realistic solution is to repeat the whole input process. A RUN instruction begins the program all over again. The RUN command is the programming equivalent of washing your hands and starting over.

With the *filespec* option, RUN begins execution of another program stored on disk. This process, called *chaining,* is discussed in Chapter 19, "Managing Memory."

Conditional Testing

Just as decision making is an important and frequent part of your daily life, decision making is a perpetual programming theme. Like a fork in the road, a *logic juncture* is a place in your program where the subsequent execution path can go different ways.

When programming a logic juncture, your thought process goes like this: "If such and such is True, I want this to happen. If not, then that should happen instead."

You choose the program path based on the evaluation of a test condition. Depending on the type of test condition, QBasic offers two flexible program structures. The IF-THEN statement tests whether a condition is True or False and then directs logic flow depending on the result. The SELECT structure tests whether a value lies in specified ranges, and then branches accordingly.

Testing with the *IF* Instruction

With an IF instruction, you can test whether an expression is True or False and direct logic flow accordingly. With a block IF instruction, you can perform successive True and False tests.

The IF instruction has many forms, but they all can be classified into two categories: single-line IF and multiline IF.

Single-Line *IF*

Here are the two classic IF-THEN-ELSE single-line forms.

<table>
<tr>
<td>S
T
A
T
E
M
E
N
T</td>
<td>

IF *expression* THEN *thenclause*

or

IF *expression* THEN *thenclause* ELSE *elseclause*

where

    expression is any expression that evaluates to True or False,

    thenclause is the action to perform if *expression* is True,

and

    elseclause is the action to perform if *expression* is False.

The ELSE *elseclause* phrase is optional.

</td>
</tr>
</table>

An IF-THEN instruction can take many forms. Let's start with a simple example:

```
INPUT "What is the temperature outside"; Temp!
IF Temp! > 100 THEN PRINT "It's hot"
PRINT "So long for now"
```

Here are two sample runs of this program. The first time the user replies 106 when asked for the temperature. The second time the reply is 84.

```
What is the temperature outside? 106
It's hot
So long for now


What is the temperature outside? 84
So long for now
```

The INPUT line of the program displays the question What is the temperature outside? and waits for you to respond. When you type in a value, the program stores your reply in the variable Temp!. An INPUT instruction accomplishes all this. (INPUT was explained briefly in Chapter 3, "A Hands-On Introduction to Programming," and it is discussed further in Chapter 16, "Using Hardware Devices.")

Look at the IF-THEN instruction in the second program line. Do you see how it works? If the value of the variable Temp! is greater than 100, then the program prints the message It's hot. (Remember that the > character is a relational operator meaning "greater than." Relational operators were introduced in Chapter 6, "Language Building Blocks," and are discussed again later in this chapter.)

Now look at the two sample runs of the program. The first time, we gave the temperature as 106. Because 106 is greater than 100, the program dutifully displays the It's hot message.

But the second time we input the temperature as 84. What happened? Did the computer just ignore the part of the IF-THEN instruction that followed the THEN?

That's exactly what happened. When the test condition of an IF-THEN instruction is false, the computer disregards the part of the instruction after THEN. The program moves immediately down to the next program line.

In the second run, the value of Temp! is 84. The test condition is False because 84 is not greater than 100. As a result, the computer ignores the part of the instruction after THEN (the PRINT clause) and moves down to the next program line. In this case, the next line is the PRINT instruction that displays the So long for now message.

Adding an *ELSE* Clause to *IF-THEN*

Suppose you want to do one thing if the test condition is True but another thing if the test condition is False. No problem. A second form of the IF-THEN statement adds an ELSE clause just for this purpose.

To demonstrate this form, change the IF-THEN instruction so that the new program looks like this:

```
INPUT "What is the temperature outside"; Temp!
IF Temp! > 100 THEN PRINT "It's hot" ELSE PRINT "Not too bad"
PRINT "So long for now"
```

Now let's try those two runs again:

```
What is the temperature outside? 106
It's hot
So long for now


What is the temperature outside? 84
Not too bad
So long for now
```

When we give the temperature as 104, the result is the same as before. But now when we give the temperature as 86, the computer displays the Not too bad message.

By adding an ELSE clause to an IF-THEN instruction, you specify what to do when the testing condition is False—the ELSE part—as well as what to do when the testing condition is True—the THEN part (see Figure 7.1).

Figure 7.1.

The IF-THEN-ELSE instruction.

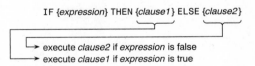

```
IF {expression} THEN {clause1} ELSE {clause2}
```

→ execute *clause2* if *expression* is false
→ execute *clause1* if *expression* is true

THEN and *ELSE* Clauses

How fancy can the THEN and ELSE clauses get? For starters, each clause can be any single QBasic instruction. Here are a few sample instructions:

```
IF A = B THEN PRINT "Same" ELSE PRINT "Different"

IF A = B THEN GOTO Identical ELSE GOTO Unequal

IF A = B THEN BEEP

IF A = B THEN END

IF A = B THEN Profit! = 20 ELSE Profit! = Cost! * Discount!
```

The THEN or ELSE clause also can contain multiple instructions. Simply separate each instruction with a colon. For example:

```
IF Score > 500 THEN Rate = 3.5: Num% = 29: Winner$ = "Debby"
```

This instruction tests whether the value of the variable Score is greater than 500. If so, then the values of Rate, Num% and Winner$ are assigned the values 3.5, 29, and "Debby" respectively. If the value of Score is not greater than 500, control passes directly to the next line without assigning values to any of the three variables.

GOTO is one of the most common statements to place in a THEN or ELSE clause. That way, you can branch to different lines depending on the result of a testing expression. For example:

```
IF Age% > 20 THEN GOTO 500
```

If the value of Age% is greater than 20, the program proceeds directly to line 500. Perhaps Age% is the age of a person. If the person is an adult (at least 21 years old), the program branches directly to line 500 to begin the instructions found there. There might be several instructions between the IF instruction and line 500. Those instructions execute if the person is a minor (that is, under the age of 21).

GOTO is so common in THEN and ELSE clauses that QBasic provides a special short-ened form of the IF statement for such cases. If the THEN or ELSE clause consists of GOTO and a line number, you can omit the THEN keyword or the GOTO keyword. For example, you can write the last instruction in either of the following ways:

```
IF Age% > 20 GOTO 500
```

```
IF Age% > 20 THEN 500
```

Table 7.1 summarizes the various allowable forms of THEN and ELSE clauses in an IF instruction.

Table 7.1. Syntax forms for *THEN* and *ELSE* clauses.

Syntax	Action Taken
instructions	One or more QBasic instructions separated with colons. After the instructions execute, control passes to the line following the IF instruction.
GOTO *label*	*label* is a valid line label. Control passes to the line designated by the label. In such a clause, the THEN or ELSE keyword is optional.
GOTO *linenum*	*linenum* is a valid line number. Control passes to the line designated by the line number. In such a clause, the THEN or ELSE keyword is optional.

continues

Table 7.1. Continued	
Syntax	**Action Taken**
linenum	*linenum* is a valid line number. Control passes to the line designated by the line number. In such a case (when the GOTO keyword is omitted), the THEN or ELSE keyword must appear.

Types of Testing Expressions

Now let's take a closer look at the testing expressions you can place in an IF instruction.

The testing expression must be a *Boolean expression,* which simply means an expression that evaluates to True or False.

Most often, the expression is a *relational expression.* Such expressions use the equality and inequality operators to form natural conditional tests. Here are a few examples:

```
IF Num% < 0 THEN PRINT "Number is negative"

IF Num% <= 0 THEN PRINT "Number is not positive"

IF Animal$ = "Dog" THEN PRINT "It's a pooch"

IF (MyScore + HerScore) > YourScore THEN PRINT "You lose"
```

The first line uses the "less than" operator (<) to test the value of the variable Num%. If Num% has a value less than zero, the line displays the message Number is negative. If the value of Num% is zero or positive, the line displays no message at all.

The second line has a subtle difference from the first line. The second line uses the "less than or equal to" operator (<=). Here, the condition is True whenever Num% is negative *or* zero. Notice that the first and second lines both display their messages when Num% is negative. Neither line displays a message when Num% is positive. The difference arises when Num% is exactly zero. Then the second line displays its message but the first line does not.

T I P   Boolean Expressions Are Really Just Numbers

Internally, QBasic needs a way to represent Boolean values; that is, a way to represent True or False. In fact, QBasic uses simple integer numbers: 0 for False and –1 for True. As a result, Boolean expressions are really just special cases of numeric expressions.

When QBasic evaluates a Boolean expression, False becomes 0 and True becomes –1. (When converting a number to a Boolean value, QBasic evaluates 0 as False and any nonzero number as True.) You can demonstrate this conversion with this short test:

```
NumItems% = 0
IF NumItems% THEN PRINT "Nonzero" ELSE PRINT "Zero"
```

In the `IF` instruction, the variable `NumItems%` is a Boolean expression all by itself. The output of this program is `Zero`, which demonstrates that 0 is treated as False. Now change the assignment instruction so that the value of `NumItems%` has any nonzero value. For example:

```
NumItems% = 22
```

The program now displays `Nonzero` because the Boolean expression has become True.

Another way to see the arithmetic conversion is to try this instruction:

```
PRINT 129 > 45
```

Does that instruction look funny? What do you think the output is? Try it. Then try `PRINT 45 > 129`.

The third example in the preceding list demonstrates that testing expressions can be string as well as numeric. Here, the "equals" operator (=) tests whether the string stored in `Animal$` is `Dog`. If so, the line displays the message `It's a pooch`. In relational expressions, the equal sign really means "equals" (as opposed to the equal sign in assignment instructions, which means "is assigned the value"). Also, notice that the expression is True only when there is an exact match. If `Animal$` has the value `DOG` (all capital letters), the result is False. `Dog` and `DOG` are *not* identical strings.

The final line shows an expression involving parentheses. Here the values of `MyScore` and `HerScore` are added together. This sum is then compared with the value in `YourScore` to decide whether the expression is True or False.

The Relational Operators

QBasic provides six relational operators for your testing expressions. The operators were briefly mentioned in the previous chapter and are listed again in Table 7.2.

Table 7.2. Relational operators.

Symbol	Name	Example
=	Equals	`4 = (3 + 1)`
<>	Not equal	`"Dog" <> "Cat"`
>	Greater than	`8 > 5`
<	Less than	`3 < 6`
>=	Greater than or equals	`9 >= 9`
<=	Less than or equals	`"Hi" <= "Ho"`

Each example in the last column of the table is True. Notice that some of the operators consist of two individual characters which together make one symbol. For example, the "less than or equals" operator is the "left-angle bracket" symbol (Shift-comma on most keyboards) followed by the equal sign.

Compound Testing Expressions

Sometimes you need to test two or more conditions. For example, suppose you want to assign the value Perfect to Result$ only if *both* of the following conditions are True:

- The value of Score% is 300
- The value of Game$ is Bowling

The following instruction does the trick:

```
IF (Score% = 300) AND (Game$ = "Bowling") THEN Result$ = "Perfect"
```

This instruction uses a compound expression for the test. Notice that the two conditions are combined with the logical operator AND. Both conditions must be True so that the variable Result$ is assigned the value Perfect. If only one condition is True (or if neither condition is True), the test fails and program flow proceeds directly to the next line.

The parentheses in this sample IF instruction are not required. You can remove the parentheses and QBasic still interprets the line correctly. However, the parentheses make the line easy to read and understand. In similar instructions, we recommend that you use parentheses for clarity.

Relational Operators Work on Strings

All the relational operators work on strings as well as numbers. One string "equals" another string only if both strings contain exactly the same sequence of characters. That's easy enough to understand.

But how can one string be "greater than" or "less than" another string? How does the last example in Table 7.2 work?

Every string character has an associated numeric value from 0 to 255. These values conform to an established code known as ASCII (American Standard Code for Information Interchange). For example, in ASCII, the letter *A* is 65 and an asterisk (*) is 42. (ASCII is discussed in Chapter 11, "Manipulating Strings," and all the ASCII values are listed in Appendix B, "ASCII Character Set.")

Using ASCII, you can compare two strings character by character. The details are explained in Chapter 11, but here is the essence of the method: Characters at the same position in each string are compared (first character with first character, second with second, and so on). As soon as one pair of characters are different, the comparison stops. The ASCII values of the two characters (in the pair) are compared. One character must have a larger ASCII value than the other. The string containing the "larger" character is considered to be the "larger" string.

Consider the last example in Table 7.2, which compares Hi with Ho. Both strings have H as their first character. The second characters, however, are different. The ASCII value of i is 105 and o has a value of 111. Therefore, o is larger than i and Ho is larger than Hi.

The Logical Operators

The sample IF instruction uses AND to combine the two conditions. AND is one of QBasic's six logical operators. The logical operators combine Boolean expressions to create one large Boolean expression. (Remember that a Boolean expression is an expression that can be evaluated to True or False.)

The most common logical operators are AND, OR, and NOT. They work as follows:

- AND combines two expressions. Each expression must be True for the entire (composite) expression to be True.

- OR combines two expressions. Either expression (or both expressions) must be True for the entire expression to be True.

- NOT negates a single expression.

Here's an example of NOT:

```
IF NOT (Score% = 300) THEN Result$ = "Could do better"
```

QBasic has three other logical operators: XOR, EQV, and IMP. Figure 7.2 shows the results returned by all the logical operators. In the figure, A and B represent Boolean operands that have a value of T (True) or F (False). The figure has four lines because there are four possible "truth configurations" for the two combined expressions:

- A and B are both True
- A is True but B is False
- A is False but B is True
- A and B are both False

OPERAND VALUE		VALUE OF LOGICAL OPERATION					
A	B	NOT A	A AND B	A OR B	A X OR B	A EQV B	A IMP B
T	T	F	T	T	F	T	T
T	F	F	F	T	T	F	F
F	T	T	F	T	T	F	T
F	F	T	F	F	F	T	T

Figure 7.2.

Results of logical operators.

Multiple *IF* Instructions

A single IF instruction is fine when your condition is nothing more than one True or False test. But suppose you have a condition with several possible outcomes.

For example, reconsider the golf problem discussed earlier in this chapter. Recall that you wanted to examine the value of the variable Strokes% and display a different message depending on the value. Here's how we programmed that task using an ON-GOTO instruction and line labels:

```
ON Strokes% GOTO HoleInOne, Eagle, Birdie, Par
    PRINT "You got a bogie.": GOTO Done
HoleInOne:
    PRINT "You got a hole in one!": GOTO Done
Eagle:
    PRINT "You got an eagle.": GOTO Done
Birdie:
    PRINT "You got a birdie.": GOTO Done
Par:
    PRINT "You got par."
Done:
    REM   The program continues here
```

Another way to program this problem is with consecutive IF instructions. For example:

```
IF Strokes% = 1 THEN PRINT "You got a hole in one!"
IF Strokes% = 2 THEN PRINT "You got an eagle."
IF Strokes% = 3 THEN PRINT "You got a birdie."
IF Strokes% = 4 THEN PRINT "You got par."
IF Strokes% > 4 THEN PRINT "You got a bogie."
REM       The program continues here
```

Notice that any particular value of Strokes% can satisfy only one of the IF conditions. That guarantees that only one of the messages prints when you run this program fragment.

Sometimes you want to test a variable for different value ranges. For example, suppose a program stores the age of a person in the variable Age%. You want to print out whether the person is a child, teenager, or adult. Here's how you might program that with multiple IF instructions.

```
    IF Age% < 0 THEN PRINT "Error in age": GOTO Done
    IF Age% <= 12 THEN PRINT "Child": GOTO Done
    IF Age% < 20 THEN PRINT "Teenager": GOTO Done
    PRINT "Adult"
Done:
    REM Program continues here
```

Do you see why the GOTO instructions are necessary in the three IF instructions? Without the GOTO statements, you erroneously get extra messages for some values of Age%. For example, suppose Age% is 10 and the program has none of the GOTO instructions. Follow the logic and you'll see that the Child, Teenager, and Adult messages will all print.

You can eliminate the GOTO statements in these kinds of IF blocks by placing multiple tests in appropriate IF instructions. Here, for example, is another way to successfully program the last example:

```
IF Age% < 0 THEN PRINT "Error in age"
IF (Age% >= 0) AND (Age% <= 12) THEN PRINT "Child"
IF (Age% > 12) AND (Age% < 20) THEN PRINT "Teenager"
IF Age% >= 20 THEN PRINT "Adult"
REM    The program continues here
```

The second and third IF instructions contain multiple conditions.

Nested *IF* Instructions

You can nest IF instructions to two or more levels. The basic form looks like this:

```
IF expr1 THEN IF expr2 THEN clause
```

With ELSE clauses, the form looks like this:

```
IF expr1 THEN IF expr2 THEN clause1 ELSE clause2 ELSE clause3
```

Nested IF statements provide another way to write compound tests. Once again, here's an IF instruction shown earlier that contains a compound testing expression:

```
IF (Score% = 300) AND (Game$ = "Bowling") THEN Result$ = "Perfect"
```

With nested IF statements, the following instruction is equivalent:

```
IF Score% = 300 THEN IF Game$ = "Bowling" THEN Result$ = "Perfect"
```

We recommend that you avoid using nested IF instructions. As the previous example suggests, such instructions quickly become confusing. Furthermore, things get even more muddled when nested IF instructions contain ELSE clauses.

Multiline *IF*

IF instructions need not be confined to a single line. QBasic extends the IF concept to a multiple-line block. Such a structure creates more understandable program instructions anytime one of the following situations occurs:

- The *thenclause* or *elseclause* contains two or more instructions
- IF instructions are nested
- An IF instruction extends past one physical line

We recommend that you use a single-line IF instruction only when the *thenclause* and *elseclause* each contain only one instruction and the entire IF instruction fits easily in one physical line.

The single-line IF form is never mandatory. You can always write any IF-THEN-ELSE instruction using the multiline form.

The syntax of the multiline IF looks like this.

```
IF expression THEN
      {instructions}
ELSEIF expression THEN
      {instructions}
ELSEIF expression THEN
      {instructions} ...
ELSE
      {instructions}
END IF
```

where

> expression is a Boolean expression (any expression that evaluates to True or False),

and

> instructions is a block of one or more instructions placed on separate program lines.

ELSEIF blocks are optional. You can have none, one, or several ELSEIF blocks. Furthermore, the ELSE block is also optional.

**S
T
A
T
E
M
E
N
T**

Here is a simple example of a multiline IF:

```
IF Amount! > 100.0 THEN
  NumLargeChecks% = NumLargeChecks% + 1
  PRINT "Another large check"
ELSE
  NumSmallChecks% = NumSmallChecks% + 1
  PRINT "Just a small check"
END IF
```

The multiline IF always begins with an IF clause on the first line. This first line terminates with the THEN keyword. Nothing can follow THEN on this first line; that's how QBasic differentiates a multiline IF structure from the single-line IF.

The last line is always END IF. Notice that a space separates the two keywords END and IF.

You can use any number of ELSEIF clauses. Notice that ELSEIF is one keyword; there is no internal space. Only one ELSE clause can appear.

Clauses evaluate sequentially. First, QBasic checks the initial IF clause. If True (nonzero), the first set of instructions executes (that is, the group of instructions following the THEN), and control passes to the line after END IF. If False (zero), each ELSEIF clause is tested one at a time.

As soon as one ELSEIF clause is True, the associated set of instructions executes, and then control passes to the line after the END IF.

If every ELSEIF clause is False or if there are no ELSEIF clauses, the instructions associated with the ELSE clause execute. If no ELSE clause appears, program flow resumes at the line after the END IF.

Notice that the ELSE and ELSEIF clauses are optional.

You can place a series of individual instructions on multiple lines, creating an instruction block. Each set of *instructions* can be one or more instruction. Multiple instructions are placed on distinct lines creating an instruction block.

Further, any such instruction can be another multiline IF structure. You can nest IF structures to any level.

Here's an example of a block IF construction that demonstrates the use of ELSEIF clauses. This program fragment evaluates the value of MyNumber% and displays an appropriate message.

```
IF MyNumber% = 0 THEN
    PRINT "Zero"
ELSEIF MyNumber% = 1 THEN
    PRINT "One"
ELSEIF MyNumber% >= 2 THEN
    PRINT "Greater than one"
ELSE
    PRINT "Negative"
END IF
```

Testing with *SELECT CASE*

Whereas the IF structure tests for True and False conditions, the SELECT structure tests whether the value of an expression falls within predetermined ranges. Use SELECT to conditionally execute instructions depending on the value of a test expression.

```
SELECT CASE expression
    CASE testlist
        {instructions}
    CASE testlist
        {instructions} ...
    CASE ELSE
        {instructions}
END SELECT
```

where

    expression is any general numeric or string expression,

    testlist is one or more test ranges, separated by commas,

and

    instructions is a block of one or more instructions placed on separate program lines.

CASE blocks are optional. You can have none, one, or several CASE blocks. Furthermore, the CASE-ELSE block is also optional.

S T A T E M E N T

The following example should give you the flavor of using SELECT:

```
SELECT CASE Age%
    CASE 1 TO 12
        PRINT "Child"
        NumChildren% = NumChildren% + 1
    CASE 13 TO 19
        PRINT "Teenager"
        NumTeens% = NumTeens% + 1
    CASE IS > 19
        PRINT "Adult"
        NumAdults% = NumAdults% + 1
    CASE ELSE
        PRINT "Impossible"
END SELECT
```

The testing expression can be numeric or string. The value of *expression* is tested against the ranges in the various test lists. The *expression* and the test expressions in each *testlist* must agree in type—either all numeric or all string.

Each *testlist* specifies a range of values against which the value of *expression* is compared.

There are three general forms for `testlist`:

■ `testexpr1 TO testexpr2`

The test is True if the value of `expression` lies within the range from `testexpr1` to `testexpr2`.

■ `IS rel-oper testexpr`

`rel-op` is one of the six relational operators: =, >, <, <>, >=, <=. The test is True if the value of `expression` satisfies the relational expression.

■ `testexpr`

The test is True if the value of `expression` equals the value of `testexpr`.

The expressions `testexpr`, `testexpr1`, and `testexpr2` are any expressions that agree in type (string or numeric) with the `expression` on the SELECT CASE line. Table 7.3 shows some sample test ranges.

Table 7.3. Sample test ranges.

Type	Example
Relational	CASE IS >= 39
Equality	CASE IS = 21.6
Equality (implied "=")	CASE 21.6
Explicit range	CASE -7 TO 7
Multiple	CASE IS <> 14, IS < 101

Notice that `testlist` can be comprised of two or more test ranges separated by commas. A multiple test evaluates to True if any of the individual tests are True.

SELECT evaluates each CASE clause sequentially, looking for a match. The first time `expression` is within one of the ranges specified by a `testlist`, the associated instructions block executes. Control then passes to the line following the END SELECT.

If every CASE test is False, the instruction block following the CASE ELSE executes. If no CASE ELSE clause is present, program control passes to the line following END SELECT.

Any meaningful SELECT structure contains at least one CASE test. However, no error occurs if you write a SELECT structure containing no CASE test. In such a situation, control passes to the line following END SELECT.

The SELECT structure is a flexible programming tool not found in BASICA or GW-BASIC. With SELECT, you can often replace multiple IF constructions with more elegant, understandable instructions. Use SELECT liberally. Anytime you're contemplating convoluted IF tests, you should probably use SELECT instead.

The following program fragment displays information about the first character of a test string. The test string is stored in the variable MyString$. (The expression LEFT$(MyString$, 1) returns the first character of MyString$. See Chapter 11, "Manipulating Strings.")

```
SELECT CASE LEFT$(MyString$, 1)
   CASE ""
     PRINT "Null String"
   CASE "A", "E", "I", "O", "U", "a", "e", "i", "o", "u"
      PRINT "Vowel"
   CASE "A" TO "Z", "a" TO "z"
      PRINT "Consonant"
   CASE "0" TO "9"
      PRINT "Numeric Digit"
   CASE ELSE
      PRINT "Special Character"
END SELECT
```

Notice how this example works when MyString$ begins with a letter. If the letter is a vowel, the second CASE clause is True. Even though the third CASE clause includes all letters (and thus the vowels), the vowels are intercepted earlier by the second CASE clause.

Summary

Normal program flow progresses line by line down your program. Often, however, you need to alter this sequential order.

The most straightforward way to alter the program flow is with a *branch*. A branch is the direct transfer from one location in your program to another. With GOTO, you can make an *unconditional branch* to any instruction in your program. ON-GOTO provides *conditional branching,* where you branch to one of several instructions depending on the value of a particular expression.

An END, STOP, or SYSTEM instruction immediately terminates your program. These instructions can be placed in the middle of a program as well as at the bottom.

Frequently programs need to make decisions. Often a condition is tested and the program takes different actions depending on the result of the test. IF-THEN-ELSE instructions provide a versatile tool for conditional testing.

Looping

A *loop* is any group of instructions that execute repeatedly. For example, this short program contains a loop:

```
   PRINT "Begin beeping"
DoBeeps:
   BEEP
   PRINT "Still beeping"
   GOTO DoBeeps
PRINT "How can I get here?"
```

The loop begins with the label DoBeeps: in the second line. The end of the loop is the GOTO instruction in the fifth line. In this case, we have an *endless loop*. Do you see why?

The loop is endless because there is no way out. The GOTO instruction always returns the program back to the DoBeeps label in the second line. The loop and the beeping go on forever. The PRINT instruction in the final line never gets a chance to do its thing! You'll have to hit Ctrl-Break to interrupt this program, or turn off your computer, or stop paying your electric bills and wait until your power is disconnected!

A useful loop must have a way to end. When a loop has an ending mechanism, we call the loop a *controlled loop*. A controlled loop executes until a predetermined condition is satisfied. Some form of controlled loop occurs in most nontrivial programs.

QBasic provides three special structures for the programming of controlled loops: FOR-NEXT, WHILE-WEND, and DO-LOOP. The characteristics of each structure are similar, but different.

When programming a controlled loop, you need to choose between FOR-NEXT, WHILE-WEND, and DO-LOOP. As shown in Figure 8.1, your choice generally depends on the answers to the following two questions:

- Do you know how many times you must go through the loop before the loop ends?

- Must the loop execute at least one time?

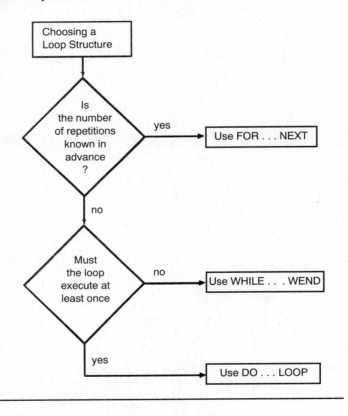

Figure 8.1.

Selecting the appropriate loop structure.

Using *FOR-NEXT* Loops

A FOR-NEXT loop uses a numeric variable to control the number of repetitions. This special variable is called a *counter variable* or *control variable*.

An Example of *FOR-NEXT*

Let's write a program that displays a table of the squares of the numbers from 0 to 6. (The square of a number is simply the number multiplied by itself.) This kind of task is perfect for a FOR-NEXT loop (as seen in Listing 8.1).

Listing 8.1. The Squares program that displays the squares of numbers.

```
REM - Display Squares of Numbers
PRINT "Number", "Square"
FOR Number% = 0 TO 6
    Square% = Number% * Number%
    PRINT Number%, Square%
NEXT Number%
PRINT "End of table"
```

Here's the output from Listing 8.1.

```
Number       Square
  0            0
  1            1
  2            4
  3            9
  4            16
  5            25
  6            36
End of table
```

Let's go over the program. The second line displays the title for the table. Notice that the comma in the PRINT instruction forces the output (Number and Square) to align in predefined columns or *print zones*. We discussed print zones in Chapter 3, "A Hands-On Introduction to Programming," and discuss them in depth in Chapter 12, "Writing Text on the Video Screen."

The loop starts in the line beginning with FOR. Number% is the counter variable. The value of Number% changes each time through the loop. This line sets the first value of Number% to 0 and the final value to 6.

The line beginning with NEXT marks the end of the loop. In a FOR-NEXT loop, all the instructions between the FOR instruction and the NEXT instruction are called the *body* of the loop.

The body of a loop can have any number of instructions. Occasionally a loop has over 100 instructions. Here, the body of our more modest loop is the two instructions between the FOR and NEXT instructions.

Do you see how the loop works? The body of the loop executes repetitively. In succession, Number% takes on the values 0, 1, 2, 3, 4, 5, and 6. The single PRINT instruction (in the line above the NEXT instruction) displays every one of the numeric lines in the table. (Again, the comma aligns the output into columns.)

The first time through the loop, Number% is zero. The assignment statement (just below the FOR statement) computes the square of Number%. Because Number% is zero, the value of Square% is also zero. The ensuing PRINT instruction displays the first line of the table. The NEXT instruction then effectively says "now it's time to increase the value of Number%."

By default, the value of a counter variable increases by one each time through a FOR-NEXT loop. Therefore, the new value of Number% becomes 1 (0 + 1 equals 1).

The program now returns to the beginning of the loop, at the FOR instruction. Here the new value of Number% (1) is compared against the final value of the loop (6 in this case). Because the final value is not yet exceeded, the body of the loop executes again. Number% is 1 and Square% becomes 1 also (1 times 1 is 1). The PRINT instruction displays the second line of the table.

This looping process continues, with Number% continually increasing by 1. Eventually Number% reaches 6. The body of the loop still executes because Number% has equalled—but not yet exceeded—the final value of the loop.

The NEXT instruction then increases the value of Number% to 7. Now, when control returns back to the FOR instruction, the value of Number% is finally greater than the maximum loop value of 6. This signals that the loop is over. The program then proceeds with the first line after the NEXT instruction. In our case, control passes to the final line of the program, which displays the closing message.

The *STEP* Clause

By default, the counter variable increments by 1 each time through a FOR-NEXT loop. You can alter this increment by adding a STEP clause to the end of the FOR instruction. For example, Listing 8.2 is the Squares program from Listing 8.1 with the FOR instruction modified to include a STEP clause.

Listing 8.2. The Squares program with a *STEP* clause.

```
REM - Display Squares of Numbers
PRINT "Number", "Square"
FOR Number% = 0 TO 6 STEP 2
    Square% = Number% * Number%
    PRINT Number%, Square%
NEXT Number%
PRINT "End of table"
```

The following is the output of Listing 8.2:

```
Number      Square
  0           0
  2           4
  4           16
  6           36
End of table
```

The STEP clause specifies an increment of 2 each time through the loop. As a result, Number% becomes successively 0, 2, 4, and 6.

With certain increments, you may not hit the final value of the loop exactly. For example, suppose we wrote the FOR instruction as follows:

```
FOR Number% = 0 TO 6 STEP 4
```

The successive values of Number% increase by 4 (0, 4, 8, and so on). Number% never becomes 6, the designated final value of the loop. In such a case, the loop terminates whenever the counter variable becomes greater than the final value. In this example, the body of the loop executes only when the value of Number% is equal to 0 and 4. The loop terminates when Number% becomes 8. The output is as follows:

```
Number      Square
  0           0
  4           16
End of table
```

You can specify negative increments. When the increment is negative, the counter variable decreases each time through the loop. For a proper "negative" loop, specify the final value of the counter variable to be smaller than the initial value.

For example, Listing 8.3 shows the Squares program rewritten with the FOR instruction now specifying a negative STEP clause.

Listing 8.3. The Squares program with a negative *STEP*.

```
REM - Display Squares of Numbers
PRINT "Number", "Square"
FOR Number% = 3 TO -2 STEP -1
   Square% = Number% * Number%
   PRINT Number%, Square%
NEXT Number%
PRINT "End of table"
```

The output of Listing 8.3. is

```
Number        Square
  3             9
  2             4
  1             1
  0             0
 -1             1
 -2             4
End of table
```

Bypassing the Loop

QBasic bypasses a FOR-NEXT altogether if one of these two conditions is met:

- The starting loop value is greater than the final loop value when the STEP increment is positive.
- The starting loop value is smaller than the final loop value when the STEP increment is negative.

Suppose we change the FOR instruction as follows:

```
FOR Number% = 5 TO 2
```

Here the starting value of the loop (5) is less than the final value (2). Because no STEP clause appears, the default increment is 1. QBasic "realizes" that you can't count upward from 5 and reach 2! Therefore, the loop doesn't execute at all—not even once. The program output becomes

```
Number        Square
End of table
```

Syntax of FOR-NEXT

To summarize, here is the general syntax of a FOR-NEXT loop:

```
FOR countervar = start TO end STEP increment
     .
     .      'body of loop
     .
NEXT countervar
```

where

> *countervar* is a numeric variable acting as the counter variable,
>
> *start* specifies the initial value of *countervar*,
>
> *end* specifies the final value of *countervar*,
>
> *increment* specifies how much to increase *countervar* each time through the loop,

and

> body of loop is a block of QBasic instructions.

The STEP *increment* clause is optional. Also, you can omit *countervar* in the NEXT instruction.

S T A T E M E N T

Using Variables in a *FOR* Instruction

You can specify the loop limits and/or the STEP increment with variables, or with an entire expression. For example, the following FOR instructions are all acceptable:

```
FOR Number% = 2 TO Final%

FOR Number% = First% TO Last%

FOR Number% = First% TO Last% STEP Increment%

FOR Number% = First% TO Last% STEP (Last% - First%) / 10

FOR Number% = (Value1% - Value2%) TO 100
```

By using variables, a program can have different loop boundaries from run to run. For example, Listing 8.4 is the Squares program modified to ask the user for the loop boundaries. When prompted, you type values for the first and last entries in the table.

Listing 8.4. The Squares program with variables as loop ranges.

```
REM - Display Squares of Numbers (Get Limits from user)
INPUT "Please input first value"; First%
INPUT "Please input last value"; Last%
PRINT "Number", "Square"
FOR Number% = First% TO Last%
    Square% = Number% * Number%
    PRINT Number%, Square%
NEXT Number%
PRINT "End of table"
```

The output from Listing 8.4 is

```
Please input first value? 4
Please input last value? 7
Number        Square
   4             16
   5             25
   6             36
   7             49
End of table
```

Notice how the FOR instruction now specifies the loop limits with the variables First% and Last%. The values for First% and Last% are supplied by the user with the aid of the two INPUT instructions.

What happens if you type a larger number for the first value than for the last value? Try it and find out.

Including the Counter Variable in a *NEXT* Instruction

In a NEXT instruction, the counter variable is optional. That is, you can write the NEXT instruction as simply

```
NEXT
```

We recommend, however, that you always include the counter variable in NEXT instructions. That way, you make perfectly clear what the looping variables are.

We discuss nested loops a little later in this chapter. When two or more loops are active simultaneously, NEXT instructions are much easier to understand if they include counter variables.

Placing a Loop in a Single Line

You can specify an entire FOR-NEXT loop in one program line. You don't have to isolate the loop components into separate physical lines. Simply use a colon (:) to separate the individual instructions. For example:

```
FOR Item% = 1 TO LastItem%: PRINT Item%: NEXT Item%
```

The preceding line has the same effect as the following three lines:

```
FOR Item% = 1 TO LastItem%
    PRINT Item%
NEXT Item%
```

Of course, the body of the loop must be relatively small for a single-line loop to be feasible.

Using the Counter Variable

The counter variable can be any numeric type. So far, most of our counter variables have been of type integer (they're integer because of the percent sign at the end of the variable names).

The following loop works fine, however, with a single-precision counter variable named Value!:

```
FOR Value! = 1 TO 4
    PRINT Value!
NEXT Value!
```

The output is just what you would expect:

```
1
2
3
4
```

188

Sometimes you *need* the counter variable to be single- or double-precision. For example, suppose the loop increment has a fractional value:

```
FOR Counter! = 0 TO 1 STEP 1 / 4
    PRINT Counter!
NEXT Counter!
```

The output now contains fractional numbers:

```
0
.25
.5
.75
1
```

If possible, use integer variables for your counter variables. Unless absolutely needed, avoid single- or double-precision counter variables.

First of all, loops with integer counter variables execute faster than loops with noninteger counter variables. Secondly, mathematical errors can occur when counter variables or STEP increments are single- or double-precision. Remember that QBasic cannot represent most single- and double-precision numbers exactly, only approximately. In a loop that contains a fractional STEP clause (or fractional loop limits), accuracy errors can cause the loop to execute an incorrect number of times.

NOTE | ## An Example of a Round-Off Error

Try the following loop (which has a negative step):

```
FOR Counter! = 0 TO 1 STEP 1 / 3
    PRINT Counter!
NEXT Counter!
```

Here's the unexpected output:

```
0
.3333333
.6666667
```

What happened to the fourth line with a value of 1?

A round-off error, that's what. QBasic can only approximate the single-precision number one-third. Just before the fourth time through the loop, the value of Counter! is greater than 1—trivially greater than 1, but still greater than 1.

However, any value of Counter! greater than 1 tells QBasic that the FOR-NEXT loop is complete. As a result, the loop only executes three times, and a programming error results.

We repeat the warning: Use integer counter variables if at all possible.

Nesting *FOR* Loops

FOR-NEXT loops can be nested to any level. Many practical programming projects take advantage of nested loops. When nesting loops, be sure that each such loop uses a unique counter variable.

Innermost loops execute the fastest. This means that the NEXT instruction for an inner loop must occur before the NEXT instruction for an outer loop. Figure 8.2 shows the right and wrong way to nest loops. A NEXT without FOR error message is displayed when nested loops are crossed incorrectly.

```
FOR A% = 1 TO 8
   FOR B% = 3 TO 6
      PRINT Q(A%, B%)
   NEXT B%
NEXT A%
```

The Right Way

```
FOR A% = 1 TO 8
   FOR B% = 3 TO 6
      PRINT Q(A%, B%)
   NEXT A%
   NEXT B%
```

The Wrong Way

Figure 8.2.

Examples of nested *FOR-NEXT* loops—the right way and the wrong way.

As an example of nested loops, Listing 8.5 prints a multiplication table.

Listing 8.5. A program that demonstrates nested loops by displaying a multiplication table.

```
REM Program: MULTABLE.BAS (Demonstrate nested loops)
Max% = 4                  'Maximum value in table
PRINT "Value 1", "Value 2", "Product"
FOR A% = 1 TO Max%
   FOR B% = A% TO Max%
      Product% = A% * B%
      PRINT A%, B%, Product%
   NEXT B%
   PRINT
NEXT A%
```

The following is the output of Listing 8.5:

Value 1	Value 2	Product
1	1	1
1	2	2
1	3	3
1	4	4
2	2	4
2	3	6
2	4	8
3	3	9
3	4	12
4	4	16

The second FOR instruction begins an inner loop while the outer loop is still active. The counter variables for the outer and inner loops are A% and B% respectively. Notice how the second FOR instruction uses A% (the counter variable from the outer loop) as the lower limit of the inner loop. That is why Value 1 in the output table increases each time the inner loop restarts.

You can edit the second program line to change the value of Max%. By doing so, you can create larger (or smaller) multiplication tables.

T I P   Indenting Loops

We suggest that you indent the body of each of your loops. This is not a requirement of QBasic, but merely common sense. Consistent indentation makes programs easier to read. The result is programs that are easier to understand and easier to troubleshoot.

Our preferred style is to place the FOR and NEXT keywords for each loop at the same indentation level. We indent the body of the loop three spaces. Nested loops are further indented to reflect the levels to which they are nested.

Omitting Counter Variables on *NEXT* Instructions in *FOR-NEXT* Loops

When nesting FOR-NEXT loops, using counter variables with your NEXT instructions is especially prudent. By using counter variables, you can easily identify which FOR instruction matches each NEXT instruction. This facilitates the readability of your programs and makes debugging easier.

If you don't use counter variables on the NEXT instructions, each NEXT instruction is matched with the innermost (that is, the most recently activated) FOR instruction. For example, consider the following program fragment which does not include counter variables on the NEXT instructions:

```
FOR A% = 1 TO 2
   FOR B% = 1 TO 3
      FOR C% = 1 TO 4
         PRINT A% * B% * C%
      NEXT
   NEXT
NEXT
```

The following program fragment—which uses the appropriate counter variables on the NEXT instructions—is much easier to follow because it clearly identifies the matching NEXT and FOR instructions:

```
FOR A% = 1 TO 2
   FOR B% = 1 TO 3
      FOR C% = 1 TO 4
         PRINT A% * B% * C%
      NEXT C%
   NEXT B%
NEXT A%
```

Both programs produce the same results, although the second one is much clearer.

Common Traps in *FOR* Loops

Here are four "Don'ts" involving FOR-NEXT loops:

1. Don't redefine the control variable inside the loop.

Never explicitly change the value of the counter variable inside the body of the loop. This is asking for problems. Beware of the common ways you can fall into this trap:

a. Using the counter variable on the left side of an assignment instruction.

b. Making the counter variable the object of an INPUT instruction.

c. Reusing the same counter variable in a nested loop.

If you ever find yourself needing to write a program using any of these techniques, throw some water on your face, and rethink your logic. There is bound to be a better way.

2. Don't depend on the value of the control variable outside the loop.

Think of the counter variable as undefined once the loop terminates. You may reuse the counter variable for another purpose—often as a counter variable in a subsequent loop. But don't assume that the counter variable has any particular value once the loop terminates.

3. Don't branch into or out of loops.

It's okay to use GOTO instructions that branch within the body of a loop. But don't branch into a loop from outside the loop. If you do, the limits of the loop are not properly defined. The loop might run indefinitely.

4. Don't use more than one NEXT with each control variable.

Pair each FOR instruction with a single NEXT instruction. For example, the following loop (which contains two NEXT instructions) causes a NEXT without FOR error in the final line.

```
FOR Num% = 5 TO 15
    IF Num% >= 10 THEN GOTO PrintAsIs
    PRINT " "; Num%    'PRINT with a leading space
NEXT Num%
PrintAsIs:
    PRINT Num%         'PRINT without leading space
NEXT Num%
```

Instead, branch to a single NEXT at the end of the loop. The preceding loop should be written as follows (with a new label and GOTO added):

```
FOR Num% = 5 TO 15
    IF Num% >= 10 THEN GOTO PrintAsIs
    PRINT " "; Num%    'PRINT with a leading space
GOTO CloseLoop
PrintAsIs:
    PRINT Num%         'PRINT without leading space
CloseLoop:
NEXT Num%
```

Terminating Loops with the *EXIT FOR* Statement

Sometimes you might want to terminate a loop before the final value of the counter variable is reached. Use the EXIT FOR statement. Execution resumes just after the NEXT statement.

Consider the following example of EXIT FOR. Suppose that you want to display the names contained in the array EmployeeName$. The array is dimensioned from 1 to 500. The exact number of employees is unknown, but it is less than 500. Therefore, the array contains names from element 1 up to some (unknown) array element. The remainder of the array values are just null strings.

The following loop displays the names. EXIT FOR terminates the loop when the first null string is detected. (The subsequent discussion of WHILE-WEND loops shows a more elegant way to solve this problem.)

```
FOR Counter% = 1 TO 500
   IF EmployeeName$(Counter%) = "" THEN
      EXIT FOR            'prematurely branches out of the loop
   ELSE
      PRINT EmployeeName$(Counter%)
   END IF
NEXT Counter%
```

Using *WHILE-WEND* Loops

WHILE-WEND loops are controlled by a *condition* rather than a counter variable. Think of the condition as a True or False test placed at the top of the loop. The body of the loop continues to execute as long as the condition remains True.

```
WHILE boolexp
   .
   .         'body of loop
   .
WEND
```

where

    boolexpr specifies the condition as a Boolean (True or False) expression,

and

    body of loop is any group of QBasic instructions.

S
T
A
T
E
M
E
N
T

Typically, the Boolean expression is a relational expression that QBasic automatically evaluates to True or False. Such relational expressions are just like the True or False expressions used as tests in IF instructions.

Here are two examples of WHILE conditions:

```
WHILE TermX% < 100                      'relational expression

WHILE (Day$ = "Mon") OR (Day$ = "Tue")   'compound logical
```

The WEND statement is used to terminate the body of the loop.

Before entering the body of a WHILE-WEND loop for the first time, QBasic evaluates the condition in your WHILE instruction. If the condition is False, QBasic bypasses the loop entirely and continues to execute on the line immediately following WEND.

If the condition is True, the body of the loop executes. Control then returns to the WHILE instruction, and the condition is reevaluated. As long as the condition remains True, the loop continues to execute.

Obviously, instructions inside the loop must do something to affect the testing condition, or the loop is in danger of executing forever. Usually the body of the loop modifies one or more variables that occur in the testing expression.

Consider the WHILE-WEND loop in Listing 8.6, a program that mimics a launching countdown:

Listing 8.6. The COUNTDWN.BAS program.

```
REM Program: COUNTDWN.BAS (Demonstrates WHILE-WEND)
TimeLeft% = 5
WHILE TimeLeft% >= 1                'Boolean condition
    PRINT TimeLeft%
    TimeLeft% = TimeLeft% - 1
WEND
PRINT "Blast off"
END
```

The following is the output of Listing 8.6:

```
5
4
3
2
1
Blast off
```

The two instructions between WHILE and WEND contain the body of the loop. Notice how the instruction immediately above the WEND statement decrements the value of TimeLeft% with each pass through the loop. The condition in the WHILE instruction is True as long as TimeLeft% has a value greater than or equal to 1.

Sometimes you can create a useful loop with an empty body of instructions. For example, the following WHILE-WEND loop pauses program execution until the user presses a key. (The INKEY$ function, discussed in Chapter 16, "Using Hardware Devices," detects characters typed at the keyboard.)

```
WHILE INKEY$ = ""
WEND
```

(The first line ends with two consecutive double quotation marks. The pair of quotation marks denotes an empty string—that is, a string containing no characters. The INKEY$ function returns an empty string as long as no key is typed at the keyboard.)

To demonstrate this loop, try the following program:

```
PRINT "I'm waiting for you to press a key"
WHILE INKEY$ = ""
WEND
PRINT "You finally pressed a key"
```

This program first displays the message in the top line. Next, the computer continuously executes the WHILE-WEND loop as long as you don't press a key. (The condition in the WHILE instruction remains True as long as you don't press a key.)

Effectively, the computer waits for you to press a key. When you finally do press a key, the condition in the WHILE instruction becomes False and the loop terminates. The program then continues with the bottom line, which displays the ending message.

Like FOR-NEXT loops, WHILE-WEND loops can be nested to any level; simple WHILE-WEND loops can be written on a single line (with the instructions separated by colons).

For example, you can write the waiting loop in a single line like this:

```
WHILE INKEY$ = "": WEND
```

In the previous section on FOR-NEXT loops, we discussed the programming problem of displaying employee names in an array dimensioned from 1 to 500. Here is a solution using a WHILE-WEND loop and a compound testing condition. The test for the end of the array is assimilated into the WHILE condition with a logical AND operator.

```
Counter% = 1
WHILE (EmployeeName$(Counter%) <> "") AND (Counter% <= 500)
   PRINT EmployeeName$(Counter%)
   Counter% = Counter% + 1
WEND
```

Using *DO-LOOP* Loops

With the DO-LOOP, you can create flexible loops which extend the capabilities of WHILE-WEND loops. Like WHILE-WEND, DO-LOOP uses a condition to control the loop.

However, DO-LOOP is more flexible than WHILE-WEND because you can place the condition at the beginning of the loop (the top-test form) or at the end (the bottom-test form). Furthermore, you have more options for each testing condition.

S T A T E M E N T

The top-test form:

```
DO WHILE boolexpr
   .
   .        'body of loop
   .
LOOP
```

or

```
DO UNTIL boolexpr
   .
   .        'body of loop
   .
LOOP
```

where

  boolexpr specifies the condition as a Boolean (True or False) expression,

and

  body of loop is any group of QBasic instructions.

The bottom-test form:

```
DO
      .
      .      'body of loop
      .
LOOP WHILE boolexpr
```

or

```
DO
      .
      .      'body of loop
      .
LOOP UNTIL boolexpr
```

where

boolexpr specifies the condition as a Boolean (True or False) expression,

and

body of loop is any group of QBasic instructions.

S
T
A
T
E
M
E
N
T

Notice that for both the top-test and bottom-test forms the loop begins with a DO statement and ends with a LOOP statement.

Each testing condition must begin with WHILE or UNTIL. With WHILE, the loop continues if the condition is True but terminates if the condition is False. UNTIL has the opposite effect; the loop continues if the condition is False and terminates if the loop is True. Table 8.1 summarizes the effect of the WHILE and UNTIL keywords.

Table 8.1. Use of *WHILE* and *UNTIL* in *DO* loops.

Value of Testing Condition

Keyword	True	False
WHILE	Continue loop	Terminate loop
UNTIL	Terminate loop	Continue loop

The top-test form of a DO loop is similar to a WHILE-WEND loop. In fact, the following two loop constructions are equivalent:

```
DO WHILE boolexpr

    .
    .      'body of loop
    .

LOOP
```

```
WHILE boolexpr

    .
    .      'body of loop
    .

WEND
```

A bottom-test DO loop must execute the loop body at least once. Such loops often terminate with an UNTIL condition. For example, the following loop displays the square root of a series of numbers input by the user. When the user types 0, the loop terminates. (See Chapter 10, "Manipulating Numbers," for the SQR function, and Chapter 16, "Using Hardware Devices," for the INPUT statement.)

```
DO
    INPUT "Type a number"; Number!
    PRINT "The square root of"; Number!; "is"; SQR(Number!)
LOOP UNTIL Number! = 0
```

Just as you can prematurely exit a FOR-NEXT loop with an EXIT FOR instruction, you can prematurely exit a DO-LOOP block with an EXIT DO instruction.

Summary

Loops are instruction blocks that execute repetitively. Loops are one of the most common and useful programming structures. Many programming tasks involve repetitive calculations that are ideal for looping.

A controlled loop executes a limited number of times. QBasic has special statements for three kinds of controlled loops:

■ FOR-NEXT loops, which execute a specified number of times,

■ WHILE-WEND loops, which execute as long as a Boolean (logical) condition remains True, and

■ DO-LOOP loops, which execute as long as a condition remains True or until a condition becomes True.

Managing Large Amounts of Data

Ordinary variables store only a single value. Such variables are certainly quite useful, but ultimately limiting. Many programming projects require the storage and manipulation of large amounts of information.

For example, suppose you want to write an inventory control program for an automobile parts company. You might need to deal with thousands of different parts. How are you going to manipulate such large amounts of data with ordinary variables? The simple truth is, you're not.

To handle such sizable data requirements, you need *arrays*. Arrays are like super variables, storing multiple data values under a single name. Arrays were introduced in Chapter 6, "Language Building Blocks," and are explored in depth here. The *record,* or user-defined data type, is also introduced.

The other main topic of this chapter concerns getting large amounts of data into your program. That's when READ and DATA statements play a major role.

Storing Data in Programs with *DATA* and *READ*

Of course, if your program is going to manipulate data, first you must somehow get the data into your program. There are three general techniques to cross this fundamental bridge:

1. Request the data from the user at run-time.

This is the backbone of interactive programs. Usually a program prompts the user to type the relevant data from the keyboard. (Refer to the INPUT statement in Chapter 16, "Using Hardware Devices.")

2. Read the data from a disk file.

    Data can be saved on disk and then read while the program is running. This technique is common in business applications. Perhaps your program processes monthly sales figures that are stored on disk. (See Chapter 14, "Using Sequential Disk Files.")

3. Store the data as part of the program.

    This is the most straightforward technique. What is simpler than storing the data as part of the program? Assignment instructions are one way to store data in a program. After all, the instruction MyDOS! = 5.0 stores the value 5.0 directly inside the program.

Another way to store data inside the program is with DATA instructions. To explain DATA, we must first introduce a representative programming task.

The Baseball Coach—A Case Study

Let's say you're the coach of the Mudville Nine—a little league baseball team. Like most baseball fans, you're obsessed with the players' statistics. At the end of the season, the league office sends you a report showing how each of your batters fared (see Figure 9.1).

You want to calculate each player's batting average. (For you non-baseball fans, a batting average is the number of hits divided by the number of times at bat. For example, if Babe Ruth has 2 hits in 8 at bats, his batting average is 2 divided by 8, or 0.250.)

You decide to write a program that displays each player's name along with his or her batting statistics. You want a four-column table. The first column is the player's name. Columns two through four are each player's hits, times at bat, and batting average.

Computing the batting average for each player is easy. You just divide each player's hits by the number of times at bat. The problem is getting the data into the program in the first place.

You *could* write a program that looks something like this:

```
.
.
.
Player$ = "Johnny"
Hits% = 21
```

```
AtBats% = 82
BatAve! = Hits% / AtBats%
PRINT Player$, Hits%, AtBats%, BatAve!
Player$ = "Melanie"
Hits% = 15
AtBats% = 66
BatAve! = Hits% /AtBats%
PRINT Player$, Hits%, AtBats%, BatAve!
Player$ = "Slugger"
     .
     .
     .
```

This works correctly, but makes for a needlessly long program containing too many repetitious instructions.

Listing 9.1, the BASEBALL.BAS program, places data in the program a much better way—with DATA instructions:

Team Name: Mudville Nine

Player	Hits	Times at Bat
Johnnie	21	82
Melanie	15	66
Slugger	34	95
Casey	16	88
Babe	31	79
Christine	29	74
Solly	21	74
Debbie	14	58
Rick	8	84

Figure 9.1.

Batting statistics for the Mudville Nine.

Listing 9.1. The BASEBALL.BAS program.

```
REM Program: BASEBALL.BAS
REM -- Display Batting Averages for the Mudville Nine
DATA Johnny, 21, 82
DATA Melanie, 15, 66
DATA Slugger, 34, 95
DATA Casey, 16, 88
DATA Babe, 31, 79
DATA Christine, 29, 74
DATA Solly, 21, 74
DATA Debbie, 14, 58
DATA Rick, 8, 84
REM
PRINT "Season Stats for the Mudville Nine"
PRINT
PRINT "Player", "Hits", "At Bats", "Batting Average"
FOR J% = 1 TO 9
   READ Player$, Hits%, AtBats%
   BatAve! = Hits% / AtBats%
   PRINT Player$, Hits%, AtBats%, BatAve!
NEXT J%
END
```

Here is the output of Listing 9.1, the BASEBALL.BAS program:

```
Player      Hits      At Bats      Batting Average
Johnnie     21        82           .2560976
Melanie     15        66           .2272727
Slugger     34        95           .3578947
Casey       16        88           .1818182
Babe        31        79           .3924051
Christine   29        74           .3918919
Solly       21        74           .2837838
Debbie      14        58           .2413793
Rick        8         84           .0952381
```

Do you get the general idea of how DATA works? The DATA instructions contain the data values that the program uses. The READ instruction (in the FOR-NEXT loop) "reads" the data and assigns appropriate values to the variables: Player$, Hits%, and AtBats%. The FOR-NEXT loop eventually reads all the data contained in the DATA instructions. Let's take a closer look at DATA and READ.

Understanding *DATA* and *READ*

DATA instructions store numeric or string literals in a data list. READ instructions then assign the data values to variables.

DATA *literals*

where

   literals is a list of data values (numeric and/or string) separated by commas.

S T A T E M E N T

READ *varnames*

where

   varnames is a list of variable names separated by commas.

S T A T E M E N T

A DATA instruction can contain one or more values. Use a comma to separate multiple values. For example:

DATA 25

DATA 40, 23.677

DATA 510, 31.33, 1.67E-21, 92

As these examples show, numbers can be in any form: integers, numbers with decimal points, or scientific notation with the E symbol (but not expressions with operators such as 14 * 6).

NOTE **DATA Instructions Are Nonexecutable**

DATA instructions don't really *do* anything. In QBasic terminology, DATA instructions are *nonexecutable*. The sole purpose of DATA instructions is to specify values so that READ instructions can assign these values to variables.

Each READ instruction contains one or more variable names. Again, separate multiple variable names with commas:

```
READ Num!
READ A%, B%, C!
```

You can have any number of DATA instructions in a program. Regardless of the number of DATA instructions, or the number of values in each DATA instruction, think of all the DATA instructions as creating one long list of values. The list begins with the values in the first DATA instruction. The list grows by adding the literals from each successive DATA instruction in the order the DATA instructions appear in your program.

QBasic maintains a pointer to the current item in the data list. This pointer keeps track of which value in the DATA instructions was last read. Each READ instruction plucks as many data values from the list as necessary—one data value for each variable in the READ instruction. For example, even though the variable names are spread across two READ instructions, the following program fragment still assigns the numbers 1 through 5 to the five variables Mon, Tue, Wed, Thu, and Fri.

```
DATA 1, 2, 3, 4, 5
READ Mon, Tue, Wed
READ Thu, Fri
```

The following example works just as well:

```
DATA 1, 2
DATA 3, 4
DATA 5
READ Mon, Tue, Wed, Thu, Fri
```

Where to Place *DATA* Instructions

You can place DATA instructions before or after the associated READ instructions. When a READ instruction occurs, QBasic "finds" the DATA instructions, regardless of whether the DATA instructions occur above or below the READ instruction. Programmers usually place DATA instructions in one of these three locations:

1. In a block near the beginning of the program.
2. In a block near the end of the program.
3. Near the READ instruction(s).

Your program doesn't have to read all the values in your DATA instructions:

```
DATA 4, 7, 9
READ D%, E%
```

D% and E% have the values 4 and 7, respectively. The data value of 9 never gets assigned to any variable. That's okay, no harm is done.

However, it's another story if you try to read past the end of your data list:

```
DATA 4, 7
READ D%, E%, F%
```

This causes your program to terminate with the error message

```
Out of DATA
```

That makes sense. You tried to read three data values with the READ instruction but only two values were available.

Storing Strings with *DATA*

As the BASEBALL.BAS program demonstrated, DATA and READ work with strings as well as with numbers. You can freely mix string and numeric values in the same DATA instruction.

Separate string values with commas, just as you do with numeric values. For example:

```
READ City$, State$
DATA Dallas, Texas
PRINT City$
PRINT State$
```

The result is

```
Dallas
Texas
```

Notice that you don't have to enclose the string data values with quotation marks as you do in the following assignment instruction:

```
City$ = "Dallas"
```

However, you *can* use the quotation marks. You can write the previous DATA instruction as follows:

```
DATA "Dallas", "Texas"
```

The result is the same.

You *have* to use quotation marks with DATA in these cases:

1. Your string contains a comma or colon.

2. Your string contains leading or trailing blanks.

Consider this example:

```
READ Who$, What$, Where$
DATA "Elvis Presley", "      Concert", "Toledo, Ohio"
PRINT Who$
PRINT What$
PRINT Where$
```

The result is

```
Elvis Presley
      Concert
Toledo, Ohio
```

Now, stay on your toes because this gets tricky. Suppose you try the same program but change the DATA instruction to remove the quotation marks (notice the blank spaces before Concert):

```
DATA Elvis Presley,      Concert, Toledo, Ohio
```

The result is now

```
Elvis Presley
Concert
Toledo
```

The blank space between Elvis and Presley causes no problems. But the blank spaces before Concert are stripped away (DATA does that). And the comma between Toledo and Ohio just makes the city and the state two separate data values.

NOTE **Mixing Strings and Numbers**

When mixing strings and numbers in DATA instructions, be careful that each READ variable is assigned a data value of the proper type. If a variable has a numeric data type, the corresponding data value must be numeric. A string variable causes a run-time error (Syntax error).

For a string variable, the corresponding data value should be string. However, a numeric value does not produce an error. Instead, QBasic treats the numeric value as a string value (a simple sequence of text characters).

In a DATA instruction, you can't use the apostrophe (single quotation mark) to indicate a comment. Instead, the apostrophe is treated just like any other string character. To place a comment at the end of a DATA instruction, use :REM. For example:

```
DATA 7631.45, 5558.33, 6711.72    :REM Quarterly Sales
```

This DATA instruction shows why you must use quotation marks around any string data value that contains a colon. In a line with a DATA instruction, as in any other program line, the colon separates multiple instructions.

Adjusting the Data List Pointer with *RESTORE*

Occasionally you might want a program to read the same data list more than once. You can "manually" adjust the data list pointer with RESTORE.

RESTORE
or
RESTORE *linenum*
or
RESTORE *label*
where
linenum is the line number of a DATA instruction
and
label is the line label of a DATA instruction.

S
T
A
T
E
M
E
N
T

Without a line number or label parameter, RESTORE reinitializes the data pointer back to the top of the list. The next READ instruction gets the first data value of the first DATA instruction.

For example:

```
DATA 1, 2
DATA 3, 4
READ A%, B%, C%
RESTORE
READ D%
PRINT A%, B%, C%, D%
```

The result is

```
1           2           3           1
```

With a line number or line label parameter, RESTORE moves the data pointer to the beginning of the designated line.

Using Arrays

In most of our program examples so far, the variables have been simple variables—"simple" because each variable stores a single value. In the following instructions, for example, the variables Month1$, Month2$, and Month3$ are separate variables that store separate values:

```
Month1$ = "January"
Month2$ = "February"
Month3$ = "March"
```

Simple variables can be numeric or string. The value of a variable might change during a program. However, at all times, each simple variable "houses" a single data value.

Arrays change all that. *Arrays*—or more properly, *array variables*—consist of several data values maintained under a common name. With arrays, you can easily manipulate large amounts of related data. With only a few program lines, you can recalculate hundreds of data values or print a large table. You'll see how shortly.

Just as with ordinary variables, every array has a name that you create. Array names follow the same conventions as ordinary variables, including the optional %, &, !, #, or $ suffix that identifies the data type of the array. Once you give an array a data type, every element of an array conforms to that data type.

The distinguishing feature of an array is the *subscript* (or *index number*) that immediately follows the name (see Figure 9.2). The subscript is enclosed in parentheses.

```
VALUE! = COST!(38)
```
Array Name   Subscript

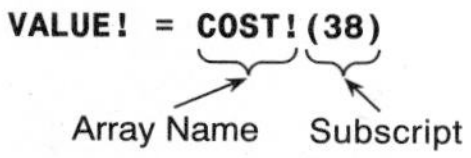

Figure 9.2.

The syntax of an array.

The parentheses "tell" QBasic that this is an array rather than an ordinary variable. The value of the subscript identifies a single element of the whole array. For example, our collection of month names can be written as an array like this:

```
Month$(1) = "January"
Month$(2) = "February"
Month$(3) = "March"
```

Here you have an array named Month$. It is a string array because the name ends with a dollar sign. Each individual element of Month$ contains a string value. The first element of the array, Month$(1), has the value January. The second element, Month$(2), has the value February.

Arrays can be string or numeric. Just as with ordinary variables, numeric arrays can be integer (%), long integer (&), single-precision (!), or double-precision (#). For each array, every element of the array contains data of the same type (string, integer, single-precision, or double-precision).

In the BASEBALL.BAS program, for example, you might create an array called Average! that represents each player's batting average. You could consider each player to have a number from 1 to 9. The batting average of player number 6, for example, would be stored in element Average!(6) of the array.

An array subscript is always enclosed in parentheses placed immediately after the array name. The subscript can be an explicit number, a variable, or even an expression that evaluates to a number. See Table 9.1 for some examples.

Table 9.1. Sample array subscripts.

Array Element	Type of Subscript
Month$(2)	Explicit number
Salary!(Employee%)	Variable name
Cost#(23 + J%)	Simple expression
Cost#((J% - 1) * 3)	Expression containing parentheses

Subscript values must be whole numbers. If not, QBasic rounds the value to the nearest integer. For example, if Salary! is an array containing the salaries of a company's employees, Salary!(433.2) references employee number 433 and Salary!(228.8) references employee 229.

A Sample Program with Arrays

Let's look at arrays in action. The following program demonstrates that a few simple FOR-NEXT loops can manipulate a lot of data.

Suppose you own Ace Accordian Supply. Your 1992 monthly sales figures have finally arrived. You want to write a program that lists the monthly sales and computes the yearly total.

Listing 9.2, the SALES.BAS program, does the job.

Listing 9.2. The SALES.BAS program for the Ace Accordian Supply company.

```
REM Program: SALES.BAS (Monthly sales for Ace Accordian Supply)
DIM Month$(12), NumSold%(12)   'Set limits of each array
REM
DATA Jan, Feb, Mar, Apr, May, Jun, Jul, Aug, Sep, Oct, Nov, Dec
DATA 28, 21, 14, 32, 25, 26, 20, 16, 23, 19, 29, 26
FOR J% = 1 TO 12
    READ Month$(J%)             'Read string data for each month
NEXT J%
FOR J% = 1 TO 12
    READ NumSold%(J%)           'Read number sold each month
NEXT J%
REM
PRINT "Ace Accordian Supply - 1992 Sales"
PRINT "MONTH", "NUMBER SOLD"    'Display table heading
FOR J% = 1 TO 12
    PRINT Month$(J%), NumSold%(J%)
NEXT J%
PRINT
Total% = 0
FOR J% = 1 TO 12               'Calculate yearly sales total
    Total% = Total% + NumSold%(J%)
NEXT J%
PRINT "YEARLY TOTAL", Total%
END
```

The output of Listing 9.2 looks like this:

```
Ace Accordian Supply - 1992 Sales
MONTH           NUMBER SOLD
Jan             28
Feb             21
Mar             14
Apr             32
May             25
Jun             26
Jul             20
Aug             16
Sep             23
Oct             19
Nov             29
Dec             26


YEARLY TOTAL    279
```

Let's examine this program. The first thing you might notice is the DIM instruction in the second line. The DIM instructions (short for DIMension) tell QBasic the names and sizes of the arrays that will be used in a program. The details of DIM are discussed a little later. But, for now, this DIM instruction informs QBasic that the program uses two arrays:

1. A string array named Month$

2. An integer array named NumSold%

Each of these arrays contains 12 elements. DIM only establishes the names and dimensions of the arrays. You still must get data values into the individual array elements.

The two DATA instructions contain the data values that will be stored into the array elements. The first DATA instruction has 12 data strings—the abbreviations for each of the 12 months. The second DATA instruction contains the month-by-month accordian sales (28 sold in January, 21 sold in February, and so on).

Next, the two FOR-NEXT loops read the data values into the arrays. Look how these two simple loops read all the data values. That's the power of array subscripting. After these loops execute, each array contains 12 data values in preparation for the rest of the program. In the NumSold% array, for example, NumSold%(1) is 28, NumSold%(2) is 21, and so on.

NOTE

READ and *DATA* Work Well with Arrays

The FOR-NEXT loops of the SALES.BAS program demonstrate just how well READ and DATA work with arrays. By placing a READ instruction inside a loop, you can assign data to all elements of an array in a few simple program lines.

The program now displays the output. A two-column table is created.

After displaying the heading for the table, the ensuing FOR-NEXT loop displays the monthly sales figures. These values are nothing more than the data values picked up from the DATA instructions. But, again, notice how easily a simple loop can display a whole array full of data.

Finally, the program calculates Total%, the total sales over the whole year. First, the instruction Total% = 0 initializes Total% with a value of 0.

The ultimate value of Total% is the sum of the monthly sales figures. That is, Total% should be the sum of all the elements of the NumSold% array:

NumSold%(1) + NumSold%(2) + ... + NumSold%(12).

Again, a simple loop is the answer. The final FOR-NEXT loop calculates the value of Total%. Notice how the assignment instruction inside this loop adds one array element at a time to the current value of Total%. When the loop finishes, Total% contains the desired sum, which is displayed by the final PRINT instruction.

The SALES.BAS program demonstrates the power of arrays. With a few simple loops, you can easily manipulate array elements. Notice how the FOR-NEXT counter variable (J% in this program) is often used as an array subscript. This practice is commonplace in programs with arrays.

Loops and arrays naturally work well together. Loop counter variables increment sequentially, which is exactly how array elements are subscripted.

Dimensioning Arrays with *DIM*

As the second line of SALES.BAS demonstrates, you use DIM to declare the arrays that a program utilizes. DIM permits an extended syntax with several options. For now, we consider only the simple form of the DIM instruction. (Extensions to the syntax of DIM are explained later in this chapter.)

The simple form of the DIM instruction accomplishes four things:

1. Establishes the name of the array
2. Establishes the data type of the array
3. Specifies the number of elements in the array
4. Initializes the value of each element of the array: numeric array elements become zero and string array elements become the null string

Here is the syntax of the simple form of the DIM instruction.

DIM *arrayname(subscriptrange)*

where

    arrayname is the name for the array,

and

    subscriptrange specifies the index range for the elements in the array.

S
T
A
T
E
M
E
N
T

Array names follow the same conventions as variable names. In particular, a data type suffix (!, #, %, &, or $) establishes the data type for each element of the array (recall that every element of an array must be the same data type). If you don't use a suffix on the array name, the data type defaults to single-precision.

The *subscriptrange* parameter establishes the lowest and highest values allowed for the array subscript. There are two forms of the *subscriptrange* parameter: a single value, or two values separated by the keyword TO.

In the former case, the single value of *subscriptrange* establishes the highest permissible value of the array subscript. QBasic automatically considers the lowest legal subscript value to be 0 (not 1). For example, the following instruction

```
DIM NumVotes%(10)
```

establishes an integer array named NumVotes%, which has 11 elements:

```
NumVotes%(0), NumVotes%(1), ... , NumVotes%(10).
```

In the latter case (with the TO keyword), the *subscriptrange* parameter directly specifies the lowest and highest permissible values of the subscript. The lowest value does not have to be 0 or 1; the value can even be negative.

A DIM instruction can declare two or more arrays. In these cases, use a comma to separate the array names. Table 9.2 shows some sample DIM instructions.

Table 9.2. Sample *DIM* instructions.

Instruction	Description
DIM Client$(200)	String array with 201 elements: Client$(0) to Client$(200)
DIM Profit!(1975 TO 1992)	Single-precision array with 17 elements: Profit!(1975) to Profit!(1992)
DIM Shares&(-40 TO 15)	Long integer array with 56 elements: Shares&(-40) to Shares&(15)
DIM Tax!(30), Cost(30)	Two single-precision arrays, each with 31 elements.
DIM A%(45), B%(34), C$(21)	Three arrays: (1) An integer array with 46 elements: A%(0) to A%(45) (2) Another integer array with 35 elements: B%(0) to B%(34). (3) A string array with 22 elements: C$(0) to C$(21).

T I P   Where To Put DIM Instructions

A DIM instruction can appear anywhere before the first use of the array. However, when possible, you should place all your DIM instructions together near the beginning of the program. That way, you can quickly identify the names and sizes of all the program's arrays.

Changing the Base Subscript—*OPTION BASE*

An OPTION BASE instruction changes the default lower array subscript from zero to one.

```
OPTION BASE basesub
```

where

   basesub specifies the lowest array subscript for subsequent DIM
   instructions.

The only legal values for *basesub* are zero and one.

Consider the following program fragment:

```
OPTION BASE 1
DIM MyArray!(200)
```

The first line changes the default lower array bound from zero to one. As a result, the DIM instruction creates an array with elements from MyArray!(1) to MyArray!(200).

"What's the big deal?" you ask. Not much, really. Even if an array has a zero subscript, you don't have to use it. Changing the base from 0 to 1 does conserve a small amount of memory storage. This isn't too important until we come to two-dimensional arrays (later in this chapter).

Dimensioning with Small Arrays

You can use an array without making an "official" declaration in a DIM instruction. In such a case, QBasic assigns a default element range from 0 to 10. For example, suppose the following lines are the first two lines of a program:

```
DATA 21, 45, 18, 32
READ Lotto%(1), Lotto%(2), Lotto%(3), Lotto%(4)
```

Notice that no DIM instruction appears even though the program uses Lotto% as an integer array. This *does* work. QBasic treats Lotto% as an integer array with elements from 0 to 10. It's just as if you dimensioned Lotto% with the following instruction:

```
DIM Lotto%(10)
```

Array and Variable Naming Conflicts

You can give an array and an ordinary variable the same name. However, it is poor programming practice to do so. In such a case, the array and the variable are two distinct entities that can coexist in the same program. Consider this:

```
DIM Client$(200)
Client$ = "Donald Trump"
```

The ordinary variable named Client$ is totally distinct from the array of the same name. Throughout the program, QBasic can always distinguish the array from the variable because the array has a subscript and the variable does not.

Although you can get by without DIM for small arrays, we discourage such "nondeclarations." Good programmers use DIM with every array, including small arrays. You want to make your programs easy to read, verify, and modify—take advantage of every opportunity to do so.

Using Variables and Constants as Array Dimensions

So far, our example DIM instructions specify the number of array elements with numeric literals. But you can use variable names and constants also.

Variables and constants provide a convenient way to alter array boundaries between successive runs of a program. For example, suppose you have a program that displays results of your track club's road races. The program dimensions arrays as follows:

```
DIM LastName$(300), FirstName$(300)
DIM Age%(300), Weight!(300)
DIM RaceTime!(300)
```

A more flexible solution is to use a variable name like this:

```
MaxRunners% = 300
DIM LastName$(MaxRunners%), FirstName$(MaxRunners%)
DIM Age%(MaxRunners%), Weight!(MaxRunners%)
DIM RaceTime!(MaxRunners%)
```

Not only is the name MaxRunners% easier to understand than the literal 300, you only need to modify the single line that assigns a value to MaxRunners% (instead of modifying all the DIM instructions) if you need to change the number 300 between successive runs of the program.

You can use this same technique with constants as well as variables. For example, the first line of the preceding program fragment might establish MaxRunners% as a constant, as follows:

```
CONST MaxRunners% = 300
```

Does it matter whether MaxRunners% is a constant or a variable? There is a subtle distinction that is related to the way memory for the array is allocated. This advanced topic of static and dynamic memory allocation is discussed in Chapter 19, "Managing Memory." For now, the distinction between a variable and constant is unimportant.

You can ask the user to supply the array boundaries. For example, you might assign a value to MaxRunners% with this instruction:

```
INPUT "How many runners in the race"; MaxRunners%
```

Remember, in DIM instructions, you can use variable and constant names (as well as literals) for the subscript limits.

Table Lookup—A Sample Program with Arrays

Suppose you want to write a program that asks the user for a telephone area code. After the user enters the area code, the program responds with the name of the state or province associated with that area code. For example, if the user enters the number 213, the program displays California.

Imagine that you have a job requiring you to respond with a state name whenever given an area-code number. How would you tackle this task *without* a computer? Think for a minute before you continue reading.

Most likely, you would first find a list or table of all the area codes and the corresponding states. Then, whenever anyone asks about a particular area code, you scan your list for that code. If you find a match, you respond with the corresponding state name. If you don't find a match, you reply that there is no such area code on your list.

This general technique is known as *table lookup.* You look through a table to find a specific entry. When you find it, you get the corresponding information from an adjacent "column" of the table.

The AREACODE.BAS Program

Listing 9.3 contains a program, named AREACODE.BAS, which does precisely the same table lookup. To keep the program relatively short, we have not included the entire area code list.

Listing 9.3. The AREACODE.BAS program.

```
REM Program: AREACODE.BAS (Show the state for any area code)
DIM Code%(150), State$(150)
REM ===================================
REM Read the Codes and States into arrays
REM ===================================
Num% = 0
DO
   Num% = Num% + 1
   READ Code%(Num%), State$(Num%)       'Read data into arrays
LOOP UNTIL Code%(Num%) = 999
Num% = Num% - 1    'Adjust Num% to actual number of table values
REM =============================================
REM Get Code and look up corresponding state name
REM =============================================
DO
   INPUT "Enter area code (use 0 to end program)"; Entry%
   IF Entry% = 0 THEN EXIT DO
   Message$ = "No such area code found"
   FOR J% = 1 TO Num%
      IF Entry% = Code%(J%) THEN Message$ = State$(J%)
   NEXT J%
   PRINT Message$
LOOP
PRINT "All done"
END
REM ===================================
REM The area codes and state names follow
REM ===================================
DATA 201, New Jersey
DATA 202, D.C.
DATA 203, Connecticut
DATA 204, Manitoba
DATA 205, Alabama
DATA 206, Washington
DATA 207, Maine
DATA 208, Idaho
DATA 209, California
DATA 212, New York
DATA 213, California
DATA 214, Texas
DATA 999, End of list
```

Here is some sample output from Listing 9.3:

```
Enter area code (use 0 to end program)? 201
New Jersey
Enter area code (use 0 to end program)? 212
New York
Enter area code (use 0 to end program)? 714
No such area code found
Enter area code (use 0 to end program)? 0
All done
```

The DATA instructions at the end of the program provide the area code list. The first DO-LOOP block reads the area codes and state names into arrays that the program can later search for matches. The second DO-LOOP block asks the user for an area code, searches through the area code array until a match is found, and then displays the corresponding state name.

Table 9.3 shows how the area codes and state names are stored in the Code% and State$ arrays.

Table 9.3. Partial contents of the area code and state name arrays.

Element Number	Area Code (Code%)	State Name (State$)
1	201	New Jersey
2	202	D.C.
3	203	Connecticut
4	204	Manitoba
5	205	Alabama

How the Program Works

Let's examine AREACODE.BAS to see how the program works. Some of this explanation is review, but you should find the details helpful in understanding a typical application of arrays.

The DIM instruction sets aside 150 elements for the Code% and State$ arrays. (Actually, the line reserves 151 elements for each array because QBasic gives the first array element an index of 0, not 1. This program, however, uses only the elements from 1 upward.) Because fewer than 150 area codes exist, 150 elements provide ample space for every possible area code.

Before the first DO-LOOP, the value of Num% is set equal to zero. This variable is destined for big things. Num% will point to each array element while the data is read into the arrays; afterward Num% will help count the number of area codes found in the DATA instructions. Num% is set to zero in preparation for reading the first values into the arrays. (This line could be omitted because QBasic automatically initializes each new variable with a value of zero. However, including the line makes the program logic easier to follow.)

The DO-LOOP initializes the arrays. *Initializing* means setting (in the beginning of a program) the program's variables to the values they will need during the main part of the program. The DIM instruction reserves memory space for the arrays, but does not put the DATA instruction values into the arrays.

The first instruction of the DO block adds one to Num% in preparation for reading the next pair of data items and storing the values into the subsequent pair of array-element slots. Because the initial value of Num% is zero, the first time this line executes, the value of Num% increases to one.

The READ instruction reads each pair of data items (area code and state) and stores that information in the two arrays. The LOOP UNTIL instruction checks whether the final pair of data items has been read. The program uses the nonexistent area code 999 to indicate that no more area codes are in the list. If the last item in the list *has not* been read (that is, Code%(Num%) does not equal 999), the program simply continues the DO-LOOP, which bumps up the value of Num% and reads the next pair of data values. If the last item in the list *has* been read (that is, Code%(Num%) equals 999), the program ends the DO-LOOP block.

When the DO-LOOP terminates, the arrays are filled with all the area-code and state-name data, and the program can continue with its processing. However, one necessary chore must be done first.

We need to subtract one from Num% to have an accurate count of the number of area codes in the Code% array. Do you see why? When the DO-LOOP finishes, the Num% element of the Code% array contains 999. This special "flag" value is not part of the actual data. After subtracting one from Num%, the Num% element of Code% contains the last real area code value.

The second DO-LOOP block does the "user input" section of the program. This loop asks the user for an area code, displays the corresponding state name, and then repeats the process until the user tells the program to stop—by entering 0 as an area code. After the INPUT instruction, the IF instruction checks whether the user entered the value of 0; if so, the program branches out of the loop to conclude the program.

The variable Message$ stores the response that the user eventually will see. At first, Message$ is set to report that a match is not found. If a match is subsequently found, Message$ is later updated appropriately.

The FOR-NEXT loop searches through the area codes in the Code% array attempting to match the entered area code. When the loop finds a match (in the IF instruction), the counter variable J% contains the number of the matching element from the Code% array. At this point, Message$ is assigned the proper state name from the State$ array. Notice that the same index value of J% points to the proper corresponding value in the State$ array. That's table lookup in action.

When the FOR-NEXT loop finishes, the PRINT instruction displays the program's response. Notice that Message$ contains the appropriate message whether or not a match was found. If a match was found, Message$ contains the matching state name; if no match was found, Message$ contains the "no match" message originally set before the FOR-NEXT loop.

The DO-LOOP continues executing to process each request by the user. Even if the previous request results in a match, the value of Message$ reinitializes in anticipation of a possible failure this time around.

The DO-LOOP continues until the user inputs a value of 0. This triggers the EXIT DO (in the IF Entry% instruction) to branch out of the loop. Notice that this is the only way out of this DO-LOOP block. The PRINT "All done" instruction then displays the concluding message and the END terminates the program.

The remainder of the program is the DATA instructions that list the area code and state name.

Now try making some changes to the program. First, consult your phone book and add DATA instructions for more area codes. Insert your new DATA instructions just before the final 999 entry. You might want to add more messages, perhaps a line before the second DO-LOOP that displays Num%, the number of area codes in the array. If you feel really ambitious, change the program to ask for the state name, not the area code, and then have the program respond by displaying all the area codes for that state.

Using Multidimensional Arrays

So far, our sample arrays have been one-dimensional—a list of values. For example, the array Salary!(Employee%) contains salary information as a function of an employee number. One-dimensional arrays use only a single subscript to span all the values of the array.

Suppose, however, that you have data in the form of a table (a spreadsheet, for example). Such data has a two-dimensional, row-and-column structure.

Two-Dimensional Arrays

QBasic supports two-dimensional arrays to represent such two-dimensional data. You need two subscripts to specify an element of a two-dimensional array—one subscript for the row number and one subscript for the column number. Use a comma to separate the two subscripts.

For example, a chessboard can be considered a two-dimensional array. Figure 9.3 shows a chess game in progress. Each square of the 8-by-8 board has a row number from 1 to 8 and a column number from 1 to 8.

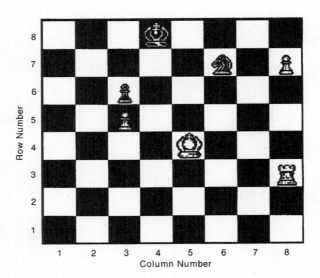

Figure 9.3.

A chess game in progress.

For the chessboard, a two-dimensional array named `Piece$` contains the name of the chess piece currently occupying each square. The following instructions represent the board shown in Figure 9.3:

```
DIM Piece$(8, 8)
FOR Row% = 1 TO 8
   FOR Column% = 1 TO 8
      Piece$ (Column%, Row%) = "None"
   NEXT Column%
NEXT Row%
Piece$(3, 5) = "White Pawn"
Piece$(8, 7) = "White Pawn"
Piece$(8, 3) = "White Rook"
Piece$(5, 4) = "White King"
Piece$(3, 6) = "Black Pawn"
```

```
Piece$(6, 7) = "Black Knight"
Piece$(4, 8) = "Black King"
```

The first line dimensions the `Piece$` array with a `DIM` instruction. The array is designated to be two-dimensional by the use of two subscripts. This `DIM` instruction tells QBasic the following information:

- `Piece$` is a two-dimensional string array.
- The first dimension has subscript values ranging from 0 to 8.
- The second dimension has subscript values ranging from 0 to 8.

Notice that each dimension actually spans nine values (because the lowest value in each dimension is 0, not 1). So altogether, there are 81 (9 by 9) elements in the `Piece$` array.

In this program fragment, two nested `FOR-NEXT` loops initialize the value of each array element with the string value `None`. Notice how nested loops quickly reference an entire two-dimensional array.

The remaining lines assign specific string values to the array elements that represent squares containing pieces. In each array reference, the first subscript is a column number and the second subscript is a row number. So, for example, `Piece$(3, 5)` refers to the piece at column 3 and row 5.

Just as with one-dimensional arrays, you can use the `TO` parameter to specify the subscript range of a two-dimensional array. For example, the following instruction declares that the two-dimensional string array `Title$` has index ranges from 10 to 25 and 30 to 64:

```
DIM Title$(10 TO 25, 30 TO 64)
```

Clothing Sales—A Case Study of Two-Dimensional Arrays

Suppose you manage the clothing department of Bizarre's Department Store. You sell only three kinds of garments: raincoats, swimsuits, and underwear. (Now you see why the store is named Bizarre's.)

At the end of the year, the sales figures look like Figure 9.4. You want to write a program that displays this information and totals the seasonal sales.

Bizarre's Department Store

	Winter	Spring	Summer	Fall
Raincoats	522	309	101	486
Swimsuits	82	334	623	111
Underwear	362	295	384	244

Figure 9.4.

Annual clothing sales.

Listing 9.4 contains that program—GARMENT.BAS:

Listing 9.4. The GARMENT.BAS program.

```
REM Program: GARMENT.BAS (Demonstrate 2-D Arrays)
DIM Garment$(3)
DIM Sales%(3, 4)        '3 items by 4 seasons
REM ===================================================
FOR Item% = 1 TO 3: READ Garment$(Item%): NEXT Item%
FOR Item% = 1 TO 3
   FOR Season% = 1 TO 4
      READ Sales%(Item%, Season%)
   NEXT Season%
NEXT Item%               'Done reading data
REM ===================================================
PRINT , "Winter", "Spring", "Summer", "Fall"
FOR Item% = 1 TO 3
   PRINT Garment$(Item%),
   FOR Season% = 1 TO 4
      PRINT Sales%(Item%, Season%),   'Print sales data
   NEXT Season%
NEXT Item%
PRINT
REM ===================================================
FOR Season% = 1 TO 4    'Store total sales in 0 element
   Sales%(0, Season%) = 0
   FOR Item% = 1 TO 3
      Temp% = Sales%(Item%, Season%)
      Sales%(0, Season%) = Sales%(0, Season%) + Temp%
   NEXT Item%
NEXT Season%
```

```
PRINT "All Garments",
FOR Season% = 1 TO 4
    PRINT Sales%(0, Season%),    'Total sales by season
NEXT Season%
END
REM =================================================
DATA Raincoats, Swimsuits, Underwear
REM Winter, Spring, Summer, & Fall sales data follow
DATA 522, 309, 101, 486: REM Raincoats (W, S, S, F)
DATA 82,  334, 623, 111: REM Swimsuit sales by season
DATA 362, 295, 384, 244: REM Underwear sales by season
```

The output looks like this:

	Winter	Spring	Summer	Fall
Raincoats	522	309	101	486
Swimsuits	82	334	623	111
Underwear	362	295	384	244
All Garments	966	938	1108	841

Let's examine GARMENT.BAS to see how the program works.

The two DIM instructions dimension the two arrays. Garment$ is a one-dimensional array containing the string names of the three garments.

The key array is Sales%, a two-dimensional array containing the seasonal sales for the three garments. This array represents the number of items sold as a function of the garment *and* the season. There are 3 garments (raincoats, swimsuits, and underwear) and 4 seasons (winter, spring, summer, and fall). Therefore, Sales% is dimensioned 3 by 4.

The next block of instructions reads the array. The data itself is in the DATA instructions at the end of the program. Notice that the nested FOR-NEXT loops read all the data for the Sales% array.

After the FOR-NEXT loops read all the data, the PRINT instruction displays the column headings for the table. The first comma moves the column headings one extra print zone to the right. The commas at the end of the two subsequent PRINT instructions move the cursor to the next print zone but keep the cursor on the same line. (For more information on PRINT and print zones, see Chapter 12, "Writing Text on the Video Screen.")

Next, the program totals the garments sold in each season. Here we take advantage of zeroth elements in the Sales% array. When referring to each garment, the first dimension of Sales% varies from 1 to 3 (1 = raincoats, 2 = swimsuits, 3 = underwear). The program uses the zeroth element to refer to total garment sales.

For example, `Sales%(1, 2)` refers to the spring sales of raincoats (1 = raincoats, 2 = spring). `Sales%(0, 2)` refers to the spring sales of all garments (0 = all garments, 2 = spring).

The nested `FOR-NEXT` loops compute the zeroth element for each season. The assignment instruction for `Sales%(0, Season%)` initializes the value to 0. (Strictly speaking, this line is not necessary because QBasic automatically initializes each numeric array element with a value of 0.) For each item, the inner loop over `Item%` increments the value of `Sales%(0, Season%)` by `Sales%(Item%, Season%)`.

All that remains is to display the bottom line of output—the total sales of each garment in each season. That's the job of the final `FOR-NEXT` loop.

SALES.BAS demonstrates the power of two-dimensional arrays with nested `FOR-NEXT` loops. Although the array bounds in this program were modest (3 items, 4 seasons), managing a much larger array (like 2000 items by 15 stores) is no more complicated. With a few program lines, arrays can manipulate tremendous amounts of information.

By the way, SALES.BAS represents the beginning of a two-dimensional spreadsheet program. You might be familiar with commercially available spreadsheets such as Lotus 1-2-3 or Excel. Of course, SALES.BAS is much simpler than these products, but the same programming themes prevail.

Extending Arrays to Higher Dimensions

Arrays are not limited to two dimensions. QBasic allows arrays with as many as 60 dimensions! In practice, arrays with more than three dimensions are rare. The maximum number of elements per dimension is 32,768. To declare a multidimensional array, just specify the array bounds with a `DIM` instruction.

For example, the following instruction specifies a three-dimensional array:

```
DIM Profit!(6, 15, 12)
```

This array might represent the profits of a department store chain as a function of the individual store, the department, and the month. For example, `Profit!(2, 8, 11)` refers to the profit from store #2 (let's say the Miami store), department #15 (maybe cosmetics), in the 11th month (November).

Using the Extended *DIM* Instruction

QBasic extends the power of the `DIM` statement, providing the statement more capability than is available in BASICA/GW-BASIC. `DIM` can also specify a data type for arrays and for ordinary variables.

```
DIM SHARED varname(subscriptrange) AS type,
          varname(subscriptrange) AS type ...
```

where

    varname is the name of an ordinary variable or an array,

    subscriptrange specifies array dimensions when *varname* is an array,

and

    type declares the data type of *varname*.

The keyword SHARED is optional. The AS *type* clause is also optional. Further, the *subscriptrange* parameter is optional because *varname* can be an ordinary variable as well as an array name.

S T A T E M E N T

The optional SHARED keyword paves the way for variable sharing within a program module. See Chapter 17, "Modular Programming."

The optional AS clause specifies the data type of *varname*. To use the AS clause, *varname* must not contain a type-declaration suffix. The *type* parameter must be one of the terms listed in Table 9.4.

Table 9.4. *AS clause data declarations.*

Term	Variable Type
INTEGER	Integer
LONG	Long integer
SINGLE	Single-precision
DOUBLE	Double-precision
STRING	Variable-length string
STRING * *num*	Fixed-length string of length *num*
user-defined	User-defined

Notice that *varname* can be an ordinary variable or an array. For example, the following DIM instructions declare Population to be a long integer variable and StreetName to be a 100-element array of fixed-length strings of length 25:

```
DIM Population AS LONG

DIM StreetName(1 TO 100) AS STRING * 25
```

The user-defined data type, or *record,* is discussed later in this chapter.

Determining Array Bounds with *LBOUND* and *UBOUND*

The LBOUND and UBOUND functions provide a convenient way to determine the lower and upper bounds of an array.

F U N C T I O N	LBOUND(*arrayname*, *dimension*)
	
	 UBOUND(*arrayname*, *dimension*)
	
	 where
	
	    arrayname is the name of the array,
	
	 and
	
	    dimension is an integer expression specifying one of the dimensions of the array.
	
	 The *dimension* parameter is optional.

The value of *dimension* can range from 1 to the number of dimensions in the array (with a maximum of 60). For example, suppose that you create a three-dimensional array with the following DIM instruction:

```
DIM My3DArray%(50, -10 TO 18, 1 TO 4)
```

Table 9.5 shows the values displayed by various calls to the LBOUND and UBOUND functions.

Table 9.5. Values returned by *LBOUND* and *UBOUND*.

Function Call	Output
PRINT LBOUND(My3DArray%, 1)	0
PRINT LBOUND(My3DArray%, 2)	-10
PRINT LBOUND(My3DArray%, 3)	1
PRINT UBOUND(My3DArray%, 1)	50
PRINT UBOUND(My3DArray%, 2)	18
PRINT UBOUND(My3DArray%, 3)	4

If you omit the dimension parameter, QBasic uses 1 by default. Therefore, you need only the *arrayname* parameter for one-dimensional arrays. Consider this program fragment:

```
DIM Velocity#(-30 TO 89)
PRINT LBOUND(Velocity#)
PRINT UBOUND(Velocity#)
```

The output is

```
-30
 89
```

Advanced Array Topics

The following topics concerning array management are deferred to later chapters:

- Sharing arrays between procedures: See Chapter 17, "Modular Programming."

- Static and dynamic array allocation: See Chapter 19, "Managing Memory."

- Erasing and reallocating arrays: See Chapter 19, "Managing Memory."

Using Records

One shortcoming of arrays is that every element of an array must be the same data type. Sometimes you want to assemble diverse data types under a common name.

QBasic introduces a new data type (not available in BASICA/GW-BASIC) called a *record* or *user-defined data type*. Records give you a free hand to custom design an individualized data type for a particular application. (One common use of records is in the manipulation of random-access disk files. See Chapter 15, "Using Random and Binary Disk Files.")

Like an array, a record is a structured data type made up of multiple elements. Unlike an array, elements of a record can be different data types. Use a TYPE-END TYPE block structure to define each record.

For example, suppose that you are writing a payroll program. For each employee, you need to work with his or her name, company ID number, and salary. The following TYPE block establishes a record called Employee:

```
TYPE Employee
   FullName AS STRING * 35
   IDNumber AS INTEGER
   Salary AS SINGLE
END TYPE
```

Employee is a record made up of three pieces of information: FullName, which stores the employee's name; IDNumber, which stores the employee's identification number; and Salary, which stores the employee's salary.

Before continuing with this example, let's take a more detailed look at TYPE-END TYPE blocks.

Defining a Record

Place the TYPE instruction on the first line of the block and the END TYPE instruction on the last line. Between those two lines, each component of the record appears on a separate line.

STATEMENT

```
TYPE recordname
   elementname AS type
   elementname AS type
   elementname AS type
END TYPE
```

where

recordname is the name for the data type,

elementname is the name for each component of the record,

and

type specifies the data type of the corresponding elementname.

The names for recordname and elementname are defined by you. The normal variable-naming conventions apply, except that you cannot use the type-declaration suffixes (%, &, !, #, or $).

Notice that recordname gives a name to the data type itself, not to a variable having this data type. In the payroll example, Employee is the name of the data type. No actual variable having this data type has been created yet. (We'll do so shortly.)

The type parameter must be one of the data types listed in Table 9.6.

Table 9.6. Data types in record declarations.

Type	Description
INTEGER	Integer
LONG	Long integer
SINGLE	Single-precision
DOUBLE	Double-precision
STRING * *num*	Fixed-length string of length *num*
user-defined type	Record (another record type)

Notice that strings must be fixed-length. You specify the length with an asterisk followed by *num,* where *num* is an integer literal (or constant). *type* cannot be a variable-length string or an array name. However, *type* can be another record. That is, one component of a record can be an another entire record of a different type.

Declaring Variables of a Record Type

After you define a record with TYPE, use DIM (or REDIM, COMMON, STATIC, or SHARED) to declare a variable as having that data type. For example, the following instruction declares Boss to be a variable of the record type Employee:

```
DIM Boss AS Employee
```

Arrays of records are permissible. The following instruction declares Salesmen to be an array of 75 elements. Each element of the array is a record.

```
DIM Salesmen(1 TO 75) AS Employee
```

Specifying Components of a Record Variable

You isolate individual components of a record variable by separating the root from the element name with a period. For example, the following program fragment assigns values to the three components of Boss:

```
Boss.FullName = "George M. Honcho"
Boss.IDNumber = 122
Boss.Salary = 3530.50
```

Similarly, you can define the 34th element of the Salesmen array like this:

```
Salesmen(34).FullName = "Ed Closer"
Salesmen(34).IDNumber = 399
Salesmen(34).Salary = 2650.75
```

Nesting Records

You can nest records by defining the component of one record to have the data type of another record. When records are nested, use two or more periods to create a path down to the desired element. Consider the NESTREC.BAS program, Listing 9.5:

Listing 9.5. The NESTREC.BAS program.

```
REM Program: NESTREC.BAS (Demonstrate Nested Records)

TYPE Employee                   'Define Employee record
    FullName AS STRING * 35
    IDNumber AS INTEGER
    Salary AS SINGLE
END TYPE

TYPE Committee                  'Define record
    ProjectName AS STRING * 30  ' -This component is a string.
    Chairman AS Employee        ' -This component is a record.
    Treasurer AS Employee       ' -This component is a record.
    Budget AS SINGLE            ' -This component is a number.
END TYPE

DIM President AS Employee       ' ------------------------
DIM Salesman AS Employee        ' Give variables record type.
DIM UrbanRenewal AS Committee   ' ------------------------

President.FullName = "Whitney Crabtree"
President.IDNumber = 1000
President.Salary = 823.18


UrbanRenewal.Chairman = President   'Assign a record to a record.

PRINT UrbanRenewal.Chairman.FullName  ' --------------------
PRINT UrbanRenewal.Chairman.IDNumber  ' - Note nested paths -
PRINT UrbanRenewal.Chairman.Salary    ' --------------------
END
```

The output is

```
Whitney Crabtree
 1000
 823.18
```

Notice that the record type `Committee` has two components that are themselves records of the type `Employee`. After the `DIM` instructions, the next three lines assign values to the record variable `President` using the descriptors `President.FullName`, `President.IDNumber`, and `President.Salary`.

The next line assigns the entire `President` record to the `Chairman` component of the `UrbanRenewal` record. The point is that this one instruction transfers all three components of `President`. As proof, the `PRINT` instructions use the nested path structure to display the transferred values.

Summary

The array is your primary tool for managing large amounts of related data. Arrays are like super variables that store multiple elements under a common array name. You refer to the individual array elements with a subscript or subscripts. Arrays can be single- or multidimensional.

Arrays and loops work well together. Inside a loop, the loop's counter variable is often used as a subscript in array references. A simple `FOR-NEXT` loop can manipulate all the data in a huge array.

With `DATA` instructions, you can conveniently store numerous data values as part of your program. `READ` instructions can then assign the data values to individual array elements. `DATA` and `READ` work with ordinary variables as well as arrays.

You can customize your own structured data type with a record. A record can group components of different data types under a common name.

Manipulating Numbers

M ost programs manipulate data. After all, when you program routine tasks (such as assigning values to variables, calculating numeric quantities, or printing results), you're manipulating data.

Indeed, the term *data manipulation* could be a title for the rest of this book. In one way or another, nearly all programming topics relate to data manipulation.

This chapter explores various ways of manipulating numbers. The next chapter focuses on string manipulation.

Two main topics are covered in this chapter:

■ Using QBasic's numerical functions

■ Converting values from one data type to another

Introduction to Functions

A *function* manipulates one or more arguments in a predetermined way to produce a single value. For example, the SQR function returns the square root of a single argument.

QBasic supports two kinds of functions:

■ Built-in functions (these are automatically available to any program)

■ User-defined functions

T I P   A Word about User-Defined Functions

As the name implies, a user-defined function is created by *you*. You define such functions with FUNCTION-END FUNCTION blocks and with DEF FN instructions. After you define your functions, your program can invoke them over and over again. User-defined functions are discussed in Chapter 17, "Modular Programming." Until that chapter, the word *function* refers to built-in functions.

This chapter and the next chapter examine only the built-in functions. These functions are predefined in QBasic. You can use a built-in function in any program at any time.

You have already briefly used a few of QBasic's built-in functions (for example, the SQR function in Chapter 3, "A Hands-On Introduction to Programming"). As you will soon see, the wealth of QBasic functions provides an invaluable programming tool.

Each function call consists of a reserved word and, usually, one or more arguments (parameters) enclosed in parentheses (see Figure 10.1). Most functions use a single argument, but some functions require two or more arguments. (A special form of the random number function RND actually has no arguments, but that's a unique case. The RND function is discussed later in this chapter.) When a function has multiple arguments inside the parentheses, the arguments are separated by commas.

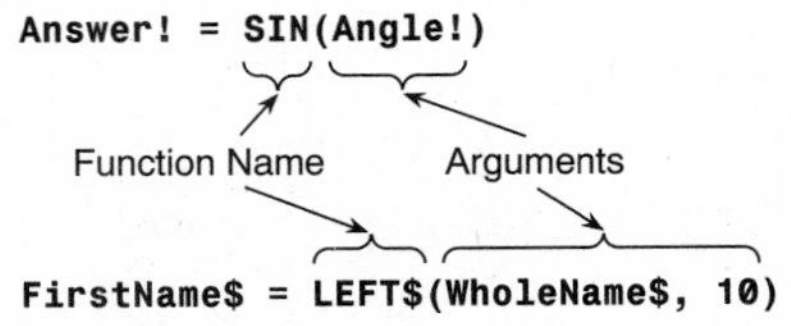

```
Answer! = SIN(Angle!)
```

Function Name   Arguments

Figure 10.1.

Two typical function calls.

```
FirstName$ = LEFT$(WholeName$, 10)
```

Regardless of the number of arguments, every function returns a single value. The available functions can be divided into two categories:

■ *String functions.* These functions return a string value. The function name always ends with a dollar sign. Some string functions require numeric arguments, others require string arguments.

■ *Numeric functions.* These functions, naturally enough, return a numeric value. The function name never ends with a dollar sign. Most numeric functions require numeric arguments, some require string arguments.

Notice that the argument (or arguments) of a function is not necessarily the same data type as the value returned by the function. For example, the LEN function returns a numeric value equal to the length of its string argument:

```
Num! = LEN(MyString$)
```

(LEN is discussed in the next chapter.)

In general, you can call a function anywhere a single value is acceptable. For example, Table 10.1 shows a few places where you might use the SQR function.

Table 10.1. Sample function calls.

Instruction	Comment
Num! = SQR(55)	Right-hand side of assignment instruction
PRINT SQR(MyNum!)	In a PRINT instruction
A! = SQR(SQR(24))	As an argument of another function
IF SQR(A%) < 5 THEN...	In an IF-THEN instruction

Using the Numeric Functions and Statements

When we discuss the numeric functions and statements, we often use the term *general numeric expression,* or simply *numeric expression.*

A numeric expression is any expression that evaluates to a single numeric value. The expression can contain any combination of literals, variables, array elements, and function calls. The final value can have any of the four numeric data types (integer, long integer, single-precision, or double-precision).

Table 10.2 shows a few examples of numeric expressions.

Table 10.2. Sample numeric expressions.

Numeric Expression	Comment
435	Simple numeric literal
(Cost! * NumItems%) / 12.2	Expression with variables
Salary!(Employee%)	Simple array reference
SQR(Side1# - Side2#)	Expression containing a function call

Obviously, the numeric functions and statements are mathematical. We recognize that many programmers are not math wizards and don't intend to write programs that do fancy mathematical manipulation. In fact, many programmers get along fine writing programs that require no more math than the simple arithmetic provided by the addition, subtraction, multiplication, and division operators (+, −, *, and /).

If you expect your programs to utilize only simple arithmetic, feel free to skim the following material. Later, if the need arises, you can always come back for reference.

As Table 10.3 shows, QBasic provides a host of numerical functions and statements.

Table 10.3. Mathematical functions and statements.

Name	Type	Description
	Trigonometric	
SIN	Function	Sine of an angle
COS	Function	Cosine of an angle
TAN	Function	Tangent of an angle
ATN	Function	Arctangent of a number
	Logarithmic	
EXP	Function	Exponential
LOG	Function	Natural logarithm
	Conversion	
CINT	Function	Convert a number to integer
CLNG	Function	Convert a number to long integer
CSNG	Function	Convert a number to single-precision
CDBL	Function	Convert a number to double-precision
	Rounding	
FIX	Function	Truncate to integer
INT	Function	Round to lower integer
	Random Numbers	
RANDOMIZE	Statement	Seed random-number generator
RND	Function	Generate a random number

Name	Type	Description
Arithmetic		
ABS	Function	Absolute value
SGN	Function	Sign of a number
SQR	Function	Square root

Unless you specify otherwise, each mathematical function returns a single-precision result—even when the argument(s) is double-precision.

Using the Trigonometric Functions

The trigonometric functions SIN, COS, and TAN return the sine, cosine, and tangent of an angle, respectively. QBasic also includes the ATN function, which returns the arctangent (or inverse tangent) of a number.

SIN*(angle)*

COS*(angle)*

TAN*(angle)*

ATN*(numexpr)*

where

    angle specifies an angle in radians

and

    numexpr is a general numeric expression.

**F
U
N
C
T
I
O
N**

Angles are specified in radians because radians are mathematically more convenient than degrees. One radian is approximately 57.3 degrees. There are 2π radians in a complete circle (that is, 2π radians equal 360 degrees; as a result, π is approximately 3.14). Figure 10.2 shows the mapping between radians and degrees.

The value of *angle* can be positive, negative, or zero. The SIN and COS functions always return a value between –1.0 and +1.0. The TAN function returns values ranging from large negative numbers to large positive numbers.

The arctangent of *numexpr* is the angle whose tangent has the value of *numexpr*. Therefore, ATN is the inverse function to TAN. The result of the ATN function is an angle expressed in radians. This angle is confined to the range from –π/2 to +π/2.

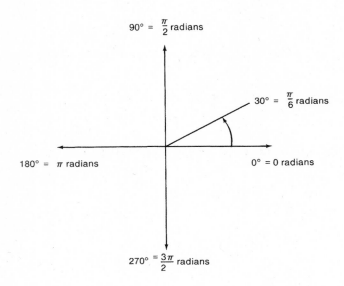

Figure 10.2.

Specifying angles in radians and degrees.

T I P   Using ATN to Find the Value of π

Many trigonometric programs need to work with the value of π. The ATN function provides a convenient way to store the value of π in a variable. Here's how.

The tangent of (π/4) is exactly 1. This means that the arctangent of 1 is π/4. The following program fragment demonstrates how to calculate π to single- and double-precision accuracy. The program stores the values in the variables Pi! and Pi#, and displays the results.

```
Pi! = 4 * ATN(1)
Pi# = 4 * ATN(1#)
PRINT Pi!
PRINT Pi#
```

Here is the output:

```
3.141593
3.141592653589793
```

Notice that ATN(1#) returns a double-precision result. The technique of placing a type suffix (the pound sign in this example) at the end of a numeric literal is discussed later in this chapter.

Using the Logarithmic Functions

LOG returns the natural logarithm. The EXP function, the inverse function of LOG, returns the exponential.

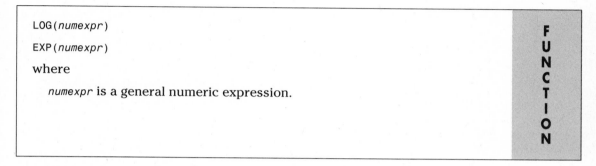

LOG(*numexpr*)

EXP(*numexpr*)

where

    numexpr is a general numeric expression.

F
U
N
C
T
I
O
N

For the LOG function, *numexpr* must be positive, or an Illegal function call error occurs. (Mathematically, a logarithm is undefined for a negative argument.)

For the EXP function, *numexpr* can be positive, negative, or zero. The largest permissible value of *numexpr* depends on the numeric data type of the argument. If *numexpr* is double-precision, the upper limit of *numexpr* is 709. If *numexpr* is single-precision, integer, or long integer, the upper limit is 88. (A value of *numexpr* above the limit creates numeric overflow because, mathematically, the exponential returns a value larger than the maximum value for that data type.)

LOG and EXP are based on the natural logarithms, also called logarithms to the base *e*. The mathematical constant *e* has a value of approximately 2.71828. You can see QBasic's value of *e* in single- and double-precision with the following experiment:

```
PRINT EXP(1)
PRINT EXP(1#)
```

The result is

```
2.718282
2.718281828459045
```

You might need logarithms to the base 10, sometimes called common logarithms. The following instruction uses the LOG function to calculate the common logarithm of X!:

```
ComLog! = LOG(X!) / LOG(10)
```

You can duplicate the exponential function with the exponential operator ^ (the caret, or up-arrow symbol—Shift-6 on most keyboards). Mathematically,

EXP(X) is e^x (*e* raised to the power of X). Another way to express the same thing in QBasic is EXP(1) ^ X. For example, consider the following program fragment:

```
X! = 4.9
PRINT EXP(X!)
PRINT EXP(1) ^ X!
```

Here is the output:

```
134.2898
134.2898
```

Use 10 ^ X to calculate the base 10 exponential of X (10 raised to the X power).

Using the Conversion Functions

QBasic has several functions that convert a number from one numeric type to another (such as from single-precision to integer). These are the conversion functions: CINT, CLNG, CSNG, and CDBL.

CINT, CLNG, CSNG, and CDBL convert a given numeric expression in any format into the equivalent number in a specified numeric format.

F U N C T I O N

CINT(*numexpr*)

CLNG(*numexpr*)

CSNG(*numexpr*)

CDBL(*numexpr*)

where

   numexpr is a general numeric expression.

CINT converts to integer. The value of *numexpr* must be in the range from –32,768 to +32,767. If *numexpr* contains a fractional part, CINT rounds to the closest integer. If *numexpr* has a fractional part of exactly .5, CINT rounds to the closest whole integer. (By contrast, the CINT function in GW-BASIC and BASICA rounds to the next higher whole number.)

CLNG converts to long integer. The value of *numexpr* must be in the range from –2,147,483,648 to 2,147,483,647. The rounding of a fractional number works exactly like CINT.

CSNG converts to single-precision. The value of *numexpr* must be in the range from (approximately) –3.37E+38 to +3.37E+38.

CDBL converts to double-precision. The value of *numexpr* must be in the range from (approximately) −1.67D+308 to +1.67D+308.

Table 10.4 shows the results of some conversion instructions.

Table 10.4. Sample commands using the conversion functions.

Direct-Mode Command	Result
PRINT CINT(-1.8)	-2
PRINT CINT(29.4)	29
PRINT CINT(29.8)	30
PRINT CLNG(48324.5)	48324
PRINT CLNG(48325.5)	48326
PRINT CSNG(1.23456789#)	1.234568
PRINT CSNG(1 / 7)	.1428571
X! = 1 / 7:PRINT CDBL(X!)	.1428571492433548
PRINT CDBL(1# / 7)	.1428571428571428

In Table 10.4, compare the results of the two CDBL examples with the last CSNG example. Although CDBL calculates to 16 digits of precision, only the first 7 digits are accurate. The variable X! has only single-precision accuracy, and CDBL cannot convert a single-precision expression to double-precision accuracy. However, the expression (1# / 7) produces double-precision accuracy, and CDBL processes this expression to full accuracy.

You *do not* need conversion functions when you assign a numeric expression to a variable. Consider these instructions:

MyInt% = CINT(1234.5 * 4)

MyLng& = CLNG(15 ^ 7)

MySng! = CSNG(23.8# / 9)

MyDbl# = CDBL(38.23 * 14.7)

In each case, you get exactly the same result by omitting the conversion function. The assignment of a numeric expression to a numeric variable forces the appropriate type conversion. No conversion function is necessary.

Numeric type conversion and the use of suffixes on numeric literals are discussed later in this chapter. You will see how the type conversion functions can prevent certain overflow errors.

Data type conversion can be somewhat confusing at first. Rest assured that, unless you are doing sophisticated mathematical computation, your numeric results will be correct most of the time if you just write your mathematical expressions naturally.

Using the Rounding Functions

In addition to CINT and CLNG, QBasic has two other functions that convert a general numeric expression into a whole number.

<table>
<tr><td rowspan="2">F
U
N
C
T
I
O
N</td><td>FIX(numexpr)</td></tr>
<tr><td>INT(numexpr)

where

    numexpr is a general numeric expression.</td></tr>
</table>

FIX simply strips off the fractional part of *numexpr*. This is called *truncation*. FIX(8.9) is 8, and FIX(-8.9) is –8.

INT returns the largest whole number that is less than or equal to the value of *numexpr*. This is called *rounding down* or *flooring*. INT(8.9) is 8 and INT(-8.9) is –9.

Recall that CINT and CLNG return the whole number closest to *numexpr*. Rounding is either up or down, as appropriate. CINT(4.2) is 4, and CINT(4.8) is 5.

FIX and INT are similar functions. Each returns the same value when *numexpr* is zero or positive. However, when *numexpr* is negative, the functions produce different results.

Unlike CINT and CLNG, FIX and INT can work with values outside the range of QBasic's integer and long integer numbers. Although FIX and INT return whole numbers, the results are single- or double-precision. If *numexpr* is single-precision, then FIX and INT return single-precision results. If *numexpr* is double-precision, then FIX and INT return double-precision results. For example, PRINT FIX(123456.7) and PRINT INT(123456.7) each return 123456.

Contrast that with PRINT CINT(123456.7), which causes an overflow error because 123456.7 is too large for QBasic's integer data type.

Listing 10.1 demonstrates the differences between values returned by CINT, FIX, and INT.

Listing 10.1. The ROUND.BAS program.

```
REM Program: ROUND.BAS (Demonstrate the rounding functions)

PRINT "X", "CINT(X)", "FIX(X)", "INT(X)"
FOR X! = -2.8 TO 2.8 STEP 1.4
   PRINT X!, CINT(X!), FIX(X!), INT(X!)
NEXT X!
```

Here's the output from Listing 10.1:

X	CINT(X)	FIX(X)	INT(X)
-2.8	-3	-2	-3
-1.4	-1	-1	-2
0	0	0	0
1.4	1	1	1
2.8	3	2	2

Using Random Numbers

The RND function returns a single-precision *random* number between 0 and 1.

RND

or

RND(*numexpr*)

where

   numexpr is a general numeric expression.

The argument, *numexpr*, is optional.

F U N C T I O N

How can a number be random? Just what does a "random" number mean?

A random number is simply an unpredictable number—a number that cannot be predetermined.

Many scientific simulations and game-playing programs use random numbers regularly. As a simple example, the following instruction tosses a simulated coin:

```
IF RND > .5 THEN PRINT "Heads" ELSE PRINT "Tails"
```

RND returns values that are not truly random, but rather are computed by a numeric formula that creates *pseudorandom* numbers. Pseudorandom numbers, though derived from a mathematical computation, emulate the unpredictability of random numbers. QBasic keeps the required formula internally and you don't have to worry about it.

However, the formula does depend on an initial starting value, sometimes called a *seed*. By default, QBasic provides the same seed each time you run a program. Therefore, unless you reseed the random-number generator, RND produces the same sequence of random numbers each time the program is run.

To reseed the random-number formula, QBasic provides the RANDOMIZE statement.

S T A T E M E N T

RANDOMIZE *seed*

or

RANDOMIZE

where

    seed is a general numeric expression.

The *seed* parameter is optional.

RANDOMIZE is not a function, but a full-fledged QBasic statement. Notice that the *seed* parameter is not enclosed in parentheses.

Typically, you use a single RANDOMIZE instruction at the beginning of every program that uses RND. In order to change the random-number sequence each time a particular program is run, you must alter the value of *seed* with each run. QBasic's TIMER function provides a handy way to seed the random number generator unpredictably. (TIMER is a special function that returns the number of elapsed seconds since midnight. TIMER is discussed further in Chapter 16, "Using Hardware Devices.") Use the following instruction:

```
RANDOMIZE TIMER
```

A RANDOMIZE instruction without the *seed* parameter causes QBasic to prompt you for a seed value by displaying the following message:

```
Random-number seed (-32768 to 32767)?
```

You must provide the numeric seed before execution resumes.

RND operates differently depending on the value of the *numexpr* argument (see Table 10.5). Notice that the argument, *numexpr*, is optional.

Table 10.5. Operation of *RND* function.

Value of Argument	Action Performed
numexpr > 0	Returns the next random number in the current sequence.
numexpr omitted	Same effect as *numexpr* > 0.
numexpr = 0	Returns the previous random number.
numexpr < 0	Reseeds the random-number generator using *numexpr* and returns the first number of the new sequence.

The following program demonstrates the type of random numbers returned by the RND function:

```
RANDOMIZE TIMER
FOR J% = 1 TO 5
    PRINT RND
NEXT J%
```

Here is the output from a typical run. (Your results will differ, of course. After all, these are random numbers.)

```
.5473383
.6511793
.9765581
.277216
.9823589
```

Notice that RND always returns a decimal fraction between 0 and 1. What if you need a random integer, for example, from 10 to 35?

With the aid of RND and INT, the following formula produces a random integer in the range from *lowinteger* to *highinteger*:

```
INT((highinteger - lowinteger + 1) * RND + lowinteger)
```

For example, the instruction PRINT INT(26 * RND + 10) displays a random integer in the range from 10 to 35.

To demonstrate this technique, the program in Listing 10.2 calculates and displays five random rolls of a pair of dice.

Listing 10.2. The DICEROLL.BAS program.

```
REM Program: DICEROLL.BAS (Roll dice 5 times)

RANDOMIZE TIMER
FOR Roll% = 1 TO 5
   Die1% = INT(6 * RND + 1)
   Die2% = INT(6 * RND + 1)
   PRINT "Roll"; Roll%; "is"; Die1% + Die2%
NEXT Roll%
```

Here are some typical results of Listing 10.2. (Again, your results will differ because of the use of the RANDOMIZE instruction.)

```
Roll 1 is 8
Roll 2 is 12
Roll 3 is 7
Roll 4 is 10
Roll 5 is 4
```

(The PRINT instruction inside the FOR-NEXT loop uses semicolons to separate displayed items. This technique was mentioned in Chapter 3, "A Hands-On Introduction to Programming." The PRINT instruction is discussed thoroughly in Chapter 12, "Writing Text on the Video Screen.")

Using the Arithmetic Functions

Three miscellaneous numeric functions remain—ABS, SGN, and SQR.

FUNCTION

ABS(*numexpr*)

SGN(*numexpr*)

SQR(*numexpr*)

where

numexpr is a general numeric expression.

The ABS function returns the absolute value of *numexpr*. The absolute value of a number is the magnitude of the number without regard to sign. For example, the absolute value of −21.7 and the absolute value of +21.7 are both 21.7.

Many calculations require that you find the difference between two numbers, regardless of which number is larger. For example, suppose you have two variables named A! and B!. You want to set Diff! to the positive difference between A! and B!. However, you don't know whether A! or B! has the larger value. You could use a messy IF instruction like this:

```
IF A! > B! THEN Diff! = A! - B! ELSE Diff! = B! - A!
```

There is a better way. Rather than fool around with cumbersome IF instructions, use ABS to calculate the positive difference as follows:

```
Diff! = ABS(A! - B!)
```

The SGN function returns the sign of *numexpr*, not to be confused with the trigonometric SIN function discussed previously. As Table 10.6 shows, the SGN function returns −1, 0, or +1 depending on the value of *numexpr*.

Table 10.6. The *SGN* function.

Value of *numexpr*	Result of *SGN(numexpr)*
Positive (> 0)	1
Zero (= 0)	0
Negative (< 0)	−1

The SQR function, which you've already seen, returns the square root of *numexpr*. Negative arguments are not allowed, and the value of *numexpr* must be greater than or equal to 0.

Calculating Square Roots

T I P

Mathematically, the square root of a number is equivalent to raising the number to the one-half (.5) power. Therefore, the following two instructions return the same result:

```
MyRoot! = SQR(MyNumber!)

MyRoot! = MyNumber! ^ 0.5
```

The SQR form tends to be easier to read when you are glancing at a program. Furthermore, QBasic executes the SQR form faster. For square roots, use SQR instead of the .5 exponent.

Type Conversion

Table 10.7 reviews QBasic's data types. Every variable has one of these six data types.

Table 10.7. The six data types.

Data Types	Sample Variable Name
Variable-length string	MyName$
Fixed-length string	TodayDate$
Integer	MyAge%
Long integer	NumPeople&
Single-precision	Price!
Double-precision	Mass#

Mixing Data Types

When you assign a value to a variable, QBasic checks that the value matches the variable's type. What happens if there is a mismatch?

Most of the time, QBasic is quite forgiving. QBasic tries to convert the value of the data to match the variable's data type. This process, whereby QBasic converts a value of one data type into another data type, is known as *type conversion.*

You can assign a string value to a variable of either string data type. Also, you can assign any numeric value to a variable of any numeric type. If necessary, QBasic makes the required type conversion.

For example, the following instructions are perfectly legal:

```
MyAge% = 39.9999
```

```
TAX! = 23456
```

```
Value# = Cost&
```

QBasic converts the numeric value on the right-hand side into the data type required by the variable. When numeric variables are involved, the type conversion is called, naturally enough, *numeric type conversion.* Several more examples are discussed shortly. (See Chapter 11, "Manipulating Strings," for a discussion of string type conversion.)

However, strings and numbers are like water and oil: You just can't mix them. You can't assign string data to a numeric variable or numeric data to a string variable. Each of the following instructions causes a run-time error (Type mismatch):

```
MyAge% = "Too much"

YourAge& = BigNumber$

MySize$ = YourSize!

YourSize$ = 38
```

Numeric Type Conversion

QBasic can convert a numeric value from one type to another in the following two situations:

- When you assign a value to a variable
- When evaluating a numeric expression

Type Conversion During Variable Assignment

If necessary, when you assign a value to a numeric variable, QBasic converts the value to the data type of the variable.

The following rules apply:

1. Rounding occurs when you assign a number with a fractional part to an integer variable. For example:

   ```
   MyNum% = 34.84
   BigNum! = -53411.2
   Value& = BigNum!
   PRINT MyNum%
   PRINT Value&
   ```

   The result is

   ```
    35
   -53411
   ```

   A fractional number is rounded (up or down) to the closest whole number. If the number ends in exactly .5, QBasic rounds (up or down) to the closest whole integer.

2. Rounding occurs when you assign a value of more than seven significant digits to a single-precision value. For example:

```
Population& = 132354861
Population! = Population&
TestNum# = 7.436921342D+20
TestNum! = TestNum#
PRINT Population!
PRINT TestNum!
```

The result is

```
1.323649E+08
7.436921E+20
```

(In the literal assigned to `TestNum#`, the `D` is the exponential indicator for double-precision numbers. That is, the number on the right of the equal sign is double-precision. See Chapter 6, "Language Building Blocks," for more information.)

3. An `Overflow` error occurs if you try to assign a value outside the allowable range of the variable. For example, the following instructions are illegal:

```
MyNum% = 63111.5
```

```
MyNum! = 4.563D+75
```

The first instruction is illegal, not because `63111.5` has a fractional part, but because the rounded value is too large for an integer variable (remember that an integer variable cannot be larger than 32,767). The second instruction is illegal, not because a double-precision literal is assigned to a single-precision variable, but because the value of the double-precision literal is too large for a single-precision number.

4. Loss of precision can occur when you assign a single-precision value to a double-precision variable. Only the first seven digits (rounded) of the result are valid. For example:

```
MyNum! = .11
MyNum# = MyNum!
PRINT MyNum#
```

The result is

```
.1099999994039536
```

The digits after the sequence of nines are inaccurate.

Type Conversion During Expression Evaluation

During the evaluation of an arithmetic expression, as QBasic performs each operation, the operands must be at the same level of precision. If necessary QBasic converts operands to the same level of precision.

Here's a simple example:

```
TotalCost! = Num% * UnitCost!
```

The expression Num% * UnitCost! multiplies an integer value (Num%) and a single-precision value (UnitCost!). The result is assigned to a single-precision variable (TotalCost!). To do the multiplication, QBasic needs both operands at the same level of precision. Therefore, before multiplying, QBasic automatically converts the value of Num% to single-precision.

Why doesn't QBasic convert UnitCost! to integer instead? What determines which operand gets converted?

QBasic converts the less-precise operand to the precision of the more-precise operand. Table 10.8 shows the precision order of numeric data types.

Table 10.8. Precision of numeric data types.

Data Type	Precision
Double-precision	Most precise
Single-precision	
Long integer	
Integer	Least precise

Two problems can arise during the evaluation of expressions:

- Loss of accuracy
- Overflow

Loss of Accuracy

Ready for something challenging? The following example is tricky, so you need to stay alert. Consider this program fragment:

```
A% = 5: B! = 1.5: C# = 1000
Temp! = A% / B!
PRINT Temp! * C#
PRINT A% / B! * C#
```

Look closely at the two PRINT instructions. They compute and display essentially the same thing. After all, Temp! in the first instruction is equivalent to the expression A% / B! that occurs in the second instruction.

Therefore, you might reasonably expect that these two PRINT instructions produce the same result. But here is the output:

```
3333.333253860474
3333.333333333333
```

What's going on? Notice that both results display as double-precision numbers (with 16 digits). However, only the second number has double-precision accuracy. (The first number is inaccurate after the string of threes.)

To see why, look at the second line of the program fragment. The variable Temp! is single-precision and QBasic computes the expression on the right-hand side to single-precision accuracy (that is, to 7 digits of precision). In the subsequent PRINT instruction, the value of Temp! is multiplied by the double-precision quantity C#. The net result is a double-precision value (16 digits) with only single-precision accuracy (7 digits). That's why you see the nonsignificant digits (253860474) after the third decimal place.

The second PRINT instruction is similar, but different. Here, QBasic recognizes that the presence of a double-precision operand (C#) requires the entire expression to have double-precision accuracy. Therefore, the values of A% and B! are converted to double-precision during the expression evaluation. As a result, the final value has full double-precision accuracy.

Overflow

The following instruction generates an overflow error. Why?

```
MyNum! = 2 * 25000
```

The two operands—2 and 25000—are integer numbers, so QBasic does the multiplication expecting an integer result. However, the outcome (50000) is too large for the integer data type, and overflow occurs. (Recall, from Chapter 6, "Language Building Blocks," that the maximum value for an integer number is 32,767.)

You can avoid this overflow error by using one of the type conversion functions (discussed earlier in this chapter). For example, you could rewrite the instruction as follows:

```
MyNum! = CLNG(2) * 25000
```

Now the instruction works fine. In this modified instruction, the CLNG function converts the regular integer 2 to a long integer and thus avoids the integer overflow. Notice that CSNG or CDBL would work also.

However, don't make this mistake:

```
MyNum! = CLNG(2 * 25000)
```

The expression inside the parentheses causes integer overflow before CLNG has a chance to act.

The following section discusses another way to prevent such overflow errors.

Using Type-Declaration Characters on Numeric Literals

You can attach a type-declaration suffix to a numeric literal. This suffix specifies the data type of the literal. Table 10.9 shows some examples.

Table 10.9. Examples of numeric literals.

Literal	Precision
2	Integer
2&	Long integer
2!	Single-precision
2#	Double-precision
1.5	Single-precision
1.5#	Double-precision

The following instruction avoids the overflow error previously mentioned:

```
MyNum! = 2& * 25000
```

Now 2& is a long integer, and the multiplication by 25000 has long-integer precision. The result, 50000, is well within the range of long integer values. Note that 2! or 2# would work as well as 2&.

Certain literals that you type in your program are converted by QBasic into an alternate form that contains a type-declaration suffix. For example, type this:

```
TWO! = 2.0
```

When you press Enter, the editor converts the line to look like this:

```
TWO! = 2!
```

Table 10.10 shows some more examples of how the editor reformats certain numeric literals.

Table 10.10. Examples of numeric literal conversion.	
You Type This...	**Editor Gives You This...**
2.0	2!
1.23456789	1.23456789#
9876543210	9876543210#
1.3D+05	130000#
0.4	.4
1.2e20	1.2E+20
476%	476

Summary

QBasic provides an abundance of built-in functions. Each function takes one or more arguments and returns a single value (which can be numeric or string).

The numeric functions solve mathematical problems. QBasic has functions for arithmetic (SQR), trigonometry (SIN), logarithms (LOG), rounding (INT), and random numbers (RND).

Numeric expressions can contain numbers of different data types. When evaluating expressions, if necessary, QBasic converts parts of a numeric expression from one data type to another (for example, from single-precision to integer). Occasionally your final results lose some accuracy during this process.

This chapter concentrates on the manipulation of numbers. The next chapter discusses the manipulation of strings.

Manipulating Strings

You learned about the manipulation of numbers in the previous chapter. Now turn your attention to the other side of the data coin: strings (text).

This chapter covers three main topics:

- Using QBasic's string functions
- Forming string expressions
- Performing string type conversion

Fundamental String Concepts

Before learning the string functions, you need to understand a few fundamental concepts of string manipulation, namely:

- Length of a string
- The null string
- Joining strings
- Forming string expressions

Length of a String

Every data string has a *length*. This length is simply the number of text characters (including blank spaces and punctuation characters) that comprise the string. For example, the string `Hello` has a length of five. The string `Paris, Texas` has a length of 12 (including the comma and blank space). The maximum-length string is 32,767 characters.

A string variable also has a length. The length of a string variable is simply the length of the data string currently stored in the variable.

The Null String

A string can have a length of zero! In QBasic jargon, a zero-length string is called a *null string*. You form a null string by placing two double quotation marks together. For example:

```
MyText$ = ""
```

`MyText$` has a length of 0 (the null string).

Don't confuse the null string with a string consisting of a single blank space. The latter string has a length of 1. When you "display" the null string with `PRINT` instruction, you do not get any characters at all (not even a blank space). Here's an example:

```
Part1$ = "check"
Part2$ = "book"
Middle$ = ""                        'null string
PRINT Part1$; Middle$; Part2$
Middle$ = " "                       'one blank space
PRINT Part1$; Middle$; Part2$
```

The result is

```
checkbook
check book
```

Joining Strings

As discussed in Chapter 6, "Language Building Blocks," you use the plus (+) operator to join two strings together. This process, called *concatenation,* forms a new string made up of the first string immediately followed by the second string.

The length of the new string is simply the sum of the lengths of the two operand strings.

Consider this program fragment:

```
FirstPart$ = "Don't rock"
Result$ = FirstPart$ + "the boat."
PRINT Result$
```

The output is

```
Don't rockthe boat.
```

Concatenation does not do any formatting, trimming, or padding with blank characters. In the present example, to add a blank space between `rock` and `the`, you must change the program. Here is one solution (with the second line changed):

```
FirstPart$ = "Don't rock"
Result$ = FirstPart$ + " the boat."    'blank space before the
PRINT Result$
```

Now the output is more readable:

```
Don't rock the boat.
```

String Expressions

Just as you can form numeric expressions, you can also form string expressions. The term *string expression* refers to any expression that evaluates to a single string value.

A string expression can be as simple as a single variable name or as complex as a combination of string literals, variables, functions, and the plus sign. Table 11.1 shows some examples of string expressions.

Table 11.1. Some sample string expressions.

Expression	Comment
`"Bob and Ray"`	Single literal
`Title$`	Single variable
`LEFT$(Title$, 3)`	String function
`"Mortimer" + LastName$`	Combination expression

Using the String Functions and Statements

QBasic's functions are not all mathematical. Far from it. As Table 11.2 shows, QBasic provides several built-in functions and statements that manipulate strings.

Table 11.2. String functions and statements.

Name	Type	Description
Finding String Length		
LEN	Function	Returns length of string.
Converting Case		
LCASE$	Function	Converts string to lowercase.
UCASE$	Function	Converts string to uppercase.
Returning a Substring		
LEFT$	Function	Returns leftmost characters.
RIGHT$	Function	Returns rightmost characters.
MID$	Function	Returns substring.
LTRIM$	Function	Strips blank spaces from left of string.
RTRIM$	Function	Strips blank spaces from right of string
Converting to and from ASCII		
ASC	Function	Returns the ASCII value of a character.
CHR$	Function	Returns a character, given its ASCII value.
Converting Strings to Numbers		
VAL	Function	Converts a string to a number
STR$	Function	Converts a number to a string form
HEX$	Function	Converts a number to a hex string
OCT$	Function	Converts a number to an octal string

Name	Type	Description
	Searching for Substring	
INSTR	Function	Searches for a substring.
	Generating Strings	
STRING$	Function	Constructs a string of identical characters.
SPACE$	Function	Constructs a string of blank spaces.
	Modifying a String Variable	
LSET	Statement	Left-justifies a string.
RSET	Statement	Right-justifies a string.
MID$	Statement	Merges one string into another.

All these functions and statements work with strings. Some of the functions return numeric values and some return string values. The functions that return string values have a dollar sign at the end of the function name. Functions that return numeric values do not end with a dollar sign. The functions that return numeric values take string arguments.

Finding String Length

To find the length of a string, use LEN.

LEN(*string*)

where

    string is a string expression.

F
U
N
C
T
I
O
N

Consider the following program:

```
Null$=""          'The double quotes form a null string
PRINT LEN(Null$)
```

```
MyName$ = "Phil Feldman"
PRINT LEN(MyName$)
PRINT LEN("You had to be there")
```

The output is

```
0
12
19
```

Converting Case

Use LCASE$ and UCASE$ to convert strings to lower- or uppercase.

F U N C T I O N	LCASE$(*strexpr*) UCASE$(*strexpr*) where *strexpr* is a general string expression.

The LCASE$ function returns a copy of *strexpr* that has all uppercase letters converted to lowercase. Nonalphabetic characters, such as digits and punctuation symbols, remain unchanged. Similarly, UCASE$ converts all the lowercase letters of *strexpr* to uppercase.

Here is a program fragment that shows LCASE$ and UCASE$ in action:

```
Test$ = "Learning QBasic is as easy as 1-2-3."
PRINT Test$
PRINT LCASE$(Test$)
PRINT UCASE$(Test$)
```

The output is

```
Learning QBasic is as easy as 1-2-3.
learning qbasic is as easy as 1-2-3.
LEARNING QBASIC IS AS EASY AS 1-2-3.
```

UCASE$ is handy when you need to test a user's response. For example, suppose your program asks users whether they need instructions. You want to display instructions if the user replies affirmatively. The following program fragment tests the response with one simple IF instruction:

```
INPUT "Do you want instructions (Yes or No)"; Response$
IF UCASE$(Response$) = "YES" THEN
    REM Display the instructions here
END IF
```

Now the instructions display if the user's response is Yes, YES, yes, or even yEs. There is no need to test for each of the various capitalizations.

Returning a Substring

The LEFT$, RIGHT$, and MID$ functions return a portion of a string. A portion of a larger string is called a *substring* of the larger string. For example, water is a substring of Clearwater.

To use LEFT$, RIGHT$, or MID$, you must specify the length of the desired substring (the number of characters you want returned) and the position in the original string where the substring begins.

LEFT$(*string, stringlength*)

RIGHT$(*string, stringlength*)

MID$(*string, startposition*)

or

MID$(*string, startposition, stringlength*)

where

   string is a string expression,

   stringlength specifies the length of the substring to return,

and

   startposition specifies the position in *string* where the substring starts.

The *stringlength* parameter is optional for MID$.

F U N C T I O N

The *LEFT$* and *RIGHT$* Functions

The LEFT$ function returns a substring copied from the leftmost characters in *string*. Similarly, RIGHT$ extracts the rightmost characters in *string*. The *stringlength* parameter must be in the range from 0 to 32,767. If *stringlength* is zero, a null string is returned. If *stringlength* is greater than the length of *string,* the entire *string* is returned.

Here is a simple example of LEFT$ and RIGHT$:

```
Test$ = "Phil says hello to Tom"
PRINT LEFT$(Test$, 15)      'leftmost 15 characters of Test$
PRINT RIGHT$(Test$, 12)     'rightmost 12 characters of Test$
```

The output looks like this:

```
Phil says hello
hello to Tom
```

The *MID$* Function

The MID$ function extracts a substring from the interior of *string*. The *stringlength* and *startposition* parameters must be in the range from 1 to 32,767.

MID$ returns a substring that begins at *startposition* and has a length of *stringlength* characters. For example, if *startposition* is 6 and *stringlength* is 4, MID$ returns the sixth through ninth characters of *string*.

An example should clarify just how MID$ works:

```
Test$ = "Every good boy does fine"
PRINT MID$(Test$, 7, 8)     'characters 7,8,9,10,11,12,13,14
PRINT MID$(Test$, 12, 3)    'characters 12,13,14
PRINT MID$(Test$, 12)       'characters 12 to end of string
PRINT MID$(Test$ + " work in school", 12, 18)
```

The output is

```
good boy
boy
boy does fine
boy does fine work
```

Notice that MID$ has two forms: with and without the *stringlength* parameter. If you omit *stringlength*, MID$ returns all characters from *startposition* to the end of *string*. You get the same effect in the three-parameter form when *string* contains less than *stringlength* characters from *startposition* to the end of *string*.

In the present example, the first, second, and fourth lines use the three-parameter form of `MID$`. The third line uses the two-parameter form.

If *startposition* is greater than the length of *string*, `MID$` simply returns a null string.

Here's a tricky example. Can you follow what happens?

```
FOR Start% = 1 TO 7
    PRINT MID$("QBASIC", Start%, 2)
NEXT Start%
PRINT "Done"
```

Here is the output:

```
QB
BA
AS
SI
IC
C

Done
```

Notice that there is a blank line of output (the seventh line) just before the `Done` message. The seventh line is blank because the start position (given by `Start%` with a value of 7) is beyond the length of the six-character string `QBASIC`.

The *LTRIM$* and *RTRIM$* Functions

The `LTRIM$` and `RTRIM$` functions strip blank spaces from the left and right sides, respectively, of a string.

LTRIM$(*strexpr*)

RTRIM$(*strexpr*)

where

    strexpr is a general string expression.

F U N C T I O N

For example, the instruction `PRINT LTRIM$("        Goodnight")` displays `Goodnight` (the leading blanks are removed).

Converting Strings to ASCII

Every string character has an associated numeric value from 0 to 255. These values conform to a special code known as ASCII (*A*merican *S*tandard *C*ode for *I*nformation *I*nterchange). For example, the uppercase letter *A* has an ASCII value of 65. The lowercase letter *a* is 97. A blank space is 32. Appendix B, "ASCII Character Set," lists all the ASCII values and the associated characters.

The functions ASC and CHR$ convert between string characters and numeric ASCII values—ASC returns the ASCII value for a given string character and CHR$ returns the string character corresponding to a given ASCII value.

<table>
<tr><td>F
U
N
C
T
I
O
N</td><td>

ASC(*strexpr*)

CHR$(*ASCIIcode*)

where

    strexpr is a string expression

and

    ASCIIcode is an ASCII code value in the range from 0 to 255.

</td></tr>
</table>

Notice that CHR$ ends with a dollar sign but ASC does not. The CHR$ function is a string function that takes a numeric argument but returns a string value. ASC, on the other hand, takes a string argument but returns a numerical value.

The ASC function returns the ASCII value of the first character in the *strexpr* argument. If *strexpr* is a null string, a run-time error occurs (Illegal function call). Here is an example of the ASC function in action:

```
PRINT ASC("A")
PRINT ASC("Apples")
PRINT ASC("2")
Motto$ = "23 Skidoo"
PRINT ASC(Motto$)
```

The result is

```
65
65
50
50
```

The CHR$ function complements the ASC function. The CHR$ function returns the single-character string corresponding to the value of *ASCIIcode*. For example, CHR$(65) returns A.

The CHR$ function enables you to easily display characters that have special meanings in QBasic. For example, suppose you want to display a double quotation mark. PRINT """ doesn't work. You cannot put a double quotation mark in a string literal because the character itself has a special meaning (as a string delimiter).

However, CHR$ comes to the rescue. The ASCII value for the double quotation mark is 34. The following program uses CHR$(34) to display double quotation marks around a string:

```
Proverb$ = "A rolling stone gathers no moss."
PRINT Proverb$
PRINT CHR$(34); Proverb$; CHR$(34)
```

The result is

```
A rolling stone gathers no moss.
"A rolling stone gathers no moss."
```

NOTE **A Tour of the ASCII Character Set**

If you browse through Appendix B, you see many special "characters" in addition to the normal letters, digits, and punctuation marks. For example, you find graphics characters at the ASCII values from 128 to 255. You can beep the speaker or clear the screen with some of the "special effects" characters below ASCII 32. Try this program for a little fun:

```
FOR J = 1 TO 255
    PRINT CHR$(J);          'The semicolon is important
NEXT J
```

You just displayed the entire ASCII character set! What you see on your screen represents the characters from 13 up (you "displayed" the lower characters but CHR$(12) cleared the screen).

Did you hear the speaker beep when you ran the program? The "bell" character is ASCII 7. You can actually beep your speaker with PRINT CHR$(7).

Notice how easily CHR$ lets you get characters into your programs that are unavailable on your keyboard. Your keyboard doesn't have a key for the Greek letter alpha, for example, but CHR$(224) can take its place.

For further discussion of PRINT with the special ASCII characters, see Chapter 12, "Writing Text on the Video Screen."

Converting Strings to Numbers

Sometimes you need to treat a numeric quantity (such as the value of a variable) as a string. That is, you want to convert a number into a string. At other times, you need the opposite capability—interpreting a string as a number. The STR$ and VAL functions do these conversions.

F U N C T I O N

STR$(*numexpr*)

VAL(*stringexpr*)

where

   numexpr is a general numeric expression,

and

   stringexpr is a string expression.

The STR$ function converts *numexpr* into string form. If *numexpr* is positive, STR$ adds a leading space. Here's an example:

```
Number! = 1.8
Num$ = STR$(Number!)
PRINT "XXXXX"
PRINT Num$
PRINT LEN(Num$)
```

The output is

```
XXXXX
 1.8
4
```

The STR$ function in the second line converts the number 1.8 into the string "1.8" (with a blank space before the 1). The output confirms the leading space and shows the string length of Num$ is 4. (The four characters are the leading space plus the three characters in 1.8.)

Why would you want to convert a number into a string? Using the string form, you can manipulate numbers with the various string functions, and often you can format output more easily. For example, the following program fragment prints the amount of a check surrounded by three dashes on each side:

```
Amount! = 458.62
Amount$ = STR$(Amount!)          'Convert Amount! to string
NewAmount$ = LTRIM$(Amount$)
```

```
' Note: Above line strips the leading blank from Amount$
PRINT "Check amount is ---"; NewAmount$; "---"
```

The output looks like this:

```
Check amount is ---458.62---
```

The second line converts Amount! to string form. Remember, the string in Amount$ now contains " 458.62" (with a blank space before the 4).

The third line creates NewAmount$, which is simply Amount$ with the leading blank space removed. The LTRIM$ function makes trimming the blank space easy.

The point of this exercise is that if the PRINT instruction uses Amount! or Amount$ rather than NewAmount$, the output contains an annoying blank space just before the number:

```
Check amount is --- 458.62---
```

The VAL function complements STR$. VAL converts a string into a numeric value. VAL works by examining *stringexpr* from left to right until reaching the first character that cannot be interpreted as part of a number. (Blank spaces are ignored.) For example VAL("76 trombones") returns 76.

If the first nonblank character of *stringexpr* is nonnumeric, VAL returns the value of 0. Table 11.3 shows examples of results of the VAL function.

Table 11.3. Results of the *VAL* function.

String	VAL(String)	Comment
"43.21"	43.21	VAL converts the string to the number.
"28,631,409"	28	VAL does not "understand" commas; conversion stops at the first comma.
" 14"	14	Leading blanks are ignored.
"-19"	-19	Negative numbers are fine.
"- 1 9"	-19	Internal blanks are ignored.
"Twelve"	0	VAL returns 0 when the string is non-numeric.
"Lotus123"	0	VAL does not find embedded numbers. The "L" immediately signals a nonnumeric string.

T I P **Converting Numbers to Hexadecimal and Octal Strings**

Like binary numbers, hexadecimal and octal numbers are specialized numbering systems appropriate for manipulating memory addresses and byte values. Two specialized functions, HEX$ and OCT$, convert regular decimal numbers into hexadecimal and octal strings, respectively.

Such number systems are an advanced subject that are discussed in Chapter 19, "Managing Memory."

Searching for a Substring

Many string-processing programs need to search a large string (or several different strings) to check whether a particular substring is present. For example, a program that handles full names of employees might need to find everyone with the last name of Smith.

The INSTR function searches a string for a specified substring and returns the position where the substring is found. QBasic has two forms of the INSTR function.

FUNCTION

INSTR(*targetstr*, *substr*)

or

INSTR(*startposition*, *targetstr*, *substr*)

where

startposition specifies the character position where the search begins,

targetstr is the string being searched,

and

substr is the string being searched for.

The *startposition* parameter is optional.

INSTR searches the target string left to right for the first occurrence of *substr*. In the two-parameter form of INSTR (without the *startposition* parameter), the search begins at the first character of the target string. In the three-parameter form (with *startposition*), you can specify at which character in the target string the search should begin.

Notice that INSTR returns a numeric value. This value indicates whether or not a match is found and, if so, where. A value of 0 means that no match is found (or that a special condition has occurred; see Table 11.4, which shows how to interpret a value returned by INSTR). A positive value indicates the position in *targetstr* where the substring begins.

Table 11.4 shows how to interpret a value returned by INSTR.

Table 11.4. The results of *INSTR*.

Condition	Result of *INSTR*
Match is found	Position where the match occurs
No match is found	0
startposition greater than LEN*(targetstr)*	0
targetstr is null ("")	0
substr is null	Value of *startposition* if given; otherwise 1

For example:

```
Target$ = "The one and only one"
PRINT INSTR(Target$, "one")
PRINT INSTR(7, Target$, "one")
```

The output is

```
5
18
```

Generating Strings of Repeated Characters

The STRING$ function generates a specified number of identical characters.

F
U
N
C
T
I
O
N

```
STRING$(strlength, ASCIIcode)
```

or

```
STRING$(strlength, strexpr)
```

where

> *strlength* specifies the length of the string to return,
>
> *ASCIIcode* specifies the ASCII code (0 to 255) of the repeating character,

and

> *strexpr* is a string expression whose first character specifies the repeating character.

For example, the ASCII code for the plus sign is 43. Thus STRING$(8, 43) creates a string of eight plus signs. STRING$ is often used to embellish output, as in the following example:

```
Plus$ = STRING$(8, 43)
PRINT Plus$; " Today's News "; Plus$
```

The output looks like this:

```
++++++++ Today's News  ++++++++
```

Notice that the repeating character can be specified with an explicit ASCII value or with a string expression. That is, the second argument for STRING$ can be a numerical ASCII code or a string. Here is the previous program fragment using the latter form of STRING$:

```
Plus$ = STRING$(8, "+")
PRINT Plus$; " Today's News "; Plus$
```

Both versions of STRING$ create the identical output.

When the repeating character is a blank space, a special function is available.

F
U
N
C
T
I
O
N

```
SPACE$(numspaces)
```

where

> *numspaces* specifies the number of spaces to return in the range from 0 to 32,767.

Because the ASCII code for a blank space is 32, the function SPACE$(*numspaces*) returns the same string as STRING$(*strlength*, 32) assuming that the values of *numspaces* and *strlength* are the same.

Modifying a String Variable

The MID$ statement replaces part of a string variable's value with another specified string.

MID$(*strvar*, *position*, *length*) = *strexpr*

or

MID$(*strvar*, *position*) = *strexpr*

where

    strvar is a string variable whose contents are to be modified,

    position is an integer expression specifying the position in *strvar* where the replacement begins,

    length is an integer expression specifying the number of characters to be replaced,

and

    strexpr is a general string expression specifying the replacement string.

The *length* parameter is optional.

S T A T E M E N T

For example, consider the following instruction:

```
MID$(Check$, 7, 4) = "highway"
```

This instruction replaces the seventh through tenth characters of Check$ with the string high.

When the length of *strexpr* is greater than the value of *length* (as in the present example), only the first *length* characters are replaced.

If you omit the optional *length* parameter, all of *strexpr* is substituted into *strvar*. However, MID$ never modifies the original length of *strvar*. The replacement of characters terminates at the final character position of *strvar*.

If *position* is past the end of *strvar*, an Illegal function call error occurs.

Table 11.5 shows various examples of MID$ in use. In each case, the initial value of Test$ is Days of wine and roses.

Table 11.5. Example *MID$* instructions.

Instruction	Final Value of *Test$*
MID$(Test$, 9) = "soda"	Days of soda and roses.
MID$(Test$, 9, 4) = "sodapop"	Days of soda and roses.
MID$(Test$, 14) = "not"	Days of wine not roses.
MID$(Test$, 18) = "carnations."	Days of wine and carnat

Don't confuse the MID$ statement being discussed here with the MID$ function that was discussed earlier in this chapter. The MID$ statement replaces text within an existing string variable. The MID$ function returns text extracted from a string variable.

The LSET and RSET statements left-justify and right-justify, respectively, a string expression within a given string variable.

S T A T E M E N T

```
LSET strvar = strexpr

RSET strvar = strexpr
```

where

   strvar is a string variable,

and

   strexpr is a general string expression.

LSET and RSET assign the value of *strexpr* to the variable *strvar*. The length of *strvar* does not change. If the length of *strexpr* is less than the length of *strvar,* blank spaces pad the remaining character positions. If the length of *strexpr* is greater than the length of *strvar,* the extra characters are truncated.

LSET and RSET can format columnar output. For example, the following program fragment right-justifies three strings in successive 15-character fields:

```
Field1$ = SPACE$(15): Field2$ = Field1$:  Field3$ = Field1$

RSET Field1$ = "Gilda"
```

```
RSET Field2$ = "Jeanette"
RSET Field3$ = "Mary"

PRINT Field1$; Field2$; Field3$

RSET Field1$ = "Phil"
RSET Field2$ = "Jim"
RSET Field3$ = "Jesse"

PRINT Field1$; Field2$; Field3$
```

The output consists of three right-justified columns:

```
    Gilda      Jeanette         Mary
     Phil           Jim        Jesse
```

LSET and RSET are also used to assign values to field variables in conjunction with random-access disk files (see Chapter 15, "Using Random and Binary Disk Files").

Comparing Strings

In Chapter 7, "Program Flow and Decision Making," you saw that the relational operators (Table 7.2) can compare two strings as well as two numbers. For example, you can write an IF instruction that compares strings, such as

```
IF MyName$ > "Joe" THEN . . .
```

just as you can write IF instructions that compare numbers, such as

```
IF MyAge% > 32 THEN . . .
```

When comparing two strings, QBasic compares the ASCII values of corresponding characters. The ranking order of the two strings depends on the first character position in which the two strings differ. The higher ASCII value determines the "larger" string.

Anytime a longer string begins with the identical characters of a shorter string, the longer string is considered "larger." Two strings are equal only if each string is the same length and both strings consist of the identical sequence of characters.

Each of the following expressions is "True":

```
"upper" > "Upper"
```

```
"Apples" <> "Oranges"
```

```
"Foot" < "Football"
```

```
"Chocolate cake" < "Chocolate ice cream"

("Big" + "Deal") = "BigDeal"

"3" >= "3"

"36" > "3245"
```

String Type Conversion

Variable-length string variables are elastic. As the name implies, such string variables can be assigned any string (including a fixed-length string). The length of the variable expands or contracts as necessary.

Also, you can assign any string value to a fixed-length string variable. Type conversion occurs as follows:

- If the length of the variable is greater than the length of the string, the extra rightmost positions of the variable become blank spaces.

- If the length of the variable is less than the length of the string, QBasic truncates the string value, keeping only the leftmost portion of the string.

The following program demonstrates string type conversion:

```
MyName$ =  "Rumplestiltskin"    'MyName$ is variable-length
DIM YourName AS STRING * 6      'YourName is fixed-length

YourName = MyName$              'Truncation occurs
PRINT YourName

YourName = "Al"                 'Blank padding occurs
PRINT YourName; "XXX"

MyName$ = "Al"                  'Variable-length reassignment
PRINT MyName$; "XXX"
```

Here is the output:

```
Rumple
Al    XXX
AlXXX
```

Notice the four blank spaces in the middle line of the output. The (fixed-length) string variable YourName is six characters long (the two letters Al followed by four blank spaces).

Summary

The length of a string is simply the number of characters in the string. Every string character has an associated numeric value from 0 to 255. These values comprise the ASCII character code. With ASCII, you can compare strings and determine which string is "larger." This lets you use strings, as well as numbers, in relational expressions.

The string functions make fancy manipulations a snap. QBasic includes functions that find a string length (LEN), convert ASCII values to strings (CHR$), find a substring (MID$), and convert a string to a number (VAL).

Data manipulation is a prevailing programming theme. The last two chapters concentrate on working with numbers and strings. Numeric and string data are often assigned to variables, combined into expressions, and displayed on-screen.

Intermediate Programming

P A R T

III

O U T L I N E

Now that you possess a sound understanding of QBasic's funda-mentals, it is time to dig deeper. Part III explores more of the language—especially subjects relating to input and output (that is, how QBasic interacts with the external environment).

Here are some of the topics explored in Part III:

- Writing text on the video screen, including format control and colors
- Storing and retrieving data from disk files
- Creating graphics
- Using the keyboard interactively
- Producing music and sound effects
- Constructing modular programs with subprograms and functions

Writing Text on the Video Screen

Q Basic can take full advantage of your computer hardware to create dazzling video screens of text and graphics. This chapter focuses on text; graphics is deferred to Chapter 13, "Creating Graphics."

Maybe the word *text* doesn't conjure up the glamorous images associated with *graphics,* but QBasic has powerful text features. Text can be written in specialized formats, placed anywhere on-screen, "colorized," and even animated.

Regardless of the video adapter and monitor attached to your computer, you can display text. In fact, by default, QBasic programs put your video screen in text mode.

In text mode, PRINT instructions produce white characters on a black background. Your screen can display up to 2000 characters—80 characters per line and 25 total lines. (EGA and VGA systems can display even more.) As you will see later in this chapter, you can change these defaults with COLOR and WIDTH instructions.

Understanding the Text Screen

To understand text mode, think of the screen as an imaginary 80 by 25 grid of cells as shown in Figure 12.1. The lines or rows are numbered from 1 to 25 from the top of the screen to the bottom. The horizontal positions or columns are numbered from 1 to 80 from left to right.

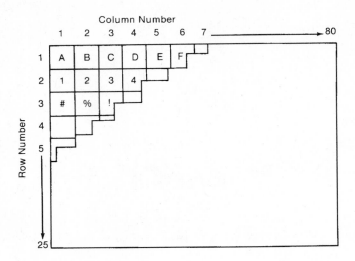

Figure 12.1.

The default text screen.

Each grid cell can be occupied by one text character. There are 256 different characters available as shown in the ASCII character set (see Appendix B, "ASCII Character Set").

The ASCII character set includes not only the standard numbers, letters, and punctuation symbols, but also some foreign letters, special symbols, cursor-movement "characters," and even some line-graphics characters.

In general, you can position the cursor at any cell in this imaginary grid and then use a PRINT instruction to write text beginning at that spot. If text is written in column 80, the cursor does an automatic "carriage return" and moves down to column 1 of the next line. When a carriage return occurs on the 25th line, all screen text scrolls up one line and subsequent text is written on the now-blank 25th line. Text formerly on the top line scrolls off the screen.

T I P   **Using the 25th Line as a Status Line**

Actually, the 25th line is a special case. By using the KEY statement, discussed in Chapter 16, "Using Hardware Devices," you can make the bottom screen row a status line that displays keystroke sequences assigned to the function keys. In this case, you can write to rows 1 to 24 only, and scrolling occurs after line 24 rather than line 25.

Using the *PRINT* Statement

The workhorse of the text-mode display is the PRINT statement. PRINT writes both string and numeric values to the video screen.

PRINT *expressionlist punctuation*

where

    expressionlist is a list of expressions separated by commas and semi-colons,

and

    punctuation is either a comma or a semicolon.

Both *expressionlist* and *punctuation* are optional parameters.

S T A T E M E N T

Each expression in *expressionlist* must be in numeric or string form and can consist of a literal, constant, variable, function, or a more general construct combining two or more individual components with appropriate operators. In all cases, each individual expression in your expression list must reduce to a single value, which is then displayed. Here are five simple PRINT instructions:

```
PRINT "Hello, my friend"      'String literal

PRINT X&                      'Numeric variable

PRINT Sales!(Factory%)        'Numeric array element

PRINT 4.6 * SQR(Area#)        'Mathematical expression

PRINT LEFT$(LastName$, 10)    'String function
```

Use PRINT by itself (without *expressionlist*) to force a carriage return. This causes the cursor to reposition itself at column one of the next lower line ("lower" in the sense that it is toward the bottom of the screen). If the cursor is already in column one, you get a blank line on-screen.

The use of a semicolon or comma for punctuation is explained later in this chapter under the headings "The Semicolon Delimiter" and "The Comma Delimiter and PRINT Zones."

NOTE

Using ? for Printing

For compatibility with earlier versions of BASIC, QBasic recognizes the question mark (?) as an abbreviation for the keyword PRINT. However, the editor immediately does the conversion. For example, if you type the instruction ? MyValue#, when you press Enter the editor converts the instruction to

```
PRINT MyValue#
```

String *PRINT* Formats

PRINT displays a string value straightforwardly; each character from the string occupies one character position on-screen. For example:

```
Message$ = "There is no"
PRINT Message$              'PRINT contents of variable
PRINT "place like home."    'PRINT a string literal
```

The output is

```
There is no
place like home.
```

Notice that, in a PRINT instruction, a string literal must be enclosed in quotation marks.

Numeric *PRINT* Formats

When displaying numbers, PRINT uses special formats:

- Every number prints with a trailing space.
- Negative numbers have a leading minus sign (-).
- Positive numbers (and zero) have a leading space.

The printed degree of precision depends on the numeric format.

Integer and Long Integer

The following program fragment shows how PRINT displays integer and long integer variables:

```
ExampleInt% = -123
ExampleLng& = 12345678
PRINT ExampleInt%
PRINT ExampleLng&
```

The output demonstrates the leading space in front of the positive (long integer) value:

```
-123
 12345678
```

Single-Precision

PRINT displays single-precision values in fixed-point format, if possible, or exponential format otherwise. Fixed-point format uses only the digits and, if necessary, a decimal point and a minus sign. The maximum degree of precision is seven digits.

The following program fragment demonstrates how PRINT formats some single-precision numbers using fixed-point representation:

```
Example1! = 2.5 * 4
Example2! = 1 / 1000
Example3! = -1 / 3
Example4! = 100000 / 3
Example5! = 123 + .456
PRINT Example1!
PRINT Example2!
PRINT Example3!
PRINT Example4!
PRINT Example5!
PRINT 1 / 7
```

The output looks like this:

```
 10
 .001
-.3333333
 33333.33
 123.456
 .1428571
```

Notice that the fixed-point display uses up to 7 digits of precision. As a result, the largest possible value is 9999999 and the smallest possible (positive) value is .0000001.

To display values outside these limits, PRINT resorts to exponential format. Again, the maximum degree of precision is 7 digits. But the exponential indicator, E, can set the decimal point through the full range of single-precision numbers (approximately −1.0E-38 to 1.0E+38).

The following program fragment demonstrates exponential format:

```
Example1! = 10 ^ 8          '10 * 10 * 10 *  10 * 10 * 10 * 10 * 10
Example2! = Example1! / 3
Example3! = 1 / Example1!
Example4! = -1.234 * Example3! * Example3!
PRINT Example1!
PRINT Example2!
PRINT Example3!
PRINT Example4!
```

Here is the output:

```
 1E+08
 3.333333E+07
 1E-08
-1.234E-16
```

Double-Precision

For double-precision values, PRINT extends the fixed-point format up to 16 digits. The exponential indicator for double-precision is D, rather than E. Consider the following program fragment:

```
A# = 1# / 3#
B# = 10# ^ 20#
C# = -A# / B#
D# = 1.23456789# * 1000000000     '9 zeroes in second number
E# = D# * 1000000000              '9 zeroes in second number
PRINT A#
PRINT B#
PRINT C#
PRINT D#
PRINT E#
PRINT 1# / 7#
```

Notice how the pound sign (#) is used on numeric literals to specify full double-precision accuracy. The output is

```
 .3333333333333333
 1D+20
-3.333333333333333D-21
 1234567890
 1.23456789D+18
 .1428571428571428
```

Multiple Expressions

You can PRINT multiple values on one screen line by placing two or more elements in *expressionlist*. The number of blank spaces displayed between each element depends on the delimiter used to separate the elements in the PRINT instruction.

The Semicolon Delimiter

If a semicolon separates the two items, no blank spaces are inserted and the items are juxtaposed. Notice the semicolon in the second line of the following code fragment:

```
MyString$ = "This is a note"
PRINT MyString$; "worthy achievement"
```

The PRINT instruction causes the following output:

```
This is a noteworthy achievement
```

You must be careful with numeric output. Recall that numbers automatically print with a trailing blank space. Positive numbers and zero display with a leading blank space; negative numbers have a leading minus sign.

The program in Listing 12.1 demonstrates how these conventions can either help or annoy you as you display multiple expressions with one PRINT instruction.

Listing 12.1. A program that demonstrates numeric formatting.

```
REM Demonstrate numeric formatting
HighTemp% = 47
LowTemp%  = -12
PRINT "The high today was"; HighTemp%; "degrees"
PRINT "and the low was"; LowTemp%; "degrees."
```

288

The output of Listing 12.1 is

```
The high today was 47 degrees
and the low was-12 degrees."
```

The Space Delimiter

You can also separate multiple items in *expressionlist* with one or more blank spaces. However, the editor inserts semicolons between the items. For example, if you type the following line,

```
PRINT "I see" 76 "trombones"
```

the editor converts the line to this:

```
PRINT "I see"; 76; "trombones"
```

The output is

```
I see 76 trombones
```

The Comma Delimiter and *PRINT* Zones

A PRINT instruction can align output into predefined fields or zones.

Picture each potential 80-character line of screen output divided into five zones. Each zone, except the last, is 14 characters wide. The zones begin at column positions 1, 15, 29, 43, and 57.

By separating the elements of *expressionlist* with commas, you display the items of *expressionlist* in successive zones. Consider this instruction:

```
PRINT "Zone1", "Zone2", "Zone3"
```

The result is the following zoned output:

```
Zone1         Zone2         Zone3
```

Numbers still print with the usual leading and trailing spaces. One convenient use of comma separators is to display simple tables with a PRINT instruction, as in Listing 12.2.

Listing 12.2. The SHOWZONE.BAS program.

```
REM Program: SHOWZONE.BAS (Demonstrate PRINT zones)
PRINT , "Position", "Batting Ave."
PRINT
```

```
PRINT "Rose", "First Base", .347
PRINT "DiMaggio", "Center", .287
PRINT "Ruth", "Right Field", .301
PRINT "Uecker", "Catcher", .106
```

Listing 12.2. prints the following aligned table:

```
          Position     Batting Ave.

Rose      First Base      .347
DiMaggio  Center          .287
Ruth      Right Field     .301
Uecker    Catcher         .106
```

Notice how the beginning comma in the first PRINT instruction forces Position to print in the second print zone.

If a particular item is longer than 14 characters (and, as you've seen, some numbers display 16 or more characters), a comma tabs the next item to the beginning of the subsequent print zone. You must be careful not to ruin your table's alignment. The PRINT USING statement, discussed shortly, can correct such problems.

Trailing Punctuation

If you terminate a PRINT instruction with a semicolon or a comma, you suppress the final carriage-return and line-feed.

A final semicolon keeps the cursor on the same display line right after the last printed item. Then a subsequent PRINT instruction resumes printing from this point. For example, the following program produces only one line of output:

```
PRINT "A stitch in time saves";
PRINT 9
```

The result is

```
A stitch in time saves 9
```

A trailing comma on a PRINT instruction tabs the cursor to the beginning of the next print zone. A subsequent PRINT instruction resumes printing from that point.

The *TAB* and *SPC* Functions

TAB and SPC provide additional control over the horizontal cursor position. The two functions can be used only as part of the expression list in a PRINT instruction (or a PRINT# or LPRINT instruction).

F U N C T I O N

TAB(*column*)

where

    column is an integer expression in the range from 1 to 255.

The TAB function advances the cursor to the specified column position on the same line. If the cursor is already positioned beyond *column,* the cursor drops down to the next line at the position specified by *column.*

You can use TAB to display aligned columnar output at tab positions of your choosing. For example, suppose that you keep track of clients' names in an array called ClientName$ and billable hours in an array called BillHours%. The following program fragment displays a summary table:

```
PRINT "#"; TAB(6); "Client Name" TAB(35); "Billable Hours"
PRINT
FOR J% = 1 TO NumClients%
   PRINT J%; TAB(6); ClientName$(J%); TAB(35); BillHours%(J%)
NEXT J%
```

SPC displays a given number of blank spaces.

F U N C T I O N

SPC(*numspaces*)

where

    numspaces is an integer expression in the range from 1 to 255.

Consider the following example:

```
PRINT "Heave"; SPC(20); "Ho"
```

This displays the following output (with 20 embedded blank spaces):

```
Heave                   Ho
```

If either TAB or SPC occurs at the end of the expression list in a PRINT instruction, the cursor remains at the end of the line (that is, no carriage-return is
issued). In essence, an implied semicolon follows each SPC or TAB function,
regardless of whether you explicitly include the semicolon.

For example, consider this program fragment:

```
FOR Num% = 1 TO 7
    PRINT Num%; SPC(Num%)
NEXT Num%
PRINT "Done"
```

The result is this single line of screen output:

```
 1  2   3    4     5      6       7        Done
```

Notice that the number of blank spaces between successive digits successively
increases by one.

Controlling Formats with *PRINT USING*

Sometimes PRINT does not provide sufficient formatting. With PRINT USING, you
can specify a format string for enhanced control over your output. The following are some of the things you can do with PRINT USING:

- Align columns of numbers on the decimal point
- Display a partial string
- Place a dollar sign immediately before a number
- Display any number in scientific notation
- Restrict the number of decimal digits that you display

PRINT USING *formatstring*; *expressionlist punctuation*

where

formatstring is a string containing formatting instructions,

expressionlist is a list of expressions separated by semicolons or commas,

and

punctuation is a comma or semicolon.

The *punctuation* parameter is optional.

The expression list contains the list of items to be displayed, just as in the regular PRINT instruction. PRINT USING, however, does not distinguish between the different punctuation delimiters contained inside *expressionlist*. Commas are treated just like semicolons in the sense that no tabbing to specific columns occurs. Either a trailing comma or a trailing semicolon for punctuation produces the identical effect; the cursor remains just after the last displayed item (no carriage-return or line-feed occurs).

The *formatstring* parameter describes how to format the strings and numbers contained in the expression list. The format string can be specified by a string constant enclosed in double quotation marks. Alternatively, you can store the format string in a string variable and then use the name of the string variable in the PRINT USING instruction.

Various special characters in *formatstring* cause special printing effects, as shown in Table 12.1.

Table 12.1. PRINT USING format characters.

Character	Effect
Numbers	
#	Holds place for a single digit
.	Prints a decimal point
,	Places a comma every three digits
+	Prints the sign of the number
-	Prints negative numbers with a trailing minus sign
**	Places leading asterisks before the number
$$	Places a dollar sign before the number

Character	Effect
**$	Places leading asterisks and a dollar sign
^^^^	Specifies exponential notation
Strings	
&	Displays the entire string
!	Displays the first character of the string
\ \	Displays a specified number of characters from the beginning of the string
_(underscore)	Displays the next character of the format string verbatim
<Any>	Any other character not in this table is displayed verbatim

Let's look at several examples to see how PRINT USING works.

Displaying Numbers with *PRINT USING*

The format string sets up a numeric field that specifies exactly how the number will look. Each # in the format string indicates a digit position. Such a position is always filled by a digit or a leading minus sign. A period indicates where the decimal point should go.

A plus sign in a format string means that the sign (plus or minus) should display with the number. The sign prints before the number if the plus sign is at the beginning of the format string or after the number if the plus sign is at the end of the format string. A minus sign at the end of the format string indicates that negative numbers should display with a trailing minus. Listing 12.3 demonstrates this.

Listing 12.3. A program demonstrating the *PRINT USING* instruction with numbers.

```
REM Demonstrate PRINT USING with numbers
MyNumber! = 39.82
PRINT USING "######"; MyNumber!
PRINT USING "####.#"; MyNumber!
PRINT USING "###.###"; MyNumber!
PRINT USING "+###.###"; MyNumber!
PRINT USING "###.###-"; MyNumber!
PRINT USING "###.###-"; -MyNumber!
```

Here is the output from Listing 12.3:

```
   40
 39.8
39.820
+39.820
39.820
39.820-
```

Notice that if the format allocates extra digits before the decimal point, the number is right-justified (with leading blank spaces). Extra # characters after the decimal point cause zeroes to fill the field. Insufficient # characters after the decimal point cause rounding.

If the number requires more than the allocated number of digits before the decimal point, a leading percent sign (%) indicates insufficient formatting. For example,

```
PRINT USING "##.###"; 1234.5678
```

The result is

```
%1234.568
```

Four carets signify exponential notation. (You can also use five carets, ^^^^^, to print E+xxx for the display of large numbers that requires three-digit exponents. The four-caret form restricts exponents to a maximum of two digits.) Any decimal position can be specified. However, significant digits are left-justified, and the exponent adjusts accordingly. For example:

```
PRINT USING  "##.###^^^^"; 4592.9
PRINT USING "##.###^^^^"; -0.00000148
```

The output is

```
 4.593E+03
-1.480D-06
```

The comma, if it appears anywhere before a decimal point, causes a comma to print between every three digits. For example:

```
PRINT USING  "#####,####"; 1234567
```

produces the following output:

```
1,234,567
```

The * and $ formats are used to specify monetary values in financial programs. Each * and $ character in the format string counts as one digit position in the numeric field. Therefore, $$### specifies a five-character numeric field of which one character will be the dollar sign. Table 12.2 shows some monetary formats.

Table 12.2. Examples of *PRINT USING* monetary formats.

Format	Number	Displayed Result
`"**######"`	987.65	`*****988`
`"**######.##"`	987.65	`*****987.65`
`"$$######.##"`	987.65	`$987.65`
`"$$#,####.##"`	37823.19	`$37,823.19`
`"**$#####.##"`	101	`****$101.00`
`"**$#####.##"`	.478	`******$0.48`
`"**$#####.##"`	-32.45	`****-$32.45`

Displaying Text with *PRINT USING*

The !, &, and \ formats display text strings. The exclamation point (!) indicates that only the first character of the data string should be displayed. The ampersand (&) specifies the entire string.

Two backslashes (\ \) indicate that the first *n* characters should be displayed, where *n* is two plus the number of spaces that appear between the backslashes. Thus \\ (no intervening spaces) means the first two characters should be displayed, and \ \ (one intervening space) means three characters should be displayed. If the format field specifies more positions than occur in the string, the output string is padded with spaces to the right.

Listing 12.4 demonstrates some string formatting.

Listing 12.4. A program demonstrating the *PRINT USING* instruction with strings.

```
REM Demonstrate PRINT USING with strings
MyString$ = "QBasic"
PRINT USING "!"; MyString$
PRINT USING "&"; MyString$
PRINT USING "\\"; MyString$      'No spaces between backslashes
PRINT USING "\  \"; MyString$    '2 spaces between backslashes
```

The following output is the result of Listing 12.4:

```
Q
QBasic
QB
QBas
```

PRINT USING with Multiple Fields

The true power of PRINT USING manifests itself when your expression list contains several expressions displayed under the control of one format string.

The format string can (and does, in most practical cases) contain several juxtaposed formats. This sets up a one-to-one correspondence between successive formats and items in the expression list. If the number of formats exceeds the number of items, the extra formats are simply ignored. If the number of items exceeds the number of formats, the formats recycle until all the items are displayed.

Consider this program fragment:

```
FormStr$ =  "&###&"
PRINT USING FormStr$; "Car", 54, "Where are you?"
PRINT USING FormStr$; "Fahrenheit", 451
PRINT USING FormStr$; "A", 1, "and", "a", 2,  "and", "a", 3
```

The output looks like this:

```
Car 54Where are you?
Fahrenheit451
A  1anda  2anda  3
```

When nonspecial characters (that is, characters not listed in Table 12.1) appear in your format string, those characters are displayed verbatim. This enables you to add any desired annotation to your format strings. Consider the following example:

```
FormStr$ = "Check Number##### was for **$####.##"
PRINT USING FormStr$; 1033, 544.67
```

The result is

```
Check Number 1033 was for ***$544.67
```

Notice that a blank space is treated just like any other general character. Each blank space in your format string creates a corresponding blank space in the final output.

Use the underscore (_) to display one of the special formatting characters as part of your text output. The underscore in a format string says to treat the next character as displayable text, not as a formatting character. For example:

```
PRINT USING "I saw Romeo _& Juliet # times"; 5
```

The result is

```
I saw Romeo & Juliet 5 times
```

Without the underscore, the ampersand indicates that a string value, not a number, is expected. This causes a run-time error (Type mismatch).

One additional warning: Don't use any punctuation (such as commas, semicolons, or even blank spaces) to separate items in a format string. All punctuation has a special effect.

Recall that a comma is reserved for displaying commas in large numbers and thus has meaning only in numerical formats. A semicolon or blank space is treated like any other general character and therefore is displayed verbatim in your final output.

Using the *WRITE* Statement

The WRITE statement is similar to PRINT.

WRITE *expressionlist*

where

    expressionlist is list of expressions separated by commas.

The *expressionlist* parameter is optional.

S
T
A
T
E
M
E
N
T

WRITE works like PRINT except that

- Commas are displayed between output items
- Strings are displayed with surrounding quotation marks
- No space is placed before positive numbers
- No tabbing is supported, and all output is contiguous

Listing 12.5 demonstrates the difference between PRINT and WRITE:

Listing 12.5.   A program contrasting the *PRINT* and *WRITE* statements.

```
REM Contrast PRINT with WRITE
Units$  = "square yards"
Amount! = 497.1
PRINT "That lot is"; Amount!; Units$
WRITE "That lot is", Amount!, Units$
```

The output of Listing 12.5 is

```
That lot is 497.1 square yards
"That lot is",497.1 ,"square yards"
```

WRITE is seldom used for screen displays. However, the companion statement, WRITE#, is frequently used for sequential file output. See Chapter 14, "Using Sequential Disk Files," for a discussion of WRITE#.

Controlling the Cursor

When writing full-screen displays, you often need to display text at a specific screen position. QBasic provides extensive cursor controls. You can do the following:

- Position the cursor at a specified row and column
- Turn the cursor on or off
- Change the shape of the cursor
- Determine the current cursor position

Using the *LOCATE* Statement

The LOCATE statement positions the cursor and changes the cursor shape.

LOCATE is most often used with the *row* and/or *column* parameters to position the cursor before a subsequent PRINT instruction. For example, the following program fragment displays Hello in the center of the screen:

```
LOCATE 13, 38
PRINT "Hello"
```

LOCATE *row, column, cursorflag, startline, stopline*

where

    row is the cursor's desired row number (1 to 25),

    column is the column number (1 to 80),

    cursorflag makes the cursor visible or invisible,

    startline specifies the first scan line for the cursor shape,

and

    stopline specifies the final scan line for the cursor shape.

Each of the five parameters is an integer expression and each of the parameters is optional.

The cursor usually is invisible as your program executes. (One common exception is during INPUT prompts.) You can turn the cursor on with the *cursorflag* parameter. Use 1 to turn the cursor on, 0 to turn it back off. Thus the following instruction causes the cursor to appear:

```
LOCATE , , 1
```

When the cursor is made visible, you can change its shape. The cursor occupies a rectangular cell consisting of horizontal scan lines numbered from 0 at the top to 7 at the bottom. (Monochrome systems go from 0 to 13.) Try adjusting the values of *startline* and *stopline* to see the effect. If *stopline* is less than *startline,* a two-tiered cursor results.

Listing 12.6 demonstrates various capabilities of the LOCATE statement. Your name prints vertically on-screen.

Listing 12.6. A program using the *LOCATE* statement.

```
REM Demonstrate the LOCATE statement
LOCATE , , 1, 3, 5          'Turn cursor on and change the shape
INPUT "What's your name (note the cursor shape)";  YourName$
CLS                              'Blanks the screen
Column% = 25
FOR Row% = 1 TO LEN(YourName$)
   LOCATE Row%, Column%
   PRINT MID$(YourName$, Row%, 1)
NEXT Row%
```

Determining the Current Cursor Position

You can determine the cursor's current position with the CSRLIN and POS functions.

F U N C T I O N

CSRLIN

CSRLIN returns the current row of the cursor as an integer from 1 to 25. POS returns the horizontal position of the cursor as an integer from 1 to 80. The POS function requires a dummy argument.

F U N C T I O N

POS(*dummyargument*)

where

> *dummyargument* is a dummy argument that can have any value.

The restriction that POS requires a dummy argument and CSRLIN does not is an unfortunate inheritance from BASICA and GW-BASIC. QBasic conforms (for compatibility) with the earlier versions of BASIC.

You can use CSRLIN and POS with LOCATE to move the cursor relative to its current location. For example, the following instruction moves the cursor 3 rows down and 10 positions to the left:

```
LOCATE CSRLIN + 3, POS(0) - 10
```

Adding Color to Text Screens

So far, text displays have been drab—nothing but black and white. You can display text in color, assuming you have a color monitor and one of the following video adapters: Color Graphics Adapter (CGA), Enhanced Graphics Adapter (EGA), Multi-Color Graphics Array (MCGA), or Video Graphics Array (VGA).

The COLOR statement creates colored text. For now, the discussion of COLOR is confined to text screens. The next chapter discusses how to use the COLOR statement with graphics modes.

The *COLOR* Statement in Text Mode

Use the COLOR statement in text mode to control the foreground and background colors of your text characters. With COLOR, you also can specify the border color of your text screen.

COLOR [*foreground*] [, [*background*] [, *border*]]

where

    foreground is an integer expression (0 to 31) that specifies the color and attribute of the text character,

    background is an integer expression (0 to 15) that specifies the color of the background,

and

    border is an integer expression (0 to 15) that specifies the color of the screen border.

S T A T E M E N T

A COLOR instruction does not change text already on-screen. COLOR only defines the characteristics of subsequent text written with PRINT instructions. Any color specifications you select remain in effect until you change them with another COLOR instruction. In general, the procedure to display colored text involves three steps:

1. Choose text colors with a COLOR instruction.

2. If necessary, move the cursor with a LOCATE instruction.

3. Display the text with a PRINT instruction.

You specify colors for *foreground, background,* and *border* by using the integer values shown in Table 12.3.

Table 12.3. Available colors.

Code	Color	Code	Color
0	Black	8	Gray
1	Blue	9	Light blue
2	Green	10	Light green
3	Cyan	11	Light cyan
4	Red	12	Light red
5	Magenta	13	Light magenta
6	Brown	14	Yellow
7	White	15	High intensity white

Think of the text screen as an 80 by 25 grid of rectangular cells. Within each cell, you can place one character. The screen displays each character with a foreground color and a background color. The foreground is the character itself; the background is the rest of the cell in which the character resides.

The value of *foreground* controls the color of the character and whether the character blinks. A foreground color from 0 to 15 selects the color indicated in Table 12.3. By adding 16 to a color code value, a blinking character of the appropriate color occurs. For example, a value of 25 for *foreground* produces a light blue, blinking character.

The allowable range of *background* is actually from 0 to 15, but values from 8 to 15 map into the same colors selected by values from 0 to 7. Thus you have only eight choices for the background color.

The value of *border* controls the perimeter of your screen—that is, the region outside the normal text area. This border can be painted a solid color, but only on some CGA systems. (The *border* parameter, if present, is ignored on most EGA and VGA systems.) You can select any of 16 border colors according to the values in Table 12.3. A border color changes immediately on execution of the COLOR instruction; you don't have to issue a PRINT instruction to consummate the effect.

On EGA and VGA systems, you can modify the 16 available colors with the PALETTE statement. See the discussion of PALETTE and PALETTE USING in the next chapter.

Each of the three parameters in a COLOR instruction is optional, but at least one must appear. Unspecified parameters retain their previous values. By default, the initial values are COLOR 7, 0, 0 (white text on a black background with a black border).

Here are some examples of COLOR instructions:

```
COLOR 2, 8, 14    'Green text, gray background, yellow border.

COLOR , 1         'Change background to blue.

COLOR Hue%, , 4   'Change text color to value of Hue%, red border.

COLOR 22          'Change text color to blinking brown.

COLOR , , 9       'Change border to light blue.

COLOR             'Illegal; no parameters are specified.

COLOR 22, 23      'Illegal; value of background (23) is too large.
```

Be wary of making your foreground and background colors the same. Your subsequent text will be invisible!

A Colorful Program

To whet your appetite for the possible effects, try running Listing 12.7 on your color system:

Listing 12.7.   A program demonstrating the *COLOR* instruction.

```
REM Try different text colors and attributes
FOR Fore% = 0 TO 31
   FOR Back% = 0 TO 7
      COLOR Fore%, Back%
       PRINT "-Wow-";           'Don't forget the semicolon
   NEXT Back%
NEXT Fore%
```

Text Colors on Monochrome Systems

With the Monochrome Display Adapter (MDA), the COLOR statement produces special character attributes rather than colors. The possible effects are normal text (white-on-black), underlining, reverse video (black-on-white), invisible text (black-on-black), high intensity text, and blinking. Many, but not all, of these effects can be combined. Table 12.4 shows the values of *foreground* and *background* that produce these attributes.

Table 12.4. Character attributes on monochrome systems.		
Effect	*foreground*	*background*
Normal (white-on-black)	7	0
Reverse (black-on-white)	0	7
Invisible (black-on-black)	0	0
Underlining	1	0
High intensity	Add 8	No change
Blinking	Add 16	No change

Effects in the upper part of Table 12.4 cannot be combined. For example, underlined reverse video is impossible. However, you can use high intensity or blinking (or both) with any of the four basic effects from the upper part of the table. Simply add the indicated amount to the value of the foreground parameter (add 8 for high intensity, 16 for blinking, or 24 for both).

Other possible values of *foreground* and *background* result in one of the afore-mentioned effects. A *foreground* value from 2 to 6 produces white, 10 to 15 produces high intensity, and 26 to 31 produces blinking. A *background* value from 1 to 6 produces black.

The *border* parameter has no effect with MDA video cards.

Determining the Character at a Specific Location

Sometimes you need to know what character is at a given screen location. This requirement often arises in interactive programs, such as games or text editors, where the user is entering information displayed on-screen.

The SCREEN function determines what character, if any, is at any given screen location and also determines the character's color attributes. (Don't confuse the SCREEN function with the SCREEN statement. The SCREEN statement is discussed in the next chapter.)

SCREEN(*row, column, optionflag*)

where

row is the screen row from 1 to 25,

column is the column position from 1 to 80,

and

optionflag is a numeric expression specifying which information to return.

The *optionflag* parameter is optional. If you do not include *optionflag* in a SCREEN instruction, omit the comma after *column*.

When you omit *optionflag*, the SCREEN function returns the ASCII value (an integer from 0 to 255) corresponding to the character at the specified screen row and column. If no character has been written to the specified location, SCREEN returns 32 (the ASCII value for a blank space). Appendix B, "ASCII Character Set," contains a table of the ASCII codes and their corresponding characters.

The following program fragment counts the number of asterisks currently displayed on-screen:

```
Number% = 0
Code% = 42                 'ASCII Code for an asterisk (*)
FOR Row% = 1 TO 25
   FOR Column% = 1 TO 80
      IF SCREEN(Row%, Column%) = Code% THEN Number% = Number% + 1
   NEXT Column%
NEXT Row%
```

If *optionflag* is present and evaluates to a nonzero value, SCREEN returns the attribute (color) of the referenced character.

The attribute is expressed as an integer number from 0 to 255. The number can be deciphered to reveal these attributes of the character: foreground color, background color, and whether the character is blinking. Listing 12.8 shows how to use SCREEN to decipher this information for a character at the location (Row%, Column%).

Listing 12.8.   A program using the *SCREEN* function.

```
REM Print attributes of character at (Row%, Column%)

Attribute% = SCREEN (Row%, Column%, 1)
PRINT "Foreground color ="; Attribute% MOD 16
PRINT "Background color ="; (Attribute% AND &H70) \ 16
PRINT "Blinking         =";
Blink% = (Attribute% AND &H80) \ 128
IF Blink% = 1 THEN PRINT " Yes" ELSE PRINT " No"
```

Switching to an Alternative Text Mode

To this point, the text screen has been 80 characters wide by 25 lines high. Depending on your system's video adapter card, your computer is capable of other text modes. Table 12.5 shows the possibilities (MCGA is the Multi-Color Graphics Array).

Unless you have a monochrome monitor, your computer is capable of a 40 by 25 text mode. In this mode, each character is twice as wide (horizontally) as in the standard 80 by 25 mode. The wider characters create more dramatic screen displays.

Table 12.5. Available text modes.

Mode	Supporting Adapters			
40 by 25	CGA	EGA	MCGA	VGA
40 by 43		EGA		VGA
40 by 50				VGA
80 by 25	CGA	EGA	MCGA	VGA
80 by 43		EGA		VGA
80 by 50				VGA
80 by 60				VGA

To switch to one of the alternate text modes, use the WIDTH statement.

```
WIDTH numcolumns, numrows
```
where

   numcolumns is the maximum number of characters per line,

and

   numrows is the maximum number of characters per column.

The *numcolumns* and *numrows* parameters are optional.

The only legal values for *numcolumns* are 40 and 80. On an MDA system, only 80 is legal. The only legal values for *numrows* are 25 (CGA or MCGA), 25 or 43 (EGA), and 25, 43, 50, or 60 (VGA). You can specify *numcolumns*, *numrows*, or both. However, WIDTH by itself (with no parameters) is not a legal instruction.

When the width changes, the screen clears and the cursor returns to the upper left corner.

Notice that all locating instructions adjust correctly to each mode. Consider, for example, a 40-column mode. LOCATE and POS refer to the horizontal location using a number from 1 to 40. PRINT still uses 14-column print zones for comma-delimited lists. There are effectively only two print zones: columns 1 through 14, and 15 through 28. The third zone would stretch to column 42—too far!

Other Uses of *WIDTH*

T I P

The next chapter discusses the WIDTH statement with respect to graphics modes. Also, WIDTH has an expanded syntax for use with files and devices. These topics are discussed in Chapters 16, "Using Hardware Devices," and 22, "Understanding Advanced QBasic Topics."

Creating a Text Viewport

You can restrict text to a rectangular slice of the screen by using the VIEW PRINT statement. This creates a text viewport. When a text viewport is in effect, you can display text and scroll only within the viewport.

<table>
<tr>
<td>

**S
T
A
T
E
M
E
N
T**

</td>
<td>

`VIEW PRINT` *toprow* `TO` *bottomrow*

or simply

`VIEW PRINT`

where

    toprow is an integer expression defining the top row of the viewport,

and

    bottomrow is an integer expression defining the bottom row of the viewport.

</td>
</tr>
</table>

The viewport extends from *toprow* to *bottomrow* across the entire width of the screen. The instruction `VIEW PRINT` reinstates the entire screen as the viewport. Listing 12.9, VIEWTEXT.BAS, demonstrates the use of a text viewport.

Listing 12.9. The VIEWTEXT.BAS program.

```
REM Program: VIEWTEXT.BAS (Demonstrate text viewport)
LOCATE 5, 1: PRINT "No scrolling above the viewport"
LOCATE 6, 1: PRINT STRING$(50, 205)    'Print above the viewport.
LOCATE 16, 1: PRINT STRING$(50, 205)   'Print below the viewport.
LOCATE 17, 1: PRINT "No scrolling below the viewport"
VIEW PRINT 7 TO 15              'Set viewport from line 7 to 15.
FOR LineNum% = 1 TO 100
   PRINT "This is line number"; LineNum%
NEXT LineNum%                          'Scroll inside viewport
END
```

First the program displays text above and below the upcoming viewport. Then the text viewport is opened. The `PRINT` instruction inside the `FOR-NEXT` loop causes text to scroll, but only inside the confines of the viewport. Figure 12.2 shows the screen after the program finishes.

Clearing the Text Screen

You can clear the screen of text with a `CLS` instruction. (`CLS` is a mnemonic for *CLear Screen.*) For text displays, two forms of the `CLS` instruction are relevant (see Table 12.6).

```
No scrolling above the viewport
This is line number 93
This is line number 94
This is line number 95
This is line number 96
This is line number 97
This is line number 98
This is line number 99
This is line number 100


No scrolling below the viewport
```

Figure 12.2.

The output of the VIEWTEXT.BAS program.

Table 12.6. Using *CLS* with text screens.

Instruction	Effect
CLS	Clears text within the text viewport only.
CLS 0	Clears the entire screen.

The default viewport is the entire screen. If you haven't issued a VIEW PRINT instruction, CLS and CLS 0 both clear the entire screen. The screen clears to the background color, and the cursor returns to the upper left corner of the current viewport.

There are a few other parameter options that have to do with graphics screens. See the discussion of CLS in Chapter 13, "Creating Graphics."

Creating Text Graphics

Does the term *text graphics* seem contradictory? That oxymoron means special effects that you generate with PRINT by utilizing characters in the extended ASCII set. Indeed, you can create graphics-like effects from text mode.

Appendix B, "ASCII Character Set," contains a table of ASCII codes and characters. In addition to the normal letters, numbers, and punctuation, the extended ASCII set includes the following "characters":

- Foreign language letters and symbols
- Cursor movement characters
- Math, technical, game, and music symbols
- Speaker-beeping codes
- Outlining and graphing symbols

Most of these special characters cannot be accessed directly from the keyboard. For example, to display the heart symbol (ASCII code = 3), there is no easy way to specify the heart symbol between the PRINT instruction's quotation marks.

However, the CHR$ function (discussed in the previous chapter) provides access to the full character set. To get a heart symbol, PRINT CHR$(3) does the trick. So, if you're a "chocoholic," you might type an instruction like this:

```
PRINT "I "; CHR$(3); "  chocolate."
```

Two-Dimensional Object Strings

The real power of text graphics comes from strings that describe two-dimensional objects. Because the ASCII character set includes cursor movement in all four orthogonal directions (see Table 12.7), you can build complex strings that print as various shapes.

Table 12.7. ASCII values of cursor movement characters.

ASCII Value	Effect
28	Cursor right
29	Cursor left
30	Cursor up
31	Cursor down

The general technique of using two-dimensional text strings consists of these steps:

1. Build a string variable using CHR$.

2. Move the cursor with LOCATE.

3. PRINT the string variable.

Listing 12.10, SHOWMAN.BAS, which displays three stick-figure men, is a simple example of this.

Listing 12.10. The SHOWMAN.BAS program.

```
REM Program: SHOWMAN.BAS (Draw 2-D Text Strings)

DATA 1, 29, 31, 197, 29, 31, 94:        'ASCII Codes for man
```

```
Man$ = " "                              'Initialize Man$
FOR Count% = 1 TO 7
  READ Char%
  Man$ = Man$ + CHR$(Char%)             'Build Man$ String
NEXT Count%
LOCATE 3, 9: PRINT Man$                 'Stick Figure 1
LOCATE 17, 25: PRINT Man$               'Stick Figure 2
LOCATE 10, 50: PRINT Man$               'Stick Figure 3
END
```

Figure 12.3 shows the output of SHOWMAN.BAS.

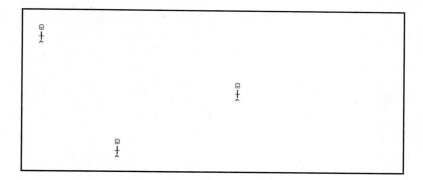

Figure 12.3.

The output of
SHOWMAN.BAS.

Text Animation

Even animation is possible with two-dimensional text strings. Here is the basic technique:

1. Build string variable(s) using CHR$.

2. Use LOCATE to position the cursor for drawing.

3. PRINT the string variable to display your shape.

4. Pause for a short time (approximately one tenth of a second).

5. Erase the shape drawn in step 3.

6. Go back to step 2.

Text animation is just an extension of the ideas used to draw two-dimensional objects.

Step 5 requires that you erase the previously drawn figure. There are many ways to do this. One method is to define an "erasing" string for each shape-drawing string. The erasing string contains a blank space, CHR$(32), everywhere the drawing string contains a printable character. Cursor movement "characters" are retained in the erasing string at the same positions they occur in the drawing string.

You can erase a shape by PRINTing the erasing string at the same cursor position used to draw the original shape. If necessary, remember to use LOCATE to reposition the cursor at the same screen position where the original shape was drawn.

Step 4 requires a pause. The upcoming sample program, JUMPMAN.BAS, uses the TIMER function inside a DO-LOOP to accomplish a delay. See Chapter 16, "Using Hardware Devices," for more on the TIMER function.

To get the flavor of text animation, try the JUMPMAN.BAS program in Listing 12.11. The same stick figure used in SHOWMAN.BAS now jumps up and down. The string variable Man$ displays the stick figure while the corresponding variable WipeOut$ erases the man.

Listing 12.11. The JUMPMAN.BAS program.

```
REM Program: JUMPMAN.BAS (Text Animation of Jumping Man)

DATA 1, 29, 31, 197, 29, 31, 94:        'ASCII Codes for man
Man$ = ""                               'Initialize Man$
FOR Count% = 1 TO 7
   READ Char%
   Man$ = Man$ + CHR$(Char%)            'Build Man$ String
NEXT Count%

DATA 32, 29, 31, 32, 29, 31, 32:        'ASCII Codes to erase man
WipeOut$ = ""                           'Initialize WipeOut$
FOR Count% = 1 TO 7
   READ Char%
   WipeOut$ = WipeOut$ + CHR$(Char%)    'Build WipeOut$ String
NEXT Count%

FOR Row% = 20 TO 1 STEP -1              'Jump up
   LOCATE Row%, 40: PRINT Man$
      Now! = TIMER                      'DO LOOP
      DO                                'delays for
      LOOP UNTIL TIMER < Now! + .1      '1/10 second
   LOCATE Row%, 40: PRINT WipeOut$
```

```
NEXT Row%

FOR Row% = 1 TO 20                'Jump down
    LOCATE Row%, 40: PRINT Man$
        Now! = TIMER              'DO LOOP
        DO                        'delays for
        LOOP UNTIL TIMER < Now! + .1   '1/10 second
    LOCATE Row%, 40: PRINT WipeOut$
NEXT Row%
END
```

You can extend this technique to create more sophisticated animation. One idea is to have your figure drawn in several different stances or postures. For example, a waving man might raise and lower his hand as he "walks." This requires two or more string variables, which are alternated as the man moves. (Of course, you will need a corresponding erasing variable for each such string variable.)

Summary

This chapter examined ways to display text information on the video screen. The primary tool was the PRINT statement. You saw how PRINT displays both numbers and character text, and how to use PRINT's automatic tabbing. When you need further control over output appearance, PRINT USING provides customized formatting.

The location of the cursor indicates the screen position where text will be displayed. You saw how to move the cursor with LOCATE and also how to determine the current cursor location.

Finally, the chapter explored some advanced but fun techniques. You displayed text in color and opened text viewports. You were introduced to text graphics by creating, displaying, and even animating text strings and figures.

Creating Graphics

This chapter is going to be fun. (Not that you haven't been having a good time so far!) Everyone enjoys creative graphics. You are going to learn how to "light up" your video screen with dots, lines, circles, colors, and even animated figures.

Effective graphics can enhance almost any program by providing easy-to-view output, friendliness, animation, and just plain amusement. Fortunately, QBasic has a wealth of tools to access your PC's graphics modes and bring out the creative graphics artist in you.

Here are some of the things you can do with graphics:

- Set one of several graphics modes
- Use colors
- Draw points, lines, and shapes
- Animate figures
- Mix text and graphics

Most IBM PCs and compatibles are capable of several different graphics modes. Your particular hardware determines which modes you have available.

Standard Video Configurations

To produce graphics, your computer must have the appropriate video hardware. QBasic supports all the popular graphics hardware for the IBM PC and compatibles. Make sure that you understand your particular hardware configuration. If you're unsure, the following discussion might help.

Inside your computer is a *video display adapter*. This piece of hardware controls the type of video signals that are sent to your video screen. This adapter can be built into your computer's motherboard or be on a "card" attached to your motherboard. Table 13.1 lists the six kinds of video display adapters in popular use.

Table 13.1. Video adapters.

Name	Features
MDA (Monochrome Display Adapter)	Text in black and white (no graphics)
HGA (Hercules Graphics Adapter)	Text and graphics in black and white
CGA (Color/Graphics Adapter)	Text and graphics in 4 colors
EGA (Enhanced Graphics Adapter)	Text and graphics in 16 colors
MCGA (Multi-Color Graphics Array)	Text and graphics in 256 colors
VGA (Video Graphics Array)	Text and graphics in 256 colors

NOTE

Obtaining Graphics with a Hercules Adapter

To use the graphics modes of the Hercules adapter (HGA), you must first load the Hercules driver (MSHERC.COM) before running QBasic. Type **MSHERC** from your DOS prompt to load the driver. (The file MSHERC.COM must be in your DOS directory path.) In text mode, QBasic is fully compatible with the Hercules emulation of the MDA even if MSHERC.COM is not loaded.

Video monitors, sometimes called *displays,* are the actual video screens on which you see the text and graphics. (In other words, the video adapters are hardware chips that send video signals that the monitors display.) Just as there are several types of video adapters, there are also several kinds of monitors and displays. Here are the most common types of monitors and displays:

- Monochrome display (for MDA and HGA Adapters)
- RGB monitor (for CGA Adapters)
- Composite monitor (for CGA Adapters)
- Enhanced monitor (for EGA Adapters)
- Analog display (for MCGA and VGA Adapters)

A *monochrome display* produces sharp text but can produce only black-and-white output. (Actually, most monochrome displays produce green and black, or amber and black, but the "colors" traditionally are called black and white.)

An *RGB monitor* (the RGB stands for red, green, blue) produces color images that are generally sharper than those produced by a *composite monitor*. (Most television sets are, in effect, composite monitors.) RGB monitors and composite monitors use different technologies to produce video output. Simply stated, RGB monitors produce color signals with three different components whereas the composite monitors blend color information into one signal.

An *enhanced monitor* is required to utilize the full capabilities of EGA Adapters.

An *analog display* is required to utilize the full capabilities of MCGA and VGA Adapters.

For the remainder of this chapter, we assume that you have the most appropriate monitor attached to your particular video adapter. Table 13.2 lists these default configurations.

Table 13.2. Default video configurations.

Name for Configuration	Adapter	Monitor
MDA	MDA	Monochrome
HGA	HGA	Monochrome
CGA	CGA	RGB
EGA	EGA	Enhanced
MCGA	MCGA	Analog
VGA	VGA	Analog

Other configurations are possible. For example, you can attach a monochrome monitor to an EGA adapter. But unless stated otherwise, Table 13.2 shows the assumed configurations.

Introduction to Graphics Modes

With a CGA, EGA, MCGA, or VGA video adapter, your computer can produce graphics. (MDA cannot produce graphics unless special added hardware is attached to your system. As the section "Obtaining Graphics with a Hercules Adapter" earlier in this chapter explained, HGA can produce graphics when the Hercules driver MSHERC.COM is loaded.) The available graphics modes differ with each hardware configuration. However, all graphics modes have two things in common:

■ A video screen image consists of many individual dots

■ You have control over each of the dots

Think of yourself as a graphics artist. Your video screen is your canvas. Your computer canvas consists of many small dots that you can turn on or off.

Each dot on the screen is called a *pixel* (picture element). You create graphics by designating a color for each pixel. When the color of the pixel is black (the background color), the dot appears to be off. The *resolution* (number of pixels on the screen) and available colors for each pixel depend on the graphics mode in effect.

To get a feeling for graphics in general, and the size of one pixel in particular, run this program:

```
SCREEN 2
PSET (320, 100)
```

The screen clears to black. You see the normal Press any key to continue message in the lower left corner. Your computer is now in screen mode 2, one of several graphics modes. Look closely at the center of your screen. Do you see the single white pixel near the center? You might have to look hard to see it. Except for the normal Press any key to continue message in the lower left corner, all the other pixels are black, producing a dark background. (A PSET instruction turns on a single pixel at a particular location. The PSET instruction is examined shortly.)

As you can see, a single pixel is small. And you have many pixels to control. Even in the graphics mode with the crudest resolution, the screen consists of some 64,000 pixels.

Does this mean that creating graphics is a mind-boggling task? After all, you have to set each pixel to a particular color.

Well, yes and no. You *do* have to control many pixels, but QBasic has a variety of statements and functions that simplify the process.

To whet your appetite for graphics, try the following program, which produces the "bull's-eye" pattern shown in Figure 13.1. This one simple program creates an interesting graphics design. Look at the program line between the FOR and NEXT instructions. It's not hard to guess that CIRCLE instructions draw circles of various sizes. CIRCLE and other graphics statements are examined throughout this chapter.

```
SCREEN 2
FOR J% = 10 TO 200 STEP 10
   CIRCLE (320, 100), J%
NEXT J%
```

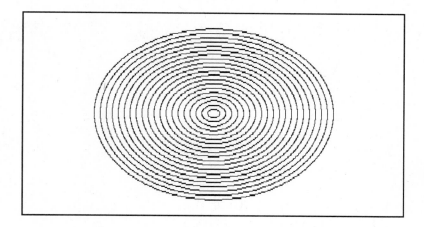

Figure 13.1.

Concentric circles drawn with CIRCLE.

If you feel adventurous, change the first line to SCREEN 1 and rerun the program. This change puts the computer in a lower resolution graphics mode. The circles now appear larger, moved to the right, and too big to be fully displayed. You will understand why before the end of the chapter.

The Available Graphics Modes— the *SCREEN* Statement

A SCREEN instruction initializes a graphics mode. This chapter considers only the simple (one-parameter) form of the SCREEN instruction. (As discussed in Chapter 20, "Using Advanced Graphics," SCREEN accepts other optional parameters.)

<table>
<tr><td>

**S
T
A
T
E
M
E
N
T**

</td><td>

SCREEN *modecode*

where

modecode is an integer expression setting the graphics mode as shown in Table 13.3.

</td></tr>
</table>

Table 13.3. The graphics modes.

modecode	Adapter	# Pixels	Colors
0	CGA,EGA,MCGA,VGA	Text Mode	16
0	HGA	Text Mode	2
1	CGA,EGA,MCGA,VGA	320 by 200	4
2	CGA,EGA,MCGA,VGA	640 by 200	B/W
3	HGA	720 by 348	B/W
4	Special	640 by 400	2
7	EGA,VGA	320 by 200	16
8	EGA,VGA	640 by 200	16
9	EGA,VGA	640 by 350	16
10	EGA,VGA	640 by 350	2
11	MCGA,VGA	640 by 480	2
12	VGA	640 by 480	16
13	MCGA,VGA	320 by 200	256

The second column of Table 13.3 shows which adapters support each screen mode. An error (Illegal function call) occurs if there is a mismatch—such as SCREEN 7 with a CGA system.

The third column shows the number of pixels associated with the particular screen mode. This column is the pixel resolution expressed as the number of horizontal pixels by the number of vertical pixels.

The last column shows the number of colors you have available for each pixel. *B/W* means that only black and white are available. In general, a COLOR instruction—discussed later in this chapter—selects colors.

Here is a synopsis of each graphics mode:

- ■ 0—Text mode: returns the display to text mode from one of the graphics modes. If the graphics mode was 1, 7, or 13, SCREEN 0 results in 40-column text mode; otherwise, 80-column text mode results.

- ■ 1—Medium-resolution CGA graphics: sets text width to 40.

- ■ 2—High-resolution CGA graphics: sets text width to 80.

- ■ 3—Hercules graphics: sets text width to 80.

- ■ 4—Special graphics mode for Olivetti and AT&T 6300 computers: sets text width to 80. You can select one of 16 colors. The background color is fixed at black.

- ■ 7—Medium-resolution graphics on an EGA (but with more colors than CGA allows): sets text width to 40.

- ■ 8—High-resolution graphics on an EGA (but with more colors than CGA allows): sets text width to 80.

- ■ 9—Enhanced high-resolution EGA graphics. You can select 16 colors from 64 available colors. Sets text width to 80.

- ■ 10—Enhanced high-resolution EGA graphics for systems with a monochrome display: sets text width to 80.

- ■ 11—VGA two-color graphics. You can select the two colors from 262,144 available colors. Sets text width to 80.

- ■ 12—VGA color graphics: You can select 16 colors from 262,144 available colors. Sets text width to 80.

- ■ 13—Medium-resolution graphics in 256 colors: You can select 256 colors from 262,114 available colors. Sets text width to 40.

For the remainder of this chapter, graphics discussions are confined to CGA graphics—that is, SCREEN modes 1 and 2. These two graphics modes are available with *any* graphics video adapter (CGA, EGA, VGA, or MCGA).

If you have an EGA, VGA, or MCGA system, see Chapter 20, "Using Advanced Graphics." That chapter discusses the graphics modes and features that your system can produce.

Coordinate Systems

The location of each graphics pixel is identified by two values: an x (horizontal) coordinate and a y (vertical) coordinate. Such coordinates often are specified as an x,y pair and enclosed in parentheses. For example, (130, 89) identifies the pixel at x-coordinate 130 and y-coordinate 89.

Location (0, 0) identifies the pixel at the upper left corner of the screen. Notice that, in graphics modes, numbering starts with 0 (not with 1 as in text mode). The x-coordinates increase moving horizontally to the right, and y-coordinates increase moving vertically down.

If you are familiar with mathematical graphs, you are probably accustomed to graphs with origins in the lower left corner and y values increasing upward. Does it seem strange that, in QBasic's graphics modes, the origin is in the upper left corner and y values increase downward? Most likely, it does.

The origin in the upper left corner is a computing tradition, and traditions die hard. (However, y values increasing down the graph is similar to the way you think about row numbers increasing down a text screen.) In Chapter 20, "Using Advanced Graphics," you learn how to correct this "problem" by redefining the standard coordinate system.

The coordinates of the upper left corner of the screen are (0, 0). What are the coordinates of the lower right corner of the screen?

The answer is, "It depends." The coordinates of the lower right corner depend on the SCREEN mode selected. For example, the coordinates of the lower right corner are (319, 199) for medium-resolution (SCREEN 1), (639, 199) for high-resolution (SCREEN 2), and (639, 349) for enhanced high-resolution (SCREEN 9).

Figure 13.2 shows the layout of a high-resolution screen with the coordinates of a few pixels specified.

Specifying Coordinates

Most graphics statements and functions require one or more coordinate pairs as parameters. In general, there are three ways you can specify a coordinate pair:

- Absolute coordinates
- LPR (Last Point Referenced)
- Relative coordinates

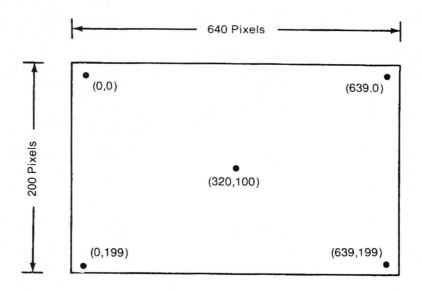

Figure 13.2.
Coordinate system of a
high-resolution screen.

Absolute Coordinates

The simplest way to designate a pixel location is to specify the x- and y-coordinates explicitly.

For example, a PSET instruction (discussed shortly) plots a pixel at a specified location. Using absolute coordinates, the following instruction turns on the pixel at x-coordinate 214 and y-coordinate 89:

```
PSET (214, 89)
```

LPR (Last Point Referenced)

In graphics modes, QBasic keeps track of where the last point is displayed. The position of this last point is called the *LPR* (Last Point Referenced).

Many graphics instructions accept the LPR as a default coordinate point. For example, one form of the LINE instruction accepts only a destination parameter. A line is then drawn from the current LPR to this destination point. After the line is drawn, the destination point becomes the new LPR.

Relative Coordinates

A third option, available with most graphics statements, is to specify coordinates as a displacement from the LPR. Such coordinates are called *relative*.

You use the keyword STEP to specify this form. Here is a typical example:

```
PSET STEP (-24, 18)
```

This instruction directs QBasic to plot a point 24 pixels to the left and 18 pixels below the LPR. If the LPR happens to be at (140, 75), the new point plots at (116, 93). Notice that relative coordinates can be positive or negative. Positive *x* values are to the right and negative *x* values to the left. Positive *y* values are down and negative *y* values are up.

Initializing a Graphics Mode

When you initialize a graphics mode with a SCREEN instruction, three things happen:

- The video screen clears to a black background.
- The default graphics color becomes white.
- The LPR becomes the middle of the screen.

However, nothing happens if a SCREEN instruction specifies the graphics mode that is currently in effect. In this case, the screen does not clear and the LPR does not change. Effectively, QBasic just ignores the SCREEN instruction.

Drawing Simple Shapes in Black and White

Now let's create some graphics. The following statements produce points, lines, and circles:

- PSET, PRESET (single points)
- LINE (straight lines)
- CIRCLE (circles)

Start with the simplest forms of these statements. For now, you will use black and white graphics. Later in this chapter, you learn how to add optional parameters that produce color graphics and create fancier shapes such as rectangles and pie slices.

Plotting Points—*PSET* and *PRESET*

The PSET statement turns on a pixel at a given screen location. "Turns on" means that the pixel color changes to white from the formerly black background color.

You can specify the coordinates of the pixel in absolute or relative form.

```
PSET (x-coord, y-coord)        'Absolute form
PSET STEP(x-coord, y-coord)    'Relative form
where
    x-coord specifies the x-coordinate of the pixel to turn on,
and
    y-coord specifies the y-coordinate.
```

S
T
A
T
E
M
E
N
T

The first form, without STEP, indicates that the coordinates are in absolute form. For example, the following instruction turns on the pixel located at x-coordinate 319 and y-coordinate 103:

```
PSET (319, 103)
```

The second form, with STEP, indicates that the coordinates are in relative form. For example, the following instruction turns on the pixel located 20 pixels to the right of the LPR and 18 pixels below the LPR:

```
PSET STEP (20, 18)
```

The companion statement, PRESET, turns off a pixel. Here, "turns off" means to make the pixel color black (the background color). As with PSET, you can use absolute or relative coordinates.

```
PRESET (x-coord, y-coord)        'Absolute form
PRESET STEP(x-coord, y-coord)    'Relative form
where
    x-coord specifies the x-coordinate of the pixel to turn off,
and
    y-coord specifies the y-coordinate.
```

S
T
A
T
E
M
E
N
T

Try the following program to get a better feel for PSET and PRESET:

```
SCREEN 1
CLS
PSET (160, 100)
    WHILE INKEY$ = "": WEND
PSET STEP(-25, 10)
    WHILE INKEY$ = "": WEND
PRESET (160, 100)
    WHILE INKEY$ = "": WEND
PRESET STEP(-25, 10)
```

The first two instructions initialize SCREEN mode 1 (medium-resolution graphics) and clear the screen.

T I P Clearing a Graphics Screen

Just as in text mode, CLS clears a graphics screen. CLS sets all pixels to the background color (usually black). See the end of this chapter for a discussion of some special forms of the CLS instruction.

The PSET (160, 100) instruction turns on a pixel near the center of the screen. Do you see it?

The WHILE INKEY$ = "": WEND loop simply pauses the program execution until you press any key. (The INKEY$ function was introduced in Chapter 7, "Program Flow and Decision Making," and is discussed thoroughly in Chapter 16, "Using Hardware Devices.")

The program is waiting for you to press a key. When you do, QBasic executes the following PSET instruction:

```
PSET STEP(-25, 10)
```

Another pixel turns on 25 pixels to the left and 10 pixels below the first pixel. The STEP keyword means the coordinates are relative to the LPR rather than absolute coordinates. The first PSET instruction established the LPR at absolute location (160, 100). The new pixel is at (160 - 25, 100 + 10) or absolute coordinates (135, 110).

Now let's erase these two pixels. First press a key to execute this instruction:

```
PRESET (160, 100)
```

The first pixel turns back to black and fades into the background. The LPR is once again at this location (160, 100). To erase the second pixel, press any key to execute the program's final instruction:

```
PRESET STEP(-25, 10)
```

Remember, relative coordinates can be positive or negative. Positive *x* coordinates are to the right and negative *x* coordinates are to the left. Positive *y* coordinates are down and negative *y* coordinates are up.

Listing 13.1, DRAWGRID.BAS, demonstrates PSET and PRESET with coordinate parameters specified by variables. First, PSET displays a grid of dots. Then, after you press a key, PRESET erases the grid.

Listing 13.1. The DRAWGRID.BAS program.

```
REM Program: DRAWGRID.BAS (Demonstrate PSET and PRESET)
SCREEN 1
CLS                          'Clear the screen
FOR X% = 5 TO 315 STEP 5
   FOR Y% = 5 TO 195 STEP 5
      PSET (X%, Y%)          'Turn on pixel
   NEXT Y%
NEXT X%
REM
WHILE INKEY$ = "": WEND       'Pause until user hits key
REM
FOR X% = 5 TO 315 STEP 5
   FOR Y% = 5 TO 195 STEP 5
      PRESET (X%, Y%)        'Turn off pixel
   NEXT Y%
NEXT X%
END
```

NOTE

What about Fractional Coordinates?

Because coordinates can be variables or general expressions, what happens if a coordinate value has a fractional component? Suppose, for example, you try this:

```
NUMBER! = 49.33
PSET (NUMBER!, 2 * NUMBER!)
```

No problem. It's true that every graphics pixel is located at an integral value of *x* and *y*. However, if your coordinate expression has a fractional component, QBasic simply rounds the value to the nearest integer. This fractional rounding takes place with all graphics instructions.

The PSET and PRESET instructions use variables for the coordinate specifications. In general, you can use any expression for your *x* and *y* values.

As you saw earlier in this chapter, the WHILE-WEND loop pauses the program until you press any key.

Drawing Straight Lines—*LINE*

The LINE statement draws a straight line. The line can be short, long, horizontal, vertical, or at any angle. You just specify the two end points, and QBasic does the rest.

```
LINE startpoint - endpoint
```

where

>   *startpoint* is the *x,y* location of the starting point of the line

and

>   *endpoint* is the *x,y* location of the end point of the line.

The *startpoint* parameter is optional, but the *endpoint* parameter is mandatory. If you omit *startpoint*, the line begins at the LPR.

For example, the following instruction draws a line from the point (100, 30) to the point (210, 80):

```
LINE (100, 30) - (210, 80)
```

Listing 13.2, MOUNTAIN.BAS, shows LINE in action. The program draws the simple "mountain" shape shown in Figure 13.3:

Listing 13.2.   The MOUNTAIN.BAS program.

```
REM Program: MOUNTAIN.BAS (Demonstrate simple lines)
SCREEN 2
CLS
FOR Xbottom% = 10 TO 610 STEP 30
   LINE (310, 20)-(Xbottom%, 180)
NEXT Xbottom%
```

In MOUNTAIN.BAS, all the lines start at x-coordinate 310 and y-coordinate 20. This point is the top of the mountain. The FOR-NEXT loop variable Xbottom% controls the *x* coordinate at the bottom of the mountain. Notice how the Xbottom% changes values to draw the various lines in the mountain.

In a LINE instruction, you can specify the beginning and ending points in absolute coordinates (without STEP) or relative coordinates (with STEP). As MOUNTAIN.BAS demonstrates, the components of *startpoint* and *endpoint* can be variables (or even expressions).

For example, the following instruction draws a line from (30, 42) to a point with an x-coordinate given by Xvalue and a y-coordinate given by the expression Yvalue + 28.

```
LINE (30, 42) - (Xvalue, Yvalue + 28)
```

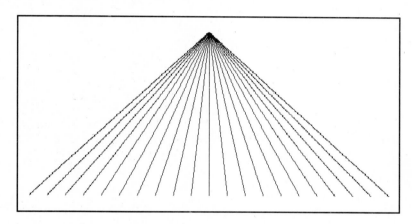

Figure 13.3.

The "mountain" drawn by MOUNTAIN.BAS.

To specify a relative coordinate, you can use STEP with *startpoint*, *endpoint*, or both parameters.

Here are some examples of instructions that use relative coordinates:

```
LINE STEP(10, -30)-(65, 70)
```

The line begins at the point 10 pixels to the right and 30 pixels above the LPR. The line ends at the point with absolute coordinates (65, 70).

```
LINE (X%, Y%)-STEP(50, 40)
```

The line begins at the point specified by the absolute coordinates (X%, Y%). This point becomes the LPR. The line ends at the point 50 pixels to the right and 40 pixels below the newly established LPR (X%, Y%).

```
LINE STEP(-10, 20)-STEP(60, 85)
```

The line begins 10 pixels to the left and 20 pixels below the LPR. This starting point becomes the LPR. The line ends at the point 60 pixels to the right and 85 pixels below the starting point.

The last two instructions demonstrate how relative coordinates work with the *endpoint* parameter. When STEP appears with the *endpoint* parameter, the LPR for determining the end point is simply the beginning of the line.

The starting point parameter is optional in a LINE instruction. Here is an example:

```
LINE -(80, 120)
```

This instruction draws a line from the LPR to absolute location (80, 120). When you omit the *startpoint* parameter, the line begins at the LPR. It's just as though you specified the starting point with the parameter STEP(0, 0).

One last example:

```
LINE -STEP(60, 0)
```

This instruction draws a horizontal line beginning at the LPR and extending 60 pixels to the right.

Drawing Circles—*CIRCLE*

Use CIRCLE to draw circles. (Now that certainly makes sense.) For now, we consider only the simplest form of CIRCLE, drawing a complete circle in black and white. Later in the chapter, you see how optional parameters produce ellipses, arcs, and pie-shaped wedges.

S T A T E M E N T

```
CIRCLE (xcenter, ycenter), radius        'Absolute form
```
or
```
CIRCLE STEP (xcenter, ycenter), radius   'Relative form
```
where

    xcenter is the x-coordinate of the circle's center,

    ycenter is the y-coordinate of the circle's center,

and

    radius specifies the radius of the circle.

For example, the following instruction draws a circle centered at absolute location (75, 60) with a radius of 28 pixels:

```
CIRCLE (75, 60), 28
```

The *xcenter* and *ycenter* parameters determine the location of the circle's center. As usual, you can use absolute coordinates (without STEP) or relative coordinates (with STEP).

A circle's radius is the distance from the center of the circle to the perimeter. With the *radius* parameter, you specify the radius length (in pixels) of the circle you want QBasic to draw.

However, drawing circles on a video screen presents a complication. Standard video monitors have a different inter-pixel spacing horizontally and vertically. To draw true-looking circles, the radius must continually adjust as the circle is drawn.

QBasic makes this adjustment automatically so that CIRCLE instructions produce accurate circles. With the *radius* parameter, you specify the pixel length *along the x axis*. If the value of *radius* is negative, an error results (Illegal function call).

Listing 13.3, RINGS.BAS, demonstrates CIRCLE by drawing the five-circle symbol of the Olympic games. Figure 13.4 shows the result.

Listing 13.3. The RINGS.BAS program.

```
REM Program: RINGS.BAS (Draw the Olympic rings)
SCREEN 1
CLS
Radius% = 40
FOR X% = 50 TO 250 STEP 100
    CIRCLE (X%, 80), Radius%
NEXT X%
FOR X% = 100 TO 200 STEP 100
    CIRCLE (X%, 120), Radius%
NEXT X%
```

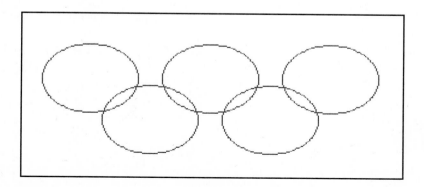

Figure 13.4.

The "Olympic" symbol drawn by RINGS.BAS.

Creating Color Graphics

Enough of this drab black and white. It's time to put some color into your graphics. For starters, try the following experiment:

1. Modify the first CIRCLE instruction of RINGS.BAS as follows (there's an added parameter at the end of the instruction):

   ```
   CIRCLE (X%, 80), Radius%, 1
   ```

2. Run the modified program. The top three circles are now cyan instead of white. (Cyan, by the way, is a bluish-green color.)

3. Modify the second COLOR instruction to look like this:

   ```
   CIRCLE (X%, 120), Radius%, 2
   ```

4. Run the program again. The bottom two circles are now magenta.

By adding a simple parameter to the CIRCLE instructions, you drew colored circles. The details of this technique are discussed soon enough. But first, a general discussion of graphics colors is in order.

 **NOTE** **CGA Color Graphics**

Of the two CGA graphics modes, only SCREEN mode 1 supports color. (SCREEN mode 2 produces only black-and-white graphics.) In this chapter, the detailed discussion of color graphics is confined to SCREEN mode 1. Chapter 20, "Using Advanced Graphics," discusses color graphics in relation to the EGA and VGA modes: SCREEN modes 7 through 13.

Foreground and Background Colors

In graphics modes, just as in text mode, there are both *foreground* colors and *background* colors. However, for graphics modes, the distinction between foreground and background is a bit vague.

After all, in graphics modes, the screen is simply a grid of pixels with each pixel having a particular color. Technically speaking, you cannot always say that one pixel is in the foreground and another pixel in the background.

Consider a quilt pattern with pixels alternating in color. Who is to say that one color is the foreground color and another color the background color? This question is similar to the old conundrum, "Is a zebra black with white stripes or white with black stripes?"

Nevertheless, we *do* speak of foreground and background colors. Practically speaking, most graphics consist of images drawn on a uniform background. In this light, we distinguish between foreground and background colors as follows:

- The *foreground* color is the color of a drawn object. For example, you draw a red circle by turning each pixel of the circle into red. In this case, red is the foreground color.

- The *background* color, naturally enough, is the color of all the background pixels. When you initialize a graphics mode, the background is solid black.

Specifying Pixel Colors

QBasic provides two primary ways of specifying pixel colors.

1. The *color* parameter. You can add an optional color parameter to PSET, PRESET, LINE, and CIRCLE instructions. This parameter specifies the foreground color with which the pixels are drawn.

2. The COLOR statement. Just as in text mode, you can specify default foreground and background colors with a COLOR instruction.

We now discuss color in terms of SCREEN modes 1 and 2.

Color Graphics in *SCREEN* Mode 1

As you have seen, a SCREEN 1 instruction activates medium-resolution graphics mode. This mode is available with any video adapter (CGA, EGA, VGA, or MCGA). If you have a CGA system, this is the *only* graphics mode that supports color.

Mode 1 has the following characteristics:

- The screen is 320 pixels horizontally by 200 pixels vertically.

- Background pixels can be any of 16 possible colors.

- Up to four colors can be on-screen at the same time. (Black and white each count as one color.)

- Two different palettes are available. Each palette consists of three foreground colors preselected by QBasic and one background color that you can select.

The *palette* concept requires some explanation. Think of yourself, the programmer, as a graphic artist. You paint from a palette that contains four cups of different colored paint. These cups are labeled numerically from 0 to 3. Whenever you draw a point, line, or circle, you choose the color by selecting one of the four cups. You indicate your choice of cup with a number from 0 to 3.

Table 13.4 shows the default colors in each cup.

Table 13.4. Default palette colors.	
Cup Number	**Color**
0	Black (background color)
1	Cyan
2	Magenta
3	White

Later in this chapter, you learn how to put any of the 16 available colors into cup 0 and also how to select an alternate palette with three different colors in cups 1 through 3. For now, let's see how to work with this default palette.

Specifying the *color* Parameter

PSET, PRESET, LINE, and CIRCLE instructions accept an optional parameter that specifies the pixel color by designating which color cup to use.

S T A T E M E N T

Color Graphics Instructions in Mode 1

PSET (*x-coord, y-coord*), *color*

PRESET (*x-coord, y-coord*), *color*

LINE *startpoint - endpoint, color*

CIRCLE (*xcenter, ycenter*), *radius, color*

where

   color specifies the drawing color with a value from 0 to 3.

(The *x-coord, y-coord, startpoint, endpoint, xcenter, ycenter*, and *radius* parameters work as explained previously.)

Now you can understand how the modified RINGS.BAS program works. Remember, you changed the two COLOR instructions in RINGS.BAS to appear as follows:

```
CIRCLE (X%, 80), Radius%, 1

CIRCLE (X%, 120), Radius%, 2
```

The first COLOR instruction specifies color cup 1 (cyan), and the second instruction specifies color cup 2 (magenta).

Specifying *color* with Variables

In PSET, PRESET, LINE, and CIRCLE instructions, you can specify the *color* parameter with a variable or expression. Listing 13.4 uses a variable named Cup% for the *color* parameter.

Listing 13.4. The LINES.BAS program.

```
REM Program: LINES.BAS (Draw 4 horizontal lines)
SCREEN 1
CLS
FOR Cup% = 0 TO 3
   Y% = 40 * Cup%
   LINE (20, Y%)-(200, Y%), Cup%
NEXT Cup%
```

Notice that the LINE instruction specifies the *color* parameter with the variable Cup%.

LINES.BAS actually draws four horizontal lines, but you see only three! The first time through the loop, Cup% has the value of 0. The LINE instruction draws a horizontal line using color 0, which is black. The screen background, however, is already black. As a result, the line is invisible. The next three times through the loop, Cup% has the values of 1, 2, and 3, which result in lines of cyan, magenta, and white, respectively.

Erasing Graphic Figures

You can use color 0 to "erase" something previously drawn with another color. For example, try this program:

```
SCREEN 1
CLS
```

```
CIRCLE (100, 90), 30, 1    'Draw cyan circle
WHILE INKEY$ = "": WEND
CIRCLE (100, 90), 30, 0    'Erase the circle
```

The program draws a cyan circle with the first CIRCLE instruction and waits for you to press a key. When you do press a key, the second CIRCLE instruction erases the circle. This second CIRCLE instruction actually redraws the previous circle using black. The effect is to erase the circle.

Using *PSET* and *PRESET* with Colors

PSET and PRESET are equivalent when you include a *color* parameter. Each instruction changes the designated pixel to the indicated color. For example, either one of the following two instructions makes the pixel at (X%, Y%) magenta:

```
PSET (X%, Y%), 2
```

```
PRESET (X%, Y%), 2
```

> ### Illegal *color* Values
>
> What happens if you specify a *color* parameter outside of the range from 0 to 3?
>
> If *color* has a value from 4 to 32,767, or from –32,764 to –1, QBasic acts like the value was 3. In other words, the graphics color is white. Values of color from –32,768 to –32,765 act like color values from 0 to 3.
>
> However, if *color* has a value less than –32,768, or greater than 32,767, the instruction is illegal. Your program terminates with the error message Overflow.

Using the *COLOR* Instruction in Mode 1

Similar to a COLOR instruction in text mode (see Chapter 12, "Writing Text on the Video Screen"), a COLOR instruction in graphics mode lets you redefine the default colors. However, graphics COLOR instructions work quite differently from text mode COLOR instructions.

COLOR *background*, *palette*

where

> *background* specifies the background color

and

> *palette* specifies one of two color palettes for foreground color selection.

Each of the parameters is optional.

With a COLOR instruction, you can do either or both of the following:

- Choose any one of 16 colors to be the background color—that is, the color in cup number 0.

- Select an alternate palette that contains green, red, and brown in color cups 1, 2, and 3, respectively. (This alternate palette replaces the default palette that contains cyan, magenta, and white in cups 1, 2, and 3.)

Notice that each of the parameters is optional. You can specify 0, 1, or 2 parameters with each COLOR instruction. The parameters can be variables or numeric expressions. Here are some sample COLOR instructions:

```
COLOR 2, 3      'Both parameters are specified

COLOR Hue%      '2nd parameter retains its current value

COLOR , 1       '1st parameter retains its current value

COLOR           'Both parameters retain their current value
```

Now let's see how each parameter (*background* and *palette*) works.

Changing the Background Color

With the *background* parameter in a COLOR instruction, you can designate cup 0 to be any of the 16 colors indicated in Table 13.5. As shown in the table, each of the 16 colors has a color code value ranging from 0 to 15.

By default, QBasic uses black as the background color. In other words, when you initialize graphics, cup 0 (the cup with the background color) contains color 0 (black).

Table 13.5. Available colors.

Code	Color	Code	Color
0	Black	8	Gray
1	Blue	9	Light blue
2	Green	10	Light green
3	Cyan	11	Light cyan
4	Red	12	Light red
5	Magenta	13	Light magenta
6	Brown	14	Yellow
7	White	15	Bright white

To change the background color, specify the first parameter in a COLOR instruction. You can choose any of the 16 colors for the background. For example, the following instruction changes the background to blue:

```
COLOR 1
```

Want to see the various background colors? Listing 13.5, BACKGRND.BAS, cycles through the available colors. Just press Enter to watch the background change.

Listing 13.5.   The BACKGROUND.BAS program.

```
REM Program: BACKGRND.BAS (Cycle through background colors)
SCREEN 1
CLS
FOR Hue% = 0 TO 14
    COLOR Hue%
    PRINT "Background color is now color"; Hue%
    INPUT "Press Enter to see the next color", Dummy$
NEXT Hue%
```

Notice that the FOR loop makes 14, not 15, the final value of Hue%. Why? The text color is bright white. If Hue% is 15, the text color and background color are identical. The result is invisible text!

Recovering from an Invisible Screen

On occasion, you might inadvertently have a graphics program paused with identical colors for the background and foreground. This is a quandary because the screen text becomes invisible, and you might not know what to do next. Help!

Fortunately, QBasic provides a convenient way out. Simply press Ctrl-Break. Your program terminates immediately, and control returns to the editing environment.

Regardless of the background color, the color parameter in PSET, PRESET, LINE, and CIRCLE instructions draws shapes in cyan, magenta, or white (1 = cyan, 2 = magenta, 3 = white). In these instructions, however, color 0 refers to the current background color. This means that you can use color 0 to erase a previous image without having to know the current background color. For example, consider the following instructions:

```
CIRCLE (100, 50), 20, 1
```

```
CIRCLE (100, 50), 20, 0
```

The first of these two instructions draws a cyan circle regardless of the current background color. The second instruction draws a circle in the current background color, *whatever that color happens to be.* In effect, the second instruction erases the circle drawn by the first instruction.

A Secret about the Default Color Cups

The cyan, magenta, and white colors found in color cups 1, 2, and 3 are actually the light cyan, light magenta, and bright white colors in Table 13.5. (That is, the three drawing colors correspond to codes 11, 13, and 15 rather than codes 3, 5, and 7.)

To demonstrate this, draw a cyan shape with a CIRCLE or LINE instruction. For example

```
CIRCLE (100, 50), 20, 1
```

Now change the background color. COLOR 3 produces a cyan background, but you can still see the circle. That's because the circle is really light cyan on the cyan background. To erase the circle, use COLOR 11 (light cyan), which makes the background the same color as the circle.

Changing the Palette

Ready for more? Now it is time to change the palette. By doing so, a new set of four drawing colors becomes available.

QBasic provides two color palettes, known as the *odd* palette and the *even* palette. You can work with only one palette at a time. So far, you have worked with the odd palette, which is the default palette. This palette draws with the familiar colors of cyan, magenta, and white. By contrast, the even palette draws with green, red, and brown. Table 13.6 summarizes the colors in each palette.

Table 13.6. Palette colors.

Cup Number	Palette 0 (even)	Palette 1 (odd)
0	Background color	Background color
1	Green	Cyan
2	Red	Magenta
3	Brown	Bright white

To select a palette, you specify the second parameter in a COLOR instruction. This parameter is the *palette* parameter. When *palette* has the value of 1 (or any odd number), you select the default palette containing cyan and magenta. When *palette* is 0 (or any even number), you select the alternate palette containing green and red.

Here are some sample COLOR instructions that select a palette. Notice that, if you want to specify the palette but leave the background color unchanged, you insert a comma between the COLOR keyword and the *palette* parameter.

```
COLOR 1, 0     'Background color blue, select palette 0

COLOR , 1      'Background color same, select palette 1
```

When you switch palettes, you instantly change the colors already on-screen. Images drawn with color cup 1 of the old palette switch immediately to the color in color cup 1 of the new palette. (The same holds true for color cups 2 and 3.)

Remember the LINES.BAS program that drew four horizontal lines? Let's modify the program to try the alternate palette. Listing 13.6 adds a COLOR instruction after the CLS instruction.

Listing 13.6. The modified LINES.BAS program.

```
REM Program: LINES.BAS (Draw 4 horizontal lines)
SCREEN 1
CLS
COLOR , 0      'This instruction is now added
FOR Cup% = 0 TO 3
   Y% = 40 * Cup%
   LINE (20, Y%)-(200, Y%), Cup%
NEXT Cup%
```

To see how palettes work, try this experiment:

1. Run this modified version of LINES.BAS. Notice that the horizontal lines are now green, red, and brown. The uppermost line is still invisible because it is drawn in black (the background color). Also notice that the on-screen text characters are now brown. With the even palette, brown replaces white as the default color.

2. Press any key to return to the QBasic editor.

3. Press F6 to move the input focus to the Immediate window.

4. Change the palette back to the default palette with the following immediate-mode command:

   `COLOR , 1`

   QBasic shifts the screen back to the output graphics window. Notice that the horizontal lines have changed to cyan, magenta, and white.

5. Press any key to return to the editor.

6. Try some immediate-mode COLOR commands that change the palette and/or background. Here is one to get you started:

   `COLOR 9, 0`

"Color" Graphics in *SCREEN* Mode 2

SCREEN 2 selects high-resolution graphics (640 pixels horizontally by 200 pixels vertically). Color graphics in this mode are simple: There aren't any!

All graphics in mode 2 must be in black and white (white drawing on a black background). If you try a COLOR instruction in this mode, your program terminates with the error message Illegal function call.

However, you do not get an error message if you specify the `color` parameter in a `PSET`, `PRESET`, `LINE`, or `CIRCLE` instruction. QBasic simply ignores this `color` parameter and always draws with white.

> **NOTE**   **Color Graphics in Higher Screen Modes**
>
> `SCREEN` modes 7 through 10 work only on systems equipped with EGA, VGA, or MCGA video adapters. `SCREEN` modes 11 through 13 work only on VGA systems. CGA systems cannot utilize these screen modes.
>
> These modes support extended color capability. The modes are discussed in Chapter 20, "Using Advanced Graphics."

Painting Enclosed Areas—the *PAINT* Statement

`PAINT` pours color into any enclosed region.

S T A T E M E N T

PAINT (*x-coord, y-coord*), *paint, bordercolor*

where

    x-coord and *y-coord* specify the *x,y* location where painting begins,

    paint is the paint color,

and

    bordercolor designates the color of the boundary region.

The *paint* and *bordercolor* parameters are optional.

`PAINT` works from a single point outward. Imagine a painter with a spray gun containing color *paint*. The painter begins at the single point given by (*x-coord, y-coord*) and sprays paint slowly in all directions. Whenever a point or area of color *bordercolor* is encountered, painting stops in that direction.

The (*x-coord, y-coord*) parameter specifies the initial painting position. This is the only mandatory parameter. As usual, these coordinates are absolute (without STEP) or relative (with STEP). For example:

```
PAINT (80, 50)      'Begin painting at absolute location (80, 50)

PAINT STEP (80, 50) 'Begin painting at relative location (80, 50)
```

The integer expression *paint* specifies the color in the spray gun. If you don't specify the *paint* parameter, QBasic uses the default value of 3. The value of *paint* corresponds to the number of the selected color cup. As such, *paint* should have a value from 0 to 3. (QBasic allows values from –32,764 to –1 and from 4 to 32,767. Other values result in a run-time error: `Illegal function call`.)

The *bordercolor* parameter defines the color of the boundary region. Painting stops wherever the border color is encountered. If you don't specify *bordercolor*, the default is the same color as the *paint* parameter.

Make sure that the region you want to paint is completely enclosed by a boundary of the border color. Otherwise, the paint can leak into undesired areas.

Notice that the default color for *bordercolor* is the *paint* color, not color 3 (white). Suppose that you are using cyan paint in a region outlined by white. Your PAINT instruction, assuming SCREEN 1, should look something like this:

```
PAINT (100, 50), 1, 3    '1 = cyan paint, 3 = white border
```

Don't make the mistake of omitting the *bordercolor* parameter in such a case. The following instruction paints with cyan until a border region of cyan is reached (not until a white border is reached):

```
PAINT (100, 50), 1
```

This instruction causes the paint to encroach onto and through a white border.

Listing 13.7, DOPAINT.BAS, demonstrates PAINT. Intersecting circles are drawn in white. Then regions are painted various colors. Notice that the second PAINT instruction omits both the *paint* and *bordercolor* parameters. Therefore, QBasic uses the default value for each parameter, namely 3. This PAINT instruction fills the area with white until the specified boundary is reached.

Listing 13.7. The DOPAINT.BAS program.

```
REM Program: DOPAINT.BAS (Demonstrate PAINT statement)
SCREEN 1
'

CIRCLE (150, 100), 50      'Draw a white circle
CIRCLE (200, 100), 50      'Draw an intersecting circle
CIRCLE (175, 100), 100     'Draw an outer circle
'

PAINT (110, 100), 1, 3     'Paint left hemisphere cyan
PAINT (240, 100)           'Paint right hemisphere white
PAINT (170, 100), 2, 3     'Paint inside magenta
PAINT (100, 190), 2, 3     'Paint outside magenta
```

Drawing Boxes and Circles

The LINE and CIRCLE instructions accept optional parameters that enable you to draw boxes, arcs, ellipses, and wedges.

Drawing Boxes with *LINE*

To draw a box, use the optional B parameter in a LINE instruction. With BF instead of just B, the box fills with color.

STATEMENT

LINE *startpoint* - *endpoint*, *color*, B

or

LINE *startpoint* - *endpoint*, *color*, BF

where

   B draws an outlined box,

and

   BF draws a box and paints the interior a solid color.

The *startpoint*, *endpoint*, and *color* parameters have been explained previously.

When drawing a box (that is, a rectangle), the *startpoint* and *endpoint* parameters establish the diagonally opposite corners of the box.

You can paint the interior of the rectangle by using BF rather than B. (BF stands for *Box Filled*.) The *color* parameter determines the paint color. If you omit *color*, QBasic uses the default color cup value of 3.

Listing 13.8, SHOWLINE.BAS, demonstrates LINE with some simple line and rectangle drawing. Because it's hard to show color in a black-and-white book, the *color* parameter is not used in the LINE instructions.

Listing 13.8. The SHOWLINE.BAS program.

```
REM Program: SHOWLINE.BAS (Show lines and rectangles)
SCREEN 1
CLS
Delta% = 25
'
LINE (10, 20)-(35, 20)
```

```
LINE -STEP(Delta%, Delta%)
LINE -STEP(Delta%, -Delta%)
LINE -STEP(Delta%, 0)              'Completes a "flying V"
'
LINE (150, 20)-(200, 45), , B              'An outlined box
LINE (230, 20)-STEP(50, Delta%), , BF      'A filled box
END
```

Notice how the final two LINE instructions use two consecutive commas to omit the *color* parameter. By omitting the *color* parameter, the value of *color* defaults to 3 in each instruction.

Figure 13.5 shows the result of Listing 13.8.

Figure 13.5.

Lines and rectangles drawn by SHOWLINE.BAS.

Drawing Arcs, Ellipses, and Wedges with *CIRCLE*

You can add three optional parameters (*start*, *end*, and *aspect*) to the end of a CIRCLE instruction. With these parameters, you can draw not only a circle but a partial circle, partial ellipse, complete ellipse, or a pie-shaped wedge. (An ellipse is a squashed-in circle resembling the outline of a football.)

CIRCLE (*xcenter*, *ycenter*), *radius*, *color*, *start*, *end*, *aspect*

where

    xcenter, *ycenter*, *radius*, and *color* have been explained previously,

    start specifies the beginning point of an arc as an angle in radians,

    end specifies the ending point of an arc as an angle in radians,

and

    aspect specifies the aspect ratio of the x-radius to the y-radius.

S T A T E M E N T

A CIRCLE instruction can contain up to seven parameters! That might seem imposing, but actually you can quickly learn the syntax of CIRCLE. Remember, with CIRCLE, you need to specify only the *xcenter*, *ycenter*, and *radius* parameters. The other four parameters are optional.

Use *start* and *end* to draw a partial circle (that is, an arc). The *start* and *end* parameters identify each terminus of the arc as an angle in radians (not degrees) from the horizontal. Each angle must be in the range from -2π to $+2\pi$ (or the value is normalized into this range). The angles are located in the conventional geometric manner with 0 to the right, 0.5π straight up, π to the left, and 1.5π straight down (see Figure 10.2). Recall that 360 degrees equals 2π radians (see Chapter 10, "Manipulating Numbers").

QBasic draws each arc counterclockwise. Consider the drawing "pen" to be raised above the screen and moving in a circle with the prescribed center and radius. The pen sweeps counterclockwise. When the *start* angle is reached, the pen "drops" to the screen and begins drawing. When the *end* angle is reached, the pen "lifts" from the screen to complete the desired arc. If you specify either *start* or *end*, but not both, the absent parameter defaults to a value of zero.

If *start* or *end* is negative, QBasic draws a straight line from the respective terminus of the arc to the center of the circle. Thus, by making both parameters negative, you generate a pie-shaped wedge. To locate an arc, the minus sign is stripped from the parameter to form a positive number (that is, the absolute value of the parameter determines the location angle).

By adjusting *aspect*, you create an ellipse (or partial arc of an ellipse) rather than a true circle. When drawing an ellipse, the *radius* parameter specifies the length of the major (larger) axis of the ellipse. When *aspect* is less than 1, *radius* is the x-radius, and the ellipse has a larger x-radius than y-radius. When *aspect* is greater than 1, *radius* is the y-radius, and the ellipse has a larger y-radius than x-radius. If *aspect* is negative, the results are unpredictable, but no fatal error occurs. You have to experiment with your particular hardware to determine appropriate values of *aspect* for your desired circles and ellipses.

When a complete circle or ellipse is drawn, the LPR becomes the center of the circle or ellipse. When an arc is drawn, the LPR becomes the center that the circle or ellipse would have if the arc were completed.

Listing 13.9, DOCIRCLE.BAS, demonstrates many features of CIRCLE.

Listing 13.9. The DOCIRCLE.BAS program.

```
REM Program: DOCIRCLE.BAS (Demonstrate the CIRCLE statement)
SCREEN 2                    'Select high-resolution graphics
CLS
PI = 4 * ATN(1)             'Calculate the value of Pi
'
CIRCLE (100, 30), 30                            'Shape A
CIRCLE (200, 30), 30, , PI / 10, PI / 2         'Shape B
CIRCLE (300, 30), 30, , PI / 2, PI / 10         'Shape C
CIRCLE (100, 140), 30, , -PI / 10, -PI / 2      'Shape D
```

```
CIRCLE (200, 140), 30, , , , .2                  'Shape E
CIRCLE (300, 140), 30, , , , 2                   'Shape F
'
LOCATE 8, 13: PRINT "A"; TAB(26); "B"; TAB(38); "C"
LOCATE 23, 13: PRINT "D"; TAB(26); "E"; TAB(38); "F"
```

Figure 13.6 shows the results of DOCIRCLE.BAS. The screen image contains six shapes, in two rows of three. Shapes A through C are in the top row, and shapes D through F are in the bottom row.

Shape A is a complete circle. Shapes B and C are partial circles that demonstrate the flip-flopping of the *start* and *end* parameters. Shape D is a pie-shaped wedge created with negative values for *start* and *end*. Shapes E and F demonstrate how changing *aspect* creates different ellipses.

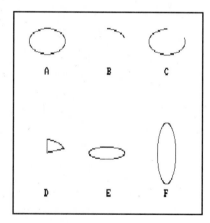

Figure 13.6.

Output from the
DOCIRCLE.BAS program.

Notice that the LOCATE and PRINT instructions in the final two program lines work fine in graphics mode. One nice feature of QBasic's graphics mode is that you can mix text and graphics on the same screen.

A Graphics Language— the *DRAW* Statement

As you can see, QBasic certainly has an impressive repertoire of graphics statements. With PSET, LINE, COLOR, and PAINT, you can readily create a variety of graphic images.

But there is more. You also can describe graphic images with DRAW instructions. A DRAW instruction consists of the keyword DRAW followed by a string expression. The string expression expresses graphic images according to a special graphics language.

S T A T E M E N T

DRAW *stringexpression*

where

stringexpression is a string expression conforming to the conventions of the graphics language.

The DRAW language contains strings that can do the following:

- Produce lines
- Set colors
- Paint areas
- Rotate images
- Scale shapes

With these capabilities, DRAW can do some things, such as image rotation and scaling, which are difficult with QBasic's "regular" graphics statements. On the other hand, DRAW cannot easily produce certain shapes, especially circles and arcs.

Fortunately, DRAW works smoothly with the other QBasic graphics statements. The result is a powerful, integrated graphics capability.

Each DRAW string expression contains one or more fundamental *command string*. The fundamental DRAW command strings consist of a one- or two-letter abbreviation followed, in most cases, by an optional numeric argument. Table 13.7 shows the fundamental DRAW commands.

Table 13.7. Fundamental *DRAW* commands.

Command	Action
U*n**	Move up
D*n*	Move down
L*n*	Move left
R*n*	Move right
E*n*	Move diagonally up and right
F*n*	Move diagonally down and right
G*n*	Move diagonally down and left
H*n*	Move diagonally up and left
M*x*,*y*	Move to point *x,y*
B	Raise pen (move without plotting)
N	Move, but return to original LPR when done
A*n*	Set rotation angle
TA*n*	Set turn angle
C*n*	Set color
S*n*	Set scale factor
P	Paint area
X	Execute substring

* n is an optional numeric argument designating the number of pixels to move for the movement commands, the size of the angle in the rotation commands, the foreground color in the color command, or the scaling factor in the scaling command.

Before using DRAW, you must put the computer in one of QBasic's graphics modes with a SCREEN instruction.

Using Movement Commands

The M command draws a line from the LPR to the point specified by *x,y*. For example, the following instruction draws a line from the LPR to the point (85, 99):

```
DRAW "M 85,99"
```

This has the same effect as the instruction

```
LINE -(85, 99)
```

You can express movement in relative coordinates by preceding the *x* destination with a plus (+) or minus (−) sign. Such a sign designator establishes both the *x* and *y* coordinates as relative. Here are some examples:

```
DRAW "M  23, 48"    'Move to absolute coordinate (23,48)
DRAW "M +23, 48"    'Move 23 pixels right, 48 down from LPR
DRAW "M +23,-48"    'Move 23 pixels right, 48 up from LPR
DRAW "M -23, 48"    'Move 23 pixels left, 48 down from LPR
DRAW "M -23,-48"    'Move 23 pixels left, 48 up from LPR
```

Relative Movement

For relative moves, you can move in any of the eight basic compass directions (see Figure 13.7).

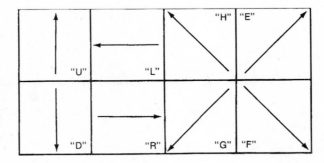

Each of the eight relative movement commands takes an integer argument (*n*) that specifies how many pixels to move. If you omit the argument, a single pixel is drawn in the specified direction. If the argument is negative, movement occurs in the opposite (180 degree) direction. Here are some examples:

```
DRAW "R16"    'Draw a 16-pixel line from LPR to the right
DRAW "E"      'Draw 1 pixel "northeast" from the LPR
```

```
DRAW "U8"      'Draw an 8-pixel line from LPR upward
DRAW "U-8"     'Draw an 8-pixel line from LPR downward
```

After any movement command, the LPR is set to the destination point.

Movement Prefixes

Two prefixes are available to modify a movement command:

- ■ B Move without plotting; for example, DRAW "BD14"

- ■ N Move without updating LPR; for example, DRAW "NM8,29"

Use B to adjust the LPR without drawing any line. Use N to draw a line without updating the LPR.

Forming Command Strings

The fundamental command strings can be, and usually are, grouped together to form one string expression. For example, the following program produces the kite shown in Figure 13.8. Notice how the individual command strings are joined into one string literal.

```
SCREEN 1          'Must be in graphics mode to use DRAW
DRAW "H25 E25 F25 G25 D10 NL5 NR5 D10"      'Draw Kite
```

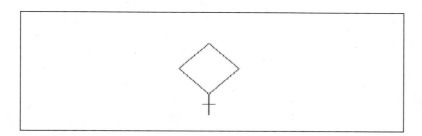

Figure 13.8.

A kite produced by DRAW.

In DRAW strings, blank spaces are not significant between the fundamental command strings. You can use spaces to separate commands for readability, but such spaces are not required. Also, semicolons are optional delimiters. Upper- and lowercase are interchangeable for the command letters. For example, you could write the kite command as follows:

```
DRAW "H25 e25f25G 25; D10 N L5; Nr5d10"
```

It sure is harder to read that way, but it's legal.

Using Rotation Commands

The A*n* command causes all subsequent images to be rotated at the angle (*n* * 90) degrees where *n* can be 0, 1, 2, or 3. For example, DRAW "A2" rotates subsequent images 180 degrees.

The TA*n* command (Turn Angle) sets the rotation angle to *n* where *n* can range from –360 to +360 degrees. Negative *n* causes clockwise rotations, and positive *n* causes counterclockwise rotations.

Notice that these commands specify angles in degrees. This is a departure from the usual QBasic standard of angles measured in radians.

Figure 13.9 shows the kite rotated clockwise 30 degrees. Notice in the following program fragment that a TA command is added to cause the rotation:

```
SCREEN 1
DRAW "TA-30"                     'Set 30-degree rotation
DRAW "H25 E25 F25 G25 D10 NL5 NR5 D10"      'Draw Kite
```

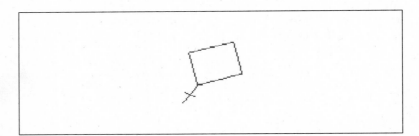

Figure 13.9.

The kite is rotated 30 degrees.

Scaling an Image

S*n* makes subsequent images larger or smaller. The parameter *n* sets the scale factor to *n*/4. Thus "S12" creates images three times larger, and "S2" halves the size. The value of *n* can range from 1 to 255. The default for *n* is 4, which sets the scaling to unity (that is, no scaling).

To see the scaling effect, try adding a DRAW "S8" instruction in either kite drawing program just after the SCREEN 1 instruction. The kite now becomes twice the original size.

Colorizing and Painting

You can adjust the foreground (drawing) color with the C*n* command. Here, as usual, *n* can assume any value consistent with the current SCREEN mode and your system's video hardware.

In either kite program, try adding the following instruction immediately after the SCREEN instruction:

```
DRAW "C2"
```

You will see a magenta kite.

One use of the C command is to erase all or part of an already drawn figure. Just set the drawing color to the background color (usually black). Then redraw the figure. Bingo, the figure disappears.

Use the P command to paint the interior of any enclosed shape.

P *paintcolor, bordercolor*

where

   paintcolor specifies the color to use for painting.

The entire area is painted until a boundary of the color *bordercolor* is reached. Painting begins at the current LPR.

S T A T E M E N T

To demonstrate the P and C commands, the following program draws the kite in magenta with the interior painted cyan:

```
SCREEN 1
DRAW "C2"                            'Set color to magenta
DRAW "H25 E25 F25 G25 D10 NL5 NR5 D10"    'Draw Kite
DRAW "BU25"                          'Move LPR inside kite
DRAW "P1, 2"                         'Paint interior cyan
```

Using Variables with *DRAW*

So far, all our example DRAW strings and numeric arguments have been literals, but you also can use variables.

For numeric variables as parameters, however, the syntax requires the command letter to be followed by an equal sign and then a string representation of the numeric variable's memory address. QBasic's VARPTR$ function returns such a string. (Don't confuse VARPTR$, which returns a string, with VARPTR, which returns an integer numeric value.)

Table 13.8 shows some DRAW instruction written with numeric literals and the equivalent instructions using numeric variables.

Table 13.8. Using numeric variables with *DRAW*.	
Instruction	**Equivalent Form with Numeric Variables**
DRAW "R65"	Span% = 65: DRAW "R =" + VARPTR$(Span%)
DRAW "P1,2"	C% = 1: B% = 2:
	DRAW "P ="+ VARPTR$(C%) +", =" + VARPTR$(B%)
DRAW "U3 L6"	X% = 3: Y% = 6
	DRAW "U =" + VARPTR$(X%) + "L =" + VARPTR$(Y%)

T I P   **Use String Variables for *DRAW* Arguments**

DRAW arguments can be any string expressions, including string variables. You can assign an entire command string to a string variable and then DRAW the variable directly. For example, here is an alternative way to draw the diamond part of the kite:

```
Diamond$ = "H25 E25 F25 G25"
```

```
DRAW Diamond$
```

Take advantage of string variables to store frequently used command strings. Then you can "draw" the strings with simple string variables rather than lengthy string literals.

Using Substrings

The X subcommand specifies that a secondary string variable be executed from within the primary string. This is like a GOSUB. The primary string makes a "call" to a secondary string command.

The syntax of the X subcommand, like numeric variables, requires that the memory location of the secondary string variable be identified with VARPTR$.

For example, the following instruction draws two enlarged, cyan diamonds (assuming that Diamond$ is defined as shown in the previous sidebar):

```
DRAW "S8 C1 X" + VARPTR$(Diamond$) + "BR15 X" + VARPTR$(Diamond$)
```

The X subcommand is awkward. You can duplicate the effect of the X subcommand simply by concatenating direct strings. For example, the following instruction draws the same two diamonds:

```
DRAW "S8 C1" + Diamond$ + "BR15" + Diamond$
```

The *POINT* Function

The POINT function returns information about a given pixel. There are two distinct forms of POINT: the color form and the coordinate form.

The Color Form of the *POINT* Function

In this form, POINT returns the color of the pixel at the specified location.

```
POINT(xycoordinates)
```
where

    xycoordinates specify an *x* and *y* position.

The returned value is the color cup number from 0 to 3. If *xycoordinates* specify a location off the screen, POINT returns a value of –1.

For example, the following instruction assigns to Hue% the color of the pixel at location (65, 30):

```
Hue% = POINT(65, 30)
```

You can use POINT to specify the *color* parameter in various graphing instructions. For example, the following instruction turns the pixel at location (233, 108) into the same color as the pixel at (44, 21):

```
PSET(233, 108), POINT(44, 21)
```

The Coordinate Form of the *POINT* Function

In the second form of the POINT function, only one parameter appears. The parameter can have the value of 0 or 1. POINT returns LPR information as shown in Table 13.9.

Table 13.9. *POINT* function options.	
Function	**Meaning**
POINT(0)	Returns x-coordinate of LPR
POINT(1)	Returns y-coordinate of LPR

Actually, POINT can accept the parameter values of 2 and 3 as well as 0 and 1. The parameter values of 2 and 3 apply when you change the graphics coordinate system. This topic is discussed in Chapter 20, "Using Advanced Graphics."

Clipping

What happens if you try to graph outside the normal screen boundary? For example, suppose that you specify LINE coordinates above the upper edge of the screen. Is this an error?

No. Most graphics instructions, such as LINE and CIRCLE, permit graphics coordinates outside the screen boundaries. Such instructions draw only the portion of the image lying inside the screen boundaries.

This process of suppressing out-of-bounds graphics is called *clipping*. To understand clipping, think of your video screen lying inside a much larger imaginary canvas. This large canvas permits coordinates extending past those of your video screen.

LINE and other graphics instructions work on this large canvas. Whenever part of the image comes into your screen area, the graphics become visible. Anything solely on the imaginary canvas is clipped.

The following program demonstrates the clipping of a circle and a box. Notice that the center of the circle lies above the upper edge of the video screen. The LINE instruction draws a rectangle with one side lying to the left of the screen boundary.

```
SCREEN 2
CIRCLE (300, -50), 200
LINE (-90, 50)-(150, 150), , B
```

Adjusting the Viewport— the *VIEW* Statement

With a VIEW instruction, you confine graphics within a specified rectangular area of your video screen. This area is called a *viewport*. Anything drawn outside the viewport is clipped.

VIEW has two forms, with and without the SCREEN keyword.

VIEW *(upleftxy)*-*(lowrightxy)*, *viewcolor*, *bordercolor*

or

VIEW SCREEN *(upleftxy)*-*(lowrightxy)*, *viewcolor*, *bordercolor*

where

upleftxy specifies the upper left corner of the viewport in absolute coordinates,

lowrightxy specifies the lower right corner of the viewport in absolute coordinates,

viewcolor specifies the color to paint the viewport,

and

bordercolor specifies a border color to draw around the viewport.

The *viewcolor* and *bordercolor* parameters are optional.

S
T
A
T
E
M
E
N
T

When you establish a viewport, PSET, PRESET, LINE, CIRCLE, and DRAW work only within the viewport. However, text printing and related functions, such as LOCATE, still operate on the full screen.

If *viewcolor* is present, the entire rectangular area of the viewport is painted the specified color. If *bordercolor* is present and if there is screen space available, a one-pixel-wide border is drawn around the viewport in the specified color.

When you omit the SCREEN keyword, subsequent coordinate references are relative to the upper left corner of the viewport. Graphic images are thus translated (displaced) into the viewport. When you include SCREEN, coordinate references remain relative to the upper left corner of the video screen. In either case, graphics outside the viewport are clipped.

CLS clears only the viewport area, not the entire screen (see the discussion of CLS later in this chapter).

You can activate only a single viewport at any one time. A second VIEW instruction redefines the viewport.

VIEW without any arguments restores the entire screen as the viewport. Using a SCREEN instruction to change video modes also cancels any previous viewport setting.

The *upleftxy* and *lowrightxy* parameters actually designate *any* two diagonally opposite corners, not necessarily the upper-left and lower-right corners.

Listing 13.10, VIEWPORT.BAS, demonstrates the use of viewports with and without the SCREEN keyword. Notice that the LOCATE instructions position text relative to the whole screen. The output of this program is shown in Figure 13.10.

Listing 13.10.   The VIEWPORT.BAS program.

```
REM Program: VIEWPORT.BAS (Demonstrate viewports and clipping)
SCREEN 1
CLS
VIEW (20, 20)-(300, 180), , 1             'Cyan border
   CIRCLE (140, 80), 120                   'x,y relative to viewport
   LOCATE 4, 14
   PRINT "Outer Viewport"
VIEW SCREEN (50, 45)-(270, 155), 0, 2     'Magenta border
   CIRCLE (160, 100), 80                   'x,y relative to screen
   LOCATE 12, 14
   PRINT "Inner Viewport"
END
```

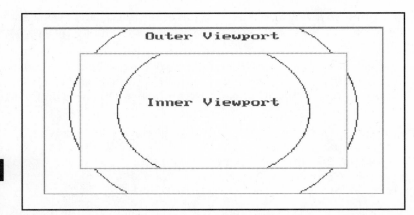

Figure 13.10.

The output of the VIEWPORT.BAS program.

Mixing Text and Graphics

As you have seen throughout this chapter, you can mix text with graphics. The normal text statements, such as PRINT and LOCATE, work correctly in the graphics modes. You can superimpose text onto graphic images and graphic images onto text.

Scrolling text (by printing on the bottom line with a carriage return) causes the entire screen to scroll. Graphics and text scroll upward together.

A WIDTH instruction can toggle the screen mode. A WIDTH 80 instruction issued from SCREEN mode 1 causes the graphics mode to switch to mode 2—just as though you issued a SCREEN 2 instruction. Similarly, a WIDTH 40 instruction from SCREEN mode 2 acts just as if you had issued a SCREEN 1 instruction.

Clearing the Screen—*CLS* Revisited

You can append an optional argument to CLS to control which viewport (text or graphics) clears.

CLS *clearmode*

where

    clearmode is an integer number from 0 to 2 that specifies which viewport to clear (see Table 13.10).

The *clearmode* parameter is optional.

S T A T E M E N T

Table 13.10. Results of various *CLS* instructions.

Instruction	Effect
CLS 0	Clears the entire screen of text and graphics
CLS 1	Clears the graphics viewport
CLS 2	Clears only the text viewport

continues

Table 13.10. Continued

Instruction	Effect
CLS	Clears the graphics viewport if a graphics viewport is active (that is, if a VIEW instruction has been executed)
	Clears the text viewport if no graphics viewport is active
	Clears the entire screen if no viewport is active (that is, if no VIEW SCREEN instruction and no VIEW PRINT instruction has been executed)

Advanced Graphics

Much material has been covered in this chapter, but the surface has barely been scratched. Hold on, that's not true—this certainly has "scratched the surface." However, QBasic provides many graphics features that have not yet been mentioned.

Chapter 20, "Using Advanced Graphics," introduces the following advanced graphics topics:

- Drawing stylized lines
- Filling areas with patterned tiles
- Animating graphic images
- Customizing the coordinate system
- Using the graphing options available with EGA, VGA, and MCGA video adapters
- Storing images on alternate screen "pages"

Summary

QBasic provides extensive graphics capability. You initialize graphics with a SCREEN instruction. In graphic modes, the screen is a rectangular grid of tiny dots called *pixels*. You have control over each pixel. By turning the pixels on or off (white or black), or making them various colors, you can create exciting visual screens.

Of course, to use graphics, your computer must have the appropriate hardware. QBasic supports CGA (medium- and high-resolution graphics), EGA, VGA, and MCGA video adapters. With a color monitor, QBasic can produce color graphics.

A number of special instructions aid you in drawing images. LINE draws straight lines and rectangles. CIRCLE draws circles, ellipses, and arcs. PSET and PRESET turn on any individual pixel. Each of these instructions works with color as well as black and white.

Speaking of color, the COLOR instruction adjusts the default colors. In medium-resolution graphics (mode 1), you can make the background any one of 16 colors. A COLOR instruction also selects one of two color palettes; each palette has three predefined colors for drawing objects.

High-resolution graphics (mode 2) does not support color. Only black-and-white graphics are possible. However, the screen has twice as many pixels, so you can create finer detailed drawings than with mode 1.

DRAW provides a separate facility for specifying graphic images. With DRAW instructions, you specify graphics parameters using special string expressions. DRAW can scale and rotate images.

Graphics modes provide full text support. The various text mode statements like PRINT and LOCATE work smoothly in graphics modes. You can integrate text and graphics with text superimposed directly onto graphic images.

Using Sequential Disk Files

As a programmer, you face a recurring challenge: getting data into your programs. Most programs manipulate data in one way or another. After all, you are manipulating data when you simply add two numbers or when you display text on-screen. Take a moment and think about the ways you get data into your programs.

You are already familiar with two fundamental techniques for inputting data in your programs:

■ *Store the data directly in the program.* This is the simplest method. An assignment instruction such as

```
City$ = "Phoenix"
```

stores the data ("Phoenix" in this case) as part of the program itself. Also, DATA and READ instructions (see Chapter 9, "Managing Large Amounts of Data") store data directly in the program.

■ *Ask the user for the data.* When the person running the program must supply data, your program can prompt the user to type in the data from the keyboard. Your primary tool for this method is the INPUT statement (introduced in Chapter 7, "Program Flow and Decision Making," and discussed in depth in Chapter 16, "Using Hardware Devices").

These methods work fine but they're only appropriate when the amount of data is relatively small. What if your data requirements become more demanding? Suppose you want to write a program that manages a large database such as your baseball card collection, a mailing list, or the inventory of a hardware store. It's just not feasible to store all the necessary data inside the program or to ask the user to supply the data when the program runs. Furthermore, the data changes with time and therefore needs periodic updating.

The common solution to these problems is data files on disk. The data file can be on a floppy disk or a hard disk. Once a data file exists, your program can read the data directly from the file, process the data, and then write a new (or updated) data file directly to the disk.

By storing data on disk files, independently from the programs, you derive many tangible benefits:

■ Data files can be maintained and updated.

■ Large databases can be accessed conveniently.

■ Programs are kept intact and relatively small.

■ Files can be shared by several programs.

■ Data files created from external sources (such as a word processor or spreadsheet) can be read.

QBasic supports three kinds of data files: *sequential, random-access,* and *binary.* This chapter and the next discuss how to use each file type and the advantages and disadvantages of each. This chapter covers sequential files; the following chapter covers random-access and binary files.

Of course, if you work with disk files, you become immediately involved with disk directories. This is normally the domain of DOS, but QBasic furnishes a number of file maintenance tools.

Here are the main topics covered in this chapter:

■ Maintaining disk directories from QBasic

■ Using sequential files

Files and Directories in DOS: a Brief Tutorial

As a user of QBasic, you are unavoidably involved with PC DOS or MS-DOS. DOS places certain demands on what you can and cannot do with disk files. Substantial discussion of DOS is beyond the scope of this book. However, in the interests of establishing some common ground and terminology, a brief tutorial on DOS file maintenance is included here. For more details, consult your DOS documentation or one of the many excellent books on DOS, such as *Using MS-DOS 5,* published by Que Corporation.

Your computer has one or more disk *drives*. Each drive is designated with a letter followed by a colon. Floppy disk drives (into which you insert floppy disks) are usually designated A: and B:; fixed (hard) disk drives are usually designated C: and D:. For the purposes of this discussion, the term *drive* refers not only to the hardware drive, but also to the media currently in the drive. Thus, "storing a file on the A: drive" means storing a file on the disk in drive A:.

Each drive is organized in a *directory* structure. The base directory is called the *root*. The root can spawn one or more *subdirectories,* each of which can also have one or more subdirectories, and so on. (The terms directory and subdirectory are used interchangeably.)

A *file* is a collection of bytes given a name and stored in a directory. Two different directories can contain files with the same name. Such files, however, are independent and can contain completely different data.

To uniquely identify a file, you must specify not only the name of the file, but also the *path* to the file. The path consists of the drive and the chain of directories from the root to the directory containing the file.

Directory names are one to eight characters long. In a path, the backslash character (\) separates directory names and also indicates the root directory at the front of the chain.

Filenames also have one to eight characters, but optionally can include an extension of zero to three characters. If included, the extension is separated with a period. Thus MYPROG, MYPROG.BAS, M.ME, and ABC123. all are valid filenames. In a file or directory name, upper- and lowercase letters are not differentiated; MyProg.Bas and MYPROG.BAS are the same file.

A *filespec* is the complete specification of a file. As mentioned, this includes the path to the file as well as the name of the file. Here are some examples:

A:\QBASIC\MYPROG.BAS

B:\MYPROG.BAS

C:\LISTINGS\HOMES\3BEDRM\SALES.DTA

In each case, the filename appears after the last backslash. The path name is the portion up to but not including the filename. The path name consists of the drive designation and the directory chain.

At all times, DOS maintains a default drive and a default path on each drive. Filespecs can be given relative to these defaults. For example, A:BASEBALL\CARDS.DTA refers to a file named CARDS.DTA that resides on the A: drive in the subdirectory BASEBALL.

The key point is that BASEBALL is a subdirectory of the current (or default) directory on the A: drive. Notice that no backslash appears immediately after the drive designator; this indicates a relative path. The simple filespec ROSTER.DTA means that the file resides in the default directory of the default drive.

When you first turn on your computer, the default directory on each drive is the root directory.

File and Directory Maintenance in QBasic

QBasic has six statements that perform DOS-like commands (see Table 14.1). Use these statements to do file and directory manipulation from within your programs or directly from QBasic's Immediate window.

Table 14.1. QBasic's DOS-like statements.

QBasic Statement	Equivalent DOS Command	DOS Abbreviation	Effect
MKDIR	MKDIR	MD	Creates a directory
RMDIR	RMDIR	RD	Removes (deletes) a directory
CHDIR	CHDIR	CD	Changes current directory
FILES	DIR		Lists files in a directory
KILL	ERASE	DEL	Deletes a file
NAME	RENAME	REN	Renames a file

The syntax of these six statements is straightforward.

STATEMENT

MKDIR *pathname*

RMDIR *pathname*

CHDIR *pathname*

FILES *filespec*

KILL *filespec*

NAME *oldfilespec* AS *newfilespec*

where

pathname is a string expression specifying a path;

filespec, *oldfilespec*, and *newfilespec* are string expressions that specify a file.

For FILES, the *filespec* parameter is optional; for the other statements, the parameters are mandatory.

Using *MKDIR, RMDIR,* and *CHDIR*

In a MKDIR, RMDIR, or CHDIR instruction, the *pathname* parameter can optionally include a drive designator. If you omit the drive in *pathname*, QBasic assumes the default drive (from where you invoked QBasic). Standard DOS path-naming conventions apply.

Notice that *pathname* must be a string—either a literal (in double quotation marks) or a string variable. For example, to create a directory called \CLIENTS on your B: drive, you could use

```
MKDIR "B:\CLIENTS"        'Notice the quotation marks
```

or

```
NewDir$ = "B:\CLIENTS"
MKDIR NewDir$             'The path is stored in a string variable
```

but not

```
MKDIR B:\CLIENTS          'The path is not a string
```

pathname has a limit of 127 characters. If *pathname* is the null string, or if *pathname* does not designate a valid directory, a run-time error occurs (Path not found or Bad file name).

The statements MKDIR, RMDIR, and CHDIR operate just like their DOS counter-parts. Refer to your DOS documentation for additional information. Notice that if you change the directory (with CHDIR) on the drive from which you invoked QBasic, you will be in that default directory when your program terminates.

Using *FILES, KILL,* and *NAME*

In a FILES, KILL, or NAME instruction, the *filespec* parameter can optionally include a drive and path specification. If omitted, the default (or current) path is selected. Again, standard DOS naming conventions apply. There is a 63-character limit on a *filespec*. Except with the NAME instruction, wildcard characters (* and ?) are permitted in a *filespec*. If you're not familiar with wildcard characters, see your DOS documentation for details.

Using the *FILES* Statement

FILES displays on-screen a list of files and subdirectories in a disk drive. The effect is similar to the DOS command DIR/W. Multiple files are shown on one line. Subdirectories are indicated with the notation <DIR>. The listing termi-nates with the number of free bytes on the drive referenced by the *filespec* parameter. If you omit the *filespec* parameter, all the files in the current directory are listed.

368

Here are some examples of FILES instructions:

```
FILES "B:\HOMES\*.*"       'Lists all files in subdirectory

FILES "VERSION?.TXT"       'Lists all 8-character files whose
                           'names start with "VERSION" and
                           'have a ".TXT" extension

FILES                      'Lists all files on current directory

FILES "A:"                 'Lists all files in the current
                           'directory of drive A:

FILES "A:\"                'Lists all files in root directory of
                           'A: drive
```

Using the *KILL* Statement

KILL deletes only files, not directories. Use a RMDIR instruction to delete directories.

Be careful when using wildcard characters in a *filespec*. You might accidentally erase more than you bargained for. If you try to KILL a file that is open, a File not found error occurs. (Opening and closing files is discussed in this chapter.)

Using the *NAME* Statement

NAME renames a file. The *oldfilespec* parameter identifies the existing file; *newfilespec* is the new name for the file. When *oldfilespec* and *newfilespec* specify the same path, NAME simply renames the file on the same drive. After the NAME instruction, the file exists in the same location on the disk, but with a new name. As such, NAME performs the same function in QBasic that RENAME does in DOS.

However, NAME can do something that the DOS RENAME command cannot. NAME can move a file to a different directory on the same drive. (Be careful that you don't confuse directory paths.) For example:

```
NAME "\QB\GAMES\PINGPONG.BAS" AS "TENNIS.BAS"
```

This instruction moves the file named PINGPONG.BAS from the \QB\GAMES subdirectory on the current drive to the default directory on the current drive. After the move, the file is renamed TENNIS.BAS and no longer exists in any form on the \QB\GAMES directory. The point is that unless \QB\GAMES is the default directory on the current drive, the file changes directories.

To simply rename a file on the same drive, you should include the path with each filespec. The example at hand becomes

```
NAME "\QB\GAMES\PINGPONG.BAS" AS "\QB\GAMES\TENNIS.BAS"
```

Manipulating Directories Directly with the *Immediate* Window

Although you certainly can use MKDIR, RMDIR, CHDIR, FILES, KILL, and NAME inside your programs, these instructions are also quite useful directly from the Immediate window.

For example, try this. Place a formatted disk containing some files into your B: drive. (If your machine does not have a B: drive, you can use the A: drive or the C: drive if your machine has a hard disk. Simply replace the letter B: in the following instructions with A: or C: as appropriate.) Now press F6 until the Immediate window becomes active. Type the following instruction and press Enter:

```
FILES "B:\"
```

QBasic responds by displaying a listing of the files (and subdirectories) on the root directory of your disk.

For example, our test disk contained two files: the QBasic program TEST.BAS and another file named OURSTUFF.DAT. Here's our output:

```
FILES "B:\"
B:\
TEST    .BAS      OURSTUFF.DAT
 360448 Bytes free
```

The notation 360448 Bytes free indicates the amount of unused disk space on the specified drive. This amount and the names of the actual files will vary on your test disk.

Now let's create a subdirectory named QUE. You can use MKDIR and then FILES to verify the directory's creation:

```
MKDIR "B:\QUE"
```

```
FILES "B:\"
B:\
TEST    .BAS      OURSTUFF.DAT      QUE        <DIR>
 359424 Bytes free
```

QBasic displays the annotation `<DIR>` to indicate that QUE is a subdirectory rather than a filename. The number of free bytes is less than before because some disk space was necessary to store the new subdirectory.

Last, remove the new subdirectory with `RMDIR` and return the disk back to its original configuration. Remember that you are now typing and issuing these instructions directly from the `Immediate` window.

```
RMDIR "B:\QUE"

FILES "B:\"
TEST    .BAS      OURSTUFF.DAT
 360448 Bytes free
```

Manipulating Data Files—General Techniques

Now that we've established a background of DOS file and directory maintenance, let's refocus our attention to data files on disk. As mentioned, QBasic supports three types of data files.

Sequential files store data as ASCII text. Information is written to the file in much the same way as information is displayed on the video screen.

Random-access files store data in special QBasic internal formats. Such files require a rigid file structure.

Binary files store data as individual bytes. No file structure exists and no special internal formats are assumed.

Which file type is best? As you might expect, each type is better in certain situations.

In general, programs that manipulate sequential files are relatively easy to write and understand, but reading and writing the files is relatively slow. Random-access files require more programming complexity, but the I/O operations are relatively fast. Binary files provide maximum flexibility, but impose the greatest demands on the programmer to keep track of the file organization. In the next two chapters, much more is said about the trade-offs.

Whether a program uses sequential, random-access, or binary files, some general techniques are common to all three file types. To communicate with a disk file, a program must follow these essential steps:

1. Open the data file. With the `OPEN` statement, you inform QBasic of the filename, file type, and how the program expects to use the file.

2. Read data from and/or write data to the file. QBasic provides a variety of statements to perform I/O operations.

3. Close the data file. With the CLOSE statement, your program terminates I/O operations on the data file.

Using the *OPEN* Statement

Before using any disk file, you must establish a communication link. An OPEN instruction serves several purposes:

- Declares the name and path of the data file
- Establishes the file type and the I/O mode
- Opens a communications channel between the program and the file
- Associates an integer number with the data file

The various forms of the OPEN instruction are examined in detail throughout this chapter and the next as each file type is examined.

Using the *CLOSE* Statement

After your program concludes I/O activity on a data file, use a CLOSE instruction to cancel the communications link. CLOSE terminates the association between the data file on disk and the corresponding file number. The CLOSE statement is studied in detail as each file type is studied.

Using Files for Database Maintenance

The most common application for sequential files and random-access files is database maintenance. A *database* is simply a collection of related information. For our purposes, each database is stored on a disk file.

A database consists of a series of *records*. Each record is divided into one or more *fields*. For example, in a personnel list, each employee becomes a record in the database file. The fields for each employee might include name, department, salary, and service date.

Or consider a database of your stock investments. Each stock you own is a record. The fields might be the name of the stock, date of purchase, purchase price, and the current value.

A Coin Collection—a Sample Database

To provide a common thread for the next two chapters, a sample database is needed. Let's use a coin collection. As a budding numismatist, you decide to create a database file to maintain a list of your coin assets.

Each coin is a record in your database. For every coin, you want to maintain four items of information:

- The year the coin was minted
- The category of coin (penny, dime, quarter, and so on)
- The value of the coin
- Any additional pertinent information about the coin

Let's assume your coin collection consists of three coins. (Okay, you're not Donald Trump yet, but you've got to start somewhere!)

Your database file will have three records, one record for each coin. You could organize the three records in this database as shown in Table 14.2.

Table 14.2. A coin collection database.

Year	Category	Value	Comments
1910	Lincoln penny	$ 70.00	S mint mark, uncirculated
1916	Mercury dime	$ 47.25	
1935	Silver dollar	$200.00	Bought at auction for $75

As you examine sequential and random-access files in this and the following chapter, you learn to write programs that manipulate this database.

Sequential Files

Sequential files are written as ASCII text. This gives the files a degree of portability; many word-processing programs and other applications programs can read and write ASCII files. Also, you can use the TYPE command from DOS to display a sequential file on your screen.

Within a record, fields are separated by commas. Record boundaries are maintained automatically. QBasic provides several statements to read and write sequential files conveniently. Therefore, programming is relatively easy.

However, there are two main drawbacks to sequential files:

■ You must read records sequentially. For example, if you want information in the 50th record, you must read through the initial 49 records first. This process is relatively slow.

■ You cannot read and write to a sequential file simultaneously. You must open the file for either reading or writing and close the file before reopening it in the other mode.

You might think of a sequential file as something like a cassette music tape (see Figure 14.1). Individual songs on the tape are like records on the file. To listen to a song in the middle of the tape, you must first play through the previous songs. To read a record in the middle of the file, you must first read the previous records.

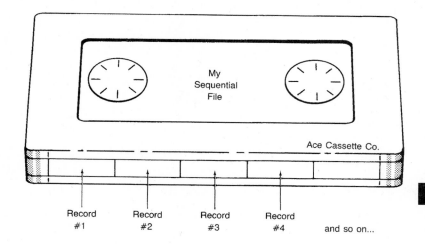

Figure 14.1.

A sequential file is like a cassette music tape.

Creating a Sequential File

When creating a sequential file, your program must follow these steps:

1. OPEN the file as a sequential file for writing.

2. Prepare your data for writing to the file.

3. Use the WRITE# instruction to write data to the file.

4. CLOSE the file.

Let's examine each step and then try a sample program.

Opening the File

The OPEN statement has many forms. Here is the fundamental syntax you use when creating a new sequential file.

<table>
<tr>
<td>
S
T
A
T
E
M
E
N
T
</td>
<td>

OPEN *filespec* FOR OUTPUT AS #*filenum*

where

    filespec is a string expression that specifies the name (and optionally the path) of the new sequential data file

and

    filenum is an integer expression from 1 to 255 that associates a numeric value with the opened file.

</td>
</tr>
</table>

For example, the following instruction opens a file named MYDATA.QUE (on the root directory of the B: drive) as a sequential file that is being created. A file number of 35 is assigned to this file.

```
OPEN "B:\MYDATA.QUE" FOR OUTPUT AS #35
```

The pound character (#) is optional before the filenum parameter. That is, you could also write the previous instruction as follows:

```
OPEN "B:\MYDATA.QUE" FOR OUTPUT AS 35   'No # before file number
```

The phrase FOR OUTPUT tells QBasic that this file is a sequential file to which the program will be writing output. (As you will see later, OPEN accepts other phrases with other meanings.)

When you open a file for OUTPUT, that file does not need to be one that already exists. In fact, the file should *not* be one that already exists. Why? Because if the file already exists, QBasic completely erases the old file contents. Don't open an existing file FOR OUTPUT unless you intend to create a brand new file.

Make sure your OPEN instruction specifies the path and file correctly. You don't want to lose data inadvertently by specifying the wrong file. Of course, it's a good idea to have a backup version of your important files for such emergencies.

The file number (35 in our present example) provides a convenient way to refer to the file in later program instructions. As you will see, when you want to write data to the file, you instruct QBasic to write on file number 35 rather than specifying the full-blown file name. The OPEN instruction tells QBasic exactly what file you mean by file number 35.

Preparing the Data

When you first create a database file, you must somehow get the data into your program. The trick here is to decide the best way to enter the data. Several methods exist. You usually will use one or a combination of the following techniques:

- Enter data explicitly in DATA instructions; use READ instructions.

- Prompt the user for data with INPUT instructions. (The sample program that follows uses this technique.)

- Read data from other data files or devices.

- Compute data values using various QBasic functions.

Writing the Data

When each record is ready to write, use a WRITE# instruction to actually write the record to the disk file. WRITE# works with both strings and numbers.

```
WRITE #filenum, expressionlist
```

where

    filenum is the file number

and

    expressionlist is a list of expressions separated by commas.

S T A T E M E N T

Each WRITE# instruction writes one record to the file. Each expression in *expressionlist* is the data for one field of the record.

WRITE# does some special formatting, which is examined in the sample program. WRITE# sends data to a file in the same form that WRITE sends output to the video screen. See the discussion of WRITE in Chapter 12, "Writing Text on the Video Screen," for more details.

Often you place the WRITE# instruction inside a loop. This loop processes all the records in the data file.

Closing the File

After all the records are written to the file, close the file with a CLOSE instruction.

**S
T
A
T
E
M
E
N
T**

CLOSE #*filenum*

where

   filenum is an integer expression that specifies the file to close.

As with OPEN instructions, the pound sign (#) is optional.

For example, use the following instruction to close file number 35 (that was previously opened for output):

CLOSE #35

CLOSE terminates the association of the file number with the data file. As a result, the file number becomes available for a subsequent OPEN instruction. CLOSE also flushes the file buffer, which means that all information written to the file is properly processed.

The Sample Program SFCREATE.BAS

Now let's put these QBasic statements into action. Remember the coin collection? Listing 14.1 is a program called SFCREATE.BAS, which creates a new sequential data file called MYCOINS.SEQ. The user responds to various prompts to supply the data.

Listing 14.1. The SFCREATE.BAS program.

```
REM Program: SFCREATE.BAS (Create a sequential file)

PRINT "Creating Sequential Data File: B:MYCOINS.SEQ"
PRINT
OPEN "B:MYCOINS.SEQ" FOR OUTPUT AS #1
```

```
DO
    INPUT "Year (or <Enter> when all done)"; Year%
    IF Year% = 0 THEN EXIT DO      'End input loop
    INPUT "Category of Coin"; Category$
    INPUT "Value"; Value!
    LINE INPUT "Comments (if any)? "; Comment$
    WRITE #1, Year%, Category$, Value!, Comment$
    PRINT
LOOP                  'Get data for next coin

CLOSE #1
PRINT "All done - B:MYCOINS.SEQ is created"
END
```

The OPEN instruction declares that the file will be written on drive B:. Because no specific path is specified, QBasic assumes that the file should appear in the current directory on drive B:. This directory is the root directory (unless you changed the default directory before starting QBasic). You can (and often do) specify an explicit directory path in the OPEN instruction such as B:\DATA\MYCOINS.SEQ or B:\MYCOINS.SEQ (root directory). The OPEN instruction assigns the file number 1 to the newly opened file.

Each data record corresponds to one coin in the collection. Each record contains four fields: the year the coin was minted, the category of the coin, the value of the coin, and any pertinent comments about the coin. Two of the fields (Year and Value) are numeric, and two fields (Category and Comment) are string.

The year is a whole number, such as 1976, suitable for an integer variable: Year%. The value is expressed in dollars and cents, such as 47.25, suitable for a single-precision variable: Value!. The category and comment are stored in the string variables Category$ and Comment$, respectively.

The main work of the program is done inside the DO-LOOP block. For each coin, an INPUT or LINE INPUT instruction prompts you for each of the four pieces of information. You must input the value as a number in dollars. However, the dollar sign is not part of the input. Thus, if the value of the coin is $103.50, you must type 103.50, not $103.50.

The comment field uses a LINE INPUT instruction because commas might be used as part of the input string. A regular INPUT instruction would treat such commas as input delimiters.

For each coin, the program prompts you for the necessary information and stores the values in the variables Year%, Category$, Value!, and Comment$. Then the WRITE #1 instruction inside the DO-LOOP writes the record to the data file.

Notice that all four data fields are written with a single WRITE# instruction. The #1 is the same file number you assigned to the file in the OPEN instruction.

When all the data is entered, you simply press the Enter key in response to the next Year prompt. This assigns a value of zero to the variable Year%. Notice how the IF instruction tests for this condition and terminates the loop when Year% has the value zero.

Here is a sample run of SFCREATE.BAS. Boldface type indicates what you type.

```
Creating Sequential Data File: B:MYCOINS.SEQ

Year (or <Enter> when all done)? 1910
Category of Coin? Lincoln Penny
Value? 70
Comments (if any)? S mint mark, uncirculated

Year (or <Enter> when all done)? 1916
Category of Coin? Mercury Dime
Value? 47.25
Comments (if any)?

Year (or <Enter> when all done)? 1935
Category of Coin? Silver Dollar
Value? 200
Comments (if any)? Bought at auction for $75

Year (or <Enter> when all done)?
All done - B:MYCOINS.SEQ is created
```

Examining a Sequential Data File

You've now created the sequential data file MYCOINS.SEQ. What does the file look like? Let's find out.

Examining the file is easy. Because sequential files are standard ASCII text files, you can use the TYPE command in DOS to view the file contents. Or you can view and modify the file with most word processors and text editors.

Try QBasic's editor to see what MYCOINS.SEQ looks like. From the Main menu, select the Open option in the File submenu. Specify the file B:MYCOINS.SEQ (or whatever path and name you have used). You should see the following:

```
1910,"Lincoln Penny",70,"S mint mark, uncirculated"
1916,"Mercury Dime",47.25,""
1935,"Silver Dollar",200,"Bought at auction for $75"
```

The three records (lines) of this file were created with QBasic's WRITE# statement. Notice how WRITE# formats the output. Within a record, WRITE# places a comma between adjacent fields.

String values are enclosed in double quotation marks. This avoids ambiguity if a string value contains an embedded comma. A null string appears as two consecutive quotation marks—for example, the comment field (final field) of the second record. Numbers do not contain any leading or trailing blank spaces. This saves disk space by minimizing the file size.

As you will soon see, you can read sequential files with INPUT# instructions. WRITE# creates records in the exact form that INPUT# expects.

Appending a Sequential File

Suppose you acquire some new coins. To accommodate your growing collection, you want to write a program that adds new records to the end of your existing sequential file, MYCOINS.SEQ. The process of adding new records is called *appending* the file.

Appending sequential files is easy with QBasic. You open the file in a special mode called APPEND. In your OPEN instruction, use the phrase FOR APPEND rather than FOR OUTPUT. For example, the OPEN instruction of SFCREATE.BAS would now look like this:

```
OPEN "B:MYCOINS.SEQ" FOR APPEND AS #1
```

Here are the four steps necessary to append records to an existing sequential data file:

1. OPEN the file FOR APPEND.

2. Prepare your data for writing to the file.

3. Use the WRITE# instruction to write additional data records at the end of the file.

4. CLOSE the file.

Only the first step differs from the process of creating a new file. Opening a file for APPEND readies a previously existing file to receive additional records.

If the OPEN instruction specifies a nonexistent file, the file is created just as though the file was OPENed for OUTPUT.

Reading a Sequential File

You have seen how to create a database file and then how to write or append records to the file. Now you will learn how to read information from a file that already exists on disk.

Obviously, a database file is not very useful unless the information can be read and processed. You might need the data for any number of reasons. For a mailing list file, you might want to print mailing labels. Perhaps you need to read a file containing weekly sales figures to identify peak sales periods. For the coin collection, you might want to write a program to calculate the total value of all the coins.

Reading information from a sequential file involves the following steps:

1. OPEN the file FOR INPUT.

2. Use the INPUT# instruction to read data into variables.

3. Process the data.

4. CLOSE the file.

The first step introduces the third way to open a sequential data file: FOR INPUT. (Opening a file FOR OUTPUT and FOR APPEND have already been discussed.) By opening a file FOR INPUT, you tell QBasic that you intend to *read from* the file rather than *write to* the file. When you open a file FOR INPUT, you can only read records from the file. You cannot write any records to the file.

To open the file for input, simply use the phrase FOR INPUT in your OPEN instruction. For example, the following instruction opens the MYCOINS.SEQ sequential database file for input and specifies 1 to be the file number:

```
OPEN "B:MYCOINS.SEQ" FOR INPUT AS #1
```

Of course, when you open a file for input, that file must already exist. If QBasic cannot find your specified file, you get a File not found error.

The *INPUT#* Statement

After you open a file for input, use an INPUT# instruction to read records from the file. INPUT# and WRITE# are complementary statements. Whereas WRITE# writes a data record to a file opened for output, INPUT# reads a data record from a file opened for input.

INPUT# is designed for reading sequential files created with WRITE#. An INPUT# instruction reverses the process of a WRITE# instruction.

As you have seen, a WRITE# instruction contains a variable list whose values are written to a record in the sequential file. An INPUT# instruction also contains a variable list. INPUT# reads a data record from a sequential file and stores the data values into the variables in the variable list.

To use INPUT#, you must know the number of fields in each record and the type of data in each field. The variables in *variablelist* should match the file data. You guarantee correct matching if the variable list in the INPUT# instruction is exactly the same as the variable list used in the WRITE# instruction that created the file record.

With INPUT#, you can read numeric data into a string variable, but you cannot read string data into a numeric variable. Of course, if you read numeric data into a string variable, you can subsequently process the data only in string form.

Even if you need only some of the information in a record, you should read all the fields of the record to make sure that QBasic keeps your place in the file correctly.

Usually *variablelist* consists of the same variable names used in the complementary WRITE# instruction that created the file. Such consistency ensures the data file is read successfully.

The Sample Program DOVALUE.BAS

Now let's open a data file FOR INPUT and see INPUT# in action.

What's the total value of your coin collection? You have three coins: a penny worth $70, a dime worth $47.25, and a silver dollar worth $200. The total value should be $317.25.

You can write a program to confirm this total. Listing 14.2, DOVALUE.BAS, opens MYCOINS.SEQ for input, reads the data with INPUT#, and calculates the total value of all the coins in the collection.

Listing 14.2. The DOVALUE.BAS program.

```
REM Program: DOVALUE.BAS (Find Total Value of Coins)

OPEN "B:MYCOINS.SEQ" FOR INPUT AS #1

TotalValue! = 0!
DO UNTIL EOF(1)
    INPUT #1, Year%, Category$, Value!, Comment$
    TotalValue! = TotalValue! + Value!
LOOP

CLOSE #1
PRINT USING "Total Value is $$####.##"; TotalValue!
END
```

Running this program produces the following output:

```
Total value is    $317.25
```

The total is verified!

Notice that the INPUT# instruction reads all four fields of each record (Year, Category, Value, Comment) even though only Value! is actually used in the calculations. This follows the practice of making the variable list of your INPUT# instruction duplicate the variable list of the WRITE# instruction that created the file. By matching the variable lists exactly, you make sure that QBasic retains the correct place in the file as you read each record.

The *EOF* Function

What's that EOF in the DO UNTIL instruction? How does the DO-LOOP block work?

EOF (*E*nd *O*f *F*ile) is a QBasic function that tests whether the end of a sequential file was reached.

EOF returns a logical value: True (–1) if the end of file was reached, or False (0) otherwise. This means that you can use EOF with IF, DO UNTIL, and WHILE instructions. By using EOF, you don't have to know beforehand how many records are in your data file.

```
EOF( filenum)
```

where

    filenum is the file number.

In the present case, you know that three records are in the data file. Therefore, you could write the loop as follows:

```
FOR J% = 1 TO 3
    INPUT #1, Year%, Category$, Value!, Comment$
    TotalValue! = TotalValue! + Value!
NEXT J%
```

This method works just fine. But suppose that you didn't know beforehand how many records are in the data file. Then you wouldn't know what loop values to use in the FOR instruction.

You need some way to read all the records in a file and know when you reach the end. EOF provides this capability.

Be sure that you test for EOF before attempting to read past the end of the file. A run-time error occurs (Input past end of file) if you try to execute an INPUT# instruction when the last record has already been read.

Modifying a Sequential Data File

Suppose now that you want to update some information in your data file. Let's say that some information in a database changes and you want to modify some of the records.

Updating presents a complication because you can't open a sequential file for reading and writing at the same time. Furthermore, the OUTPUT and APPEND modes enable you only to add records, not edit existing records.

There are three basic solutions to this problem:

■ OPEN two data files simultaneously—the original file FOR INPUT and a new file FOR OUTPUT. Read each record from the old file into variables. Update the values of these variables as necessary. Then rewrite the updated record to the new file.

■ OPEN the original file FOR INPUT. Read all the records into arrays. CLOSE the file. Update the data in the arrays as necessary. OPEN the file again, this time FOR OUTPUT. Write all the data back to the file.

■ Use a word processor or text editor to modify the data file.

Back to the coin collection. As time passes, the values of the coins change (upward, you hope). Let's say that you want to modify MYCOINS.SEQ to update the value field of each record. The following sections describe how to do this using each of the three techniques.

Opening Two Files Simultaneously

Listing 14.3 uses the first technique.

Listing 14.3. The UPDATE1.BAS program.

```
REM Program: UPDATE1.BAS (Update Coin Values into a Second File)

PRINT "Update Coin Values to new file B:MYCOIN2.SEQ"
OPEN "B:MYCOINS.SEQ" FOR INPUT AS #1
OPEN "B:MYCOIN2.SEQ" FOR OUTPUT AS #2

DO UNTIL EOF(1)
   PRINT
   INPUT #1, Year%, Category$, Value!, Comment$
   PRINT "    Year:"; Year%
   PRINT "Category: "; Category$
   PRINT "Comments: "; Comment$
   PRINT USING "   Value:#####.##"; Value!
   INPUT "New Value (Press <Enter> if unchanged)"; NewValue!
   IF NewValue! <> 0 THEN Value! = NewValue!
   WRITE #2, Year%, Category$, Value!, Comment$
LOOP

PRINT
PRINT "All Done — B:MYCOIN2.SEQ created"
CLOSE #1
CLOSE #2
END
```

The first OPEN instruction opens MYCOINS.SEQ in preparation for reading from the file. The following OPEN instruction opens a new file, MYCOIN2.SEQ, which this program creates.

The main work of the program takes place in the DO-LOOP block. The INPUT #1 instruction reads the next record from MYCOINS.SEQ. Subsequent program lines display the values of the four fields on-screen. Then the INPUT instruction prompts you to type in the new value for the coin. (If the value remains unchanged, you can just press Enter.) If you type in a new value, the IF instruction updates the value of Value! accordingly. Finally, the WRITE #2 instruction writes the updated record to the new sequential file MYCOIN2.SEQ.

Notice that by opening two files and writing only to the new file, the original data file remains intact. This provides a measure of redundancy and safety. You always have the old data file if you make a mistake or suffer one of those "always at the worst time" power failures.

Opening Multiple Files

TIP

You can have several files open at the same time. Of course, each file must have a unique file number.

QBasic limits the maximum number of files you can open simultaneously to 15. Furthermore, your hardware configuration and DOS version can limit you to less than 15 simultaneously opened files. From DOS, you can use the FILES command in your CONFIG.SYS file to change the default maximum number of opened files. Refer to your DOS documentation for more details.

Sometimes, in a program that opens multiple files, you might not know what file numbers are already in use when you need to open a new file. For example, this might occur when files are opened as a result of IF tests.

The QBasic FREEFILE function returns the lowest unused file number. The function accepts no parameters, so the syntax is simply

FREEFILE

The FREEFILE function guarantees to return a *filenum* value that is not currently in use. The following program fragment shows a typical application of FREEFILE:

```
MyFileNumber% = FREEFILE
OPEN "B:MYFILE.DTA" FOR OUTPUT AS MyFileNumber%
```

Using Arrays

As Listing 14.4 shows, another way to update your data file is by using arrays:

Listing 14.4. The UPDATE2.BAS program.

```
REM Program: UPDATE2.BAS (Update Coin Values Using Arrays)

PRINT "Update Coin Values Using Arrays"
DIM Year%(100), Category$(100), Value!(100), Comment$(100)
OPEN "B:MYCOINS.SEQ" FOR INPUT AS #1

Count% = 0
DO UNTIL EOF(1)
   Count% = Count% + 1
   PRINT
   INPUT #1, Year%(Count%), Category$(Count%), _
            Value!(Count%), Comment$(Count%)   'This is one line
   PRINT "    Year:"; Year%(Count%)
   PRINT "Category: "; Category$(Count%)
   PRINT "Comments: "; Comment$(Count%)
   PRINT USING "   Value:#####.##"; Value!(Count%)
   INPUT "New Value (Press <Enter> if unchanged)"; NewValue!
   IF NewValue! <> 0 THEN Value!(Count%) = NewValue!
LOOP
CLOSE #1

OPEN "B:MYCOINS.SEQ" FOR OUTPUT AS #1    'Reopen file for output

FOR J% = 1 TO Count%
   WRITE #1, Year%(J%), Category$(J%), Value!(J%), Comment$(J%)
NEXT J%

PRINT "All done — B:MYCOINS.SEQ updated and rewritten"
CLOSE #1
END
```

 NOTE The INPUT #1... instruction is shown on two physical lines for typographic purposes in this book. The QBasic editor, however, will remove the underscore character and create one long line.

In this program, four arrays replace the four simple variables. When using this technique, be sure to dimension your arrays sufficiently.

The DO-LOOP block reads all the data from MYCOINS.SEQ into these arrays. Notice how the variable Count% keeps track of the total number of data records.

For each coin, the user sees the old information and can update the coin's value, just as in the previous program. Now, however, the updated information goes into the Value! array.

The file is closed, then immediately reopened for OUTPUT. The process of opening the file for output erases the whole previous file. If a program error occurs at this point, you can lose all the data information. Therefore, when you use this method, it's a good idea to have a backup copy of your data file.

The FOR-NEXT loop writes the updated information. The value of Count% indicates how many records to write. The net result is a completely updated version of MYCOINS.SEQ.

Modifying the File Externally

You can modify your data file with a word processor or text editor. This is somewhat dangerous because you must be sure to preserve the file formatting. Be careful to keep the delimiters intact and make sure your word processor does not add any extraneous control characters.

Some file modifications are easier to do externally than with a QBasic program. As an example, suppose that you want to delete an entire record from your data file.

Use the QBasic editor. Simply load in the data file, position the cursor over the record to be zapped, and press Ctrl-Y. Save the file, and the job is complete.

Other Sequential File Tools

You have learned the essential tools of sequential file handling in QBasic, namely:

■ Opening a file for INPUT, OUTPUT, or APPEND

■ Writing a record with WRITE#

■ Reading a record with INPUT#

■ Testing for the end of the file with the EOF function

But there's more. QBasic offers other statements and functions for use with sequential files in special situations. Here is a brief review of these other tools with an emphasis on when you might need to use them.

Using the *LINE INPUT#* Statement

LINE INPUT# reads an entire record into a single string variable.

<table>
<tr>
<td>

**S
T
A
T
E
M
E
N
T**

</td>
<td>

LINE INPUT #*filenum*, *stringvar*

where

    filenum is the file number,

and

    stringvar is a string variable.

</td>
</tr>
</table>

Each record is read in its entirety, including any commas or quotation marks. For example, the first record from MYCOINS.SEQ looks like this:

```
1910,"Lincoln Penny",70,"S mint mark, uncirculated"
```

You might read this record with the following instruction:

```
LINE INPUT #1, MyData$
```

This instruction assigns to MyData$ an exact copy of the entire record, including the quotation marks and commas.

Use LINE INPUT# when a file has a special structure or an unknown structure. Perhaps the file was not created with WRITE# or you don't know the exact WRITE# instruction that was used to create the file. Another possibility is that the number of fields varies from record to record.

In such cases, the programmer is responsible for analyzing the data in *stringvar* appropriately. Depending on the situation, your program might have to search for meaningful delimiters or otherwise break down *stringvar* into usable components.

Reading with the *INPUT$* Function

INPUT$ is a special form of the INPUT function. With INPUT$, you read only a specified number of characters from the current record.

F
U
N
C
T
I
O
N

```
INPUT$(numchar, #filenum)
```

where

numchar is an integer expression that specifies how many characters
should be read,

and

filenum is the file number.

The pound sign (#) before the file number is optional.

For example, the following instruction reads the next 12 characters from the
current record of file number 1 into the string variable NextDozen$:

```
NextDozen$ = INPUT$(12, #1)
```

Using the *LOF* Function

The LOF function (*L*ength *O*f *F*ile) returns the number of bytes (length) of a data
file. LOF is handy in certain critical disk-storage situations. One application of
LOF is testing whether a file has become too large to save on disk.

F
U
N
C
T
I
O
N

```
LOF( filenum)
```

where

filenum is the file number of an opened file.

As an example of LOF, the following instruction displays the length of file
number 8:

```
PRINT "Size of file 8 is"; LOF(8)
```

Using the *PRINT#* and *PRINT# USING* Statements

In addition to using WRITE#, you can write data to a sequential file with the PRINT# and PRINT# USING statements.

<table>
<tr>
<td>

S
T
A
T
E
M
E
N
T

</td>
<td>

PRINT #*filenum*, *expressionlist*

or

PRINT #*filenum*, USING *formatstring*; *expressionlist*

where

   filenum is the file number,

   expressionlist is a list of expressions separated by commas and semicolons (and optionally ending with a comma or semicolon),

and

   formatstring is a string containing formatting instructions.

</td>
</tr>
</table>

PRINT# and PRINT# USING send data to a file in the same form that PRINT and PRINT USING send data to the screen. See Chapter 12, "Writing Text on the Video Screen," for a detailed discussion of PRINT and PRINT USING (and the required format strings).

However, PRINT# generally does not write information in a form suitable for subsequent reading by INPUT# because PRINT# does not automatically place quotation marks around strings and does not separate fields with commas. Look at this program fragment:

```
A$ = "I ate"
B$ = "pizzas"
N% = 2
PRINT #1, A$; N%; B$
```

The PRINT# instruction generates a file record that looks like this:

```
I ate 2 pizzas
```

There are no quotation marks around the strings and no commas delimiting the fields. The instruction INPUT #1, A$, N%, B$ does not read this record successfully. Without a comma delimiter in the data, A$ becomes I ate 2 pizzas. N% and B$ are not read correctly.

So why would you ever want to use PRINT# and PRINT# USING? Actually, you wouldn't if you're writing to files that INPUT# is going to read later in another QBasic program.

But there are other reasons to create sequential files. You might want to generate a file destined to be read by people, or into a word processor, or into another application such as a spreadsheet. Such applications require files designed in specialized formats. PRINT# and PRINT# USING supply this control.

Setting and Determining the File Position with *SEEK* and *LOC*

The SEEK statement resets the file position pointer for the next read or write. The SEEK and LOC functions return the current position within the file. To use these features, you must consider the file as a sequence of data bytes. The first byte of the file is 1.

The SEEK statement sets the file pointer to a specified position.

SEEK #*filenum*, *position*

where

   filenum is the file number of an open file,

and

   position specifies the file position as a byte in the range from 1 to 2,147,483,647.

The pound sign (#) before the file number is optional.

S T A T E M E N T

The SEEK function returns the current file position.

SEEK(*filenum*)

where

   filenum is the file number of an open file.

F U N C T I O N

The LOC function returns the last byte written or read, but in a modified form.

<table>
<tr><td>

**F
U
N
C
T
I
O
N**

</td><td>

LOC(*filenum*)

where

    filenum is the file number of an open file.

</td></tr>
</table>

LOC considers a sequential file to be divided into 128-byte blocks. LOC returns the block number of the file position. For example, if the last byte read from or written to is byte 287, LOC returns 3; the byte is inside the third 128-byte block.

By convention, LOC returns 1 (not 0) for a file opened but not yet read from or written to.

The SEEK statement and SEEK function are QBasic enhancements that do not exist in BASICA or GW-BASIC. A version of LOC does exist in BASICA and GW-BASIC, but is incompatible with the QBasic version.

Because sequential files usually are not handled byte by byte, SEEK and LOC are not particularly useful with such files. However, as you see in the next chapter, SEEK and LOC become important with random-access and binary files.

Summary of Statements and Functions for Sequential Files

Table 14.3 summarizes the statements and functions available for sequential file processing.

Table 14.3. Sequential file statements and functions.

Keyword	Type	Effect
OPEN	Statement	Opens a file in specified mode
CLOSE	Statement	Closes a file
WRITE#	Statement	Writes comma-delimited information
INPUT#	Statement	Reads comma-delimited information

Keyword	Type	Effect
PRINT#	Statement	Writes space-delimited information
PRINT# USING	Statement	Writes formatted information
INPUT$	Function	Reads given number of characters
LINE INPUT#	Statement	Reads entire record
EOF	Function	Tests for end of file
LOF	Function	Returns size of file
SEEK	Statement	Sets file position pointer
SEEK	Function	Returns current file position
LOC	Function	Returns current file position

Summary

QBasic has several statements that provide DOS-like file and directory management. Some of the things your programs can do are delete or rename files, and create, delete, or change subdirectories.

A common application of disk files is the database. A database is a body of related information, such as the names of students in a school or a hobbyist's collection of postage stamps.

When creating a disk file, you can choose between three different file types: *sequential, random-access,* and *binary.* A sequential file is organized into a series of primary records, with each record containing one or more fields. For a stamp collection database, each record would probably be a stamp and the fields might be the country, denomination, condition, and price of the stamp. To use any of the three file types, you OPEN the file, read or write records (or bytes) as appropriate, and finally CLOSE the file.

The next chapter discusses random-access and binary files. After exploring each type of disk file, you will be in a better position to judge the merits and disadvantages of each of the three types of files.

Using Random and Binary Disk Files

A rmed with a knowledge of sequential disk files from the previous chapter, it's time to venture into the realms of random-access and binary disk files.

Here are the main topics of this chapter:

- Using random-access files
- Using binary files
- Understanding the general forms of OPEN and CLOSE
- Using disk files in networked environments

Using Random-Access Files

Moving on from sequential files, the second kind of disk data file is the random-access (or simply *random*) file. Random files meet the needs of large database file applications.

If you are a beginner with QBasic, or just getting your feet wet programming disk data files, we recommend that you master sequential files before tackling random files.

Random files require more complex programming than sequential files. Random files (and later in this chapter, binary files) are covered at a quicker pace than sequential files were covered in the last chapter. You can skip ahead to the next chapter without any loss of continuity.

Compared to sequential files, random files offer these significant advantages:

■ Two-way I/O activity. When opened, a random file can be read from and written to.

■ Random-access. You can access any record quickly and conveniently.

■ Record modification. You can modify individual records without rewriting all other records.

As you have seen, reading a particular record of a sequential file requires reading all the previous records first. For example, if your program wants only the information in the 75th record, you first must read all the information in the initial 74 records. If your program wants the fifth record, you need to read only the initial four records. The further into the file the record you want to retrieve is located, the longer it takes to access that record.

By contrast, random files are organized more like a compact disc player, which can locate any song on a compact disc with equal aplomb. Random files reference individual records by number. By simply specifying a record number, you can access that record's information quickly. The access time is virtually the same for the first record, the 50th record, or the 2,000th record. Random files are the only practical choice for large database applications.

Furthermore, once you read a random file record, you can modify the data and rewrite the record directly—no need to close and reopen the file. Appending records is also straightforward.

By this time, you're probably thinking random files are the cure-all for disk database programming. After all, random file records are swiftly read anywhere in the file and the file can be opened for input and output simultaneously. Why would anyone use sequential files?

Computing, like life, involves a series of trade-offs. Here is the price you must pay to use random files:

■ Rigid file structure. Each record of a random file must have the same configuration: the number of fields and data type for each field cannot vary from record to record.

■ Lack of portability. You cannot easily read random files with non-BASIC programs such as word processors and spreadsheets. The TYPE command in DOS does not display random files.

■ Increased programming effort. Programming random files is more complex than programming sequential files.

Like a sequential file, a random file is a series of records, and each record consists of data fields. Unlike a sequential file, each random file record has a predetermined size that cannot change throughout the file.

Designing a Random-Access File

You might think of a random-access file record as something like a survey form—the kind of form where you provide data in marked boxes. As Figure 15.1 shows, such forms often provide one box for each data character.

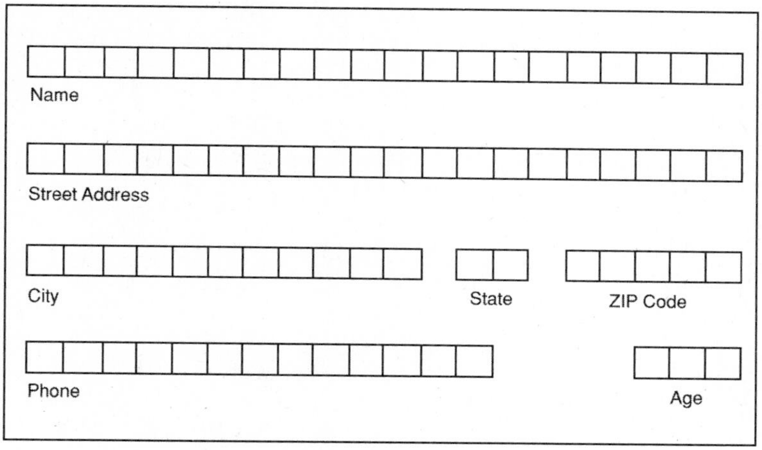

Figure 15.1.

A fixed-field data form.

Notice that each field in the form has its own fixed size. It's okay if the data for one field requires less than the allocated number of characters, but it's not okay to use more characters than allocated. For example, the sample form has a name field of 20 characters. You can enter a name of less than 20 characters, but you cannot use more than the 20 allotted characters.

This fixed-field size requirement is exactly the situation with random-access files. You must determine a template form for each record. The number of fields and the size of each field must remain constant throughout the file. You can make each field whatever size you want, but once you specify the size you must stick to it.

As a result, the size (number of bytes) of each record is constant in a random-access file. That's why QBasic can access any record quickly. Because the record size is constant, when a record number is given, the position of the data on the disk is readily computed. For any record in the file, the computer takes essentially the same time to determine where the data is, to find the data, and then to read the information.

Before using a random-access file, you must design the template for each record. Decide how many fields each record will have. Then decide the size of each field. You need to treat text fields and numeric fields a little differently.

Creating Text Fields in a Random-Access File

For a text field, simply determine the maximum number of text characters allowed for that field. For each record in the file, you allocate that maximum size for the field, whether or not all the characters are actually used.

For example, you might determine that a field reserved for a customer's name should be allocated 30 characters. Whether the actual data is I. M. Sly, Ace Accordion Supply, or Rumplestiltskin Meriweather, that field always occupies 30 bytes (characters) in the data file.

Creating Numeric Fields in a Random-Access File

Random-access files save numbers in the internal binary formats that QBasic uses to store the numbers in memory. This means that for each numeric field, you designate one of QBasic's four numeric types: integer, long integer, single-precision, or double-precision.

Be careful that you choose the numeric type of each field wisely. The numeric type of each field must accommodate every entry for that field. If a field contains a number with a fractional component, such as 34.67, that field must be single-precision or double-precision. For whole numbers, the integer type is limited to 32,767. Use long integer if your values might be larger than 32,767.

Because numbers are stored in their binary form, the size (in bytes) of each numeric field is determined by the numeric type (see Table 15.1).

Table 15.1. Size of numeric types.

Number Type	Size (Bytes)
Integer	2
Long integer	4
Single-precision	4
Double-precision	8

For example, a field reserved for a single-precision number is allocated four bytes. Whether the actual data is 10, 28.699, or 6.04E-28, the number is stored in four bytes, just as it would be in the machine's RAM memory.

A Sample Record

Suppose you want to design a random file database for the coin collection introduced in the previous chapter. Each record (coin) requires four fields: Year, Category, Value, and Comment.

Year is a whole number expressed in four digits, such as 1947. Such numbers are well within the range of the integer data type, so the first field is type integer and requires two bytes.

Category is a text field. Twenty characters should be enough to describe each coin's category, so the second field is 20 bytes.

Value is a numeric field expressed in dollars and cents, such as 135.50. No coin will be worth more than 3000 dollars. Single-precision numbers easily satisfy this data range, so the third field is four bytes long.

Comment is a text field. The data for this field varies widely from coin to coin. Let's limit each comment to 50 characters, so the length of the fourth field is 50 bytes.

The Comment field typifies the squandering of disk space that can occur with random-access files. For many coins, the Comment field will be short or blank, yet a full 50 bytes is still reserved. This squandering is the price that must be paid to maintain rigid file structure. Typically, a database stored as a random file takes more room on disk than the same database stored as a sequential file.

Figure 15.2 shows the template form for each record of the coin collection database. The total size of each record is fixed at 76 bytes.

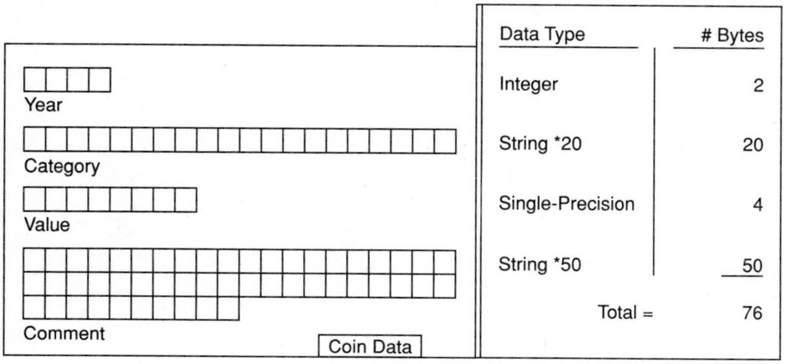

Data Type	# Bytes
Integer	2
String *20	20
Single-Precision	4
String *50	50
Total =	76

Year

Category

Value

Comment

Coin Data

Figure 15.2.

The random-access record for each coin.

Using a Random-Access File with User-Defined Data Types

Compared to BASICA and GW-BASIC, QBasic streamlines the process of reading and writing random files.

In BASICA and GW-BASIC, you need the artifice of field variables and FIELD instructions to transfer data between your program and a random file on disk. This awkward technique is discussed later in this chapter. (QBasic supports field variables for compatibility with BASICA and GW-BASIC.)

However, QBasic introduces the user-defined data type, which lets you create natural data structures to describe your database records (see Chapter 9, "Managing Large Amounts of Data"). After you create a user-defined data type, you can designate variables—called *record* variables—to possess your created data type.

When you associate a user-defined variable with your database record template, transferring data to and from random files is easy.

Use the following steps to process random files with record variables:

1. Define a record variable matching your database template.

2. OPEN the file FOR RANDOM.

3. Use the GET and PUT instructions to read and write data with the record variables.

4. CLOSE the file.

There are some new concepts in these four steps. Let's take a look at each step.

Defining the Record Variable

Recall from Chapter 9 that you use a TYPE-END TYPE block to create a record (user-defined) data type. For example, the following block creates a data type called CoinType appropriate for the coin collection database. The ensuing DIM instruction declares the record variable Coin to have the data type CoinType.

```
TYPE CoinType
    Year AS INTEGER
    Category AS STRING * 20
    Value AS SINGLE
    Comment AS STRING * 50
```

```
END TYPE

DIM Coin AS CoinType      'Declare Coin to be a variable
                          'of type CoinType
```

Opening the File

You can open a sequential file in INPUT, OUTPUT, or APPEND mode. By contrast, you always open a random file FOR RANDOM. The OPEN instruction adds a LEN clause that specifies the length of each record in the file.

OPEN *filespec* FOR RANDOM AS #*filenum* LEN = *recordlength*

where

    filespec specifies the name and path of the data file,

    filenum is the file number,

and

    recordlength is an integer expression specifying, in bytes, the size of each record.

The pound sign (#) in front of the *filenum* parameter is optional. The FOR RANDOM and LEN clauses are optional, as this section explains.

S T A T E M E N T

A single OPEN instruction opens a random file for any or all I/O activities—reading, writing, and appending.

Suppose you design a random-access database file for your coin collection. You will describe each coin (record in the file) with a variable of the user-defined type CoinType. Remember, the size of each record is 76 bytes (2 for the year, 20 for the category, 4 for the value, and 50 for the comments). So 76 is the value for the *recordlength* parameter in the LEN clause of the OPEN instruction.

Let's say that you call the file MYCOINS.RAN (the file extension .RAN is used for random files), and the file is on a disk in the B: drive. Then the following instruction opens MYCOINS.RAN as file number 1:

```
OPEN "B:MYCOINS.RAN" FOR RANDOM AS #1 LEN = 76
```

The FOR RANDOM clause is optional because random-access is the default mode for the OPEN instruction. If you do not include a FOR clause in an OPEN instruction, QBasic opens the file for random access, just as if you had specified FOR RANDOM. This means you could open the coin database file as follows:

```
OPEN "B:MYCOINS.RAN" AS #1 LEN = 76
```

However, you should always include the FOR RANDOM clause for clarity.

As you have seen, the LEN clause specifies the length, in bytes, of each random-access record. For optimal efficiency, the value in the LEN clause should precisely match the record length. Although wasteful of disk space, the value in the LEN clause can be larger than the actual record length.

Here's a trick to help you specify LEN clauses in your random-access OPEN instructions. QBasic provides the LEN function to calculate the length (number of bytes) of any variable, including a record variable.

F U N C T I O N

```
LEN(variable)
```

where

    variable is any variable.

Notice that this is a second form of the LEN function. Chapter 11, "Manipulating Strings," introduced the alternate form, which returns the number of characters in a string.

As an example of LEN, the instruction PRINT LEN(Coin) displays 76. This confirms that the length of the record is 76 bytes.

The trick is to use the LEN function in the LEN clause of the OPEN instruction. That way, you don't have to know or supply the exact length of the record data type. For example:

```
OPEN "B:MYCOINS.RAN" FOR RANDOM as #1 LEN = LEN(Coin)
```

Remember that the LEN clause is optional. If you omit the LEN clause in an OPEN instruction, the record length defaults to 128 bytes.

Writing and Reading Records

Use the PUT statement to write a random file record.

PUT #*filenum*, *recordnum*, *variable*

where

    filenum is the file number,

    recordnum is a numeric expression (from 1 to 2,147,483,647) specifying the record to be written,

and

    variable specifies the variable containing the data to be written to the file.

The *recordnum* parameter and the pound sign (#) are optional.

---

recordnum can specify any record in the file: an old record whose data is to be rewritten or a new record receiving data for the first time. Furthermore, your record numbers don't have to be continuous. For example, you can write record number 15 when only records 1 through 4 have been written previously.

If you omit *recordnum*, the default record number is 1 plus the last record written (using PUT) or read. Thus you can write incrementally increasing record numbers with successive PUT instructions that omit *recordnum*. You can also have a single PUT instruction inside a loop. When you omit the *recordnum* parameter, use two consecutive commas in the PUT instruction. For example, the following instruction writes the next consecutive record to the coin database file, which was opened as file number 1:

```
PUT #1, , Coin
```

variable is usually a variable of the appropriate user-defined data type. However, you can use any variable as long as the length of the variable is not more than the length of the record. QBasic simply writes all the bytes of the variable.

Before writing a record, you must assign the proper values to each component of your record variable. Recall that QBasic record variables use a period notation to identify individual components (see Chapter 9, "Managing Large Amounts of Data").

The following program fragment demonstrates writing a sample record of the coin database:

```
Coin.Year = 1910
Coin.Category = "Lincoln Penny"
Coin.Value = 70.00
Coin.Comment = "S mint mark, uncirculated"

PUT #1, 5, Coin          'Write record number 5
```

Use the GET statement to read a record.

S T A T E M E N T

```
GET #filenum, recordnum, variable
```

where

    filenum is the file number,

    recordnum is the record number,

and

    variable specifies the variable to receive the data.

The *recordnum* parameter and the pound sign (#) are optional.

As with PUT, *recordnum* can specify any record. If you omit *recordnum*, the default record number is the last record read or written plus one.

The following instruction reads record number 5 from the coin database into the record variable named Coin:

```
GET #1, 5, Coin          'Read record number 5
```

Each component of the record variable Coin now contains the appropriate data.

Closing the Random-Access File

When I/O activity is finished, use the CLOSE statement as usual.

Example of a Random-Access File Program

Suppose you have the coin database on a random-access file named MYCOINS.RAN. The coin market is favorable, and prices are rising. You decide to update the database file by increasing the value of each coin by 10 percent. (In the previous chapter, the programs UPDATE1.BAS and UPDATE2.BAS solved a similar problem for sequential files.)

Listing 15.1, UPDATE3.BAS, modifies the random file MYCOINS.RAN to reflect the increase in values.

Listing 15.1. The UPDATE3.BAS program.

```
REM Program: UPDATE3.BAS   (Increase coin values by 10%)

TYPE CoinType
    Year AS INTEGER
    Category AS STRING * 20
    Value AS SINGLE
    Comment AS STRING * 50
END TYPE

DIM Coin AS CoinType
OPEN "B:MYCOINS.RAN" FOR RANDOM AS #5 LEN = 76

FOR Record% = 1 TO 3                'File has only 3 records
    GET #5, Record%, Coin
    Coin.Value = 1.1 * Coin.Value   'Increase value by 10%
    PUT #5, Record%, Coin
NEXT Record%

CLOSE #5
END
```

This program demonstrates one of the great advantages of random files over sequential files: You can read and write random files without closing and reopening the file.

Furthermore, you can read or write records in any order. For example, you could have Record% loop from 3 down to 1 and the program would still work fine.

Using *SEEK* and *LOC* with Random-Access Files

For random files, SEEK and LOC deal with record numbers, not bytes.

The SEEK statement positions the file pointer at the next record you want to read or write. For example:

```
SEEK #9, 23   'Move pointer to the 23rd record of file number 9
```

After this SEEK instruction, a GET or PUT instruction without a *recordnum* parameter operates on this newly reset file position. For example, the following instruction writes on the newly set record number 23:

```
PUT #9, , Coin
```

The SEEK function returns the next record to be read or written. The LOC function returns the last record read or written. For example:

```
GET #9, 2, Coin                             'Read record number 2
PRINT "Last record read was  "; LOC(9)      'Displays last record
PRINT "Next record to read is"; SEEK(9)     'Displays next record
```

The output is

```
Last record read was    2
Next record to read is 3
```

Using the *EOF* Function
with Random-Access Files

With random files, the EOF function returns a True value (–1) if the most recent GET instruction did not read an entire record. This happens when GET reads beyond the end of the file.

Using Field Variables

For compatibility with existing BASICA and GW-BASIC programs, QBasic supports the older, more cumbersome method of random-access file I/O—the field variable technique. It is recommended that you use record variables, not field variables, in any new programs you write.

Use the following steps to process random files with field variables:

1. Open the file FOR RANDOM.

2. Establish field variables with a FIELD instruction.

3. Use the GET and PUT instructions to read and write data that is transferred in the field variables.

4. Close the file.

Steps 1 and 4 (opening and closing the file) work just like random-access file processing with record variables. The ensuing discussion focuses on steps 2 and 3.

Establishing Field Variables

Transferring data between your QBasic program and the random file uses special string variables called field variables. You assign one field variable to each data field of your record template—that is, one field variable for each component of your database record.

The coin database, for example, has four fields (Year, Category, Value, and Comment). Therefore, any program using the coin database must define four field variables—one field variable for each field in the database.

To define field variables, you use a FIELD instruction.

```
FIELD #filenum, fieldwidth AS stringvar,
                fieldwidth AS stringvar, ...
```

where

   filenum is the file number,

   fieldwidth is an integer expression specifying the number of bytes (characters) allocated to the corresponding field variable,

and

   stringvar declares a string variable or specified element in a string array to be a field variable.

The pound sign (#) before the *filenum* parameter is optional.

S T A T E M E N T

FIELD simply associates a field variable in your program with each field of a record in your random file. Because all records of a random file have the same fields, one set of field variables suffices for the entire file.

Field variables are a kind of two-way conduit for the data flow between your programs and the random file. When you write a record, you first store the data for each field in the appropriate field variable. (The technique for doing this is explained shortly.) A PUT instruction then writes the record on the file.

Similarly, a GET instruction transfers data from a record into the appropriate field variable. Then you decode the data from the field variables for use within your program. Later in this chapter, the section titled "Reading a Record with GET" shows you the decoding technique.

A FIELD instruction declares the name and length of each field variable. Field variables are always string variables. As you will see in the next few sections, all data, whether text or numeric, transfers with string operations.

Recall that when you design a random file, you allocate a fixed size (in bytes) for each field. The *fieldwidth* parameter designates these sizes.

One FIELD instruction defines *all* the field variables for each record of your random file. In the FIELD instruction, you repeat the *fieldwidth* AS *stringvar* clause as many times as there are fields in each record.

For example, the following FIELD instruction establishes field variables for the coin collection database:

```
FIELD #1, 2 AS FieldYear$, 20 AS FieldCategory$, _
         4 AS FieldValue$, 50 AS FieldComment$
```

(For typographic purposes in this book, this instruction is divided into two lines. However, in the QBasic editor, the instruction occupies one line without the underscore character.)

Let's examine this instruction closely. The #1 means that this FIELD instruction defines the field variables for file number 1, the same file number opened with the OPEN instruction. There are four *fieldwidth* AS *stringvar* clauses, one clause for each of the four fields in the database. The first of these clauses, 2 AS FieldYear$, defines the field variable FieldYear$ and assigns the variable a length of two bytes (characters). The next three clauses define the other three field variables and assign the appropriate length for each variable. The field variables are FieldYear$, FieldCategory$, FieldValue$, and FieldComment$. Notice that each field variable is a string.

A given FIELD instruction can contain any number of *fieldwidth* AS *stringvar* clauses. Use as many clauses as necessary to define all the field variables for the particular file. The coin database file has four fields per record. But another file might have only one field in each record (therefore, one clause in the FIELD instruction) or perhaps ten fields in each record (therefore, ten clauses in the FIELD instruction). You separate each clause with a comma.

Writing and Reading Records

As with record variables, use a PUT instruction to write a random file record and a GET instruction to read a record. The syntax differs slightly from that used with record variables.

Writing a Record with *PUT*

Before you write a random record with PUT, you must transfer the data values for the record into the appropriate field variables. You might think of this as moving the data for each record to a loading dock. Suppose you have a data value for each field of the record you intend to write. You bring the data value for each field to the loading dock and then transfer each data value into the corresponding field variable. When each field variable contains the proper data, a single PUT instruction writes the entire record to the file.

But how do you transfer data values to the field variables? QBasic provides the LSET and RSET statements for this purpose. Each LSET or RSET instruction transfers the data for one field to the appropriate field variable.

LSET *fieldvar* = *stringexpr*

SET *fieldvar* = *stringexpr*

where

    fieldvar is a string variable previously defined as a field variable,

and

    stringexpr is a string expression representing the text data to be stored in the field variable.

**S
T
A
T
E
M
E
N
T**

For each field variable, you use either an LSET or RSET instruction. The technique varies depending on whether the data field is text or numeric.

When the data field is text, an LSET or RSET instruction is straightforward. Because both the field variable and the data itself are text, an LSET or RSET instruction moves the string data directly into the field variable.

For example, *either* of the following instructions moves the data field Midnight into the field variable FieldTime$:

```
LSET FieldTime$ = "Midnight"
```

```
RSET FieldTime$ = "Midnight"
```

The only difference between LSET and RSET is that, if necessary, LSET left-justifies the data string within the field variable whereas RSET right-justifies the data string. Leftover positions are padded with blank spaces. In practice, most of the time you will use LSET instructions rather than RSET.

In the preceding example, the data field Midnight has a string length of eight characters. Suppose the FIELD instruction that defines the field variable FieldTime$ specifies FieldTime$ to have a length of 10. Then the LSET instruction assigns to FieldTime$ the 10-character string consisting of Midnight followed by two blank spaces. RSET produces the 10-character string consisting of two blank spaces followed by Midnight.

If the string expression is longer than the size of the field variable, the rightmost portion of the string expression is truncated as necessary. Notice that the length of the field variable always remains precisely the length defined in the FIELD instruction, regardless of the length of *stringexpr*.

When a data field is numeric, things get a little more complicated. Numeric data must be converted into the proper string form before being assigned to a field variable. The "MK$" group of string functions does this conversion.

FUNCTION

MKI$(*integerexpr*)

MKL$(*longintegerexpr*)

MKS$(*numexpr*)

MKD$(*numexpr*)

where

    integerexpr is a general numeric expression resolving to a value within the integer range (–32,768 to +32,767),

    longintegerexpr is a general numeric expression resolving to a value within the long integer range (–2,147,483,648 to 2,147,483,647),

and

    numexpr is any general numeric expression.

There is a separate function for each numeric data type: MKI$ for integer, MKL$ for long integer, MKS$ for single-precision, and MKD$ for double-precision.

The "MK$" functions convert numbers into the string forms required by the field variables. The field variables must still be assigned with LSET or RSET instructions.

For example, the coin collection database has two numeric fields: Year and Value. Year is integer, and Value is single-precision. The following instructions use MKI$ and MKS$ to assign the numeric data in the variables Year% and Value! to the corresponding field variables FieldYear$ and FieldValue$:

```
LSET FieldYear$  = MKI$(Year%)
LSET FieldValue$ = MKS$(Value!)
```

Notice that each "MK$" function is a string function ending with a dollar sign. MKI$ converts an integer number into the appropriate two-character string, MKL$ converts a long integer number into the appropriate four-character string, MKS$ converts a single-precision number into the appropriate four-character string, and MKD$ converts a double-precision number into the appropriate eight-character string. These string lengths should match exactly with the length of the corresponding field variables. Therefore, you can use either an LSET or RSET instruction with these functions.

Now back to writing a record. After you assign all the field variables for a record (with LSET or RSET), use the PUT statement to actually write the random file record on disk.

PUT #*filenum*, *recordnum*

where

   filenum is the file number,

and

   recordnum specifies the record number being written.

The pound sign is optional. Also, the *recordnum* parameter is optional. If you omit *recordnum*, QBasic uses the next higher record number from the last record written or read.

S
T
A
T
E
M
E
N
T

A PUT instruction always writes a complete record. When you execute a PUT instruction, QBasic assumes that you have previously assigned a value to each field variable using LSET or RSET. The PUT instruction writes the record in the template form you established with the FIELD instruction.

The first record in a random file is considered to be record number 1. Successive records increase numerically up to a maximum record number of over two billion. (Yes, random files certainly can accommodate large databases!)

The *recordnum* parameter can specify any record in the file: an old record whose data is being rewritten, or a new record receiving data for the first time. Furthermore, your record numbers don't have to be continuous. For example, you can write record number 15 when only records 1 through 4 have previously been written. In this case, QBasic automatically creates records 5 through 14, although each such record would contain unknown data.

If you omit the *recordnum* parameter, the default record number is simply one more than the last record written. As a result, you can write incrementally increasing record numbers with successive PUT instructions that omit *recordnum*.

The following program fragment demonstrates writing a sample record of the coin database:

```
Year% = 1910
Category$ = "Lincoln Penny"
```

```
Value! = 70.00
Comment$ = "S mint mark, uncirculated"

LSET FieldYear$ = MKI$(Year%)
LSET FieldCategory$ = Category$
LSET FieldValue$ = MKS$(Value!)
LSET FieldComment$ = Comment$

PUT #1, 5                'Write record number 5
```

Reading a Record with *GET*

GET and PUT are complementary statements. You write a record with PUT; you read a record with GET.

S T A T E M E N T	GET #*filenum*, *recordnum*
	
	where
	
	    filenum is the file number
	
	and
	
	    recordnum specifies the record number being read.
	
	The pound sign is optional. Also, the *recordnum* parameter is optional. If you omit *recordnum*, QBasic uses the next higher record number from the last record read or written.

GET and PUT are exact opposites. Whereas PUT writes a record from data stored in the field variables, GET reads a record and places the data into the field variables. You then must decipher the string information in the field variables to finally derive the actual data in the record.

As with PUT, text fields are easy and numeric fields are more complicated. After a GET instruction, a field variable for a text field contains the actual data read from the record.

Numeric data, however, must be reconverted from the string form of the field variable back to the proper numeric format. The "CV" group of numeric functions performs this conversion. Whereas the "MK$" functions convert numbers to field variable strings, the CV functions convert the field variable strings back to numbers.

```
CVI(string2$)
CVL(string4$)
CVS(string4$)
CVD(string8$)
where
    string2$ is a two-byte string,
    string4$ is a four-byte string,
and
    string8$ is an eight-byte string.
```

F
U
N
C
T
I
O
N

You must know which numeric data type corresponds to each field variable. Then use the appropriate CV function: CVI for integer, CVL for long integer, CVS for single-precision, and CVD for double-precision.

Here is a sample program fragment that reads the third record of the coin database and transfers the data from the field variables into normal program variables:

```
GET #1, 5            'Read record number 5

Year% = CVI(FieldYear$)
Category$ = FieldCategory$
Value! = CVS(FieldValue$)
Comment$ = FieldComment$
```

CAUTION

Field variables have a special status. They cannot be used as normal program variables. Use only LSET and RSET instructions to assign data to field variables.

In particular, never use a field variable on the *left* side of an assignment instruction, such as

```
FieldComment$ = "Uncirculated"
```

or with an INPUT instruction. Such transgressions cause the field variable to be disassociated with the file buffer and render the field variable useless for further file I/O.

Of course, field variables often appear on the *right* side of assignment statements to extract data after a GET instruction.

Closing the File

When I/O activity is finished, use a CLOSE instruction as usual.

Compatibility with BASICA and GW-BASIC

Random files created with QBasic are almost but not quite compatible with random files created with BASICA or GW-BASIC.

The discrepancy occurs with single- and double-precision numeric fields. QBasic uses IEEE formats to store such numbers but BASICA (and GW-BASIC) use an older Microsoft proprietary format. As a result, you must convert formats when transporting files between the different versions of BASIC. Fortunately, QBasic includes a complete set of conversion functions.

CVSMBF and CVDMBF replace CVS and CVD respectively when you use QBasic to read a random file created with BASICA or GW-BASIC. Similarly, MKSMBF$ and MKDMBF$ replace MKS$ and MKD$ respectively when you use QBasic to create a random file that is later to be read with a BASICA or GW-BASIC program.

F U N C T I O N

CVSMBF(*str4$*)

CVDMBF(*str8$*)

MKSMBF$(*numexpr*)

MKDMBF$(*numexpr*)

where

> *str4$* is a four-byte string representing a single-precision number in Microsoft's proprietary format,

> *str8$* is an eight-byte string representing a double-precision number in Microsoft's proprietary format,

and

> *numexpr* is a general numeric expression.

No special conversion is necessary for integer or text fields. QBasic, BASICA, and GW-BASIC use the same internal formats for such data.

BASICA and GW-BASIC do not support long integers. You cannot use MKL$ in QBasic when you create files destined to be read with a BASICA or GW-BASIC program.

Summary of Statements and Functions for Random-Access Files

Table 15.2 summarizes the statements and functions that work with random-access files.

Table 15.2. Random-access file statements and functions.		
Keyword	**Type**	**Effect**
OPEN	Statement	Opens a file FOR RANDOM
CLOSE	Statement	Closes a file
TYPE	Statement	Defines a record data type
PUT	Statement	Writes a record
GET	Statement	Reads a record
EOF	Function	Tests for the end of a file
LOF	Function	Returns the size of a file
SEEK	Statement	Sets file pointer to desired record
SEEK	Function	Returns next record to read or write
LOC	Function	Returns last record read or written
FIELD	Statement	Defines field variables
LSET	Statement	Assigns data to a field variable
RSET	Statement	Assigns data to a field variable
MKI$	Function	Converts integer to field form
MKL$	Function	Converts long integer to field form
MKS$	Function	Converts single-precision number to field form
MKD$	Function	Converts double-precision number to field form
MKSMBF$	Function	Converts single-precision numbers to Microsoft format
MKDMBF$	Function	Converts double-precision numbers to Microsoft format
CVI	Function	Converts field variable to integer
CVL	Function	Converts field variable to long integer

continues

Table 15.2. Continued

Keyword	Type	Effect
CVS	Function	Converts to single-precision number
CVD	Function	Converts to double-precision number
CVSMBF	Function	Converts single-precision numbers from Microsoft format
CVDMBF	Function	Converts double-precision numbers from Microsoft format

Using Binary Files

In addition to sequential files and random-access files, QBasic offers a third type of data file—the binary file. At the most elemental level, any file is just a sequence of byte values. You can open any file in binary file mode to read or write such bytes directly. No particular structure is assumed; the entire file is treated as one long sequence of bytes.

When working with such files, you usually need to know how the file data is organized to make any sense of the data. Does the data represent ASCII values, memory maps, numeric formats? Something else?

Binary mode is useful to interpret files created in formats alien to QBasic, such as spreadsheets or non-ASCII word-processing documents. You can read or modify any part of the file, including control characters, end-of-file indicators, or anything else.

A file position pointer is associated with each binary file. At any given time, the pointer identifies which byte is the next to be read or written. The file bytes are considered to be numbered sequentially: one for the first byte, two for the next byte, and so on. You can move the pointer anywhere in the file and then read or write however many bytes you want.

After a file is opened in binary mode, you can both read and write to the file.

Working with a Binary File

Use the following steps to work with a binary file in a QBasic program:

1. OPEN the file FOR BINARY.

2. Use GET instructions to read data or PUT instructions to write data.

3. CLOSE the file.

Opening the File

For binary files, the OPEN instruction simply declares the file as BINARY.

For example, this instruction opens a file residing on the A: drive as file number 3:

```
OPEN "A:MYFILE.BIN" FOR BINARY AS #3
```

A single OPEN instruction opens a binary file for reading, writing, or appending.

Reading and Writing Data

Use GET to read from the file, and PUT to write to the file.

```
GET #filenum, startbyte, variable

PUT #filenum, startbyte, variable
```

where

  filenum is the file number,

  startbyte is a numeric expression specifying the byte in the file where I/O begins,

and

  variable is any variable, array element, or record variable to receive or transmit the data values.

The pound sign is optional. As this section explains, the *startbyte* parameter is optional.

S T A T E M E N T

If you omit *startbyte*, the current file pointer establishes a default value. Successive GET and PUT instructions automatically adjust this pointer. Also, you can use SEEK to adjust the pointer explicitly.

GET reads the necessary number of bytes required to satisfy the length of *variable* (two bytes for a variable of integer type, eight bytes for a double-precision variable, and so on). If *variable* is a user-defined type or a fixed-length string, GET simply reads the number of bytes required to satisfy the length of the variable. If *variable* is a variable-length string, the length of *variable* is considered to be the length of the data currently stored in *variable*. Similarly, PUT writes the number of bytes equal to the length of *variable*.

The following instruction reads eight bytes from file number 1 into the double-precision variable MyData# (eight bytes are read because double-precision variables occupy eight bytes):

```
GET #1, , MyData#
```

The omission of the second parameter indicates that reading begins from the current position of the file pointer. After the read, the file pointer advances eight bytes.

What happens if you try to read past the end of the file? No error occurs, but only bytes within the file are read. Bytes past the end of the file are "read" as binary 0.

For example, suppose the file pointer is at byte 28, the last byte in the file is 30, and you execute the preceding GET instruction. Only three bytes transfer to MyData# (bytes 28, 29, and 30). The file pointer remains at the end of the file.

Here are some examples of PUT instructions:

```
PUT #1, 45, MyName$    'Writes string beginning at byte 45

PUT #1, , Coin         'Writes coin record at default location
```

Use PUT to modify existing data or to write new information past the end of the file.

Closing the File

Close the file in the usual way.

Using the *SEEK* Statement

Use the SEEK statement to adjust the file pointer. For example, the following instruction sets the pointer position to byte number 50 of file number 3:

```
SEEK #3, 50
```

The position can range from 1 to 2,147,483,647.

After you use SEEK, a GET or PUT instruction without a *startbyte* parameter uses the newly specified file position.

You can SEEK to any file position—even a position past the end of the file. In such cases, PUT appends data and increases the file size.

Using the *SEEK* and *LOC* Functions

With binary files, the SEEK and LOC functions return a file position in number of bytes from the beginning of the file. SEEK returns the current file pointer, which is always at the next byte to be read or written. LOC returns the last byte read or written.

```
PUT #3, 30, MyAge%       'Last byte written is byte number 31
PRINT "File pointer is at byte number"; SEEK(3)
PRINT "Last byte written was number"; LOC(3)
```

The output is

```
File pointer is at byte number 32
Last byte written was number 31
```

Using the *EOF* Function

The EOF function works the same as with random files. EOF returns True (–1) if a GET statement tries to read past the end of the file.

A Sample Program—A Quick File Analyzer

Suppose that a friend approaches you one day with a disk in hand. Somewhat chagrined, she says "I've got a problem. There's a strange file on this disk. I think it's a data file of some sort, but I don't know what program generated the file or even what format the file is in. Can you help me?"

QBasic's binary file mode is useful in this situation. You can write a program to read the file in binary and "dump" the contents for analysis. For starters, you might try the program in Listing 15.2, SHOWFILE.BAS. Assume that the file is named ALIEN.XXX and that you place the disk in your B: drive.

Listing 15.2. The SHOWFILE.BAS program.

```
REM Program: SHOWFILE.BAS   (Dump the contents of a file)

FileName$ = "B:ALIEN.XXX"
OPEN FileName$ FOR BINARY AS #4

DIM Byte AS STRING * 1     'Define Byte as a 1-character string
```

continues

Listing 15.2. Continued

```
FOR Index% = 1 TO LOF(4)    'Loop through each byte in file
   GET #4, , Byte
   SELECT CASE ASC(Byte)
      CASE IS < 32: Byte = CHR$(3)     'ASCII   3 = heart  symbol
      CASE IS > 127: Byte = CHR$(236)  'ASCII 236 = infinity sign
      CASE ELSE
      REM                                  Leave Byte alone
   END SELECT

   PRINT Byte;
   IF (Index% MOD 40) = 39 THEN PRINT
NEXT Index%

PRINT
CLOSE #4
END
```

This program interprets the contents of the file as ASCII characters. To avoid certain control characters disrupting the screen display, all bytes with ASCII values less than 32 are displayed as the heart symbol. All bytes with ASCII values greater than 127 are displayed as the infinity sign. "Normal" text characters (in the ASCII range from 32 to 127) display verbatim.

Of course, this program is only a first cut at analyzing the data. You can extend this technique to print each byte in hexadecimal form and to search for special file control characters such as carriage-return (ASCII 13) and line-feed (ASCII 10).

What happens if you try using SHOWFILE.BAS on the coin database files? Figures 15.3 and 15.4 show the results when FileName$ is set to B:MYCOINS.SEQ and to B:MYCOINS.RAN, respectively. (MYCOINS.SEQ is in its original form—before using either update program.)

Figure 15.3.

Dumping
B:MYCOINS.SEQ with
SHOWFILE.BAS.

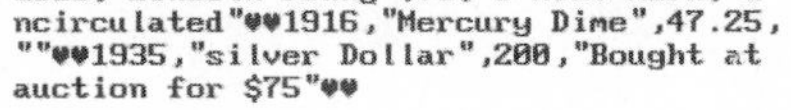

```
1910,"Lincoln Penny",70,"S Mint mark, u
ncirculated"♥♥1916,"Mercury Dime",47.25,
""♥♥1935,"silver Dollar",200,"Bought at
auction for $75"♥♥
```

Notice that B:MYCOINS.SEQ produces compact output. Both text and numeric fields are readable. By contrast, B:MYCOINS.RAN produces spacious output with unreadable numeric fields. The continuous blank regions are due to unused (blank) positions in the 50-character Comment field. The unreadable numbers are due to the fact that random files store numbers in internal binary formats, not as ASCII text.

```
v♥Lincoln Penny      ♥♥∞BS mint mark u
ncirculated                        !♥M
ercury Dime       ♥♥=B
                                 ∞♥Silve
r Dollar       ♥♥HCBought at auction for
   $75
```

Summary of Statements and Functions for Binary Files

Table 15.3 summarizes the statements and functions used to process binary files.

Table 15.3. Binary file statements and functions.

Keyword	Type	Effect
OPEN	Statement	Opens a file FOR BINARY
CLOSE	Statement	Closes a file
PUT	Statement	Writes data to a file
GET	Statement	Reads from a file
EOF	Function	Tests for end of file
LOF	Function	Returns the size of a file
SEEK	Statement	Sets the file position pointer
SEEK	Function	Returns current byte pointer
LOC	Function	Returns pointer to last byte I/O

Another Look at the *OPEN* Statement

As you have seen, the first step in programming with a data file is to OPEN the file. Let's review the general syntax of an OPEN instruction.

The General Syntax of *OPEN*

The general syntax of an OPEN instruction is as follows:

<table>
<tr>
<td>
S
T
A
T
E
M
E
N
T
</td>
<td>

OPEN *filespec* FOR *mode* AS #*filenum* LEN = *recordlength*

where

    filespec is a string expression that specifies the name (and optionally the path) of the data file,

    mode is one of the five terms shown in Table 15.4,

    filenum is an integer expression from 1 to 255 and associates a numeric value with the opened file,

and

    recordlength is an integer expression specifying the size (in bytes) of each record in a random-access file.

</td>
</tr>
</table>

The *mode* parameter establishes the file type and the I/O mode as shown in Table 15.4.

Table 15.4. File modes.

mode	File Type	I/O Activity
INPUT	Sequential	Reading from beginning of file
OUTPUT	Sequential	Writing new file
APPEND	Sequential	Writing after end of old file
RANDOM	Random	Reading and writing on a new or old file
BINARY	Binary	Reading and writing on a new or old file

The entire FOR *mode* clause is optional. If you omit the clause, QBasic opens the file as a random access file—just as if the OPEN instruction specified FOR RANDOM.

Use the LEN = *recordlength* clause with a random file to specify the length of each record in the file. Like the FOR clause, the LEN clause is also optional. If you omit the LEN clause, the record length defaults to 128 bytes (characters).

Normally, you specify a LEN clause with any random file, and omit the LEN clause with a sequential or binary file. (A LEN clause with a sequential file adjusts the length of the file buffer. File buffers are managed by DOS and, generally speaking, are not something you need to concern yourself about. Consult your DOS documentation for more information about file buffers. QBasic simply ignores a LEN clause with a binary file.)

As an example of OPEN, the following instruction opens the file CARDS.SEQ (on the current directory of the A: drive) as a sequential file to be read from. A file number of 18 is assigned to this file.

```
OPEN "A:CARDS.SEQ" FOR INPUT AS #18
```

The following instruction opens a random file named CARDS.RAN (on the current directory of the A: drive) as file number 3. The length of each file record is 93 bytes.

```
OPEN "A:CARDS.RAN" FOR RANDOM AS #3 LEN = 93
```

The following instruction opens a binary file named TEST.BIN (on the \BIN directory of the C: drive) as file number 7:

```
OPEN "C:\BIN\TEST.BIN" FOR BINARY AS #7
```

Succinct Syntax of *OPEN*

The OPEN statement has a second, more succinct syntax. This second form is like an abbreviated, stripped-down version of the general syntax.

```
OPEN modestring, #filenum, filespec, recordlength
```
where

> *modestring* is a string expression establishing the file type and I/O mode.

The *filenum*, *filespec*, and *recordlength* parameters have the same meanings as in the original syntax. The pound sign and the *recordlength* parameter are optional.

S T A T E M E N T

Only the first character of *modestring* is meaningful; therefore *modestring* is usually just a single character. Table 15.5 lists the possible values of *modestring* and their *mode* equivalents from the general syntax.

Table 15.5. Values for *modestring*.

modestring	Equivalent Mode
"I"	INPUT
"O"	OUTPUT
"A"	APPEND
"R"	RANDOM
"B"	BINARY

Here are the three previous instructions written with the succinct syntax.

```
OPEN "I", #18, "A:CARDS.SEQ"

OPEN "R", #3, "A:CARDS.RAN", 93

OPEN "B", #7, "C:\TEST.BIN"
```

The general and succinct forms of the OPEN instruction are equivalent—just different ways of expressing the same thing. Take your pick. The general syntax is easier to read in actual programs, but the succinct form saves a few typing keystrokes.

Opening Files in a Network Environment

Our discussion of OPEN's general syntax is not quite complete. OPEN accepts some optional parameters useful when designing file-handling programs for a network environment.

On a network, such as a local area network, two users running independent programs might want to open a specific file at the same time. When working in a network environment, you need control over which files can be shared and what privileges (reading and writing) you grant other users on your files.

QBasic accommodates network needs with two optional items in the OPEN instruction: the ACCESS clause and the *lockmode* parameter. Also, the LOCK and UNLOCK statements provide additional network control.

Declaring Access Permissions in an *OPEN* Instruction

In an OPEN instruction, the optional ACCESS clause and the optional *lockmode* parameter are placed as follows:

```
OPEN filespec FOR mode ACCESS accessmode lockmode
AS #filenum LEN = recordlength
```

where

    filespec, *mode*, *filenum*, and *recordlength* have the same meanings as described previously in the general syntax for the OPEN instruction.

    accessmode and *lockmode* are described subsequently in Tables 15.6 and 15.7.

S T A T E M E N T

Use the ACCESS *accessmode* clause to declare your intentions on a public file. Table 15.6 shows the three possible values for *accessmode*.

Table 15.6. Access parameters in an *OPEN* instruction.

accessmode	Meaning
READ	Opens the file for reading only
WRITE	Opens the file for writing only
READ WRITE	Opens the file for reading and writing (legal only if mode is APPEND, RANDOM, or BINARY)

For example, the following instruction specifies that you are opening a public file for reading only:

```
OPEN "C:SALES.DTA" FOR INPUT ACCESS READ AS #4
```

Use the *lockmode* parameter to specify the type of access other users can have to a file that you open. Table 15.7 shows the possible values of *lockmode*.

Table 15.7. Values for *lockmode* in an *OPEN* instruction.

lockmode	Meaning
(default)	Only one user can open the file at a time.
SHARED	Multiple users can open the file jointly.
LOCK READ	No other user can read from the file.
LOCK WRITE	No other user can write to the file.
LOCK READ WRITE	No other user can access the file.

Using the *LOCK* and *UNLOCK* Statements

Use LOCK to deny other programs access to an opened file. The companion statement, UNLOCK, removes the restrictions.

S T A T E M E N T

```
LOCK #filenum, recordnum

LOCK #filenum, start TO end

UNLOCK #filenum, recordnum

UNLOCK #filenum, start TO end
```

where

   filenum is the file number,

   recordnum is the record or byte to be locked,

   start is the number of the first record or byte to be locked,

and

   end is the number of the last record or byte to be locked.

The pound sign is optional. Also, all information after the *filenum* parameter is optional. Further, you can omit the *start* parameter from the *start* TO *end* clause.

Notice that LOCK and UNLOCK instructions each have two forms: one form that specifies a single record or byte to be locked, and a second form that specifies a range of records or bytes to be locked.

For random-access files, *recordnum*, *start*, and *end* refer to a record number. Record number 1 is the first record of the file. For binary files, the three parameters refer to a byte location with byte number 1 being the first byte in the file.

Use *recordnum* to specify a single record or byte to be locked or unlocked. Use *start* and *end* to specify a range of records or bytes. If you omit *start*, the default value is 1. If you omit all record arguments, the complete file becomes locked.

Here are some example LOCK instructions. The file number parameter is 7, and a binary file is assumed.

```
LOCK #7              'Lock the complete file

LOCK #7, 49          'Lock only byte 49
```

```
LOCK #7, 18 TO 39      'Lock bytes 18 through 39

LOCK #7, TO 99         'Lock bytes 1 through 99
```

To remove a lock, UNLOCK requires the identical parameters used in the companion LOCK instruction. You cannot use UNLOCK to remove only some of the restrictions imposed by LOCK.

For example, if you lock records numbered 10 to 25 with a LOCK instruction, a subsequent UNLOCK instruction must also specify the records numbered from 10 to 25. You could not unlock only the records numbered from, say, 15 to 20.

Using the *FILEATTR* Function

The FILEATTR function returns the attributes of any opened file.

FILEATTR(*filenum, attribute*)

where

   filenum is the file number,

and

   attribute is an integer expression specifying which information to return.

F U N C T I O N

The value of *attribute* can be 1 or 2. When *attribute* is 1, FILEATTR returns a number that indicates the mode of the opened file (see Table 15.8).

Table 15.8. Mode values returned by the *FILEATTR* function.

Returned Value	File Mode
1	INPUT
2	OUTPUT
4	RANDOM
8	APPEND
32	BINARY

When attribute is 2, FILEATTR returns the DOS-internal file number assigned to the opened file. This number is sometimes referred to as the DOS file handle.

More on Closing Files

As you have seen, a CLOSE instruction cancels your program's communication link with an open file. In the examples so far, each CLOSE instruction closed a single file by specifying the file number with which the file was opened.

However, a single CLOSE instruction can close two or more files. To do so, specify all the desired file numbers, separating each with a comma. For example, the following instruction closes files numbered 2, 3, and 8:

```
CLOSE #2, #3, #8
```

Furthermore, CLOSE with no file number arguments closes *all* open files. The RESET statement, which accepts no arguments, has the same effect. END and RUN statements also close all open files.

After closing a file, the file number previously associated with the file becomes available for a subsequent OPEN instruction. Similarly, after closing a file, you can reopen the file with the same or with a different file number as long as the new file number doesn't conflict with the file number of another opened file.

Here are some examples of instructions that close files:

```
CLOSE #1            'Close file number 1

CLOSE #2, #3        'Close files 2 and 3

CLOSE 2, 3          'Close files 2 and 3 (no pound signs)

CLOSE MyFile%       'Close file specified by variable

CLOSE               'Close all opened files

RESET               'Close all opened files
```

Summary

In the last two chapters, you learned how to manage external disk files from within your programs. External files give you the power to store data separately from programs. That way, programs that regularly use data files can remain unchanged even though the data files are modified. Furthermore, one program can read or write a data file used by other programs.

Similar to a sequential file, a random file database is organized into a series of primary records, with each record containing one or more fields. A binary file, by contrast, is treated as a series of data bytes with no assumed structure.

Sequential files are easy to program. However, reading and writing records are relatively slow. For large databases, random-access files have many advantages. Any record in a random-access file can be read or written quickly. However, programming random-access files is more complicated. Binary files provide great flexibility, but demand that you keep track of both the file organization and the meaning of each data byte.

Using Hardware Devices

The last four chapters attest to the considerable control you have over the video screen and the disk drives. But QBasic also supports other hardware devices. This chapter shows you how to control the following hardware devices:

- Line printer
- Keyboard
- Speaker
- Date and time RAM
- Joysticks
- Light pen

You can "trap" activity on many of these devices; that is, you can specify that if a certain event—such as the pressing of a key or the use of the light pen—takes place while your program is running, a branch to a designated subroutine occurs. See Chapter 21, "Trapping Errors and Events," for a discussion of event trapping.

Using the Printer

Your computer system probably includes a line printer—perhaps a dot-matrix, ink jet, or laser printer. You can control your printer inside QBasic programs or generate program listings from the development environment.

Of course, your printer must be on before you can produce any printed output. You cannot turn your printer on or off directly from QBasic. You have to flip your printer's power switch (or press your printer's power button) the old-fashioned way—by hand.

Sending Output to the Printer

Often you want to produce printed output. Some programs produce financial or inventory reports, for example. You can easily direct your output to the printer rather than to the video screen. QBasic has two statements that direct output to the printer.

<table>
<tr>
<td>

**S
T
A
T
E
M
E
N
T**

</td>
<td>

`LPRINT expressionlist punctuation`

and

`LPRINT USING formatstring; expressionlist punctuation`

where

    `expressionlist` is a list of expressions separated by commas and semi colons,

    `formatstring` is a string expression containing formatting instructions,

and

    `punctuation` is either a comma or a semicolon.

In an `LPRINT` instruction, `expressionlist` is optional. In either an `LPRINT` or `LPRINT USING` instruction, `punctuation` is optional.

</td>
</tr>
</table>

`LPRINT` and `LPRINT USING` send data to your printer in much the same way that `PRINT` and `PRINT USING` send data to your video screen:

- Comma separators delineate multiple expressions into print zones.

- A trailing semicolon in the expression list suppresses the carriage return/line feed.

- The simple instruction `LPRINT` (without any expression list) prints a blank line on the printer.

- `LPRINT USING` works with format strings in exactly the same way `PRINT USING` does.

- The `TAB` and `SPC` functions work within `LPRINT` and `LPRINT USING`.

The essential point is that just as any PRINT instruction creates output on the video screen, the equivalent LPRINT instruction produces the same output on the line printer. Similarly, LPRINT USING duplicates on your printer the results that PRINT USING produces on your video screen.

 What Does the L Stand for?

You can think of the *L* in LPRINT as an abbreviation for *Line* printer.

See Chapter 12, "Writing Text on the Video Screen," for a complete discussion of PRINT, PRINT USING, TAB, and SPC.

Adjusting the Printer Width

By default, QBasic assumes that your printer has a width of 80 characters. This means that you cannot print past column 80. After printing in column 80, QBasic "tells" the printer to do a carriage-return and line-feed. As a result, printing continues at the leftmost column in the next line down.

The WIDTH LPRINT statement, however, lets you adjust the default printer width.

WIDTH LPRINT *width*

where

    width is a numeric expression specifying the default width for the line printer. The *width* parameter should have a value from 1 to 255.

S
T
A
T
E
M
E
N
T

You might want to make *width* larger or smaller than 80. If you have a wide carriage printer, you can set *width* to 136 (or whatever your actual printer width is) to enable wide-carriage printing. For printer emulation of 40-column SCREEN mode, set *width* to 40. However, by setting *width* to the maximum value of 255, QBasic no longer checks the length of a printed line.

Listing 16.1, the PRNWIDTH.BAS program, demonstrates the effect of adjusting the printer width:

Listing 16.1.   The PRNWIDTH.BAS program.

```
REM Program: PRNWIDTH.BAS (Adjust the printer's default width)

Motto$ = "A stitch in time saves nine."
WIDTH LPRINT 80             'Set printer width to 80
LPRINT Motto$
LPRINT                      'Print a blank line

WIDTH LPRINT 20             'Set printer width to 20
LPRINT Motto$
LPRINT

WIDTH LPRINT 10             'Set printer width to 10
LPRINT Motto$
END
```

The output of PRNWIDTH.BAS looks like this on the printer:

```
A stitch in time saves nine.

A stitch in time sav
es nine.

A stitch i
n time sav
es nine.
```

Using the *LPOS* Function

Use LPOS to determine the horizontal (column) position of the print head. LPOS does for the printer what POS does for the screen.

FUNCTION

LPOS(*printernumber*)

where

   printernumber is a numeric expression specifying the printer number.

The value of *printernumber* specifies the DOS line-printer designation. Most single-printer systems configure the line printer as device LPT1:. Systems with two or three printers also have LPT2: and/or LPT3:. A value of 0 or 1 for *printernumber* refers to LPT1:, 2 refers to LPT2:, and 3 refers to LPT3:.

The vast majority of computer systems have a single printer (which is almost always configured as LPT1:). If your system is in this large group, use 0 or 1 as the value for *printernumber*.

LPOS is handy when you print multiple items on a single line. At a given point in your program, you might need to know whether the current printer line has enough room to print the next item. If there is enough room, you want to print the item. If not, you want to issue a carriage return before you print the item.

As an example, the following program fragment checks whether the current line of an 80-column printer has sufficient room to print the value of Item$. If not, the IF instruction issues a printer carriage return (LPRINT) before the subsequent program line prints Item$.

```
IF (LPOS(1) + LEN(Item$)) > 80 THEN LPRINT
LPRINT Item$
```

It is not quite accurate to say that LPOS returns the current column position of the printer head. Many printers buffer output. LPOS actually returns the number of characters sent to the printer since the last carriage return was sent.

LPOS and *TAB* Don't Mix

Be aware that LPOS might not work correctly if you use the TAB function in your LPRINT instructions. TAB characters are not recognized correctly by LPOS because LPOS does not expand TAB functions into individual characters. Avoid TAB if you intend to use LPOS.

Generating Program Listings

You can generate a printed listing of your current program any time the program is loaded in the QBasic editor environment. You do so through the Print option on the File menu. The necessary steps are explained in Chapter 5, "Using the QBasic Editor."

Using the Keyboard

Now it is time to turn your attention to an extremely important part of your computer—the keyboard. This section examines the following ways that you can control this device with which your fingers are so familiar:

■ Accept input from the user while the program is running.

■ Detect a user keystroke.

■ Define the function keys to produce specified strings.

■ Manipulate the Function Key Display on the bottom of your screen.

Obtaining User Input

Frequently, you want the user to supply information while your program is running. QBasic provides three similar ways to request and accept input data—the INPUT statement, the LINE INPUT statement, and the INPUT$ function.

You are already familiar with the INPUT and LINE INPUT statements:

■ INPUT prompts the user for numeric or string data (or both). The INPUT statement was introduced in Chapter 3, "A Hands-On Introduction to Programming," and has been used frequently in the program examples.

■ LINE INPUT stores an entire line typed by the user into a single string variable. The LINE INPUT statement was introduced in Chapter 14, "Using Sequential Disk Files," in conjunction with disk files.

This chapter condenses what you have learned about INPUT and LINE INPUT, and presents some further details. The INPUT$ function is also introduced.

The *INPUT* Statement

An INPUT instruction enables your program to prompt the user for one or more data values.

```
INPUT ; "promptstring"; variablelist
```

where

   promptstring is a string literal displayed on-screen to prompt the user for input,

and

   variablelist is a comma-delimited list of variables to which the user's input is assigned.

The semicolon after INPUT is optional. The semicolon after "promptstring" can be replaced with a comma. Different punctuation causes different effects, as this section will explain.

You can omit the entire promptstring clause, yielding this simpler form of INPUT:

```
INPUT variablelist
```

INPUT takes several forms.

In INPUT instructions, the semicolon and comma have the following meanings:

- A semicolon after the keyword INPUT makes the cursor stay on the same line after the user presses Enter.

- No semicolon (or other punctuation character) after the keyword INPUT causes the cursor to move down to the next line after the user presses Enter.

- A semicolon after "promptstring" causes the INPUT instruction to display the prompt string followed by a question mark.

- A comma after "promptstring" causes the INPUT instruction to display the prompt string, but no question mark is added to the prompting string.

When you don't include a prompt string with INPUT, only a question mark (with no message displayed) prompts the user.

Here is an example of the simplest form of INPUT instruction:

```
INPUT UserNumber!
```

The results of this instruction are the following:

1. The screen displays a question mark.

2. The program pauses for the user to supply a number. After typing the number, the user must press Enter.

3. The numeric value typed by the user is assigned to the variable
   `UserNumber!`.

4. The program continues.

You can display a prompting message by including a *promptstring* parameter,
as in the following example:

```
INPUT "Please enter a number";  UserNumber!
```

Now the message `Please enter a number?` prompts the user to enter a number.
Notice the question mark at the end of the message. If you use a comma rather
than a semicolon after `"promptstring"`, the question mark does not appear.

You can prompt for multiple values by using multiple variables in your variable list. The user must separate each typed-in value with a comma. Listing
16.2, AREARECT.BAS, is a simple example of prompting for two input values:

Listing 16.2. The AREARECT.BAS program.

```
REM Program: AREARECT.BAS (Demonstrate INPUT with two variables)

PRINT "Area of a rectangle given two connecting sides."
INPUT "Please enter the lengths of the 2 sides"; Side1!, Side2!
Area! = Side1! * Side2!
PRINT "The area is"; Area!
```

Here is sample output from this program:

```
Area of a rectangle given two connecting sides.
Please enter the lengths of the 2 sides? 10.6, 3.9
The area is 41.34
```

Variables in *variablelist* can be string variables as well as numeric variables.
For example, the following instruction requests the user's name:

```
INPUT "Please type your name"; UserName$
```

When you type string input in response to an INPUT prompt, you don't have to
enclose your response in double quotation marks. However, just as with
numeric input, a comma acts as a separator between distinct data values. By
using double quotation marks around a string, a single input string can contain
embedded commas. See the upcoming discussion of LINE INPUT for an example
of string input containing an embedded comma.

Leading blank spaces and tab characters are ignored in the typed input unless
double quotation marks are used around string data.

In addition to simple string or numeric variables, *variablelist* can also include
array elements or elements of records.

When responding to an INPUT prompt, your input must match *variablelist* both in number and type. That is, the number of input responses and their type (string or numeric) must correspond exactly to the number and type of variables in the variable list. If there is any discrepancy, QBasic displays the following message:

```
Redo from start
```

You then must reenter the entire line of data.

The *LINE INPUT* Statement

LINE INPUT is similar to INPUT.

LINE INPUT ; "*promptstring*"; *stringvariable*

where

    promptstring is a string literal displayed on-screen to prompt the user for input,

and

    stringvariable is a string variable to which the user's input is assigned.

The semicolon after LINE INPUT is optional.

You can omit the entire *promptstring* clause, yielding this simpler form of LINE INPUT:

LINE INPUT *stringvariable*

S T A T E M E N T

If included, the semicolon after LINE INPUT causes the cursor to stay on the same line after the user presses Enter.

LINE INPUT differs from INPUT in the following ways:

- You can assign data input from the keyboard to only one variable and the variable must be of the type string.

- No question mark prints automatically. You must explicitly include a question mark in *promptstring* when you want one to appear.

- Delimiters (such as commas) in the user's input have no special meaning. Everything the user types (up to 255 characters) before pressing Enter is transferred as a single string value in *stringvariable*.

Use `LINE INPUT` when commas are required as part of the input. Consider these two instructions:

```
INPUT "What is your full name"; FullName$
```

```
LINE INPUT "What is your full name? "; FullName$
```

Either instruction works if the input is **John Wesley Harding**. But suppose that the input is **Harding, John Wesley**. Now `LINE INPUT` works okay (the comma is accepted), but the `INPUT` instruction fails because the comma after `Harding` separates the input into two values (when only one value was expected).

The *INPUT$* Function

Chapter 14, "Using Sequential Disk Files," contains a discussion of the `INPUT$` function in relation to files. A simplified form of `INPUT$` reads characters typed from the keyboard.

F U N C T I O N

`INPUT$(`*numcharacters*`)`

where

numcharacters is an integer expression specifying how many characters to read.

For example, the following instruction assigns to `MyString$` the next five characters typed at the keyboard:

```
MyString$ = INPUT$(5)
```

More precisely, `INPUT$` reads from the keyboard buffer. Any characters waiting in the buffer are processed. If necessary, `INPUT$` pauses execution until the required number of characters is typed.

The `INPUT$` function does not echo the typed characters on-screen.

Detecting a Keystroke

Suppose that in a particular program you need to display two screens full of information one after the other. You want the first screen to remain visible until the user is ready to read the second screen.

One solution is to display a message with the first screen that instructs the user to press a key to view the second screen.

That's fine, but how do you pause your program's execution and detect when the user presses a key? Well, we wouldn't ask this question if QBasic didn't provide a way, would we?

If you simply want to detect a single keystroke, use the INKEY$ function.

INKEY$

The INKEY$ function examines the keyboard buffer to determine whether a key was pressed. Even if multiple characters are waiting in the buffer, only the first keystroke is recognized. INKEY$ returns a zero-, one-, or two-character string interpreted as follows:

- *Null string*: No character is in the keyboard buffer; that is, no character has been pressed yet.

- *One-character string*: The string contains the actual character read from the keyboard buffer. For example, if the user pressed the g key, INKEY$ returns "g"; if the user pressed Shift-g, INKEY$ returns "G".

- *Two-character string*: This indicates that a special key was pressed, such as one of the function keys (F1 through F10, Home, or Del, for example) or a key combination (Alt-Q, for example). Such a two-character string is called an *extended key code*. The first character always has an ASCII value of 0. See Appendix C, "Keyboard Scan Codes," for a list of the extended codes.

The Keyboard Is Buffered

T I P

Whenever you press a key, whether you are using QBasic or some other application, DOS records the keystroke in the *keyboard buffer*. This buffer is simply an area of memory that retains the values of the most recent keystrokes. (As your application "reads" and processes your keystrokes, they are removed from the buffer. Typically, the buffer has room to record up to 16 keystrokes. This process of recording and removing the keystrokes from the buffer usually happens so fast that you don't notice any delay.)

While a QBasic program is running, keystrokes usually are not removed from the buffer (except by INPUT and other specialized instructions). Any keys you press build up in the buffer.

INKEY$, unlike INPUT, does not wait for the user to press a key. INKEY$ simply removes the first keystroke found in the keyboard buffer, if the buffer contains any keystrokes at all. Try the following demonstration program to see the effect of keyboard buffering and INKEY$:

```
PRINT "Start"
   FOR J = 1 TO 10000: NEXT J        'Waste time
   PRINT INKEY$          'Display 1st character in buffer
   PRINT INKEY$          'Display 2nd character in buffer
PRINT "Done"
```

The FOR-NEXT loop in the second line simply wastes time—about five seconds on an AT-class machine. (If you are using a PC with a 386 or 486 processor, you might want to raise the upper loop bound from 10,000 to 30,000.) During this wait, you can press a key to store a keystroke in the buffer.

For starters, run the program (press Shift-F5). Don't press any key after pressing Shift-F5. This is what you should see:

```
Start


Done
```

Notice the time delay (caused by the FOR-NEXT loop) from when the Start message displays until the Done message appears. The two blank lines between Start and Done are the result of the two PRINT INKEY$ instructions. Because you didn't press any keys while the program was running, the keyboard buffer is blank and INKEY$ returns a null string that is displayed as a blank line.

Now run the program again. Quickly press the h key (the unshifted letter H) after you see Start, but before Done appears. You now see the following:

```
Start
h

Done
```

Notice how the h keystroke remains in the buffer while waiting for the FOR-NEXT loop to terminate. The INKEY$ function then "pulls" this keystroke from the buffer and the first PRINT INKEY$ instruction dutifully displays it. No other character is in the keyboard buffer, so the second PRINT INKEY$ instruction once again results in a blank line of output.

Now for the big finish. Run the program one last time. Quickly press the h, j, and k keys in rapid succession, before the Done message displays. Here's the result:

```
Start
h
j
Done
```

The h, j, and k keystrokes were all stored in the buffer. The first PRINT INKEY$ instruction pulls out and displays the h. The second PRINT INKEY$ similarly detects and displays the j.

So what happens to the k? Actually, QBasic flushes (removes all characters from the buffer) immediately on starting a program and immediately after terminating a program. Therefore, the k was in the buffer while the program was running, but was "lost" when the program terminated. Notice also that if any keys are in the buffer when you start a program, those keys are flushed when you press Shift-F5.

The most frequent use of INKEY$ is, undoubtedly, to pause program execution until the user presses a key.

Remember the problem we posed of displaying two screens of information and waiting for the user to press a key to view the second screen? One solution is to place the following instructions between the program sections that display each screen:

```
PRINT "Press a key to see the next screen."
DO
LOOP WHILE INKEY$ = ""
```

The last two instructions form a simple DO loop that executes until the user presses any key. As long as the user doesn't press a key, INKEY$ continually returns the null string and the loop keeps going.

As soon as the user presses a key, INKEY$ returns some character, and the condition in the DO loop fails. The loop now terminates and the program continues with the next line (which in this case presumably begins displaying the second screen).

As this program demonstrates, INKEY$ is used most effectively in some kind of loop.

Defining the Function Keys

One exotic keyboard technique at your disposal is to redefine the F1 through F12 function keys. You can associate your own designated string values with the function keys. That way, when the user presses one of your preassigned function keys, out pops the string you defined for the key. You will feel like an honest-to-goodness programming wizard.

The KEY statement does the trick.

```
KEY funckeynumber, stringexpression
```

where

funckeynumber is an integer expression designating a particular
function key,

and

stringexpression is a general string expression.

KEY assigns the value of stringexpression to the designated function key. Now when the function key is pressed during program execution, the effect is as if stringexpression were typed instead.

Values of 1 through 10 for funckeynumber correspond to the function keys F1 through F10. On keyboards with F11 and F12, the corresponding values for funckeynumber are 30 and 31, respectively.

The text for stringexpression can be up to 15 characters. Characters beyond 15 are ignored.

Use KEY when specific strings or substrings are repeated frequently during user input. For example, suppose you're writing a program that prints invitations and seating cards for a dinner dance. The user must input a list of the attendees. (INPUT instructions prompt for the names.) Consider the benefits of adding these lines to the program:

```
KEY 1, "Dr. "
KEY 2, "Mr. "
KEY 3, "Mrs. "
KEY 4, "Ms. "
KEY 5, "Mr. and Mrs. "
```

Now, for example, rather than typing **Mr. and Mrs. John Hannan**, only F5 followed by **John Hannan** is necessary. This is quite a time-saver.

Here's a short program that reassigns the F2 key:

```
KEY 2, "The honorable "    'Blank space before the final quote
INPUT "Who are you anyway"; Person$
PRINT
PRINT "You are: "; Person$
```

Try the program. It's fun. When you are prompted for input, press F2 before typing your name. Kind of neat, isn't it?

NOTE

Key Trapping

Imagine this: A program interrupts itself to perform a special task whenever the user presses a particular key. For example, a program might display a help screen whenever the user presses F1.

This capability of instant response to a keystroke is called *key trapping*. In effect, you set a trap for a particular key. If the user "falls into the trap" by pressing the "hotkey," the program responds appropriately.

Key trapping is discussed in Chapter 21, "Trapping Errors and Events."

Displaying the Values of the Function Keys

QBasic provides some special statements that display values you might have assigned to the function keys.

You can optionally use the bottom (25th) line of the output screen as a Function Key Display. When so used, the bottom screen line perpetually displays the text strings assigned to the function keys F1 through F10. In this mode, only the upper 24 lines of the output screen display regular program output. Scrolling occurs at the 24th line because the 25th line is reserved for the Function Key Display.

Three special forms of the KEY statement enable you to display the key strings on-screen (see Table 16.1).

Table 16.1. Alternate forms of the *KEY* statement.

Instruction	Meaning
KEY ON	Turns on the Function Key Display on the bottom (25th) line of the output screen. The display shows the first six characters assigned to each of the F1 through F10 function keys.
KEY OFF	Removes the Function Key Display from the bottom line of the output screen.
KEY LIST	Displays the complete string value of each function key in a vertical list.

KEY ON and KEY OFF turn the Function Key Display on and off, respectively. The display consists of the numbers 1 through 10 spread out across the bottom screen line. Next to each number are the first six characters of the text string assigned to the corresponding function key (F1 through F10).

When a KEY ON instruction executes, the Function Key Display turns on for the remainder of the program (unless a subsequent KEY OFF instruction removes the display).

Try the following program to get a feel for the Function Key Display:

```
INPUT "Press Enter to turn on the Function Key Display", Dummy$
KEY ON
INPUT "Press Enter to reassign the F5 function key", Dummy$
KEY 5, "Wow"
INPUT "Press Enter to end the program", Dummy$
```

Press Enter in response to the first prompt. The bottom line of the output screen becomes the Function Key Display. Notice that no string values are preassigned to the function keys. Now press Enter again. The string "Wow" is now assigned to the F5 key, and you see the value reflected on the display line. Notice that when you press Enter to end the program, the Press any key to continue message is displayed right over the Function Key Display.

When you first invoke QBasic, no values are preassigned to the function keys. However, if you run a program that assigns a value to a function key, that value remains assigned when the program terminates and remains assigned even if you load a new program. You must exit and reenter QBasic to once again automatically blank out any assigned function keys.

NOTE

The Function Key Display with BASICA and GW-BASIC

If you have experience with BASICA or GW-BASIC, you'll notice that QBasic treats the Function Key Display differently than those earlier versions of BASIC.

With BASICA and GW-BASIC, the Function Key Display is on by default and certain values are preassigned to each of the F1 through F10 function keys. In contrast, QBasic has the Function Key Display off by default and no values are preassigned to any of the function keys.

For more about the Function Key Display with GW-BASIC or BASICA, see Chapter 23, "Learning the GW-BASIC (BASICA) Programming Environment."

Using the Speaker

The sound capability of IBM personal computers is rather modest. The speaker is limited to one voice in a single timbre. Furthermore, you can't adjust the volume. Still, the speaker can produce music and various sound effects.

Creating Sound Effects with *BEEP* and *SOUND*

As you have seen (heard?), BEEP creates a short (about a quarter-second) tone. The statement accepts no arguments, so the syntax is straightforward:

```
BEEP
```

Use BEEP to get your user's attention. You might use this when requesting input and when displaying an error message. Here's an example:

```
PRINT "Sorry, your checkbook is out of balance."
BEEP
```

SOUND instructions generate more sophisticated sound effects.

SOUND *frequency, duration*

where

    frequency is a numeric expression specifying the pitch of the sound in Hz (cycles per second),

and

    duration is a numeric expression specifying the length of time (in "clock ticks") to play the tone.

S
T
A
T
E
M
E
N
T

The *frequency* parameter can range from 37 to 32,767. In practice, you should avoid frequencies above 7000 because frequencies in the high range tend to cause poor response in most speakers. Above 7000, the tones tend to dwindle in volume until they become inaudible around 12,000 Hz.

The value of *duration* is measured in clock ticks. There are approximately 18.2 clock ticks per second. The following instruction plays a tone of 440 Hz for five seconds:

```
SOUND 440, 91
```

The SOUND instruction does not suspend program execution until the tone completes. Instead, the tone begins, and execution proceeds immediately with the subsequent instruction. The tone continues for the prescribed duration while other instructions execute simultaneously.

If a second SOUND instruction occurs while a tone is still playing, and the second SOUND instruction has a duration of zero, the speaker is turned off (canceling all sounds). If the duration is greater than zero, the first tone completes before the new SOUND instruction executes.

You can use SOUND to create special effects. Listing 16.3 contains a program that produces the sound effect of a spinning coin falling on a flat surface.

Listing 16.3. The COINFALL.BAS program.

```
REM Program: COINFALL.BAS (Sound effect of a falling coin)

FOR Index% = 20 TO 1 STEP -1
   SOUND 500, 1
   SOUND 32000, Index% * .1
NEXT Index%
```

This program uses a trick. The second SOUND instruction specifies a frequency of 32,000. As mentioned previously, a frequency this high is inaudible. As a result, the effect of this instruction is a short pause between sounds generated by the first SOUND instruction.

Playing Music with the *PLAY* Statement

Although SOUND can generate music, QBasic provides a much more flexible facility for playing tunes. With the PLAY statement, you can define musical passages with specialized string expressions and then play the music through the speaker.

STATEMENT

PLAY *stringexpression*

where

stringexpression is a string expression conforming to the conventions of the music macro language.

PLAY uses a special string language in much the same way that DRAW creates graphics with its specialized string language.

There are 84 notes available spanning seven octaves. The lowest note, note 1, is the C three octaves below middle C. Note 37 is middle C. The highest note, note 84, is the B note on the seventh octave.

You can specify notes by number or by letter. For example, the following instruction plays note 37:

PLAY "N37"

Similarly, the following instruction plays the same note (the C in octave 3):

PLAY "O3 C"

With the PLAY language, you can do the following:

- Play individual notes.
- Play rests (musical pauses).
- Adjust the tempo.

Fundamental PLAY command strings consist of a one- or two-letter mnemonic followed, in some cases, by a numeric argument. Table 16.2 lists the PLAY commands.

Table 16.2. *PLAY* commands.

Command	Action
O*n* *	Set *n* as the current octave.
>	Increase the octave by 1.
<	Decrease the octave by 1.
N*n*	Play note *n*.
A	Play the A note in the current octave.
B	Play the B note in the current octave.
C	Play the C note in the current octave.
D	Play the D note in the current octave.
E	Play the E note in the current octave.
F	Play the F note in the current octave.
G	Play the G note in the current octave.
L*n*	Set *n* as the duration of each subsequent note.
MS	Set "Music Staccato."

continues

Table 16.2. Continued

Command	Action
MN	Set "Music Normal."
ML	Set "Music Legato."
P*n*	Pause for *n* number of beats.
T*n*	Set *n* as the music tempo.
MF	Play music in foreground.
MB	Play music in background.
X	Execute substring.
+	Suffix to indicate a sharp.
#	Suffix to indicate a sharp (same effect as +).
-	Suffix to indicate a flat.
.	Suffix to increase note duration by 50 percent.

* n is an optional numeric argument used with several PLAY commands.

You can place multiple commands in a single string literal. For example, PLAY " T150 O4 CDE" plays three notes (C, D, and E) at a specified tempo. Within strings, spaces are irrelevant. Use spaces to clarify the components of your command strings.

Upper- and lowercase letters can be used interchangeably in the command strings.

Setting the Octave

There are seven octaves numbered from zero to six. Each octave ranges from a C note to the higher B note. Middle C is the first note in octave number 3 (which is actually the fourth octave, because the octaves are numbered from 0).

The O*n* (letter "oh") command sets the current octave with *n* ranging from zero to six. Setting the octave establishes the default octave for all notes to follow. Unless you specify otherwise, each subsequent note plays from the current octave.

The greater-than sign (>) increases the current octave by one; the less-than sign (<) decreases the current octave by one. However, you cannot set the octave to less than zero or greater than six. The default octave is four.

Playing an Individual Note

A letter from A to G specifies which note to play in the current octave. By adding a pound (#) or plus (+) symbol after the note, you change the note to a sharp. By adding a minus (-) symbol, you create a flat. The following instruction plays the entire 12 note sequence of octave 5:

```
PLAY "O5 C C# D D+ E F F# G A- A B- B"
```

With the N*n* command, you can specify notes by number rather than letter. Here, *n* is a number from 0 to 84 specifying which note to play. If *n* is zero, the program plays a rest (or pause) rather than a tone.

Adjusting the Length of Each Note

The L*n* command sets the length for all notes to follow. The note length is 1/*n*. For example, L1 is a whole note, and L4 is a quarter note. *n* can range from 1 to 64. The default for *n* is 4 (a quarter note).

A numeric length argument can follow a particular note to change the length of only that note. For example, the following instruction plays a B flat eighth note, an E eighth note, an F half note, and a C eighth note:

```
PLAY "L8 B-EF2C"
```

A period after an individual note plays a dotted note. This means that the length of the note is multiplied by 3/2. More than one dot can appear after each note, with each dot specifying another 3/2 multiplier to the total length. For example, PLAY "L4 C.." plays a C that is 9/4 as long as a quarter note. Dots can appear after a note even if a numeric length designator appears (for example, PLAY "A8.").

Use the P*n* command to specify a pause or rest. *n*, which can range from 1 to 64, determines the length of the pause, using the same scale as for the L command. You can use dots after a P command to extend the pause length.

Although the L command specifies the time for each note, the note actually plays only a percentage of this time. The three commands MS, MN, and ML specify this percentage. MS plays each subsequent note 3/4 of the time specified by L. The remaining 1/4 time is silent. With MN, each note is on 7/8 of the time and off 1/8. ML plays each note the full period specified by L (no delay between notes). The MS, MN, and ML abbreviations stand for the musical terms "music staccato" (quick), "music normal," and "music legato" (slow).

Adjusting the Tempo

The T*n* command adjusts the tempo for the subsequent music. This command sets *n* to the number of quarter notes per minute. The value of *n* can range from 32 to 255. The default is 120 (a quarter note plays for half a second).

Setting Foreground and Background Music

By default, music plays in the foreground. This means that any PLAY instruction must conclude before any subsequent instruction (PLAY or otherwise) executes.

You can also specify background music. In this mode, a PLAY instruction places music into a buffer. Subsequent program instructions execute while the music *simultaneously* plays from the buffer. The buffer can accept up to 32 notes at a time. If more than 32 notes stack up, music plays in the foreground until the number of notes in the buffer drops to 32.

Use MB to initialize background music. The MF command resets music to the foreground.

Using Variables with *PLAY*

So far, all the example PLAY strings and numeric arguments have been literals. But you can use variables instead.

Numeric variables can be used as parameters. The syntax, however, requires that the command letter be followed by an equal sign and then a string that identifies the memory location of the numeric variable. QBasic's VARPTR$ function determines the correct memory location. Table 16.3 shows some PLAY instructions written with numeric literals and the equivalent instructions using numeric variables.

Table 16.3. Using numeric variables with *PLAY*.

Instruction	Equivalent Form with Numeric Variables
PLAY "N45"	NoteNum% = 45: PLAY "N =" + VARPTR$(NoteNum%)
PLAY "O5 L8"	X% = 5: Y% = 8
	PLAY "O =" + VARPTR$(X%)
	PLAY "L =" + VARPTR$(Y%)

You can assign an entire command string to a string variable, and then PLAY the string variable. For example, you can play the natural notes from C to B by entering the following:

```
Scale$ = "CDEFGAB": PLAY Scale$
```

Using Substrings

The X subcommand specifies that a secondary string variable be executed from within the primary string. As with numeric variables, you must identify the memory location of the secondary string variable by using VARPTR$. For example, the following instruction plays the natural-note scale at two different tempos (assuming Scale$ is defined as in the previous example):

```
PLAY "T50 X" + VARPTR$(Scale$) + "T200 X" + VARPTR$(Scale$)
```

The X subcommand is awkward. You can get the same effect more directly. For example, the following instruction plays the same two musical scales as does the previous instruction:

```
PLAY "T50" + Scale$ + "T200" + Scale$
```

BASICA and GW-BASIC Compatibility

If you have BASICA or GW-BASIC programs containing instructions, be careful when converting these programs to QBasic. QBasic's PLAY is not quite compatible with BASICA's PLAY. Unlike BASICA, QBasic requires the VARPTR$ function to use the X subcommand and to embed variables in DRAW strings.

This incompatibility arises because, unlike an interpreter, the QBasic compiler cannot resolve variable names during program execution. With QBasic, variable names are converted into addresses at compile time. For more information, see Chapter 24, "Comparing the GW-BASIC (BASICA) Language to QBasic."

Sample Music

Let's put it all together. As an example of a complete tune, the program PLAYTUNE.BAS, Listing 16.4, plays the classic melody from *The Beautiful Blue Danube* by Johann Strauss, Jr., in the key of D. Run the program, sit back, and enjoy!

Listing 16.4. The PLAYTUNE.BAS program.

```
REM Program: PLAYTUNE.BAS (Play the Blue Danube Waltz)

TunePart$ = "DF#AL2 O4 D L4 O5 DDP4"
PLAY "T180 DF#A L2 AL4 O4 AAP4F#F#P4 O3 D"
PLAY "DF#A L2 A L4 O4 AAP4GGP4 O3 C+"
PLAY "C#EB L2 B L4 O4 BBP4GGP4 O3 C+"
PLAY "C#EB L2 B L4 O4 BBP4F+F+P4 O3 D"
PLAY TunePart$
PLAY "O4 AAP4 O3 D"
PLAY TunePart$
PLAY "O4 BBP4EEG L8 BP8 ML B1 L4 MN G+A ML L2 O5 F#1"
PLAY "L4 MN D O4 F# ML L2 F+ MN L4 E ML L2 B MN L4 A"
PLAY "DP8D8D4"
END
```

Using the *PLAY* Function

The PLAY function returns the number of unplayed notes in the background music buffer.

F U N C T I O N

PLAY(*dummyargument*)

where

   dummyargument can be any numeric expression.

The value of *dummyargument* has no effect on the operation of the PLAY function. The argument is required solely to satisfy conventional syntax.

The background music buffer is limited to 32 notes. Before adding notes to the buffer, you can use the PLAY function to be sure there is enough room.

For example, the following instruction checks that the music buffer can accommodate eight additional notes:

```
IF PLAY(1) <= 24 THEN PLAY "CDEFGAB>C"
```

If music is playing in the foreground or if no music is playing, the PLAY function returns a value of zero.

NOTE

Music Trapping

As mentioned previously, you can play background music while your program does other things. The background music buffer holds as many as 32 notes. Suppose that you want to continuously play a 60-note tune in the background. Is this possible?

Yes. The technique is known as *music trapping* because you set a trap for the background music buffer. When the number of notes in the buffer becomes small, the program automatically interrupts whatever it's doing to refill the buffer with more notes.

For additional information on playing music continually from the background music buffer, see the discussion of event trapping in Chapter 21, "Trapping Errors and Events."

Handling Dates and Times

Manipulating the date and time is often important. You might have a program that prints periodic inventory reports. You want to print the current date on the report but don't want to have to type the date each time you run the program.

You can retrieve the current date with a simple QBasic function. QBasic includes several statements and functions that make dealing with dates and times quite convenient. You can do the following:

- Set or retrieve the current calendar date.
- Set or retrieve the current time of day.
- Measure elapsed time.

Manipulating the Date with *DATE$*

DOS maintains the current date. On most of today's computers, this date is generated by a clock-calendar chip. When you start your computer, this chip sends the current date information to DOS. On older computers, you must explicitly provide the date when you boot the system.

Retrieving the Current Date

The DATE$ function, which retrieves the current date, takes no arguments:

DATE$

DATE$ returns the current date as a 10-character string. This string has the following form:

mm-dd-yyyy

where *mm* is the month (from 01 to 12), *dd* is the day of the month (from 01 to 31), and *yyyy* is the year (from 1980 to 2099).

For example, on the fourth of July in 1993, the instruction PRINT DATE$ displays the following output:

07-04-1993

Setting the Current Date

The DATE$ statement changes the date maintained by DOS.

<table>
<tr>
<td>

**S
T
A
T
E
M
E
N
T**

</td>
<td>

DATE$ = *datestring*

where

   datestring is a string expression specifying the date.

</td>
</tr>
</table>

You can format *datestring* in any of the following four ways:

mm-dd-yy

mm/dd/yy

mm-dd-yyyy

mm/dd/yyyy

Four-character year values must be within the range from 1980 to 2099. Two-character year values must range from 80 to 99—representing the years from 1980 to 1999.

The instruction DATE$ = "12-25-93" sets the system date to Christmas Day of 1993.

The following program fragment asks the user to input the current date and then displays the date for confirmation:

```
INPUT "Please type today's date in the form MM-DD-YY"; NewDate$
DATE$ = NewDate$
PRINT "Today's date is "; DATE$
```

Manipulating the Current Time of Day

DOS also maintains the time of day. You can retrieve and set this time in a manner similar to that used for the date.

Retrieving the Current Time

The TIME$ function, which retrieves the current time, takes no arguments.

```
TIME$
```

TIME$ returns the current time of day as an eight-character string. This string has the following form:

hh:mm:ss

where *hh* is the hour from 00 to 23, *mm* is minutes from 00 to 59, and *ss* is seconds from 00 to 59.

For example, at 10 seconds before 2 o'clock in the afternoon, the instruction PRINT TIME$ displays the following output:

```
13:59:50
```

Notice the use of military time (hours from 00 to 23).

Setting the Current Time

The TIME$ statement resets the current time maintained by DOS.

`TIME$` = *timestring*

where

    timestring is a string expression specifying the time.

You can format *timestring* in any of the following three ways:

hh

hh:*mm*

hh:*mm*:*ss*

If you omit minutes or seconds, the values of the missing parameters default to zero. Again, military time is used, so hours past noon have values greater than 12.

The instruction `TIME$` = `"17:30:15"` sets the time of day to 15 seconds after 5:30 p.m.

Measuring Elapsed Time with the *TIMER* Function

The `TIMER` function returns the number of seconds elapsed since midnight (or since the computer was booted, if the time of day was not set with the DOS `TIME` command or with QBasic's `TIME$` statement).

The instruction `PRINT TIMER` displays the elapsed time. Here's a sample of the elapsed time that `PRINT TIMER` might display:

`39601.11`

That's a lot of seconds, but it's only about 11 o'clock in the morning! (How many seconds are there in a day? Believe it or not, exactly 86,400.)

NOTE

How Accurate Is TIMER?

PRINT TIMER displays a single-precision number (usually expressed with two decimal digits). Because the IBM PC's internal clock is updated approximately 18.2 times a second (actually every 0.0549255 seconds), the resolution of the TIMER function is accurate to a little better than one-tenth of a second.

Timing Program Execution

Sometimes you need to know the elapsed time between two points in a program. For example, in an educational testing program, you might want to know how long the user takes to respond to questions.

The TIMER function does the job. Here are the required steps to measure the elapsed time between two points in a program:

1. Assign the value of TIMER to a variable; for example, StartTime! = TIMER.

2. Begin the process to be measured and complete the process.

3. Immediately assign the value of TIMER to a second variable; for example, EndTime! = TIMER.

4. Subtract the values of the two variables to determine the elapsed time.

As an example, the program in Listing 16.5 determines and displays the time required to calculate the square roots of the first 5,000 integers.

Listing 16.5. The ELAPTIME.BAS program.

```
REM Program: ELAPTIME.BAS (Measure computing time)

StartTime! = TIMER
FOR Index% = 1 TO 5000          'Loop to be timed
   MyVal! = SQR(Index%)
NEXT Index%
EndTime! = TIMER

PRINT "Elapsed time (seconds) ="; EndTime! - StartTime!
```

The following is the output of this program on one particular IBM AT-compatible computer. (Is your computer faster or slower?)

```
Elapsed time (seconds) = 4.171875
```

The precision of this output is deceptive. Because the TIMER function is accurate to one-tenth of a second, the accuracy of this output must be considered the same, namely 4.2 seconds.

How fast can you type? The program in Listing 16.6, HOWFAST.BAS, asks you to type the alphabet and then times your typing speed:

Listing 16.6. The HOWFAST.BAS program.

```
REM Program: HOWFAST.BAS (Measure typing time)
REM
StartTime! = TIMER
PRINT "Type the alphabet from a to z as fast as you can"
INPUT Stuff$
EndTime! = TIMER
PRINT "You took"; EndTime! - StartTime!; "seconds"
```

Here's what one of your nimble-fingered authors produced:

```
Type the alphabet from a to z as fast as you can
? abcdefghijklmnopqrstuvwxyz
You took 7.421875 seconds
```

How about you?

Pausing Execution for a Specified Time Period

You might want a program to pause for a specified time period. Let's say that you are programming a "slide show" that displays several consecutive screens of text and graphics. For the viewer to absorb each screen, you need the program to pause about 10 seconds between displays of each screen.

Time delays are another use for the TIMER function. One technique consists of invoking TIMER inside a WHILE-WEND loop until the specified time period elapses.

Suppose, for example, that you want to produce two speaker beeps spaced five seconds apart. The program in Listing 16.7 does just that.

Listing 16.7. The TWOBEEPS.BAS program.

```
REM Program: TWOBEEPS.BAS (Pause 5 seconds between beeps)

WaitTime! = 5            'Length of pause time (in seconds)
```

```
StartTime! = TIMER        'Store the starting time
BEEP                      'First beep

WHILE (TIMER - StartTime!) < WaitTime!
WEND                      'Loop for WaitTime! seconds

BEEP                      'Second beep
END
```

The critical component is the WHILE-WEND loop. The WHILE instruction continually invokes TIMER until the total elapsed time is greater than or equal to the value of WaitTime!.

This TIMER technique has the benefit of working correctly on a computer with any CPU chip (8088, 8086, 80286, or 80386) and at any clock speed.

CAUTION

The Midnight Problem

If you intend to time long events (lasting several hours), or you work in the wee hours, you should become familiar with the "midnight problem."

TIMER, as you know, returns the number of seconds since midnight. There are 86,400 seconds in a day (24 hours). So, just before midnight, TIMER returns values around 86,000. But, as soon as midnight passes, TIMER suddenly returns very small numbers.

Therefore, if midnight occurs while you are timing an event, the WHILE-WEND loop in the TWOBEEPS.BAS program no longer works. The dramatically decreased values returned by TIMER automatically satisfy the test condition. The loop perpetuates too long.

To solve this problem, you need a fancier WHILE-WEND loop that checks for the bewitching hour. Here is such a loop (if you want, you can substitute the following six program lines for the two WHILE-WEND instructions of TWOBEEPS.BAS):

```
Now! = StartTime!
WHILE (Now! - StartTime!) < WaitTime!
   OldTime! = Now!
   Now! = TIMER
   IF (Now! < OldTime!) THEN Now! = Now! + 86400!
WEND
```

The IF instruction checks for midnight and updates the value of Now! if necessary.

Using Joysticks

The IBM PC family can support two joysticks. Each joystick has a two-dimensional stick and one or two buttons (sometimes called triggers). For the purposes of the following discussion, consider the two joysticks labeled A and B, and the buttons on each joystick labeled 1 and 2.

Many computer systems use a single joystick. In this case, the joystick is A. Some joysticks have only one button, designated as button 1.

Reading the Joystick Coordinates with the *STICK* Function

Use the STICK function to determine current joystick coordinates.

<table>
<tr><td>F U N C T I O N</td><td>

STICK(*stickoption*)

where

    stickoption is a numerical expression specifying which joystick coordinate to return.
</td></tr>
</table>

The value of *stickoption* must resolve to an integer in the range from 0 to 3. Table 16.4 shows the coordinate returned for each value of *stickoption*.

Table 16.4. *STICK* function arguments.	
stickoption	Coordinate Value Returned
0	X coordinate of joystick A
1	Y coordinate of joystick A
2	X coordinate of joystick B
3	Y coordinate of joystick B

The value of each coordinate ranges from 1 to 200.

The values returned by STICK(1), STICK(2), and STICK(3) are not the current values of the respective coordinates but, instead, the values of the respective coordinates the last time STICK(0) was called. This clumsy circumstance is simply a quirk of the joystick interface.

A call to STICK(0) actually does double duty. Besides returning the X coordinate of joystick A, the call also stores each of the other joystick coordinates. To get the most accurate reading, call STICK(0) immediately before initiating a call to STICK(1), STICK(2), or STICK(3).

The following program fragment displays the value of the Y coordinates of each joystick:

```
Dummy! = STICK(0)      'Call STICK(0) to store all coordinates
PRINT STICK(1), STICK(3)
```

Reading the Joystick Buttons with the *STRIG* Function

The STRIG function returns information on the status of the joystick trigger buttons.

STRIG(*buttonoption*)

where

  buttonoption is a numerical expression specifying which button information to return.

F
U
N
C
T
I
O
N

The value of *buttonoption* must resolve to an integer in the range from 0 to 7. Table 16.5 shows the information returned for each value of *buttonoption*.

Table 16.5. *STRIG* function arguments.

buttonoption	Value Returned
0	−1 if button 1 on joystick A was pressed since the last STRIG(0) call; otherwise 0

continues

Table 16.5. Continued

buttonoption	Value Returned
1	−1 if button 1 on joystick A is currently pressed; otherwise 0
2	−1 if button 1 on joystick B was pressed since the last STRIG(2) call; otherwise 0
3	−1 if button 1 on joystick B is currently pressed; otherwise 0
4	−1 if button 2 on joystick A was pressed since the last STRIG(4) call; otherwise 0
5	−1 if button 2 on joystick A is currently pressed; otherwise 0
6	−1 if button 2 on joystick B was pressed since the last STRIG(6) call; otherwise 0
7	−1 if button 2 on joystick B is currently pressed; otherwise 0

Notice that the STRIG function always returns a value of −1 or 0. These values correspond to the Boolean (logical) values of True (−1) and False (0). As a result, you can conveniently use STRIG in IF instructions. For example, the following instruction prints Down if button 1 of joystick B is currently pressed or prints Up if the button is not being pressed:

```
IF STRIG(3) THEN PRINT "Down" ELSE PRINT   "Up"
```

Using a Light Pen

A light pen is one of the few optional peripheral devices supported by both the computer hardware and the operating system. Depending on the individual model you use, you activate the pen by pressing it against the screen or by using a switch on the stylus.

F U N C T I O N

QBasic's PEN function can monitor where the pen is located and whether the pen is activated.

PEN(*penoption*)

where

penoption is a numerical expression specifying which light pen information to return.

The value of *penoption* must resolve to an integer in the range from 0 to 9. Table 16.6 shows the information returned for each value of *penoption*.

Table 16.6. *PEN* function arguments.

penoption	Value Returned
0	−1 if pen was activated since the last call to PEN; otherwise 0
1	X pixel coordinate (0-319 or 0-639) the last time the pen was activated
2	Y pixel coordinate (0-199) the last time the pen was activated
3	−1 if pen is currently activated; otherwise 0
4	Current X pixel coordinate (0-319 or 0-639)
5	Current Y pixel coordinate (0-199)
6	The character row position (1-24) the last time the pen was activated
7	The character column position (1-40 or 1-80) the last time the pen was activated
8	The current character row position (1-24)
9	The current character column (1-40 or 1-80)

Before using the PEN function in a program, you must issue one PEN ON instruction. (See Chapter 21, "Trapping Errors and Events," for additional discussion of the PEN ON statement.)

The following program fragment checks whether the light pen is activated and, if so, displays the pen's coordinates:

```
PEN ON
IF PEN(3) THEN
    PRINT "X coordinate ="; PEN(4)
    PRINT "Y coordinate ="; PEN(5)
END IF
```

There is a possible conflict between the use of a light pen and a mouse. If you have a mouse installed, the mouse driver probably uses the same BIOS calls as the PEN function. This conflict causes the PEN function to malfunction. In such cases, you might need to disable your mouse before you can use the light pen successfully.

Summary

QBasic certainly gives you extensive control over your computer hardware. In previous chapters, you learned how to program your disk drives and fill your video screen with text and graphics. In this chapter, you learned how to write programs that manipulate the rest of your computer hardware: the printer, keyboard, speaker, and the internally maintained date and time.

With your printer, you can write programs that *print* the output (rather than display the output on the screen). You can also print program listings. This way, you can permanently save important results and view them at your leisure.

The keyboard is more intriguing than you might first imagine. Of course, you can have users type information when they are prompted by your program. But you can also assign string values to function keys and detect whenever the user presses a key.

Although the speaker is a simple piece of hardware, it is a gold mine for creative programmers. You can create sound effects and musical melodies. With PLAY, you can perform real music—your own compositions or popular favorites.

QBasic can manipulate the date and time maintained by DOS. You can print the current date and time as part of a sales report. In an educational testing program, you might time how long the user takes to provide particular answers.

Modular Programming: Subprograms, Functions, and Subroutines

D ivide and conquer. Guided by this maxim, men and women have traveled to the moon, waged war, created epic movies, and accomplished many other goals. The idea is simple: tackle a large-scale task by partitioning the single task into a group of subtasks. It's much easier to solve a collection of smaller tasks than one large task.

So it is with programming projects. A complex programming job can seem bewildering, almost impossible. You might hardly know where to begin. But if you concentrate on breaking the whole project into a collection of smaller projects, the job suddenly seems much less formidable. Each subtask isn't so bad. The whole is merely the sum of the parts.

The idea of breaking a large program into isolated chunks is the foundation behind *modular structured programming*. Structured programming is a modern coding philosophy, explored in-depth throughout this chapter.

True, it's one thing to philosophize and another to put the ideas into practice. To write structured programs, our programming language must provide the necessary tools. This is where BASICA and GW-BASIC fall short.

BASICA and GW-BASIC are unstructured languages. Each program written with BASICA or GW-BASIC is one self-contained unit. Subtasks cannot be individually programmed, debugged, and maintained. You must always think in the context of the whole program, even when working on an isolated part. That's why BASICA and GW-BASIC are not well-suited for large-scale programming tasks.

QBasic changes all that. Compared to BASICA and GW-BASIC, QBasic offers several language extensions that implement the modern philosophy of modular structured programming.

The most important of these language extensions (arguably) is the user-defined procedure. By using procedures, you can write individualized program units that are as simple or as complex as you like. These procedures can then be invoked from your mainline. It's like having a group of "right-hand men" you can summon whenever you need them.

Introducing Procedures

QBasic supports two kinds of procedures: subprograms and user-defined functions. Essentially, a *procedure* is a technique for defining your own statements and functions to supplement the statements and functions built into QBasic. (Recall that a statement is a keyword verb such as PRINT or LINE.) A *subprogram* is like a user-defined statement. A *user-defined function* is just that—a function that you define.

What's so special about procedures? Here are the three main features of procedures; these concepts are elaborated on throughout this chapter:

- *Procedures are isolated from your main program.* Procedures enjoy a unique dual status. They're part of a program and also distinct entities. When you save a program containing procedures, the procedures are saved along with the main program as a single file. However, within the editor environment, QBasic maintains procedures as distinct entities that can be individually tested and edited.

- *Procedures use local variables.* Variables established inside a procedure have meaning only inside the procedure. Such variables are "invisible" to the main program or to other procedures. If a variable in the main program (or in another procedure) coincidentally has the same name as a variable in a particular procedure, the two variables are distinct entities. Local variables maintain the autonomy of a procedure.

- *Procedures can pass parameter values back and forth to the main program.* Such parameters can be variables or expressions. Each call to a procedure can pass different values to the procedure.

Using Subprograms

A subprogram is a block of instructions that begins with a SUB statement and ends with an END SUB statement. Use a CALL instruction to invoke the subprogram. Before delineating the formal syntax for SUB and CALL, let's plunge right into an example.

Consider the program in Listing 17.1, QUIZ.BAS. This program is a knowledge test of three translations between Spanish and English.

Listing 17.1. The QUIZ.BAS program.

```
REM Program: QUIZ.BAS (Spanish to English quiz)

DATA La Pluma, The Pen, Saber, To Know, Rojo, Red

FOR Word% = 1 TO 3
   READ SpanishWord$, EnglishWord$
   PRINT
   PRINT "Translate: "; SpanishWord$;
   CALL WaitKey                        'Invoke the subprogram
   PRINT "Answer is: "; EnglishWord$
NEXT Word%
END


SUB WaitKey
   PRINT TAB(30); "Press a key to see the answer."
   DO
   LOOP UNTIL INKEY$ <> ""      'Wait for user to press a key
   PRINT
END SUB
```

Listing 17.1 contains a subprogram named WaitKey. The SUB-END SUB block defines the subprogram. WaitKey displays a message (Press a key to see the answer.) and then waits until the user presses a key. Inside the main program, the CALL WaitKey instruction invokes the subprogram.

Entering a Subprogram into QBasic

Type QUIZ.BAS into QBasic using the QBasic editor. You're going to be in for a surprise!

Nothing unusual happens until you type the SUB instruction. Figure 17.1 shows your screen at the point of typing the SUB instruction. In the figure, you have not yet pressed the Enter key—the cursor is at the end of the line.

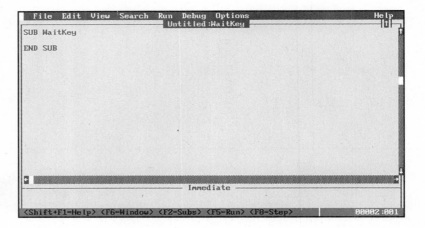

```
 File  Edit  View  Search  Run  Debug  Options                    Help
                         Untitled
REM Program: QUIZ.BAS (Spanish to English quiz)

DATA La Pluma, The Pen, Saber, To Know, Rojo, Red

FOR Word% = 1 TO 3
    READ SpanishWord$, EnglishWord$
    PRINT
    PRINT "Translate: "; SpanishWord$;
    CALL WaitKey                         'Invoke the subprogram
    PRINT "Answer is: "; EnglishWord$
NEXT Word%
END

SUB WaitKey



                         Immediate
<Shift+F1=Help> <F6=Window> <F2=Subs> <F5=Run> <F8=Step>    00014:012
```

Figure 17.1.

Typing the **SUB** instruction.

Now press Enter and watch what happens. Your screen suddenly looks like Figure 17.2.

```
 File  Edit  View  Search  Run  Debug  Options                    Help
                      Untitled:WaitKey
SUB WaitKey

END SUB










                         Immediate
<Shift+F1=Help> <F6=Window> <F2=Subs> <F5=Run> <F8=Step>    00002:001
```

Figure 17.2.

Entering a subprogram.

The QBasic editor enters a separate mode in which you're to type the subprogram. Notice that your main program has temporarily vanished. Also, the END SUB instruction is provided automatically. Press the Enter key and type the subprogram. When you finish, your screen should look like Figure 17.3.

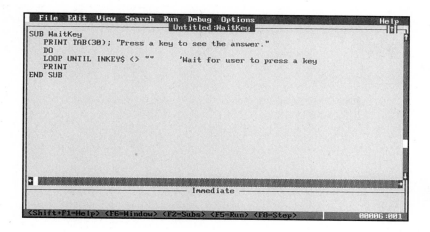

Figure 17.3.

Typing the subprogram.

Press Shift-F2 (more on this keystroke later). The screen reverts to the main program. But where is the subprogram WaitKey?

QBasic maintains each subprogram and user-defined function in a separate window. The subprogram is there and remains associated with your main program. You will see how to view the subprogram shortly. First, are you ready for another surprise?

Save the program on disk. Follow these steps:

1. Invoke the File menu (Alt-F).

2. Select Save As... (press A or use the arrow keys and Enter).

3. Name the program QUIZ in the dialog box, and press Enter.

QBasic saves the program and returns to the editor. Your screen should now look like Figure 17.4. Look closely at the program. There's a new first line. QBasic added the following DECLARE instruction:

```
DECLARE SUB WaitKey ()
```

The DECLARE instruction signifies that your main program has a subprogram named WaitKey. DECLARE also provides information about parameters passed to the subprogram. DECLARE is discussed in-depth later in this chapter.

Running QUIZ.BAS

Run QUIZ.BAS to see how the subprogram works. The first line of output you see looks like this:

```
Translate: La Pluma          Press a key to see the answer.
```

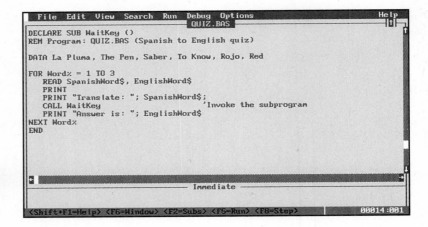

Figure 17.4.

The QUIZ.BAS program after saving.

At this point, execution is looping inside the WaitKey subprogram until you press a key. When you think you know the answer (or you give up), press a key to see the answer and get the next question. After you press a key, your screen looks like this:

```
Translate: La Pluma        Press a key to see the answer.

Answer is: The Pen

Translate: Saber           Press a key to see the answer.
```

Again, WaitKey is patiently waiting for you to press a key.

The program continues for three questions and answers. Try it.

Passing Parameters—the *Cross* Subprogram

QBasic provides the CIRCLE statement to draw circles and the LINE statement to draw rectangles. Suppose you want a CROSS statement that draws crosses. Well, QBasic doesn't provide such a statement. So write your own!

The program in Listing 17.2, SEECROSS.BAS, uses a subprogram called Cross.

Listing 17.2. The SEECROSS.BAS program.

```
REM Program SEECROSS.BAS (Draw pattern of crosses)


SCREEN 1
Xside% = 25              'Change these values
Yside% = 15             ' to see the effect
```

```
REM Draw the central cross
CALL Cross(160, 100, 120, 80)                        'CALL #1

REM Draw the smaller crosses
FOR Xcenter% = 100 TO 220 STEP 120
   FOR Ycenter% = 60 TO 140 STEP 80
      CALL Cross(Xcenter%, Ycenter%, Xside%, Yside%)    'CALL #2
   NEXT Ycenter%
NEXT Xcenter%
END

SUB Cross (X%, Y%, LengthX%, LengthY%)
   LINE (X%, Y%)-STEP(LengthX%, 0)
   LINE (X%, Y%)-STEP(-LengthX%, 0)
   LINE (X%, Y%)-STEP(0, LengthY%)
   LINE (X%, Y%)-STEP(0, -LengthY%)
END SUB
```

Try running SEECROSS.BAS. Figure 17.5 shows the result. Your computer system must have a graphics adapter; the program does not work on monochrome (MDA) systems.

Look at the Cross subprogram, especially the SUB declaration:

```
SUB Cross (X%, Y%, LengthX%, LengthY%)
```

This SUB instruction defines Cross to be a subprogram with four parameters. Here, each parameter is an integer variable.

In a SUB instruction, the parameters specify variables inside the subprogram. These specified variables communicate values to and from the calling program. Parameters specified as part of the definition of a procedure are called *formal* parameters.

Now look inside the main program at the two instructions that call Cross:

```
CALL Cross(160, 100, 120, 80)
```

```
CALL Cross(Xcenter%, Ycenter%, Xside%, Yside%)
```

Each of these two CALL instructions passes a value to the corresponding formal parameters. For example, the first CALL instruction passes the values 160, 100, 120, and 80 to the variables X%, Y%, LengthX%, and LengthY% inside the Cross subprogram.

In a CALL instruction, each passed value is called an *actual parameter* (see Figure 17.6).

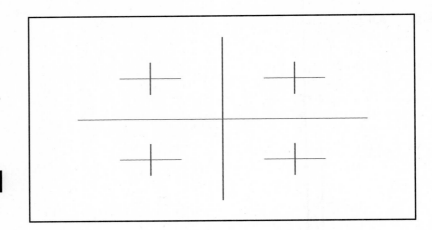

Figure 17.5.

Crosses produced by
SEECROSS.BAS.

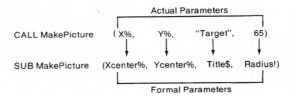

Figure 17.6.

Actual and formal
parameters.

Notice that the actual parameters can be literals or variables. The first CALL instruction uses literals; the second CALL uses values specified by variables.

Parameter passing is covered in depth later in this chapter. At that time you'll discover how to pass other data types (including arrays and records) and how a procedure can pass values back to the main program.

Using User-Defined Functions

A user-defined function is similar to a subprogram, with one major difference: a user-defined function returns a value in exactly the same way that a built-in function returns a value.

After you define a function, you invoke that function the same way you invoke one of QBasic's built-in functions. That is, you can specify the function name in expressions, in PRINT instructions, or anywhere else you can use a built-in function.

Writing a User-Defined Function

Consider an example. The built-in function SQR returns the square root of its argument. The instruction PRINT SQR(16) displays 4 because 4 is the square root of 16.

Suppose that you want a function called SQUARE that returns the square of its argument. (The *square* of a number is the number multiplied by itself.) You can define SQUARE with the following FUNCTION-END FUNCTION block:

```
FUNCTION SQUARE! (Value!)
    SQUARE! = Value! * Value!
END FUNCTION
```

With SQUARE now defined, the instruction PRINT SQUARE!(4) returns 16 because 16 is the square of 4.

Notice that the SQUARE! function uses the single-precision type-declaration suffix (!) on both the name of the function (SQUARE!) and the formal parameter (Value!).

Because every function returns a value, you must designate a data type for the function itself. In this case, SQUARE! indicates that the function returns a single-precision result. The parameter Value! indicates that the actual parameter passed to the function must also be a single-precision number or variable.

Just as with variable names, the data type of a function is considered to be single-precision unless the function name ends with a type-declaration suffix. Therefore, this function could be named SQUARE (no suffix) as well as SQUARE! (with the exclamation point suffix).

Inside every user-defined function, an assignment instruction must specify the resulting value returned by the function. The left side of this assignment instruction consists simply of the name of the function.

Introducing a String Function—*MIRROR$*

SQUARE! is a rather simple function. The body of SQUARE! consists of nothing more than the single assignment instruction that specifies the resulting value. You can write complicated functions that require many instructions to define.

Here's a slightly more complicated function:

```
FUNCTION Mirror$ (Value$)
    Temp$ = ""
    FOR Char% = LEN(Value$) TO 1 STEP -1
        Temp$ = Temp$ + MID$(Value$, Char%, 1)
    NEXT Char%
    Mirror$ = Temp$
END FUNCTION
```

Mirror$ is a string function. You pass Mirror$ a string argument and Mirror$ returns the reverse string. That is, if you pass to Mirror$ the value NATURES, Mirror$ returns SERUTAN. If you pass Hello out there, you get back ereht tuo olleH.

Just like subprograms, user-defined functions employ local variables. Any such variable has meaning only inside the function. A variable with the same name in the main program or in another procedure is a distinct entity.

Using Procedures

That concludes an intuitive introduction to procedures. More detail is now in order.

Defining a Subprogram

Here is a subprogram definition in skeletal form:

**S
T
A
T
E
M
E
N
T**

```
SUB subname [(paramlist)] [STATIC]
        [instructions]
[EXIT SUB]
        [instructions]
END SUB
```

where

   subname is the name of the subprogram,

   paramlist is the list of formal parameters,

and

   instructions is a block of QBasic instructions.

The square brackets ([ ]) denote an optional item. As such, the following items are all optional in a subprogram definition: the list of parameters, the STATIC keyword, the EXIT SUB instruction, and the block of instructions.

The subprogram name is a unique name associated with the subprogram. You cannot give any other procedure the same name, nor can you give a main-program variable the same name. The name does not convey any data type. In fact, *subname* cannot have a type-declaration suffix. *subname* is limited to 40 characters.

The parameter list, if present, consists of a comma-delimited list of the formal parameters. Each formal parameter can be a simple variable, an array, or a variable with a user-defined (record) data type.

Here is the syntax for *paramlist* when no arrays or records are involved. Passing arrays and records is deferred until later in the chapter.

```
formalparam [AS type] [, formalparam [AS type]] ...
```

where

    formalparam is the name of a formal parameter,

and

    type identifies the data type of the formal parameter.

The square brackets denote an optional item. *type* can be any one of the following keywords: INTEGER, LONG, SINGLE, DOUBLE, or STRING. The STRING type is always a variable-length string.

S T A T E M E N T

For example, the following subprogram definition uses two formal parameters (an integer and a string):

```
SUB ShowName (NumTimes AS INTEGER, LastName AS STRING)
```

Each formal parameter must have an assigned data type. If you don't use an AS clause, the data type is specified in one of two ways:

- A type-declaration suffix in the formal parameter

- A default data type specified by an active DEF*type* declaration. Using DEF*type* with procedures is deferred until Chapter 22, "Understanding Advanced QBasic Topics."

For example, you could write the preceding subprogram declaration as follows:

```
SUB ShowName (NumTimes%, LastName$)
```

Some programmers prefer the type-declaration suffixes, others prefer the AS clause. Take your pick.

The STATIC keyword, when present, specifies that all variables local to the subprogram are *static*. Static variables retain their values between successive calls. Without STATIC, the local variables are reinitialized each time the subprogram is called.

For example, consider this program containing the subprogram MeAgain:

```
FOR Counter% = 1 TO 3
   CALL MeAgain
NEXT Counter%
END


SUB MeAgain STATIC
   NumCalls% = NumCalls% + 1
   PRINT "You called me again--this is call number"; NumCalls%
END SUB
```

Here's the output:

```
You called me again--this is call number 1
You called me again--this is call number 2
You called me again--this is call number 3
```

The STATIC declaration in the MeAgain subprogram causes the value of NumCalls% to be preserved between calls. Remove the STATIC keyword so that the SUB declaration is simply SUB MeAgain. Now the output becomes:

```
You called me again--this is call number 1
You called me again--this is call number 1
You called me again--this is call number 1
```

Within the subprogram, *instructions* is any number of valid instructions subject only to the following proviso: You cannot nest a function or subprogram declaration inside another procedure. In other words, *instructions* cannot include a SUB-END SUB, FUNCTION-END FUNCTION, or DEF FN-END DEF block. (DEF FN is discussed later in this chapter.)

The SUB and END SUB statements delineate the physical beginning and end of the subprogram. When execution flows into the END SUB statement, the subprogram ends and control returns to the point where the subprogram was called.

An EXIT SUB statement creates an early termination of the subprogram. When QBasic encounters EXIT SUB, the subprogram ends immediately and control returns to the calling location.

The following subprogram uses an EXIT SUB:

```
SUB ShowFirstAndLast (Value$)
   IF LEN(Value$) < 2 THEN
      PRINT "Your string is less than 2 characters"
      EXIT SUB
   END IF
   PRINT "First character is: "; LEFT$(Value$, 1)
   PRINT " Last character is: "; RIGHT$(Value$, 1)
END SUB
```

Calling a Subprogram

Use a CALL instruction to invoke a subprogram. CALL has both an explicit and an implicit form.

CALL *subname* (*argumentlist*)   'Explicit form

or

   subname *argumentlist*   'Implicit form

where

   subname is the name of the subprogram,

and

   argumentlist is a list of the arguments (actual parameters).

In either the explicit or implicit form, *argumentlist* is optional.

S T A T E M E N T

The subprogram name must be the same name used to define the subprogram in the SUB-END SUB definition. The argument list, if present, is a comma-delimited list of the arguments passed to the subprogram. Each argument can be a variable or an expression. For example, consider the following subprogram declaration:

```
SUB StarSearch (LastName$, Age%, Weight!)
```

Each of the following instructions is a valid call to StarSearch:

```
CALL StarSearch("Fonda", 38, 145.5)

CALL StarSearch(Actor$, 39 - 10, Heft!)

CALL StarSearch(UCASE$(First$ + Last$), CINT(Age!), 159.5)
```

Notice how the last example uses the built-in functions UCASE$ and CINT to form expressions used as arguments.

Notice that the implicit form omits the CALL keyword. Simply specifying the subprogram name is sufficient to invoke the subprogram.

When you invoke a subprogram without CALL, do not place parentheses around the argument list. For example, using the implicit form, the three previous calls to StarSearch would look like the following:

```
StarSearch "Fonda", 38, 145.5

StarSearch Actor$, 39 - 10, Heft!

StarSearch UCASE$(First$ + Last$), CINT(Age!), 159.5
```

We recommend that you use the explicit form (with CALL and parentheses around arguments) rather than the implicit form (with no CALL and no parentheses around arguments). Subprogram calls are easier to identify when CALL is used.

You can call a subprogram from the main program, another subprogram, a user-defined function, or even from within the subprogram itself. The latter form is known as a *recursive* call. Recursion is discussed later in this chapter.

Defining a Function

Here is a skeletal look at a user-defined function:

<table>
<tr>
<td>

S T A T E M E N T

</td>
<td>

```
FUNCTION funcname [(paramlist)] [STATIC]
       [instructions]
funcname = expr
       [instructions]
END FUNCTION
```

where

    funcname is the name of the user-defined function,

    paramlist is the list of formal parameters,

    instructions is a block of QBasic instructions,

and

    expr is any general expression having a value of the same data type as *funcname*.

The square brackets denote optional items.

</td>
</tr>
</table>

As with a subprogram name, *funcname* is a unique name associated with the function. You cannot give any other procedure the same name, nor can you give a main-program variable the same name.

Unlike a subprogram name, however, *funcname* establishes a data type for the value returned by the function. The same rules used to designate the data type of a variable apply:

- Use a type-declaration suffix on *funcname*.

- Use a DEF*type* instruction before the FUNCTION declaration to establish a default data type for *funcname*. This technique is discussed in Chapter 22, "Understanding Advanced QBasic Topics."

■ Do nothing. The data type defaults to single-precision.

User-defined functions and subprograms are quite similar. For user-defined functions, the *paramlist*, *instructions*, and STATIC declaration work exactly as they do with subprograms. An EXIT FUNCTION instruction in a user-defined function is analogous to the EXIT SUB instruction used in subprograms.

The main difference, of course, is that a function assigns a value to the name of the function itself. To have your function return a value properly, you must execute (within the function block) an assignment instruction that has the name of the function on the left side. If *funcname* has a type-declaration suffix, don't forget to use the same suffix in the assignment instruction.

In the assignment instruction, only the root name of the function is on the left side. That is, do not include any parenthetical arguments after the function name. The right side of the assignment instruction can be any general expression consistent with the data type of *funcname*.

If no such assignment instruction executes, the function returns a default value (0 for numeric functions, the null string for string functions).

Your function can contain more than one assignment instruction assigning a value to *funcname*. When the function terminates, the returned value comes from the assignment executed most recently.

The following function returns the string value "BETWEEN", "BOUNDARY", or "OUTSIDE", depending on whether the value of Target! is between, equal to, or outside the two boundary values Bound1! and Bound2!.

```
FUNCTION ShowLocation$ (Target!, Bound1!, Bound2!)
   SELECT CASE SGN(Bound1! - Target!) * SGN(Target! - Bound2!)
      CASE IS > 0
         ShowLocation$ = "BETWEEN"
      CASE IS < 0
         ShowLocation$ = "OUTSIDE"
      CASE ELSE
         ShowLocation$ = "BOUNDARY"
   END SELECT
END FUNCTION
```

Invoking a Function

You invoke a user-defined function in exactly the same way as you invoke one of QBasic's regular built-in functions. You can use the name of the function in an expression. You can place the function name anywhere a variable of the same data type might go.

For example, each of the following instructions invokes the ShowLocation$ function:

```
PRINT ShowLocation$(Age!, 13, 18)

Abbrev$ = LEFT$(ShowLocation$(Goal!, High!, Low!), 2)

IF ShowLocation$(A!, B!, C!) = "OUTSIDE" THEN PRINT "Unbounded"
```

Just as with subprograms, you can invoke a function from your main program, from a subprogram, from another function, or even from within the function itself.

Passing Parameters

For both subprograms and functions, there are two fundamental rules of parameter passing:

■ The number of arguments in *argumentlist* must be the same as the number of formal parameters in *paramlist*.

■ The data type of each argument must match the data type of the corresponding formal parameter.

Suppose you declare a subprogram with three formal parameters, as follows:

```
SUB MySub (SmallNum%, BigNum#, Word$)
```

Each of the following calls is illegal:

```
CALL MySub(MyNum%, YourNum#)               'Not enough arguments

CALL MySub(NumA%, NumB#, Title$, NumC!)    'Too many arguments

CALL MySub(MyNum%, YourNum#, HerNum!)      'HerNum! is not string
```

Passing by Reference

Parameters pass between a procedure and the calling program along a two-way street. In the examples so far, data has passed from the calling program to the procedure. Through the parameter list, however, a subprogram or function can pass values back to the calling program as well.

Recall that the parameter list in the procedure declaration designates the formal parameters. Each formal parameter is a variable name local to that particular procedure.

Recall also that an actual parameter passed to the procedure is either

- A variable name local to the calling program
- A literal, constant, or expression

In the former case, the parameter passes by reference. This means that QBasic passes the address of the variable to the procedure. Inside the procedure, the corresponding formal parameter is also assigned this same address.

As a result, if the procedure modifies the value of a formal parameter, the change occurs at the same address that the calling program associates with the actual parameter. Therefore, the procedure effectively passes a value back to the calling program. That is, when control passes back to the calling program, the value of the actual parameter retains the value assigned to the corresponding formal parameter in the procedure.

When an actual parameter is a variable (as opposed to a literal or an expression), parameter passing is by reference.

Consider the program in Listing 17.3, REFPASS.BAS, for example.

Listing 17.3. The REFPASS.BAS program.

```
REM Program: REFPASS.BAS (Demonstrate passing by reference)
X% = 10
Y! = 25.5
PRINT "Main Program: X% ="; X%; SPC(5); "Y! ="; Y!
CALL MySub(X%, Y!)      'Variables passed by reference
PRINT "Main Program: X% ="; X%; SPC(5); "Y! ="; Y!
END


SUB MySub (A%, B!)
   PRINT "Subprogram: A% ="; A%; SPC(5); "B! ="; B!
   A% = 50
   B! = 13.8
   PRINT "Subprogram: A% ="; A%; SPC(5); "B! ="; B!
END SUB
```

Here's the output of REFPASS.BAS. Notice how the subprogram effectively changes the values of X% and Y! in the main program:

```
Main Program: X% = 10     Y! = 25.5
Subprogram: A% = 10     B! = 25.5
Subprogram: A% = 50     B! = 13.8
Main Program: X% = 50     Y! = 13.8
```

Passing by Value

When an actual parameter is a literal, a constant, or an expression, parameter passing is by value. QBasic passes the value of the parameter rather than the address.

To simulate true passing by value, QBasic uses the following steps to pass a copy of the expression:

1. The value of the expression is calculated.
2. The result is stored in a temporary memory location.
3. The address of this temporary location is passed to the procedure.

If the procedure modifies the value, the change occurs only in the temporary location. As a result, no variables in the main program change.

To force QBasic to pass a variable by value, enclose the variable in parentheses. This makes the argument an expression. In such a case, even if the procedure modifies the parameter, the change occurs only in the copy of the variable. The original variable remains unmodified.

For example, consider the program in Listing 17.4, VARPASS.BAS, which is a modified version of REFPASS.BAS. The subprogram MySub is unchanged from the identical subprogram in Listing 17.3, REFPASS.BAS.

Listing 17.4.   The VARPASS.BAS program.

```
REM Program: VARPASS.BAS (Demonstrate passing by value)
X% = 10
Y! = 25.5
PRINT "Main Program: X% ="; X%; SPC(5); "Y! ="; Y!
CALL MySub(10, (Y!))          'Arguments passed by value
PRINT "Main Program: X% ="; X%; SPC(5); "Y! ="; Y!
END

SUB MySub (A%, B!)
   PRINT "Subprogram: A% ="; A%; SPC(5); "B! ="; B!
   A% = 50
   B! = 13.8
   PRINT "Subprogram: A% ="; A%; SPC(5); "B! ="; B!
END SUB
```

Here is the output. In the CALL instruction, parentheses were placed around the actual parameter Y%. That forces QBasic to pass Y% by value rather than by reference. Notice that, after calling the subprogram, the values of X% and Y! do not change.

```
Main Program: X% = 10     Y! = 25.5
Subprogram:   A% = 10     B! = 25.5
Subprogram:   A% = 50     B! = 13.8
Main Program: X% = 10     Y! = 25.5
```

Passing a String

A fixed-length string cannot be a formal parameter in a procedure declaration. Any such string parameter must be variable-length. Consider these function declarations:

```
FUNCTION Char%(Target$)                 'OK--variable length

FUNCTION Char%(Target AS STRING)        'OK--variable length

FUNCTION Char%(Target AS STRING * 20)   'Illegal--fixed length
```

When you invoke a subprogram or function, variable-length strings are fine as actual parameters (arguments).

Passing an Array

You can pass an entire array. Use the array name followed by an empty set of parentheses. The corresponding formal parameter also has an empty set of parentheses.

Inside the procedure, do not DIM the array. You can use the LBOUND and UBOUND functions to determine the lower and upper bounds of the array. (See Chapter 9, "Managing Large Amounts of Data," for LBOUND and UBOUND.) For example:

```
DIM Sales% (1 TO 8, 0 TO 10)
   .
   .
   .
PRINT "Total Sales ="; SumArray%(Sales%()) 'Note empty ()
END

FUNCTION SumArray% (A%())
   Total% = 0
   FOR FirstDim% = LBOUND(A%, 1) TO UBOUND(A%, 1)
      FOR SecondDim% = LBOUND(A%, 2) TO UBOUND(A%, 2)
         Total% = Total% + A%(FirstDim%, SecondDim%)
      NEXT SecondDim%
   NEXT FirstDim%
   SumArray% = Total%
END FUNCTION
```

To pass an individual array element, place the appropriate subscripts inside the parentheses. For example, the following instruction calls a subprogram and passes a single array element:

```
CALL ShowValue(MyArray(23))      'Single array element
```

Passing a Record

Follow these steps to pass an entire record:

1. Define the record type with a TYPE-END TYPE block in the calling program. For example:

   ```
   TYPE BaseballPlayer
       FullName AS STRING * 40
       BattingAverage AS SINGLE
       HomeRuns AS INTEGER
   END TYPE
   ```

2. Use a DIM instruction to give a variable your user-defined type:

   ```
   DIM Mantle AS BaseballPlayer
   ```

3. When you invoke the procedure, pass your declared variable:

   ```
   CALL GetStats(Mantle)
   ```

4. In the procedure declaration, give the formal parameter your record type:

   ```
   CALL GetStats (Person AS BaseballPlayer)
   ```

To pass an individual record element, use the element descriptor when you invoke a procedure:

```
CALL HitTotal(Mantle.HomeRuns)
```

Understanding the *DECLARE* Instruction

Earlier you saw that, when you save a program, QBasic adds to your main program one DECLARE instruction for every procedure contained within the program.

You can also write your own DECLARE instructions.

A DECLARE instruction accomplishes the following:

- Specifies the name of a procedure invoked within the program
- Specifies the named procedure as a FUNCTION or SUB
- Indicates the number of parameters and the data type of each parameter

DECLARE instructions must occur in the main program, never inside a subprogram or function. Place the DECLARE before any call to the associated procedure—usually near the beginning of the program.

DECLARE SUB *procname* (*paramlist*)

or

DECLARE FUNCTION *procname* (*paramlist*)

where

    procname is the name of the procedure,

and

    paramlist is a comma-delimited list of the parameters passed to the procedure.

The parameter list is optional.

S T A T E M E N T

For *procname*, use the name of the procedure exactly as the name appears in the SUB or FUNCTION declaration. For a FUNCTION, *procname* may or may not include the type-declaration suffix.

paramlist indicates the number of arguments and the data type of each argument passed to the procedure. The list consists of dummy variables, in the sense that only the data type of each variable name is significant. To specify a data type, use a type-declaration suffix (%, &, !, #, or $) or an AS *type* clause (where *type* is INTEGER, LONG, SINGLE, DOUBLE, STRING, or a user-defined type).

For an array parameter, use an empty set of parentheses after the variable name.

If the procedure has no arguments, *paramlist* does not appear, but you still need an empty set of parentheses after *procname*.

Here are some sample declarations:

```
DECLARE SUB BigDeal (NumPlanets%, NumStars AS DOUBLE)

DECLARE FUNCTION ShowMotto$ ()
```

```
DECLARE SUB FastSort (MyValue!(), Index%)

DECLARE SUB DoIt ()
```

These declarations indicate the following:

- BigDeal is a subprogram called with two parameters: the first parameter is integer, the second is double-precision.

- ShowMotto$ is a string function called with no parameters.

- FastSort is a subprogram called with two parameters: the first parameter is a single-precision array, the second is an integer.

- DoIt is a subprogram that passes no parameters.

As you've seen, QBasic automatically generates DECLARE instructions when you save a program. QBasic generates a DECLARE instruction for each SUB or FUNC-TION called and defined within the program, provided you have not explicitly written such a DECLARE yourself. As a result, you can write each DECLARE yourself or rely on QBasic to provide the DECLARE instructions for you.

Technically, DECLARE is optional. If you run a program containing no DECLARE instructions, QBasic executes the procedures fine. But DECLARE instructions provide a way to cross-check the number, name, and parameters expected by each procedure.

Sharing Variables

By default, variables inside a procedure are local to the procedure. In programming terminology, the *scope* of the variable is limited to the procedure block. A variable in your main program (or another procedure) might have the same name; the two variables are distinct and have no relationship to each other.

For example, Listing 17.5 contains a variable named Hue$ in the main program and another Hue$ inside the ShowIt subprogram. The program in Listing 17.5 demonstrates that the two variables are independent.

Listing 17.5. The SHOWHUE.BAS program.

```
REM Program: SHOWHUE.BAS (Demonstrate local variables)
Hue$ = "Red"       'Assign Hue$ in the main program
CALL ShowIt
PRINT "Main Program: Hue$ = "; Hue$
END
```

```
SUB ShowIt
   Hue$ = "Blue"      'This Hue$ is local to ShowIt
   PRINT "Subprogram:    Hue$ = "; Hue$
END SUB
```

The output is

```
Subprogram:    Hue$ = Blue
Main program: Hue$ = Red
```

You can share variables between procedures and your main program. Shared variables are global in scope. In effect, sharing variables is an alternative way of passing parameters to procedures.

As a general rule, use parameter-passing rather than variable-sharing. Excessive use of variable sharing goes against the grain of modular, localized procedures. Remember that you want to maximize the readability and "modifiability" of your programs. Table 17.1 shows the available degrees of variable sharing.

Table 17.1. Sharing variables in procedures.

Effect	Technique
Sharing between an individual procedure and the main program	Use SHARED *instruction* inside the procedure
Sharing between all procedures and the main program	Use SHARED *attribute* in the main program
Sharing between multiple procedures	Use COMMON instruction

The *SHARED* Instruction

A SHARED instruction unites a procedure-level variable with a main-program variable of the same name.

```
SHARED varname AS type, varname AS type ...
```

where

   varname is a simple variable name, or an array name followed by empty parentheses (),

and

   type specifies the variable's data type.

The AS type clause is optional. A SHARED instruction can contain one or more varname specifications. If more than one varname occurs, separate each varname clause with a comma.

A variable name specified by varname must be identical to the variable name used in the main program. This applies with equal force to type-declaration suffixes as well as to the root name. If you use an AS clause to type the variable in your main program, you must use the same AS clause in the SHARED instruction.

type can be INTEGER, LONG, SINGLE, DOUBLE, STRING, STRING * length, or a user-defined (record) type.

The SHARED instruction is valid only inside a subprogram or user-defined function, not in the main program.

The program in Listing 17.6, SHOWHUE2.BAS, demonstrates the SHARED instruction:

Listing 17.6.   The SHOWHUE2.BAS program.

```
REM Program: SHOWHUE2.BAS (Demonstrate shared variables)
Hue$ = "Red"        'Assign Hue$ in the main program
CALL ShowIt
CALL ShowItAgain
PRINT "Main Program: Hue$ = "; Hue$
END


SUB ShowIt
   SHARED Hue$        'Share Hue$ in ShowIt with the main program
   Hue$ = "Blue"      'Changes Hue$ in main program also
   PRINT "ShowIt:      Hue$ = "; Hue$
END SUB
```

```
SUB ShowItAgain
   Hue$ = "Green"        'This Hue$ is local in ShowItAgain
   PRINT "ShowItAgain:  Hue$ = "; Hue$
END SUB
```

The output is

```
ShowIt:        Hue$ = Blue
ShowItAgain:   Hue$ = Green
Main Program: Hue$ = Blue
```

Compare the output of SHOWHUE2.BAS with the output of the SHOWHUE.BAS program discussed previously.

The *SHARED* Attribute

Use the SHARED keyword in a DIM or REDIM instruction to make a main-program variable global to all procedures. (For details on REDIM, see Chapter 19, "Managing Memory.") The variable can be a simple variable or an array.

For example, compare Listing 17.7, SHOWHUE3.BAS, with Listing 17.6, SHOWHUE2.BAS. The SHARED instruction in ShowIt is now gone and the following DIM SHARED instruction is added to the main program:

```
DIM SHARED Hue$
```

Here is SHOWHUE3.BAS:

Listing 17.7. The SHOWHUE3.BAS program.

```
REM Program: SHOWHUE3.BAS (Demonstrate shared variables)
DIM SHARED Hue$     'Share Hue$ with all procedures
Hue$ = "Red"        'Assign Hue$ in the main program
CALL ShowIt
CALL ShowItAgain
PRINT "Main Program: Hue$ = "; Hue$
END

SUB ShowIt
   Hue$ = "Blue"              'This Hue$ is local to ShowIt
   PRINT "ShowIt:       Hue$ = "; Hue$
END SUB
```

continues

Listing 17.7. Continued

```
SUB ShowItAgain
   Hue$ = "Green"          'This Hue$ is local to ShowItAgain
   PRINT "ShowItAgain:  Hue$ = "; Hue$
END SUB
```

Here's the output of SHOWHUE3.BAS:

```
ShowIt:       Hue$ = Blue
ShowItAgain:  Hue$ = Green
Main Program: Hue$ = Green
```

The *COMMON* Instruction

The COMMON instruction provides variable sharing across multiple procedures and/or the main program. COMMON also provides a way to share variables when one program chains to another. Detailed discussion of chaining and the COMMON instruction is deferred until Chapter 22, "Understanding Advanced QBasic Topics."

Using Static Variables—the *STATIC* Instruction

Inside a procedure, use a STATIC instruction to identify particular variables as static. (The STATIC instruction is valid only inside user-created procedures.) The STATIC instruction affects a designated variable in two ways:

- Makes an otherwise shared variable local to the procedure
- Makes the variable static (preserves the value of the variable between successive invocations of the procedure)

STATIC *varname* AS *type*, *varname* AS *type* . . .

where

    varname is a simple variable name, or an array name followed by empty parentheses (),

and

    type specifies the variable's data type.

The AS *type* clause is optional. The governing rules for *varname* and *type* are akin to those for the SHARED instruction.

S
T
A
T
E
M
E
N
T

A STATIC instruction generally is used in one of two situations:

- You have declared a number of global variables with a SHARED instruction in your main program. Inside a particular procedure, you want to create a local variable with the same name as one of the global variables. Use STATIC inside the procedure to override the SHARED instruction in that one procedure.

- You want some variables, but not all variables, inside a procedure to retain their values between calls. You cannot use the STATIC attribute in the SUB or FUNCTION declaration because that would make *all* variables static. Instead, use the STATIC instruction to isolate the particular static variables.

Don't confuse the static instruction with the $STATIC metastatement. $STATIC, discussed in Chapter 19, "Managing Memory," specifies how arrays are allocated.

Using Recursive Procedures

Recursion is the ability of a procedure to call itself, or to call other procedures that, in turn, call the original procedure.

QBasic supports recursive procedures. But think twice before using recursion. If ever a programming technique was a two-edged sword, recursion is it.

Trade-offs of Recursion

Recursive programming is elegant, but often difficult to understand. This difficulty leads to future headaches when such a program needs modification.

Every program that can be written with recursion also can be written without recursion, so you face trade-offs when deciding whether to use recursion (see Table 17.2).

Table 17.2. Recursion versus nonrecursion.

Feature	Recursion	Nonrecursion
Clarity of programming	Poor	Good
Compactness of program	Good	Fair
Computational efficiency	Fair	Good

Some real-world problems have naturally recursive formulations. These are the problems that lend themselves to effective recursive solutions. Examples of such problems are binary tree searching and quick sorting.

A Recursion Example

The classic example of recursion is factorials. For those who need a math refresher, the factorial of a positive whole number is the product of all the whole numbers from one up to the number. For example, the factorial of 4 is 24 (1 * 2 * 3 * 4 = 24). The factorial of zero, by definition, is one.

A factorial can be defined recursively. The factorial of a positive whole number N is simply N times the factorial of $(N-1)$.

Here's a function that recursively computes the factorial of any non-negative whole number:

```
FUNCTION Factorial# (N%)
   IF N% > 1 THEN
      Factorial# = N% * Factorial#(N% - 1)
   ELSE
      Factorial# = 1
   END IF
END FUNCTION
```

Many books give such a function to illustrate recursion. Everyone is happy, the next topic is discussed, and nobody thinks twice. Often overlooked is the fact that a function to calculate factorials can easily be written nonrecursively. Consider this:

```
FUNCTION Factorial# (N%)
   Value# = 1!
```

```
    IF N% > 0 THEN
       FOR Counter% = 1 TO N%
          Value# = Value# * Counter%
       NEXT Counter%
    END IF
    Factorial# = Value#
END FUNCTION
```

Which function is easier to understand? Both functions are fairly simple, so you might not have much basis for choosing. We suspect, however, that the nonrecursive algorithm is clearer, especially to those who have trouble grasping recursion.

How about a speed comparison? We timed these two functions separately inside a main program. The recursive algorithm runs about 10 percent slower.

The criteria for using recursion boil down to two considerations. If the program is much easier to write with recursion and/or an important saving in program length is realized, then use recursion. Otherwise, use a nonrecursive algorithm. Recursion is clever, but don't outfox yourself.

Controlling Stack Space

Deeply nested recursive functions place a heavy demand on stack space. You might get the run-time error Out of stack space. In such a situation, you probably need to adjust the size of the stack.

The stack is an area of RAM memory maintained automatically by QBasic. The stack holds temporary quantities such as return addresses from subprogram calls. Each time you invoke a recursive function, QBasic uses the stack to hold a new copy of the function.

To adjust the stack size, use a CLEAR, , stacksize instruction. See Chapter 19, "Managing Memory," for more information on the stack and the CLEAR instruction.

However, be wary of a stack space error stemming from unintentional recursion. Unintentional recursion is a mistaken recursive instruction inside a user-defined function. The effect of such an indiscretion is runaway recursive calls until the available stack space is gobbled up.

Here are the two most likely causes of unintentional recursion:

- Using the function identifier on the right side of an assignment instruction
- Using the function identifier as an argument, especially in a PRINT instruction

The following two functions demonstrate these errors:

```
FUNCTION DoCost!
   DiscountRate! = .86
      DoCost! = 185.5
   IF Client$ = "Hilton" THEN                'Client$ is global
      DoCost! = DoCost! * DiscountRate!   'Unintentional recursion
   END IF
END FUNCTION

FUNCTION ShowValue%
   ShowValue% = 45
   PRINT "The value is"; ShowValue%        'Unintentional recursion
END FUNCTION
```

Structured Programming with Procedures

Modular structured programming was introduced early in this chapter. The central theme is simple: reduce a big programming task to a closely knit group of smaller programming tasks.

Most of this chapter has been devoted to creating and using procedures. With that background, you can now consider how to use procedures in implementing structured programs.

With suitable apologies to Moses, here are the nine commandments of structured programming, as applied to procedures:

1. Do all the detailed work in the procedures.

   Try to keep your main program short. Relegate the blood-and-guts work to the procedures.

2. Make each procedure easy to understand and maintain.

   Just because the details go into the procedures, that's no excuse for making the procedures difficult to read and, as a result, difficult to maintain. Your goal is to make each subprogram easily understood. When a procedure seems too long and complex, break it into smaller and simpler procedures.

3. Use only a top-down flow of control.

   Try to make your programs flow smoothly from the top down to the bottom. Such flow is much easier to follow than convoluted, up-and-down-and-back-up logic. Use top-down programming in procedures as well as the main program.

4. Use only the three basic structured constructs.

You can write any main program or procedure using only these three constructs:

- ■ Sequence or process (assignment and computation)

- ■ Selection (IF-THEN-ELSE or SELECT CASE)

- ■ Iteration (FOR-NEXT, DO-LOOP, or WHILE-WEND)

The iterative constructs, of course, internally branch back up to the beginning of the construct. These constructs do not, however, branch upward outside the construct. Another way to look at this restriction follows.

5. Avoid GOTO instructions.

GOTO instructions cause breaks in a smooth top-down logic flow. Occasionally a GOTO is the best solution to a programming problem, but those times are extremely rare. Break the GOTO habit. Take it as a personal challenge. It is much easier than you think.

6. Use local variables as much as possible.

Minimize references to global variables in your procedures. This keeps the procedures independent. If you pass parameters by value, the procedure can reference, but not alter, the variables. If you use global variables instead, your procedure might accidentally modify the values of global variables. Such modification can cause undesirable side effects in other procedures or the main program.

7. Avoid recursion.

8. Don't reinvent the wheel.

Keep a lookout for procedures you can borrow instead of always writing your own. Build a procedure library from your own procedures as well as from other sources, such as public domain, magazines, and books. Don't waste your time writing procedures when you can get them at little or no cost. Spend your time on the parts you cannot get elsewhere—the program design, the main program, and the specialized procedures. Work smarter, not harder.

9. The more procedures, the better.

Keep your mainline short. Like the boss whose job consists of delegating assignments to subordinates, the mainline section of your program should delegate work to the procedures. Such a mainline can be short and simple. It's not unusual, even in a large complex program, for the mainline section to be the shortest block.

A Sample Program

The following program, MORTGAGE.BAS, is an example of a structured program containing several procedures. Notice especially how a reasonably complex programming task is broken into several independent procedures. Each procedure solves a smaller, easily managed—and easily programmed—subtask.

Listing 17.8, MORTGAGE.BAS, calculates and displays complete loan repayment schedules, including interest and amortization breakdowns. You can override the normal monthly payment to study balloon payments or early payoffs.

Listing 17.8. The MORTGAGE.BAS program.

```
REM Program: MORTGAGE.BAS (Mortgage Analyzer)
  CLS
  PRINT "Mortgage - Analysis of a loan repayment"

  CALL GetTerms(Prin!, IntRate!, NumMonths%)

  PRINT
  Payment! = LoanPay!(Prin!, IntRate!, NumMonths%)
  PRINT USING "Regular payment = #######.##"; Payment!

  CALL GetOverride(Payment!)
  CALL ShowTable(Prin!, IntRate!, NumMonths%, Payment!)
END

SUB GetNumber (Value!)   'Prompt user for number and get it
  PRINT "Entry? ";
  LINE INPUT Value$
  Value! = VAL(Value$)
END SUB

SUB GetOverride (Payment!)   'Get override of monthly payment
  INPUT "Do you want to override this (Y or N)"; Reply$
  Reply$ = UCASE$(LEFT$(Reply$, 1))
  IF Reply$ = "Y" THEN
     DO
        PRINT
        PRINT "Please enter the desired payment."
        CALL GetNumber(Payment!)
```

```
        LOOP UNTIL Payment > 0!
    END IF
END SUB

SUB GetTerms (Prin!, IntRate!, NumMonths%)
    REM Get user to input the loan specifications

    DO
        PRINT
        PRINT "Please enter the principal."
        CALL GetNumber(Prin!)
    LOOP UNTIL Prin! > 0

    DO
        PRINT
        PRINT "Please enter the annual interest rate."
        CALL GetNumber(IntRate!)
    LOOP UNTIL (IntRate! > 0) AND (IntRate! < 100)

    DO
        PRINT
        PRINT "Please enter the length of the loan in months."
        CALL GetNumber(NumMonths!)
        NumMonths% = NumMonths!          'Convert to integer
    LOOP UNTIL (NumMonths% > 0) AND (NumMonths% < 2000)
END SUB

FUNCTION LoanPay! (Prin!, IntRate!, NumMonths%)
    REM Compute the monthly payment

    MonthlyInterest! = IntRate! / 1200
    Numerator! = Prin! * MonthlyInterest!
    Term! = (MonthlyInterest! + 1) ^ NumMonths%
    Denominator! = 1! - (1! / Term!)
    LoanPay! = Numerator! / Denominator!
END FUNCTION

SUB ShowHeader (Prin!, IntRate!, FirstPayment!, NumMonths%)
    REM Display the loan terms and the column headers
    CLS
    PRINT "Mortgage - Analysis of a loan repayment"
    PRINT
```

continues

Listing 17.8. Continued

```
    Format$ = "########.##"
    PRINT USING "Principal      = ########.##"; Prin!
    PRINT USING "Interest Rate   = ########.##"; IntRate!
    PRINT USING "Regular Payment = ########.##"; FirstPayment!
    PRINT USING "Term in months  = ########"; NumMonths%
    PRINT
    PRINT Tab(8); "Remaining"; Tab(20); "--Interest Paid--";
    PRINT Tab(43); "-Amount Amortized-"
    PRINT "Paymt."; Tab(9); "Balance"; Tab(20); "This time";
    PRINT Tab(32); "To date"; Tab(43); "This time";
    PRINT Tab(54); "To date"
END SUB

SUB ShowTable (Prin!, IntRate!, NumMonths%, Payment!)
    REM Compute and display month by month values

    Payment! = FIX(Payment! * 100 + .5) / 100
    FirstPayment! = Payment!
    Balance! = FIX(Prin! * 100 + .5) / 100
    IntFactor! = IntRate! / 12
    TotalPayments% = 0
    TotalInt! = 0
    TotalAmort! = 0
    LinesToShow% = 12
    LineCount% = 0
    PayNum% = 0
    CONST TRUE = -1, FALSE = 0
    WantToSeeIt% = TRUE
    CALL ShowHeader(Prin!, IntRate!, FirstPayment!, NumMonths%)

    DO
        PayNum% = PayNum% + 1
        Interest! = FIX(Balance! * IntFactor! + .5) / 100
        IF PayNum% = NumMonths% THEN Payment! = Balance! + Interest!
        Amortized! = Payment! - Interest!
        Balance! = Balance! - Amortized!
        IF Balance! < 0 THEN
            Payment! = Payment! + Balance!
            Amortized! = Amortized + Balance!
            Balance! = 0!
        END IF
```

```
         TotalPayments! = TotalPayments! + Payment!
         TotalInt! = TotalInt! + Interest!
         TotalAmort! = TotalAmort! + Amortized!
         IF WantToSeeIt% THEN
            PRINT USING "####   "; PayNum%;
            F$ = "#######.## "
            PRINT USING F$; Balance!; Interest!;
            PRINT USING F$; TotalInt!, Amortized; TotalAmort!
            LineCount% = LineCount% + 1
            IF LineCount% = LinesToShow% THEN
               PRINT
               PRINT "Press T for Totals or [Enter] for next screen";
               INPUT Reply$
               IF UCASE$(LEFT$(Reply$, 1)) = "T" THEN
                  WantToSeeIt% = FALSE
               END IF
               CALL ShowHeader(Prin!, IntRate!, FirstPayment!, NumMonths%)
               LineCount% = 0
            END IF
         END IF
      LOOP UNTIL (PayNum% = NumMonths%) OR (Balance! = 0)
      PRINT
      PRINT USING "Last payment   = ########.##"; Payment!
      PRINT USING "Total payments = ########.##"; TotalPayments!
      PRINT USING "Total number of payments = #####"; PayNum%
      PRINT "Ratio of total payments to principal =";
      PRINT USING "###.####"; TotalPayments! / Prin!
END SUB
```

Using the Mortgage Analyzer

Running MORTGAGE.BAS is simple. First the program prompts you for the
fundamental loan specifications. These are the principal, annual interest rate
(as a percentage), and length of the loan in months.

The program assumes a conventional mortgage. A payment is made every
month with all payments (except perhaps the last) equal. Interest is com-
pounded with each payment.

After you supply the input, the regular monthly payment is shown. You now
have the option of overriding this payment and, instead, specifying a different

monthly payment. This option results in a balloon payment (if you reduce the normal payment) or an early amortization of the loan (if you increase the normal payment).

Next the program presents a yearly analysis. For each month you see the current loan balance, the contribution paid toward interest, and the contribution paid toward principal.

After seeing a year's worth of information, you can get the next year of information or go immediately to the final totals.

A Sample Run

Suppose that you need a short-term second mortgage for $5,000. Your bank offers an 18-month loan at 14.5 percent interest. You initially can afford to pay only $250 a month in repayment. Because the normal payment is over $300 a month, the bank agrees to a balloon payment at the end. Figures 17.7 through 17.9 show the analysis of this loan produced by MORTGAGE.BAS.

```
Mortgage - Analysis of a loan repayment

Please enter the principal.
Entry? 5000

Please enter the annual interest rate.
Entry? 14.5

Please enter the length of the loan in months.
Entry? 18

Regular payment =     310.75
Do you want to override this (Y or N)? Y

Please enter the desired payment.
Entry? 250
```

Figure 17.7.

The loan data is entered.

Editing Subprograms and Functions

Here are various techniques for managing procedures inside the QBasic editor:

- To create a new procedure:
    1. Invoke the Edit menu (press Alt-E).
    2. Select New SUB... or New FUNCTION... as appropriate (see Figure 17.10).

```
Mortgage - Analysis of a loan repayment

Principal         =      5000.00
Interest Rate     =        14.50
Regular Payment   =       250.00
Term in months    =          18

          Remaining   --Interest Paid--    -Amount Amortized-
Paymt.    Balance     This time  To date    This time  To date
   1      4810.42       60.42      60.42      189.58    189.58
   2      4618.55       58.13     118.55      191.87    381.45
   3      4424.36       55.81     174.36      194.19    575.64
   4      4227.82       53.46     227.82      196.54    772.18
   5      4028.91       51.09     278.91      198.91    971.09
   6      3827.59       48.68     327.59      201.32   1172.41
   7      3623.84       46.25     373.84      203.75   1376.16
   8      3417.63       43.79     417.63      206.21   1582.37
   9      3208.93       41.30     458.93      208.70   1791.07
  10      2997.70       38.77     497.70      211.23   2002.30
  11      2783.92       36.22     533.92      213.78   2216.08
  12      2567.56       33.64     567.56      216.36   2432.44

Press T for Totals or [Enter] for next SCREEN ?
```

Figure 17.8.

The first year of the loan is analyzed.

```
Mortgage - Analysis of a loan repayment

Principal         =      5000.00
Interest Rate     =        14.50
Regular Payment   =       250.00
Term in months    =          18

          Remaining   --Interest Paid--    -Amount Amortized-
Paymt.    Balance     This time  To date    This time  To date
  13      2348.58       31.02     598.58      218.98   2651.42
  14      2126.96       28.38     626.96      221.62   2873.04
  15      1902.66       25.70     652.66      224.30   3097.34
  16      1675.65       22.99     675.65      227.01   3324.35
  17      1445.90       20.25     695.90      229.75   3554.10
  18         0.00       17.47     713.37     1445.90   5000.00

Last payment    =      1463.37
Total payments  =      5713.37
Total number of payments =     18
Ratio of total payments to principal =  1.1427
```

Figure 17.9.

The final six months are analyzed, and the concluding totals are shown.

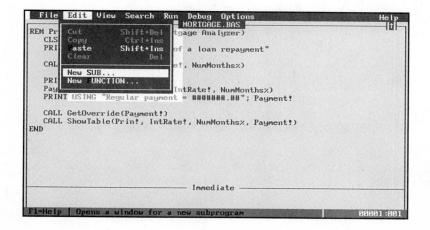

Figure 17.10.

Highlight bar on New SUB...

3. QBasic opens a dialog box. Enter the name of the procedure and press Enter.

Alternatively, while in the main program or another procedure, you can simply type the keyword SUB or the keyword FUNCTION followed by the name of the procedure. This is a shortcut for the three steps just mentioned.

In either case, QBasic temporarily clears the contents of the editing window and replaces it with a skeleton outline for the new procedure (SUB and END SUB instructions or FUNCTION and END FUNCTION instructions).

You are now set for editing and can begin typing the procedure.

■ To save a procedure:

Simply save the whole program (Alt-F followed by Save). QBasic does not save procedures as independent disk files. Instead, the main program and all the associated procedures are saved together.

■ To see a list of the procedures in a given program:

1. Invoke the View menu (Alt-V).

2. Select SUBs... and press Enter, or alternatively, just press the hotkey F2 to replace the previous two steps.

A dialog box opens showing all the procedures associated with the main program. The procedures appear in alphabetical order. Figure 17.11 shows this dialog box for the MORTGAGE.BAS program.

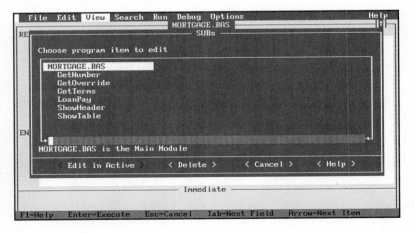

Figure 17.11.

Listing the procedures in MORTGAGE.BAS.

The main box contains a list of the procedure names indented from the name of the main program. As you move the highlight along each procedure, a message below the box indicates the type of procedure.

■ To view and edit a procedure:

    1. Follow the previous steps to highlight the desired procedure.

    2. Use the Tab key or press Alt-A to select <Edit in Active>.

    3. Press Enter.

QBasic displays the procedure in an Edit window. You can now edit the procedure.

■ To cycle through procedures:

Instead of highlighting each procedure one at a time, you can quickly cycle through the procedures (in alphabetical order). Use one of the following hotkeys:

Press Shift-F2 while editing. This hotkey brings the next procedure (in alphabetical order) into view. Repeated presses of Shift-F2 cycle from the main program through all the procedures.

Press Ctrl-F2. This has the same effect as Shift-F2 but the cycling is in reverse alphabetical order.

■ To delete a procedure from your program:

    1. Highlight the procedure name in the dialog box of the View menu. (Press F2 and move the highlight.)

    2. Use Tab or Alt-D to select <Delete>.

    3. Press Enter.

Understanding Subroutines and *DEF FN* Functions—the "Old" Way

As previously mentioned, subprograms and user-defined functions are language extensions not found in BASICA or GW-BASIC. However, BASICA and GW-BASIC have two similar constructs: *subroutines* and *DEF FN functions*. Essentially, subroutines are the old form of subprograms while DEF FN functions are the old form of user-defined functions.

QBasic supports subroutines and DEF FN functions mainly for compatibility with BASICA and GW-BASIC. Be advised that subprograms and user-defined functions are more powerful. Procedures can do everything that subroutines and DEF FN functions can do—and do it better!

We recommend that you avoid subroutines and DEF FN functions when you write new programs. Use subprograms and user-defined functions instead.

(There is one notable exception: you need subroutines for error trapping as discussed in Chapter 21, "Trapping Errors and Events.")

The remainder of this chapter has two primary purposes:

■ To provide you with a background in subroutines for the discussion of error trapping in Chapter 21.

■ To explain subroutines and DEF FN functions in case you encounter such constructions in published programs.

Using Subroutines

Don't confuse a subroutine and a subprogram. Essentially, a subroutine is a cruder version of a subprogram. When touting the merits of procedures earlier in the chapter, the following three features of subprograms were emphasized:

■ *Subprograms are isolated from your main program.*

■ *Subprograms use local variables.*

■ *Subprograms can pass parameters back and forth to the main program.*

In contrast:

■ *Subroutines are part of your main program.* A subroutine exists as a group of instructions inside your main program. The QBasic editor does not maintain subroutines as distinct entities. It does, however, maintain subprograms that way.

■ *Subroutines use global variables.* In contrast to local variables, global variables have scope throughout the entire program. A variable in the main program and a variable with the same name inside a subroutine are one and the same variable. As a result, subroutines do not enjoy the same autonomy that subprograms do.

■ *Subroutines have no explicit mechanism for passing parameters.* Subroutines can only "pass parameters" through the clumsy artifice of global variables.

Using *GOSUB* and *RETURN*

You invoke (call) a subroutine with a GOSUB instruction.

```
GOSUB linenum

or

GOSUB label

where

    linenum is a line number,

and

    label is a label.
```

S
T
A
T
E
M
E
N
T

Notice the similarity to the GOTO instruction. The crucial difference between GOSUB and GOTO is that when GOSUB executes, QBasic keeps track of the program location at which the call occurs. When the subroutine terminates, logic flow resumes at the instruction just after the GOSUB that called the subroutine.

The subroutine must begin with a label or an instruction containing a line number (so that the GOSUB destination is defined). Other than that, no special instruction indicates the beginning of the subroutine.

For a subroutine, GOSUB serves the same purpose that CALL does for a subprogram. Like a subprogram, you can call a subroutine any number of times. These calls can come from the same GOSUB instruction (possibly inside a loop) or from different GOSUB instructions.

Within the subroutine itself, use a RETURN instruction to indicate the logical end of the subroutine.

```
RETURN

or

RETURN linenum

or

RETURN label

where

    linenum is a line number,

and

    label is a label.
```

S
T
A
T
E
M
E
N
T

A RETURN instruction signifies the conclusion of the subroutine. RETURN for a subroutine is analogous to EXIT SUB or END SUB for a subprogram.

If no arguments are specified with RETURN, program control returns to the instruction immediately after the invoking GOSUB statement. If a line number or label is included, program control diverts to the indicated location instead.

The program in Listing 17.9, HYPOT.BAS, finds the hypotenuse of three different right triangles. A subroutine identified by the label GetHypotenuse calculates and displays the value of the hypotenuse given the two sides Side1! and Side2!.

Listing 17.9. The HYPOT.BAS program.

```
REM Program: HYPOT.BAS (Calculate hypotenuses)
Side1! = 3: Side2! = 4
GOSUB GetHypotenuse

Side1! = 3.5: Side2! = 5.5
GOSUB GetHypotenuse

Side1! = 5: Side2! = 7
GOSUB GetHypotenuse
END                     'What happens if this END is missing?

GetHypotenuse:   'Subroutine to compute and display hypotenuse
   Hypotenuse! = SQR(Side1! * Side1! + Side2 * Side2!)
   PRINT "Hypotenuse =" ; Hypotenuse!
RETURN
```

Here is the output of HYPOT.BAS:

```
Hypotenuse = 5
Hypotenuse = 6.519202
Hypotenuse = 8.602325
```

Separating Subroutines from the Main Program

Did you notice the questioning remark in the END instruction of HYPOT.BAS? If the END is removed, the main part of the program "falls into" the subroutine. This results in an extra (unwanted) line of output as follows:

```
Hypotenuse = 5
Hypotenuse = 6.519202
```

```
Hypotenuse = 8.602325
Hypotenuse = 8.602325
```

After displaying this output, a run-time error occurs (RETURN without GOSUB). The error results because, after falling into the subroutine, QBasic encounters the RETURN instruction with no prior GOSUB statement call.

You must avoid falling into subroutines inadvertently. The program design shown in Figure 17.12 eliminates the potential problem. Notice that the main body of the program terminates with an END instruction, and the subroutines are placed below.

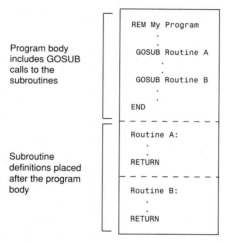

Program body includes GOSUB calls to the subroutines

```
REM My Program
    .
    .
GOSUB Routine A
    .
    .
GOSUB Routine B
    .
    .
END
```

Subroutine definitions placed after the program body

```
Routine A:
    .
RETURN

Routine B:
    .
RETURN
```

Figure 17.12.

Skeleton form of a program with subroutines.

Using the *ON GOSUB* Instruction

The ON GOSUB instruction works analogously to the ON GOTO instruction.

ON *numexpr* GOSUB *labellist*

or

ON *numexpr* GOSUB *linenumlist*

where

   numexpr is a general numeric expression,

   labellist is a list of one or more labels separated by commas,

S
T
A
T
E
M
E
N
T

and

> *linenumlist* is a list of one or more line numbers separated by commas.

ON GOSUB works just like the ON GOTO instruction except that with ON GOSUB each branch is to a subroutine. For more details, refer to the discussion of the ON GOTO instruction in Chapter 7, "Program Flow and Decision Making."

Using *DEF FN* Functions

DEF FN is an alternative to FUNCTION-END FUNCTION. The single-line DEF FN function is the only form of user-defined function available in BASICA or GW-BASIC. QBasic supports DEF FN and even extends the DEF FN concept to a multiline form. Keep in mind, however, that the more powerful user-defined FUNCTION declaration can do everything DEF FN can, and then some.

DEF FN creates a user-defined function that, like a FUNCTION block, returns a value. Unlike FUNCTION, however, DEF FN exists as part of your main program. You cannot place DEF FN inside a procedure. Further, DEF FN functions cannot be recursive.

S T A T E M E N T

Single-line form:

```
DEF FNfuncname (paramlist) = expr
```

Multiline form:

```
DEF FNfuncname (paramlist)
     instructions
FNfuncname = expr
     instructions
END DEF
```

where

> *funcname* preceded by FN constitutes the name of the function,
>
> *paramlist* is a comma-delimited list of the formal parameters,
>
> *expr* is a general expression specifying the value of the function,

and

> *instructions* is a block of valid instructions.

The *paramlist* and *instructions* block are optional.

To call the function, use FN*funcname*. The data type of the function is determined by a type-declaration suffix on *funcname* (or by any DEF*type* instruction in effect).

paramlist cannot include arrays, records, or fixed-length strings. You can use an AS *type* clause to specify the data type of any individual parameter. Place parentheses around the parameter list. If a function does not use a parameter list, no parentheses appear after the function name.

The following program fragment defines a single-line function and calls it from a PRINT instruction:

```
DEF FNAverage! (A!, B!, C!) = (A! + B! + C!) / 3!
        .
        .
        .
PRINT FNAverage!(134.8, MyNumber!, 89)
```

The multiline DEF FN is governed by these considerations:

- Variables inside the DEF FN block (but not in *paramlist*) are global to the main program. Use a STATIC instruction to declare variables local to the DEF FN block.

- All arguments are passed by value.

- Use EXIT DEF to exit the function block prematurely.

Summary

With user-defined procedures, you can add statements and functions to those predefined by QBasic. A subprogram is a sort of customized statement; a user-defined function is a sort of customized function.

Procedures are programming islands. From anywhere in your main program, you can "fly" to one of the islands and then "fly" back. For a subprogram, the CALL instruction is your airplane. For a user-defined function, you fly by merely invoking the function as you would one of QBasic's predefined functions.

The QBasic editor maintains procedures independently from the main program. Inside a procedure, local variables provide autonomy with respect to the "outside world" of the main program and other procedures.

A procedure can communicate with the calling instruction by passing needed parameters. A user-defined function returns a value in the same way that a regular, predefined function does.

One advantage of procedures is that you don't have to write a block of instructions over and over. You write the instructions once, making a subprogram or function out of the instruction block. You then invoke the procedure as needed.

Perhaps the most significant advantage of procedures is that they provide the primary tool for tackling major programming projects. Large-scale programs are best handled by modular programming. You divide the large task into several smaller tasks, or modules. To create the final program, you write several smaller modules that you piece together into the final program.

Subroutines and DEF FN functions represent the older (BASICA and GW-BASIC) way of modular programming. QBasic supports the two techniques for compatibility—so that you can run existing BASICA and GW-BASIC programs with QBasic.

Subroutines are needed for error trapping, as explained in Chapter 21, "Trapping Errors and Events." In general, however, you should prefer subprograms and user-defined functions over subroutines and DEF FN functions.

Toward Advanced Programming

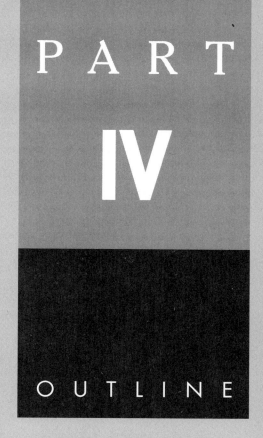

PART

IV

OUTLINE

By now, you have a solid foundation in QBasic programming. In fact, with only your present knowledge, you can write successful programs for most of your day-to-day programming tasks.

But QBasic is a rich language with a wealth of additional features. Part IV presents an eclectic mix of more advanced programming topics.

The following topics are included in Part IV:

- Trapping events and errors
- Animating graphics
- Reading and writing data values directly to memory
- Communicating with hardware devices as files
- Debugging and testing: what to do when things go wrong

Interactive Debugging and Testing

Beginning programmers often are surprised when they learn that most programs don't work correctly the first time. Some beginners get frustrated and lose confidence, mistaken in the belief that no one makes as many errors as they do. It's often comforting to know that even expert programmers frequently make programming mistakes.

In fact, you can gauge a programmer's experience by his or her attitude toward testing and debugging. Experienced programmers realize that for any program to work properly, thorough testing is essential.

Some programmers detest testing and are bugged by debugging. They'd rather spend endless hours in the design and planning stages. By the time they actually type their programs, they feel confident that no bugs could have crept in.

Programmers at the other extreme say to themselves, "Let me just type anything halfway close. I can fix the errors later." These programmers tend to produce sloppy, jumbled programs that are needlessly difficult to debug.

A middle ground between these two extremes, of course, is preferable.

The sloppy-program trap is easy to fall into! QBasic's interactive nature and impressive debugging tools can lead you to think that you can readily debug your way out of any mess. Here are some debugging techniques that you can utilize when troubleshooting:

■ Display the values of variables or expressions after you stop your program (PRINT from the Immediate window)

■ Execute your program one line at a time (Debug menu)

■ Determine the location of nonspecific error messages (ON ERROR GOTO)

■ Repeatedly suspend and resume execution (Breakpoints, STOP, CONT, Ctrl-Break)

■ Trace your program's logic flow (Debug menu)

In this chapter, the example programs are deliberately short and contain conspicuous errors. We recognize that your difficult problem-solving tasks will occur in larger programs where the errors are not so apparent. Our main concerns are showing errors and demonstrating debugging techniques. We believe short, to-the-point examples are the best teaching method.

NOTE

The First "Bug"

"Bug" and "debug" are well-known terms in the programming vernacular. A *bug* is an error or problem in a program. When a program doesn't work correctly, the program is said to have a "bug." The process of finding and correcting the bug is called *debugging the program,* or simply *debugging.*

Did you ever wonder how the colorful terms "bug" and "debug" originated?

The story goes that, when computers were in their infancy, some computer operators were having hardware problems. The setting was the late 1940s at an East Coast naval installation. The computers, which were less powerful than the one on your desk, were vacuum tube devices that required warehouse-sized rooms.

A computer was malfunctioning and the operators went to take a look. They found a dead moth lodged in one of the electric circuits. The moth apparently was killed from the heat of the vacuum tubes or from contact with one of the exposed circuits. When they removed the moth, the computer worked again. By eliminating the bug, the operators solved the problem. Imagine that! The earliest "bug" was, in fact, a real insect.

This first "debugging" was actually the correction of a hardware problem. But somehow, over the years, debugging has come to mean the elimination of programming (software) errors.

A Debugging Philosophy

To write successful programs, you must perform the interrelated actions of testing and debugging:

- *Testing* refers to the actions that determine whether a program runs correctly.

- *Debugging* is the subsequent activity of finding and removing the errors, or bugs.

Some programmers lump both activities together under just one name—either testing or debugging—but we think the distinction is important.

Sometimes a test run shows clearly that a program has errors. The testing part can be easy, but the debugging process might be much more difficult. In a sense, testing and debugging never end. Every time you run a program, you're testing.

Programmers (cautious programmers, anyway) often say that every nontrivial program has a bug waiting to be found. And when the bug is found and fixed, another remains. Figure 18.1 depicts the process of programming a project from beginning to end. As the figure lightheartedly demonstrates, you never really reach the end.

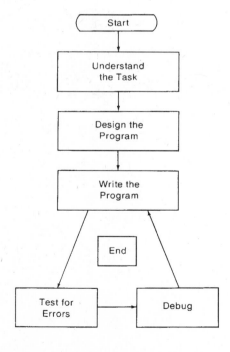

Figure 18.1.

The programming process.

Here are some principles of a sound debugging philosophy:

- *Assume that your program has errors.* No one is perfect, and no one writes perfect programs all the time. Expect to find errors. Exposing the errors—all of them—is your purpose in testing and debugging. Enjoy the detective work.

- *No single test run can prove a program to be bug-free.* Plan to run many test cases and to use a variety of test data. A program running to completion and producing expected output is a good sign, but that's only the beginning of testing.

- *Try to make your programs fail during testing.* Don't rely on "friendly" data when you test. If the program is destined to be used by other users who must supply data, try all kinds of unreasonable values. Your users might type almost anything when prompted for input. Your goal should be a "bulletproof" program—one that cannot "crash" (produce a QBasic error message) or generate an incorrect result, no matter what users try.

- *Write structured programs.* Follow the procedures outlined in Chapter 17, "Modular Programming." Make liberal use of functions and subprograms. Several smaller components are easier to understand, program, test, and debug than one larger component. Divide and conquer.

Dealing with Run-time Errors

Errors are a fact of programming life. All programmers make mistakes, so don't feel bad when the inevitable errors occur. Recognize that errors are bound to happen, learn from them, and forge ahead.

Understanding Run-time Errors

Errors that you don't discover until you run a program are called *run-time* errors. There are three fundamental types of run-time errors:

- *Syntax errors.* A syntax error occurs when an instruction doesn't follow the rules of QBasic. For example, you might spell a keyword incorrectly, use improper punctuation, or combine keywords in an illegal way. In such a case the instruction is meaningless. As a result, QBasic cannot even *attempt* to execute it. The editor catches some syntax errors as you type. Any remaining syntax errors are caught when you actually run the program.

- *Execution errors.* An execution error occurs when QBasic cannot perform a program instruction. The syntax of the instruction is fine, but the action requested by the instruction is impossible. For example, you might divide a number by zero, a mathematically illegal operation. When an execution error occurs, QBasic interrupts the program. It highlights the offending line in the program and displays an error message. In general, the error message quickly points out the problem (although sometimes the cause of the problem is not obvious).

■ *Logic errors.* A logic error occurs when a program runs to completion but the results are just not right. All the instructions have legal syntax, and QBasic executes the program and terminates normally. As far as QBasic is concerned, everything went fine. However, the program just doesn't produce correct results. Logic errors are the hardest types of errors to debug. Fortunately, QBasic's special debugging features are most helpful with these types of *errors.*

Recognizing Run-time Errors

This section presents a very simple example of each type of run-time error. Of course, in real life your errors are bound to occur in more complex programs.

An Example of a Syntax Error

At this point in your programming career, you are unavoidably familiar with syntax errors. Syntax errors usually arise from simple typing mistakes. When a syntax error occurs, QBasic stops running your program and informs you of the guilty line.

Try the following experiment. Type the second line exactly as shown, with PRINT incorrectly spelled as PRNT.

```
PRINT "Hello"
PRNT "Goodbye"
```

Notice that nothing special happens when you type the incorrect line. This is an example of a syntax error that is not caught by QBasic until you actually try to run the program.

Now run the program. To do so, press Shift-F5 (or select Start from the Run menu). QBasic finds the syntax error. The screen shifts back to the editor and a message box pops open. Inside the box is a message indicating that a syntax error is present. The offending line is highlighted in your program. Press Enter to close the message box. The cursor is on the incorrect word PRNT. You can now edit PRNT to read PRINT.

QBasic insists that you follow its rules. You might think that PRNT is close enough to PRINT that QBasic should be able to "figure out" what you mean. No such luck. PRNT is indecipherable to QBasic, and a syntax error results.

An Example of an Execution Error

When an execution error occurs, QBasic stops your program and displays an explanatory error message. Try typing the following example program exactly as shown:

```
FindBatAve:
    INPUT "Number of hits"; NumHits
    INPUT "Number of times at bat"; NumAB
    PRINT "Batting average is"
    PRINT NumHits / NumAB
    PRINT
    GOTO FindBatAve
```

This program computes baseball batting averages. (In baseball, a player's batting average is the number of hits divided by the number of times at bat.) The program loops so that multiple batting averages can be computed.

Suppose you use this program to calculate the following three batting averages:

■ A player had 128 hits in 523 at bats for an entire season.

■ A player had 27 hits in 79 at bats in one month.

■ A player had 8 hits in 30 at bats in one week.

Let's say you make a mistake when running this program, inadvertently entering 0 at bats during the third calculation. Here's the resulting output:

```
Number of hits? 128
Number of times at bat? 523
Batting average is
 .2447419

Number of hits? 27
Number of times at bat? 79
Batting average is
 .3417721

Number of hits? 8
Number of times at bat? 0
Batting average is
```

The first calculation results in a batting average of .2447419. In baseball terminology, batting averages are rounded to three digits, so this batting average is .245. The second batting average is .3417721, or .342 when rounded to three digits.

When the third calculation is tried, a problem develops. You inadvertently enter 0 rather than 30 for the number of times at bat. This means that the value of the variable NumAB becomes 0 and, in the fifth program line, QBasic tries to divide by zero. Division by zero is an illegal mathematical operation.

What happens? QBasic switches your screen back to the editor, displays a Division by zero error message, and highlights the line in your program that caused the error. You can now press Enter to clear the error message box and retry the program. After computing the correct result, press Ctrl-Break to exit from the program.

An Example of a Logic Error

As with the other types of errors, logic errors often result from simple typing mistakes. Look at the following short program, which contains just such a logic error:

```
Items% = 50
UnitCost = 2.25
PRINT "Total cost ="; UnitCost * Item%
```

Here's the output:

```
Total cost = 0
```

That can't be right. Do you see the problem? The PRINT instruction contains the variable Item% when Items% was intended. When the PRINT instruction executes, QBasic uses the default value of 0 for Item% because no other line assigned any other value to Item%. So the PRINT instruction displays the product of UnitCost (2.25) and Item% (0), which produces the result of zero.

The program has no syntax errors or execution errors, only a logic error.

More often than not, logic errors result from those typing mistakes that don't produce syntax or execution errors. When you find that a program has a logic error, the first thing to do is carefully check your typing. Make sure your program reads as you intended.

General Debugging Tips

Here are some general tips for debugging the trickier types of errors—the execution errors and logic errors that don't have evident causes.

■ *Start by looking for the obvious.* Most errors result from obvious, not subtle, causes. Look for simple mistakes, such as careless typing errors. Here are a few common errors:

1. Interchanging the colon and semicolon characters.

2. Improperly nesting parentheses in an expression.

3. Typing a capital I or a lowercase letter l when you mean to type the numeral 1.

4. Interchanging the less than (<) and greater than (>) signs.

Obvious errors often are the hardest ones to find because you can't believe you could make such a stupid mistake. Take heart, all programmers make them.

■ *Reasonable-looking output can be wrong.* Usually, incorrect output is so wrong that it leaps out at you and screams, "I'm wrong!" But beware of reasonable-looking output. The worst kind of error causes slightly incorrect results, which can lead you to carelessly assume that everything is working correctly. Be suspicious.

■ *Verify that QBasic's statements and functions work as you expect.* You might have an incorrect assumption about how a QBasic statement or function works. LOG, for example, works with natural, not common, logarithms. Use this book and your QBasic manual for confirmation.

■ *Make sure that your algorithms are correct.* An *algorithm* is simply a step-by-step procedure for solving a problem. If you use algorithms from books and magazines, be skeptical of what you read. Printed algorithms and program listings contain errors more often than you might guess. Look for a second source, if possible. Goodness knows, in spite of our tireless efforts, a programming error could be lurking somewhere in this book.

■ *Learn QBasic's debugging features and techniques.* They're explained throughout this chapter.

Debugging Execution Errors

Here's a situation familiar to all programmers. Your program aborts with an explanatory error message and a highlight on the offending line. But you can't figure out what's wrong. What do you do now?

This question has many answers, depending on what the error message is and what the program line contains. Here are some things to try, and tips about a few of the more common error messages:

■ *Look again for typing errors.* This cannot be stressed enough: Look for simple errors first—and the most common simple errors are typing errors.

Watch for These Typing Errors

Here are the characters that are most frequently typed incorrectly—
either omitted, or interchanged with other characters (which are listed):

Alphabetic	I l	O
Numeric	1	0
Special	., :; ([ )] < > ' " / \ $	

Are you accustomed to typing the lowercase letter *l* rather than the numeral *1*? If so, beware. The two characters look almost identical when
you type them, but QBasic treats them very differently. The letter *O* and
the numeral *0* can be confused until you get used to the slash that is displayed in the zero.

■ PRINT *the current values of your main variables.* When your program
aborts with an error message, you can use QBasic's Immediate window to
display (PRINT) the values of variables. This technique is discussed later
in this chapter.

■ *Split up multi-instruction program lines.* If you get a Subscript out of range
error message for a line containing half a dozen subscript references
spread over several instructions, you won't know which instruction is the
culprit. Put each instruction on a separate program line, or split a long
instruction into smaller components.

■ *Look in other parts of the program that manipulate the same variables.* If
QBasic indicates a program line is doing something illegal, the problem
often stems from a previous line that erroneously computed the variable.
The following error messages are frequently caused by incorrect manipulation of a variable elsewhere in the program:

```
Illegal function call

Subscript out of range

Division by zero
```

■ *Add an* ON ERROR GOTO *instruction.* This technique lets you branch to a
special subroutine whenever an error occurs. This is an advanced topic
which is discussed in Chapter 21, "Trapping Errors and Events."

■ *Check the punctuation in your* DATA *instruction when you get an* Out of DATA
error. Even though this error message always refers to a line with a READ
instruction, the problem is most likely either in your DATA instructions or
in a loop around the READ instruction. In either case, your program tried
to read more data elements than remained in your data list. Often the
cause is simply a mistyped comma in a DATA instruction. See the sample
debugging session later in this chapter for an example of this type of
error.

Debugging with the Immediate Window

One of the big advantages of QBasic's interactive environment is that, after your program stops with an error message, you can do detective work from the Immediate window. Most importantly, you can print the values of important variables to help determine what went wrong.

When a program stops, whether normally or due to an error condition, QBasic retains the current values of all the variables. By issuing PRINT instructions from the Immediate window, you can display the value of any variable or array element.

For example, suppose your program aborts with the following error message:

```
Illegal function
```

The highlight is on a program line which reads

```
Length! = SQR(Area!)
```

Apparently the SQR function fails because something is wrong with the value of Area!. To find out, all you have to do is go to the Immediate window (press F6), type the instruction PRINT Area!, and press Enter. QBasic then displays the current value of AREA!.

You'll probably discover that Area! has a negative value. If so, that's the problem. QBasic's SQR function works only with positive arguments (or zero).

Of course, if you do find that the value of Area! is negative, that's only the beginning of the whole solution. Now you must find out how Area! was calculated. If Area! was manipulated several times before the line where the error occurred, you need to backtrack to determine how Area! erroneously became negative. More PRINT commands should narrow down the problem.

Interrupting a Program with Ctrl-Break

You can suspend execution at any time while your program is running by pressing Ctrl-Break. QBasic returns to the editor screen and highlights the line that was executing at that moment.

You can now toggle the output screen with F4 or use the Immediate window (F6).

Resuming a Program—the Continue Command

From the Immediate window, you can display the values of key variables with PRINT. But here's the kicker: You can resume execution of your program from the point where it was interrupted. All you have to do is select the Continue command from the Run menu. The hotkey for Continue is F5.

Think about that. You can interrupt a program, display variable values, and then resume the program from wherever the interruption occurred. That's impressive debugging capability.

An Example of Ctrl-Break and Continue

Ctrl-Break is handy when a program seems to be executing for an unduly long time. Usually the problem is an endless loop.

For example, suppose you write a program that computes the sum of all the odd integers from 1 to 99. Here's your program:

```
Increment = 2
Sum = 0
FOR J = 1 TO 99 STEP Incrment
    Sum = Sum + J
NEXT J
PRINT Sum
```

This seems reasonable. The counter variable J in the FOR-NEXT loop assumes all odd integer values from 1 to 99. The loop computes the desired sum. But when you run the program, a strange thing happens: the program "hangs." No answer is displayed and no error message occurs.

You press Ctrl-Break. QBasic interrupts the program with the highlight, probably, on the Sum = Sum + J instruction. You display the value of Sum with a PRINT Sum instruction from the Immediate window. QBasic displays a large number which seems plausible. Next you display the value of J. Lo and behold, the value of J is 1. That's funny, the loop doesn't seem to be getting anywhere.

You now press any key to return to the editor, then press F5 to continue the program. The program resumes execution but still hangs. So you press Ctrl-Break again. You redisplay Sum and J, just as you did before, to see whether the values change. The problem persists: Sum has a larger value but J is still 1. Apparently the counter variable is not increasing.

Then you see it. Of course! In the `FOR` instruction, you typed `Incrment` instead of `Increment`. Your typing error created an endless loop with `J` always having a value of 1. (If you examine the program, you'll see that the value of `Sum` actually indicates how many times the loop has executed.)

You edit the `FOR` instruction to spell `Increment` correctly. The program now runs fine.

NOTE

Sometimes You Cannot Continue after Editing Your Program

After interrupting your program with Ctrl-Break, you can issue Immediate window instructions and then resume execution with the Continue command. However, Continue *sometimes* does not work.

If you edit a program line that results in QBasic being unable to continue your program, a dialog box opens to inform you of that fact. You then have a choice of going ahead with the modification or leaving the program intact so that you can continue execution.

Debugging Logic Errors

Let's say you have written a program, cleaned up all the syntax errors, and eliminated all execution errors. But the program doesn't do what you intended. It runs to completion but the results look wrong. You have the dreaded *logic error*. Now what?

■ Look *again* for typing errors.

■ Display the contents of variables after the program ends.

■ Look for variable conflicts. QBasic makes it easy to create new variables, but this convenience sometimes fosters program bugs. Here are the two variable conflicts most likely to introduce logic errors into your programs:

1. Accidentally using a not-quite-the-same variable name. Make sure that you spell a variable name consistently throughout the program. Pay special attention to the consistent use of suffixes.

2. Reusing a temporary variable that's still in use. Suppose a variable occurs in one part of a program. Another part of the program subsequently uses the same variable name during an independent calculation. The first part of the program then regains control and needs the old value of the variable—but the old value isn't there.

   The programmer might have neglected to check whether or not this variable name was already in use, or have simply forgotten that it would still be needed by the first part of the program. This kind of error is common with subroutines. It's one reason you should avoid subroutines in favor of subprograms and user-defined functions.

■ Verify that QBasic's statements and functions work the way you think they do.

■ Redesign troublesome parts of the program. Use subprograms and user-defined functions to isolate program chunks into smaller units.

■ Use the special debugging features found on the Debug menu. That's the subject of the rest of this chapter.

Introducing the *Debug* Menu

The nerve center of QBasic's debugging toolbox is the Debug menu (see Figure 18.2). Press Alt-D from the editor to pop up the Debug menu.

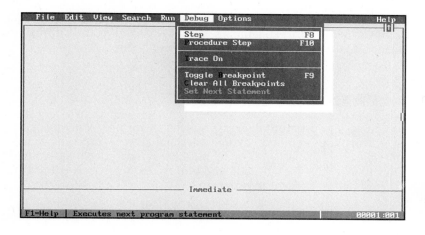

Figure 18.2.

The Debug menu.

The following two terms are central to QBasic's debugging terminology:

■ *Trace:* a line-by-line examination of your program's logic flow. QBasic includes options to single-step through your program or animate tracing at continual slow-motion speed.

■ *Breakpoint:* a designated program line where you want execution to halt temporarily. When the execution is interrupted, you can examine the values of variables or make other tests before you resume *execution.*

Testing and Debugging: A Case Study

The best way to get a feel for the tools found on the Debug menu is to follow a case study. Suppose that you must tackle the following programming task:

Task:

Write a function to find the mean, or average, of the values in an integer array. The array, which has one dimension, is the only parameter passed to the function. The main program dimensions the array and assigns a value to every array element. Therefore, inside the function, you can use QBasic's LBOUND and UBOUND functions to determine the size of the array.

Also, write a subprogram named MinMax. This subprogram is passed an integer array and returns the minimum and maximum elements in the array. Use three parameters. The first parameter is the array. The second and third parameters, Min% and Max%, contain the minimum and maximum values, respectively. Min% and Max% must be passed back to the main program.

To test your procedures, write a main program called GETSTATS, which dimensions a three-element integer array. Assign the values 15, 25, and 10, respectively, to the array's three elements. Use your function and subprogram to display the array's minimum, maximum, and mean values.

Designing the Program

After some planning and program design, you write your program and type it in the QBasic editor. You are not a keyboard wizard, however, so you make a few typing mistakes that are caught by the editor's syntax checking feature. At last, however, the program is complete, and you're ready to try the first run. Listing 18.1 contains the completed program.

Listing 18.1. The GETSTATS.BAS program.

```
REM Program: GETSTATS.BAS (Compute statistics on an array)

DECLARE SUB MinMax (IntegerArray%(), Minimum%, Maximum%)
DECLARE FUNCTION Mean% (IntegerArray%())

CLS
DIM MyArray%(3)
FOR Index% = 1 TO 3
   READ MyArray%(Index%)
NEXT Index%
```

```
DATA 15. 25, 10

CALL MinMax(MyArray%(), Smallest%, Largest%)
PRINT "Minimum value ="; Smallest%
PRINT "Maximum value ="; Largest%

PRINT "Mean ="; Mean%(MyArray%())
END

FUNCTION Mean% (MyArray%())
REM Compute the mean of the values in MyArray%
   Sum% = 0
   FOR Index% = LBOUND(MyArray%) TO UBOUND(MyArray%)
      Sum% = Sum% + MyArray%(Index%)
   NEXT Index%
   NumElements% = UBOUND(MyArray%) - LBOUND(MyArray%)
   Mean% = Sum% / NumElements%
END FUNCTION

SUB MinMax (MyArray%(), Min%, Max%)
REM Return Min and Max elements in MyArray%
   Min% = MyArray%(LBOUND(MyArray%))
   Max% = MyArray%(LBOUND(MyArray%))
   FOR Index% = LBOUND(MyArray%) TO UBOUND(MyArray%)
      IF MyArray%(Index%) < Min% THEN Min% = MyArray%(Index%)
      IF MyArray%(Index%) > Max% THEN Max% = MyArray%(Index%)
   NEXT Index%
END SUB
```

Can we coax you into trying this example? Type the program exactly as it appears. The program has some errors. After all, that's the point of this exercise. By following along on your computer, you'll learn several debugging techniques.

Testing and Debugging the Program

In glorious anticipation, you press Shift-F5 to run the program. What happens? You quickly get an Out of DATA error (see Figure 18.3). Notice that the READ instruction is highlighted. Something seems to be wrong with the assignment of the array values.

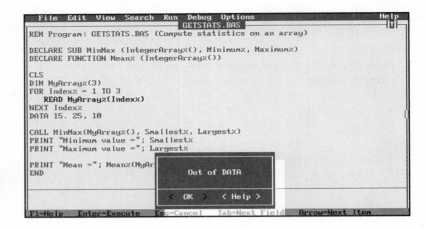

Figure 18.3.

An Out of DATA
error.

Using the *Immediate* Window

To track down the error, examine the values stored in the array. The Immediate window makes this procedure easy. Follow these steps:

1. Press Enter to remove the error message.

2. Press F6 to move the input focus to the Immediate window.

3. Type the following line in the Immediate window:

   ```
   FOR Q = 1 TO 3: PRINT MyArray%(Q): NEXT Q
   ```

4. Press Enter to see the results.

QBasic shifts to the output screen and displays the following output:

```
15
10
0
```

These values are suspicious because the expected array values are 15, 25, and 10. What happened to 25? Look back at the data to find out. First, follow these steps:

1. Press any key to return to the editor screen.

2. Press F6 to move the input focus from the Immediate window back to the View window.

Correcting the *DATA* Instruction

Because you have suspicious data, the DATA instruction is a natural place to look. Sure enough, it has a typo. Here's the offending instruction:

```
DATA 15. 25, 10
```

The period should be a comma.

Do you see what happened when the program ran?

The period effectively created a data instruction containing only two values: 15.25 and 10. When QBasic needed a third value, no third value was available.

Edit the DATA instruction to replace the period with a comma. The corrected line should look like this:

```
DATA 15, 25, 10
```

Now rerun the program: press Shift-F5 (or select Start from the Run menu). This time the program runs to completion and displays the following output:

```
Minimum value = 0
Maximum value = 25
Mean = 17
```

Unfortunately, you have more errors to track down. Only the maximum value is correct. The minimum value should be 10, not 0. The mean should be 16 2/3 (or approximately 16.6667), not 17. Notice that the mean is (15 + 25 + 10) / 3, or 50/3.

You can use QBasic's debugging tools to track down the errors. First, press any key to return to the editor.

Tracing a Program

Tracing reveals the logic flow of a program. While your program runs, QBasic highlights each instruction as it executes. Table 18.1 shows the various forms of tracing.

Table 18.1. Tracing options.

Action	Invocation	Effect
Single Step	F8, or Step (Debug menu)	Executes only the highlighted instruction; branches to functions and subprograms as necessary
Procedure Step	F10, or Procedure Step (Debug menu)	Similar to Single Step except that a function or subprogram executes as a single instruction
Animated Trace	Trace On (Debug menu)	Runs the entire program in slow motion

Using Single Step and Procedure Step

In this part of the exercise, we briefly digress to demonstrate tracing. The actual debugging resumes shortly.

To begin a Single Step trace or a Procedure Step trace, follow these steps:

1. Invoke the Run menu (Alt-R).

2. Select Restart. Use the cursor keys or press R (see Figure 18.4).

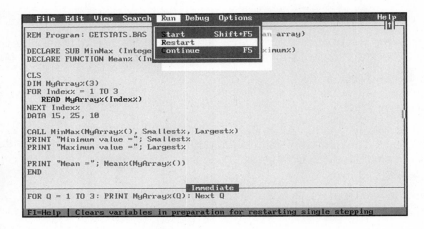

Figure 18.4.

Selecting Restart on the Run menu.

Restart clears all variables, reinitializes your program, and highlights the first executable instruction—in this case, the CLS instruction (see Figure 18.5).

Press F8 or F10. QBasic executes the CLS instruction and moves the highlight down to the following DIM instruction:

```
DIM MyArray%(3)
```

Press F8 or F10 three more times. Notice how the highlight moves a line at a time, from the FOR instruction to the READ instruction and, finally, to the following NEXT instruction:

```
NEXT Index%
```

Watch carefully as you press F8 the next time. The highlight jumps back up to the READ instruction. Press F8 a few more times and watch the highlight toggle between the READ and the NEXT instruction.

QBasic is executing the FOR-NEXT loop. After three iterations (Index% loops from 1 to 3), the highlight moves from the NEXT instruction down to the following CALL instruction:

```
CALL MinMax(MyArray%(), Smallest%, Largest%)
```

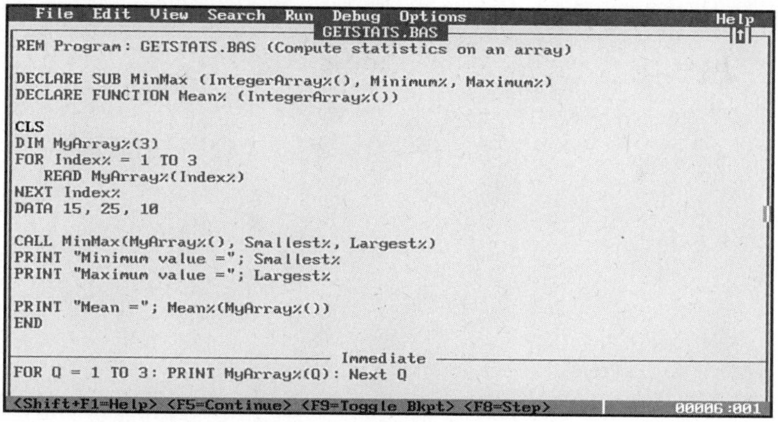

```
  File  Edit  View  Search  Run  Debug  Options                    Help
                         GETSTATS.BAS
REM Program: GETSTATS.BAS (Compute statistics on an array)

DECLARE SUB MinMax (IntegerArray%(), Minimum%, Maximum%)
DECLARE FUNCTION Mean% (IntegerArray%())

CLS
DIM MyArray%(3)
FOR Index% = 1 TO 3
   READ MyArray%(Index%)
NEXT Index%
DATA 15, 25, 10

CALL MinMax(MyArray%(), Smallest%, Largest%)
PRINT "Minimum value ="; Smallest%
PRINT "Maximum value ="; Largest%

PRINT "Mean ="; Mean%(MyArray%())
END
                         Immediate
FOR Q = 1 TO 3: PRINT MyArray%(Q): Next Q
<Shift+F1=Help> <F5=Continue> <F9=Toggle Bkpt> <F8=Step>      00006:001
```

Figure 18.5.

The screen after restarting.

The highlight skips the nonexecutable DATA instruction. Tracing stops only on the executable instructions.

Now, for the first time, it matters whether you next press F8 or F10. Don't press F10. If you were to press F10, QBasic would execute the entire MinMax subprogram as one step and move the highlight down to the subsequent PRINT instruction. Instead, press F8. QBasic places the MinMax subprogram on the screen and highlights the first executable instruction (see Figure 18.6).

Continue to press F8 or F10 to cycle through MinMax. Eventually, the subprogram terminates. Control passes back to the main program at the first PRINT instruction:

```
PRINT "Minimum value ="; Smallest%
```

Now watch the screen closely as you press F8. Did you detect a flicker? As QBasic executes the PRINT instruction, your video screen toggled quickly to the output screen and then back to the editor. Press F4 to view the output screen. You should see the following line:

```
Minimum value = 0
```

This line confirms that QBasic executed the PRINT instruction. Press any key to return to the editor. The second PRINT instruction is highlighted:

```
PRINT "Maximum value ="; Largest%
```

Press F8 to execute this instruction. Then press F4 to view the output screen, which now displays the following two lines:

```
Minimum value = 0
Maximum value = 25
```

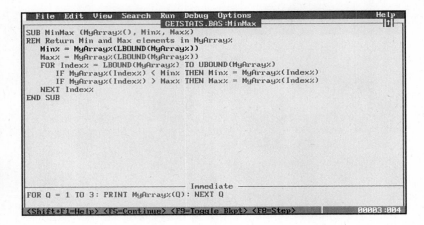

Figure 18.6.

Tracing the `MinMax` subprogram.

Press a key to return to the editor. The final PRINT instruction is highlighted:

```
PRINT "Mean ="; Mean%(MyArray%())
```

Notice that this PRINT instruction invokes the Mean% function. This time, don't press F8. If you were to press F8, QBasic would display the Mean% function in preparation for tracing. Instead, press F10. This step executes, as a single step, the PRINT instruction, which includes the entire Mean% function. The highlight moves down to the END instruction. Press F4 to see the output screen, which now includes the final PRINT instruction.

```
Minimum value = 0
Maximum value = 25
Mean = 17
```

Press any key to return to the editor. Then press F8 to complete single-step tracing of the program. Notice that no line is highlighted. This is because the program has terminated.

Using Animated Trace

Animated trace provides a continuous, slow-motion trace of your program. Each instruction is highlighted in turn. The effect is the same as repeatedly pressing F8. Here are the steps for generating an animated trace:

1. Invoke the Debug menu by pressing Alt-D.

2. Select Trace On either by pressing T or by moving the highlight down to Trace On and pressing Enter.

3. Run the program by pressing Shift-F5.

QBasic single-steps through the program. As each subprogram and function executes, it is displayed on-screen.

Trace On is a toggle. You turn off the automatic animated trace by repeating the preceding three steps. Try it. Notice that when you activate the Debug menu, you see a dot next to Trace On (see Figure 18.7). The dot indicates that animated tracing is currently active.

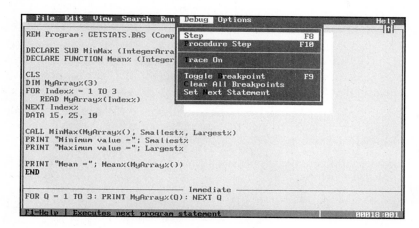

Figure 18.7.

Activating Trace On.

Here are the main features of animated tracing:

- Your program's general logic flow is shown, including any procedure invocations.

- You can press Ctrl-Break at any time to suspend the tracing and the program execution. After such a pause you can use the Immediate window, view the output screen with F4, or Single Step with F8. You can resume the trace by pressing F5.

- Another way you can invoke animated tracing is by placing a TRON instruction in the program. TRON is a mnemonic for *TRace ON*. When QBasic executes a TRON instruction, it turns tracing on just as though you selected Trace On from the Debug menu. The companion instruction, TROFF, turns tracing off. These instructions provide compatibility with BASICA and GW-BASIC. The tracing options available from the Debug menu make TRON and TROFF outmoded.

Setting Breakpoints

A breakpoint is a debugger's best friend. A breakpoint is a specified program line where you want to suspend execution. By setting breakpoints, you can halt execution at strategic locations. After the program suspends at a breakpoint, you can set new options from the Debug menu, or use the Immediate window to display the values of variables and expressions.

To set a breakpoint:

1. Move the cursor to the target line.

2. Select Toggle Breakpoint from the Debug menu; or simply press F9 and don't use the Debug menu at all.

QBasic shows the breakpoint by highlighting the line in red or reverse video.

Follow the identical procedure to remove a breakpoint. As the name implies, Toggle Breakpoint alternately sets and removes an individual breakpoint. You can remove all breakpoints in one fell swoop by selecting Clear All Breakpoints from the Debug menu.

Now let's use a breakpoint as you get back to debugging the program. Recall that something is wrong with the calculation of the mean—the program displays 17 when 16 2/3 is expected.

A reasonable next step is to set a breakpoint at the end of the Mean% function. To do so, follow these steps:

1. Bring the Mean% function to the View window by pressing F2 and then selecting Mean (or press Shift-F2 as many times as necessary).

2. Move the cursor down to the END FUNCTION line at the bottom of the procedure.

3. Press F9. QBasic highlights the line in red or reverse video to indicate a breakpoint.

4. Return the main program to the View window by pressing F2 (or Shift-F2) again.

Make sure that Trace On is off. Now press Shift-F5 to start program execution. The program executes up to the breakpoint and suspends.

Press F4 to see the output. Notice that the bottom line reads Mean =. You don't yet see any value for the mean because the Mean% function has not yet returned a value to the main program.

Press F4 to return to the editor. Now press F6 to utilize the Immediate window. Type the following line:

```
PRINT Sum%, NumElements%, Sum% / NumElements%
```

You see the following values displayed on the output screen: 50, 3, and 16.66667. The 50 is correct (15 + 25 + 10). The 3 is also correct.

Sum% / NumElements% is 16.66667. This is the expected result. So why does the Mean% function return 17 instead? The evidence indicates that the function's value is being assigned incorrectly. Return to the editor screen and look at the program line that assigns the value of Mean%:

```
Mean% = Sum% / NumElements%
```

The right-hand side is a floating-point expression, even though the variables are all of type integer. You inadvertently made the function name, Mean%, an integer function.

Correct the error by changing all occurrences of Mean% to Mean!. You can use the Change... command from the Search menu. (There are a total of four changes to be made.)

Now remove the breakpoint (by pressing F9) and run the program by pressing Shift-F5. The following output appears:

```
Minimum value = 0
Maximum value = 25
Mean = 16.66667
```

Progress! The mean now is correct. The minimum value, however, should be 10, not 0. Press any key to return to the editor. Bring the MinMax subprogram to the View window. Set a breakpoint in MinMax at the FOR instruction. Press Shift-F5 to rerun the program. QBasic pauses just after executing the following two instructions:

```
Min% = MyArray%(LBOUND(MyArray%))
Max% = MyArray%(LBOUND(MyArray%))
```

You expect the lower array bound to be 1. Min% and Max% each should be 15 because 15 is the expected value of MyArray%(1). Find out: Press F6 to move to the Immediate window, then type the following line:

```
PRINT Min%, Max%, LBOUND(MyArray%), UBOUND(MyArray%)
```

Press Enter. QBasic displays the following result:

```
0           0           0           3
```

What happened? Min% and Max% are each 0, not 15. Furthermore, the value of LBOUND(MyArray%) is 0, not 1. The problem is evident: the array has been dimensioned from 0 to 3, not from 1 to 3.

Press any key to return to the editor, and then place the main program in the View window. The culprit is the DIM MyArray%(3) instruction. You forgot that the default minimum array index is 0, not 1. Edit the DIM instruction to look as follows:

```
DIM MyArray%(1 TO 3)
```

Remove the breakpoint. Try Clear All Breakpoints from the Debug menu. Press Shift-F5 to try another run. The output now looks like this:

```
Minimum value = 10
Maximum value = 25
Mean = 25
```

This result is disturbing! You seem to have taken one step forward and one step backward. Now the minimum and maximum values are correct. But the mean, which you just corrected, is suddenly misbehaving again.

Finding the Last Bug

To track down the problem, reset a breakpoint at the END FUNCTION line in the Mean! function. Press Shift-F5 to run the program to this breakpoint.

Now go to the Immediate window and type the following line:

```
PRINT Sum%, NumElements%, Sum% / NumElements%
```

You see the following result:

```
        50                2              25
```

The value of 50 for Sum% is correct (15 + 25 + 10 = 50). NumElements%, however, is 2, not 3 as expected. Do you see the problem?

Look at the instruction that calculates NumElements%. The UBOUND and LBOUND functions return 3 and 1, respectively. You can use the Immediate window to confirm these values. That's why NumElements% is 2, (3–1 = 2).

The instruction is in error. The correct formula for NumElements% requires the addition of 1. To fix the problem, edit the instruction to appear as follows:

```
NumElements% = UBOUND(MyArray%) - LBOUND(MyArray%) + 1
```

This bug was subtle. When the array was dimensioned incorrectly, from 0 to 3, LBOUND returned 0. As a result, the original, incorrect formula for NumElements% serendipitously returned 3, the correct value in this case!

Only when you corrected the dimensioning error did the bug in the NumElements% calculation become apparent. Some logic errors are indeed tricky.

Final Testing

Select Clear All Breakpoints from the Debug menu. Now press Shift-F5 to run the program. You should see the following output:

```
Minimum value = 10
Maximum value = 25
Mean = 16.66667
```

Finally, the results are correct. Listing 18.2 contains the debugged program:

Listing 18.2. The debugged GETSTATS.BAS program.

```
REM Program: GETSTATS.BAS (Compute statistics on an array)

DECLARE SUB MinMax (IntegerArray%(), Minimum%, Maximum%)
DECLARE FUNCTION Mean! (IntegerArray%())

CLS
DIM MyArray%(1 TO 3)
FOR Index% = 1 TO 3
   READ MyArray%(Index%)
NEXT Index%
DATA 15, 25, 10

CALL MinMax(MyArray%(), Smallest%, Largest%)
PRINT "Minimum value ="; Smallest%
PRINT "Maximum value ="; Largest%

PRINT "Mean ="; Mean!(MyArray%())
END

FUNCTION Mean! (MyArray%())
REM Compute the mean of the values in MyArray%
   Sum% = 0
   FOR Index% = LBOUND(MyArray%) TO UBOUND(MyArray%)
      Sum% = Sum% + MyArray%(Index%)
   NEXT Index%
   NumElements% = UBOUND(MyArray%) - LBOUND(MyArray%) + 1
   Mean! = Sum% / NumElements%
END FUNCTION

SUB MinMax (MyArray%(), Min%, Max%)
REM Return Min and Max elements in MyArray%
   Min% = MyArray%(LBOUND(MyArray%))
   Max% = MyArray%(LBOUND(MyArray%))
   FOR Index% = LBOUND(MyArray%) TO UBOUND(MyArray%)
      IF MyArray%(Index%) < Min% THEN Min% = MyArray%(Index%)
      IF MyArray%(Index%) > Max% THEN Max% = MyArray%(Index%)
   NEXT Index%
END SUB
```

Is the program *fully* debugged? An old programming adage says that, except for trivial programs, bug-free programs don't exist. That's a little heavy-handed. But only a little.

Even when a program does not contain any outright errors, you can usually find changes that make the program execute more efficiently, display the output clearer, or make the program's logic easier to understand.

Reread the original programming task. Can you see any potential snags if the data changes? Here's one lurking problem: Suppose the three integer data values change to 15000, 25000, and 10000. Look what happens to the variable Sum% in the Mean! function. Overflow, that's what. Sum% should not have been an integer variable. Single-precision or perhaps long integer would have been a better choice.

The lesson is simple: Rigorous testing is required to shoo away the inevitable bugs. If you don't look for bugs, the bugs will look for you.

Other Debugging Tools

Besides the major debugging tools already discussed, QBasic has some additional debugging features. This section presents the following three debugging aids:

■ Selecting the next instruction to execute

■ Executing up to a designated instruction

■ Using the STOP instruction

Using Set Next Statement

After pausing execution, you can designate which instruction executes next with the Set Next Statement option on the Debug menu. Rather than execute any instructions, this command simply moves the highlight. When you resume execution with F5, F8, or F10, the new instruction executes first. The effect is like a GOTO.

Follow the next four steps to try Set Next Statement:

1. Pause a program with the highlight on a particular instruction.

2. Move the cursor to whatever instruction you want to execute next. This instruction can be anywhere in the main program or in any procedure.

3. Invoke the Debug menu (Alt-D).

4. Select Set Next Statement either by using the cursor keys and pressing Enter, or by simply pressing the N key.

The highlight moves to your selected instruction. Now press F5 to resume execution at this new instruction.

Executing to the Cursor

Pressing F7 causes your program to execute from the highlighted line to the line on which you place the cursor. If the cursor is on a line not in the subsequent program flow, the effect is the same as pressing F5.

Using *STOP*

QBasic provides the STOP instruction for compatibility with BASICA and GW-BASIC. STOP is the "old" way of setting a breakpoint.

When QBasic encounters a STOP instruction, execution suspends with the highlight on the STOP instruction. You can now use the Immediate window, set options with the Debug menu, or do anything normally associated with suspended programs. As usual, you can resume the program with F5.

Essentially, STOP is like a breakpoint set at the STOP instruction itself. If you run old BASICA or GW-BASIC programs that contain STOP instructions, that's fine. But QBasic's breakpoint features make STOP an outmoded technique for new programs.

A Summary of Debugging Tools

Tables 18.2 through 18.5 summarize QBasic's debugging facilities.

Table 18.2. Commands that control execution.

Action	Menu	Hotkey
Continue	Run	F5
Start	Run	Shift-F5
Restart	Run	
Set Next Statement	Debug	
Execute to Cursor		F7
Suspend Execution		Ctrl-Break

Table 18.3. Tracing commands.

Action	Menu	Hotkey
Trace On	Debug	
Step	Debug	F8
Procedure Step	Debug	F10

Table 18.4. Breakpoint commands.

Action	Menu	Hotkey
Toggle Breakpoint	Debug	F9
Clear All Breakpoints	Debug	

Table 18.5. Viewing commands.

Action	Menu	Hotkey
Subs...	View	F2
Next sub		Shift-F2
View previous sub		Ctrl-F2
Output Screen	View	F4

Summary

Experienced programmers realize that testing and debugging are a necessary part of successful programming. As a general rule, nontrivial programs contain bugs that must be found and eliminated. Many programmers dislike testing and debugging. But actually, testing and debugging can be kind of fun. Much depends on your state of mind. After all, most people like solving puzzles and being "detectives."

Three kinds of errors crop up in programs:

- *Syntax* errors, which are incorrectly worded instructions that seem like gibberish to QBasic

■ *Execution* errors, which cause diagnostic messages as the result of (correctly worded) instructions that QBasic just cannot execute successfully

■ *Logic* errors, which occur when your program runs to completion but yields incorrect results

Fortunately, QBasic provides several debugging features and techniques. The most important is the ability to suspend program execution, perform detective work with the Immediate window, and then resume the program.

With breakpoints, you can suspend a program at any line. You can display the values of crucial variables and expressions from the Immediate window. You can also reassign the value of any variable.

Tracing provides a way to observe the logic flow of your program. You can see the order in which each instruction executes. While tracing, you can suspend execution and use the Immediate window.

Most programming errors stem from simple mistakes rather than obscure bugs. Look for the obvious before the subtle. By far the most likely source of any error is a simple typing mistake. When errors occur, double- and triple-check your typing.

Occasionally you can get stuck tracking down an elusive bug. We advise you to walk away for a while. Do something relaxing. Watch TV, take a walk, jog, play Ping-Pong, or just nap. It's amazing how some nagging bugs are swiftly found after a rejuvenating break.

Managing Memory

As a QBasic programmer, you generally write programs without even thinking about memory management. QBasic automatically supervises your machine's memory to handle variable storage, string management, array allocation, heap maintenance, and stack maintenance.

Occasionally, however, you need to exert explicit control over memory resources. Perhaps large arrays are gobbling up available memory, and you must squeeze out some extra bytes. Maybe you want to write directly into the memory-mapped video areas.

This chapter examines ways in which you can control memory. Here are some of the topics discussed:

- Using hexadecimal notation
- Identifying a memory address with a segment and offset
- Allocating arrays (both dynamically and statically)
- Reading and writing the value of an individual memory location
- Explicitly controlling the heap and stack
- Saving and reloading memory contents to a disk file
- Locating a variable in memory
- Incorporating machine language routines in QBasic programs

Before delving into the details of controlling memory, let's discuss two subjects for background:

■ *Using alternate number systems*

With QBasic, you can express integer numbers with octal or hexadecimal notation as well as with the conventional decimal notation. Hexadecimal is especially important because memory addresses are conveniently expressed in hex notation.

■ *Understanding the memory architecture of the IBM PC*

If you're going to manipulate memory, you need to understand the organization of your machine's memory and how QBasic utilizes the memory resources.

Using Alternate Number Systems— Binary, Octal, and Hexadecimal

You've probably heard of binary numbers. In *binary* you represent integer numbers using only the digits 0 and 1. Counting from 0, the first six binary numbers are 0, 1, 10, 11, 100, and 101, which represent the decimal numbers 0, 1, 2, 3, 4, and 5, respectively.

Compared with our familiar decimal notation, the binary representation of a number generally requires many more digits. There must be a trade-off. Why ever use binary numbers? As it turns out, binary numbers are quite natural in computer applications. Why? Because a binary digit has only two states (0 or 1) and can be represented easily by an electric circuit being either off or on.

Hexadecimal is another numbering system frequently used in programming. Each hexadecimal digit represents four binary digits. Because a binary digit has 2 states (on or off), 4 binary digits represent 24 (2 * 2 * 2 * 2), or 16 values. It follows that hexadecimal is a base 16 numbering system. This means there are 16 hexadecimal digits. By convention, these digits are the ten numerals 0 through 9 followed by the six letters A through F.

In other words, to count from 0 in hexadecimal, you count up to 9 as usual. However, the decimal number 10 is simply the single hexadecimal digit A. The next hexadecimal number is B. The hexadecimal digit F is the decimal number 15. At this point, you run out of hexadecimal digits and must go to two-digit numbers. The hexadecimal number 10 is decimal 16.

Octal notation is yet another numbering system. Octal is a base 8 system using the digits 0 through 7. The decimal number 8 becomes 10 in octal, and so on.

Table 19.1 shows the binary, octal, and hexadecimal conversion of the decimal numbers from 0 to 16.

Table 19.1. Conversion of decimal numbers to binary, octal, and hexadecimal.

Decimal	Binary	Octal	Hexadecimal
0	0	0	0
1	1	1	1
2	10	2	2
3	11	3	3
4	100	4	4
5	101	5	5
6	110	6	6
7	111	7	7
8	1000	10	8
9	1001	11	9
10	1010	12	A
11	1011	13	B
12	1100	14	C
13	1101	15	D
14	1110	16	E
15	1111	17	F
16	10000	20	10

In QBasic you can write integer (and long integer) literals with hexadecimal notation. Just use the prefix &H before the hexadecimal value. For example, the literal &H10 refers to the hexadecimal number 10, which is 16 in decimal.

To see how this works, type the instruction PRINT &H10. QBasic displays the result: 16.

You can write the H or the hexadecimal letters (A through F) in upper- or lowercase, for example, &H2E or &h2e. However, the editor converts the lowercase letters to uppercase: &H2E.

NOTE The following discussion is concise and might get a little too technical for some readers. If so, you can jump ahead to the section "Understanding the Memory Architecture of the IBM PC" without much loss of continuity. Also, Chapter 22, "Understanding Advanced QBasic Topics," contains further discussion of manipulating integers as hexadecimal numbers at the bit level.

Because each hexadecimal digit directly corresponds to four binary bits, hexadecimal notation is convenient when working with bit patterns or, as you'll see later in this chapter, memory addresses.

For example, the literal &H3B evaluates to the bit pattern 0011 1011, which in turn evaluates to the decimal integer 59. In the bit pattern, the first four bits correspond to the hex digit 3, and the second four bits correspond to the hex digit B.

For regular (short) integers, the range for hexadecimal literals is from &H0 to &HFFFF. Table 19.2 gives some examples. Notice that QBasic uses a special scheme for negative numbers. In QBasic, the literals from &H0 to &H7FFF correspond to the decimal numbers from 0 to 32,767. However, the literals from &H8000 to &HFFFF correspond to the negative decimal numbers from −32,768 to −1.

Table 19.2. Examples of (short) integer hexadecimal literals.

Hex Literal	Binary Bit Pattern	Decimal Value
&H4ACE	0100 1010 1100 1110	19150
&H2	0000 0000 0000 0010	2
&H7FFF	0111 1111 1111 1111	32767
&H8000	1000 0000 0000 0000	−32768
&H8001	1000 0000 0000 0001	−32767
&HFFFF	1111 1111 1111 1111	−1

Long integer hexadecimal values can contain up to eight hexadecimal digits (32 binary bits). If the literal contains four or fewer hexadecimal digits, use a trailing & to signify that the literal is a long integer (as opposed to a short integer). For example, &H3B& specifies the long integer value 59. The range of long integer hexadecimal literals is from &H0& to &HFFFFFFFF. Table 19.3 gives some examples.

Table 19.3. Examples of long integer hexadecimal literals.

Hex Literal	Bit Pattern	Decimal Value
&H2A&	0000 0000 0000 0000 0000 0000 0010 1010	42
&HBADFACE	0000 1011 1010 1101 1111 1010 1100 1110	195951310
&H7FFFFFFF	0111 1111 1111 1111 1111 1111 1111 1111	2147483647
&H80000000	1000 0000 0000 0000 0000 0000 0000 0000	–2147483648
&HFFFFFFFF	1111 1111 1111 1111 1111 1111 1111 1111	–1

You can also specify an (integer) octal literal with the prefix &0 (the letter "oh," not the numeral "zero"). Octal values use only the digits from 0 to 7. The range of integer octal literals is from &00 to &0177777. The range of long integer octal literals is from &00& to &037777777777.

Two specialized QBasic functions, HEX$ and OCT$, convert numbers into hexadecimal and octal strings, respectively.

HEX$(*numexpr*)

OCT$(*numexpr*)

where

    numexpr is a general numeric expression.

F
U
N
C
T
I
O
N

If the value of *numexpr* is not a whole number, QBasic rounds the value to the nearest integer or long integer, as necessary.

Listing 19.1, HEXOCT.BAS, displays a short table of decimal numbers and their hexadecimal and octal equivalents.

Listing 19.1. The HEXOCT.BAS program.

```
REM Program: HEXOCT.BAS
PRINT "Decimal", "Hexadecimal", "Octal"
FOR Num% = 100 TO 500 STEP 100
   PRINT Num%, HEX$(Num%), OCT$(Num%)
NEXT Num%
```

Here is the output of Listing 19.1:

```
Decimal        Hexadecimal    Octal
   100         64             144
   200         C8             310
   300         12C            454
   400         190            620
   500         1F4            764
```

Understanding the Memory Architecture of the IBM PC

To establish some common ground and introduce some terminology, here's a whirlwind tour of memory architecture in the IBM PC family.

Memory Bytes

Memory is a collection of 8-bit units called *bytes*. At a given instant, each bit in the computer's memory is either on or off (1 or 0). Therefore, at any moment, each byte is in one of 28 (or 256) possible configurations.

You can consider any given byte configuration to be a number ranging from 0 (all bits off) to 255 (all bits on). For example, Figure 19.1 depicts some sample byte configurations and the number that each configuration represents.

```
        0 0 0 0 0 0 0 0   =  0 0   =     0
        0 0 0 0 0 1 0 0   =  0 4   =     4
        0 0 1 0 1 1 0 0   =  2 C   =    4 4
        1 0 0 1 1 0 0 1   =  9 9   =   1 5 3
        1 1 1 1 1 1 1 1   =  F F   =   2 5 5

          Binary            Hex      Decimal
```

Figure 19.1.

Some sample memory bytes.

Physically, each memory byte is one of two types:

- RAM (random-access memory)
- ROM (read-only memory)

RAM memory can be written to and read from—that is, the configuration of a RAM byte can change. When properly instructed, your computer's processor can alter the value of any RAM byte. QBasic stores all variable values in RAM because the values frequently change during the execution of a program.

ROM memory, on the other hand, is "hard-wired." Each byte of ROM has an unchangeable configuration set at the factory. The processor can read the value of a ROM byte but cannot change the bit configuration. As you might expect, ROM memory stores essential information that must not vary, such as most of your computer's operating system.

Memory Addresses

Each byte, whether RAM or ROM, has a unique *address*. The address is the memory location of that particular byte.

Early IBM PC models, and competitors' "clone" models, utilize the Intel 8088 (or 8086) microprocessor. The hardware design of these computers allots 20 signal lines to specify an address value. Like a bit, each signal line can have a value of 1 or 0. Quick arithmetic shows that the number of possible addresses is 220, which is 1,048,576 (1 megabyte). The actual address values range from 0 to 1,048,575.

When programmers discuss memory addresses, hexadecimal number notation is more convenient than decimal. Because a hex digit has one of 16 possible values (from 0 to 9 and A to F), each 20-bit address value can be expressed with a 5-digit hex number (165 = 220). In hex notation, memory addresses range from 00000 to FFFFF.

For convenience, you can consider the 1 megabyte address space to be divided into 16 blocks of 64 kilobytes each. The first block has addresses from 00000 to 0FFFF, the second block from 10000 to 1FFFF, the last block from F0000 to FFFFF. The first hex digit identifies the block in which that address appears. Figure 19.2 shows the organization of this memory.

All would be relatively simple if not for the fact that the 8088 is a 16-bit microprocessor and cannot work directly with numbers larger than 16 bits. With 16 bits, you get only 216, or 65,536 (64K), possible values.

F 0 0 0 0	Permanent System ROM
E 0 0 0 0	Other Use (Cartridge ROM)
D 0 0 0 0	Other Use (Cartridge ROM)
C 0 0 0 0	ROM Expansion
B 0 0 0 0	Standard Video Memory
A 0 0 0 0	Extended Video Memory (EGA)
9 0 0 0 0	Working RAM, up to 640K
8 0 0 0 0	Working RAM, up to 576K
7 0 0 0 0	Working RAM, up to 512K
6 0 0 0 0	Working RAM, up to 448K
5 0 0 0 0	Working RAM, up to 384K
4 0 0 0 0	Working RAM, up to 320K
3 0 0 0 0	Working RAM, up to 256K
2 0 0 0 0	Working RAM, up to 192K
1 0 0 0 0	Working RAM, up to 128K
0 0 0 0 0	Working RAM, up to 64K

Figure 19.2.

Memory block structure.

NOTE

What's a *K* and a Kilobyte?

K is short for *kilo* which, in computing terminology, stands for 1,024, the power of 2 with the value closest to 1,000. Therefore, 64K means 64 times 1,024, which is 65,536.

In computer literature, 64K bytes (64 kilobytes) often is abbreviated 64KB, and sometimes just 64K. However, using "K" to mean "kilobytes" is dangerous. Why? Because K often is used to mean 1,024 of something other than bytes, such as bits, memory locations, or memory configurations. Here, we use K to mean 1,024. When referring to bytes, we just say "64 kilobytes" rather than 64K.

This creates a dilemma. The processor uses 16-bit numbers (four hex digits), but the addressing system accommodates 20-bit numbers (five hex digits). The solution is an addressing scheme involving *segmented addresses*.

Segmented Addresses

A segmented address specifies a memory location with two 16-bit numbers: a *segment* and an *offset*.

Each segment begins at a memory location evenly divisible by 16. As a result, the last hex digit of each segment's first location is 0. For example, each of the following addresses specifies the beginning of a segment: 00010, FEDC0, 382A0, FFFF0. Notice that because the last digit is always 0, you can identify each segment by specifying only the first four digits.

Four hex digits is a 16-bit number, so you're halfway home.

To complete an address, the offset specifies the relative location from the beginning of the segment. Each offset address is also a 16-bit number (four hex digits). Therefore each offset is within 64 kilobytes of the beginning of the segment.

Therefore, you use two 16-bit numbers to specify an address: a segment and an offset. Each number usually is represented by four hex digits. In conventional notation, you place a colon between the two values. For example, the address 38CE:A22B means the segment address is 38CE0, and the offset from this segment is A22B (remember the segment has an implied 0 at the end). To find the absolute address, you must add the two values together (see Figure 19.3).

Notice that you can specify a particular memory location with several different segmented addresses. Because a segment begins every 16 bytes and an offset ranges up to 64 kilobytes, there is considerable overlap in the 64 kilobyte address space of each segment.

Given a particular segmented address, you can specify the same location by decreasing the segment part and increasing the offset part, or vice versa. For each unit decrease in the segment, you must raise the offset value by 16. For example, the following segmented addresses all refer to the identical memory location: 2345:8F23, 2344:8F33, 2335:9023, 3C37:0003.

```
Segmented Address                    38 C E : A 2 2 B

— — — — — — — — — — — — — — — — — —

Segment (Add 0)                          3 8 C E 0

Offset                                   + A 2 2 B

Absolute Address                         4 2 F 0 B
```

Figure 19.3.

Calculating an absolute address.

Addresses on Machines with 286 and 386 Processors

The IBM PC AT, the high-numbered models of the PS/2 line, and various manufacturers' clone models use advanced central processor chips, namely the 80286, 80386, or 80486. These newer chips have additional address-signal lines and can address more memory than the 8088 (see Table 19.4).

Like the 8088, the 80286 uses a segmented address architecture with 64 kilobyte segments. The 80386 and 80486 use full 32-bit registers and 32-bit signal lines and can address 4 GB (4 gigabytes = 4 billion bytes).

Table 19.4. Addressable memory of CPU chips.

CPU	Signal Lines	Addressable Memory
8088 (8086)	20	2^{20} = 1 MB (megabyte)
80286	24	2^{24} = 16 MB
80386	32	2^{32} = 4 GB (gigabytes)
80486	32	2^{32} = 4 GB

However, when running QBasic under DOS (or under OS/2 in the DOS-compatibility mode), the more advanced chips just emulate the 8088. Memory addresses are limited to 1 megabyte with the same segment and offset architecture.

Allocation of Variables

With some understanding of memory addressing under your belt, you're now ready to explore how QBasic utilizes your machine's memory.

QBasic maintains two distinct regions of RAM memory where the values of variables are stored:

- DGROUP—the default data segment
- Far heap—available memory

DGROUP is a 64-kilobyte memory segment. The distinctive feature of DGROUP is that its segment address is loaded into DS, the data segment register of the CPU. The machine-language instructions generated by QBasic need only to specify offsets into this segment to locate data stored in DGROUP.

This offset-only addressing (the segment is implied) is called *near addressing*. The advantage of near addressing is efficiency and speed; the disadvantage is a 64-kilobyte limit for the address space.

The far heap is essentially all the RAM left unused after your program, DGROUP, and QBasic itself are allocated in memory. The size of the far heap depends on your machine configuration: how much total RAM you have, the size of your working program, and whether you have any TSR (Terminate-and-Stay-Resident) programs installed. On a machine with 640 kilobytes of RAM, a modest program loaded and running, and no sizable TSR programs, the far heap is approximately 300 kilobytes.

The advantage of using the far heap to store variables is that the heap has a larger memory area than DGROUP. The disadvantage is that addressing into the heap requires both a segment and offset; this is slower than using DGROUP. Addressing requiring both a segment and an offset is called *far addressing*.

What determines whether a variable is stored in DGROUP or in the far heap? To answer that question, you must first understand static and dynamic allocation.

Static and Dynamic Allocation

The memory location of a stored variable can be allocated by QBasic either when you start the program or while the program is running (executing). The former is called *static allocation,* the latter *dynamic allocation.* Once again, the trade-offs involve flexibility versus efficiency.

Dynamic allocation is flexible because storage is allocated and deallocated while the program runs. If a dynamic variable is no longer needed, the memory can be freed for another use. (With GW-BASIC, BASICA and earlier versions of BASIC, *all* allocation is dynamic.)

Static allocation, on the other hand, is less flexible but more efficient. Static variables are allocated to fixed memory locations before the program runs and remain so allocated throughout the execution of the program. This is efficient because, before the program begins, QBasic resolves the necessary addresses. As a result, the machine language instructions produced by QBasic already contain the appropriate addresses.

Notice that to allocate statically, QBasic must be able to determine the variable's exact size before the program runs. This is always the case for any simple variable or record, and these data items are always allocated statically inside DGROUP.

Array Allocation

Arrays are the critical case for storage allocation because a large array can require considerable memory.

You should allocate an array statically inside DGROUP if possible. But a large array can gobble up too much of DGROUP's precious 64-kilobyte memory limit. Large arrays are better allocated dynamically (so that the storage can be returned) and in the far heap (where more memory is available).

By default, QBasic statically allocates any array that you dimension with literal subscripts (or constants defined with CONST instructions) and dynamically allocates any array that you dimension with variables. For example:

```
DIM MonthlyProfit!(1 TO 12)      'Literal subscript

CONST MaxItems = 520
DIM Invoices%(MaxItems)          'Constant subscript

DIM Salary!(NumEmployees%)       'Variable subscript
```

Notice that QBasic has no choice but to use dynamic allocation when an array is dimensioned with a variable subscript. Static allocation is impossible because the value of the variable (and therefore the size of the array) is not known until the program runs.

Storing a Variable

Here's the answer to whether QBasic puts a variable in DGROUP or in the far heap:

- Simple variables are statically allocated in DGROUP.
- Record variables are statically allocated in DGROUP.
- Static arrays in COMMON are allocated in DGROUP (see Chapter 22, "Understanding Advanced QBasic Topics," for more information on COMMON).
- Variable-length string arrays, whether static or dynamic, are allocated in DGROUP.
- Other arrays, whether static or dynamic, are allocated in the far heap.

Declaring Arrays Static or Dynamic

You can force any array to be statically or dynamically allocated with the $STATIC and $DYNAMIC metacommands.

STATEMENT

```
REM $STATIC

or

' $STATIC
```

```
REM $DYNAMIC
```

or

```
' $DYNAMIC
```

To form one of these metacommands, place the metastatement (`$STATIC` or `$DYNAMIC`) after a comment designator (`REM` or the apostrophe). That is, the following two lines are the equivalent forms of the `$STATIC` metacommand:

```
REM $STATIC
```

```
' $STATIC
```

After a `$STATIC` metacommand executes, QBasic allocates subsequent arrays statically. However, if an array is dimensioned with variable subscripts, allocation is necessarily dynamic.

The complementary metacommand, `$DYNAMIC`, instructs QBasic to allocate subsequent arrays dynamically. The only exceptions are small, implicitly dimensioned arrays (without `DIM` or `REDIM` instructions), which are always allocated statically.

The following program fragment forces `MyArray%` to be dynamic. Without the metacommand, `MyArray%` would be static.

```
REM $DYNAMIC
DIM MyArray%(1000)
```

Use `$STATIC` and `$DYNAMIC` to gain some control over array allocation. By deftly manipulating arrays, you can sidestep potential `Out of memory` errors.

Erasing Arrays—the *ERASE* Instruction

An `ERASE` instruction affects designated arrays; the effect depends on whether the arrays are static or dynamic.

ERASE *arraylist*

where

arraylist is a list of array names separated by commas.

If *arrayname* refers to a static array:

- Each element is reinitialized (elements of numeric arrays are reset to 0; elements of string arrays are reset to the null string).

- Each element in an array of records is reset to 0 (even fixed-length string elements).

  The effect is simply to reset the value of every array element to a default value.

If *arrayname* refers to a dynamic array:

- The array is deallocated. This frees the memory used by the array.

The following program fragment demonstrates reinitializing a static array:

```
DIM MyArray%(1000)        'Static array by default
MyArray%(500) = 18

PRINT MyArray%(500)
ERASE MyArray%            'Reset all elements to 0
PRINT MyArray%(500)
```

The output is

```
18
0
```

When working with arrays, remember that QBasic requires considerable memory resources to store large arrays (especially large, multidimensional arrays). For example, QBasic needs more than 15,000 bytes of memory to store the following array:

```
DIM Salary!(300, 12)
```

(Because of the 0 subscript, the Salary! array is actually 301 elements by 13 elements. This is 3,913 elements altogether—301 times 13. Each single-precision element requires four memory bytes. So the total memory requirement is 15,652 bytes—3,913 times 4.)

When working with dynamic arrays, use the ERASE instruction to "erase" an array from memory. The array elements become permanently lost. However, QBasic can now use the array's previous memory space for other purposes, such as dimensioning a new array.

When you specify one or more arrays in an ERASE instruction, use only the root names of the arrays, with no parentheses or subscripts. For example, the following instruction erases previously dimensioned arrays named Price! and Client%:

```
ERASE Price!, Client%
```

There are two primary reasons to erase a dynamic array:

1. Your program no longer uses the dynamic array. By erasing the array, you free memory for other purposes.

2. You want to redimension an array. You get an Array already dimensioned error if you execute a second DIM instruction with the same array name. By first erasing the array, you can DIM the array again (although you must use the same number of subscripts). Keep in mind, however, that the ERASE instruction permanently removes the old contents of the array. Also, the REDIM instruction, discussed shortly, redimensions arrays.

Determining the Available Array Memory

The FRE function returns the amount of RAM available for arrays.

FRE(*strexpr*)

or

FRE(*numexpr*)

where

    strexpr is any string expression,

and

    numexpr is a general numeric expression.

F U N C T I O N

Because QBasic manages string space independently from the space for numeric data, the FRE function takes several forms. Table 19.5 shows the different values that FRE returns.

Table 19.5. Values returned by the *FRE* function.

Argument	Value Returned
−1	Available memory for numeric arrays
−2	Available stack memory
Other numeric value	Available string memory before compression
Any string expression	Available string memory after compression

The stack is a portion of memory where QBasic stores intermediate results, return addresses for subprograms, and other run-time necessities. The stack is discussed later in this chapter.

QBasic actively manages string space during program execution. The location of string data changes frequently while your program executes. As your program reassigns values to string variables and string array elements, "holes" often crop up in the string space.

When you call FRE with a string expression, QBasic compresses the string space by removing all holes and relocating existing strings to achieve one continuous block of free string memory. *strexpr* can be any string argument; the value acts only as a dummy argument.

When you call FRE with a numeric argument other than −1 or −2, QBasic returns the amount of unallocated string space without doing any compression. This returned value might be less than the value returned by FRE with a string argument.

Listing 19.2, SHOWFREE.BAS, uses FRE to show the available numeric array space before and after the allocation of a dynamic array:

Listing 19.2. The SHOWFREE.BAS program.

```
REM Program: SHOWFREE.BAS (Show free memory)

REM $DYNAMIC

PRINT "-- Available array memory in bytes --"
PRINT
PRINT "Before dimensioning the array:"; FRE(-1)

DIM MyArray%(20000)
PRINT " After dimensioning the array:"; FRE(-1)

ERASE MyArray%          'Deallocate the array
```

```
PRINT " After deallocating the array:"; FRE(-1)
END
```

The output values depend on your particular hardware and software configuration. Here's a typical result:

```
-- Available array memory in bytes --

Before dimensioning the array: 159876
After dimensioning the array: 119860
After deallocating the array: 159876
```

Reallocating a Dynamic Array with *REDIM*

Use REDIM to reallocate a dynamic array.

```
REDIM SHARED arrayname(subscriptrange) AS type,
             arrayname(subscriptrange) AS type ...
```
where

    arrayname is the name of an array,

    subscriptrange specifies the new dimensions for the array,

and

    type declares the data type of *arrayname*.

The keyword SHARED is optional. The AS *type* clause is also optional.

S T A T E M E N T

The optional SHARED keyword provides for sharing the variable between the main program and procedures (see Chapter 17, "Modular Programming"). The optional AS clause specifies the data type of *arrayname*.

It's okay if *arrayname* is not the name of an active array. REDIM simply allocates the array in exactly the same way as a DIM instruction (see Chapter 9, "Managing Large Amounts of Data").

If *arrayname* is the name of a currently dimensioned array, REDIM deallocates the old array and reallocates the array with the new dimensions. All the old array values are lost during this process. New array values reinitialize to 0 (for numeric arrays) and null strings (for string arrays).

REDIM can change the size of each dimension but cannot change the number of dimensions. For example, the following is a typical use of REDIM:

```
' $DYNAMIC
DIM MyArray!(20, 20, 20)
    .
    .
    .
REDIM MyArray!(30, 20, 10)
    .
    .
    .
```

This works because MyArray! has three dimensions in both the DIM and REDIM instructions. However, change the REDIM instruction to REDIM MyArray!(5000), and the result is a Wrong number of dimensions error.

You do not need to ERASE an array before redimensioning.

The syntax of REDIM closely parallels that of DIM. See Chapter 9, "Managing Large Amounts of Data," for a full discussion of the syntax for DIM.

Tips for Saving Array Space

You might get Array too big or Out of data space errors in programs that use large arrays. Here are some tips on optimizing array space to accommodate larger arrays:

- Use $DYNAMIC to make arrays dynamic.
- Turn variable-length string arrays into fixed-length string arrays.
- Make array dimensions smaller. This might sound trite, but perhaps your arrays are larger than necessary.
- Use a more economical data type if possible—integer rather than long integer, single-precision rather than double-precision.
- Reduce the size of the stack to allow more memory in the far heap. You can adjust stack size with a CLEAR instruction. (CLEAR is discussed in the next section.)

Controlling the Stack with *CLEAR*

CLEAR reinitializes memory and sets the size of the stack.

S
T
A
T
E
M
E
N
T

```
CLEAR
or
CLEAR, , stacksize
```
where

 stacksize specifies the new size for the stack.

CLEAR performs the programming equivalent of a spring cleaning. Without the optional *stacksize* parameter, CLEAR by itself does the following:

- Resets all numeric variables, array elements, and record elements to 0

- Resets all string variables, array elements, and record elements to the null string

- Closes all files (the same as a CLOSE instruction; see Chapter 14, "Using Sequential Disk Files")

- Clears all COMMON variables (for a description of the COMMON instruction, see Chapter 22, "Understanding Advanced QBasic Topics")

- Reinitializes the stack (destroys data stored in the stack)

CLEAR is valid only in your main program. An Illegal function call error occurs if you place CLEAR inside a procedure.

With the *stacksize* parameter, CLEAR also changes the size of the stack to the value of *stacksize*. Recall that FRE(-2) returns the current size of the unused stack space. The *stacksize* parameter can be any general numeric expression having a value within the range of long integers.

QBasic stores many temporary quantities in the stack, including return addresses from GOSUB and subprogram calls. CLEAR demolishes data in the stack, so don't use CLEAR when any such data is active. You might need to increase the stack size for certain programs—for example, programs that utilize intensive recursion.

Why the funny syntax with two commas before *stacksize*? Once again, this is for GW-BASIC and BASICA compatibility. In GW-BASIC and BASICA, CLEAR permits an additional first parameter not necessary in QBasic. With the given syntax, the same CLEAR instructions in QBasic also work with GW-BASIC and BASICA.

Listing 19.3, CLEARIT.BAS, demonstrates adjusting the stack size:

Listing 19.3. The CLEARIT.BAS program.

```
REM Program: CLEARIT.BAS (Demonstrate the CLEAR statement)

PRINT "Before CLEAR: Available stack space (bytes) ="; FRE(-2)
MyNumber! = 1.42
MyString$ = "Last laugh"

CLEAR , , 5000       'Reset variables and set stack size to 5000

PRINT
PRINT " After CLEAR: Available stack space (bytes) ="; FRE(-2)
PRINT "MyNumber! ="; MyNumber!
PRINT "MyString$ ="; MyString$
END
```

The output is as follows (your numbers may vary):

```
Before CLEAR: Available stack space (bytes) = 1188

After CLEAR: Available stack space (bytes) = 4950
MyNumber! = 0
MyString$ =
```

Referencing Memory Locations

Occasionally you need to exert explicit control over memory resources. QBasic provides the following statements and functions which require a memory address as an argument:

- The PEEK function, which examines a memory location

- The POKE statement, which changes the value stored in a RAM memory location

- The DEF SEG statement, which sets the memory segment within which PEEK and POKE operate

- The BSAVE statement, which creates a disk file containing an image of a specified portion of memory

- The BLOAD statement, which loads back into memory the values previously saved on disk with BSAVE

■ The CALL ABSOLUTE statement, which supports the incorporation of machine language routines into a QBasic program

Setting the Segment Address: *DEF SEG*

PEEK, POKE, BSAVE, BLOAD, and CALL ABSOLUTE require that you specify memory addresses. However, the syntax of these statements and functions require only the offset portion of the address. To specify the full address, you must also designate a segment address. This is the job of DEF SEG.

When you first start QBasic, the default segment address is set to DGROUP (the data segment). However, you don't know what that address is. The exact memory address of the DGROUP segment depends on your computer configuration, the size of DOS, and any resident programs.

Often, when using BLOAD, BSAVE, CALL ABSOLUTE, PEEK, or POKE, this default segment address is just what you want. But what if you want to work with memory locations outside of DGROUP's 64-kilobyte chunk of memory? The answer is to use DEF SEG before using one of the other statements or functions. A DEF SEG instruction changes the segment address to a value that you specify.

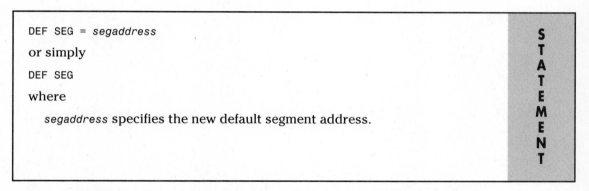

```
DEF SEG = segaddress
```
or simply
```
DEF SEG
```
where

    segaddress specifies the new default segment address.

S T A T E M E N T

For example, the following instruction sets the default segment address to the upper 64-kilobyte memory area (the F block):

```
DEF SEG = &HF000
```

When the *segaddress* parameter is present, the segment address must resolve to a whole number in the range from 0 to 65,535 (&H0 to &HFFFF). If the value is larger than 65,535, a run-time error occurs (Overflow). If the value of *segaddress* contains a fractional part, the value is rounded to the closest whole number.

DEF SEG with no argument restores the default segment to the original value (DGROUP).

Segment values are commonly specified as hexadecimal literals because hexadecimal is a convenient notation for memory addresses. The hex values from &H0 to &HFFFF map directly into decimal memory addresses from 0 to 65,535.

When a DEF SEG instruction executes, the specified segment address stays in effect until a subsequent DEF SEG instruction occurs.

Be sure to leave a blank space between DEF and SEG. The following instruction refers to a variable named DEFSEG, not to the DEF SEG statement:

```
DEFSEG = &HB800
```

The discussion of memory management throughout the rest of this chapter contains several examples of DEF SEG instructions.

Examining the Contents of Memory Locations with *PEEK*

Use the PEEK function to examine the contents of any memory location.

FUNCTION

PEEK(*offset*)

where

    offset specifies an offset address.

The value of *offset* must be within the range from 0 to 65,535 (&H0 to &HFFFF). However, *offset* does not have to be a hex literal. Variables, expressions, and decimal literals are fine, too. The given offset address supplements the segment address to fully specify the memory address. (Use the DEF SEG instruction to set the segment address.)

PEEK returns an integer value in the range from 0 to 255. This value represents the eight-bit memory byte at the designated address.

One use of PEEK is to examine special locations in ROM (read-only memory). On IBM computers, the ROM memory byte at address F000:FFFE contains a value that indicates the computer model. Not surprisingly, this memory location is known as the *model identification byte*.

Here's a user-defined string function named SysID$ that examines F000:FEEE and reports the results:

```
FUNCTION SysID$
REM Function: SysID$ (Returns Computer System ID)
    DEF SEG = &HF000          'Set segment address before PEEK
    ID% = PEEK(&HFFFE)        'Peeks address F000:FFFE
    SELECT CASE ID%
       CASE IS = 255: SysID$ = "255 - PC"
       CASE IS = 254: SysID$ = "254 - XT (or Portable PC)"
       CASE IS = 253: SysID$ = "253 - PCjr"
       CASE IS = 252: SysID$ = "252 - AT, XT286, PS/2 with 80286"
       CASE IS = 251: SysID$ = "251 - late model XT"
       CASE IS = 250: SysID$ = "250 - PS/2 Model 30"
       CASE IS = 249: SysID$ = "249 - PC Convertible"
       CASE IS = 248: SysID$ = "248 - PS/2 with 80386"
       CASE ELSE: SysID$ = "Unknown"
    END SELECT
END FUNCTION
```

You might try SysID$ on various computers. IBM has not been completely consistent in the numbers used in the system identification byte, but the values are generally reliable.

The fun part is testing "compatible" computers. Some clone makers use the same indicators as IBM, but other manufacturers use entirely different values or no special value.

Changing the Contents of Memory with *POKE*

The POKE statement complements the PEEK function. Whereas PEEK examines a memory byte, POKE writes a value at a specified memory location.

POKE *offset, databyte*

where

    offset specifies an offset address,

and

    databyte specifies the value to be written.

S T A T E M E N T

The following program uses POKE to write directly into video memory. The program displays a character on-screen.

```
SCREEN 0              'Set text mode
DEF SEG = &HB800      'Beginning of CGA/EGA/VGA video RAM
POKE 2000, 3          'Displays ASCII 3 (heart character)
```

The result is a single heart symbol in the approximate center of the screen. The POKE instruction writes at offset 2000 (decimal), which maps into the character position where the heart displays. The 3 represents the ASCII character to display—a heart symbol. Appendix B, "ASCII Character Set," lists these numbers and characters.

In a POKE instruction, *offset* can be any general numeric expression specifying a value in the range from 0 to 65,536. The value of *databyte* also can be any numeric expression, this time in the range from 0 to 255. If either parameter contains a fractional part, rounding occurs.

Use DEF SEG to specify the segment address of the referenced memory location. In the example program, the DEF SEG instruction points to the start of the RAM area used for the video display.

 NOTE The program will not work on a computer using the monochrome display adapter, which maps its video into the RAM area starting at segment &HB000.

You must be careful anytime you use POKE. Be sure that you correctly specify the memory address—both segment and offset. Because POKE has access to any RAM location, you can accidentally "step on" part of DOS, QBasic, or some other sensitive location. A system crash is possible, meaning that you might have to turn the power off and back on again to restart. Be sure to save any program that uses POKE before you run it.

Saving Memory Images in Disk Files

BSAVE creates a disk file that contains a byte-by-byte image of a continuous portion of memory. The companion statement, BLOAD, loads such a disk file back into memory.

S
T
A
T
E
M
E
N
T

```
BSAVE filespec, offset, length

BLOAD filespec, offset
```

where

    filespec specifies the name of the file that stores the data,

    offset specifies an offset address,

and

    length specifies the number of bytes to save.

In a BLOAD instruction, *offset* is optional.

You typically use BSAVE and BLOAD to save and restore machine language programs and graphic screen images.

Look at BSAVE first. The *filespec* is a string expression that specifies the file to which the memory image will be saved. The *filespec* optionally can include a drive designation and/or path. If the file already exists, the new data replaces the old data. QBasic creates a new file if necessary. An invalid *filespec* results in a run-time error (Path not found).

You designate the area of memory to save by specifying a beginning address and a length. The address and length values are stored in the disk file along with the data. The *offset* and *length* parameters can be any general numeric expressions.

The segment part of the address comes from the most recently executed DEF SEG instruction. (The data segment, DGROUP, is the default if no DEF SEG instruction appears.) *offset* specifies the offset part of the address. The range of *offset* is from 0 to 65,535 (64 kilobytes). QBasic rounds to the closest integer if necessary.

The *length* parameter specifies the number of bytes to save. Again, the range is from 0 to 65,535 and QBasic rounds if necessary.

Now for BLOAD. BLOAD restores memory values previously saved with BSAVE. Because BSAVE uses a special format to save files, BLOAD can read only files saved with BSAVE. The *filespec* designates the file to be read. If the file cannot be found, a File not found error occurs. If the file is of the wrong type (not created with BSAVE), you get a Bad file mode error.

You can load the file into any continuous portion of memory. The segment part of the address comes from the most recently executed DEF SEG instruction (or the default data segment if no DEF SEG is present).

For BLOAD, the *offset* parameter is optional. If present, *offset* naturally enough specifies the offset part of the address. If you omit *offset*, QBasic examines the file to find and uses the offset address specified when the file was saved with BSAVE. If you do specify offset, QBasic overrides the offset saved with the file.

QBasic does not check the range of the address. This means that you can load the file anywhere into memory. You must be careful not to overwrite sensitive areas such as your program, the operating system, or critical data. You could inadvertently hang your computer and force a complete reboot.

Listing 19.4 demonstrates saving and restoring a CGA graphic image:

Listing 19.4. The BSAVEIT.BAS program.

```
REM Program: BSAVEIT.BAS (Save and restore a video image)

SCREEN 1                        'Low-resolution graphics
CLS
Radius% = 40
FOR X% = 50 TO 250 STEP 100
   CIRCLE (X%, 80), Radius%
NEXT X%
FOR X% = 100 TO 200 STEP 100
   CIRCLE (X%, 120), Radius%
NEXT X%                         'The "Olympic" rings are drawn

DEF SEG = &HB800                'Beginning of video RAM
BSAVE "IMAGE.CGA", 0, &H4000    'Save image on disk file

PRINT "Press a key to erase the image"
WHILE INKEY$ = "": WEND
CLS

PRINT "Press a key to restore the image"
WHILE INKEY$ = "": WEND
CLS

BLOAD "IMAGE.CGA"               'Restore the image from disk file
END
```

The program begins by drawing the same "Olympic" rings shown in Figure 13.4. The BSAVE instruction saves the image to a file named IMAGE.CGA. Notice that a CGA graphics image takes &H4000 bytes (16 kilobytes).

After the image is erased, the BLOAD instruction restores the video RAM with the image saved on the disk file. The result is a regeneration of the original video image.

This technique works for CGA and monochrome. (Use DEF SEG = &HB000 for monochrome.) However, EGA and VGA screen images cannot be easily saved with BSAVE. For one thing, these screen images take at least 128 kilobytes of memory, which is twice the amount BSAVE can store (although you theoretically could save one visual screen on multiple files). More troublesome, however, is the fact that EGA and VGA do not directly map video memory; this causes undesirable results when BLOAD attempts to restore the saved files.

Locating a Variable in Memory with *VARSEG* and *VARPTR*

Occasionally you need the memory address where QBasic stores a particular variable. The VARSEG and VARPTR functions return, respectively, the segment and offset address of a designated variable.

Each returned value is an unsigned, two-byte integer ranging from 0 to 65,535. (Notice that PRINT interprets such numbers as signed integers and displays a negative number for unsigned values above 32,767.)

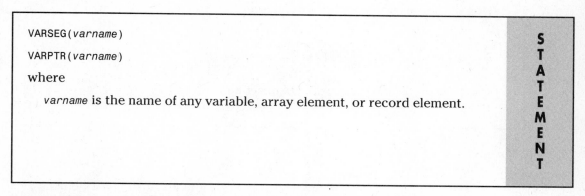

VARSEG(*varname*)

VARPTR(*varname*)

where

    varname is the name of any variable, array element, or record element.

S
T
A
T
E
M
E
N
T

The functions work differently depending on the data type of the variable being referenced.

For a numeric variable:

- ■ VARSEG returns the segment address of the variable.

- ■ VARPTR returns the offset address of the variable.

For a string variable:

- **VARSEG** returns the segment address of the string descriptor.
- **VARPTR** returns the offset address of the string descriptor.

The string descriptor does not contain the string data but instead contains the length of the string and a pointer to where the data is stored. A string descriptor is always four bytes long (see Appendix F, "Internal Data Formats").

Here are some examples:

```
PRINT VARSEG(MyVariable%)      'Displays segment and
PRINT VARPTR(MyVariable%)      'offset of MyVariable%

PRINT VARPTR(MyArray!(6))      'Offset of array element
```

Take note: Use a value returned by VARPTR, VARSEG, or VARPTR$ immediately after returning a value. (VARPTR$ is discussed shortly.) QBasic reorganizes variable storage frequently. Any instructions you place between the function call and the use of the returned value can cause the location of the variable to change and thus nullify the returned value.

For the most part, QBasic manages variable storage transparently to the programmer. You don't need these functions during ordinary QBasic programming. When incorporating machine language routines into your QBasic programs, however, you might need to pass address arguments of variables to the alien routines. That's when VARSEG and VARPTR are most useful. See the discussion of CALL ABSOLUTE later in this chapter.

Using the *VARPTR$* Function

VARPTR$ returns, in string form, the offset address of a variable.

FUNCTION

VARPTR$(*varname*)

where

varname is the name of any variable, array element, or record element.

VARPTR$ exists to provide a way for DRAW and PLAY instructions to include variable names within command strings (see Chapter 13, "Creating Graphics," for more information on DRAW and Chapter 16, "Using Hardware Devices," for more information on PLAY).

Incorporating Machine Language Routines with *CALL ABSOLUTE*

QBasic provides the flexibility to communicate with routines written in assembly (machine) language. Of course, to successfully blend machine language procedures, you must have a thorough understanding of programming and parameter passing in machine language.

NOTE

Why Use Machine Language Routines?

Here are some reasons to use machine language routines (assuming, of course, that you know machine language):

- A critical procedure must execute at the peak of efficiency. Although QBasic programs generally execute quickly, nothing beats a well-written machine language routine for speed.

- You already have routines written in machine language. Why reprogram in QBasic? If you already have debugged procedures written in machine language, use them as is.

- It's easier to write certain routines in machine language. You might find it more convenient to write a particular procedure in machine language, so you can take advantage of the special features of machine language. For example, low-level programming is easier in machine language than in QBasic.

You invoke a machine language routine from QBasic with a CALL ABSOLUTE instruction. Obviously, machine language programming is an advanced subject that this book cannot cover in detail. However, an overview of CALL ABSOLUTE is included to provide an introduction to the techniques involved.

```
CALL ABSOLUTE(argumentlist, offset)
```

where

> *argumentlist* is a comma-delimited list of arguments to pass to the machine language routine,

and

> *offset* is an integer variable that specifies the offset address of the start of the machine language routine.

The *argumentlist* parameter is optional. However, *offset* is mandatory. If *argumentlist* does not appear, do not use a comma before the *offset* parameter.

CALL ABSOLUTE operates as follows:

- Using QBasic instructions (POKE statements), the machine language routine is poked into a reserved section of memory.

- CALL ABSOLUTE branches to that section of memory and executes the bytes there as machine language instructions.

Use DEF SEG to specify the segment address of the start of the machine language routine.

Arguments from *argumentlist* are passed as offset addresses from DGROUP (the current data segment). Notice that a DEF SEG instruction does not change the segment address of DGROUP.

When CALL ABSOLUTE executes, QBasic passes only *argumentlist*; *offset* is not passed.

How do you reserve a section of memory for the machine language routine? Here is the simplest technique:

1. Dimension an array that reserves enough memory to store the machine language routine. For example, DIM MyRoutine(1 TO 20) reserves 80 bytes (20 elements at 4 bytes per element).

2. Use DEF SEG and VARSEG to set the segment address for the routine:

   ```
   DEF SEG = VARSEG(MyRoutine(1))
   ```

3. Use VARPTR to set a pointer to the offset address for the routine:

   ```
   StartPoint% = VARPTR(MyRoutine(1))
   ```

4. Use POKE instructions to store the machine language routine into memory:

   ```
   POKE(StartPoint%), Byte1%
   ```

```
POKE(StartPoint% + 1), Byte2%
.
.
.
```

5. Use CALL ABSOLUTE and VARPTR to invoke the routine:

    ```
    CALL ABSOLUTE(Arg1%, Arg2%,  VARPTR(MyRoutine(1))
    ```

6. Restore the default segment: DEF SEG

Summary

QBasic manages your computer's memory resources "behind the scenes." Most of the time you don't need to concern yourself with the details of how memory is being used.

Occasionally, however, you need to (literally) "address" memory issues. Large arrays can be a concern because of their hunger for more and more memory. By controlling the static and dynamic allocation of arrays, you can exert a measure of control.

Memory consists of eight-bit bytes located at consecutive memory addresses. The addressing scheme on the IBM PC uses a segment and offset address to specify an absolute memory location. Memory is logically organized into 64-kilobyte chunks. Hexadecimal notation is convenient for specifying addresses.

QBasic provides the ability to directly access memory. With PEEK and POKE, you can examine and reset the value at any memory location. It is possible to read and write disk files containing an image of an area of memory. You can even invoke a machine language routine that you have placed in a designated section of memory.

Using Advanced Graphics

C hapter 13, "Creating Graphics," discussed graphics in some depth. Here we pick up where that chapter left off. This chapter discusses the following advanced graphics features:

■ Animating graphic images

■ Storing images on alternate screen "pages"

■ Customizing your coordinate system

■ Graphing options available with EGA, VGA, and MCGA video adapters

■ Drawing stylized lines

■ Filling areas with patterned tiles

Animation with *GET* and *PUT*

Animating graphic images is fairly easy. Use GET and PUT instructions. GET takes a "snapshot" of any rectangular screen area and saves the image in a numeric array. PUT reproduces the image anywhere on the screen. You can create multiple copies of an image or smoothly move an image along the screen.

**S
T
A
T
E
M
E
N
T**

```
GET (upleftxy)-(lowrightxy), arrayname(indices)
```

where

> *upleftxy* is the x,y location of the upper left corner of the rectangular area to save,
>
> *lowrightxy* is the x,y location of the lower right corner of the rectangular area to save,
>
> *arrayname* is the name of the numeric array to store the image,

and

> *indices* specifies the array element where storage of the image begins.

The *indices* parameter is optional. If *indices* does not appear, no parentheses should appear after *arrayname*.

**S
T
A
T
E
M
E
N
T**

```
PUT (upleftxy), arrayname(indices), drawoption
```

where

> *upleftxy* is the x,y location of the upper left corner of the rectangular area to receive the stored image,
>
> *arrayname* is the name of the numeric array holding the image,
>
> *indices* specifies the array element where storage of the image begins,

and

> *drawoption* specifies how the information in *arrayname* is drawn on the screen.

The *indices* parameter is optional. If *indices* does not appear, no parentheses should appear after *arrayname*. Also, the *drawoption* parameter is optional.

With GET, *upleftxy* and *lowrightxy* can actually specify any two diagonally opposite corners. For most applications, *upleftxy* is the upper left corner, which provides consistency with subsequent PUT instructions because PUT requires that *upleftxy* be the upper left corner.

You can define the location of the image area with absolute or relative coordinates. For example, the following instruction takes a snapshot of the rectangular area defined by the diagonally opposite corners (45, 18) and (125, 78):

```
GET (45, 18) - (125, 78), Image%
```

Here are a few examples of relative coordinates:

```
GET (45, 18) - STEP(80, 60), Image%       'Same as previous example

GET STEP(20, 42) - STEP(10, 10), Image% 'Both corners relative

PUT STEP(38, -12), Image%                 'Top left corner relative
```

In these examples, the array `Image%` holds the graphics information. You can use any numeric array with GET as long as the array was previously dimensioned with a DIM instruction.

Normally, you use a one-dimensional array for *arrayname* and begin the image storage with the lowest array element (usually element 0). However, by including the optional *indices* arguments, you can specify another array element to begin the storage. For example:

```
GET (1, 1)-(30, 30), Image%(38)   'Begin storage at element 38

GET (1, 1)-(30, 30), Im2D(6, 3)   'Begin at element (6,3) of 2D array
```

The *indices* parameters can be variables and constants as well as literals. Be careful that whatever *indices* you use in a GET instruction you also use in corresponding PUT instructions.

In our subsequent examples, *arrayname* is a one-dimensional array with no *indices* argument. Thus storage begins, by default, with element 0 of the array. This is the most common and straightforward technique.

Don't Confuse Graphics *GET* and *PUT* with File *GET* and *PUT*

QBasic has two entirely different sets of GET and PUT instructions. The graphics GET and PUT instructions, discussed in this chapter, are entirely different from the file-access GET and PUT instructions discussed in Chapter 15, "Using Random and Binary Disk Files."

Determining the Array Size

The numeric array, *arrayname*, can be any numeric type but must be dimensioned large enough to hold the graphics information. The minimum acceptable dimensioning depends on the size of the image area, the SCREEN mode, and the numeric data type of *arrayname*.

We recommend that you use integer arrays to hold your images. As a rule of thumb, a snapshot of the entire screen in SCREEN modes 1 or 2 requires an integer array of approximately 8,000 elements. You can proportion the dimension size downward based on the size of your image.

If you need more precision in determining the array size, Listing 20.1, CALCSIZE.BAS, calculates the minimum array dimensions required to store a given snapshot. For simplicity, the program assumes integer arrays.

Listing 20.1. The CALCSIZE.BAS program.

```
REM Program: CALCSIZE.BAS (Calculate size for GET array)
INPUT "X value of upper left corner"; X1
INPUT "Y value of upper left corner"; Y1
INPUT "X value of lower right corner"; X2
INPUT "Y value of lower right corner"; Y2
INPUT "SCREEN mode (1,2,7,8,9,10,11,12, or 13)"; Mode%

SELECT CASE Mode%
    CASE 2
        NumBits% = 1
    CASE 1, 10
        NumBits% = 2
    CASE 13
        NumBits% = 8
    CASE ELSE
        NumBits% = 4
END SELECT

XRange% = X2 - X1 + 1: YRange% = Y2 - Y1 + 1
NumBytes% = 4 + INT((XRange% * NumBits% + 7) / 8) * YRange%
PRINT
PRINT "Dimension an integer array at least"; (NumBytes% - 1) / 2
END
```

This program assumes the default minimum array element is zero—that is, that no OPTION BASE instruction exists.

Be aware that the value returned by CALCSIZE.BAS represents only a minimum array size. In some cases, you might need to slightly increase the dimensioning beyond the value displayed by CALCSIZE.BAS.

In a program using GET, QBasic generates an Illegal function call error if *arrayname* is insufficiently dimensioned. In such a case, simply increase the dimension size until the error goes away.

A Test Case—Stick Figures

Let's try an example. The following program draws the stick figure depicted in Figure 20.1:

```
SCREEN 1
CIRCLE (20, 20), 6
PAINT (20, 20)
DRAW "D16 NE8 NH8 D4 NF8 NG8"
```

Figure 20.1.

A simple stick figure.

Now suppose you want to store the stick figure and reproduce the image at various screen locations. First you must save the stick figure into an array. A box with diagonally opposite corners (8, 8) and (31, 51) would surround the stick figure. (You can verify this by actually drawing the box. Simply add the instruction LINE (8, 8)-(31, 55), , B to the end of the program.) This box is the snapshot area that you will save into the array.

How large must the array be? That's a job for the CALCSIZE.BAS program. Running CALCSIZE.BAS produces the following output:

```
X value of upper left corner? 8
Y value of upper left corner? 8
X value of lower right corner? 31
Y value of lower right corner? 55
SCREEN mode (1,2,7,8,9,10,11,12, or 13)? 1

Dimension an integer array at least 145
```

Therefore, the storage array, named Image%, must be dimensioned at least 145.

Before animating the figure, try using PUT to produce multiple copies of the stick figure. Edit the program to look as follows:

```
DIM Image%(145)                'Dimension the storage array
SCREEN 1
CIRCLE (20, 20), 6
PAINT (20, 20)
DRAW "D16 NE8 NH8 D4 NF8 NG8"
GET (8, 8)-(31, 55), Image%    'Store the snapshot in Image%
```

```
FOR X% = 50 TO 250 STEP 50
   FOR Y% = 50 TO 150 STEP 50
      PUT (X%, Y%), Image%         'Draw a copy
   NEXT Y%
NEXT X%
```

This program draws 15 new stick figures in three rows of five each.

Adding Animation

Now try some true animation. You will move a single stick figure across a complex background. Once the image is stored and the background is drawn, animation requires these steps:

1. PUT the image on-screen.

2. Calculate the next position of the image.

3. PUT the image on-screen at the old location (this removes the original image).

4. Go back to step 1, using the new position.

This technique uses a process called XOR animation. (XOR and the other *drawoption* alternatives of the PUT statement are discussed shortly.)

XOR animation has the remarkable property that when an image is PUT a second time at the same location, the original background is restored, including all colors. PUT uses XOR animation by default if you omit the *drawoption* parameter.

The ANIMATE.BAS program in Listing 20.2 demonstrates XOR animation. A stick figure "walks" across a background consisting of various colored squares.

Listing 20.2.   The ANIMATE.BAS program.

```
REM Program: ANIMATE.BAS (Demonstrate XOR Animation)
DIM Image%(145)
SCREEN 1

CIRCLE (20, 20), 6
PAINT (20, 20)
DRAW "D16 NE8 NH8 D4 NF8 NG8"
GET (8, 8)-(31, 55), Image%
CLS

LINE (100, 60)-STEP(20, 20), 1, BF
LINE (150, 60)-STEP(20, 20), 3, BF       'Draw a background of
```

```
LINE (100, 90)-STEP(20, 20), 3, B        'various colored boxes
LINE (150, 90)-STEP(20, 20), 2, BF

FOR X% = 20 TO 200 STEP 2
   PUT (X%, 60), Image%, XOR            'Draw stick figure
      Now! = TIMER
      DO                                 'Pause execution
      LOOP UNTIL TIMER > Now! + .15      'for .15 seconds
   PUT (X%, 60), Image%, XOR            'Erase stick figure
NEXT X%
END
```

The first PUT instruction draws the stick figure at the updated X% position. The second PUT instruction erases the stick figure and restores the original background.

Notice the delay loop between the two PUT instructions (see Chapter 16, "Using Hardware Devices," for the TIMER function). You need a delay loop to reduce screen flicker and to let the eye adjust to the just-drawn image. In general, you want a short delay between the drawing and erasing of the image. However, you also want the shortest possible time between the erasure and the redrawing of the next image.

Other *drawoption* Values

The optional PUT parameter *drawoption* defines how the image interacts with the background over which the PUT takes place. There are five possible values of *drawoption*: PSET, PRESET, AND, OR, and XOR. Table 20.1 shows the resulting effects.

Table 20.1. The effects of the *drawoption* parameter.

drawoption	Effect
PSET	Places the image in all cases
PRESET	Places the complementary image in all cases
AND	Places image only if background exists
OR	Superimposes the image on the background
XOR	Reverses image only if background exists

The PSET option simply draws the stored image, obliterating any background. PRESET does the same thing, but the stored image is drawn with inverted colors (for example, in the four colors available in SCREEN mode 1, black would be substituted for white, and cyan for magenta).

To understand the effect of one of the logical operators (AND, OR, or XOR), you must calculate the result of each interaction between an image pixel and the corresponding background pixel.

For example, consider XOR in medium resolution (SCREEN 1). Four attribute values (colors) are possible for each pixel: 0, 1, 2, or 3. These values correspond to black, cyan, magenta, and white respectively. The binary equivalents are 00, 01, 10, and 11.

 If you need some brushing up on how binary numbers and bit patterns work, see Chapter 19, "Managing Memory," and Chapter 22, "Understanding Advanced QBasic Topics."

At every point in the PUT frame, a foreground pixel from the image is written over a corresponding background pixel. The logical XOR operation on the foreground and background attributes determines the attribute of the resultant pixel. Table 20.2 shows the resulting values.

Table 20.2. *XOR* results in medium resolution.				
Background	**Foreground**			
	00	01	10	11
00	00	01	10	11
01	01	00	11	10
10	10	11	00	01
11	11	10	01	00

Try adding various *drawoption* parameters to either or both PUT instructions in the ANIMATE.BAS program. Experiment with the different effects. The following modification to the first PUT instruction produces interesting results when the animated figure interacts with the colored squares:

```
PUT (X%, 60), Image%, OR
```

Redefining Coordinate Systems

Let's face it: The coordinate systems used in the various SCREEN modes are somewhat arbitrary and unnatural. You might prefer a coordinate system that's more natural to certain applications. As a simple example, you might like *y* values to increase as you move up the screen rather than down the screen.

The *WINDOW* Statement

WINDOW maps the default screen coordinates into a coordinate system of your own choosing. For example, you can define the lower left corner of the screen to be location (0, 0) and the upper right corner of the screen (1, 1). Then you can reference all pixels with an x and a y value between 0 and 1. The x values increase toward the right, and y values increase upward. With this system, the center of the screen is always (0.5, 0.5), regardless of the SCREEN mode.

WINDOW has two forms: with and without the SCREEN keyword.

WINDOW (*leftxy*) - (*rightxy*)

or

WINDOW SCREEN (*leftxy*) - (*rightxy*)

where

    leftxy specifies the x,y location of either the upper left corner or the lower left corner,

and

    rightxy specifies the x,y location of either the upper right corner or the lower right corner.

S
T
A
T
E
M
E
N
T

When you include SCREEN, *leftxy* refers to the upper left corner of the screen and *rightxy* refers to the lower right corner. The y values increase down the screen in the normal way. When you omit SCREEN, *leftxy* refers to the lower left corner of the screen and *rightxy* refers to the upper right corner. The y values increase moving up the screen.

You specify *leftxy* and *rightxy* as pairs of single-precision numbers. This gives you great range in designing a coordinate system.

If your coordinate system permits *leftxy* and *rightxy* to be integer numbers, objects subsequently will be drawn significantly faster than if *leftxy* and *rightxy* are single-precision numbers.

Consider this instruction:

```
WINDOW (-30000, -.2)-(30000, .2)
```

This instruction causes the entire screen to map into a numeric range from –30,000 to +30,000 in the x direction but only from –0.2 to +0.2 in the y direction.

Notice that subsequent coordinate references can be single-precision numbers that specify exact points in the y direction. For example, assuming the previous WINDOW instruction is in effect, the following instruction plots a point centered horizontally but 7/8 of the way up the screen:

```
PSET (0, .15)
```

To illustrate WINDOW and the effect of SCREEN, Figures 20.2, 20.3, and 20.4 compare the default coordinate system with two WINDOW-created coordinate systems. High resolution (SCREEN 2) is assumed.

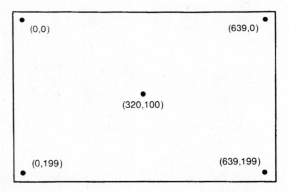

Figure 20.2.

The default coordinate system.

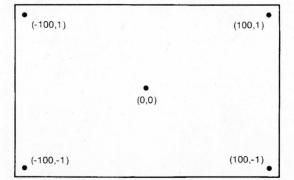

Figure 20.3.

Coordinates after
*WINDOW (-100,
-1)(-100, -1)*.

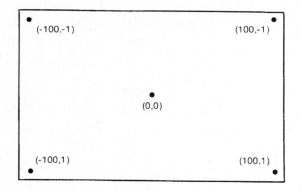

Figure 20.4.

Coordinates after
WINDOW SCREEN
(-100, -1)
(-100, -1).

Physical and World Coordinates

For any particular SCREEN mode, default coordinates are called *physical* coordinates. For example, in SCREEN mode 1, the center of the screen is (160, 100) in physical coordinates.

User-defined coordinates, established with a WINDOW statement, are called *world* coordinates. Thus, after WINDOW (-1, -1)-(1, 1), the center of the screen is (0, 0) in world coordinates.

User-Defined Coordinate Systems

T I P

You might discover many applications for user-defined coordinate systems. Here are two common applications:

- Converting graphics from one SCREEN mode to another.

- Creating natural coordinate systems for mathematical graphs.

Suppose you have a program that does graphics in SCREEN mode 1. The program is full of absolute coordinate references in the standard (320 by 200) coordinate system. You then upgrade your hardware to a VGA (or EGA), and you want to convert your program to the enhanced resolution (640 by 350) available in SCREEN mode 9. Instead of changing every coordinate reference, all you need is a WINDOW (0, 0)-(319, 199) instruction after the initial SCREEN 9 instruction. Quite a time-saver!

Using *WINDOW* and *VIEW* Together

WINDOW and VIEW instructions often are paired together. This permits various effects including the scaling and displacement of images.

When WINDOW comes first, a subsequent VIEW instruction establishes the viewport using the world coordinates. This means that a graphic image is displaced and scaled down to fit inside the viewport. The viewport becomes the microcosm of the whole screen, and the complete extent of the world coordinates is superimposed on the viewport.

As an example, consider Listing 20.3, WINDVIEW.BAS. The output of Listing 20.3 is shown in Figure 20.5.

Listing 20.3.   The WINDVIEW.BAS program.

```
REM Program: WINDVIEW.BAS (Scaling with WINDOW and VIEW)
SCREEN 1
WINDOW (0, 0)-(50, 50)    'Remove this line to see the effect
CIRCLE (10, 40), 5

VIEW (180, 60)-(250, 140), , 3    'Establish the viewport
CIRCLE (10, 40), 5
END
```

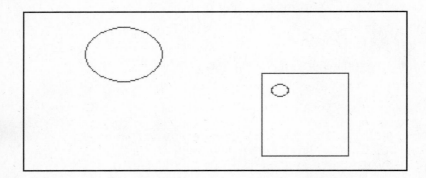

Figure 20.5.

The output of the WINDOW.BAS program.

The first circle is drawn near the upper left corner of the screen. Then a viewport is established in the right half of the screen. The second circle is drawn near the upper left corner of the viewport. Even though the two CIRCLE instructions are identical, the second circle is scaled down. The point is that each circle has the same size and location, relative to the viewport in which it is drawn. (The viewport for the first circle is the entire screen.)

Without the WINDOW instruction, no scaling takes place. Instead, both circles are the same size and are located the same physical distance from the top of their respective viewports. Try deleting the WINDOW instruction to see the effect.

Notice that the coordinates in the VIEW instruction are the physical coordinates. VIEW always specifies the viewport using physical coordinates, regardless of any prior WINDOW instruction.

When VIEW comes first, a subsequent WINDOW instruction applies the world coordinates to the viewport rather than to the entire screen.

The *PMAP* Function

The PMAP function provides a way to translate between physical coordinates and world coordinates when a WINDOW instruction is in effect. If you know a coordinate in one system and need to find the equivalent coordinate in the other system, PMAP does the job.

PMAP(*coordinate*, *mapoption*)

where

    coordinate specifies a world or physical coordinate for x or y,

and

    mapoption is an integer expression from 0 to 3.

F
U
N
C
T
I
O
N

The value of *mapoption* determines what the *coordinate* parameter specifies and what the output of the PMAP function is (see Table 20.3).

Table 20.3. *PMAP* options.

mapoption	coordinate	Result
0	World coordinate x	Physical coordinate x
1	World coordinate y	Physical coordinate y
2	Physical coordinate x	World coordinate x
3	Physical coordinate y	World coordinate y

For example, if the variable WorldY! is a world y-coordinate, the following instruction prints the value of the world coordinate translated into the physical y-coordinate:

```
PRINT PMAP(WorldY!, 1)
```

Using World Coordinates in the *POINT* Function

You might recall from Chapter 13, "Creating Graphics," that the POINT function returns information about a given pixel. The coordinate form of POINT can return information about world coordinates as well as physical coordinates. Here's the complete syntax for the coordinate form of the POINT function:

<table>
<tr>
<td>

F
U
N
C
T
I
O
N

</td>
<td>

POINT(*pointoption*)

where

    pointoption can range from 0 to 3.

</td>
</tr>
</table>

Table 20.4 shows the various options. (In the table, "LPR" is Last Point Referenced.)

Table 20.4. *POINT* function options.

pointoption	Meaning
0	Returns physical x coordinate of LPR
1	Returns physical y coordinate of LPR
2	Returns world x coordinate of LPR
3	Returns world y coordinate of LPR

The world coordinates and physical coordinates are distinct only if a WINDOW instruction is in effect. Otherwise, the world and physical coordinates are identical.

EGA, MCGA, and VGA Considerations

If your computer system has an EGA, VGA, or MCGA video adapter, you have more graphics options than Chapter 13 discusses. On EGA (and VGA and MCGA) systems, SCREEN modes 7, 8, 9, and 10 become available. Also, you can utilize more colors and options with SCREEN modes 1 and 2.

On VGA systems, SCREEN modes 11, 12, and 13 become available. MCGA systems can utilize SCREEN modes 11 and 13, but not SCREEN mode 12.

EGA Colors

You can access 64 colors altogether, identified with the numbers from 0 to 63. The program in Listing 20.4, EGACOLOR.BAS, cycles through the various colors. Each color number is displayed below the corresponding color box. The colors change every five seconds.

Listing 20.4. The EGACOLOR.BAS program.

```
REM Program: EGACOLOR.BAS (Cycle through the 64 EGA colors)
SCREEN 9
PRINT "EGA Colors"
FOR J% = 1 TO 9
   LINE (J% * 63, 50)-STEP(40, 70), J%, BF
NEXT J%

FOR Page% = 0 TO 6
   FOR Box% = 1 TO 9
      Value% = Page% * 9 + Box%
      LOCATE 11, Box% * 8 + 1
         PRINT Value%
      PALETTE Box%, Value%            'Change colors
   NEXT Box%
      Now! = TIMER
      DO
      LOOP UNTIL TIMER > Now! + 5   'Pause for 5 seconds
NEXT Page%
END
```

VGA Colors

VGA increases your options even further. SCREEN modes 11, 12, and 13 become available. All told, you can access 262,144 colors.

The MCGA supports SCREEN modes 11 and 13, but not SCREEN mode 12.

With VGA, you have 262,144 different colors available. A VGA color is determined by selecting an intensity level for each of the three primary video colors: blue, green, and red. You specify the intensity level of each color with a number from 0 (lowest intensity) to 63 (brightest intensity). As such, there are 64 different intensity levels (represented by the numbers from 0 to 63) for each of the three primary colors. The number 262,144 is the product of 64 * 64 * 64.

The VGACOLOR.BAS program, presented in Listing 20.5, cycles through various VGA colors. The program displays, and continually adjusts, the colors in four on-screen boxes. The first three boxes display an intensity level for the blue, green, and red components, respectively. The program shows the numeric value of each intensity level below the appropriate colored box. The fourth box displays the composite VGA color formed with the current settings of the three primary colors. The number shown below this box is the value of the variable ColorVGA&. The next section explains the formula used to compute ColorVGA&.

Listing 20.5.   The VGACOLOR.BAS program.

```
REM Program: VGACOLOR.BAS (Cycle through VGA Colors)
SCREEN 12
PRINT "VGA Colors"
FOR J% = 1 TO 4
   LINE (J% * 125, 125)-STEP(75, 150), J%, BF
NEXT J%

LOCATE 20, 19: PRINT "Blue"
LOCATE 20, 34: PRINT "Green"
LOCATE 20, 51: PRINT "Red"
LOCATE 20, 64: PRINT "Composite"

Increment% = 7                         'Set to 1 to see all colors
FOR BlueIndex% = 0 TO 63 STEP Increment%
   LOCATE 22, 19
   PRINT BlueIndex%
   BlueVGA& = 65536 * BlueIndex%
   FOR GreenIndex% = 0 TO 63 STEP Increment%
```

```
    LOCATE 22, 34
    PRINT GreenIndex%
    GreenVGA& = 256 * GreenIndex%
    FOR RedIndex% = 0 TO 63 STEP Increment%
        LOCATE 22, 50
        PRINT RedIndex%
        RedVGA& = RedIndex%

        ColorVGA& = BlueVGA& + GreenVGA& + RedVGA&
        LOCATE 22, 64
        PRINT ColorVGA&

        PALETTE 1, BlueVGA&
        PALETTE 2, GreenVGA&
        PALETTE 3, RedVGA&
        PALETTE 4, ColorVGA&

        Now! = TIMER
        DO
        LOOP UNTIL TIMER > Now! + .5      'Pause for 1/2 second

    NEXT RedIndex%
  NEXT GreenIndex%
NEXT BlueIndex%
```

The *PALETTE* Statement

Listing 20.4 (EGACOLOR.BAS) and Listing 20.5 (VGACOLOR.BAS) use a PALETTE instruction to change colors. PALETTE, and the companion statement PALETTE USING, are valid only with an EGA, MCGA, or VGA adapter.

As you recall from Chapter 13, the colors available in any SCREEN mode are predetermined. For example, only two colors (black and white) are available in mode 2, and four colors (black, cyan, magenta, and white) are available in SCREEN mode 1. (Though in SCREEN mode 1, a COLOR instruction can toggle the palette to provide a different set of four colors.)

With advanced video (EGA, MCGA, or VGA) and PALETTE, you can extend the color capabilities of your graphing. A PALETTE instruction reorganizes the numeric color values. Previously, a *color* parameter in a graphics instruction specified a particular color. Now, think of such a parameter as an *attribute*.

For example, consider this instruction:

```
PSET (50, 30), 2
```

Think of this instruction as assigning attribute 2, not color 2, to the pixel at (50, 30). With a PALETTE instruction, you can assign whatever color you choose to attribute 2.

The situation is analogous to an artist painting from a palette of different colors. The artist's palette has a fixed number of slots. The artist can choose any color to fill each slot.

Depending on the SCREEN mode, you have a certain number of slots in your palette. These are the attributes. By default, QBasic assigns a particular color (in the range from 0 to 15) to each slot. But with a PALETTE instruction, you can put any of 64 colors (EGA) or 262,144 colors (MCGA or VGA) into each slot. (In SCREEN mode 13, you can assign any of 262,144 colors to slots numbered from 0 to 255.)

F U N C T I O N

PALETTE *attribute*, *color*

or simply,

PALETTE

where

    attribute specifies which attribute number to change,

and

    color specifies which color to assign to *attribute*.

For the EGA modes, the value of *color* can range from 0 to 63.

For the MCGA and VGA modes, you determine a *color* value by selecting an intensity level for the blue, green, and red components of the desired color. Use the following formula:

color = (65536 * *blue*) + (256 * *green*) + *red*

where *blue*, *green*, and *red* can each have a value from 0 (low intensity) to 63 (high intensity).

Notice that the range for *color* is from 0 (low intensity for *blue*, *green*, and *red*) to 4,144,959 (high intensity for each color component). However, there are many gaps in this range. The formula produces only 262,144 valid *color* values. When selecting color, use the formula to guarantee a proper value. (Don't just randomly select a value from 0 to 4,144,959.) An incorrect value causes an Illegal function call error.

For the MCGA and VGA modes, `color` requires a long integer expression. Either a long integer or regular integer suffices for the EGA modes.

A PALETTE instruction affects text and graphics already on the screen as well as subsequent text and graphics. Images drawn with `attribute` instantly change to the new color specified by `color`.

The ranges of attribute and color depend on the screen mode and video adapter (see Table 20.5).

Table 20.5. Attribute and color ranges.

SCREEN Mode	Adapter	attribute Range	color Range
0	VGA, EGA	0-15	0-63
1	VGA, EGA	0-3	0-15
2	VGA, EGA	0-1	0-15
7	VGA, EGA	0-15	0-15
8	VGA, EGA	0-15	0-15
9	VGA, EGA	0-15	0-63
10	VGA, EGA	0-3	0-8
11	VGA, MCGA	0-1	0-4,144,959
12	VGA	0-15	0-4,144,959
13	VGA, MCGA	0-255	0-4,144,959

Notice that text mode (SCREEN 0) supports PALETTE. For example, in mode 0 the following instruction assigns color 38 to attribute 3:

PALETTE 3, 38

In mode 2, `attribute` can be 0 or 1, corresponding to the background and foreground. The following instruction assigns color 27 to the foreground:

PALETTE 1, 27

Modes 7, 8, and 9 restrict the `attribute` range from 0 to 3 if your EGA has only 64K of memory.

In mode 10, for monochrome monitors, each attribute can be assigned a "color" from 0 to 8 interpreted as follows: 0 is black, 4 is white, 8 is high-intensity white, and the other values produce various blinking effects.

Mode 11 is analogous to mode 2; `attribute` can be only 0 or 1.

A PALETTE instruction with no arguments simply reassigns the default colors.

You might want to run the programs in Listings 20.4 and 20.5 (EGACOLOR.BAS and VGACOLOR.BAS) to see the actual colors associated with the various values of the *color* parameter.

The following program, Listing 20.6, demonstrates adding color to SCREEN mode 2. When prompted for a color, give a number from 0 to 15 to see what color fills the circle. Notice how the text color changes as well as the paint color.

Listing 20.6. A program demonstrating *SCREEN* mode 2.

```
REM Demonstrate colors in SCREEN mode 2
SCREEN 2
CIRCLE (300, 100), 150
DO
    LOCATE 23, 5
    INPUT "Paint color (0-15, 0 = quit)"; Hue%
    PALETTE 1, Hue%
    PAINT (300, 100), 1
LOOP UNTIL Hue% = 0
```

You can use PALETTE to display images instantly. First, assign one or more *attribute* values to the background color. Then draw a complex screen with text and/or graphics. Images drawn with the background color are temporarily invisible. Such images immediately pop into view when a PALETTE instruction reassigns *attribute* to a new color.

The *PALETTE USING* Statement

PALETTE instructions change one *attribute* at a time. With PALETTE USING, you can modify every attribute at once.

<table>
<tr>
<td>

**S
T
A
T
E
M
E
N
T**

</td>
<td>

PALETTE USING *arrayname(arrayindex)*

where

    arrayname is an integer or long integer array containing the new color assignments,

and

    arrayindex specifies the first array element containing the new color values.

</td>
</tr>
</table>

> The *arrayindex* parameter is optional. If *arrayindex* does not appear, do not use any parentheses after *arrayname*.

Be sure to dimension *arrayname* before using the array in a PALETTE USING instruction. The dimensioning must be large enough to accommodate every *attribute*. Use the array elements from *arrayindex* upwards. For example, if you want to change all 16 attributes in SCREEN mode 9, you must dimension *arrayname* at least 15 more than *arrayindex*.

arrayindex, if it appears, can be any numerical expression. If *arrayindex* does not appear, QBasic uses the default value of 0. In this case, the array must be dimensioned at least 15.

The array element at *arrayindex* specifies the new color value for attribute 0. The next array element specifies the color for attribute 1, and so on. An array value of –1 indicates no change of color for the corresponding attribute.

The VGA modes (SCREEN 11 through 13) require *arrayname* to be a long integer array because the color values range from 0 to 4,144,959 (although only 262,144 actual values are valid). For the other modes, *arrayname* can be a long integer or regular integer array.

The following program, Listing 20.7, changes 16 screen colors at once with PALETTE USING.

Listing 20.7. A program demonstrating *PALETTE USING*.

```
REM Demonstrate PALETTE USING
DIM NewColor%(63)
SCREEN 9

FOR J% = 0 TO 63
    NewColor%(J%) = J%
NEXT J%

FOR J% = 1 TO 15
    LINE (J% * 35, 50)-STEP(25, 40), J%, BF
NEXT J%

Now! = TIMER
DO
LOOP UNTIL TIMER > Now! + 3        'Pause for 3 seconds

PALETTE USING NewColor%(30)        'Try changing 30 from 0 to 49
```

Notice that the program reassigns all 16 attributes including attribute 0, the background color. That's why the background changes color. In the final instruction, *arrayindex* has a value of 30. Try changing the value of *arrayindex* to see the results.

Styling and Tiling

Straight lines and painted areas don't have to be solid. You might want a dashed line or a patterned fill. QBasic has instructions that let you design and customize such features.

The style of a line consists of the sequence of pixels that are on and off. By default, QBasic draws a solid line (all pixels in the specified color). But you might want a "textured" line such as a dotted or dashed line—in a mathematical graph, for example.

A *tile* is the two-dimensional equivalent of a line style. Normally, painted areas are filled with a solid color. But you might want to fill an enclosed area with a pattern. You can design your own tiles. Each tile has a specified arrangement of pixels that are on and off. These tiles can be laid to fill the desired area.

Styles and tiles occur in these situations:

- You specify a line style in a LINE instruction.

- You specify a tile in a PAINT instruction.

Constructing a Line Style

Consider a line fragment of 16 consecutive pixels. You can construct a line style by establishing a pattern determining which of these 16 pixels are on and which are off.

QBasic uses your line style when drawing a line. The 16-pixel pattern repeats as necessary for the entire length of the line. You specify a style with a 4-digit hexadecimal number that represents your custom pixel pattern.

Let's say you want a line style with two dashes followed by two dots. The 16-pixel sequence consists of 3 on, 2 off, 3 on, 2 off, 1 on, 2 off, 1 on, and 2 off. Figure 20.6 shows the process of determining the hexadecimal number corresponding to this line. Four steps are involved:

1. Represent the 16-pixel pattern visually.

2. Create a 16-bit binary number. A 1 represents each on-pixel, and a 0 represents each off-pixel.

3. Divide the 16 binary bits into four sets of four bits. Each set of four bits becomes a hexadecimal digit. Table 20.6 shows the conversion between four-bit groups and hexadecimal digits. Also, Chapter 19, "Managing Memory," and Chapter 22, "Understanding Advanced QBasic Topics," contain further discussions of hexadecimal numbers and bit patterns.

4. Prefix the four-digit hexadecimal number with &H in standard QBasic notation.

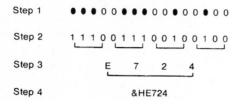

Figure 20.6.

Creating a line style.

Table 20.6. Binary to hexadecimal conversion.

Binary	Hex
0000	0
0001	1
0010	2
0011	3
0100	4
0101	5
0110	6
0111	7
1000	8
1001	9
1010	A
1011	B
1100	C
1101	D
1110	E
1111	F

The resulting hexadecimal number is suitable for the *pattern* argument (the last parameter) in a LINE instruction. The complete syntax of a LINE instruction includes the *pattern* argument.

LINE *startpoint* - *endpoint*, *color*, B, *pattern*

where

    pattern specifies the dot pattern for the line or box.

The *startpoint*, *endpoint*, *color*, and B parameters are explained in Chapter 13, "Creating Graphics."

To demonstrate the use of LINE, the following program produces the stylized boxes shown in Figure 20.7. The outer box is styled with our sample pattern.

```
SCREEN 1
CLS
LINE (10, 10) - (290, 190), , B, &HE724    'Outer box
LINE (30, 30) - (270, 170), , B, &H1111    'Dotted line
LINE (50, 50) - (250, 150), , B, &HF0F0    'Dashed line
LINE (70, 70) - (230, 130), , B, &HFFCC    'Inner box
```

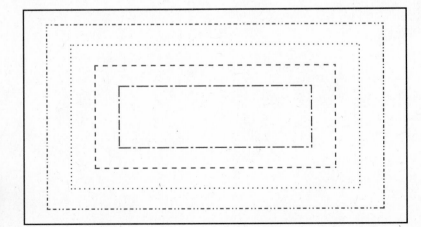

Figure 20.7.

Four line styles.

Constructing a Tile

Unlike a line style, a tile must be specified with a string. This string becomes the *paint* parameter in a PAINT instruction. (See Chapter 13, "Creating Graphics," for a general discussion of PAINT.)

The technique for constructing tiles depends on the SCREEN mode. We explain high-resolution tiles, medium-resolution tiles, EGA tiles, and VGA tiles.

High-Resolution Tiles—*SCREEN* Mode 2

For SCREEN mode 2, a tile consists of a rectangular grid of pixels—8 pixels horizontally and 1 to 64 pixels vertically. Consider each row of 8 pixels to be a binary number. An "on" pixel is represented by a 1 and an "off" pixel is represented by a 0. Every row corresponds to an 8-bit binary number of zeroes and ones. Each binary number reduces to a decimal number from 0 to 255.

You form the tile string by concatenating these numbers with the CHR$ function. Figure 20.8 shows this process for an 8 by 6 tile containing a triangle design.

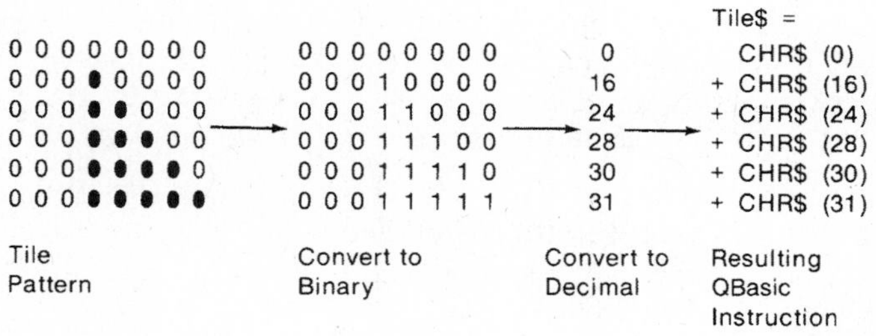

Figure 20.8.

Constructing a high-resolution tile.

The program in Listing 20.8 uses these tiles to fill the inside of a circle. The result is shown in Figure 20.9.

Listing 20.8.   A program that creates a circle with tiles.

```
REM Tile a circle with a triangle pattern
SCREEN 2
CLS
Tile$ = CHR$(0) + CHR$(16) + CHR$(24)
Tile$ = Tile$ + CHR$(28) + CHR$(30) + CHR$(31)
CIRCLE (300, 100), 150
PAINT (300, 100), Tile$
```

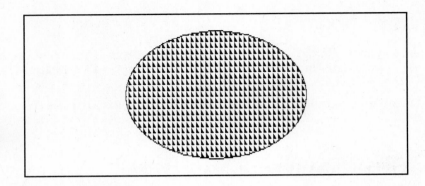

Medium-Resolution Tiles—*SCREEN* Mode 1

The situation is similar to that of high-resolution tiles, but now colors are involved. A tile is 4 pixels wide and from 1 to 64 pixels high. In a given four-pixel row, each pixel can be assigned one of the four color values from 0 to 3. Thus each row is represented by a four-digit number, each digit being 0, 1, 2, or 3.

To construct the appropriate tile string, convert each digit to a two-bit binary number (0 is 00, 1 is 01, 2 is 10, and 3 is 11). Then concatenate the bits to form an eight-bit binary number for each row. Next, convert each binary number to a decimal number (from 0 to 255). Finally, form the tile string by concatenating these numbers with CHR$, just as in high-resolution tiling.

Figure 20.10 shows a four-row tile created by this technique. Try the program in Listing 20.9, which fills a circle with these tiles:

Listing 20.9.   A medium-resolution tiling program.

```
REM Example of medium-resolution tiling
SCREEN 1
CLS
Tile$ = CHR$(24) + CHR$(36) + CHR$(130) + CHR$(130)
CIRCLE (150, 100), 100
PAINT (100, 100), TILE$
```

EGA and VGA Tiles

An EGA or VGA tile is 8 pixels horizontally and from 1 to 64 pixels vertically. In the 16-color modes (SCREEN modes 7, 8, 9, 11, and 12), each pixel is one of the 16 available colors. See Table 12.3 for a list of these colors and the decimal value associated with each color.

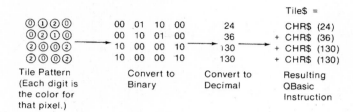

			Tile$ =
⓪①②⓪	00 01 10 00	24	CHR$ (24)
⓪②①⓪	00 10 01 00	36	+ CHR$ (36)
②⓪⓪②	10 00 00 10	₁30	+ CHR$ (130)
②⓪⓪②	10 00 00 10	130	+ CHR$ (130)
Tile Pattern (Each digit is the color for that pixel.)	Convert to Binary	Convert to Decimal	Resulting QBasic Instruction

Figure 20.10.

Constructing a medium-resolution tile.

Tiling is complicated by the fact that the EGA and VGA modes represent pixel colors with a stack of four-bit planes rather than the single plane used in the medium- and high-resolution modes. The result is that each eight-pixel tile row requires four bytes (one byte for each bit plane).

For example, consider an EGA tile composed of two eight-pixel rows. The first row consists of the colors red, red, white, white, blue, blue, black, and black. The second row consists of the colors white, white, blue, blue, black, black, red, and red.

To construct the appropriate tile string, work with each row individually. For each row, convert each color pixel into the appropriate four-bit binary number (red = 4 = 0100, blue = 1 = 0001, white = 7 = 0111, black = 0 = 0000). Stack these four-bit binary numbers into a grid of four eight-bit binary numbers. Then concatenate these four numbers with CHR$ to form the component of the tile string for each row. Finally, combine the tile strings for each row to produce the final tile string.

Figure 20.11 shows the creation of the sample two-row tile. The program in Listing 20.10 uses these tiles to fill the inside of a circle drawn in EGA mode (SCREEN 9):

Listing 20.10. An EGA tiling program.

```
REM Example of EGA Tiling
SCREEN 9
Row1$ = CHR$(60) + CHR$(48) + CHR$(240) + CHR$(0)
Row2$ = CHR$(240) + CHR$(192) + CHR$(195) + CHR$(0)
Tile$ = Row1$ + Row2$
CIRCLE (300, 150), 150
PAINT (300, 150), Tile$
```

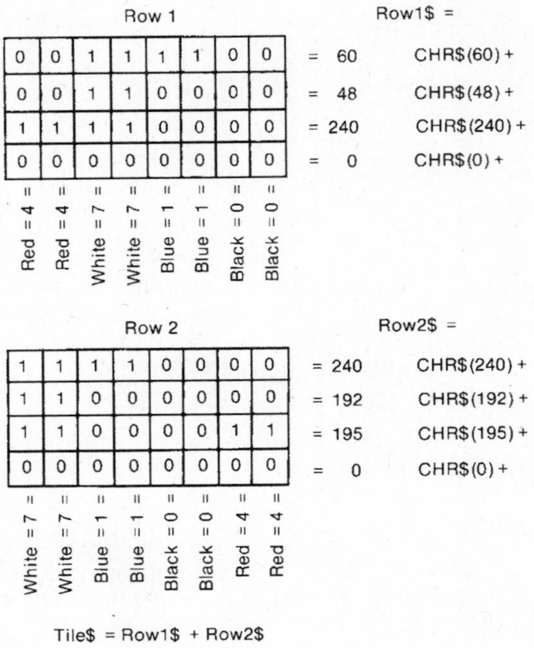

Row 1   Row1$ =

0	0	1	1	1	1	0	0	= 60	CHR$(60) +
0	0	1	1	0	0	0	0	= 48	CHR$(48) +
1	1	1	1	0	0	0	0	= 240	CHR$(240) +
0	0	0	0	0	0	0	0	= 0	CHR$(0) +

Red = 4 | Red = 4 | White = 7 | White = 7 | Blue = 1 | Blue = 1 | Black = 0 | Black = 0

Row 2   Row2$ =

1	1	1	1	0	0	0	0	= 240	CHR$(240) +
1	1	0	0	0	0	0	0	= 192	CHR$(192) +
1	1	0	0	0	0	1	1	= 195	CHR$(195) +
0	0	0	0	0	0	0	0	= 0	CHR$(0) +

White = 7 | White = 7 | Blue = 1 | Blue = 1 | Black = 0 | Black = 0 | Red = 4 | Red = 4

Figure 20.11.

Constructing an EGA tile.

Tile$ = Row1$ + Row2$

The *SCREEN* Statement Revisited— Graphics Pages

Until now, each SCREEN instruction has contained only one parameter (the graphics mode). However, the full syntax of the SCREEN instruction includes three optional parameters.

> **STATEMENT**
>
> SCREEN *modecode*, *colorswitch*, *activepage*, *visualpage*
>
> where
>
>   *modecode* sets the screen mode,
>
>   *colorswitch* is a numeric expression enabling or disabling color,
>
>   *activepage* specifies the working page,
>
> and
>
>   *visualpage* specifies the page in view.
>
> The *colorswitch*, *activepage*, and *visualpage* parameters are optional.

modecode is the only mandatory parameter; its use is discussed at length in Chapter 13, "Creating Graphics."

colorswitch has meaning only for composite monitors (including television sets) used in SCREEN modes 0 and 1. (Notice that composite monitors are rarely used today.) The *colorswitch* parameter controls whether a color signal is sent to the monitor. There are four relevant instructions:

```
SCREEN 0, 0   'Disable color in text mode (black and white only)
SCREEN 0, 1   'Enable color in text mode

SCREEN 1, 0   'Enable color in medium-resolution graphics
SCREEN 1, 1   'Disable color in medium-resolution graphics
```

colorswitch can actually range from 0 to 255. The important matter is whether the value is 0. All nonzero values act the same way.

A *page* is a screen image stored in RAM. The number of available pages depends on your hardware and the screen mode. The *active* page is the page with which text and graphic instructions are currently working. This page might or might not be visible.

The *visual* page is the page currently visible on-screen. By utilizing pages, you can build images on one page while the video screen displays another page. Then, with a SCREEN instruction, you can make a new page instantly visible. This allows animation and other effects.

Specifying Pages

Pages are designated with integer numbers from zero upward. The number of active pages depends on both the screen mode and your hardware.

CGA systems reserve 16K of RAM for paged memory. Text mode (SCREEN mode 0) supports multiple pages. SCREEN modes 1 and 2 do not support multiple pages.

EGA systems can have 64K, 128K, or 256K of memory on the EGA card. This EGA memory can store page images. SCREEN modes 7 to 10 support multiple pages. The VGA and MCGA modes (SCREEN modes 11 through 13) do not support multiple pages.

Table 20.7 shows the available pages as a function of screen mode and hardware configuration.

Table 20.7. Memory pages.

Mode	Resolution	EGA Memory	Page Size	Page Range
0	WIDTH 40		2K	0-7
0	WIDTH 80		4K	0-3
1	320 x 200		16K	0
2	640 x 200		16K	0
3	720 x 348		32K	0-1
7	320 x 200	64K	32K	0-1
7	320 x 200	128K	32K	0-3
7	320 x 200	256K	32K	0-7
8	640 x 200	64K	64K	0
8	640 x 200	128K	64K	0-1
8	640 x 200	256K	64K	0-3
9	640 x 350	64K	64K	0
9	640 x 350	128K	128K	0
9	640 x 350	256K	128K	0-1
10	640 x 350	128K	128K	0
10	640 x 350	256K	128K	0-1
11	640 x 480		64K	0
12	640 x 480		256K	0
13	320 x 200		64K	0

The rightmost column, **Page Range**, shows the range of values *activepage* and *visualpage* can assume.

Copying Screen Pages

A PCOPY instruction copies a specified screen page to another screen page.

PCOPY *sourcepage, targetpage*

where

   sourcepage specifies the page to be copied,

and

   targetpage specifies the page to receive the copy.

S T A T E M E N T

For example, the following instruction copies the contents of page 2 to page 3:

```
PCOPY 2, 3
```

The value of *sourcepage* and *targetpage* each must be within the appropriate range for the SCREEN mode and video configuration. These ranges are shown in the rightmost column of Table 20.7.

Summary

Considered as a whole, the graphics capability of QBasic is quite impressive. You can write programs that take full advantage of your video hardware to produce all kinds of shapes, colors, and animation.

If you don't have much experience with graphics, experiment a little. Even the presentation of simple reports and mundane business data can be spruced up with some attention to the graphics possibilities. Of course, games and other recreational programs provide unlimited adventures for your graphics prowess.

Trapping Errors and Events

Sometimes you want a program to execute in the "foreground" while the program simultaneously checks for the occurrence of a particular event in the "background." For example, a graphics animation might display until the user presses a key.

Trapping is the ability of a program to constantly monitor designated situations and immediately branch to a user-written routine when a particular condition occurs.

QBasic supports two similar, but different, kinds of traps: *error traps* and *event traps.* In both cases, you write a special routine (a group of program instructions) to which control is passed when the trap occurs.

With an error trap, your program immediately branches to the special routine any time a run-time error occurs. This means that your routine can deal with the error and even attempt to rectify things so that the program can continue running.

An event trap waits for a particular occurrence on one of several hardware devices. For example, you might trap the pressing of a particular key (say, one of the function keys). If the user presses that key, the program interrupts whatever it's doing and immediately executes your special routine.

Error and event trapping significantly extend your control over specialized programming situations.

Error Handling and Error Trapping

Normally, a run-time error terminates your program. QBasic displays a pertinent error message and unceremoniously dumps you back to the editing environment. From there you can use the Immediate window and other debugging techniques to track down what happened. (See Chapter 18, "Interactive Debugging and Testing.")

However, there's an alternative for dealing with run-time errors. QBasic provides *error trapping*. Error trapping lets your program intercept an error and pass control to an error-handling routine. That is, when an error occurs, instead of terminating your program, program control simply passes to your error handler. An *error handler* is a user-written group of program lines— similar to a subroutine—to which execution branches when an error occurs.

With error trapping, you can do the following:

- Pass control to an error handler when an error occurs
- Determine which line caused the error
- Determine what error occurred
- Correct the problem or prompt the user for information
- Resume execution anywhere in your program

Using Error Trapping

Error trapping is most valuable in the following situations:

- You anticipate that certain errors might occur during a program, especially when you know what the program should do if any errors materialize.
- An error-producing bug has you baffled. With error trapping as a debugging tool, you can trap the error and branch to a special routine that helps you diagnose the problem.
- You write programs that request others to input data. Your users occasionally might type bad data that causes program errors. (This situation is common with coworkers in a job environment.) Error trapping lets you intercept possible program errors. In the error handler, you can correct the problem and continue the program. Often, such remedial action involves prompting the user for new (or corrected) input data.

If nothing else, an error handler provides graceful program termination. If you cannot fix the problem that caused the error, at least you can display informative messages before the program terminates.

Table 21.1 shows the keywords involved with error trapping.

Table 21.1. Error-handling statements and functions.

Keyword	Action
ON ERROR GOTO	Enables error trapping and designates the first line of the error handler
RESUME	Branches to a designated line when the error handler finishes
ERR	Returns an error code for logic errors
ERL	Returns a number identifying the line which caused the error
ERDEV	Returns an error code for device errors
ERDEV$	Returns the device causing the error
ERROR	Simulates or creates an error

QBasic's error-trapping procedures are a bit primitive. The methods are inherited from GW-BASIC and BASICA. Branch designations and error locations use line numbers and GOTO instructions. "Primitive," however, does not mean "ineffective." Error trapping is a potent tool.

Enabling Error Trapping

The heart of QBasic's error trapping is the ON ERROR GOTO instruction. Two forms exist.

```
ON ERROR GOTO linenum
or
ON ERROR GOTO label
```
where

   linenum is the line number where the error handler begins,

and

   label is the line label where the error handler begins.

S T A T E M E N T

`ON ERROR GOTO` does two things:

- Enables error trapping; no error trap occurs until an `ON ERROR GOTO` instruction executes.

- Specifies which line gets control when an error occurs.

The error handler must exist as part of your main program. As such, *label* or *linenum* must refer to a line in your main program. You cannot branch to an error handler located in a `SUB`, `FUNCTION`, or a `DEF FN` block. However, the `ON ERROR GOTO` statement can appear anywhere in the flow of program execution, even inside a subprogram or function.

Listing 21.1, TRAPERR.BAS, shows the "bare-bones" technique of using an error handler:

Listing 21.1. The TRAPPER.BAS program.

```
REM Program TRAPERR.BAS (The World's Simplest Error Handler)

REM ON ERROR GOTO ErrorHandler    'Remove REM to try handler

NiceTry% = 1 / 0
PRINT "No way to get here"
END

ErrorHandler:
    PRINT "I think you made a boo-boo"
    END
```

Notice that the `ON ERROR GOTO` statement is inactive because the line begins with `REM`.

When you run this program, the assignment instruction causes a run-time error because division by zero is an illegal operation. QBasic aborts the program and displays the following error message:

`Division by zero`

Now remove the `REM` at the beginning of the `ON ERROR GOTO` instruction. This line now activates the error-handling routine. If a program error occurs, control branches directly to the error handler at the line beginning with the `ErrorHandler:` label.

Try running the program. The output of the program is now

`I think you made a boo-boo`

Do you understand what happened? You don't get any error message this time. When the assignment instruction tries to divide by zero, QBasic intercepts the impending error and branches directly to the error handler. Inside the handler, the PRINT instruction displays the "boo-boo" message. The final END instruction ends the program.

You can have multiple error handlers and multiple ON ERROR GOTO instructions in one program. The most recently executed ON ERROR GOTO instruction designates the active error handler. Only one error handler, of course, can be active at any one time.

If your program uses line numbers, you cannot place an error handler at line number 0 because the instruction ON ERROR GOTO 0 has special significance. The effect depends on where the instruction occurs:

- If ON ERROR GOTO 0 occurs outside the error handler, the instruction turns off error trapping. A subsequent error then halts the program in the usual way. In other words, use the instruction ON ERROR GOTO 0 to turn off error trapping that has previously been turned on.

- If ON ERROR GOTO 0 occurs inside an error handler, QBasic displays the regular error message for the current error, and the program terminates. In other words, QBasic acts as if the error occurred without an error trap.

An error handler is simply a group of lines placed somewhere in your main program. The error handler is similar to a subroutine (see Chapter 17, "Modular Programming"). QBasic, unfortunately, does not support branching directly to a subprogram when an error is trapped.

Returning from an Error Handler

Most error handlers include one or more RESUME instructions. With RESUME, an error handler passes control back to the main program in much the same way as RETURN passes control back from a subroutine. There are five different forms of the RESUME instruction.

```
RESUME              'Standard form
RESUME 0            'Zero form
RESUME NEXT         'NEXT form
RESUME linenum      'Line number form
RESUME label        'Label form
```

where

linenum is a line number in the main program,

and

label is a line label in the main program.

The form of a RESUME instruction determines where execution resumes (see Table 21.2).

Table 21.2. Forms of the *RESUME* instruction.

Instruction	Return Location
RESUME	At the line that caused the error
RESUME 0	At the line that caused the error (same as RESUME)
RESUME NEXT	At the instruction immediately following the one that caused the error
RESUME linenum	At the line designated by linenum
RESUME label	At the line designated by label

To see how RESUME works, Listing 21.2 contains the original TRAPERR.BAS program from Listing 20.1 with RESUME NEXT added to the end of the error handler:

Listing 21.2. The TRAPPER.BAS program with *RESUME NEXT*.

```
REM Program TRAPERR.BAS (The World's simplest error handler)

ON ERROR GOTO ErrorHandler

NiceTry% = 1 / 0
PRINT "No way to get here"
END

ErrorHandler:
    PRINT "I think you made a boo-boo"
    RESUME NEXT
```

Now, when the error is trapped, the handler returns control to the main program at the line just after the assignment instruction that caused the error. As a result, the output of the program is

```
I think you made a boo-boo
No way to get here
```

In a RESUME instruction, *linenum* or *label* must refer to a line in your main program. You should avoid these forms of RESUME because an error can occur inside a subprogram or function. In such a case, the subprogram or function might not terminate properly. Undesirable side effects can develop. Notice that RESUME and RESUME NEXT can return program control to a SUB or FUNCTION.

RESUME instructions are valid only inside error-handling routines. A run-time error (RESUME without error) occurs if you execute a RESUME instruction outside of an error handler. Furthermore, your program cannot simply run out of instructions in a RESUME-less error handler. This mistake causes a run-time error (No RESUME).

Writing an Error Handler

Inside an error handler, you generally want to accomplish the following:

- Determine the error and which line caused it
- Display diagnostic messages
- Correct the problem
- Resume execution if feasible

The built-in functions ERR, ERL, ERDEV, and ERDEV$ provide information often useful for your error handler.

Using the *ERR* and *ERL* Functions

ERR and ERL enable your error handler to determine the type of error that occurred and which program line caused the error.

ERR

ERL

ERR returns the code of the error that invoked the error handler. Appendix F, "Error Messages," lists the errors and the associated error codes.

ERL returns the line number at which the error occurred. If the error occurs in a line without a line number, ERL returns the number of the last executed line that had a line number. If your program has no numbered lines between the start of the program and the error, ERL returns 0.

Notice that ERL works only with line numbers and not with labels. This throw-back to GW-BASIC and BASICA requires you to number all program lines so that ERL can return the most accurate information.

Using the *ERDEV* and *ERDEV$* Functions

ERDEV and ERDEV$ provide information about errors generated by hardware devices (such as the line printer or disk drive).

ERDEV

ERDEV$

ERDEV$ returns the name of the device that produced the most recent error. Table 21.3 shows some of the most likely device names that ERDEV$ might return. If an error occurs in a specialized device driver, ERDEV$ returns the name established by the device driver.

Table 21.3. Device names returned by *ERDEV$*.

Name	Device
A:	Disk drive A:
B:	Disk drive B:
C:	Disk drive C:
D:	Disk drive D:
E:	Disk drive E:
LPT1	Line printer #1
LPT2	Line printer #2
LPT3	Line printer #3
PRN	Generic printer
CON	Standard input and output (keyboard or video)
KYBD	Keyboard

Name	Device
SCRN	Video display
CLOCK$	Real time clock
AUX	Auxiliary (usually first asynchronous port)
COM1	Serial port #1
COM2	Serial port #2

ERDEV returns bit-coded information as shown in Figure 21.1.

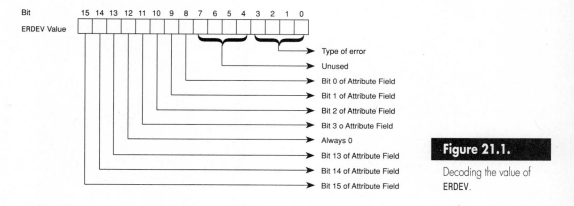

Figure 21.1.

Decoding the value of ERDEV.

The high-order eight bits from ERDEV (bits 8 through 15) map into selected bits taken from the attribute field of the device header for the particular device. You can find this information, which is quite technical, in the *DOS Technical Reference* manual or in Que's *DOS Programmer's Reference*, 3rd Edition, by Terry Dettmann and Marcus Johnson.

The lower four bits from ERDEV (bits 0 through 3) specify the type of error. To isolate this information, use the following instruction to mask the value returned by ERDEV:

```
ErrorCode% = ERDEV AND &HF
```

(For more about bit masking, see Chapter 22, "Understanding Advanced QBasic Topics.")

The variable ErrorCode% contains a number from 0 to 15 that indicates the error (see Table 21.4).

Table 21.4. Error codes returned by *ERDEV*.

Error Code	Error
0	Write-protect violation
1	Unknown unit
2	Device not ready
3	Unknown command
4	CRC error (redundancy check)
5	Bad drive request structure length
6	Seek error
7	Unknown media
8	Sector not found
9	Printer out of paper
10	Write fault
11	Read fault
12	General failure
13	(Unused)
14	(Unused)
15	Invalid disk change

Listing 21.3 demonstrates the type of information you can get from ERDEV and ERDEV$:

Listing 21.3.   A program demonstrating *ERDEV* and *ERDEV$*.

```
REM Demonstrate ERDEV and ERDEV$

ON ERROR GOTO ErrorHandler

OPEN "A:NOFILE.BAS" FOR INPUT AS #1    'Leave door open on drive A:
PRINT "All done"
END

ErrorHandler:
   PRINT "Error in device "; ERDEV$
   PRINT "ERDEV code is"; ERDEV AND &HF
   RESUME NEXT
```

If you run this program with the door on disk drive A: open, the program produces the following output:

```
Error in device A:
ERDEV code is 2
All done
```

Philosophy of Error Handlers

An error handler can be simple or complex. Especially in workplace environments, error handlers can be used to anticipate possible problems and recover smoothly.

In polished programs, most errors come from user mistakes. The likely culprits are faulty data supplied by users and silly mistakes with equipment, such as placing the wrong data disk in a disk drive or not turning on the printer.

User-supplied numeric data often is a source of errors. Bad data typed by users can lead to errors such as division by zero. You might write an error handler that checks for division by zero (among other possibilities). If that's the problem, you can redisplay the user's input and ask whether the information is correct. If the information is incorrect, branch back to where the data was entered and start over.

Disk drive errors are common when users must place a disk into a drive and type in the name of a desired file saved on the disk. Users might forget to place the disk in the drive, use the wrong disk, use the wrong drive, or supply an invalid filename. You can check for all these errors and recover without causing the program to "bomb."

Error handlers often have a series of IF instructions or a SELECT CASE block. The handler checks for various anticipated errors by using ERR, ERL, and ERDEV and executes individualized instructions that deal with each type of error.

Here's an example of such an error handler:

```
ErrorHandler:
   PRINT
   PRINT "Error"; ERR; "has occurred at line"; ERL
   SELECT CASE ERR
      CASE 11
         PRINT "You have divided by zero."
         PRINT "Please rerun the program with new values."
         END
      CASE 24
         PRINT "The printer is probably not on or is out of paper"
         PRINT "Check the printer and then press any key"
```

```
          WHILE INKEY$ = "": WEND
          RESUME
      CASE 61
          PRINT "The disk is full!"
          PRINT "The program will continue without writing to disk"
          RESUME NEXT
      CASE ELSE
          PRINT "That's an unanticipated error."
          PRINT "So long for now--stopping the program."
          END
  END SELECT
```

At the least, your error handler can display diagnostic information and solicit the user to notify you. For example:

```
MyErrorHandler:
    PRINT "A program error has occurred"
    PRINT
    PRINT "Please report the following information to"
    PRINT "Joe Programmer, Bldg. Q8, Extension 389"
    PRINT
    PRINT "Error number"; ERR; "in line"; ERL
    PRINT "Device name and problem are", ERDEV$, ERDEV
    PRINT "    - Thank you"
    PRINT "        Joe"
END
```

Simulating Errors

Use an ERROR instruction to simulate errors or create your individualized error codes.

S T A T E M E N T

ERROR *errorcode*

where

    errorcode is an integer expression that specifies an error code in the range from 0 to 255.

If *errorcode* is one of the error codes defined by QBasic (see Appendix F, "Error Messages"), ERROR causes your program to behave as though the error occurred. Control passes to your error handler from which the ERR function will return the value of *errorcode*. If you have no error handler, QBasic displays the normal error message associated with that error and terminates your program.

With ERROR, you can induce different errors while testing and developing a program. You can find out whether or not your error handler recovers suitably.

To define your own error code, use an *errorcode* value not defined by QBasic. When the ERROR instruction passes control to the error handler, you can use ERR inside the handler to test for the value of *errorcode* and take appropriate action.

If your program has no error handler, an ERROR instruction that has an invalid *errorcode* halts your program and displays the message Unprintable error.

User-defined error codes provide a way to test for special conditions or dangerous data. You can intercept potential errors and handle the problem in an error handler.

For example, here is the skeleton form of a program that asks the user to type in a password. If the user types the proper password (Swordfish), the program displays confidential information. If the typed password is invalid, program control passes to an error handler. The program defines ERROR 254, which is not a normal error number used by QBasic.

```
ON ERROR GOTO ErrorHandler
    .
    .
    .
INPUT "What is the authorizing password"; PASSWORD$
IF PASSWORD$ <> "Swordfish" THEN ERROR 254
PRINT "Strategic Plan Briefing"
    .
    .
    .
END    'of program

ErrorHandler:
    .
    .
    IF ERR <> 254 THEN GOTO MoreErrors
        PRINT "Unauthorized request"
        REM If possible, correct the problem here
            .
        RESUME NEXT
    MoreErrors:
```

```
REM Check for other errors here
  .
  .
REM End of error handler
```

Event Trapping

Event trapping is error trapping's kissing cousin. An error trap intercepts a run-time error, but an *event trap* monitors a selected peripheral device for a certain event. QBasic checks for the event between execution of each program instruction. When the event occurs, QBasic executes a specified subroutine before continuing the program.

For example, you can trap the pressing of a particular key, such as the F1 key. Once the trap is set, the program continues executing normally. However, if the user presses F1 *at any time,* the program interrupts whatever it is doing and branches immediately to your designated subroutine. (Among other things, the subroutine might display help information or request certain input.) When the subroutine concludes, the program continues from the point of interruption.

You can trap the following events:

- ■ Allowing a specific time period to elapse
- ■ Pressing a certain key (or key combination)
- ■ Depleting the background-music buffer
- ■ Receiving data at a serial communications port
- ■ Activating the light pen
- ■ Pressing a joystick trigger

To trap an event, you must do three things:

- ■ Write a subroutine, called an *event handler,* to which control branches when the event occurs.
- ■ Execute an ON *event* GOSUB instruction that associates the event handler with the desired event.
- ■ Execute an *event* ON instruction that activates the event trap.

Specifying an Event Trap

ON *event* GOSUB specifies the event to trap and the location of the associated event handler.

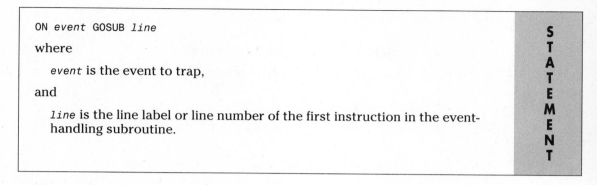

```
ON event GOSUB line
```

where

    event is the event to trap,

and

    line is the line label or line number of the first instruction in the event-handling subroutine.

S T A T E M E N T

Table 21.5 shows the possible values for *event*.

Table 21.5. "Trappable" events.

event	Trapped Event
TIMER(*numseconds*)	Elapse of a given time interval
KEY(*keynum*)	A designated keystroke
PLAY(*noteminimum*)	Background-music buffer depletion
COM(*serialport*)	Data at a serial port
PEN	Light-pen activity
STRIG(*button*)	Joystick-button activity

You can enable, disable, or suspend each event trap.

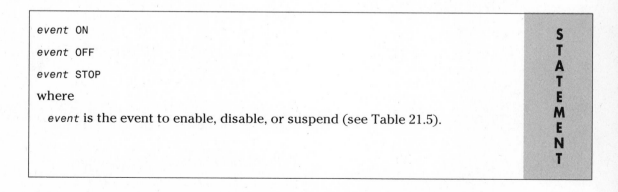

```
event ON
event OFF
event STOP
```

where

    event is the event to enable, disable, or suspend (see Table 21.5).

S T A T E M E N T

ON enables the event trap.

OFF disables an event trap previously turned on. If the event takes place, QBasic ignores the event and does not branch to the event-trap subroutine.

STOP suspends the event trap. If the event takes place, no GOSUB occurs. However, QBasic "remembers" the event. A subsequent *event* ON instruction causes an immediate trap.

The trapping of TIMER, KEY, and PLAY events is now discussed.

Trapping a *TIMER* Event

TIMER keeps track of passing time and causes an event trap whenever a designated time period elapses.

S T A T E M E N T

```
ON TIMER(numseconds) GOSUB line

TIMER ON
TIMER OFF
TIMER STOP
```

where

    numseconds specifies the number of seconds to elapse,

and

    line is a line label or line number that identifies the first line of the event-handler subroutine.

The *numseconds* parameter is a long-integer expression that must have a value from 1 to 86,400. The maximum value, 86,400, is the number of seconds in 24 hours.

Listing 21.4, PROMPTER.BAS, is an example timer trap. PROMPTER.BAS turns on a timer trap while waiting for the user to reply yes or no to a question. If the user does not respond within 15 seconds, the program beeps and displays a not-so-gentle reminder.

The ON TIMER instruction prepares the trap. This instruction does two things:

- Designates the time period interval as 15 seconds
- Specifies the label WakeUp: as the beginning of the event trap subroutine

Listing 21.4. The PROMPTER.BAS program.

```
REM Program: PROMPTER.BAS (Demonstrate TIMER trap)

ON TIMER(15) GOSUB WakeUp        'Prepare trap on 15 second interval

PRINT "Do you want instructions (Y or N)?"

TIMER ON                         'Turn on trap while waiting for reply
DO
    Reply$ = INKEY$
LOOP WHILE Reply$ = ""           'Wait for reply
TIMER OFF                        'Turn off trap once reply is made

REM Test Reply$ to continue program
END

WakeUp:                          'Event Handler Subroutine
    BEEP
    PRINT "Please reply immediately!"
    RETURN
```

Notice that the ON TIMER instruction does not actually activate the trap. That's the purpose of the TIMER ON instruction. You must specify TIMER ON before QBasic starts checking for a timer event.

The DO-LOOP block continuously loops until the user presses a key. When the user presses a key, the key's value is stored in the variable Replay$.

However, if the user does not press a key within 15 seconds, the event trap occurs. QBasic immediately GOSUBs to the WakeUp subroutine. Here the program beeps and displays a reminder. The RETURN closes the subroutine and returns control to the DO-LOOP block. If the user still doesn't press a key, the trap occurs again after 15 more seconds.

When the user does press a key, the TIMER OFF instruction turns off the event trap. Now the program no longer checks for the elapsing of 15 second intervals.

Try PROMPTER.BAS a few times. First, press a key when prompted. The program "falls past" the TIMER OFF instruction and terminates with the ensuing END instruction. On a subsequent run, don't press any key when prompted. Every 15 seconds, the program beeps and displays the message in the PRINT instruction of the WakeUp subroutine.

Trapping a *KEY* Event

With KEY, you can trap the pressing of any key or keystroke combination.

STATEMENT

```
ON KEY(keynum) GOSUB line

KEY (keynum) ON
KEY (keynum) OFF
KEY (keynum) STOP
```

where

> *keynum* identifies the key you want to trap (see Table 21.6),

and

> *line* is a line label or line number that identifies the first line of the event-handler subroutine.

Table 21.6. Trapped keys.

keynum	Key
1 to 10	Function keys F1 through F10
11	Direction key—up arrow
12	Direction key—left arrow
13	Direction key—right arrow
14	Direction key—down arrow
15 to 25	User-defined keys
30	Function key F11 (enhanced keyboard only)
31	Function key F12 (enhanced keyboard only)
0	All keys listed in this table

The following program fragment demonstrates how multiple events can share event handlers:

```
ON KEY(11) GOSUB VerticalKey:      'Up-arrow key
ON KEY(14) GOSUB VerticalKey:      'Down-arrow key
ON KEY(12) GOSUB HorizontalKey:    'Left-arrow key
```

```
ON KEY(13) GOSUB HorizontalKey:      'Right-arrow key
KEY(11) ON
KEY(12) ON
KEY(13) ON
KEY(14) ON
.
.
.
VerticalKey:
REM Subroutine to handle trapping of "vertical" keys
    PRINT "You pressed the up- or down-arrow key."
    RETURN
HorizontalKey:
REM Subroutine to handle trapping of "horizontal" keys
    PRINT "You pressed the left- or right-arrow key."
    RETURN
```

In Table 21.6, notice that key numbers from 15 to 25 identify user-defined keys. This means that you can trap any single key or a keystroke combination. You can assign any or all the key numbers from 15 to 25 to individual keys (or keystroke combinations). You can trap the space bar, Shift-Q, and Ctrl-Alt-Esc, to name a few.

Trapping user-defined keys requires three instructions.

```
KEY userkeynum, CHR$(shiftcode) + CHR$(scancode)

ON KEY(userkeynum) GOSUB line

KEY(userkeynum) ON
```

where

   userkeynum is a user-defined key number ranging from 15 to 20,

   shiftcode identifies the special keys, if any, that are being trapped,

   scancode identifies the primary key to be trapped,

and

   line is a line label or line number that identifies the first line of the event-handler subroutine.

S T A T E M E N T

The first KEY instruction is new. You use this instruction only when trapping keys not found in Table 21.6. This KEY instruction accomplishes two things:

■ Identifies the key or keystroke combination to trap by using *shiftcode* and *scancode*

■ Associates that key or keystroke combination with *userkeynum* (a number from 15 to 25)

You can determine the proper value for *shiftcode* and *scancode* this way:

■ If the trap is any single key (even a special gray key such as Esc or Num Lock), *shiftcode* is 0; *scancode* can be found in Appendix C, "Keyboard Scan Codes."

■ If the trap is a keystroke combination (such as Ctrl-Alt-K), consider the combination to have a primary key (K in this example) and secondary special keys (Ctrl and Alt). Use Table 21.7 to determine the *shiftcode* contribution for each secondary key. Add these contributions to determine the final value of *shiftcode*. Look up *scancode* for the primary key in Appendix C.

Table 21.7. Values of *shiftcode* for keystroke combinations.

Key	Value of *shiftcode*
Left Shift	1
Right Shift	2
Ctrl	4
Alt	8
Num Lock	32
Caps Lock	64
Extended Key (enhanced keyboard)	128

Here are some examples:

```
KEY 15, CHR$(0) + CHR$(57)      '/ Traps the space bar
ON KEY(15) GOSUB 2000           '¦  - 57 is scan code
KEY(15) ON                      '\  - User key number 15

200 KEY MYKEYNUM%, CHR$(3) + CHR$(57)      'Shift-space bar

200 KEY MYKEYNUM%, CHR$(0) + CHR$(1)       'Esc key

200 KEY MYKEYNUM%, CHR$(12) + CHR$(83)     'Ctrl-Alt-Del
```

The last example traps Ctrl-Alt-Del. By trapping this combination, you can disable rebooting if the user presses Ctrl-Alt-Del while your program is running.

Trapping a *PLAY* Event

With PLAY, you can trap the depletion of musical notes placed in a special music buffer.

```
ON PLAY(noteminimum) GOSUB line

PLAY ON
PLAY OFF
PLAY STOP
```

where

> *noteminimum* specifies the minimum number of notes in the background music buffer with a value from 1 to 32,

and

> *line* is a line label or line number that identifies the first line of the event-handler subroutine.

S T A T E M E N T

PLAY works only for music playing in background mode. When music plays in the background, QBasic maintains a buffer that holds the remaining notes to be played.

PLAY ON causes an event trap when the number of notes in the music buffer first decreases to *noteminimum*. No trap occurs if you execute PLAY ON when the buffer already has fewer notes than *noteminimum*. Notice that ON PLAY uses the *noteminimum* argument but PLAY ON does not.

Listing 21.5, PLAYMORE.BAS, demonstrates music trapping. The program continuously plays an up-and-down musical scale in the background while the screen fills with 500 random graphic dots.

Listing 21.5. The PROMPTER.BAS program.

```
REM Program: PLAYMORE.BAS (Play music continually)

ON PLAY(5) GOSUB PlayMore      'Trap when 5 notes left
PLAY ON                        'Try PLAY OFF to see the effect
```

continues

Listing 21.5. Continued

```
PLAY "MB"                     'Turn on background music
GOSUB PlayMore                'Use event handler to play notes

SCREEN 1                      'Low-resolution graphics
FOR Counter% = 1 TO 5000
   X = RND * 320
   Y = RND * 200
   PSET (X, Y)                'Draw random point on screen
NEXT Counter%

END

PlayMore:                     'Event handler
   PLAY "O2 C D E F G A B A G F E D"
   RETURN
```

Trapping a COM Event

The COM event recognizes when data appears in the communications buffer associated with the serial communications port.

STATEMENT

```
ON COM(serialport) GOSUB line

COM(serialport) ON
COM(serialport) OFF
COM(serialport) STOP
```

where

serialport specifies the serial port as an integer expression evaluating to 1 or 2,

and

line is a line label or line number that identifies the first line of the event-handler subroutine.

Here is the skeleton form of a program that traps a COM event:

```
ON COM(1) GOSUB DataReady    'Trap data in port number 1


COM(1) ON                    'Enable the event trap
  .
  .
DataReady:                   'Beginning of event handler
  .
  .
  RETURN
```

Trapping a *PEN* Event

PEN traps any activation of the light pen.

<table>
<tr><td>

```
ON PEN GOSUB line

PEN ON
PEN OFF
PEN STOP
```

where

    line is a line label or line number that identifies the first line of the event-handler subroutine.

</td><td>

S
T
A
T
E
M
E
N
T

</td></tr>
</table>

Trapping a *STRIG* Event

STRIG traps the pressing of a joystick button or trigger.

```
ON STRIG(button) GOSUB line

STRIG(button) ON
STRIG(button) OFF
STRIG(button) STOP
```

where

> *button* is an integer expression that specifies which joystick button to trap,

and

> *line* is a line label or line number that identifies the first line of the event-handler subroutine.

See Table 21.8 for the valid values of *button*.

Table 21.8. Joystick button values.

Value of *button*	Corresponding Joystick Button
0	Button 1, joystick A
2	Button 1, joystick B
4	Button 2, joystick A
6	Button 2, joystick B

Event Trapping Inside the Handler

QBasic executes an implied *event* STOP instruction when an event trap occurs, and control passes to the handler subroutine. When a RETURN instruction closes the handler, QBasic executes an implied *event* ON instruction to reactivate trapping of the event. Without this safeguard, the handler could get in an indefinite loop or incorrectly process multiple events if events occur while the handler is processing earlier events.

However, QBasic "remembers" an event that occurs while the handler executes. The implied *event* STOP only suspends the trap. After the handler closes, an immediate trap takes place.

NOTE | **Returning from an Event-Handler Subroutine**

An event handler is an ordinary subroutine that relinquishes control with a RETURN instruction. In many cases, you want control to resume at a specific instruction rather than immediately after the instruction that initiated the event trap.

A special form of the RETURN instruction permits a subroutine to return to *any* line number in the main program:

RETURN *line*

where *line* is any line label or line number in your program.

For example, the following instruction returns control to line number 430:

RETURN 430

Comparing Event Trapping to Error Trapping

Event trapping and error trapping are similar but not identical. Here is a comparison of the two techniques:

■ An event handler is a regular QBasic subroutine. The event handler, therefore, relinquishes control with a RETURN instruction. An error handler is a specialized routine that relinquishes control with a RESUME instruction.

■ An event trap requires an ON *event* GOSUB instruction to define the handler and an *event* ON instruction to activate the trap. To define and activate an error trap, you need only a single ON ERROR GOTO instruction.

■ You GOSUB to an event handler. You GOTO an error handler.

■ Event handlers and error handlers must be in your main program. An ON *event* GOSUB or ON ERROR GOTO instruction, however, might appear inside a subprogram or function.

■ You can trap multiple events simultaneously. Each event can have its own event handler, or multiple events can share the same event handler. On the other hand, error trapping is either on or off. Only one error handler can be active at any moment.

Summary

Error and event trapping are advantageous tools for programs with special needs.

With an error trap, your program can take measures to intercept and recover from run-time errors. One use of this technique is "bulletproofing" programs that you write for other users. You can anticipate possible errors caused by your user entering faulty input or mishandling hardware such as the disk drives. An error handler can smoothly rescue the program from these kinds of problems.

Event trapping is a similar "background" technique. Your program can monitor activity on any of several hardware devices while the regular work of the program progresses. With this technique, your program can take special action anytime one of the special events occurs.

Trapping is an advanced technique. The next chapter presents a potpourri of other advanced topics.

Understanding Advanced QBasic Topics

Bย now you have a sound understanding of QBasic programming. As you've no doubt concluded from the previous chapters, QBasic is a rich language with many statements, functions, and features. If you have mastered the material in those chapters, you should be able to successfully program almost any task.

But QBasic has even more to offer, including a number of more advanced features for specialized situations. This chapter presents a potpourri of advanced programming topics that didn't find their way into the earlier chapters.

Feel free to pick and choose the subjects that interest you. You might just want to browse and explore some new areas. Perhaps a published program in a book or magazine uses a QBasic feature with which you're not familiar. You might find the feature in this chapter.

At any rate, congratulations on coming to this point in the book. It demonstrates that you have the programming confidence to strive toward the limits of QBasic.

Here are the primary topics covered in this chapter.

- Using common blocks
- Restarting and chaining programs

■ Wholesale variable typing

■ Starting QBasic with optional settings

■ Manipulating integers at the bit level

■ Shelling to DOS

■ Communicating with I/O ports

■ Communicating with hardware devices

Using Common Blocks

A *common block* is a special area in memory where you can store the values of a designated group of variables. This provides a variable-sharing mechanism because your main program, subprograms, and functions can all access the common block. Essentially, variables in the common block can be made global to the entire program. Furthermore, as explained during the discussion of CHAIN later in this chapter, the common block provides a way to pass variables from one entire program to another.

Defining a Common Block with *COMMON*

Use a COMMON instruction to declare a common block.

<table>
<tr>
<td>

S
T
A
T
E
M
E
N
T

</td>
<td>

```
COMMON SHARED varlist
```

where

    varlist is a comma-delimited list of the variables placed into the COMMON block.

The SHARED keyword is optional.

</td>
</tr>
</table>

The variable list, *varlist*, consists of simple variable names and/or array names. Use an empty set of parentheses to denote each array name. You can specify the data type of each variable with a type-declaration suffix, or use an

AS *type* clause where *type* is INTEGER, LONG, SINGLE, DOUBLE, STRING, or a user-defined record type.

A COMMON instruction can only appear in a main program, never in the associated procedures. COMMON must appear before any executable instructions. The only statements that can precede COMMON are CONST, DATA, DECLARE, DEF*type*, DIM, OPTION BASE, REDIM, SHARED, STATIC, TYPE-END TYPE, $DYNAMIC, or $STATIC.

By including the SHARED keyword in the COMMON instruction, the variables in the common block are automatically shared with the procedures in exactly the same way that a DIM SHARED instruction in a main program shares a variable with each procedure (see Chapter 17, "Modular Programming"). The SHARED keyword makes all the variables in the common block global to the entire program.

If a COMMON instruction doesn't include the SHARED keyword, the subprograms and functions do not have access to the variables in the common block. A variable inside a procedure remains local to the procedure and independent from any variable that coincidentally has the same name in the common block. COMMON without SHARED has use when chaining, as described later in this chapter.

Here are some typical COMMON instructions:

```
COMMON SHARED Title$            'Title$ is global

COMMON SHARED Index%            'Places integer variable in common

COMMON SHARED Index AS INTEGER  'Same as above

COMMON A#, B#, C AS DOUBLE      '3 double-precision variables

COMMON SHARED BigDeal&()        'Long integer array
```

Placing Arrays in *COMMON*

When an array appears in a common block, you can place the array's DIM instruction before or after the COMMON instruction. Your choice has important ramifications depending on whether the array is statically or dynamically allocated. (See Chapter 19, "Managing Memory," for more about static and dynamic allocation.)

If the DIM instruction comes first, and the array is statically allocated, the ensuing COMMON instruction simply preserves the static allocation, as in Listing 22.1.

Listing 22.1. The Main program.

```
REM Main program
DIM Client$(1 TO 30)
COMMON SHARED Client$()
      .
      .
      .
END
```

However, if the COMMON instruction comes first, the array is dynamically allocated, even if the ensuing DIM instruction otherwise designates a static array,
as in Listing 22.2.

Listing 22.2. The revised Main program.

```
REM Main program
COMMON People$()
DIM People$(30)
```

Notice that, if the COMMON instruction were removed, the DIM instruction would
statically allocate People$. However, with the COMMON instruction first, People$
becomes a dynamic array.

COMMON Sense

Here are some guidelines for using COMMON:

■ You cannot duplicate a variable name in the same COMMON instruction.

■ Your main program can have more than one COMMON instruction. Multiple
COMMON instructions do not redefine the block. Instead, each declaration
appends variables to the existing common block. For example, the following two instructions are equivalent to the single instruction COMMON A%,
B#, C&:

```
COMMON A%, B#
COMMON C&
```

■ Remember that the SHARED attribute must appear in the COMMON instruction
to make the common block available to the program's procedures. Of
course, as Chapter 19, "Managing Memory," explained, you can use the
SHARED instruction inside a procedure to gain access to main program
variables.

■ A common block can pass variables between chained programs. Chaining is discussed in the following section.

Restarting and Chaining

Restarting begins the current program all over again. *Chaining* transfers control to a second program. You can restart the current program at any specified line, or chain to a second program and optionally share variables.

Using the *RUN* Instruction

RUN restarts the current program or transfers execution to a second program.

RUN

or

RUN *linenum*

or

RUN *filespec$*

where

linenum specifies the line number on which to begin the reexecution of the current program,

and

filespec specifies a new file to execute.

S
T
A
T
E
M
E
N
T

With or without one of the optional arguments, RUN does the following:

■ Closes all open files

■ Resets all numeric variables to zero

■ Resets all string variables to the null string

RUN by itself (with neither optional argument) simply restarts the current program. The effect is the same as terminating the original program and starting anew.

RUN provides a simple way to restart when input data is corrupt. Suppose you begin a program with a request for the user to supply some necessary data. The program checks the data and discovers input errors. Rather than have the program prompt again for corrected input, simply display an explanatory message and use a RUN instruction to begin the program all over again.

With *linenum* specified, RUN restarts the program at the designated line number. (You must use a line number; line labels are not allowed.) *linenum* must be a line number in the main program; you cannot restart execution at a line inside a function or a subprogram. Also, RUN and RUN *linenum* instructions can appear only in the main program.

With a *filespec* argument, RUN transfers control to a second program. The *filespec* optionally can include a drive and/or a path designation. If *filespec* does not include a file extension, the default extension is .BAS.

For example, the following instruction chains to a program named MYFILE.BAS:

```
RUN "MYFILE"
```

Only the RUN *filespec* form of the RUN instruction can appear inside a subprogram or a function.

When RUN chains to a second program, the original program is removed entirely from the QBasic environment before the new program loads. The effect is the same as ending the first program, selecting New on the File menu, loading the second program, and beginning execution of the second program. You cannot pass or share any variables between your first and second program. To do that, use CHAIN rather than RUN.

Using the *CHAIN* Instruction

CHAIN transfers control to a second program and permits the sharing of variables through COMMON.

STATEMENT

CHAIN *filespec*

where

filespec specifies the new file to execute.

The *filespec* argument must designate a QBasic source file (normally a file with a .BAS extension). If *filespec* has no explicit extension, .BAS is the default. CHAIN removes the original program from memory and then loads and executes the chained program.

CHAIN preserves the common block so variables can be passed along the program chain. The new program must declare the same common block as the old program.

Advantages of Chaining

Why use CHAIN at all? Here are the two most common reasons:

- Your chained-to programs already exist as independent programs. Now a new project requires some preprocessing before you invoke the old standby program or programs. You can pass necessary values from program to program with COMMON instructions. This scenario is common in production business environments using well-established programs.

- Your program exceeds available memory. Chaining provides a way to break a large program into smaller, executable chunks. Instead of creating one big program, create two or more smaller programs, each of which is small enough to fit into memory. Then store the programs on disk files, and use CHAIN to transfer control from one program to another.

Using *COMMON* with *CHAIN*

To pass a common block when chaining, you generally use the same COMMON instruction in both the old and the new program. The CHAIN instruction preserves the integrity of the common block.

Actually the COMMON instructions in the calling and chained-to programs do not have to be identical. Only the order and type of each variable specified in the respective COMMON instructions need be the same. Consider the chain skeleton in Listing 22.3.

Listing 22.3. The chain skeleton.

```
REM First program
COMMON VarA!, VarB%, ArrayC#()
   .
   .
   .
CHAIN "NewProg"
```

continues

Listing 22.3. Continued

```
END

REM NewProg     'Beginning of chained-to program
COMMON Var1!, Var2%, Array3#()
   .
   .
END
```

Now the variable VarA! in the first program corresponds through the common block to the variable Var1! in the second program. Similarly, VarB% and Var2% correspond, as do ArrayC# and Array3#.

You should use the identical number and type of variables when each program declares a shared common block. However, it's permissible to relax this requirement.

For example, suppose the first program declares a common block containing five variables. If the chained-to program requires only the first two variables in the common block, the COMMON instruction inside the second program needs to specify only the first two variables. (However, if the second program needs access to, for example, the first and fifth variables, the COMMON instruction inside the second program must declare all five variables so that the number and type of each variable match.)

Wholesale Variable Typing—*DEFtype*

By default, QBasic treats any variable without a type-declaration suffix as single precision. With a DEFtype instruction, you can change this default to one of the other data types.

The five DEFtype instructions have a similar form.

STATEMENT

```
DEFINT letterranges
DEFLNG letterranges
DEFSNG letterranges
DEFDBL letterranges
DEFSTR letterranges
```
where

  letterranges specifies a range of letters.

Each DEF*type* instruction corresponds to a particular data type (see Table 22.1).

Table 22.1. Data types of the DEFtype statements.	
Statement	**Data Type**
DEFINT	Integer
DEFLNG	Long integer
DEFSNG	Single-precision
DEFDBL	Double-precision
DEFSTR	String

A DEF*type* instruction changes the default data type for all subsequent (nonsuffixed) variables that begin with a letter included in the *letterranges* parameter. DEF*type* instructions also affect array names and user-defined FN function names.

For example, the following instruction declares that all variables beginning with the letter C are of type integer:

```
DEFINT C
```

After this instruction, variables named C, Cost, and CheckDeposit would all be type integer. Furthermore, a function defined by DEF FNCustomerID returns an integer value (*Customer* begins with *C* and is therefore affected by the DEFINT instruction).

The *letterranges* parameter is either an individual letter from A to Z or a letter range indicated by two letters separated with a dash. You can specify multiple ranges in a single instruction. To do so, separate ranges with commas.

Here are some more examples of DEF*type* instructions:

```
DEFDBL A, Q-T
```

```
DEFSTR A-Z
```

```
DEFINT C-F, R, T, W-Z
```

If you specify a lowercase letter in *letterranges*, the editor converts the letter to uppercase in the DEF*type* instruction. However, QBasic does not distinguish between upper- and lowercase letters in the subsequently affected variables. For example, after DEFINT A, variables beginning with upper- or lowercase A are considered type integer.

DEF*type* instructions affect only variables whose names have no trailing type character (%, &, !, #, or $). A type-declaration suffix on a variable takes precedence over any default(s) established with DEF. For example, consider this program fragment:

```
DEFINT N
Number = 2
Number$ = "Few"
```

There's no conflict in the two variables. The DEFINT instruction causes the first variable, Number, to be treated as an integer variable. The second variable, Number$, is a different variable and is of string type due to the explicit dollar sign suffix. (Although this program fragment works, to maximize program clarity you should avoid multiple variables with the same root name.)

However, a variable with a suffix is the same as a suffix-less variable affected by an appropriate DEF*type* instruction. For example, in the following program fragment, A and A$ are the same variable:

```
DEFSTR A
A = "Hello"
PRINT A
PRINT A$
```

The program displays Hello twice.

Because single-precision is the initial default data type, you need DEFSNG only when you want to undo the effect of a prior DEF*type* instruction.

Understanding When *DEFtype* Instructions Apply

DEF*type* instructions can appear anywhere in your program and affect the data typing of subsequent variables. Data typing is done before QBasic starts your program. Only the physical order (not the execution order) of the instructions matters. (This is different than in BASICA.)

QBasic scans instructions sequentially and, for each new variable, if no explicit type character is present, assigns the data type of the most recently applicable DEF*type*. Some situations are tricky. For example:

■ QBasic "sees" DEF*type* instructions even if the program can never execute them. You cannot bypass the effect of DEF*type* instructions by branching around them. Consider this program fragment:

```
DEFSTR A
GOTO Continue
DEFINT A
Continue:
A = "Hello"
```

This generates a Type mismatch error. Although the DEFINT A instruction is not in the execution path, the instruction is active when the variable A appears.

■ Once defined, the data type of the variable cannot be changed. Take a look at this example:

```
DEFSTR G
Continue:
Greeting = "Hello"
PRINT Greeting
DEFINT G
GOTO Continue
```

This program works in the sense that it generates an unending display of `Hello` messages. Once the data type of `Greeting` is established as string, it cannot be changed.

DEFtype and Procedures

When you create a procedure (a subprogram or function), QBasic assumes that `DEFtype` instructions in the main program apply to that procedure as well. Therefore, when the editor opens a window for typing the new procedure, you see a copy of the active `DEFtype` instructions above the `SUB` or `FUNCTION` instruction.

We have some straightforward advice on using `DEFtype` instructions: Don't! **T I P**

We recommend you use explicit data type suffixes on all your variable names (or let nonsuffixed variables always default to single-precision). This avoids possible ambiguities and errors resulting from certain typos. Many programmers balk at this advice, complaining of the extra cumbersome keystrokes needed for the suffix characters. Our counter-argument is simply that the extra keystrokes become easy and natural once you acquire the habit. And you can acquire the habit with just a few programs. Try it.

Because we recommend using the suffixes, as a general rule, we recommend against using `DEFtype` instructions. There is too much danger of programming mistakes due to confusion about which default data type is in effect at a certain point in the program.

Of course, we really shouldn't say "never." There are two programming situations in which `DEFtype` instructions make sense:

■ A relatively short program with few variables. In such a case, it is easy to keep track of every variable name.

■ A program in which *every* variable has the same data type, usually integer. A single `DEFINT A - Z` instruction takes care of all the variables.

This is important, because active DEF*type* instructions control the default data type for formal parameters and for function names that don't have an explicit type-declaration suffix. Edit these DEF*type* instructions if you want to change the defaults for any particular procedure.

Command Line Options

From the DOS prompt (C> for example), the simple command qbasic starts QBasic. The qbasic command accepts several optional arguments (see Table 22.2).

Table 22.2. Optional *qbasic* arguments.

Argument	Effect
/b	Displays in black and white
/editor	Invokes the MS-DOS Editor as a text editor
/ed	Same as /editor
/g	Disables CGA snow checking
/h	Displays highest possible resolution
/mbf	Selects Microsoft Binary Format
/nohi	Supports monitors that don't produce high-intensity
/run *sourcefile*	Loads and runs the specified source file
sourcefile	Loads the specified source file

You can specify none, one, or several options. Multiple options can be given in any order. Use at least one space to separate adjacent options. Table 22.3 gives some examples of commands used to start QBasic.

Table 22.3. Sample *qbasic* invocations.

Command	Effect
qbasic DOIT	Loads, but does not execute, DOIT.BAS
qbasic /run DOIT	Loads and executes DOIT.BAS
qbasic \prog\DOIT	Loads, but does not execute, DOIT.BAS found in the \prog directory
qbasic /b DOIT	Selects black-and-white display and loads DOIT.BAS
qbasic /mbf /b /g	Selects several options

Here's a more detailed explanation of each command option:

/b	Displays QBasic in black and white. Select this option if you use a black-and-white monitor with a CGA video card, or if you desire a black-and-white display with a color monitor.
/editor	Invokes the MS-DOS text editor rather than QBasic. This command has the same effect as typing edit directly from the DOS command line. The MS-DOS text editor, introduced with MS-DOS 5, is contained within the QBASIC.EXE file.
/g	Selects the fastest possible video I/O on systems with a CGA video card. This option can cause flicker (often called "snow") during rapid scrolling. Without this option, QBasic eliminates flicker at the expense of somewhat slower video updating. Affects CGA systems only.
/h	Selects the highest possible resolution supported by QBasic and your video hardware. Puts EGA and VGA systems in 43-line mode, for example.
/mbf	QBasic normally works with single- and double-precision numbers in IEEE format. Selecting this option causes the conversion functions MKS\$, MKD\$, CVS, and CVD to use Microsoft Binary Format rather than IEEE format when decoding numbers. Microsoft Binary Format is the default for BASICA/GW-BASIC and other older versions of BASIC.
/nohi	Some monitors do not produce high-intensity video well (or at all). This option provides a clearer display on such monitors. However, the option does not work well with some laptop computers.
/run *sourcefile*	Loads and runs the file specified by *sourcefile*. If *sourcefile* does not contain an explicit extension, .BAS is assumed.
sourcefile	Loads but does not run the file specified by *sourcefile*.

Manipulating Integers at the Bit Level

QBasic stores regular integers (short integers) in two memory bytes. A memory byte consists of eight bits, so the representation of an integer uses 16 bits altogether.

As discussed in Chapter 19, "Managing Memory," the 16-bit pattern can be interpreted as four hexadecimal digits, each hex digit consisting of four bits. For example, the decimal number 19,150 has the hexadecimal value of 4ACE. Translating to bit patterns, 4ACE becomes 0100 1010 1100 1110. In other words, QBasic stores the decimal value of 19,150 as the 16-bit number 0100101011001110.

Every integer value is represented as a *signed* 16-bit number. The high order (leftmost) bit indicates the sign of the number: 0 for a positive number, 1 for a negative number.

So, if the leftmost bit is 0, the number is positive (or zero). The remaining 15 bits express the value from 0 to 32,767.

If the leftmost bit is 1, the number is negative. QBasic uses an inverse ordering for the negative numbers: 1 followed by 15 zeroes represents the smallest negative number (–32768); 1 followed by 15 more ones represents the "largest" negative number (–1).

Long integer values are signed 32-bit numbers, which require four memory bytes to store. See Appendix E, "Internal Data Formats," for additional information.

Logical Operations on Integers

The logical operators (AND, OR, XOR, NOT, IMP, EQV) manipulate integer values at the bit level. In a logical expression, QBasic reduces each operand to a bit pattern and performs the logical operation on each pair of corresponding bits. (Refer back to Figure 7.2 to see the results of each logical operator. A 0 bit represents a "False" value and a 1 bit represents a "True" value.)

For example, the expression 23 AND 25 is equivalent to ANDing the bit pattern 0000 0000 0001 0111 together with 0000 0000 0001 1001. The result is 0000 0000 0001 0001, which has the value 17. You can demonstrate this technique with the instruction PRINT 23 AND 25. QBasic displays the result 17.

If one operand is a long integer and the other is a short integer, QBasic converts the short integer to a long integer before doing the evaluation.

Figure 22.1 shows another example of evaluating a logical expression.

```
Evaluate (NOT A%) XOR (B% IMP C%)
where A% = –312, B% = &HAF73, C% = 1482

A% = –312 = & HFEC8 =    1 1 1 1 1 1 1 0 1 1 0 0 1 0 0 0
                                                           NOT
NOT A% =                 0 0 0 0 0 0 0 1 0 0 1 1 0 1 1 1

B% =        & HAF73 =    1 0 1 0 1 1 1 1 0 1 1 1 0 0 1 1
C% = 1 4 8 2 = &H05CA =  0 0 0 0 0 1 0 1 1 1 0 0 1 0 1 0
                                                           IMP
B% IMP C% =              0 1 0 1 0 1 0 1 1 1 0 0 1 1 1 0

NOT A% =                 0 0 0 0 0 0 0 1 0 0 1 1 0 1 1 1
B% IMP C% =              0 1 0 1 0 1 0 1 1 1 0 0 1 1 1 0
                                                           XOR
Result =                 0 1 0 1 0 1 0 0 1 1 1 1 1 0 0 1

0 1 0 1 0 1 0 0 1 1 1 1 1 0 0 1 = & H54F9 = 21753
```

Figure 22.1.

Evaluating a logical expression.

Bit Masking

Sometimes you need to know whether particular bits in a variable (or function value) are 1 or 0. For example, the ERDEV function returns a 16-bit value (an integer number). However, only the rightmost four bits specify the nature of the error. (See Chapter 21, "Trapping Errors and Events," for a discussion of ERDEV.)

The task is to isolate the rightmost four bits without regard to the value of the other 12 bits. One technique that solves this problem is known as *bit masking.* A *bit mask* is a specific number (bit configuration) which, when combined with the target value using the appropriate logical operator, masks the undesired bits.

For example, consider the bit mask 0000 0000 0000 1111. The leftmost 12 bits are 0 and the rightmost four bits are 1. If you AND this bit mask with *any* 16-bit target configuration, the leftmost 12 bits of the result are always zero (because 0 ANDed with anything produces 0). Each of the rightmost four bits becomes 1 only if the corresponding target bit contains a 1.

In other words, the result consists of 12 zero bits followed by the same rightmost four bits contained in the target configuration. The leftmost 12 bits in the target configuration have been masked.

Here the bit mask consists of the hex digits 000F, which can be represented as &HF in QBasic. If you want to mask the leftmost 12 bits in the value of ERDEV, the following instruction does the trick:

```
ErrorCode% = &HF AND ERDEV
```

ErrorCode% always contains a hex value from 0 to F. If you display the value with PRINT ErrorCode%, you see a number from 0 to 15.

Similarly, you can construct other bit masks that mask any particular bit configuration.

Shelling to DOS

A *DOS shell* is a second invocation of DOS. The original invocation (or process) remains in memory.

COMMAND.COM is the default DOS command processor. When you shell, a second copy of COMMAND.COM opens to handle the new process. The original process remains suspended. When the new process terminates and closes, control passes back to the original process.

In standard terminology, the original process is called the *parent* process. The parent shells to a second process called the *child* process.

You can shell to a child process from within a program. Execution suspends while a new copy of DOS opens. Here are some things you can do with QBasic's shelling facility:

- Issue DOS commands from your QBasic program
- Execute batch or executable files in the middle of your program
- Open a temporary DOS shell so you can type interactive DOS commands
- Examine or modify the contents of the DOS-environment table

Using the *SHELL* Instruction

SHELL opens a DOS shell while retaining QBasic in memory.

STATEMENT

SHELL

or

SHELL *commandstring*

where

commandstring specifies a program (or process) to run in the new DOS shell.

By itself, SHELL invokes a new DOS shell and displays the DOS prompt. Users now can issue any series of DOS commands. Use the DOS command EXIT to close the shell and return to the QBasic program. Execution continues with the instruction following SHELL.

With the *commandstring* parameter, SHELL invokes a DOS shell and automatically runs the command specified in *commandstring*. When the DOS program terminates, the DOS shell closes, and control returns to QBasic at the instruction following SHELL.

The *commandstring* parameter is a string that can be expressed as a string literal (in quotation marks) or a string variable whose contents contain the name of the desired command. The command specified in *commandstring* can be a standard DOS command such as DIR, COPY, or SORT, or *commandstring* can specify a .COM, .EXE, or .BAT file. If you don't include an extension with the program name in your command string, DOS tries .COM, .EXE, and .BAT, in that order. For example, consider this instruction:

```
SHELL "SHOWLIST"
```

DOS first looks for a DOS command named SHOWLIST. Because there isn't such a command, DOS next looks for executable files named SHOWLIST.COM, then SHOWLIST.EXE, and finally SHOWLIST.BAT. The first one found is run. If none are found, you get the standard DOS error message: Bad command or file name. However, control returns to QBasic, and your program resumes.

A new DOS shell invokes at the directory from which you launched QBasic, which might not be the directory from which your loaded program is running. The following instruction displays a listing of the directory from which you began QBasic even if your loaded program is contained in some other directory:

```
SHELL "DIR"
```

Be sure to include any necessary parameters as part of *commandstring*. A COPY command, for example, requires at least one file parameter (and usually two file parameters). DOS requires at least one blank space between the filename and the argument string.

The following instruction copies all the files in the directory CLIENTS into the directory BACKUP. Notice the blank space after COPY:

```
SHELL "COPY \CLIENTS\*.* \BACKUP"
```

Controlling the DOS Environment with *ENVIRON* and *ENVIRON$*

DOS maintains an area in RAM called the *DOS environment table*. This area stores text information about the current DOS environment.

The table usually contains such items as COMSPEC (the name of the command processor—usually COMMAND.COM), PATH (optional paths in your directory tree), and PROMPT (the string definition of the DOS system prompt). DOS commands and user programs can examine this table to ascertain the current environment.

With an ENVIRON instruction, your QBasic program can modify the DOS environment table. The companion function, ENVIRON$, returns the table's current contents.

ENVIRON and ENVIRON$ are typically used to configure the DOS environment before issuing a SHELL instruction.

Using an *ENVIRON* Instruction

<table>
<tr>
<td>

S
T
A
T
E
M
E
N
T

</td>
<td>

ENVIRON *strexpr*

where

    strexpr is a string expression that specifies a modification to the DOS environment table.

</td>
</tr>
</table>

strexpr specifies both a DOS table parameter and a value for that parameter. You can use either an equal sign or a blank space to separate the parameter from the value. For example, the following two instructions are equivalent:

```
ENVIRON "PROMPT=Shell$g"     'Equal sign separator

ENVIRON "PROMPT Shell$g"     'Blank space separator
```

After a SHELL, each of these ENVIRON instructions change the DOS prompt to appear as follows:

```
Shell>
```

You can use ENVIRON to add a parameter to the table, modify an existing parameter, or delete a parameter.

To add a new parameter, use ENVIRON to specify a parameter not currently in the table. The new parameter and value are appended to the environment table. Be aware, however, that you usually have only a small amount of free string space in the table. You might get an Out of memory error when you try to append.

To delete an existing entry, use a null string or a semicolon as the value for the parameter. The existing parameter specification is removed from the table. Either of the following two instructions, for example, deletes the PROMPT string from the table (DOS reverts to the default prompt A> or C>):

```
ENVIRON "PROMPT="

ENVIRON "PROMPT ;"      'Note blank space before the semicolon
```

To modify an existing entry, simply specify a new value. The old value is deleted and replaced by your new entry. The following instruction, for example, replaces any PATH specification in the environment table with the new specification:

```
ENVIRON "PATH=C:\CLIENTS;C:\CONTRACT\NASA"
```

Be aware that any changes made with ENVIRON are not permanent. When your program terminates, DOS reinstates the environment table to the configuration it had when your program began.

Using the *ENVIRON$* Function

The ENVIRON$ function has two distinct forms.

```
ENVIRON$(integerexpr)          'numeric-parameter form

or

ENVIRON$(environmentstr)       'string-parameter form
```
where

    integerexpr specifies the ordinal number of the table entry to return,

and

    environmentstr is a string expression that specifies a parameter in the environment table.

F
U
N
C
T
I
O
N

In the numeric form of ENVIRON$, *integerexpr* specifies which line in the DOS environment table to return. For example, PRINT ENVIRON$(3) displays the third line in the table. If *integerexpr* specifies a line beyond the end of the table, the null string is returned. You can use any numeric expression to specify *integerexpr*; if necessary, QBasic rounds the value to the nearest integer.

The following program fragment displays the entire environment table. The effect is similar to the DOS command SET.

```
Counter% = 1
WHILE ENVIRON$(Counter%) <> ""
    PRINT ENVIRON$(Counter%)
    Counter% = Counter% + 1
WEND
```

Here's the output produced by one of our computer systems. Of course, your output probably will differ.

```
COMSPEC=C:\COMMAND.COM
PROMPT=$e[31;44;1m$p$g$e[32;44;1m
PATH=C:\;C:\DOS;C:\MOUSE;C:\BIN;C:\QBASIC
LIB=C:\LIB
```

In the string form of ENVIRON$, *environmentstr* specifies the parameter and ENVIRON$ returns the value. In our computer environment, for example, the instruction PRINT ENVIRON$("LIB") produces the following output:

```
C:\LIB
```

The following program fragment changes the PATH specification with ENVIRON and displays the results with ENVIRON$:

```
PRINT "Current PATH is "; ENVIRON$("PATH")
PRINT
ENVIRON "PATH=C:\CLIENTS;C:\CONTRACT\NASA"
PRINT "Updated PATH is "; ENVIRON$("PATH")
```

The output is

```
Current PATH is C:\;C:\DOS;C:\MOUSE;C:\BIN;C:\QBASIC

Updated PATH is C:\CLIENTS;C:\CONTRACT\NASA
```

One caution about ENVIRON$: *environmentstr* is case-sensitive. Because upper-case parameters appear in our environment table, the following function does not work:

```
ENVIRON$("path")
```

If the specified parameter is not found in the environment table, ENVIRON$ returns a null string.

Communicating with I/O Ports

Your computer's microprocessor communicates with peripherals through I/O ports. The I/O ports are hardware channels that funnel data to and from such devices as the keyboard, disk drives, and printers.

Each port is identified by a 16-bit port number that can range from 0 to 65,535. A port number frequently is called an address, even though a port "address" is part of the I/O device and not a location in main memory.

Specific port numbers are established by each computer model's designer. Many port numbers are standardized in the IBM PC family, but some port numbers differ among computer models. Consult your computer's technical documentation to determine relevant port numbers for your system.

Port addresses and communication protocols are normally the domain of DOS and especially the BIOS (Basic Input/Output System). As a QBasic programmer, you can lead a very productive programming life and not ever have to worry about I/O ports. The QBasic instructions that generate I/O automatically interface properly with the ports.

QBasic nevertheless provides some explicit port communication (see Table 22.4).

Table 22.4. Communicating with I/O ports.

Keyword	Type	Action
INP	Function	Returns the byte read from a specified port
OUT	Statement	Sends a designated byte to a specified port
WAIT	Statement	Suspends program execution until a specified port achieves a designated bit pattern

Here's the syntax for the INP function:

<table>
<tr><td>

F U N C T I O N

</td><td>

`INP(`*`portnum`*`)`

where

    portnum specifies the port number as a long integer expression in the range from 0 to 65,535.

</td></tr>
</table>

Here's the syntax for OUT and WAIT:

<table>
<tr><td>

S T A T E M E N T

</td><td>

`OUT `*`portnum`*`, `*`databyte`*

`WAIT `*`portnum`*`, `*`andbyte`*`, `*`xorbyte`*

where

    portnum specifies the port number as a long integer expression in the range from 0 to 65,535,

    databyte specifies the data to send to the designated port,

    andbyte is an integer expression from 0 to 255 to be ANDed with the data at the designated port,

and

    xorbyte is an integer expression from 0 to 255 to be XORed with the data at the designated port.

</td></tr>
</table>

In a WAIT instruction, the *xorbyte* parameter is optional.

Using the *INP* Function

The subprogram CheckLPT in Listing 22.4 checks that the line printer is ready to print. If the printer isn't ready (for example, turned off, off-line, or out of paper), the subprogram waits until you correct the problem. CheckLPT is handy for any program that directs output to the printer. Call the CheckLPT subprogram before you send data to print.

Listing 22.4. The CheckLPT subprogram.

```
SUB CheckLPT
REM Makes sure that the line printer is ready
   DEF SEG = &H40                              'BIOS data area
   StatusPort& = PEEK(9) * 256 + PEEK(8) + 1   'Get port for LPT1
   IF INP(StatusPort&) <> 223 THEN
      PRINT "Printer is not ready - Check that"
      PRINT "  1) Printer is turned on"
      PRINT "  2) Printer is online"
      PRINT "  3) Paper is loaded"
      DO
      LOOP UNTIL INP(StatusPort&) = 223         'Wait till ready
   END IF
   PRINT "Printer is ready"
   DEF SEG                                      'Restore default segment
END SUB
```

CheckLPT examines the printer's status port to determine whether the printer
is ready. The BIOS stores the two-byte base address of the printer ports at
locations 0040:0008 and 0040:0009. The status port is offset one byte from this
base address. These addresses assume your line printer is configured as LPT1
(the usual configuration). If your printer is configured as LPT2, change the
assignment of StatusPort& as follows:

```
StatusPort& = PEEK(11) * 256 + PEEK(10) + 1
```

When the status port registers 223 (bit pattern = 11011111), your printer is on-
line and ready to print. Other port values indicate a problem. Notice how
CheckLPT uses the INP function to read the status port. If the port does not
return 223, CheckLPT continues to monitor the port until 223 occurs.

 **NOTE** The value 223 is the EPSON standard for indicating that the printer
is ready. This standard, used by most printers, is recognized by
most IBM compatibles. Before using this subprogram, verify that
223 is the correct value for your system. Use the following instruction to display the value returned from your printer status port:

```
PRINT INP(StatusPort&)
```

Using the *OUT* Instruction

OUT sends a data byte to the designated port. Listing 22.5, DRIVEON.BAS, uses OUT to control disk drive A:'s motor:

Listing 22.5. The DRIVEON.BAS program.

```
REM Program: DRIVEON.BAS (Turn disk drive A: on and off)

PRINT "Now turning on the motor in disk drive A:"
PRINT "Press a key to stop the motor"

DO
    OUT &H3F2, 28         'Turns on the motor of floppy drive A:
LOOP UNTIL INKEY$ <> ""

OUT &H3F2, 12            'Turn off the motor of drive A:
END
```

The floppy disk controller is operated through several I/O ports. The port at address &H3F2 selects the various drives and turns them on and off. By sending 28 (bit pattern 00011100) to this port, the floppy controller selects drive A: and whirs the motor, which turns on the drive light. The motor is turned off by sending 12 (bit pattern 00001100).

DRIVEON.BAS simply whirs the motor in drive A: but does not engage the read and write heads. You can use this program safely regardless of whether any disks are actually in the drive.

Using the *WAIT* Instruction

WAIT suspends your program while continually monitoring the port designated by *portnum*. The byte at the port is first XORed with the *xorbyte* parameter. Then this temporary result is ANDed with the value of *andbyte*. (The *xorbyte* byte parameter is optional. QBasic uses a value of 0 for *xorbyte* if you don't explicitly specify the parameter.)

If the final result is nonzero, QBasic resumes your program at the instruction following WAIT. If the result is 0, however, QBasic rereads the port and continues the process.

andbyte and *xorbyte* represent bit masks. Each 1-bit in *andbyte* corresponds to a port bit you want to turn on. Each 1-bit in *xorbyte* corresponds to a port bit you want to turn off.

WAIT tests individual bits more effectively than it tests an entire bit pattern. Notice that *any* nonzero result, not a specific nonzero result, causes your program to resume. If any of the bits masked by *andbyte* and *xorbyte* are matched, your program resumes. Consider the following instruction, for example:

```
WAIT MyPort&, 13
```

QBasic ANDs the bit pattern at MyPort& with the bit pattern represented by 13 (00001101). Notice that the result is nonzero if any of the masked bits (bits 0, 2, and 3) are on. The *xorbyte* parameter works similarly. You cannot use WAIT to test MyPort& for the exact pattern 00001101.

Communicating with Devices

In your programs, device communication is mostly automatic. For example, PRINT instructions display information on-screen and INPUT instructions read input from the keyboard. You can use these instructions without even thinking about how the device input and output takes place. Your program doesn't have to do anything special to initialize either the screen or the keyboard.

For situations that require more demanding device communication, QBasic provides two features:

- Opening devices as files
- Interfacing with device drivers

Device Files

You can open a specific I/O (input/output) device in the same way that you open a data file on disk. Use an OPEN instruction with a device name rather than a disk file. The following instruction, for example, opens the second line printer for output:

```
OPEN "LPT2:" FOR OUTPUT AS #2
```

(See Chapter 14, "Using Sequential Disk Files," and Chapter 15, "Using Random and Binary Disk Files," for a general description of the OPEN instruction.)

Table 22.5 shows the specific devices you can open and the name QBasic uses to identify each device in the OPEN instruction.

Table 22.5. QBasic file devices.

Name	Device
COM1:	First serial port
COM2:	Second serial port
CONS:	CRT screen
SCRN:	CRT screen
KYBD:	Keyboard
LPT1:	First printer
LPT2:	Second printer
LPT3:	Third printer

Generally, you open each device for either INPUT or OUTPUT, as appropriate. (You obviously should not open the keyboard for OUTPUT or the screen for INPUT.) As discussed later in this chapter, the COM devices can be opened for simultaneous input and output.

After a device is opened, communicate with it by using PRINT#, INPUT#, and the other I/O statements described in Chapter 14. When I/O finishes, close the device with CLOSE.

Device files do not buffer I/O, but simply transmit data one character at a time. The OPEN instruction's LEN parameter is meaningless; the record length of each device file is 1.

Why use device files? Device files are the only way to send output to a second or third printer. LPRINT instructions send output only to LPT1. The following program fragment writes a short message on your second line printer (assuming you have two line printers):

```
OPEN "LPT2:" FOR OUTPUT AS #2
PRINT #2, "Hello from printer number 2"
CLOSE 2
```

Here's another problem solved by device files. Suppose your program has several PRINT instructions. At the beginning of the program, you ask users to indicate whether the output should go to the printer or to the screen. You want to route the output to the requested destination.

As a brute-force solution you could write duplicate PRINT and LPRINT instructions and set a flag to indicate printer output or screen output. Then, before each message, test the flag and branch to the appropriate instruction. This method works, but it is needlessly cumbersome.

Device files provide a better solution: simply test the flag once and open the appropriate device file. Use the same file number on each OPEN instruction. Then, for each output instruction, you need only one PRINT# instruction that directs output to this file number.

The following program fragment shows the general technique. The Destination$ variable has the value "Printer" if the user requests printed output, or "Screen" if the user requests screen output.

```
IF Destination$ = "Printer" THEN
   OPEN "LPT1:" FOR OUTPUT AS #5
ELSE
   OPEN "SCRN:" FOR OUTPUT AS #5
END IF
   .
PRINT #5, FirstMessage$
   .
PRINT #5, NextMessage$
   .
CLOSE #5
```

Using a *WIDTH* Instruction with Device Files

A special version of the WIDTH instruction adjusts the width of output devices. There are three different forms of this special WIDTH instruction.

```
WIDTH devicename, width

WIDTH #filename, width

WIDTH LPRINT width
```

where

    devicename is the device name in string form (for example, "LPT2:"),

    filenum specifies the file number under which the device was opened,

and

    width specifies the desired width on the output device.

S
T
A
T
E
M
E
N
T

Changing the width confines output to the number of columns specified by *width*. The *width* parameter can be any integer expression.

With the *filenum* parameter, you can change the width of the device while the file is open. For example, consider this program fragment:

```
OPEN "SCRN:" FOR OUTPUT AS #5
WIDTH #5, 4
PRINT #5, "My dog has fleas"
PRINT
WIDTH #5, 7
PRINT #5, "My dog has fleas"
CLOSE #5
```

The screen output is

```
My d
og h
as f
leas

My dog
has fle
as
```

Notice that this technique provides a way to set the screen width to a value other than 40 or 80.

With the *devicename* parameter, the width adjustment does not occur until the next OPEN instruction on the specified device. Here's an example instruction:

```
WIDTH "LPT1", 66    'Set the width of printer when next opened
```

The WIDTH LPRINT form sets the line width of your printer (LPT1:). See Chapter 16, "Using Hardware Devices," for more information about WIDTH LPRINT.

Using the *OPEN COM* Instruction with Device Files

QBasic gives special attention to controlling the serial ports COM1: and COM2:. The OPEN COM instruction accepts several optional parameters.

```
OPEN "COMport: options" FOR mode AS #filenum LEN = numbytes
```

where

    port is 1 or 2, designating COM1: or COM2:,

    options specifies various optional settings as explained in the text,

    mode specifies the access mode as INPUT, OUTPUT, or RANDOM,

    filenum specifies a file number to associate with the device,

and

    numbytes is the buffer length when the serial port is opened in RANDOM mode.

The *options* clause is optional. Both the FOR *mode* and LEN = *numbytes* clauses are optional. Also, the pound sign character (#) in front of the *filenum* parameter is optional.

S
T
A
T
E
M
E
N
T

The ensuing discussion of OPEN COM assumes you have some technical knowledge of communications terminology and acronyms.

The *options* clause, if present, can be broken down into two subclauses: a *primaryoptions* clause followed by a *secondaryoptions* clause. The *primaryoptions* clause specifies the baud rate, parity, data bits, and stop bits; the *secondaryoptions* clause specifies additional optional parameters.

The *primaryoptions* clause has the following form:

```
baud, parity, data, stop
```

Table 22.6 describes the primary options.

Table 22.6. Primary options in *OPEN COM.*

Option	Default	Description
baud	300	Baud rate. Typical values are 300, 1200, 2400, and 9600. Many other values are valid.
parity	E	Parity. Legal values are N, E, O, S, M, and PE, which correspond to None, Even, Odd, Space, Mark, and Enable error checking respectively.
data	7	Number of data bits. Legal values are 5, 6, 7, and 8.
stop	1	Number of stop bits. Legal values are 1, 1.5, and 2.

A comma must appear as a placeholder for any option you don't specify. For example, the following instruction opens COM1: at 1200 baud with two stop bits:

```
OPEN "COM1: 1200, , , 2" FOR RANDOM AS #7
```

Table 22.7 shows the options available in *secondaryoptions*. Unlike the primary options, you can specify selected secondary options in any order. Use commas to separate multiple entries.

Table 22.7. Secondary options in *OPEN COM*.

Option	Description
ASC	Opens the serial port in ASCII mode.
BIN	Opens the serial port in binary mode; BIN is the default if you don't select ASC.
CD*m*	Issues a device timeout if the Data Carrier Detect line is inactive for *m* milliseconds.
CS*m*	Issues a device timeout if the Clear to Send line is inactive for *m* milliseconds.
DS*m*	Issues a device timeout if the Data Set Ready line is inactive for *m* milliseconds.
LF	Appends a line-feed character to every carriage return (for serial line printers).
OP*m*	Waits up to *m* milliseconds for OPEN to succeed; if you omit *m*, the default wait is 10 seconds.
RB*b*	Sets the receive buffer to *b* bytes where *b* can be as much as 32,767; if you omit *b*, the default value is 512.
RS	Suppresses the Request to Send line.
TB*b*	Sets the transmit buffer to *b* bytes; if you omit *b*, the default is 512.

If you choose one or more secondary options, you must be sure that the entire *primaryoptions* list is present (even if the options appear with placeholders only). Look at the following example:

```
OPEN "COM2: , , , , ASC" FOR RANDOM AS #5
```

Notice that the mode parameter in the OPEN COM instruction permits random-access communications. Unlike the other device files, COM files can be opened simultaneously for input and output. Of course, serial communications with modems demand two-way data flow. RANDOM is the default mode if you omit the *mode* parameter.

In RANDOM mode, you can use any of the random-access I/O statements and functions (see Chapter 15, "Using Random and Binary Disk Files"). In particular, use GET and PUT to input and output data. Communication is buffered in RANDOM mode. The LEN parameter on the OPEN COM instruction specifies the size for this buffer.

The random-access functions EOF, LOC, or LOF return information about the communications buffer (see Table 22.8).

Table 22.8. Random-access buffer functions.

Function	Value Returned
EOF	TRUE if no characters are in the buffer
LOC	Number of characters in the buffer
LOF	Number of unused bytes in the buffer

Device Drivers

A device driver is a DOS-level program that controls a specific peripheral device, such as a particular model of a printer or mouse. Device drivers link the hardware peripheral with the general I/O routines of the DOS and BIOS. The device driver must understand the device's control codes for the device to perform as expected.

Vendors of major software products usually supply several device drivers to control devices their customers might have. Your favorite word processing or spreadsheet program, for example, probably includes several device drivers that support many kinds of printers (including yours, you hope).

Device drivers require specialized code protocols. Normally, the drivers are written in C or in assembly language. QBasic can communicate with device drivers through the IOCTL statement and the IOCTL$ function. IOCTL sends string data and IOCTL$ reads strings sent from the driver.

To communicate with a device driver, you must know that the device driver is installed and that it processes IOCTL strings. And you must know, of course, the meanings of any strings you send or receive. Furthermore, you must open the device driver with an OPEN instruction.

S
T
A
T
E
M
E
N
T

IOCTL #*filenum*, *strexpr*

IOCTL$(#*filenum*)

where

 filenum specifies the file number associated with the device driver,

and

 strexpr is a general string expression to be sent to the device driver.

The pound sign character (#) in front of *filenum* is optional.

In a typical use, IOCTL$ acknowledges that the device driver receives a string sent by IOCTL. The following example uses a (fictitious) driver to replace the normal screen driver. The string "BC2" is a request to change the screen border to color number 2. The IOCTL$ function reads a return string that specifies the border color.

```
OPEN "C:\MONITOR\MYDRIVER" FOR OUTPUT AS #9
IOCTL #9, "BC2"                        'Sets the border to color 2
IF IOCTL$(9) = "2" THEN PRINT "OK"    'Driver returns border color
 .
 .
 .
```

Summary

Sometimes the list of QBasic's features seems to go on indefinitely. Indeed, QBasic offers a wealth of programming tools and features.

This chapter is a grab-bag collection of advanced QBasic programming topics. Among other things, you learned how to use common blocks, chain programs, shell to DOS, manipulate integers as bit patterns, and communicate with ports and devices.

Explore this chapter as your time permits and your programming needs demand. Try some of the short programs. Your confidence and programming expertise will grow rapidly.

Understanding Other Versions of BASIC

P A R T

V

O U T L I N E

You now have a thorough understanding of QBasic. With this expertise, you have the power enjoyed by the programmers' fraternity: the ability to write programs for nearly all your computing needs.

But QBasic does not exist in a vacuum. Not only are there many other programming languages such as C and Pascal, there are many other versions of the BASIC language. Part V examines several popular versions of BASIC: BASICA, GW-BASIC, QuickBASIC, Visual Basic for MS-DOS, and Visual Basic for Windows. Familiarity with these other versions of BASIC increases your programming flexibility.

If you drew the BASIC family tree, BASICA and GW-BASIC would be QBasic's parents. Though you most likely won't be writing many new programs with these older versions of BASIC, you might want to convert existing BASICA and GW-BASIC programs to run under QBasic.

QuickBASIC is more like QBasic's older sibling. The programming languages are virtually identical. However, QuickBASIC offers a more professional programming environment featuring increased debugging tools, better support for managing independent program modules, and most importantly, the ability to compile programs into executable files which can run directly from DOS.

Event-driven BASIC languages represent not only the next generation, but also an evolutionary plateau. With Visual Basic for Windows, you can easily create professional-looking Windows applications complete with buttons, list boxes, and multiple windows. Visual Basic for MS-DOS provides the same type of functionality for programs written to run directly from DOS (that is, without Microsoft Windows).

Learning the GW-BASIC (BASICA) Programming Environment

G W-BASIC and BASICA are the venerable ancestors of QBasic. GW-BASIC came bundled with each version of MS-DOS until Microsoft released MS-DOS 5 in mid-1991. In that version of DOS, QBasic replaced GW-BASIC.

On IBM computers, BASICA came bundled with PC DOS. With the release of IBM DOS 5.0, IBM still bundles BASICA along with QBasic on PS/1 and PS/2 computer models.

The GW-BASIC and BASICA languages are essentially identical. (There are a few trivial differences). A program that runs successfully on one language will work 99.9 percent of the time on the other.

This chapter focuses on the GW-BASIC/BASICA programming environment. Emphasis is on the user interface and editing techniques. The next chapter explores the features in the programming language with special emphasis on how GW-BASIC/BASICA differ from QBasic.

 NOTE **BASIC = BASICA + GW-BASIC**

For notational convenience, we will use the term "BASIC" to refer to both GW-BASIC and BASICA in the rest of this chapter. So, for example, the phrase "BASIC supports full-screen editing" means that both BASICA and GW-BASIC support full-screen editing.

As a QBasic programmer, an understanding of BASIC remains important. Two situations are common:

■ You are working on a computer equipped with BASIC but not with QBasic. Such a computer would likely be running a version of DOS 3 or DOS 4. You might need to modify an existing BASIC program or write a new application.

■ You have an existing BASIC program which you would like to convert for use with QBasic. Such a program might be one you wrote previously, one obtained from a friend or coworker, or perhaps a program listing printed in a magazine.

Here are the main topics covered in this chapter:

■ Understanding the BASIC working environment

■ Executing commands in direct mode

■ Writing programs in indirect mode

■ Learning full-screen editing techniques

An Overview of BASIC

Unlike QBasic, BASIC does not feature a modern interface with pull-down menus and mouse support. Instead, BASIC works from a command line. When prompted, you type a command or a series of program lines. This command-line interface is similar to the DOS command-line interface used when typing a DOS command from the > prompt.

BASIC has two fundamental modes of operation:

■ *Direct Mode*. You enter a single command and BASIC immediately performs your requested action. This mode is similar to using the Immediate window in QBasic.

■ *Program Mode* (also called *indirect mode*). You create a program by typing a series of instructions, which are collected into a single unit. You then execute the entire program.

Installing BASIC

BASIC is usually installed as part of the normal installation of DOS. The details of installation depend on whether or not your computer has a hard disk.

Installing BASIC on a Hard Disk System

If your system has a hard disk, the installation of DOS places GW-BASIC or BASICA in the directory containing the other DOS files.

For convenience, create a working directory to store your programs. Give such a directory a descriptive name—such as \PROGRAMS or \BASIC.

Installing BASIC on a Floppy Disk System

If your computer is not equipped with a hard disk, you can run BASIC from a floppy disk. (Of course, you can run BASIC from a floppy disk even if your computer has a hard disk.) You can even save some BASIC programs on the same disk that contains the BASIC files.

With MS-DOS 4.0 or earlier, GW-BASIC is included with DOS in a file named GWBASIC.EXE. Copy this file onto another floppy disk to create a working BASIC disk.

On IBM computers, BASIC is contained in the file BASICA.COM on your DOS disk. Copy BASICA.COM onto another disk to create your working BASIC disk.

Starting BASIC

Now you're ready to start BASIC. Again, the details depend on whether you are using a hard disk system or a floppy disk system.

Starting BASIC on a Hard Disk System

First, make your BASIC work directory (\PROGRAMS in this example) the default directory. To do so, type the following command at the C> prompt:

```
C>CD \PROGRAMS
```

If you have an IBM computer, start BASIC with the following command:

```
C>BASICA
```

On a compatible, start BASIC with this command instead:

```
C>GWBASIC
```

Starting BASIC on a Floppy Disk System

Place your work disk (containing GWBASIC.EXE or BASICA.COM) in the A: drive.

If you have an IBM computer, type the following command at the A> prompt:

A>**BASICA**

If you have a compatible, type the following command instead:

A>**GWBASIC**

Understanding the Initial BASIC Screen

You have now started BASIC and your screen should look something like Figure 23.1. We say "something like" because your exact screen depends on whether you have BASICA or GW-BASIC, your version number of BASICA or GW-BASIC, and the amount of memory in your computer system.

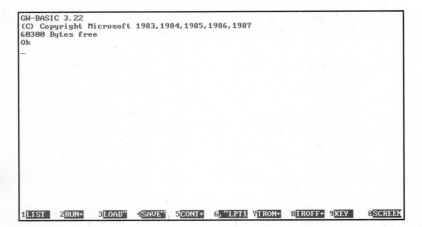

```
GW-BASIC 3.22
(C) Copyright Microsoft 1983,1984,1985,1986,1987
60300 Bytes free
Ok
_
```

```
1LIST   2RUN←   3LOAD"   4SAVE"   5CONT←   6, "LPT1   7TRON←   8TROFF←   9KEY    0SCREEN
```

Figure 23.1.

The Initial BASIC Screen on a typical computer.

Figure 23.1 shows the computer screen when BASIC is first started on an IBM-compatible machine. As you can see, this computer has version 3.22 of GW-BASIC.

Compare your screen with Figure 23.1. The first few lines on your screen identify the version of BASIC and specify various copyrights and licenses.

Your screen might display more than four lines at the top, or possibly less than four lines.

The line containing "Bytes free" indicates the amount of memory available for BASIC programs and data. The number of free bytes shown on your screen will likely be different than the 60,300 free bytes available on the example system.

The BASIC Prompt—Ok

The next line says simply Ok. Ok is the BASIC prompt. This prompt tells you that BASIC is waiting for you to enter the next command. When you enter a BASIC command, BASIC executes it (or tries to execute it), and then again displays the Ok prompt. Ok is BASIC's way of saying, "I did what you asked and I'm ready for what you want to do next."

This continual prompting represents a significant departure from QBasic. In QBasic, you work from a menu-based system in which you issue commands by selecting items from pull-down menus (or by using special hotkeys). With BASICA and GW-BASIC, you issue commands by typing them in response to an on-screen prompt—similar to the way you type DOS commands at the DOS prompt (>).

The BASIC Cursor—A Blinking Line

A blinking line appears on the line below the Ok prompt. This line, actually the underscore character, is the *cursor*. Just as with QBasic or your favorite word processor, the cursor indicates where the next character you type will appear on-screen.

The Bottom Line—The Function Key Display

The bottom line of the screen contains a list of numbers and abbreviations. This line is known as the *Function Key Display*. The abbreviations identify the purpose of each function key (F1 through F10). As you see later in this chapter—in the section titled "Reassigning the Function Keys"—you can use the function keys to rapidly execute frequently used commands.

You might recall that you can create a similar Function Key Display in QBasic with the KEY ON instruction. The difference is that, with BASIC, the Function Key Display is on by default and certain values are preassigned to each of the F1 through F10 function keys. With QBasic, in contrast, the Function Key Display is off by default and no values are preassigned to any of the function keys.

Issuing BASIC Commands

Type a command to see what happens. Try typing **hello**. Just type the word **hello** but don't press any other key.

```
Ok
hello_
```

You typed hello, but BASIC hasn't replied. To actually send a command to BASIC and get a response, you must type the command *and then press the Enter key*. Now press Enter and see what happens.

```
Ok
hello
Syntax error
OK

_
```

As you might have surmised, the Syntax error response indicates that BASIC simply doesn't understand the hello command. The message Syntax error is BASIC's way of saying, "I know you want me to do something, but I just don't understand what it is you want me to do."

After the Syntax error message, BASIC reissued the Ok prompt and the cursor. BASIC is ready for your next command.

Issuing a Direct Mode Command

Experiment with a legal BASIC command. You can make the speaker buzz with a BEEP command. Try it.

```
Ok
BEEP
Ok
```

Your computer beeps and BASIC reissues the Ok prompt. Because BEEP is a valid BASIC command, no Syntax error or other error message appears.

By typing a command in direct response to a BASIC prompt, you are using the direct mode of BASIC. This is quite similar to using the Immediate window in QBasic. When you press Enter, BASIC processes the command you typed and responds immediately.

Besides direct mode, BASIC also has an indirect mode which you use to write a program. With indirect mode, you type a series of program instructions and, only when you are finished writing all of your instructions, do you issue a command for BASIC to run your program.

Capitalization

When it comes to reserved words, BASIC is not picky about capitalization. You can type upper- or lowercase letters interchangeably. In the present example, you could type beep, BEEP, or even bEeP and the command works fine.

As you will see, BASIC does capitalize reserved words and variable names when you list your program. Unlike QBasic, however, BASIC does not edit your lines for capitalization immediately after you press Enter.

Scrolling

As you type commands, your screen invariably becomes full. Each BASIC command you type, and each response from the computer, takes at least one new line on your video screen.

When the cursor reaches the bottom line of the screen, scrolling occurs. Everything on the screen moves up one line. The cursor remains on the now blank bottom line to accommodate your next command or BASIC's next response. When the screen scrolls, the former top line "moves up" and simply disappears.

When we say the "bottom line" of the screen, we mean the line above the Function Key Display. The Function Key Display is not affected by scrolling. The Display line remains visible at all times and is immune to the upward scrolling movement of other screen lines.

If you haven't yet seen the scrolling effect, try one of these experiments:

- Continually type BEEP (followed by Enter) until the screen scrolls, or
- Just press Enter repeatedly until scrolling occurs.

Clearing the Screen

A full screen sometimes appears cluttered, and you may like to work with a fresh slate. The CLS command wipes the screen clear and returns the cursor to the upper left corner. As with QBasic, the CLS command does not erase anything in the computer's memory, but simply wipes the screen clear (except for the Function Key Display).

Try clearing your screen. Just type:

CLS

Your screen blanks and the Ok prompt appears in the upper left corner. The cursor reappears just below the prompt. BASIC waits for you to type your next command.

 NOTE **No More Cursor!**

For simplicity, we will no longer show the cursor in our examples. However, anytime you see the Ok prompt, you know that the next line contains the blinking cursor.

Correcting Typing Mistakes

Suppose you want to type BEEP, but you inadvertently type BBEP. You realize your mistake just before you press Enter. What can you do to correct this mistake?

You have three choices:

1. Do nothing special. Just press Enter. You will get the Syntax error message, of course, followed by the Ok prompt. Now you can type BEEP as you intended.

2. Use the Backspace key. Press Backspace three times. Only the first B remains. Now type EEP to complete the BEEP keyword.

3. Use the left-arrow key to reposition the cursor. Press left-arrow three times. Type E to correct the second B and complete the BEEP keyword.

The *PRINT* Command—Displaying Text On-Screen

As with QBasic, a PRINT command displays output on your video screen. However, in direct mode, the output appears immediately below your typed command. By contrast, when you type a PRINT command from the Immediate window of QBasic, the video screen switches to the independent output screen where you see the result. You then have to press any key to return to the QBasic editing environment. (For more on QBasic's Immediate window, see Chapter 4, "Learning the QBasic Environment.")

With a PRINT command in BASIC, capitalization is not important when you type PRINT but capitalization *is* important in any text you place between quotation marks following the PRINT command. The following experiment demonstrates capitalization with various PRINT commands:

```
Ok
PRINT "HELLO"
HELLO
Ok
print "hello"
hello
OK
pRiNt "hEllo"
hEllo
Ok
```

Quitting BASIC

The SYSTEM command ends BASIC and returns your computer to DOS. When you're through with a BASIC session, just type:

```
SYSTEM
```

Using Indirect Mode to Write Programs

So far, you have used the direct mode of BASIC. In direct mode, you type a command, press Enter, and BASIC executes your command. That's fine, but direct mode has an obvious limitation—you can do only one thing at a time.

You can use BASIC's indirect mode to run a collection of several BASIC instructions as a single unit—known as a program. Another name for indirect mode is program mode.

Introducing Program Mode

Listing 23.1 contains a simple BASIC program.

Listing 23.1. A simple BASIC program.

```
100 PRINT "Hello"
200 PRINT "Goodbye"
300 END
```

Notice the line numbers. With QBasic, line numbers are optional and actually discouraged. On the other hand, with BASIC, line numbers are required. BASIC does not support alphanumeric line labels, only numeric line numbers.

A line number identifies the line as being part of a program. Without the line number, the line is a command suitable for BASIC's direct mode. For more about line numbers and BASIC, see Chapter 24, "Comparing the GW-BASIC (BASICA) Language to QBasic."

To see how program mode works, try running the sample program.

Typing a Program

First, you have to enter the program into BASIC. Type the first line of the program and press Enter.

Notice that you don't see the familiar Ok prompt. You are now in BASIC's indirect (program) mode. The number at the beginning of the line (100 in this case) identifies this line as part of a program and not a direct mode command.

You get the Ok prompt only after BASIC performs a direct mode command. Here, you are entering a program rather than issuing a command.

Type the remaining two lines of the program. Your screen should look as follows:

```
Ok
100 PRINT "Hello"
200 PRINT "Goodbye"
300 END
```

BASIC stores a copy of the complete program. As you type a program line by line, BASIC retains the entire program in memory.

Running a Program

To run the program, type RUN. Don't include a line number. RUN is a direct mode command which tells BASIC to run the program stored in memory.

Type RUN and watch what happens:

```
Ok
100 PRINT "Hello"
200 PRINT "Goodbye"
300 END
RUN
Hello
Goodbye
Ok
```

The RUN command executed the program. The messages Hello and Goodbye were displayed due to lines 100 and 200, but why that last Ok prompt?

The Ok prompt simply indicates that BASIC performed your requested command (RUN in this case) and now awaits your next command. At this point, you can do one of two things:

1. Enter any direct mode command. You won't affect the program in memory. Try typing CLS or a direct mode PRINT command such as PRINT "I did it". To verify the program is unaffected, rerun your program with a RUN command.

2. Edit the program in memory. You can type new lines into your program or edit existing lines. You experiment with program editing next.

Editing a Program

Modifying a program is easy. You can add new lines, modify existing lines, or delete lines you no longer want. Try all three.

Adding a New Line

To add a new line, just type the new line. Be sure to include an appropriate line number. BASIC inserts the new line so that *all* program lines are kept in numerical order.

Our program has three lines, numbered 100, 200, and 300. You could give the program a new first line by typing a line with a line number of less than 100, a new final line with a line number greater than 300, or a new second line with a line number between 100 and 200.

Try inserting the following line and running the program:

```
150 PRINT "Still here"
```

Just type the line followed by RUN:

```
Ok
150 PRINT "Still here"
RUN
Hello
Still here
Goodbye
Ok
```

Inside the computer's memory, the program now looks like this:

```
100 PRINT "Hello"
150 PRINT "Still here"
200 PRINT "Goodbye"
300 END
```

T I P **Allow for New Program Lines**

When you write programs, avoid consecutive line numbers such as 10, 11, and 12. Why? Because you want to leave room for expansion in case you later need to add new lines between the existing lines.

A line number can be any whole number from 0 to 65529. BASIC arranges your program lines from the smallest line number to the largest.

We recommend that you leave a gap of at least 10 between successive line numbers. Many programmers use line numbers of 100, 110, 120, and so on. That way, they have room for nine new program lines between any two existing lines.

Occasionally, you might box yourself into a corner. For example you may want to insert fifteen new lines between lines 120 and 130. There *is* a way out. You can renumber program lines with the RENUM command. For more about RENUM, see the section titled "Renumbering Program Lines" later in this chapter.

Modifying an Existing Line

To alter a program line, just type the new line using the existing line number. For example, you can change line 100 by typing in a new line 100. BASIC replaces the old line 100 with the new line 100.

Try modifying the program by adding sound. Change line 100 to BEEP and rerun the program.

```
Ok
100 BEEP
RUN
Still here
Goodbye
Ok
```

Did you hear the beep when you ran the program?

Notice that the new line 100 replaces the old line 100. The program no longer displays Hello, which was the effect of the old line 100. The old line 100 is erased from the computer's memory. The program now looks as follows:

```
100 BEEP
150 PRINT "Still here"
200 PRINT "Goodbye"
300 END
```

Deleting a Line

To delete a line, just type the line number (followed by Enter). This removes the line permanently from the program.

For example, delete line 200 and run the program:

```
Ok
200
RUN
Still here
Ok
```

The program beeps and displays the message Still here. Line 200 is gone. Here is the program now:

```
100 BEEP
150 PRINT "Still here"
300 END
```

Listing a Program

When you type a program or make a program modification, you might lose track of exactly what your program looks like.

You can view the current program with the LIST command at any time. Just type LIST and press Enter. Try it now:

```
Ok
LIST
100 BEEP
150 PRINT "Still here"
300 END
Ok
```

Notice that line 200 is indeed gone.

Soon, you will see how LIST can display only selected lines of a program.

Using *END*

As with QBasic, the END instruction does just what the name suggests—it ends the program. When BASIC encounters END, the program concludes and BASIC displays the Ok prompt.

Actually, you don't need an END instruction as the final line of a program. BASIC, like QBasic, is "smart" enough to realize that your program ends after the last line. You could delete line 300 and the program would still run fine.

END does *not* indicate the physical end of the program, but rather the end of program execution. You can have more than one END instruction in a program. Whenever BASIC encounters an END instruction, your program immediately terminates.

Try this experiment to add an END instruction in the middle of the program:

```
Ok
125 END
RUN
Ok
```

You hear a beep when you run the program, but no message displays on-screen. The END instruction in line 125 terminates the program even though line 150 is still present.

Listing Parts of a Program

List the current program:

```
Ok
LIST
```

```
100 BEEP
125 END
150 PRINT "Still here"
300 END
Ok
```

You frequently use LIST immediately after making a program change. For example,

```
Ok
125
LIST
100 BEEP
150 PRINT "Still here"
300 END
Ok
```

Here, you typed 125 to erase line 125. Next, you typed LIST to see the current program. Note that line 125 is now gone.

As you have seen, LIST displays all the lines of your program. LIST works quickly; sometimes *too* quickly. Suppose your program has more than 20 lines. The early lines swiftly scroll off screen as the listing completes. You might never get a chance to examine those early lines.

Fortunately, BASIC permits you to list a specific range of lines; just specify a line number range as part of the LIST command. Use a hyphen to separate the beginning and ending range of line numbers. For example, the following instruction lists only lines 150 through 300:

```
LIST 150-300
```

If you leave off the beginning or ending line number, BASIC substitutes the first or last line, respectively. Table 23.1 shows the results of sample LIST commands.

Table 23.1. Sample *LIST* Commands.

Command	Effect
LIST	Lists all lines of a program
LIST 100-400	Lists lines numbered from 100 to 400
LIST 200-	Lists lines numbered 200 and higher
LIST -300	Lists lines numbered from 0 to 300

When listing your program, LIST displays all reserved words in uppercase, regardless of whether you originally typed them with upper- or lowercase letters. Also, LIST converts any lowercase letters in variable names to uppercase.

To see how LIST converts lowercase to uppercase, try adding the following lines to your program. Type the lines as shown, with cls and print in lowercase.

```
Ok
50 cls
120 print "Hello again"
LIST
50 CLS
100 BEEP
120 PRINT "Hello again"
150 PRINT "Still here"
300 END
Ok
```

Notice that LIST displays CLS and PRINT in uppercase (in lines 50 and 120).

T I P   **No More *Ok*, OK?**

As you have seen, BASIC displays Ok after finishing a direct mode command. After you type a line of a program, however, BASIC does not display Ok. For simplicity, we will no longer show Ok in most of our examples. However, when the context is important, we *will* show Ok for clarity or to emphasize a particular point.

Removing the Function Key Display

Many programmers find the Function Key Display (on the screen's bottom line) distracting. You can easily remove it by typing the following command:

```
KEY OFF
```

The Display line disappears. You now have extra screen space for your program listings and other work. The line remains off for the rest of your BASIC session, but will reappear when you start BASIC the next time.

You can restore the Display line with the companion command:

```
KEY ON
```

Saving and Loading Programs on Disk

As you create or modify a program, BASIC retains the program in memory. BASIC uses standard DOS filenames of 1 to 8 characters. By convention, BASIC program files have the extension .BAS. However, that extension is not mandatory. You can give your files any extension you choose (or no extension at all).

Saving a File On Disk—*SAVE*

The SAVE command saves a program on disk. Just type SAVE followed by a filename in quotation marks. BASIC saves the current program to a disk file using the filename you specify.

For example, you can save the beeping program by typing the following command:

```
SAVE "BEEP.BAS"
```

When you press Enter, BASIC saves your program with the filename BEEP.BAS. The file is saved in the directory from which you started BASIC. If you started BASIC from a floppy disk, the file is saved to that floppy disk. Similarly, if you started BASIC from your hard disk, the file is saved on the hard disk.

You don't have to use uppercase letters when typing the filename. Remember, in filenames, DOS treats lowercase and uppercase letters equivalently. And, as with all BASIC reserved words, you can type SAVE in lowercase also. So, the following command works just as well (and doesn't require so many shifted keystrokes):

```
save "beep.bas"
```

If you don't specify a file extension, SAVE automatically adds the .BAS extension. The idea is that the .BAS extension is normally used for BASIC program files. (However, you can override this default by specifying any extension you choose.)

When you save a file with the SAVE command, make sure that you don't already have a file with the same name on your directory. If you do, BASIC replaces the old disk file with the new file. You won't get any warning that your old file is about to be replaced.

Sometimes you *want* the new saved file to replace the old one. That's common when modifying an old program. In such a case, you often make changes which render the old program obsolete. So you just let the new disk file replace the old file.

You can get a listing of the files on your disk with the FILES command. The FILES command is discussed shortly.

T I P **Saving Files on Other Disk Drives (or Directories)**

By default, SAVE writes your files onto the drive (and/or directory) from which you started BASIC. You can override this default by using a drive and/or path designation as part of your filename. For example, the following command saves a file onto the B: drive

```
SAVE "B:BEEP.BAS"
```

As another example, the following command saves a file in a particular directory of a hard disk:

```
SAVE "C:\PROGRAMS\QUE\BEEP.BAS"
```

Saving a File for Use with QBasic

Normally, when you save program files on disk with the SAVE command, BASIC saves the file in a special internal format. The details of this format are not too important here. Just remember that such files cannot be read easily outside of BASIC.

You might have BASIC programs which you would like to load into QBasic. In order to do so, you must save the program file in ASCII format. That is, you must make a text file out of the BASIC program.

BASIC has a special form of the SAVE command which transfers the file into ASCII format. For details of this method, see Chapter 24, "Comparing the GW-BASIC (BASICA) Language to QBasic."

Erasing a Program from Memory—*NEW*

The NEW command erases the current program from memory. Simply type NEW. Use NEW when you're finished with one program and want to begin work on another. Of course, if your current program is important, you should save the program before typing NEW.

Try the following example. With a NEW command, you erase any current program from memory. You then type in a new program which consists of a single line. Finally, with a SAVE command, you save the new program to your disk.

```
NEW
Ok
LIST
Ok
200 PRINT "Testing, one, two, three"
RUN
Testing, one, two, three
Ok
LIST
200 PRINT "Testing, one, two, three"
SAVE "TEST"
Ok
```

Notice what happened after the first LIST. BASIC simply responded with Ok because there was no program left in memory. The NEW command erased the old program.

You then created a one-line program consisting of a single PRINT instruction. You ran the program and listed it. (Notice that the listing contains no remnants of the old program). Finally, you saved the new program. BASIC saves the file as TEST.BAS (automatically adding the .BAS extension to the filename).

Listing Filenames—*FILES*

To see a list of files saved on your work disk, type FILES. BASIC shows you all files in your default drive (and/or directory).

Type FILES now and compare your output with ours:

```
FILES
A:\
COMMAND .COM     GWBASIC .EXE     BEEP    .BAS     TEST    .BAS
 200704 Bytes free
```

The first line, A:\ in our case, indicates that the upcoming file list is for the root directory of the A: drive (the backslash, \, indicates the root directory). Next, BASIC displays the filenames. Four files are listed per line. The file list spreads to multiple lines if necessary.

The last line indicates the number of free bytes in the current directory. This number indicates how much room you have available for saving additional files.

Your FILES listing should be similar. In any case, the main point is that FILES provides proof that you have successfully saved the program files BEEP.BAS and TEST.BAS.

Loading a File from Disk—*LOAD*

LOAD is the complementary command to SAVE. Whereas SAVE stores a program from memory to a disk file, LOAD transfers a program from a disk file back into the computer's memory. LOAD erases any old program from memory before loading the new program.

After loading a program, you can run the program, list it, make modifications, or whatever. It's just as if you typed the program into your computer.

As with SAVE, a LOAD command must include the desired filename in quotation marks. Also similar, if you leave off the extension name, BASIC assumes the extension .BAS.

The following experiment shows LOAD in action:

```
NEW
Ok
LOAD "BEEP.BAS"
Ok
RUN
Hello again
Still here
Ok
LOAD "TEST"
Ok
RUN
Testing, one, two, three
Ok
LIST
200 PRINT "Testing, one, two, three"
Ok
```

Editing Techniques

So far, we have only touched on the editing methods available with BASIC. The remainder of this chapter introduces additional editing techniques such as

■ Full-screen editing

■ Insert mode

■ Special shortcut keys

■ Direct mode commands (EDIT, DELETE, AUTO, RENUM)

Line Editing

While typing a line of a program (or a command in direct mode), several special editing keys are available. Table 23.2 summarizes these special keystrokes. In the table, "Left" and "Right" denote the left arrow and right arrow keys, respectively.

Notice that each special key has an alternate form involving a Ctrl key combination. The two forms do exactly the same thing. For example, Backspace and Ctrl-H each delete the character to the left of the cursor.

Table 23.2. Special Keys for Line Editing.

Key	Alternate Key	Effect
Left	Ctrl-]	Moves the cursor one position to the left.
Right	Ctrl-\	Moves the cursor one position to the right.
Backspace	Ctrl-H	Deletes one character to the left of the cursor. All characters to the right of the cursor move one space to the left.
Del	Ctrl-Backspace	Deletes the character at the cursor. All characters to the right of the cursor move one space to the left.
Ins	Ctrl-R	Turns insert mode on or off.
Ctrl-Left	Ctrl-B	Moves the cursor to the beginning of the previous word.
Ctrl-Right	Ctrl-F	Moves the cursor to the beginning of the following word.
End	Ctrl-N	Moves the cursor to the end of the line.
Tab	Ctrl-I	Moves the cursor one tab stop to the right. Tab stops occur every eight columns.
Esc	Ctrl-[	Erases the entire line. The cursor moves to column one.
Ctrl-End	Ctrl-E	Erases all text from the cursor to the end of the line.

Line Editing Notes

Table 23.2 introduces some new features. Here are a few details:

Enter	You don't have to move the cursor to the end of a line before pressing Enter; the cursor can be anywhere on the line. Regardless of the cursor position, pressing Enter sends the *entire* line to BASIC (including the characters to the right of the cursor). The cursor can even be at the beginning of the line.
Insert mode	This mode allows you to insert characters in the middle of a line. To use insert, first move the cursor where you want to insert new characters, then press Ins. The cursor changes to a small rectangle to indicate insert mode. Characters you type are now inserted at the cursor position. Characters to the right of the cursor move right to accommodate the newly typed text. Pressing Ins a second time turns off insert mode. Also, you can automatically turn off insert mode by pressing any cursor-movement key or the Enter key.
Word movement	You can move the cursor from word to word by pressing the left or right arrow key in combination with the Ctrl key. In this context, a "word" begins with the first letter or digit following a blank space or other punctuation. Word movement provides a quick way to move the cursor along lengthy lines.
Deleting	Del and Backspace are similar, but not identical. Del deletes the character at the cursor while Backspace deletes the character to the left of the cursor. Note that, when the cursor is at the end of a line, Backspace deletes the last character but Del does not.

A Hands-On Example

Here's a short exercise to acquaint you with some of the line editing features:

1. Type NEW to erase any program in memory.

2. Type the following line but don't press Enter:

```
50 IF MYAGE = 35 THEN PRINT "Who cares?"
```

3. While holding down the Ctrl key, experiment with the left- and right-arrow keys. Watch the cursor move from word to word. Release the Ctrl key.

4. Press End to move the cursor quickly to the end of the line.

5. Move the cursor back to the M in MYAGE.

6. Press Del twice. MYAGE changes to AGE.

7. Move the cursor to the c in cares.

8. Press Ins to start insert mode. Type the heck followed by a blank space. The new text inserts into the old text. Press Ins again to turn off insert mode.

9. Press Enter. This sends the entire line to BASIC. Type LIST for confirmation. You should see the following:

```
Ok
LIST
50 IF AGE = 35 THEN PRINT "Who the heck cares?"
Ok
```

Full-Screen Editing

BASIC supports full-screen editing. You can edit any program line (or direct mode command) which you see on-screen.

To move the cursor vertically off the current line, use the up- or down-arrow key. We refer to these keys as "Up" and "Down" respectively.

Note, however, that you cannot scroll through your program by attempting to move the cursor off-screen. Nothing happens if you press Up with the cursor on the top line (or Down with the cursor on the bottom line).

To edit a line, move the cursor onto that line and make your changes. Press Enter to send the newly edited line to BASIC. The effect is just as if you had retyped the *entire* line and pressed Enter.

You must press Enter to have BASIC record your modified line. The cursor can be anywhere on the line—but you must press Enter. If you edit a line and then press Up or Down before pressing Enter, the edited line is *not* sent for processing.

Table 23.3 shows special keys for use with full-screen editing.

Table 23.3. Special Keys for Full-Screen Editing.

Key	Alternate Key	Effect
Enter	Ctrl-M	Sends the line containing the cursor to BASIC for processing. The cursor moves down to the first column of the next line.
Ctrl-Break	Ctrl-C	Aborts editing on the current line. The cursor moves down to the first column of the next line. The old line is not sent to BASIC for processing.
Up	Ctrl-6	Moves the cursor up one line.
Down	Ctrl-(hyphen)	Moves the cursor down one line.
Home	Ctrl-K	Moves the cursor to the upper-left corner of the screen.
Ctrl-Home	Ctrl-L	Clears the screen and moves the cursor to the upper-left corner. This does not erase any program lines in memory but simply clears the screen for further typing.

Using *LIST*

To edit your current program, take advantage of the LIST command in conjunction with full-screen editing. Here's how:

1. Use the LIST command to display the line(s) you want to edit. Remember, you can list only a portion of your program by designating the desired lines with LIST.

2. Move the cursor onto each line you want to edit. Make your changes and then press Enter.

A Hands-On Example

Here's another short exercise. This one familiarizes you with full-screen editing.

1. Erase any program in memory with NEW.

2. Enter the following short program.

```
10 FOR J = 1 TO 5
20     PRINT J
30 NEXT J
```

3. Move the cursor onto line 20. Edit the line to read as follows:

```
20 PRINT SIN(J)
```

4. Press Enter. This sends the edited line to BASIC.

5. Move the cursor onto line 10. Edit the line to read as follows:

```
10 FOR K = 3 TO 4
```

   Do not press Enter after editing this line.

6. Move the cursor to a line below the program. Type LIST. You should see the following:

```
LIST
10 FOR J = 1 TO 5
20      PRINT SIN(J)
30 NEXT J
Ok
```

Note that line 10 did not change because you moved off the line before pressing Enter. Line 20 *did* change because you pressed Enter after making the modifications.

Some Editing Shortcuts

T I P

You can take advantage of the full-screen editor to quickly enter repetitive instructions. Suppose, for example, that you are entering a program that will contain several occurrences of the instruction FOR INDEX% = MINVAL% TO MAXVAL%. Each time, of course, the line number is different. Let's say your program will contain this instruction in lines 140, 210, 315, 420, and 550.

Here's a shortcut. Type the instruction once using line number 140. Press Enter. Now move the cursor back up over the 1 in 140. Type 210, the next line number containing that instruction. Immediately press Enter. You've just entered the line a second time. BASIC still has a record of line 140. You can repeat this with line numbers 315, 420, and 550. The result: you've swiftly entered the five program lines.

Another shortcut: you can reissue any direct mode command that appears on-screen. Move the cursor anywhere on the line containing the desired command and press Enter; this immediately issues the command. For example, the command SAVE "MYPROGRAM.BAS" might still be on-screen, even though you have made a few program changes since issuing that SAVE command. Move the cursor onto the SAVE line and press Enter. The file is resaved.

Saving Keystrokes with the Function Keys

You can use your computer's function keys (F1 through F10) to save key-strokes when typing frequently used keywords. Each function key is preset to produce one of BASIC's keywords. You can reset these preassignments to customize the key assignments for your own application. This is a powerful technique, which can save many keystrokes and reduce typing errors.

Using the Preassigned Function Keys

Try this. With a program in memory, move the cursor to a blank line on-screen. Press F1. LIST is printed on-screen; pressing F1 produces the same result as typing the LIST command. Press Enter and you'll list your program.

Now press F2. This produces the same result as typing the RUN command and pressing Enter.

Table 23.4 shows the keystrokes preassigned to the function keys. Pressing a function key produces the keystrokes shown in the second column. In this table, the "less than" symbol (<) represents Enter. For example, pressing F2 corresponds to typing RUN followed by Enter.

Table 23.4. Function Key Preassignments.

Key	Keystrokes	Meaning
F1	LIST	Lists your program. You must press Enter after pressing F1.
F2	RUN<	Runs your program.
F3	LOAD"	Loads a program. You must type the filename and the closing quotation mark.
F4	SAVE"	Saves a program. Again, you must type the filename and the closing quotation mark.
F5	CONT<	Continues a program after pausing.
F6	,"LPT1:"<	The designation for the printer.
F7	TRON<	Turns on tracing.
F8	TROFF<	Turns off tracing.
F9	KEY	The KEY command is discussed shortly.
F10	SCREEN 0,0,0<	Returns the screen from a graphics mode back to the normal text mode.

Reassigning the Function Keys

With a KEY instruction, you can reassign the text string associated with any of the function keys. The technique is the same as that for QBasic. For details, see Chapter 16, "Using Hardware Devices."

As an example, the following command assigns the string SQR(ANGLE!) to the F5 key:

```
KEY 5, "SQR(ANGLE!)"
```

Now, while entering a program, anytime you press F5 the editor types SQR(ANGLE!) for you.

A Timesaving Tip   T I P

Before entering a lengthy program, you can reassign the function keys with the names of frequently used variables. Then, you can quickly "type" any of these variable names by simply pressing the associated function key.

Listing the Function Key Assignments

You can list the *complete* text assigned to each function key with a KEY LIST command.

Table 23.5 summarizes the special forms of the KEY command.

Table 23.5. Special Key Commands.

Command	Effect
KEY OFF	Turns off the Function Key Display.
KEY ON	Turns on the Function Key Display.
KEY LIST	Lists the complete text assigned to each function key.

Using the Alt Key Shortcuts

BASIC has yet another set of editing shortcut keys. The Alt key in combination with a letter key produces a preset keyword beginning with that letter.

For example, Alt-C issues the COLOR command. Table 23.6 lists these Alt key-strokes. To use one, press the indicated letter while simultaneously pressing Alt.

You will probably find some of these Alt keystrokes more helpful than others. Experiment with them to see which are the most timesaving. Pressing Alt-P for PRINT is convenient.

Table 23.6. The Alt Key Abbreviations.

Alt-letter	Keyword	Alt-letter	Keyword
A	AUTO	N	NEXT
B	BSAVE	O	OPEN
C	COLOR	P	PRINT
D	DELETE	Q	——
E	ELSE	R	RUN
F	FOR	S	SCREEN
G	GOTO	T	THEN
H	HEX$	U	USING
I	INPUT	V	VAL
J	——	W	WIDTH
K	KEY	X	XOR
L	LOCATE	Y	——
M	MOTOR	Z	——

Using the Direct Mode Editing Commands

BASIC features a number of direct mode commands to facilitate your program editing:

- ■ EDIT   displays a line for editing.
- ■ DELETE   deletes a range of line numbers.
- ■ AUTO   automatically generates line numbers.
- ■ RENUM   renumbers program lines.

We now discuss each of these four commands.

Displaying a Line for Editing—*EDIT*

EDIT displays a line in preparation for your editing. The command has two forms.

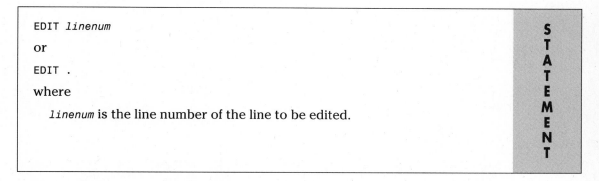

```
EDIT linenum
```
or
```
EDIT .
```
where

 linenum is the line number of the line to be edited.

S T A T E M E N T

The command EDIT 300, for example, does the following:

1. Displays line 300 on-screen.

2. Moves the cursor to the first character on the line (that is, the first digit of the line number—3 in this case).

3. Lets you then edit the line normally. When done, you press Enter to submit the line for processing.

In the second form of EDIT, the period identifies the line to edit as the current line. It is the same as specifying the current line number.

What line does BASIC consider to be the current line? Whenever you type a new program line, that line becomes the current line. BASIC considers the current line to be the last line referenced by an EDIT command, a LIST command, or an error message.

Deleting a Range of Lines—*DELETE*

You can delete a line from your program by just typing the line number and pressing Enter, but to delete a range of line numbers, you must use the DELETE command.

<table>
<tr><td rowspan="2">S
T
A
T
E
M
E
N
T</td><td>

```
DELETE startlinenum - endlinenum
```

where

    startlinenum is the first line number of a range of lines to delete,

and

    endlineum is the last line number of the range.

</td></tr>
</table>

You specify the line number range in much the same manner as with the LIST command. Table 23.7 shows some example commands.

Table 23.7. Sample *DELETE* Commands.

Command	Effect
DELETE 200	Deletes line 200.
DELETE 200-300	Deletes lines 200 through 300.
DELETE 200-	Deletes all lines numbered 200 and higher.
DELETE -200	Deletes all lines from the lowest line number up to and including line 200.
DELETE	Deletes the entire program with some versions of BASIC. Causes an Illegal function call error with other versions of BASIC. Be careful.
DELETE .-300	Deletes all lines from the current line up to and including line 300.

Notice that the last example in Table 23.7 uses the period to denote the current line. In DELETE commands, you can use the period as the *startlinenum* or *endlinenum* parameter.

T I P   Using a Period with *LIST* Commands

Just as with EDIT and DELETE commands, the period can be used with LIST commands to denote the current line. Here are a few examples:

```
LIST .        'Lists the current line

LIST .-400    'Lists from the current line to line 400

LIST -.       'Lists all lines up to the current line
```

Automatically Generating Line Numbers—*AUTO*

When writing a program, you can have BASIC automatically generate your line numbers with the AUTO command.

AUTO *linenumber, increment*

where

    linenumber is the first line number,

and

    increment is the amount to increase each successive line number.

**S
T
A
T
E
M
E
N
T**

To see how AUTO works, try this experiment:

1. Erase any current program with NEW.

2. Type AUTO 100, 20 (followed by Enter). You see:

   ```
   AUTO 100, 20
   100
   ```

   The cursor remains to the right of 100. Now you can type any BASIC instruction, press Enter, and you have entered line 100 of a new program. To continue this example, type FOR J = 1 TO 5 and press Enter

3. BASIC accepts your line 100 and prompts you with 120. You are now ready to type in line 120. Type PRINT J and press Enter.

4. You are now prompted for line 140. Note how each line number increases by 20. That's because you typed 20 for the second (*increment*) parameter in the AUTO command. Type NEXT J and press Enter.

5. The test program is complete. However, BASIC is prompting you for line 160. To stop the AUTO command, press Ctrl-Break or Ctrl-C. Try pressing Ctrl-Break now. You get the Ok prompt and BASIC returns to direct mode.

6. Type LIST to confirm that your program is entered. Your screen should look like this:

   ```
   Ok
   NEW
   Ok
   AUTO 100, 20
   ```

```
100 FOR J = 1 TO 5
120 PRINT J
140 NEXT J
160
Ok
LIST
100 FOR J = 1 TO 5
120 PRINT J
140 NEXT J
Ok
```

In an AUTO command, you can explicitly specify the line number parameter, the increment parameter, both parameters, or neither parameter. The default value for each parameter is 10. Table 23.8 shows various examples of AUTO commands.

Also, you can substitute a period (.) for the line number parameter. This tells BASIC to start with the current line number.

If you follow the line number parameter with a comma, but do not specify the *increment* parameter, BASIC assumes the last increment specified in a previous AUTO command (or 10 if there has been no previous command).

Table 23.8. Sample *AUTO* Commands.

Command	Starting line number	Increment
AUTO	10	10
AUTO 250, 35	250	35
AUTO 100	100	10
AUTO , 25	10	25
AUTO 150,	150	Last increment
AUTO ., 20	Current line number	20
AUTO .	Current line number	10

You can use AUTO to add new lines to an existing program. If AUTO generates a line number that already exists, an asterisk appears after the number as a warning. For example:

```
Ok
NEW
Ok
200 REM This is a test
```

```
AUTO 150, 50
150 REM    AUTO generated the line number
200*
```

In this example, the cursor is just to the right of the asterisk. You can now type a new instruction (which replaces the old line 200), or press Enter to maintain the old line 200 and make AUTO generate the next line number.

Renumbering Program Lines—*RENUM*

Sometimes, when editing a program, you get caught in a line number logjam. This usually happens when you want to do something like add 15 new lines between, say, lines 140 and 150.

The RENUM command is your way out of this kind of mess. RENUM renumbers all (or some) of your program lines.

RENUM *newnumber, oldnumber, increment*

where

    newnumber is the first line number for the new sequence,

    oldnumber is the line number from the existing program in which renumbering should begin,

and

    increment is the amount to increment for the new sequence of line numbers.

S T A T E M E N T

The beauty of RENUM is that the command also changes the line number references inside your program. That is, RENUM automatically corrects the line numbers that follow GOTO, GOSUB, THEN, ELSE, and other similar commands. These internal references are automatically updated with the new line n umbers.

You can explicitly specify any combination of the three parameters. The default values are 10 for *newnumber,* the first program line for *oldnumber,* and 10 for *increment.*

Table 23.9 shows some sample RENUM commands.

Table 23.9. Sample *RENUM* Commands.

Command	Effect
RENUM	Renumbers the whole program. The new first line number is 10 and successive lines increment by 10.
RENUM 200, , 50	Renumbers the entire program. The new first line number is 200 and successive lines increment by 50.
RENUM 200, 100, 50	Renumbers only the lines from 100 upward. The old line 100 becomes line 200 and successive lines increment by 50.
RENUM 200, 100	Same as previous command except that successive lines increment by 10 (the default value).
RENUM , , 5	Renumbers the entire program. The new first line number is 10 and successive lines increment by 5.

Here's a short experiment that demonstrates RENUM.

```
NEW
Ok
300 PRINT "I'm stuck in an endless loop"
302 GOTO 300
620 REM No way to get here
RENUM
Ok
LIST
10 PRINT "I'm stuck in an endless loop"
20 GOTO 10
30 REM No way to get here
Ok
```

The RENUM command renumbered the program lines as 10, 20, and 30. In line 20, note how the reference to line 10 was automatically corrected. (This program still causes an endless loop, but at least the line numbers now look better!)

Merging Files

You can merge a file saved on disk into the current program in memory. Use the MERGE command.

```
MERGE filename
```

where

> *filename* is a string expression that specifies the name (and path) of the disk file to merge.

For example, the following command merges a file named MYPROG.BAS with whatever program is already in memory (notice that the extension .BAS is assumed if no extension is specified):

```
MERGE "MYPROG"
```

To merge a file from disk, the file must have been saved with ASCII format. If not, the merge is unsuccessful and you get an error message: Bad file mode. For details on saving a BASIC program in ASCII format, see Chapter 24, "Comparing the GW-BASIC (BASICA) Language to QBasic."

Merging combines the line numbers from the disk file with the program already in memory. If any line numbers in the file duplicate line numbers already in memory, the lines from the file replace the corresponding lines in memory.

Use *MERGE* for Frequently Used Subroutines

T I P

You might develop subroutines that you use in program after program. One helpful trick is to save each of these subroutines as a separate ASCII file. Then, when you need one of the subroutines in your current program, you can merge the subroutine into your program with MERGE.

However, you must avoid line number conflicts. You might save each subroutine with a distinct range of (large) line numbers that you reserve exclusively for that subroutine.

Summary

The user interface for BASICA and GW-BASIC is more primitive than that available for QBasic. With BASICA and GW-BASIC, editing is done line-by-line. The Ok prompt indicates that BASICA/GW-BASIC is waiting for your next command.

BASICA and GW-BASIC provide two fundamental modes: direct mode and indirect mode. With direct mode, you type a command and BASICA/GW-BASIC responds immediately. This mode is similar to using the Immediate window with QBasic. With indirect mode, you type in program lines one at a time. Each program line must begin with a line number. You then type RUN to execute your program.

BASICA and GW-BASIC provide full-screen editing environments equipped with several tools. For example, you can move the cursor over the full screen to edit any visible line. Special shortcut keys save numerous keystrokes. You even can manipulate your program's line numbering with direct mode commands such as AUTO, DELETE, and RENUM.

Comparing the GW-BASIC (BASICA) Language to QBasic

The previous chapter explained the programming environment for BASICA and GW-BASIC. You learned about the user interface, line-by-line editing, and responding to the Ok prompt. This chapter discusses the programming languages of BASICA/GW-BASIC and QBasic. The focus is on the different language features of QBasic compared with the language features available with BASICA and GW-BASIC.

As a QBasic programmer, you will find a knowledge of BASICA and GW-BASIC useful in a number of situations. The most likely scenario is that you might obtain programs written in BASICA or GW-BASIC which you would like to run under QBasic. These might be programs you wrote yourself or programs obtained from other sources such as friends, coworkers, or published in books or magazines. It's also possible that you might be working on a computer system which has BASICA or GW-BASIC available, but not QBasic.

 NOTE Just as we did in the previous chapter, we will use the term "BASIC" in this chapter to refer to both GW-BASIC and BASICA.

An Overview of the QBasic and BASIC Languages

For the most part, QBasic is a *superset* of BASIC. QBasic extends the BASIC language by adding new statements, functions, and features to BASIC's core language. The result is a more powerful, feature-rich language to fuel the programmer's creativity.

Because QBasic is so firmly rooted in BASIC, many BASIC programs run under QBasic without the need for any modifications. However, because QBasic does not support some features found in BASIC (or the BASIC features work a little differently), many programs *do* require modification to run successfully under QBasic.

The primary topics of this chapter are the following:

- Language enhancements which QBasic adds to the BASIC core language
- Converting BASIC programs to run under QBasic
- BASIC statements not supported by QBasic
- Statement and function inconsistencies between BASIC and QBasic

Language Enhancements Featured in QBasic

QBasic adds several language enhancements to the BASIC language. This section examines some of the new language features found in QBasic but not in BASIC.

Line Numbers

BASIC requires that each program line begin with a line number. Further, each line must have a unique number; no two line numbers can be the same. BASIC interprets the line numbers to indicate the proper order of the lines in the program. As you type the lines of a program, BASIC puts the program lines in increasing numerical order, reordering the lines if necessary.

For example, using BASIC, suppose you type the LINENUM.BAS program shown in Listing 24.1. Type the lines in the order shown. Notice that the line numbers are not all in increasing sequence.

Listing 24.1.   The LINENUM.BAS program.

```
100 REM Program: LINENUM.BAS (Demonstrate line numbers)
400 PRINT "my"
500 PRINT "name"
300 PRINT "is"
200 PRINT "Juanita"
```

When you run and list the program, here is the result:

```
RUN
Juanita
is
my
name
Ok
LIST
100 REM Program: LINENUM.BAS (Demonstrate line numbers)
200 PRINT "Juanita"
300 PRINT "is"
400 PRINT "my"
500 PRINT "name"
Ok
```

Notice that the editor rearranged the program lines into increasing numerical sequence.

With QBasic, on the other hand, line numbers are entirely optional and, when present, are treated like any other alphanumeric label. A line number is simply a reference identifier—it is merely a way to identify (label) the line, not a numerical value. The number itself has no meaning in terms of numerical hierarchy.

So if you type the original LINENUM.BAS program into QBasic, the editor does not rearrange any of the program lines. Running the program produces the following output:

```
my
name
is
Juanita
```

Because line numbers are optional, you could type LINENUM.BAS in QBasic without any line numbers. Listing 24.2 shows how the program would look:

Listing 24.2.   The LINENUM.BAS program without line numbers.

```
REM Program: LINENUM.BAS (Demonstrate line numbers)
PRINT "my"
PRINT "name"
PRINT "is"
PRINT "Juanita"
```

Multiline Block Structures

QBasic includes several block structures which BASIC does not support. Some of QBasic's block structures extend a simpler concept offered in BASIC. For example, the IF instruction in QBasic offers multiline block components whereas an IF instruction in BASIC must be confined to a single line.

Other QBasic block structures simply do not exist in BASIC. Examples in this group are the SELECT-END SELECT, DO-LOOP, and TYPE-END TYPE blocks. Table 24.1 shows the QBasic block structures and their compatibility with BASIC.

Table 24.1. Comparison of Block Structures in QBasic and BASIC.

QBasic Block Structure	BASIC Compatibility
IF-END IF	Single-line only
SELECT-END SELECT	Does not exist
FOR-NEXT	Compatible
WHILE-WEND	Compatible
DO-LOOP	Does not exist
TYPE-END TYPE	Does not exist
FUNCTION-END FUNCTION	Does not exist
SUB-END SUB	Does not exist
DEF FN-END DEF	Single-line only

FOR-NEXT loops and WHILE-WEND loops are essentially equivalent in QBasic and BASIC. The only significant difference is that QBasic supports the EXIT FOR statement to prematurely exit a FOR-NEXT loop. BASIC does not permit the EXIT FOR statement.

In the case of IF instructions, QBasic extends the concept to a multiline block, unlike BASIC, which confines an IF instruction to a single line. Similarly, QBasic supports multiline DEF FN blocks whereas BASIC confines a DEF FN instruction to a single line.

Data Types

QBasic supports three data types not found in BASIC: long integer, fixed-length string, and the user-defined type. Long integers extend the integer data type to a wider range of whole numbers. The type-declaration suffix for long integer variables is the ampersand (&).

A fixed-length string variable stores a string value of a predetermined length. To assign a fixed length to a string variable, you use an AS clause. Although such an AS clause can appear in several different QBasic statements, the AS clause is predominantly used in DIM instructions and TYPE-END TYPE blocks. For example, the following instruction declares MyName to be a fixed-length string variable with a length of 30:

```
DIM MyName AS STRING * 30
```

The user-defined data type, or record, is a structured data type comprised of multiple elements. In that respect, a record is similar to an array. The difference is that, whereas an array is comprised entirely of elements of the same data type, a record can be comprised of elements of different data types.

You use a TYPE-END TYPE block to create a record data type. For example, the following TYPE block creates a record type called Customer:

```
TYPE Customer
    FullName AS STRING * 50
    ClientNum AS INTEGER
    BillingRate AS SINGLE
END TYPE
```

Independent Procedures

Because BASIC does not support independent code modules, every BASIC program is a complete unit. QBasic, on the other hand, permits the programmer to write independent code modules called procedures. A procedure is a self-contained code module which can be called from anywhere—from inside the main program, inside another procedure, or even inside itself.

You can develop a procedure library containing several procedures each of which accomplishes a specific purpose. Then, when writing a new program, you can include the appropriate procedures as part of your new program.

QBasic has two types of procedures: the subprogram and the user-defined function. A subprogram is a block of instructions that begins with a SUB statement and ends with an END SUB statement. You use a CALL instruction to invoke the subprogram.

A user-defined function is similar to a subprogram. The major difference between a user-defined function and a subprogram is that the user-defined function returns a value in exactly the same manner that one of QBasic's built-in functions returns a value.

You define a function with a block of instructions that begins with a FUNCTION statement and ends with an END FUNCTION statement. You invoke the function just as you invoke a built-in function: by specifying the function name in expressions, PRINT instructions, or anywhere else you can use a built-in function.

By using procedures, you can write modern, structured programs with QBasic. By developing programs in which specific tasks are delegated to specific procedures, you create modularized programs in which the logic flow is relatively easy to understand. Modifying and debugging structured programs is a breeze compared to the same chores with unstructured programs.

The main advantage of procedures is that they are isolated from the main program. The procedures can use local variables which have meaning only within the procedure. Because of this, you can write code in a procedure without worrying about variable conflicts with the main program or with other procedures. Yet you can still pass parameters—such as the values of specific variables or expressions—back and forth between the procedure and the main program. Each call to a procedure can pass different values to the procedure. So, for example, you can pass different sales data to a procedure which prints a monthly sales report.

Static Allocation of Variables and Arrays

BASIC allocates the memory addresses for stored variables (including arrays) while your program executes. Such an allocation scheme is deemed dynamic allocation because, while translating each BASIC instruction into machine language, memory locations can be modified "on the fly." Further, dynamic variables can be deallocated when no longer needed by the program. By deallocating variables, you can free memory space for other program uses. With BASIC, *all* variable allocation is dynamic.

QBasic, on the other hand, can allocate variables statically as well as dynamically. In static allocation, the memory addresses are allocated before the program executes; these addresses remain fixed throughout program execution.

Compared to dynamic allocation, static allocation is less flexible but more efficient. The efficiency comes from the fact that program instructions can be translated into machine language *before the program executes*. This is possible because the memory addresses for static variables can be determined before execution and those addresses can be included with the translated machine language instructions.

Using QBasic, you can force static allocation with the $STATIC metastatement or by using a STATIC instruction inside a user-defined procedure. For more information about static and dynamic allocation, see Chapter 19, "Managing Memory."

Converting BASIC Programs to QBasic

Because QBasic is based on BASICA and GW-BASIC, it's quite feasible to run existing BASIC programs under QBasic. If you have experience programming with BASIC, you might already have several programs which you would like to convert for use with QBasic. Further, you might find an interesting BASIC program published in a book or magazine, or even obtain a useful program from somebody else.

Most BASIC programs require little or no modification to run successfully under QBasic. However, there are some inconsistencies between BASIC and QBasic. The remainder of this chapter covers problems you might encounter when running an existing BASIC program in the QBasic environment. The discussion focuses on the following three main topics:

- Saving BASIC files in ASCII format
- BASIC statements not supported by QBasic
- Statement and function inconsistencies between BASIC and QBasic

Saving BASIC Files in ASCII Format

The previous chapter introduced BASIC's SAVE command. You learned that, with SAVE, you can store a program as a disk file. Normally, when you save BASIC programs as disk files using the SAVE command, BASIC saves the file on disk in a special internal format known as *compressed binary format.*

The problem with this special format is that such files cannot be read outside of the BASIC environment. There are several situations in which you might want to use a BASIC program file outside of BASIC. For example, while working with your word processing software, you might want to load a program into a text document. Or you might want to run your program with another version of BASIC such as QBasic.

QBasic cannot successfully load programs stored on disk in compressed binary format. Fortunately, there is a solution. With BASIC, you can save program files on disk in ASCII format. This format means that each character in the file is saved according to its ASCII code value. The result is a text file which you can successfully import into any word processor or which you can load directly into QBasic. The only disadvantage is that, on disk, an ASCII file requires a little more disk space than a compressed binary file does.

Using the *A* Parameter with the *SAVE* Command

In BASIC, you can save a program file in ASCII format by using the *A* parameter with the SAVE command. The format is as follows:

```
SAVE filename, A
```

Here, *filename* is a string expression that specifies the name (and path) of the file to save. For example, the following command saves your program in ASCII format with the name MYPROG.BAS:

```
SAVE "MYPROG", A
```

(Recall that BASIC automatically adds the extension .BAS if you do not specify any extension. See the previous chapter for details.)

Once saved in ASCII format, you can load the program directly into QBasic as you would any other QBasic program.

BASIC Statements Not Supported by QBasic

Some BASIC statements are not valid in QBasic. If your BASIC program includes program lines which contain unsupported statements, you must rewrite those lines using QBasic. The following section provides an alphabetic list of the BASIC statements not supported by QBasic along with a brief comment on the necessary program modifications.

Notice that most of the BASIC statements not supported by QBasic are direct mode BASIC commands. As such, these commands are typically used in direct mode to alter the program itself, such as modifying line numbers or deleting lines altogether.

Some of the following commands are valid as program instructions, yet rarely appear in any real program.

AUTO

AUTO is a direct mode command which instructs BASIC to provide line numbers during the typing of a program.

CONT

CONT is a direct mode command which permits the continuation of a BASIC program after execution is interrupted. Usually, the interruption is caused by pressing Ctrl-Break.

DEF USR

A DEF USR instruction specifies the starting address of an assembly (machine) language routine. BASIC and QBasic have different instructions for calling assembly language routines. In BASIC, a DEF USR instruction specifies the memory address of the assembly language routine and a CALL instruction invokes the routine. In QBasic, a single CALL ABSOLUTE instruction both invokes the assembly language routine and specifies where in memory the routine is located.

DELETE

DELETE is a direct mode command that deletes a range of program lines from memory.

EDIT

EDIT is a direct mode command which displays a program line in preparation for editing.

LIST

LIST is a direct mode command which displays all (or a specified range) of the program lines on-screen.

LLIST

LLIST is a direct mode command which lists all (or a specified range) of the program lines on the printer.

LOAD

LOAD transfers a copy of a program file from disk into memory. LOAD is most often used as a direct mode command, but occasionally appears as a program instruction. In QBasic, you can use the CHAIN instruction to transfer control from one program to another.

MERGE

MERGE is a direct mode command which merges an ASCII program file on disk into a program already stored in memory. Merge is used occasionally in programs to modify sections of code while the program is running.

MOTOR

MOTOR is an outmoded statement which turns the cassette player on or off. MOTOR is a vestige from the early days of PC programming (mid 1970s) when cassette tapes were used as the principal storage medium. (This is before hard disks and floppy disks were readily available.) It is very unlikely you will encounter a program containing MOTOR instructions.

NEW

NEW is a direct mode command which deletes the program in memory.

RENUM

RENUM is a direct mode command which renumbers program lines. Keep in mind that QBasic treats line numbers as labels and does not reorder program lines based on sequential line numbers.

SAVE

SAVE is a direct mode command which saves a program file on disk.

Statement and Function Inconsistencies

BASIC has several statements and functions which work differently in QBasic. BASIC instructions that contain the following statements and functions might need modification because of the discrepancies between BASIC and QBasic.

BLOAD, BSAVE

BASIC and QBasic use different memory locations for certain similar activities. Data files created with the BSAVE statement in BASIC might not work correctly with the BLOAD statement in QBasic.

CALL

In BASIC, the CALL statement invokes an assembly language subroutine. In QBasic, the CALL statement invokes a user-defined subprogram. Convert a BASIC CALL statement to a CALL ABSOLUTE statement in QBasic. BASIC programs that pass string arguments to assembly language routines must be rewritten for QBasic; the string descriptors in QBasic are four bytes long, unlike the string descriptors in BASIC which are only two bytes long.

CHAIN

QBasic does not support the MERGE, ALL, or DELETE options that are available with CHAIN in BASIC. Also, QBasic does not support chaining to a specific line number.

CLEAR

In BASIC, CLEAR accepts two optional parameters. The first parameter sets the size of the data segment. QBasic does not support this first parameter.

COMMON

QBasic requires that any COMMON instructions precede all executable instructions.

DEFtype, DEF FN, DIM (Static Arrays)

For any BASIC program instruction to take effect, the logic flow of the program must pass through that instruction. Should the logic flow bypass an instruction (for example, if a GOTO instruction branches the logic flow around an instruction), the bypassed instruction has no effect on the program.

By contrast, QBasic scans every program instruction before executing the first instruction of the program. During this scanning pass, QBasic internally records the references to variables and function names that occur in DEFtype, DEF FN, and DIM instructions.

For example, if a DEFINT A instruction appears, QBasic "knows" to treat variables beginning with A as integer variables. This is so even if the logic flow of the program bypasses the DEFINT A instruction. BASIC, on the other hand, never "sees" (executes) an instruction bypassed by the logic flow. In the present example, if the DEFINT A instruction is bypassed by the logic flow, BASIC does not put the DEFINT A instruction into effect.

To avoid confusing programs, it's good practice to place all DEFtype, DEF FN, and DIM instructions together near the beginning of each program.

DRAW, PLAY

QBasic requires that you use the VARPTR$ function when using an embedded variable name in a string subcommand of a DRAW or PLAY instruction. In the BASIC program, you must modify each occurrence of the X subcommand and each "= variable" construction to use VARPTR$ instead. For details on using the VARPTR$ function with DRAW and PLAY, see Chapters 13 and 16 respectively.

FIELD

In BASIC, when a random-access file is closed with CLOSE or RESET, field variables defined by FIELD statements retain the most recent values assigned by GET instructions. In QBasic, the field variables are automatically reset to null strings.

RESUME

If an error occurs while you're invoking a DEF FN function, you can use the BASIC instructions RESUME and RESUME NEXT to continue execution at the line which invoked the function. In QBasic, the RESUME and RESUME NEXT statements continue execution at the line in which the function was defined (that is, the DEF FN line itself).

SYSTEM

In BASIC, the SYSTEM command terminates the program and returns control to DOS. In QBasic, SYSTEM terminates the program and returns control to the QBasic environment. (END and SYSTEM behave differently in BASIC, but identically in QBasic.)

TAN

In BASIC, an overflow error caused by the TAN function is not fatal. Such an error is fatal in QBasic.

Reading Random-Access Data Files

BASIC and QBasic use different formats to store single- and double-precision numeric fields in random-access files. QBasic uses IEEE format, whereas BASIC uses an older proprietary format—the Microsoft-Binary-format. To automatically read BASIC data files with QBasic, use the /MBF command line option when invoking QBasic. See Chapter 22, "Understanding Advanced QBasic Topics," for more information about /MBF and command line options.

Summary

Compared to BASIC (that is, BASICA and GW-BASIC), the QBasic language represents an evolutionary plateau. QBasic adds many new instructions, features, and enhancements to the core BASIC language. Only a few statements and functions found in BASIC do not exist at all in QBasic. Some BASIC statements and functions must be modified to work correctly with QBasic.

However, for the most part, programs written in BASIC will work successfully in QBasic without any modification. As a QBasic programmer, you should be aware of the differences between BASIC and QBasic in case you need to convert an existing BASIC program to run under QBasic.

Using QuickBASIC

QuickBASIC and QBasic are closely related. Microsoft introduced the first version of QuickBASIC in the mid 1980's. Aimed at providing BASIC programmers with a more professional programming product than BASICA or GW-BASIC, QuickBASIC gained immediate popularity. QuickBASIC 4.5 is the current version of QuickBASIC.

The QBasic and QuickBASIC programming languages are virtually identical. Furthermore, the user-interface of both products has the same look and feel. For example, drop-down menus, dialog boxes, and the Immediate Window are the same in both products. However, as detailed in this chapter, QuickBASIC does offer significant features not found in QBasic. Most notable, perhaps, is that you can compile a QuickBASIC program directly into an executable file which can be run directly from DOS.

QuickBASIC is not (and has never been) bundled with any version of DOS. As a QBasic programmer, take some time to consider whether the special features offered by QuickBASIC are beneficial to you. This chapter highlights those features.

Introducing QuickBASIC's Special Features

QuickBASIC supports the following features not found in QBasic:

■ Compilation of programs into executable files

- *Modules,* which are procedures or other program fragments saved on disk

- *Libraries,* which are precompiled modules stored on disk and callable from programs

- *Include files,* which are disk files of QuickBASIC instructions that can be merged into the current program

- Named COMMON blocks

- File saving in ASCII (text) format or in a special QuickBASIC compressed format for fast loads and saves

- Enhanced, interactive debugging tools

This chapter takes you on a tour of the QuickBASIC programming environment with emphasis on the differences between QuickBASIC and QBasic.

The QuickBASIC Environment

To start QuickBASIC, type **qb** at the DOS prompt. Figure 25.1 shows QuickBASIC's opening screen. As a QBasic user, this screen should look quite familiar. The Menu bar, Title bar, Status bar, View window, and Immediate window are present in both products and work the same way.

The only significant difference you might notice is that the Menu bar contains the Calls menu which does not exist in QBasic. As explained later in this chapter, the Calls menu shows the active chain of procedure calls and is primarily used as a debugging tool.

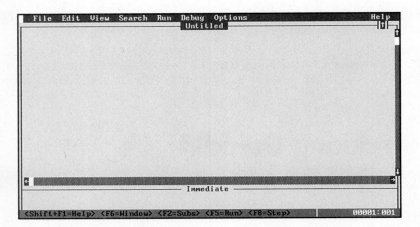

Figure 25.1.

The QuickBASIC opening screen.

Overview of the QuickBASIC Menu System

Most of the QuickBASIC menus contain options not available in QBasic. Table 25.1 lists the QuickBASIC menus and gives an overview of the QuickBASIC menu options not available with QBasic.

Table 25.1. QuickBASIC menu options not found in QBasic.

Menu	New options
File	Create, save, load, and unload individual modules. Create, save, load, and unload Include files. Shell to DOS to run a DOS command from QuickBASIC.
Edit	Restore the line being edited back to its original state.
View	View and edit an Include file. Specify the next statement to execute when a suspended program resumes.
Search	Search for selected text or for a specified label.
Run	Make an executable file. Make or modify a QuickBASIC Library. Reset the main module in a multiple module application. Modify the string passed to the COMMAND$ function.
Debug	Display the values of variables and expressions as a program executes. Set a watchpoint to halt program execution when a specified expression is True. Record the last 20 lines executed by the program. Break on most recent label in error-handling routines.
Calls	Display the sequence of nested procedure calls when a program is suspended. Resume program execution at any listed procedure.
Options	Set directory paths to QuickBASIC support files. Change the effect of clicking the right mouse button. Display the full set of menu options or display a restricted set of "easy" menu options.
Help	No substantial differences.

The remainder of this chapter discusses the most significant differences between QuickBASIC and QBasic.

Shelling to DOS

QuickBASIC provides a DOS Shell command on the File menu. With the DOS Shell command, you suspend QuickBASIC and return temporarily to DOS. From the DOS prompt, you can use DOS commands (such as DIR, COPY, or ERASE) or run a program. In general, you can do anything you normally do from a DOS prompt, yet QuickBASIC remains in memory. When you finish executing the DOS commands, you type **exit** at the DOS prompt. QuickBASIC regains control from the exact point where you left.

In order to shell, QuickBASIC needs access to the DOS file COMMAND.COM. On hard disk systems, be sure a PATH is set to this file. On floppy disk systems, you must have COMMAND.COM available on a floppy disk.

The DOS Shell command is handy for file-manipulation tasks not supported in the QuickBASIC environment, such as deleting and copying files.

NOTE

Shelling to DOS With QBasic

With QBasic, you can emulate QuickBASIC's Shell command. To do so, press F6 to access QBasic's Immediate window. Then type the following command and press Enter:

```
shell
```

You now get a DOS prompt and can execute a series of DOS commands. Type **exit** to return to the QBasic environment.

Using Modules

Modular programs are constructed from discrete units. With subprograms and user-defined functions, the QBasic and QuickBASIC programmer can isolate individual program components. Modules give the QuickBASIC programmer even greater flexibility when working with individualized program components.

A *module* is simply a group of QuickBASIC instructions saved on disk as a single file (with a .BAS extension). Modules have the following characteristics:

- A module can contain subprograms and functions.
- A module can be a complete program or a partial program.
- Every QuickBASIC program consists of one or more modules.

In a given module, the QuickBASIC instructions outside of the procedures are known as *module-level code*.

QBasic does not support multiple modules. To a QuickBASIC programmer, every QBasic program consists of a single module. As a QuickBASIC programmer, you can also work with single-module programs. Indeed, most programs *do* consist of a single module. For single-module programs, the module-level code is simply the main program (as distinguished from the procedures).

As your programs get more complex and you build a body of routines that you use repeatedly, multiple-module programming becomes quite useful.

In the QuickBASIC environment, you can simultaneously load multiple modules. One module—usually the first one you load or type—has the special status of being the *main module*. When you run a multiple-module program, execution begins at the module-level code of the main module.

Here are some of the advantages of using multiple modules:

- A tested module can be saved on disk and loaded into memory during the development of new programs. Most likely, such a module contains user-defined procedures.

- One module can invoke a procedure defined in another module.

- You can chain execution from one module to the module-level code of another module.

A Multiple-Module Example

One common application of modules is to save a group of user-defined procedures (subprograms and functions) as a module. Then, when you write a program that needs one of those functions, you simply load the appropriate module.

To illustrate working with modules, the following section looks at the steps you might use in working with a multiple-module program.

Saving a Module

Suppose that you just wrote a module named MYFUNCS.BAS. This module contains only some user-defined functions. You want to save MYFUNCS.BAS so that later you can load its modules as part of new programs.

You save a module in exactly the same way you save a program. Use the Save or Save As... option on the File menu. At this point, MYFUNCS.BAS is just like any other program saved on disk.

Loading A Module

Now suppose you want to create and run a new program which calls a function from MYFUNCS.BAS. The name of this new program is WHOOPIE.BAS. Create and save WHOOPIE.BAS with the same technique you used to create and save MYFUNCS.BAS.

You must load the MYFUNCS.BAS module so that WHOOPIE.BAS has access to the necessary function. To do so, you select the Load File... option from the File menu. A dialog box opens (see Figure 25.2).

Note that the Load as: Module option is selected. Type `myfuncs.bas` in the filename box. You must include the proper drive and/or path specification if MYFUNCS.BAS is not in the current directory. (Alternatively, if MYFUNCS.BAS appears in the list of available files, you can press Tab and the arrow keys to highlight MYFUNCS.BAS.)

You now have two modules loaded simultaneously in memory. Press F2 (the hotkey for the SUBs dialog box on the View menu). A listing of the loaded modules appears (see Figure 25.3).

Notice that the two module names appear in uppercase. Beneath each module name, you see an indented list of the procedures contained in that module. As you move the highlight up and down, the line below the box describes the highlighted item.

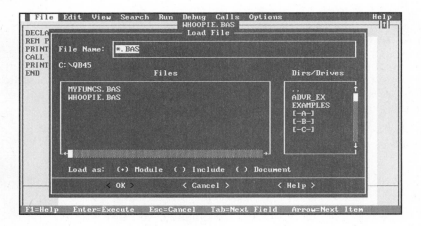

Figure 25.2.

The Load File... dialog box.

Running the Program

Before running the program, you need to do one more thing: Add a DECLARE FUNCTION instruction to WHOOPIE.BAS identifying the function in MYFUNCS.BAS that calls the main program. (DECLARE is discussed shortly.) You can now run the program.

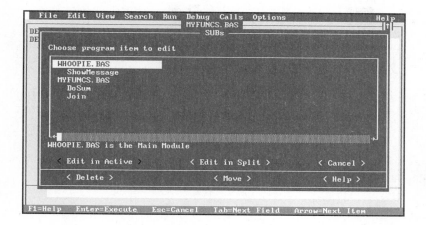

Figure 25.3.

Viewing the loaded
modules.

Saving Multiple Modules

Before finishing, save the modules. Use the Save All option on the File menu. This option saves any and all files (modules) which you edited since the last save. In this case, you modified WHOOPIE.BAS by adding a DECLARE FUNCTION instruction.

Using *DECLARE* With Multiple Modules

As you learned in Chapter 17, "Modular Programming," a DECLARE instruction in the main program identifies a subprogram or function that the main program calls. The analogy extends to multiple-module programs as well. When one module calls a subprogram or function found in other modules, you need a DECLARE instruction in the calling module.

A DECLARE instruction has scope for the entire module in which it occurs. Within that module, the procedure (identified by the DECLARE instruction) can be called from module-level code or from another procedure.

DECLARE instructions must occur in the module-level code, and never inside a subprogram or function. Place the DECLARE instruction before any call to the associated procedure—usually at the beginning of the module-level code.

When you save a program containing subprograms or user-defined functions, QBasic automatically generates DECLARE instructions in the main program to identify the embedded procedures. Similarly, when you save a QuickBASIC module containing subprograms or user-defined procedures, QuickBASIC automatically generates DECLARE instructions in the module-level code to identify the embedded procedures. Within a given module, QuickBASIC generates a DECLARE instruction for each SUB or FUNCTION called and defined within the module.

Additionally, QuickBASIC generates a DECLARE statement for each subprogram called in one module but defined in a second module. However, QuickBASIC does not generate a DECLARE statement for a user-defined function invoked from one module but defined in another module. You must write such DECLARE FUNCTION instructions yourself.

For the most part, programs can call procedures and functions without requiring DECLARE instructions. The one exception is the case just mentioned: invoking a FUNCTION defined in a different module.

You must include a DECLARE instruction for functions defined outside the main module in order to resolve a potential syntax ambiguity. Consider the following QBasic instruction:

```
MyPulse% = HeartRate(Age%)
```

Notice that the right-hand side of this assignment instruction could be interpreted two different ways: HeartRate is an array variable with Age% as the array index, or HeartRate is a user-defined function with Age% as a parameter. If HeartRate is not defined as a user-defined function in the current module, or if no DECLARE instruction exists to specify HeartRate as a user-defined function in another module, QBasic interprets HeartRate as an array variable.

Be sure to add a DECLARE FUNCTION instruction to any module which uses a user-defined function defined in another module.

Using Named **COMMON** Blocks

As you learned in Chapter 22, "Understanding Advanced QBasic Topics," a COMMON instruction collects a group of variables into a COMMON block. QuickBASIC permits COMMON blocks to work across modules. By declaring the same COMMON block in two or more modules, you make the variables global between the modules.

With QuickBASIC, unlike QBasic, you can name a COMMON block. By giving COMMON blocks different names, you can have more than one active COMMON block in a module.

To give a COMMON block a name, you place the name between two slash (/) characters. The name goes before the variable list of the COMMON block. For example, the following instruction defines a COMMON block named MyBlock.

```
COMMON /MyBlock/ MyNum!, MyString$
```

Naming a COMMON block is optional. When you specify a name, the block is known as a "named" COMMON block. When you omit the name, the block is known as a "blank" COMMON block.

COMMON declarations must always be defined in the module-level code, before any executable instructions. By including the SHARED keyword in the COMMON instruction, the variables in the COMMON block are automatically shared with each procedure in the module (in exactly the same way that a DIM SHARED instruction at the module-level shares a variable with each procedure).

The following program skeleton uses COMMON to share variables between modules:

```
REM Main program
COMMON /MyBlock/ MyNum!, MyString$

   .
   .
   .

MyNum! = 100.43
MyString$ = "It's outta here"

   .
   .
   .

REM Module-level code in a second module
COMMON /MyBlock/ MyNum!, MyString$

   .
   .
   .
```

COMMON Ground

Here are some guidelines for using COMMON declarations with multiple modules:

- You can declare any number of COMMON blocks in a given module. However, a single variable cannot appear in more than one COMMON block.

- Within a given module, multiple declarations of the same COMMON block do not redefine the block. Instead, such declarations append to the block. For example, the following two instructions are equivalent to the single instruction COMMON /MyBlock/ A%, B#, C&.

```
COMMON /MyBlock/ A%, B#
COMMON /MyBlock/ C&
```

- In multiple-module programs, the primary use of the COMMON statement is to create global variables for procedures defined in the secondary modules. Remember, though, that COMMON must appear at the module level. Use the SHARED attribute to make the variables available to the procedures (or else use the SHARED instruction inside the procedure itself).

Understanding the .MAK File

When you save a program containing multiple modules, QuickBASIC creates a special file on the current directory. This file has the base name of your main module but the extension .MAK. This .MAK file specifies the name of each module loaded with your main module.

The assumption is that, when you load the main module in a later session, you want to load all the secondary modules as well. Without the .MAK file, QuickBASIC cannot "remember" which modules were loaded with the main module. (Recall that QuickBASIC saves each module as a separate file.) If you copy program files to different directories, be sure to copy the .MAK file also.

The .MAK file is a simple ASCII file that lists each loaded module. You can edit the file with any word processor or text editor. By doing your own editing, you can add or delete modules as you wish. If you eventually decide that you don't want to load any secondary modules with the main module, delete the .MAK file altogether.

Programming with Multiple Modules

As you've seen, procedures are easily invoked between modules. However, you cannot readily transfer program flow from your main module to the module-level code in a second module. GOTO and GOSUB instructions do not work between modules.

You can use CHAIN or RUN instructions to execute a second module. But these instructions actually reload the second module as a completely new program. Your original program clears from memory.

As a result, the primary benefit of multiple-module programs is to make procedures in secondary modules available to the main module. In most cases, the secondary modules contain little or no module-level code.

Using Include Files

An *include file* is simply a disk file containing a number of QuickBASIC instructions.

During compilation of a program, an $INCLUDE metacommand merges the contents of a specified include file into the program at the specified location. These "included" instructions become part of the program and compile along with the other instructions.

Like the $DYNAMIC and $STATIC metacommands, $INCLUDE is a specialized form of comment instruction. Use the comment indicator (REM or the apostrophe) followed by the $INCLUDE metastatement and a filename.

REM $INCLUDE: *'filename'*

or

' $INCLUDE: *'filename'*

where

   filename is the name of the included file.

S
T
A
T
E
M
E
N
T

QuickBASIC recognizes this metacommand as a request to load the included file into memory during compilation. Don't forget the colon after $INCLUDE or the single quotation marks surrounding the filename.

As an example, the following metacommand loads the contents of a file named MYSTUFF.INC.

REM $INCLUDE: 'MYSTUFF.INC'

You can place any group of instructions into an include file with one significant exception: SUB and FUNCTION definitions are not permitted.

Include files can be nested. That is, an include file can itself contain an $INCLUDE metacommand which invokes a separate file.

Typical Uses of Include Files

Some programmers find that they use certain lengthy block structures (SELECT, TYPE, and DO, for example) over and over again in related programs. Such programmers often place each block structure into a distinct include file. Whenever one of the structures is needed in a new program, an $INCLUDE metacommand retrieves the structure.

Another common use of include files is to store the declarative instructions related to a particular module. For example, suppose you have an established module containing several procedures. You often load this module as part of multiple-module programs. Each time you use the module, you must place certain declarative instructions (DECLARE, COMMON, DIM, and TYPE) in the main module.

A timesaving and error-avoiding technique would be to save the declarative instructions in an include file. Give the include file the same base name as the module, but a different extension. Then, whenever you load this module into a multiple-module program, use an $INCLUDE metacommand in the main module to generate the declarative instructions. This ensures proper integration of the modules.

Creating, Saving, and Editing Include Files

Using the QuickBASIC editor, you can create, save, and edit include files. You can also load include files into memory and perform other file management tasks.

Of course, you cannot directly execute an include file—only modules can directly execute. However, once loaded into memory, you can use the F2 hotkey to select an include file for viewing. You can also split the screen to put your main program in one window and an include file in another window.

Here are some important considerations regarding include files:

- When creating an include file, be sure to identify the file as an include file. The technique for doing so is explained shortly. If you don't identify the file as an include file, QuickBASIC saves the file as a module.

- Specify the file extension when you name the file. QuickBASIC assumes no default extension for include files.

- Include files are always saved as text files, even if you request the QuickBASIC Fast Load and Save option.

- You can load an include file as a module. You can then run the include file as you would any program. However, this is dangerous and should be avoided. When you later save the program, you will generate an erroneous .MAK file.

The remainder of this section describes various editor techniques used with include files.

To create an include file, follow these steps:

1. Select Create File... from the File menu.

2. A dialog box opens. Type the name of the include file (with extension) but *don't* press Enter.

3. Tab over to the Create box.

4. Select Include by pressing *I* (or by checking the button adjacent to Include). See Figure 25.4. Press Enter.

5. A window opens for you to begin typing the file.

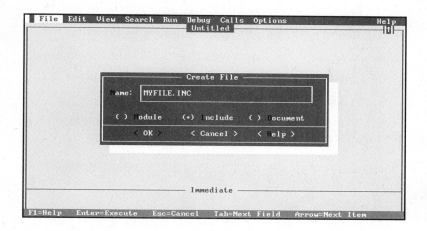

Figure 25.4.

Creating an Include File.

To save an include file on disk, follow these steps:

1. Invoke the File menu (Alt-F).

2. Select the Save option as you would for saving any file.

To load an include file into memory with other modules, follow these steps:

1. Invoke the File menu (Alt-F).

2. Select Load File... to open the Load File dialog box.

3. Type the name of the include file but don't press Enter.

4. Tab over to the Load as: option.

5. Select Include.

6. Press Enter.

To delete an include file from memory, follow these steps:

1. Select Unload File... from the File menu. A dialog box opens which lists the loaded modules and include files.

2. Move the highlight to the include file you wish to delete.

3. Press Enter.

To view and edit an include file loaded into memory, follow these steps:

1. Press F2.

2. Move the highlight to the include filename.

3. Press Enter.

To view and edit an include file not loaded in memory, but specified by an $INCLUDE metacommand in the current module, follow these steps:

1. Move the cursor to the line containing the $INCLUDE metacommand.

2. Invoke the View menu (Alt-V).

3. Select Include File (see Figure 25.5).

4. Press Enter. The included file is placed into the active window for viewing and editing.

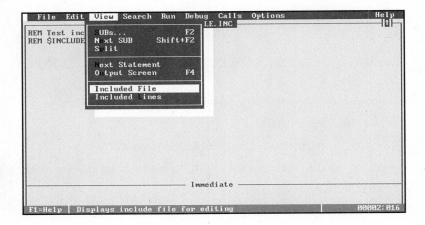

Figure 25.5.

Selecting Include File from the View menu.

To view, but not edit, the contents of an included file and the program containing the $INCLUDE metacommand, follow these steps:

1. Invoke the View menu (Alt-V).

2. Move the highlight to Included Lines.

3. Press Enter. The text of each included file now displays below the $INCLUDE metacommand which invokes the file. Included text appears in high-intensity video.

The Included Lines option is a toggle. When on, a bullet dot appears next to the option in the View menu. Selecting this option alternately turns it on and off.

When Included Lines is on, you cannot edit anywhere in your program. Attempting to edit a line, whether inside or outside an included file, opens a dialog box prompting you for the next course of action.

Merging Files

The Merge... option on the File menu inserts one file into another file. This differs from an include file in that, with Merge..., the insertion is part of the editing process. When you save the file after the merge, the merged lines become a permanent part of the updated file.

A file inserted with Merge... can include SUB and FUNCTION declarations. If included, these subprograms and functions are relegated to their normal subordinate positions in the active module. Press F2 to view the procedures in the usual manner. A file being merged must have been saved in text format.

Using Quick Libraries

A *Quick Library* is, essentially, a precompiled group of procedures. A Quick Library is saved as a file that you typically name with a .QLB extension. Each Quick Library file can consist of any number of subprograms and user-defined functions. As explained later in this chapter, you load a Quick Library into the working environment when you start QuickBASIC with the qb /1 command from DOS.

When you start QuickBASIC with a Quick Library loaded, all of the library's procedures become available to any program you run from the QuickBASIC environment. The Quick Library loads into the computer's memory independently from any part of a program. As such, the Quick Library remains loaded in memory throughout your working session, regardless of any programs you subsequently write or load from disk.

Your programs can invoke procedures defined in the Quick Library without requiring that the procedures' source code be present in any program module. This makes your programs smaller and provides considerable convenience, particularly when your body of user-defined procedures is large.

A Quick Library is already compiled and, therefore, in binary form. As such, you can distribute Quick Library files to others without dispensing any source code. This can be important if you wish to protect proprietary interests.

Creating a Quick Library

You make a Quick Library from a module or modules loaded into the QuickBASIC environment. When you save a Quick Library, all modules in the environment go into the library. You cannot designate individual procedures for inclusion or exclusion. Therefore, the first step is to manipulate your working environment until only the modules you want in the Quick Library are present. Use the Load... and Unload... options on the File menu.

If module-level code is present, that code goes into the Quick Library along with the procedures. This is wasteful because module-level code in a Quick Library cannot be invoked from programs running in the QuickBASIC environment.

When the environment contains only what you want placed into the Quick Library, you create the Quick Library by selecting the Make Library... option on the Run menu. A dialog box opens (see Figure 25.6). You type a filename for the library. If you don't specify an extension, QuickBASIC adds the default (.QLB) extension.

You can optionally add debug code by selecting the Produce Debug Code option in the dialog box. Opting to include debug code provides some error detection, but at the cost of slower execution time and a larger library file size. Most of the time, you will *not* add debug code.

To create the Quick Library, you can select Make Library or Make Library and Exit. The Make Library command returns you to the QuickBASIC environment after creating the library. The Make Library and Exit command returns you to DOS after creating the library.

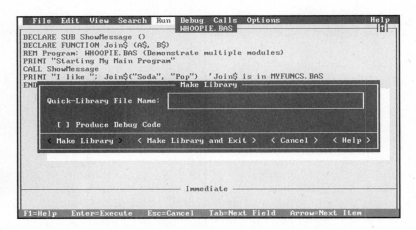

Figure 25.6.

The Make Library... dialog box.

Some notes about library creation:

- Conventionally, Quick Library filenames end with the extension .QLB. However, you can use any extension you want when naming the file.

- If you started QuickBASIC with an existing Quick Library loaded, that library merges with the current modules when you save the new Quick Library. In this manner, you can update a Quick Library with new procedures. (Starting QuickBASIC with an existing Quick Library is discussed shortly.)

- Each Quick Library is self-contained. You can't invoke a procedure in one Quick Library from a procedure in another Quick Library because QuickBASIC only allows one Quick library to be loaded at a time.

- The process of creating a Quick Library adds some additional files (with extensions .OBJ and .LIB) to your current directory.

Loading a Quick Library

You load a Quick Library at the time you start QuickBASIC from the DOS command line. Use the /l option with qb, such as

```
qb /l libname
```

where *libname* is the name of the Quick Library. The name can include a drive and/or path.

For example, the following DOS command starts QuickBASIC and loads the Quick Library MYLIB.QLB:

```
qb /l MYLIB.QLB
```

If *libname* does not include an extension, QuickBASIC assumes the default extension of .QLB.

The *libname* parameter is optional. If you specify the /l option, but don't include a library name, QuickBASIC loads the default Quick Library QB.QLB. Microsoft supplies this library on disk as part of your QuickBASIC package.

Using Procedures in a Quick Library

Once a Quick Library is installed, your programs can use the procedures contained in the library. In some ways, the situation is similar to having procedures in a secondary module. You should place the appropriate DECLARE instructions in any active module which invokes a Quick Library procedure. However, the DECLARE statement is mandatory only for user-defined functions. You do not need a DECLARE instruction in order to call a library subprogram.

A common programming practice is to create an include file associated with each Quick Library file. The include file contains a DECLARE instruction for each procedure in the library. Use $INCLUDE to merge the include file into each program that uses the library procedures.

Creating Executable Files

An *executable* file is a program that runs directly from the DOS prompt. One enticing feature of QuickBASIC is its ability to generate executable files from BASIC source programs.

For BASIC programmers who have worked exclusively with BASICA, GW-BASIC, or QBasic, making executable files is exciting. QBasic (as well as BASICA and GW-BASIC) cannot create executable files. A QBasic program must always be loaded into the QBasic environment and run directly from QBasic.

Executable files have the extension .EXE. When you run an executable file from DOS, you only need to type the base name of the file.

As a DOS user, you have run executable files many times. QBasic is an executable file named QBASIC.EXE. When you type **qbasic** to start QBasic, you are running an executable file.

With QuickBASIC, you can make an executable file either from the QuickBASIC environment or from the DOS command line through the supplied compiler (BC.EXE) and linker (LINK.EXE).

It's easy to create an executable file from a QuickBASIC program. You only need to ensure that QuickBASIC has access to a few necessary support files.

Advantages of Executable Files

Compared to running a program from the QuickBASIC environment, an executable file has the following advantages:

■ You can distribute an executable program on disk or electronically (by modem). Your users can run the program directly from DOS without the need of QuickBASIC.

■ An executable file is in binary form. This protects your proprietary interests because the source code is never distributed to the users of your program.

■ Executable files are optimized. Most programs run faster as .EXE files.

Types of Executable Files

QuickBASIC can produce two different types of .EXE files:

■ *Stand-alone .EXE files.* These .EXE files can be run directly from the DOS prompt without any additional files.

■ *.EXE files requiring BRUN45.EXE.* These .EXE files require the support file BRUN45.EXE in order to run. Microsoft provides BRUN45.EXE as part of the QuickBASIC package.

An .EXE file requiring BRUN45.EXE has the following advantages when compared to its stand-alone counterpart.

■ Smaller size. An .EXE file requiring BRUN45.EXE is considerably smaller. This is especially important if you want to distribute several .EXE files on one floppy disk. Compared to a floppy disk with stand-alone .EXE files, you can usually cram more .EXE files on one disk by making the .EXE files require BRUN45.EXE and putting BRUN45.EXE on the disk.

■ Support for CHAIN with COMMON. If your program uses CHAIN instructions with COMMON variables, create an .EXE file requiring BRUN45.EXE. Stand-alone .EXE files do not preserve COMMON variables with CHAIN. See Chapter 22, "Understanding Advanced QBasic Topics," for more information about COMMON and CHAIN.

■ Preservation of open files with CHAIN. An .EXE file requiring BRUN45.EXE does not close previously-opened files when a CHAIN instruction occurs. Stand-alone .EXE files close all open files when a CHAIN instruction executes.

As a registered owner of QuickBASIC, Microsoft grants you the right to freely distribute BRUN45.EXE with your executable files. No special license or royalty payments are required.

Necessary Support Files

In order to produce an .EXE file, QuickBASIC must have access to certain files (see Table 25.2).

Table 25.2. Support files for .EXE creation.	
File	**Description**
BC.EXE	The command-line compiler
LINK.EXE	The linker
BRUN45.LIB	Supporting library routines for .EXE files requiring BRUN45.EXE
BCOM45.LIB	Supporting library routines for stand-alone .EXE files

In addition, if your program requires routines in a Quick Library, you must make the .LIB version of the Quick Library file available.

When making a Quick Library, QuickBASIC actually produces two versions of the library—a .QLB file and a .LIB file. For example, if you create a Quick Library called MYLIB, QuickBASIC produces the files MYLIB.QLB and MYLIB.LIB. QuickBASIC uses the .QLB file when you start the environment with the `qb /1` command from DOS. QuickBASIC needs the .LIB version to make an executable file. (Note: Typically, .QLB refers to a precompiled Quick Library file while .LIB is a file containing a library of precompiled modules.)

The standard installation of QuickBASIC on a PC with a hard disk configures your system so that the support files are in the appropriate directories and paths.

Creating the .EXE File

To create an .EXE file while working in the QuickBASIC environment, select the Make EXE File.... option on the Run menu. A dialog box opens showing the filename that QuickBASIC intends to use for the executable file. This name is the base name of your source program, with an added .EXE extension. You can optionally type in a different name for the .EXE file.

From the dialog box, you can specify whether you want the executable file to include Debug code. The effects of Debug Code are discussed in the next section. You must also choose one of two file types: Stand-Alone EXE File or EXE Requiring BRUN45.EXE.

Finally, you must select whether you want to return to the QuickBASIC environment or to DOS after the .EXE file is created.

Producing Debug Code

During the .EXE creation process, you must choose whether or not to produce Debug code. Selecting Debug code makes the .EXE file larger. The extra code checks for the following list of errors and special situations.

- Arithmetic overflow and underflow.
- Array subscripts within bounds.
- RETURN instructions match GOSUB correctly.
- Messages after a run-time error include the line at which the error occurred.
- Ctrl-Break monitoring. After each line executes, the program checks whether Ctrl-Break has been pressed. If so, execution terminates.

Adding Debug code makes your .EXE file larger and your program run slower. How much larger? How much slower? That depends somewhat on the program. For most programs, including Debug code makes the program about 10 percent larger and run about 10 percent slower.

Compatibility Issues

An .EXE version of a program can produce different results than the same program run from the QuickBASIC environment. The reason is that executable files optimize source code with respect to certain arithmetic calculations. Also, .EXE files rely more on the math coprocessor or, for machines without a coprocessor, on the emulation of the math coprocessor.

The major source of incompatibility comes from single- and double-precision calculations, particularly expressions involving division. For the most part, discrepancies are small. But, of course, from the smallest inconsistencies come the most painful headaches.

Be alert for equality comparisons that contain single- and double-precision expressions. In an .EXE file, such an expression can have a slightly different value than that same expression computed in the QuickBASIC environment. This kind of small discrepancy can cause a comparison test to be unequal in an .EXE file, but equal in a .BAS file.

If you suspect a problem, try these remedies.

- Change equality comparisons to suitable inequality comparisons.

- Remove expressions from comparison tests. Instead, assign the expressions to variables before a comparison. Then, use only the simple variables as arguments in the comparison test.

- In general, break complex single- and double-precision expressions into a series of simpler expressions.

Understanding Compilation and Linking

The creation of an ..EXE file from a source program involves compilation and linking.

Compilation is the translation of each .BAS source module to an intermediate file, known as an *object* file. QuickBASIC gives an object file the .OBJ extension. Among other things, the object file assigns variable names to relative addresses, allocates storage, removes comments, and determines the order of program execution. To compile your program, QuickBASIC uses the command-line compiler BC.EXE.

Linking is the blending of each .OBJ file with the needed library routines in order to create an executable file. The linker resolves cross-reference addresses between the various components and converts relative addresses to absolute addresses. QuickBASIC links with the LINK.EXE program.

When you create an executable file, QuickBASIC runs BC.EXE and LINK.EXE automatically. On-screen, you see the calls made to these programs and the messages produced.

If you examine your default directory after creating an .EXE file, you'll find the .OBJ file produced by BC.EXE. For example, compilation of a program named TEST.BAS produces an object file named TEST.OBJ.

Introducing BC.EXE and LINK.EXE

You can run BC.EXE and LINK.EXE directly from DOS. This gives you greater control over the creation of an executable file than you have available through the QuickBASIC environment. Here are some of the reasons you might want to run BC.EXE and LINK.EXE independently.

- Your source program is too large for the QuickBASIC environment.

- You are not using the QuickBASIC editor to create your BASIC program.

- You wish to link non-BASIC object files with your QuickBASIC program.

- You want to create a map file available with BC.EXE and LINK.EXE. A map file shows a program's memory usage—including the name, memory address, and length of each program variable.

- You want to utilize options not available within the QuickBASIC environment.

For detailed information about using BC.EXE and LINK.EXE, consult the QuickBASIC documentation.

Debugging Tools

As explained in Chapter 18, QBasic offers a powerful set of tools for interactively debugging and testing your programs. For example, with tracing, you can examine a program's logic flow. You have options to single-step through your program or animate the trace at a continual slow-motion speed. By setting breakpoints, you can suspend execution temporarily. When suspended, you can examine the value of variables with the Immediate window.

QuickBASIC includes all the QBasic tools and expands the debugging capability. Most notably, by using the QuickBASIC Watch feature, you can continually monitor the value of a variable or expression as your program executes.

This section introduces several QuickBASIC debugging tools not available with QBasic.

Watching a Program

Watching means that you can observe the values of variables or expressions as your program executes. When used in conjunction with the tracing feature, watching is a powerful debugging tool.

The Debug menu provides several options related to watching, such as adding and deleting watch expressions. Also, by using the watchpoint feature, you can specify a relational expression (such as Age% > 38) and cause QuickBASIC to suspend program execution when the expression becomes True.

Whenever you watch a program, QuickBASIC opens a Watch window near the top of the screen.

Using Add Watch...

To watch the value of a variable or expression while your program executes, select the Add Watch... option from the Debug menu. A dialog box opens for you to type in any QuickBASIC expression. The expression you provide can be simple or complex. You can include any of the program's variables in your expression. Most watch expressions are fairly simple and often consist of a variable name by itself.

You can watch several expressions simultaneously by repeatedly selecting the Add Watch... option to include additional watch expressions to your list.

To watch expressions in subprograms or user-defined functions, you must first bring the appropriate procedure into the View window. Then select the Add Watch... option from the Debug menu and type in the desired expression.

Tracing a Program with Watch Expressions

With your watch expressions specified, press F8 to begin tracing. Inside the watch window, you see each watch expression on a separate line. QuickBASIC displays the procedure or module containing the expression, the expression, and the current value of the expression.

You can single-step through your program by repeatedly pressing F8. As you do so, QuickBASIC updates the value of each watch expression appropriately.

QuickBASIC watches expressions from the currently-executing procedure or main module. Other watch expressions remain dormant until execution transfers to their domain. When a watch expression is dormant, QuickBASIC displays Not watchable as the "value" of the watch expression.

Figure 25.7 shows a program being traced with an active watch window.

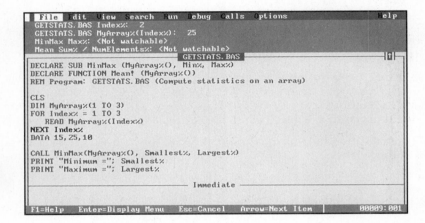

Deleting a Watch Expression

You can delete expressions from the Watch window by selecting Delete Watch... or Delete All Watch from the Debug menu. Delete Watch... opens a dialog box showing each of the watched expressions. Move the highlight bar to the expression you want to delete and then press Enter. Delete All Watch deletes all expressions from the Watch window and closes the window.

Using a Watchpoint

By selecting the Watchpoint... option in the Debug menu, you can specify a watchpoint. When you subsequently run your program, QuickBASIC suspends program execution whenever a watchpoint expression becomes True. Once suspended, you can use the Immediate window or other debugging tools, and then resume program execution.

For example, you might type Sum% / NumElements% <> 0 as a watchpoint expression. As the program runs, you will see the value of this expression in the Watch window. QuickBASIC displays the value as TRUE or FALSE. See Figure 25.8. Execution is interrupted when the expression becomes True.

```
   File  Edit  View  Search  Run  Debug  Calls  Options              Help
  GETSTATS.BAS Index%: <Not watchable>
  GETSTATS.BAS MyArray%(Index%): <Not watchable>
  MinMax Max%: <Not watchable>
  Mean Sum% / NumElements%: 16.66667
  Mean Sum% / NumElements% <> 0: <TRUE>
 ┌───────────────────────GETSTATS.BAS:Mean──────────────────────────┐
  FUNCTION Mean! (MyArray%())
     Sum% = 0
     FOR Index% = LBOUND(MyArray%) TO UBOUND(MyArray%)
       Sum% = Sum% + MyArray%(Index%)
     NEXT Index%
     NumElements% = UBOUND(MyArray%) - LBOUND(MyArray%) + 1
     Mean! = Sum% / NumElements%
  END FUNCTION




                              ─ Immediate ─
 
 <Shift+F1=Help> <F5=Continue> <F9=Toggle Bkpt> <F8=Step>      00007:004
```

Figure 25.8.

Running a program with a watchpoint.

NOTE A watchpoint expression is a logical expression that has a True or False value. Recall that, for numeric values, QBasic (and Quick-BASIC) consider 0 to be False and any nonzero value to be True. If your watchpoint expression is simply a variable name or an arithmetic expression, the watchpoint becomes True as soon as the numeric value becomes nonzero. You can therefore abbreviate the example watchpoint expression to `Sum% / NumElements%`.

Using Instant Watch

You can display the value of a variable or expression with the Instant Watch... option on the Debug menu. Instant Watch is most useful when a program is temporarily suspended. You can display a value for a variable or expression more conveniently with the Instant Watch option than you can with the Immediate window.

To use Instant Watch, place the cursor on a variable name directly in the program code. Alternatively, you can select (highlight) a variable name or expression. When you then select Instant Watch... from the Debug menu (or press Shift-F9, the equivalent hotkey), QuickBASIC displays the appropriate value. Figure 25.9 shows an example of Instant Watch.

History On

Select History On from the Debug menu to monitor logic flow. When the History On feature is activated, QuickBASIC continually keeps track of the last 20 instructions that were executed.

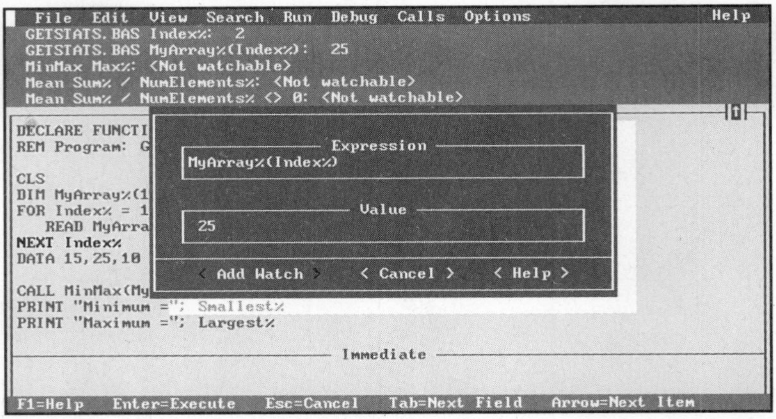

Figure 25.9.

An example of Instant Watch.

After suspending execution, you can observe the logic flow with Shift-F8 and Shift-F10. Whenever you press Shift-F8 (History Back), QuickBASIC moves the highlight to the previously executed instruction. Repeatedly pressing Shift-F8 steps backwards through your program. After you use History Back, you can then retrace the logic flow with Shift-F10 (History Forward), which undoes the effect of Shift-F8.

History On is a toggle. Select History On a second time to turn it off. A circle next to History On indicates that the option is in effect.

Using the Calls Menu

The Calls menu shows the active chain of procedure calls. If your program calls procedures from within other procedures, the Calls menu shows the stack of open procedure invocations.

For example, consider a module-level main program named SEECALLS.BAS. Three subprograms are also in this module: MySubA, MySubB, and MySubC. The main program calls MySubA. MySubA calls MySubB. Finally, MySubB calls MySubC.

Suppose you run this program and interrupt execution inside MySubC. Press Alt-C to invoke the Calls menu (see Figure 25.10).

The name at the top of the drop-down box (MySubC in this case) indicates the active procedure. Each successive entry down the box indicates the procedure which called the entry above. Finally, at the bottom of the list, is the main program name (SEECALLS.BAS in this example).

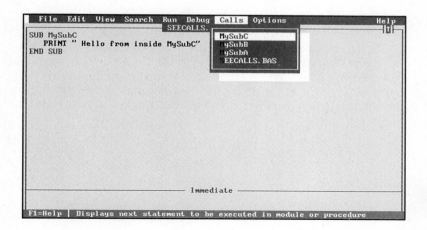

Figure 25.10.

Selecting the Calls menu.

This drop-down box is an active menu. You can use the cursor keys to move the highlight to any entry in the box. If you then press Enter followed by F7, QuickBASIC continues execution until the next instruction executes in the highlighted procedure.

Summary

QuickBASIC and QBasic are closely related. QBasic is a slightly stripped-down version of QuickBASIC. Therefore, QuickBASIC has some important features not found in QBasic. These features include compilation to executable files, multiple-module programming, procedure libraries, and enhanced debugging tools.

For a QBasic programmer, the unique features of QuickBASIC become relevant as the programmer becomes more "professional." Multiple-module programming and procedure libraries are most useful to a programmer who has a body of user-defined procedures that can be ported from program to program. Executable files are required for software released for commercial sale.

For one thing, Microsoft offers the Basic 7 Professional Development System, a high-end product for professional software developers. But more importantly, QuickBASIC is a DOS-based product, and despite the popularity and success of QuickBASIC, the product's future is cloudy. Although Microsoft intends to continue sales and support of QuickBASIC 4.5, it is unlikely that new releases of QuickBASIC will be forthcoming.

Why?

Because Microsoft QuickBASIC is a DOS-based product and the Microsoft vision of the PC future is Windows. With the release of Visual Basic in the early 1990s, the BASIC programmer has an incredible tool for developing Window's applications with relative ease. In 1992, Visual Basic for MS-DOS brought the same graphic-oriented development environment to the DOS platform. Microsoft sees Visual Basic as the future of "professional" BASIC programming. If you are not familiar with Visual Basic, the next chapter is your introduction.

Introducing Visual Basic

A new era in BASIC computing is here. As Microsoft Windows becomes the de facto operating system of today's 286-, 386- and 486-based computers, a programming challenge ensues. How can a programmer with a background in BASIC write Windows applications as painlessly as possible?

Enter Visual Basic. This revolutionary programming language from Microsoft was first released in mid-1991. With Visual Basic, you can write full-fledged Windows applications with relative ease.

Although the syntax of Visual Basic parallels that of the previous versions of BASIC, Visual Basic represents a conceptually different approach to programming called *event-driven* programming. An application developed with an event-driven program model *responds* to events which happen in the computer environment. Such events include the press of a mouse button or a call from another application running concurrently.

Though rooted in the BASIC language, Visual Basic for Windows breaks the long-standing Microsoft tradition of upward compatibility in successive versions of BASIC. Your previous BASICA, GW-BASIC, QuickBASIC, and QBasic programs will require extensive modification to work with Visual Basic.

As a Visual Basic programmer, you are something of a designer, architect, and builder. You create the user interfaces for your applications by directly manipulating on-screen objects such as control buttons and dialog boxes. You assign values for the properties of these objects by selecting various characteristics such as colors and fonts from an extensive list. You don't actually *write* any program code until you define what happens when a particular event occurs. Indeed, one of the great triumphs of Visual Basic is that you can develop complete Windows applications with a minimum of actual program instructions.

Visual Basic is not a single product, but a family of products. There are two versions for Windows: Visual Basic 2.0 for Windows, Standard Edition and Professional Edition. There are also two versions for DOS (without Windows): Visual Basic 1.0 for MS-DOS, Standard Edition and Professional Edition. The Windows products are in their second (2.0) release while the DOS products are in their first (1.0) release. Compared to the Standard Edition of each product, the Professional Edition offers a few more available objects, some advanced programming features, and a steeper price tag.

This chapter serves as an introduction to Visual Basic. The goal is to give you a feel for what programming is like in the new environments of Visual Basic for Windows and Visual Basic for MS-DOS. Here are the major topics of this chapter:

- Understanding the graphical interface revolution
- Understanding Windows from an end-user's perspective
- Understanding Windows from a programmer's perspective
- Introducing the Visual Basic computing environment
- Developing a sample Visual Basic application

 NOTE **VB/Win and VB/DOS**

Throughout the remainder of this chapter, the abbreviations VB/Win and VB/DOS refer to Visual Basic for Windows and Visual Basic for MS-DOS, respectively.

The Graphical Revolution

The ongoing trend in the PC computing environment is toward more graphical, visual user interfaces. The typical computer user is becoming accustomed to software applications which feature pull-down menus, a variety of colors and fonts, and multiple windows.

Instead of typing archaic commands from the keyboard, today's users regularly move the mouse pointer onto an appropriate icon or menu option and click the mouse button to activate a command or initiate a program.

Visual computing works because it is intuitive. We humans are visually oriented and commonly interact with our world by responding to visual clues. The more visual our computing environment, the more natural it feels.

Programming is no exception. The more visual the programming tools are, the easier it is to develop and program applications. By combining graphical design tools with a structured, event-driven language, Visual Basic defines a new level of programming capability known simply as visual programming.

NOTE **A Gooey Jargon**

Visual computing has spawned many colorful phrases and terms. Even some "graphical" acronyms have crept into everyday computer jargon. Two examples: GUI (pronounced "gooey") for Graphical User Interface and WYSIWYG (pronounced "wizzywig") for "What You See Is What You Get."

As you will see later in the chapter, it is a snap to create professional-looking user interfaces in your Visual Basic programs. Historically, programming graphics-oriented applications has been difficult. Just consider the complexity of writing a QBasic program that includes pull-down menus and dialog boxes. With Visual Basic, you can design such interfaces with a minimum of actual programming.

Introducing Microsoft Windows

Before delving into the details of VB/Win, it is important to understand the operating system environment in which it exists. Microsoft Windows has fueled the graphics-oriented computing revolution on IBM-compatible computers. This section introduces Windows from both the user's point of view and the programmer's perspective.

Windows is a software product which functions as an operating system. Windows both requires DOS and extends DOS. Windows was introduced in the mid-1980s but did not gain substantial market momentum until the release of Windows 3.0 in 1990 and Windows 3.1 a year later. Today, Windows is the number two best-selling software product of all time, behind only DOS itself. It is becoming so much of a de facto standard that most of the IBM-compatible PC manufacturers include DOS *and* Windows with their machines.

The popularity of Windows has spurred many software vendors to develop applications written specifically for the Window's environment. Such applications all have the same general look and feel. If you know how to navigate the menu structures in one Windows application, you know how to navigate menus in other Windows applications. Today, just about all the major software applications, including Lotus 1-2-3, Excel, WordPerfect, and Microsoft Word, offer versions that operate under Microsoft Windows.

Windows is visual. You manipulate on-screen objects with a mouse (or from the keyboard). The DOS prompt is gone, so you no longer have to type arcane DOS commands. One of Windows' main design goals is its ease of use.

Here are some of the main features of Windows:

- A multitasking environment in which several applications can be run simultaneously

- A consistent look and feel to all applications written specifically for Windows

- A graphical environment manipulated with a mouse (or keyboard)

- The ability to transfer data, including scanned images, spreadsheet numbers, and text, from one Windows application to another

- An assortment of accessories and utilities including a text editor, a drawing program, an appointment scheduler, a calculator, and a modem communications program

Windows From a User's Perspective

A *window* is a rectangular frame that contains a running application. You work with your applications and documents inside these windows. You can have several windows open simultaneously, which means that Windows can run multiple applications simultaneously. By switching the focus from window to window, you can work in several applications at one time. For example, you can actively work with a spreadsheet in one window while retrieving stock quotes via modem in another window.

The overriding metaphor in Windows is the *electronic desktop*. Windows tries to mimic a typical desktop. Just as you organize your real-life desktop with stacks of paper, a calendar, phone, and notepad, Windows organizes your computer screen into "electronic tools." These electronic tools might include software applications such as a word processor and spreadsheet program. Windows includes other tools such as a calendar, calculator, and program manager. You can customize your Windows environment by lumping certain applications into specific groups, called "Program Groups," which are represented on your electronic desktop by individualized icons.

Figure 26.1 shows a typical Windows screen. Three windows are visible: the Program Manager, the Accessories Window, and the Visual Basic Window. Within each window, icons represent individual programs that you can run. In this figure, the mouse pointer is positioned under the icon that reads Visual Basic 2.0. You can initiate Visual Basic by moving the mouse pointer onto the actual icon and double-clicking the mouse button.

Working with Windows

You can manipulate the size and location of visible windows. For example, you can align windows alongside each other, overlap windows, or reduce them to small icons. As such, you can organize your electronic desktop as you see fit. Figure 26.2 shows a resizing of the Program Manager and Accessories windows. The Visual Basic window has been reduced to an icon located near the lower-right corner of the screen.

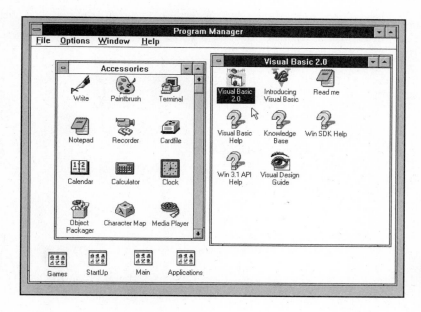

Figure 26.1.

Three typical windows.

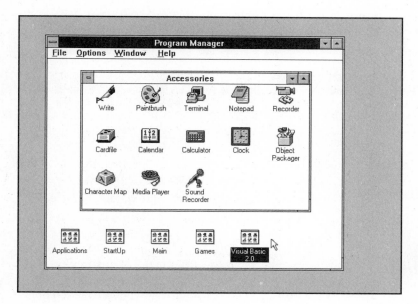

Figure 26.2.

Visual Basic reduced
to an icon.

The icons along the bottom of the screen represent groups of utilities and applications. When you click a group icon, you enlarge that group into its own window. Often, the new window contains icons for several programs or utilities. When you click one of these icons, you launch (initiate) that program.

Individual windows have many common features. Figure 26.3 shows the Visual Basic group window opened under the Program Manager. Table 26.1 discusses the window elements shown in Figure 26.3.

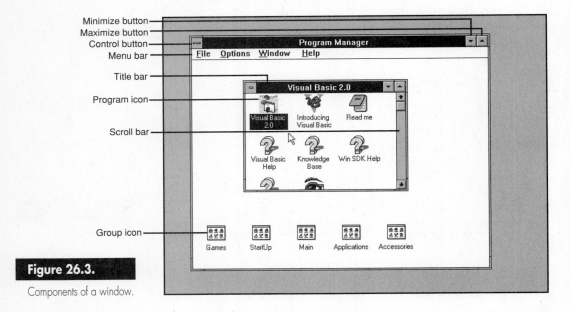

Figure 26.3.

Components of a window.

Table 26.1. The common elements found in all windows.

Element	Description
Title bar	The strip along the top of each window which contains the title for that window.
Control button	The button that opens a control menu from which you can resize, minimize, or close a window.
Minimize button	The button that reduces the window to an icon.
Maximize button	The button that enlarges a window to occupy the full screen.
Menu bar	The horizontal strip located just below the title bar that contains the titles of the menus supported by that window. Not all windows contain menu bars.
Scroll bar	When all of a window's contents cannot fit within the window, a scroll bar enables you to manipulate the mouse to pan the contents of the window horizontally and/or vertically.

Element	Description
Icon	Icons represent windows which have been mini-mized. By double-clicking an icon, you activate (or restore) the application to a window.

Windows from a Programmer's Perspective

The power and convenience of Windows is nice from a user's point of view. But there is a price to pay. Writing a full-fledged Windows program is a formidable task. The complexity of Windows requires programs which cooperate with the Windows environment. Just imagine trying to write a QBasic program that manipulates windows size and placement, pull-down menus, and other graphical objects.

Fortunately, Visual Basic shields the programmer from most of this complexity. With Visual Basic, you design the user interface for an application by selecting graphical objects from a visual toolkit (this is discussed in detail later in this chapter). The standard Windows features, such as resizing and minimizing, are automatically built into your application.

For program developers, Windows includes a body of routines known as the Windows API (Application Program Interface). Over 500 individual functions allow the programmer to interact with the Windows environment. These functions control low-level actions such as drawing visual elements, creating windows and menus, managing system memory, and communicating with the printer and other peripheral devices. These built-in functions are located in Dynamic Link Libraries (DLLs). Windows makes the DLLs available to all applications. The libraries are *dynamic* in the sense that they are dynamically linked on an "as needed" basis while the program executes.

Before Visual Basic, access to the Windows API required development tools such as Borland's Turbo C++ or the Microsoft Windows SDK (System Development Kit). The programmer had to write code utilizing the arcane syntax demanded by the Windows API.

The built-in features of Visual Basic make it unnecessary to directly access the Windows API for most applications. However, for specialized needs, such as adding sound support to your applications, you can still utilize the Windows API. But Visual Basic has tamed the wild beast of Windows programming.

Introducing Visual Basic for Windows

You start VB/Win by double-clicking the Visual Basic icon found in the Microsoft Visual Basic 2.0 group. When you start VB/Win, your screen looks like Figure 26.4.

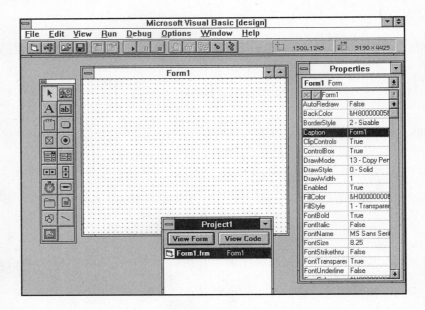

Figure 26.4.

VB/Win's opening screen.

This opening screen might seem imposing and make you feel a little bewildered. You probably notice one thing immediately: The programming environment for VB/Win is a far cry from what you are used to with QBasic.

Indeed, you are treading on unfamiliar territory. To use VB/Win, you will become familiar with a whole new terminology and will learn a whole new approach to programming. The main goals of this chapter are to introduce you to the following subjects:

- Visual Basic terminology

- The phases of developing an application

- The event-driven program model

- Object manipulation

- The design of a user interface

- A sample Visual Basic application

NOTE

A Note to Bewildered Readers

Don't worry if you don't understand everything in this chapter about Visual Basic. This chapter is merely an overview of VB/Win and VB/DOS. Because you probably have not yet worked with Visual Basic, the examples in this chapter are designed only to give you a feel for what Visual Basic programming is like, not to make you an expert. For more detailed information about programming with Visual Basic, refer to one of the popular books on Visual Basic such as *Visual Basic By Example,* by D.F. Scott, published by Que.

Understanding the Components of the Opening Screen

Look again at the opening screen shown in Figure 26.4. The major components of this screen are the Toolbar, the Toolbox, the Form window, the Properties window, and the Project window. Here is a brief introduction to each of these components. Additional details will be given later in this chapter.

Form	This window, located in the center of the screen, is the cornerstone of your application's user interface. When you design an application, you place text boxes, graphic buttons, and other objects onto a form. When the application is run, the form is what the user sees. An application can have several forms.
Toolbar	A row of icons located horizontally near the top of the screen. These icons provide instant access to fre-quently-used commands (and are also available through the menus). Example commands are opening an existing project, running an applica-tion, and single-step tracing.
Toolbox	The vertical icon group located near the left side of the screen. The Toolbox provides a set of graphic objects, called controls, which you can place onto the forms of your application.

Project Window	This window lists the files, forms, and modules that comprise the current application. By clicking a name in this window, you can activate (view) the form or see the program code associated with the form.
Properties Window	This window shows the attributes (properties) associated with a selected form or control. By manipulating values displayed in this window, you can modify the attributes of a control. For example, by changing the `BackColor` property, you can specify the color of the current object.

Thinking Like a Visual Basic Programmer

Working with VB/Win forces you to think about programming with a fresh mind set. Just as with QBasic, everything is logical and orderly, but, compared to QBasic, VB/Win adopts a *different kind* of logic and orderliness. The VB/Win programmer views the working environment in terms of object orientation, controls, forms, event-driven procedures, and methods.

Also, the VB/Win user is part artist, part programmer. You build VB/Win applications by literally drawing controls and other graphic objects onto a blank form. This form becomes the application's user interface. Indeed, beginning VB/Win programmers often feel like they are using a Windows paint program rather than a programming language.

The actual coding required to construct the graphic objects on a form is minimal, often nonexistent. That is remarkable to a QBasic programmer because, with QBasic, programming graphical objects is code intensive and error-prone. With VB/Win, it's done by interactive trial and error and involves little more than mouse movements and button clicks.

The following sections explain some of the terminology important in VB/Win.

Object-Oriented Programming

Objects are one of the hot topics in present-day programming methodology. In general, an *object* combines programming code and data into a single unit. Once defined, an object takes a life of its own. You no longer need to know how the object was created or how it works, you can simply pass information to the object. Also, you can save an object for use in other programs much as you can save QBasic subprograms for use in different programs.

In VB/Win, the primary objects are forms and controls. You draw the controls on the forms. A form defines a window on-screen. A form is what the user actually sees when running the application.

A *control* is an object you place onto a form. Each control performs a specific function. VB/Win includes several predefined controls. Typical VB/Win controls are the command button, check box, and scroll bar. Each control is represented by an icon in the Toolbox. You can also create customized controls which perform specialized functions.

Event-Driven Programs

One of the most profound differences between VB/Win and QBasic is the difference between an event-driven language and a procedural language.

QBasic, QuickBASIC, BASICA, and GW-BASIC are all *procedural* languages. With a procedural language, a program executes by proceeding logically through the program one line at a time. Sure, GOTO instructions and subprogram CALL statements can temporarily transfer logic flow so that the sequential order is interrupted, but the essence of a procedural language is that the program is in control, directing the logic flow procedurally through the program from the beginning of the program to the end.

VB/Win is completely different. Instead of being a procedural language, VB/Win is *event-driven*. Program instructions execute only when a particular event calls that section of code into action. Events are such things as pressing a key, clicking the mouse on a particular control, and the system timer reaching a particular value.

VB/Win automatically executes a SUB procedure when an application event occurs. For example, when the user clicks a command button, VB/Win executes the associated procedure. In this case, VB/Win executes the Command1_Click() procedure. Here, Command1 is the control name and Click is the event. Procedure and control names are discussed in more depth later in this chapter.

The point here is that VB/Win contains, by default, blank procedure bodies for a myriad of events which each control in your application can recognize. Here is where you finally do some actual BASIC coding. You decide which events your program will respond to, and then you write code in the appropriate procedure bodies. For example, when the user clicks the command button, your application might open a new form, display some information, and request data input. To accomplish this, you write the appropriate BASIC instructions in the Command1_Click() procedure. Should you leave this procedure blank, the application simply will not respond when the user clicks the command button.

NOTE ### The Resemblance to BASIC

You won't have much trouble with the language used to write Visual Basic procedures. It's BASIC and your QBasic training puts you in good stead here. Visual Basic contains some language extensions not found in QBasic, but Visual Basic's core language is BASIC, pure and simple.

You can think of an event-driven model as something like a mine field—not in the sense of destruction, thank goodness, but in the sense of a series of actions which take place when an event occurs. Consider that an application contains controls. Lurking "behind" these controls are a series of procedures which spring to action when the appropriate triggering mechanism takes place.

QBasic has a hint of event-driven procedures with error handling (ON ERROR GOTO) and event trapping (ON *event* GOTO). These procedures trap system events and invoke sections of code to respond to these events. For more about error handling and event trapping, see Chapter 21, "Trapping Error and Events."

Unlike a program written with a procedural language, an event-driven program does not consist of a set of instructions which execute in an orderly top-to-bottom manner. Instead, an event-driven program consists of several independent procedures. Each such procedure is associated with one of the objects defined in the application's user interface.

Methods

As stated, object-orientation programming means that objects possess data along with programming code. The program code manipulates the object to perform desired actions. In VB/Win, the program instructions associated with objects are known as *methods*.

To invoke a method in a Visual Basic instruction, you type the object name, a dot, and then the name of the method. Required or optional arguments come after the method name.

For example, the familiar QBasic PRINT instruction is transformed into a method by VB/Win. Consider the following VB/Win instruction:

```
Form1.Print "There's a method to this madness"
```

Here, Print is a method contained in the Form1 object. The Print method displays text on the form. In this case, the instruction displays There's a method to this madness on the form.

Test-Driving Visual Basic—A Sample Application

Suppose you want to write a program which lets the user type in two numbers. On the user's demand, the program displays either the sum or the product of the two input numbers. Another option lets the user quit the application.

This is a simple program, but it does demonstrate how VB/Win works. The following example is meant to give you an idea of the steps you would take to write such a program with VB/Win.

Notice that the title bar of VB/Win itself reads "Microsoft Visual Basic (design)." (You can refer back to Figure 26.4.) The word *design* is quite appropriate. In the initial stages of developing an application, you are *designing* the user interface.

Changing the Form's Caption

When you start VB/Win, the blank form has a name and a title of Form1. The *name* of the form is the identifier VB/Win uses to refer to that form. This concept is something like a variable name, but here the reference is to a VB/Win object rather than a variable or array. The title, called a *caption* in VB/Win terminology, is simply a text string you place in the title bar of the form. By default, VB/Win uses Form1 as both the name and caption for this form. Don't confuse the name and the caption—they are two similar, but different, attributes of certain objects.

Name and caption are two examples of an object's *properties*. In Visual Basic, every object (such as a form) has an associated set of attributes, called properties. Other properties of a form include its size, location, color, and whether the form is visible. Different kinds of objects have different sets of properties.

To change the caption on the form, you use the Properties window. First you click the form to select it. Then you press F4 or click the Properties window to access a list box which displays the various properties associated with the form. You can use the scroll bars on the right side of the Properties window to scroll vertically through the various properties.

When you click on a property listed in the Properties window, the current value for that property appears in the settings box located near the top of the Properties window. You can then click the displayed value and edit the value. In this example, you would click the Caption property in the Properties window, then click the text Form1 (the current value of the Caption property) that appears in the settings box. You can then type a new caption. Figure 26.5 shows the caption changed to A Number Cruncher. As you type the new caption in the settings box of the Properties window, the caption changes in the title bar of the form itself.

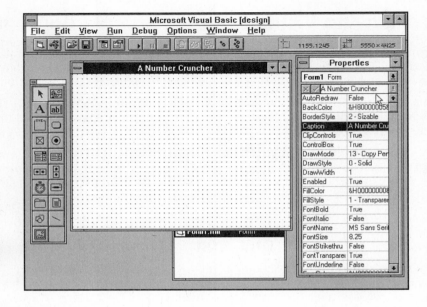

Figure 26.5.

Changing the form's caption.

Adding Text Box Controls

You can now add the desired controls to the form. First, you want to create two boxes into which the user can type the input numbers.

You use a *text box* to get input text from the user. A text box is one of several Visual Basic controls. To activate a control, you select its icon from the Toolbox located along the left side of the screen. To select an icon, you click the mouse button when the arrow pointer is on the icon. In this case the text box icon looks as follows:

Once the icon is selected, you move the pointer onto the form. When you drag the mouse over an area of the form, you see a rectangular frame change shape directly on the form. When you release the mouse button, the control appears on the form with the designated size and location. Figure 26.6 shows a text box placed near the upper-left corner of the form.

Notice that the text box control has 8 little squares along its boundaries. These are sizing handles. By clicking the mouse pointer onto a handle and then dragging the handle, you can resize a control. To move a control, you click the mouse inside the control and drag the entire control. Notice that Visual Basic displays the name of the control, Text1, inside the control.

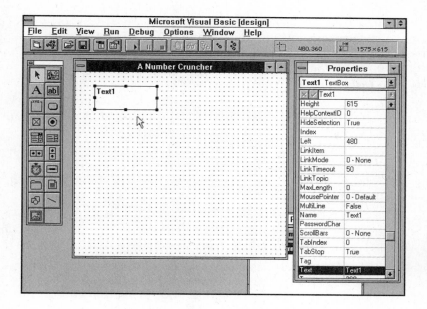

In a similar manner, you can place a second text box to the right of the first
text box. VB/Win names this control Text2.

Adding Labels

A label displays text which the user cannot change. To place a label on the
form, you first click the label icon in the Toolbox. The label icon is shown here.

Placing a label on a form involves the same technique as placing a text box.
This application uses two label controls, one below each text box. VB/Win
gives the labels the default names of Label1 and Label2.

Displaying Text Inside the Labels

When a program begins, you typically want the labels to display certain
values. In this case, the labels might read Type first number and Type second
number, respectively.

As with many other actions, VB/Win provides several ways to display text inside a label. One way involves the same technique used previously to change the caption on the form. You simply activate the Properties window and set the caption property for the label to the desired value.

To use this technique for Label1, you first activate the label by clicking the mouse inside it. Then activate the Properties window by pressing F4 or clicking the Properties window. You can find the Caption property and change the value to Type first number.

A second way to change the text inside a label is to write a procedure which displays the desired text when the program begins. VB/Win includes a Form_Load procedure which executes when the form is loaded in memory, that is, just before the form is visually displayed.

To write code for a procedure, you double-click inside the form (but not inside one of the controls located on the form). VB/Win displays a window in which you can write program code for any particular system event.

In the present example, double-clicking the current form pops open the coding window shown in Figure 26.7. The title bar for the code window reads Form1.frm. That means you are working with events recognized at the level of the form (as opposed to the level of a specific control on the form).

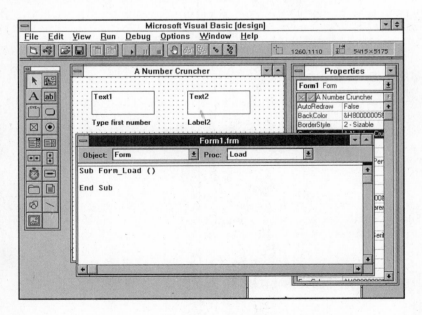

Below the title bar are two boxes labeled Object and Proc. By clicking the Object box, you can access the code procedures for any object defined in the environment. The Proc box lets you write Sub procedures for any events (such as Click) recognized by the currently-selected object.

In this case, the default procedure (Load) in the coding window is exactly the desired procedure. The Load event occurs when the form is loaded at the beginning of program execution. So this sub procedure, labeled Form_Load, activates when the form is loaded.

To specify the text contained in Label2, you can modify the Caption property of the object Label2. Typing the following instruction inside the procedure template does the trick:

```
Label2.Caption = "Type second number"
```

The left-hand side of this assignment instruction specifies the control name (Label2) separated with a dot from the property (Caption). The right-hand side specifies a value for this property which, in this case, is the string literal "Type second number".

You can also add instructions in the Form_Load procedure that initialize the two text boxes. You can specify that when the form loads, the program erases the default text displayed inside the two text boxes. The Text property specifies the text which displays inside a list box. So the following instructions erase the text contained in the two text boxes:

```
Text1.Text = ""
Text2.Text = ""
```

This would make the program start with the two text boxes empty.

Preparing for the Program Output

You can close the code window by pressing Alt-F4 or by selecting Close from the drop-down control menu in the Form1.frm window. By doing so, you return to the design environment in order to make additional modifications to the form.

The form needs a third label control. Inside this label, the program will display the results of the desired calculations. This label might be configured as a large label located in the middle of the screen. VB/Win's default name for a third label control is Label3. Using the Properties window, you can change the caption for this label to read Results will be shown here. Figure 26.8 shows this label in place on the form.

Adding the Command Buttons

The final design step is to add three command buttons near the bottom edge of the form. A *command button* is a control that triggers a specific action when the user selects the button. Typically, the user selects a command button by clicking it with the mouse. Here is the Toolbox icon for a command button:

Here are the three actions that the different command buttons initiate:

1. Display the sum of the two numbers

2. Display the product of the two numbers

3. Quit the program

After adding the command button objects to the form, you can specify the caption displayed on each command button. Once again, you can use the Properties window. VB/Win gives the command buttons the default names of Command1, Command2, and Command3.

Suppose you specify the Caption properties of the three command buttons to be Compute the sum, Compute the product, and Quit respectively. Figure 26.9 shows the completed form.

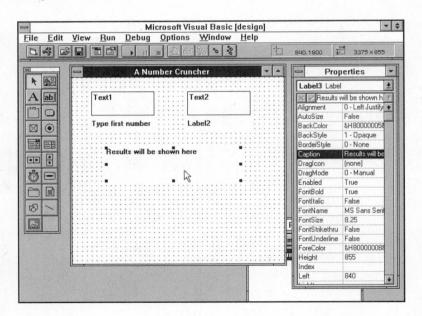

Figure 26.8.

The third label is added.

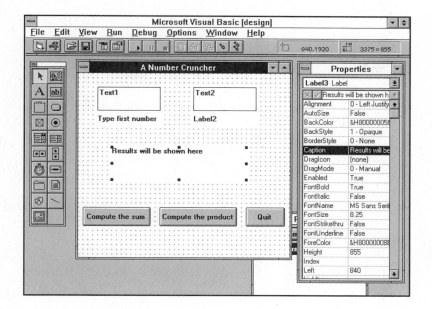

Figure 26.9.

The command buttons are added to the form.

Writing Code for the Command Buttons

The form is designed, but you still must write the event procedures which define what happens when the user clicks each command button.

For the first button, the application must display the sum of the two numbers which the user types in the text boxes. The event associated with the command button is `Click`. In other words, the `Command1_Click` procedure defines what happens when the user clicks the first command button.

To activate the code window for `Command1`, you double-click inside the button. When the code window opens, the `Click` procedure displays by default. Here are the instructions you need to type inside the procedure block:

```
Value = Val(Text1.Text) + Val(Text2.Text)
Label3.Caption = "The sum is " + Str$(Value)
```

In these instructions, `Value` is an ordinary value which stores numerical values. `Text1.Text` and `Text2.Text` refer, respectively, to the text that the user types in the two text boxes. The result of these instructions is that the caption for the third label displays the sum of the two numbers that the user types in the two text boxes.

These instructions use the `Val` and `Str$` functions which you encountered in Chapter 11, "Manipulating Strings." Notice that, with VB/Win, the keywords do not appear in all capital letters as they do with QBasic.

Similarly, the program instructions required inside the `Command2_Click` procedure are as follows:

```
Value = Val(Text1.Text) * Val(Text2.Text)
Label3.Caption = "The product is " + Str$(Value)
```

Finally, the `Command3_Click` procedure must end the program when the third button is pressed. This requires nothing more than an `END` instruction in the code block.

Running the Application

To run the program in the VB/Win environment, you can simply click the Run icon in the Toolbar. The Run icon looks like this:

When this application starts, the `Form_Load` procedure removes the default text in the two text boxes and displays the label for the second label control (`Type second number`).

To use this program, you type a number in each text box. To activate a box for typing, you click when the mouse pointer is inside the box. A cursor appears inside the box which allows you to type a number.

Once the numbers are typed, you can click one of the command buttons. If you select the calculation of the sum or product, you see a message which displays the appropriate value near the middle of the form. Figure 26.10 shows the application displaying the product of 17 and 13. You can click the third command button to end the program.

Reviewing the Sample Application

This sample application was quite simple and only touched on the capabilities of Visual Basic. This was a single-form application which used only a few of the available controls, properties, and triggering events. With Visual Basic, you can design multiple-form applications. Further, the Toolbox contains many more controls which offer a great deal more functionality than the simple controls used in this example.

However, this sample application *does* give you an idea of what working with Visual Basic involves. It is quite a departure from your familiar world of QBasic!

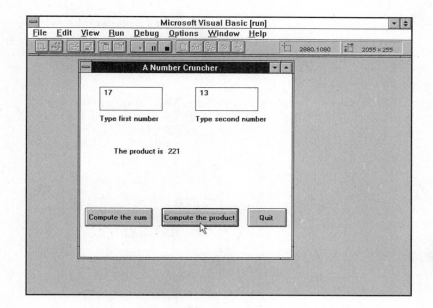

Figure 26.10.

Running the sample
application.

Introducing Visual Basic for MS-DOS

On the heels of VB/Win, Microsoft released a related product in 1992: Visual
Basic for MS-DOS (VB/DOS). This new language offers the same event-driven
program model and similar graphical development tools found in VB/Win.

VB/DOS works completely outside of the Windows environment. With VB/DOS,
you can write applications to run under DOS which have a similar look and feel
to applications that run under Windows.

The VB/DOS development environment parallels the environment of VB/Win.
To create the user interface with both products, you click controls in the
Toolbox, and then place and size those controls on a form. Just as with VB/
Win, you draw the user interface with VB/DOS to look exactly the way it should
appear to the person running your program. You write program instructions
for the pertinent event procedures.

A primary goal of VB/DOS is to act as a bridge between developers working
with VB/Win and those developing QBasic/QuickBASIC applications under
DOS. Unlike VB/Win, VB/DOS runs all code and programs developed with
QBasic/QuickBASIC. That makes Visual Basic for MS-DOS upwardly compatible
with the earlier versions of BASIC. You can consider VB/DOS to be the next
product after QuickBASIC.

The big advantage of this upward compatibility is that you can take existing GW-BASIC/QBasic/QuickBASIC applications, port them to Visual Basic for MS-DOS, and then add controls, mouse support, and user interfaces. As a result, you can overhaul existing programs and provide them with a modern, professional look.

VB/DOS and VB/Win are reasonably compatible. Microsoft provides a utility program called TRNSLATE.EXE which converts VB/DOS applications to VB/Win and vice-versa. There are some incompatibilities between the two languages, however. You typically have to do some additional programming after running TRNSLATE.EXE.

The fact that you can convert applications between VB/Win and VB/DOS means that programs written with VB/DOS can have an extended "shelf life." Should you decide to port an existing VB/DOS application to the Windows environment, you don't have a formidable task. Generally, little code modification is required. Also, it becomes relatively easy to develop applications for DOS and for Windows simultaneously.

The remainder of this chapter serves as an overview of VB/DOS. Here are the major topics presented:

- Introducing the VB/DOS programming environment
- Running a QBasic program under VB/DOS
- Converting the Number Cruncher application to VB/DOS

The VB/DOS Programming Environment

You start VB/DOS by typing **vbdos** at the DOS prompt. Figure 26.11 shows the opening screen.

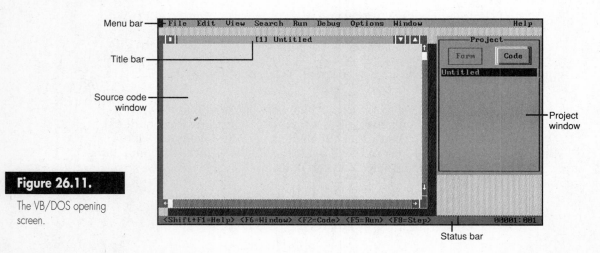

Figure 26.11.

The VB/DOS opening screen.

Notice that, unlike the VB/Win opening screen, the VB/DOS opening screen resembles the familiar QBasic programming environment. The menus along the top of the screen are the same as those in QBasic with the exception of the new Windows menu. In fact, most of the options on the VB/DOS menus are the same as the QBasic menu options. The title bar reads "Untitled" just as with QBasic.

The large window, called the View window in QBasic, is called the Code window in VB/DOS. You type program instructions in the Code window, just as you type instructions in the View window of QBasic.

Compatibility with QBasic

From the opening screen, you are in the VB/DOS editor—you can begin typing a program immediately. VB/DOS is completely compatible with QBasic in the sense that all the reserved words found in QBasic are supported by VB/DOS. However, VB/DOS does have some reserved words not found in QBasic.

At its simplest level, you can use VB/DOS to create and run procedural BASIC programs such as the programs you might develop with QBasic. (Of course, these procedural programs do not utilize the special graphical objects and event-driven procedures unique to Visual Basic.) That means you can type a QBasic program into VB/DOS, or load an existing QBasic program from disk, and run the program directly from the VB/DOS environment.

The only snags arise if your QBasic program uses any of the new VB/DOS reserved words (that is, reserved words not found in QBasic) for the names of variables, line labels, or procedures. In such cases, you must change the conflicting names to new, unique names.

When VB/DOS begins, the cursor is in the Code window and you can begin typing a program. Figure 26.12 shows the RINGS.BAS program from Chapter 13, "Creating Graphics," typed into the VB/DOS Code window. Running this program with VB/DOS produces exactly the same output as the RINGS.BAS program, shown in Figure 13.4.

Just as with QBasic, when you run RINGS.BAS from VB/DOS, the screen clears and you see the output on a separate output screen. The familiar Press any key to continue message appears along the bottom edge of the screen. When you press a key, the VB/DOS editor screen regains control.

The Windows Menu

In the menu bar, VB/DOS includes a menu not found in QBasic: the Window menu. Figure 26.13 shows the options in the Window menu. By selecting one of these options, you open a new window in the editor environment.

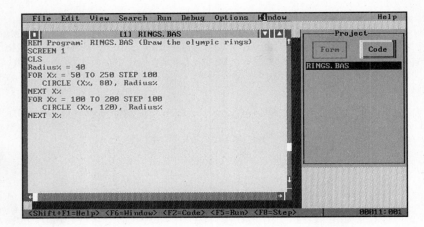

Figure 26.12.

The RINGS.BAS program typed in the VB/DOS editor.

Figure 26.13.

The Window menu.

Table 26.2 shows the various windows you can open in the editor environment.

Table 26.2. VB/DOS Windows available from the Window menu.

Window	Purpose
Calls	Displays the calling sequence of nested procedures. Similar to the Calls window in QuickBasic.
Debug	Debugging tools, including watchpoints.
Help	Displays help.
Immediate	Executes typed instructions instantly. Identical to the Immediate window in QBasic.
Output	Opens a window which is a copy of the output screen.
Project	Displays all the forms and modules in the current application.

Developing Event-Driven Applications

The real power of VB/DOS comes when you develop event-driven applications. VB/DOS includes a form design mode similar to that in VB/Win. You can create forms, place objects on these forms, and then write event procedures which respond to particular events recognized by these objects. The VB/DOS objects, properties, and associated events resemble those present in VB/Win. Indeed, the process of creating event-driven applications with VB/DOS parallels the same process you use with VB/Win.

The Form Designer

Unlike VB/Win, the form designer for VB/DOS is not available concurrently with the Code window. Instead, you must switch VB/DOS between the code-window mode and the form-design mode. To access the form designer, you select the New Form option on the File menu. Figure 26.14 shows the initial screen for the form design mode.

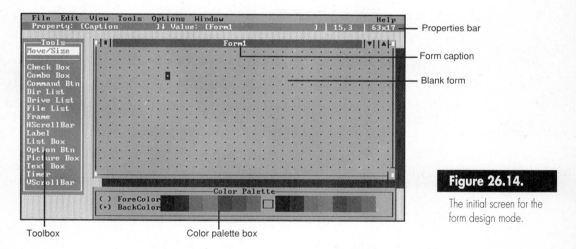

Properties bar

Form caption

Blank form

Toolbox

Color palette box

Figure 26.14.

The initial screen for the form design mode.

The Toolbox

The Toolbox lists the various controls you can add to your form. Most of these controls are similar to those in VB/Win. Notice the command button, label, and text box controls which you learned about during the discussion of VB/Win. However, VB/DOS does not represent the controls with icons. Because VB/DOS runs under DOS, the program does not support the graphical icons prevalent with Windows. As explained shortly, you use this Toolbox exactly as you do with VB/Win.

The Properties Bar

With VB/DOS, you use the Properties bar to assign values to the various properties of each object. This bar has two fields: property and value. By clicking on the property field, you can select a property from a drop-down menu. Then you can enter a value in the value field. To modify the screen colors of each object, VB/DOS has a separate color palette box along the bottom edge of the screen. You can select colors directly from this palette. VB/DOS does not have a separate Properties window as VB/Win does.

Creating a Sample Application—The Number Cruncher

To provide an overview of how you develop an event-driven application with VB/DOS—and to compare VB/DOS with VB/Win—the remainder of this chapter briefly describes the creation of the Number Cruncher application with VB/DOS. This application is identical to the application developed with VB/Win earlier in this chapter. As you'll see, the process of creating event-driven graphical applications in VB/DOS and VB/Win is similar.

Placing Controls on the Form

With VB/DOS, you place controls on the form much as you do with VB/Win. You click the mouse on the name of the control in the Toolbox. You can then move the mouse pointer onto the form, drag a rectangular frame, and drop the frame when the control is properly sized.

For example, Figure 26.15 shows a text box added to the form. Notice that VB/DOS assigns the default caption of Text1, just as VB/Win does. VB/DOS controls have four sizing handles. By manipulating these handles with the mouse, you can resize and reposition controls on the form.

Assigning Values to Control Properties

As described previously, you assign values to the object's properties with the Properties bar. Figure 26.16 shows the almost-completed form with the Caption Quit assigned to the third command button.

The drop-down list of properties appears when you click the arrow to the right of the property field (on the Properties bar). In Figure 26.16, the value Quit has been typed in the value field of the Properties bar. Notice that the form's caption has been set to A Number Cruncher. The completed form looks very similar to the companion form developed with VB/Win.

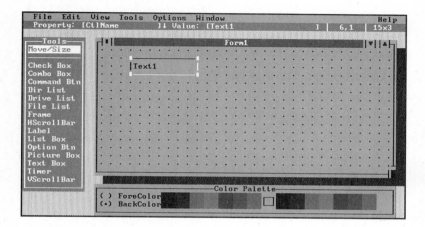

Figure 26.15.

Placing a text box on the form.

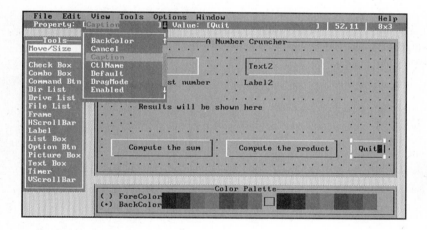

Figure 26.16.

Specifying values for the form's properties.

Adding Code for the Event Procedures

The next step is writing the program instructions that should execute when each expected event occurs. VB/DOS and VB/Win both use event procedures to create event-driven applications. To write such a procedure with VB/DOS, you first select the Event Procedures option on the Edit menu. VB/DOS displays a list of the defined objects and the events that each object can recognize. Figure 26.17 shows this list for the Number Cruncher application.

Notice that the middle box in Figure 26.17 lists the defined objects. These include the form itself, the two text boxes, the three labels, and the three command buttons. To select an object, you click on the object name. In this figure, the first command button, named Command1, is selected. The right-hand box lists the events defined for the currently-selected object. Here, the Click event is chosen.

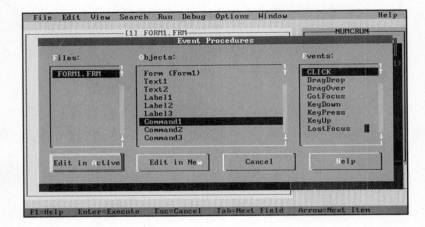

Figure 26.17.

Selecting an event procedure.

To write the code for the indicated procedure, you click the Edit in Active button. VB/DOS opens a code window with the SUB and END SUB instructions already in place. You write the instructions which comprise the body of the procedure.

Figure 26.18 shows the completed event procedure. This is the procedure that executes when the user clicks the first command button (the button which computes the sum). Notice that the procedure name is Command1_Click, just as it is with VB/Win. The instructions inside the procedure are also the same as the instructions in the companion procedure for the VB/Win application.

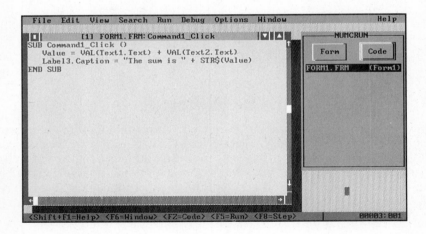

Figure 26.18.

The *Command1_Click* event procedure.

Running the Application

With all the event procedures written, you can start the program by selecting Start from the Run menu or by pressing Shift-F5, just as you do with QBasic.

The VB/DOS version of the Number Cruncher application works just like the VB/Win version. You type a number in each text box. You can then click one of the three command buttons to see the sum of the two numbers, another to see the product of the two numbers, or the third to end the program.

Figure 26.19 shows the VB/DOS application displaying the product of 17 and 13. Compare this figure with Figure 26.10, which shows the output of the same application written in VB/Win.

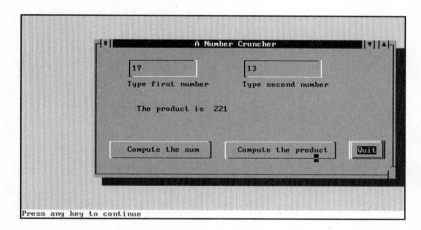

Figure 26.19.

Running the sample VB/DOS application.

In Figure 26.19, the Quit command button has just been pressed. Notice that the bottom line of the screen displays the Press any key to continue message with which you are so familiar from QBasic. When you press a key, the VB/DOS screen returns to the editing environment.

As with the VB/Win version of Number Cruncher, this VB/DOS version was a simple application which demonstrated only a few capabilities of VB/DOS. However, it does reveal how VB/Win and VB/DOS can create similar applications for the two different platforms of DOS and Windows.

Summary

VB/Win represents a radical departure from the type of programming done by a QBasic programmer. Instead of being a procedural language like QBasic, VB/Win uses an event-driven program model with objects, properties, and methods.

You design a user interface by selecting graphic controls from a toolbox and placing these controls directly onto a form. Writing actual code is minimized. The program instructions are primarily located inside event procedures.

VB/DOS is something of a link between the DOS and Windows worlds. With VB/DOS, you can develop the same type of visually oriented, event-driven programs produced by VB/Win. Further, you can port a QBasic program into VB/DOS as a way to provide a graphical front-end to an existing application.

Windows seems to be developing a stranglehold on the future of the PC computing environment. It's interesting that, when deciding on what language tool to offer Windows developers, Microsoft bypassed "trendy" languages like C and Pascal. Instead, the company went back to its roots and chose BASIC. This is nothing short of a testimonial to the popularity and flexibility of BASIC—a language that has been going strong and evolving for thirty years. With Visual Basic for Windows, BASIC has come full circle.

Instant Reference

P A R T

VI

O U T L I N E

This section is an instant reference dictionary of every QBasic keyword. This information puts at your fingertips the answers to simple questions that might arise during programming: "Is `SQR` or `SQRT` the function to calculate square roots? With what statement or function is the `USING` keyword associated? Do I need quotation marks around the file parameter in an `OPEN` instruction?"

These reference descriptions are meant to be brief but informative. They are not designed to teach new concepts or subtleties. Refer to the main text for detailed explanations.

No harm is done, of course, if you skim this material during your idle moments. As your confidence and ability with QBasic grow, such browsing might introduce you to new capabilities of the language.

Keyword Reference

T his quick reference section presents an alphabetic, dictionary-like description of every QBasic keyword. Most entries consist of the name, type, purpose, and syntax associated with the keyword plus a short example of an instruction that uses the keyword.

Description

Each keyword's description consists of the following items:

- Name (the keyword is listed in all caps)
- Type (the category to which the keyword belongs)
- Purpose (what the keyword does)
- Syntax (legal syntax including optional parameters)
- Example (a sample instruction using the keyword)

The Name, Purpose, and Example catagories are self-explanatory, but some further discussion of Type and Syntax is in order.

Types of Keywords

Each keyword is placed into one of the following categories:

- Statement
- Function
- Operator
- Metastatement
- Embedded keyword

A *statement* is a QBasic verb such as CALL or PRINT; every QBasic instruction begins with a statement. Most statements consist of a single keyword but some statements, such as OPTION BASE, consist of two or more keywords. A *function* returns a value and usually is called with one or more arguments; examples of functions are SIN and LEFT$. An *operator* connects one or more operands to form expressions; examples of operators are OR and MOD. A *metastatement* is a non-executable directive such as $DYNAMIC. An *embedded keyword* is a keyword used in conjunction with a statement to form an instruction; examples of embedded keywords include STEP (used with the FOR statement) and BINARY (used with the OPEN statement).

Functions are further subdivided into the categories shown in Table R.1.

Table R.1. QBasic functions.

Function Category	Usage
Numeric	Manipulates numbers
String	Manipulates strings
Screen	Controls video text or graphics
Conversion	Manipulates data types
Memory	Manages memory resources
File	Controls file I/O
Error handling	Processes run-time errors
Device	Controls hardware peripherals
Formatting	Controls printed output

Operators are placed into one of two categories listed in Table R.2.

Table R.2. QBasic keyword operators.

Operator Category	Usage
Logical	Creates Boolean (True/False) expressions
Arithmetic	Creates numeric expressions

Syntax Conventions

The syntax associated with each keyword is presented with the use of some specialized notation. Table R.3 shows the punctuation conventions.

Table R.3. Punctuation conventions.

Symbol	Name	Meaning
[ ]	Brackets	Enclose optional information
¦	Vertical bar	Separates two or more choices, one of which must appear
{ }	Braces	Delimit a list of choices
. . .	Ellipsis	Indicates that the previous construct can be repeated one or more times
_	Underscore	Indicates that a logical line is continued on the next physical line

Brackets, vertical bars, braces, and ellipses do not appear in actual QBasic instructions. These symbols have meaning only in the syntax descriptions. (One exception: Brackets can be used in QBasic instructions as a substitute for parentheses, but the QBasic editor converts the brackets into parentheses.)

Because of horizontal-space restrictions in this book, a syntax description of a single QBasic instruction occasionally must be broken into two physical lines. An underscore character at the end of a line indicates that a single description is continued on the next line.

Only the punctuation symbols in Table R.3 have special meaning. All other punctuation symbols used in the syntax descriptions—including commas, semicolons, and parentheses—are part of the legal syntax for the keyword being described.

As Table R.4 shows, two typographical conventions are used.

Table R.4. Typography conventions.

Typography	Meaning
UPPERCASE	Denotes a keyword
lowercase	Denotes a term that describes the required information

Uppercase words are QBasic keywords. All keywords must appear verbatim in your program instructions. Recall, however, that QBasic does not distinguish between upper- and lowercase. You can use lowercase letters when you type keywords. The editor recognizes all keywords and converts them to uppercase during program entry.

Lowercase terms in the italicized type font signify information that you must provide. These terms are descriptive. See the main text of this book for more detailed explanations about the specific information you must provide. The inside front and back covers provide the appropriate page number reference for each QBasic statement and function. For brevity, some of the italicized terms contain abbreviations (see Table R.5).

Table R.5. Abbreviations used in the lowercase terms.

Abbreviation	Meaning
bool	Boolean (logical)
char	Character(s)
expr	Expression
func	Function
num	Number (numeric)
param	Parameter
pgm	Program
proc	Procedure
seg	Segment
str	String
var	Variable

These abbreviations often are juxtaposed to form compound terms: *strexpr* (string expression), *subpgmname* (subprogram name), and *numvar* (numeric variable), for example.

Syntax Examples

A few examples of complete syntax descriptions might help you become familiar with these conventions.

```
PUT [#]filenum [, recordnum]
```

Because PUT is in uppercase, it is a keyword that must appear verbatim. The brackets around the pound character (#) signify that the pound character is optional. The term *filenum* indicates that a file number parameter must appear next. The subsequent brackets indicate that the *recordnum* (record number) parameter is optional. If *recordnum* appears, a comma must separate the *filenum* and *recordnum* parameters.

```
PEN {ON¦OFF¦STOP}
```

The combination of braces and vertical bars indicates that one of the three options must be chosen. The three acceptable forms, therefore, are PEN ON, PEN OFF, and PEN STOP.

```
CLS [{0¦1¦2}]
```

The brackets surrounding the braces indicate that one or none of the options can be chosen. The four acceptable forms, therefore, are CLS, CLS 0, CLS 1, and CLS 2.

```
READ varname [, varname] ...
```

The READ instruction consists of the keyword READ followed by one or more variable names. If more than one variable name appears, the names are separated by commas. The ellipsis indicates that the optional information between the brackets (a comma followed by a variable name) can be repeated any number of times.

Alphabetic List of QBasic Keywords

ABS   Numeric function

Purpose: Returns the absolute value of a numeric expression.

Syntax: ABS(*numexpr*)

Example: MyValue! = ABS(Number1# * Number2!)

ABSOLUTE   Embedded keyword

Purpose: Invokes a machine-language routine as part of the CALL
ABSOLUTE statement.

Syntax: `CALL ABSOLUTE([argumentlist, ] offset)`

Example: `CALL ABSOLUTE(Arg1%, Arg2%, VARPTR(MyRoutine(1)))`

ACCESS   Embedded keyword

Purpose: Specifies access privileges on an opened file in a networking
environment as part of the OPEN statement.

Syntax: `OPEN filespec [FOR mode] ACCESS accessmode _`
`[lockmode] AS [#]filenum [LEN = recordlength]`

Example: `OPEN "SALARY.DTA" FOR RANDOM ACCESS READ AS #8`

AND   Logical operator

Purpose: Creates the logical (Boolean) result of ANDing two quantities
together.

Syntax: `integerexpr1 AND integerexpr2`

Example: `IF (BigNum% > 9) AND (SmallNum% < 5) THEN PRINT "Voila"`

ANY   Embedded keyword

Purpose: Overrides type checking for a parameter of a procedure as part
of the DECLARE statement.

Syntax: `varname AS ANY`

Example: `DECLARE FUNCTION GetArea# (Side1 AS ANY, Side2 AS ANY)`

APPEND   **Embedded keyword**

Purpose: Prepares a sequential file for appending as part of the OPEN statement.

Syntax:
```
OPEN filespec FOR APPEND [ACCESS accessmode] _
[lockmode] AS [#]filenum [LEN = recordlength]
```

Example:
```
OPEN "B:MYFILE" FOR APPEND AS #1 LEN = 512
```

AS   **Embedded keyword**

Purpose: The AS keyword has several uses:

- Specifies fields as part of the FIELD statement
- Specifies a file number as part of the OPEN statement
- Renames a file as part of the NAME statement
- Specifies a variable's type in a parameter list as part of the DECLARE, FUNCTION, SUB, and DEF FN statements
- Specifies a variable's type as part of the COMMON, DIM, REDIM, SHARED, and STATIC statements
- Specifies the type of a record element as part of the TYPE statement

ASC   **Numeric function**

Purpose: Returns the ASCII code value of the first character of a string expression.

Syntax:
```
ASC(strexpr)
```

Example:
```
FirstChar% = ASC(Title$)
```

ATN   **Numeric function**

Purpose: Returns the arctangent of a numeric expression.

Syntax:
```
ATN(numexpr)
```

Example:
```
MyValue! = ATN(Number1# * Number2#)
```

BASE   **Embedded keyword**

Purpose: Adjusts the allowable range of array subscripts as part of the OPTION BASE statement.

Syntax: `OPTION BASE integerexpr`

Example: `OPTION BASE 1`

BEEP   **Statement**

Purpose: Sounds the PC's internal speaker.

Syntax: `BEEP`

Example: `BEEP`

BINARY   **Embedded keyword**

Purpose: Opens binary files as part of the OPEN statement.

Syntax: `OPEN filespec FOR BINARY [ACCESS accessmode] _`
`[lockmode] AS [#] filenum [LEN = recordlength]`

Example: `OPEN "B:MYFILE.DTA" FOR BINARY AS #3 LEN = 512`

BLOAD   **Statement**

Purpose: Loads into memory a file previously saved with BSAVE.

Syntax: `BLOAD filespec [,offset]`

Example: `BLOAD "IMAGE.CGA", &H4000`

BSAVE   **Statement**

Purpose: Saves a portion of memory onto a disk file.

Syntax: `BSAVE filespec, offset, length`

Example: `BSAVE "IMAGE.CGA", 0, &H1000`

CALL   Statement

Purpose: Invokes a subprogram.

Explicit Form:

Syntax: `CALL subpgmname[(argumentlist)]`

Example: `CALL GetCost(Item$, Price!)`

Implicit Form:

Syntax: `subpgmname[argumentlist]`

Example: `GetCost Item$, Price!`

CALL ABSOLUTE   Statement

Purpose: Invokes a machine-language routine.

Syntax: `CALL ABSOLUTE([argumentlist, ] offset)`

Example: `CALL ABSOLUTE(Arg1%, Arg2%, VARPTR(MyRoutine(1))`

CASE   Embedded keyword

Purpose: Provides comparison testing as part of the SELECT CASE statement.

Syntax:
```
SELECT CASE expr
  CASE testlist
    [instructions]
  [CASE testlist
    [instructions]]...
  [CASE ELSE
    [instructions]]
END SELECT
```

Example:
```
SELECT CASE Age%
  CASE 1 TO 17
    PRINT "Minor"
  CASE IS > 17
    PRINT "Adult"
  CASE ELSE
    PRINT "Impossible"
END SELECT
```

CDBL   Numeric function

Purpose: Converts a numeric expression into double-precision floating-point format.

Syntax: CDBL(*numexpr*)

Example: MyValue# = CDBL(TermA% + TermB%)

CHAIN   Statement

Purpose: Transfers control to another program.

Syntax: CHAIN *filespec*

Example: CHAIN "A:NEWPROG.BAS"

CHDIR   Statement

Purpose: Changes the current directory on a particular drive.

Syntax: CHDIR *pathname*

Example: CHDIR "B:\HOMES\SALES"

CHR$ String function

Purpose: Converts a numerical ASCII code into the equivalent string character.

Syntax: CHR$(*ASCIIcode*)

Example: Character$ = CHR$(65)

CINT   Numeric function

Purpose: Converts, by rounding, a numeric expression into regular (short) integer format.

Syntax: CINT(*numexpr*)

Example: MyValue% = CINT(TermA# * TermB!)

CIRCLE Statement

Purpose: Draws a full circle, ellipse, pie wedge, or part of one.

Syntax:
```
CIRCLE [STEP] (xcenter, ycenter), radius [, [color] _
[, [start], [end] [, aspect ]]]
```

Example:
```
CIRCLE STEP (MyX%, MyY%), 30, 8, , , MyAspect!
```

CLEAR Statement

Purpose: Sets numeric variables to zero and string variables to null, closes all files, and reinitializes the stack.

Syntax:
```
CLEAR [, , stacksize]
```

Example:
```
CLEAR , , 1000
```

CLNG Numeric function

Purpose: Converts, by rounding, a numeric expression into long integer format.

Syntax:
```
CLNG(numexpr)
```

Example:
```
BigInteger& = CLNG(Two%) * 25000
```

CLOSE Statement

Purpose: Ceases I/O operations (close and flush) on specified file(s) or device(s).

Syntax:
```
CLOSE [ [#]filenum [, [#]filenum] ... ]
```

Example:
```
CLOSE 2, #6
```

CLS Statement

Purpose: Clears the screen.

Syntax:
```
CLS [{0¦1¦2}]
```

Example:
```
CLS 1
```

COLOR **Statement**

Purpose: Selects colors for the CRT display (both text and graphics).

Text Mode (SCREEN 0):

Syntax: COLOR [*foreground*] [, [*background*] [, *border*]]

Example: COLOR 4, 0, 3

CGA Graphics Mode (SCREEN 1):

Syntax: COLOR [*background*] [, *palette*]

Example: COLOR Hue%, 1

EGA Graphics Mode (SCREEN 7-10):

Syntax: COLOR [*foreground*] [, [*background*]]

Example: COLOR 3, 2

VGA Graphics Mode (SCREEN 12-13):

Syntax: COLOR [*foreground*]

Example: COLOR 5

COM **Statement**

Purpose: Controls event trapping at a serial communications port.

Syntax: COM(*serialport*) {ON¦OFF¦STOP}

Example: COM(1) ON

COMMON **Statement**

Purpose: Declares a block of global variables for sharing between modules or for passing to a chained program.

Syntax: COMMON [SHARED] *varlist*

Example: COMMON MyString$, MyArray(), Price!

CONST Statement

Purpose: Declares symbolic constants.

Syntax: `CONST constname = expr [, constname = expr] ...`

Example: `CONST Pi! = 3.14159`

COS Numeric function

Purpose: Returns the trigonometric cosine of an angle.

Syntax: `COS(angle)`

Example: `MyValue# = COS(AngleInRadians#)`

CSNG Numeric function

Purpose: Converts a numeric expression into single-precision floating-point format.

Syntax: `CSNG(numexpr)`

Example: `MyValue! = CSNG(TermA%) * TermB%`

CSRLIN Screen function

Purpose: Returns the cursor's vertical position (row).

Syntax: `CSRLIN`

Example: `CursorRow% = CSRLIN`

CVD Conversion function

Purpose: Converts an eight-byte string read from a random-access file into a double-precision floating-point value.

Syntax: `CVD(str8$)`

Example: `MyValue# = CVD(MyString$)`

CVDMBF   **Conversion function**

Purpose: Converts an eight-byte string in Microsoft Binary Format to a double-precision number in IEEE format.

Syntax: CVDMBF(*str8$*)

Example: MyValue# = CVDMBF(MyString$)

CVI   **Conversion function**

Purpose: Converts a two-byte string read from a random-access file into a regular (short) integer value.

Syntax: CVI(*str2$*)

Example: MyValue% = CVI(MyString$)

CVL   **Conversion function**

Purpose: Converts a four-byte string read from a random-access file into a long integer value.

Syntax: CVL(*str4$*)

Example: MyValue& = CVL(MyString$)

CVS   **Conversion function**

Purpose: Converts a four-byte string read from a random-access file into a single-precision floating-point value.

Syntax: CVS(*str4$*)

Example: MyValue! = CVS(MyString$)

CVSMBF   **Conversion function**

Purpose: Converts a four-byte string in Microsoft-Binary-format to a single-precision number in IEEE format.

| Syntax: | CVSMBF(*str4$*) |
| Example: | MyValue! = CVSMBF(MyString$) |

DATA **Statement**

Purpose:	Stores numeric and string literals for READ statements.
Syntax:	DATA *literal* [, *literal*] ...
Example:	DATA Wade Boggs, 0.373, Reggie Jackson, 0.228

DATE$ **Statement**

Purpose:	Sets the current date.
Syntax:	DATE$ = *datestr*
Example:	DATE$ = "9/15/88"

DATE$ **String function**

Purpose:	Retrieves the current date.
Syntax:	DATE$
Example:	Today$ = DATE$

DECLARE **Statement**

Purpose:	Identifies the existence of a procedure and establishes argument type checking for that procedure.
Syntax:	DECLARE {FUNCTION¦SUB} *procname* [([*paramlist*])]
Example:	DECLARE SUB Parse (MyString AS STRING, NumChar%)

DEF FN **Statement**

| Purpose: | Names and defines a user-created function. |

Single-Line Form:

Syntax: `DEF FNfuncname [(paramlist)] = expr`

Example: `DEF FNAverage# (A#, B#, C#) = (A# + B# + C#) / 3#`

Multiline Form:

Syntax:
```
DEF FNfuncname [(paramlist)]
   [instructions]
      FNfuncname = expr
         [instructions]
END DEF
```

Example:
```
DEF FNReverseString$ (InString$)
  Temp$ = ""
  FOR Index% = LEN(InString$) TO 1 STEP -1
    Temp$ = Temp$ + MID$(InString$, Index%, 1)
  NEXT Index%
  FNReverseString$ = Temp$
END DEF
```

DEF SEG   Statement

Purpose: Assigns the default segment address for a subsequent BLOAD, BSAVE, PEEK, or POKE.

Syntax: `DEF SEG [= segaddress ]`

Example: `DEG SEG = &HB800`

DEFDBL   Statement

Purpose: Makes double-precision the default type for variables and functions that begin with specified letters.

Syntax: `DEFDBL letterrange [, letterrange] ...`

Example: `DEFDBL A, C, M-T`

DEFINT   Statement

Purpose: Makes regular integer the default type for variables and functions that begin with specified letters.

Syntax:	`DEFINT letterrange [, letterrange] ...`
Example:	`DEFINT B-E, I-N`

DEFLNG   Statement

Purpose:	Makes long integer the default type for variables and functions that begin with specified letters.
Syntax:	`DEFLNG letterrange [, letterrange] ...`
Example:	`DEFLNG F, H, Q, X-Z`

DEFSNG   Statement

Purpose:	Makes single-precision the default type for variables and functions that begin with specified letters.
Syntax:	`DEFSNG letterrange [, letterrange] ...`
Example:	`DEFSNG A-R, Y`

DEFSTR   Statement

Purpose:	Makes string the default type for variables and functions that begin with specified letters.
Syntax:	`DEFSTR letterrange [, letterrange] ...`
Example:	`DEFSTR B, S-U, Z`

DIM   Statement

Purpose:	Declares and dimensions arrays; also declares a variable and assigns a type.
Syntax:	`DIM [SHARED] varname[(subscriptrange)] [AS type] _` `[, varname[(subscriptrange)] [AS type] ]...`
Example:	`DIM ArrayA$(10 TO 20), Grid!(20 TO 52, 250 TO 320)`

DO — Statement

Purpose: Creates loops.

Top-Test Form:

Syntax:
```
DO [{WHILE boolexpr¦UNTIL boolexpr}]
 [instructions]
LOOP
```

Example:
```
DO WHILE Index% <= NumEmployees%
 PRINT LastName$(Index%)
 Index% = Index% + 1
LOOP
```

Bottom-Test Form:

Syntax:
```
DO
 [instructions]
LOOP [{WHILE boolexpr¦UNTIL boolexpr}]
```

Example:
```
DO
 PRINT LastName$(Index%)
 Index% = Index% + 1
LOOP UNTIL Index% >= NumEmployees%
```

DOUBLE — Embedded keyword

Purpose: Declares a variable's type as double-precision as part of the
COMMON, DECLARE, DEF FN, DIM, FUNCTION, REDIM, SHARED, STATIC, SUB,
and TYPE statements.

Syntax: `varname AS DOUBLE`

Example: `DIM Mass(58) AS DOUBLE`

DRAW — Statement

Purpose: Draws graphics figures specified with a special string definition
language.

Syntax: `DRAW strexpr`

Example: `DRAW "U5R5D5L5"`

ELSE   Embedded keyword

Purpose: Forms conditional tests as part of the IF statement.

Syntax: IF *expr* THEN *thenpart* [ELSE *elsepart*]

Example: IF TermA% >= TermB% THEN PRINT "Yes" ELSE PRINT "No"

ELSEIF   Embedded keyword

Purpose: Forms conditional tests as part of the multiline IF statement.

Syntax:
```
IF expr THEN
    [instructions]
ELSEIF expr THEN
    [instructions]
[ELSEIF expr THEN
    [instructions]] ...
[ELSE
    [instructions]]
END IF
```

Example:
```
IF Age% >= 65 THEN
    PRINT "Senior Citizen"
ELSEIF Age% >= 18 THEN
    PRINT "Adult"
ELSEIF Age% >= 0 THEN
    PRINT "Minor"
ELSE
    PRINT "Unborn"
END IF
```

END   Statement (program flow)

Purpose: Terminates program execution.

Syntax: END

Example: END

END   Statement (multiline structures)

Purpose: Defines the end of a multiline structure.

Syntax: `END {DEF¦FUNCTION¦IF¦SELECT¦SUB¦TYPE}`

Example:
```
IF Balance# < 0 THEN
  PRINT LastName$
  NumOverdrawn% = NumOverdrawn% + 1
END IF
```

ENDIF   Statement

Purpose: Defines the end of a multiline `IF` structure (reformatted by the editor as `END IF`).

Syntax: `ENDIF`

Example:
```
IF Balance# < 0 THEN
  PRINT LastName$
NumOverdrawn% = NumOverdrawn% + 1
ENDIF
```

ENVIRON   Statement

Purpose: Modifies the DOS-environment table before executing a child process with the `SHELL` statement.

Syntax: `ENVIRON strexpr`

Example: `ENVIRON "PATH = A:\CLIENTS"`

ENVIRON$ Memory function

Purpose: Returns a parameter from the DOS-environment table.

String-Parameter Form:

Syntax: `ENVIRON$(environmentstr)`

Example: `MyPath$ = ENVIRON$("PATH")`

Numeric-Parameter Form:

Syntax: `ENVIRON$(integerexpr)`

Example: `MyThirdEnviron$ = ENVIRON$(3)`

EOF   File function

Purpose: Tests whether the end of a sequential or communication (hardware device) file has been reached.

Syntax: `EOF(filenum)`

Example: `IF EOF(3) THEN PRINT "End of file"`

EQV   Logical operator

Purpose: Creates the logical result of the equivalence operator on two quantities (opposite of `XOR`).

Syntax: `integerexpr1 EQV integerexpr2`

Example: `IF (MyChar$ = "M") EQV (OurChar$ = "O") THEN PRINT "OK"`

ERASE   Statement

Purpose: Deallocates dynamic arrays and clears the data values in static arrays.

Syntax: `ERASE arrayname [, arrayname] ...`

Example: `ERASE MyArray#, Grid%`

ERDEV   Error-handling function

Purpose: Returns the integer error code from interrupt 24H when a device error occurs.

Syntax: `ERDEV`

Example: `ErrorCode% = ERDEV`

ERDEV$ Error-handling function

Purpose: Returns the (string) name of the device causing a device error.

Syntax: `ERDEV$`

Example: `PRINT "An error has been detected on device: "; ERDEV$`

ERL   Error-handling function

Purpose: Returns the line number (if present) of the statement causing the most recent error.

Syntax: `ERL`

Example: `PRINT "An error occurred at (or after) line number"; ERL`

ERR   Error-handling function

Purpose: Returns the error code of the most recent error.

Syntax: `ERR`

Example: `IF ERR = 11 THEN PRINT "You can't divide by zero."`

ERROR   Statement

Purpose: Simulates a run-time error or creates a user-defined error code.

Syntax: `ERROR errorcode`

Example: `ERROR 64`

EXIT   Statement

Purpose: Transfers program control from a multiline structure before the logical end of the structure.

Syntax: `EXIT {DEF|DO|FOR|FUNCTION|SUB}`

Example:
```
FOR Index% = 1 TO 100
    Sum# = Sum# + MyValue(Index%)
    IF Sum# > MaxValue# THEN
      PRINT "Maximum has been reached."
      EXIT FOR
    END IF
    PRINT Index%, Sum#
  NEXT Index%
```

EXP   Numeric function

Purpose: Returns the exponential of a number x (that is, e raised to the power x).

Syntax: EXP(*numexpr*)

Example: PRINT "The value of e is"; EXP(1#)

FIELD   Statement

Purpose: Allocates string variables as field variables in a random-access file buffer.

Syntax:
```
FIELD [#]filenum, fieldwidth AS strvar _
[, fieldwidth AS strvar] ...
```

Example: FIELD #1, 8 AS DoubPrec$, 20 AS LastName$, 2 AS Badge$

FILEATTR   File function

Purpose: Returns attributes of an opened file.

Syntax: FILEATTR(*filenum, attribute*)

Example: PRINT "Mode of file #5 is"; FILEATTR(5, 1)

FILES   Statement

Purpose: Displays the file names contained in a specified directory.

Syntax: FILES [*filespec*]

Example: FILES "B:\HOMES*.SLD"

FIX — Numeric function

Purpose: Converts, by truncation, a numeric expression into integer format.

Syntax: `FIX(numexpr)`

Example: `MyValue% = FIX(RealNum#)`

FN — Embedded keyword

Purpose: Names and defines a user-created function as part of the `DEF FN` statement.

Single-Line Form:

Syntax: `DEF FNfuncname [(paramlist)] = expr`

Example: `DEF FNAverage# (A#, B#, C#) = (A# + B# + C#) / 3#`

Multiline Form:

Syntax:
```
DEF FNfuncname [(paramlist)]
      [instructions]
   FNfuncname = expr
      [instructions]
   END DEF
```

Example:
```
DEF FNReverseString$ (InString$)
   Temp$ = ""
   FOR Index% = LEN(InString$) TO 1 STEP-1
     Temp$ = Temp$ + MID$(InString$, Index%, 1)
   NEXT Index%
   FNReverseString$ = Temp$
END DEF
```

FOR — Statement

Purpose: Defines a loop containing instructions to be executed a specified number of times.

Syntax:
```
FOR countervar = start TO end [STEP increment]
      [instructions]
   NEXT [countervar [, countervar] ... ]
```

Example:
```
FOR ItemNumber% = 1 TO LastItem%
    Sum# = Sum# + Price(ItemNumber%)
    PRINT ItemNumber%, Price(ItemNumber%), Sum#
NEXT ItemNumber%
```

FRE — Memory function

Purpose: Returns the available number of RAM bytes left in the string space, the array space, or the real-time stack.

Syntax:
```
FRE({strexpr|numexpr})
```

Example:
```
ArrayMem& = FRE(-1)
```

FREEFILE — File function

Purpose: Returns the lowest unused file number.

Syntax:
```
FREEFILE
```

Example:
```
PRINT "Lowest available file number is"; FREEFILE
```

FUNCTION — Statement

Purpose: Names and defines a function procedure.

Syntax:
```
FUNCTION funcname [(paramlist)] [STATIC]
    [instructions]
    funcname = expr
        [instructions]
END FUNCTION
```

Example:
```
FUNCTION Mean# (ValueA#, ValueB#, ValueC#)
    Sum# = ValueA# + ValueB# + ValueC#
    Mean# = Sum# / 3#
END FUNCTION
```

GET — Statement (files)

Purpose: Reads data from a random-access file into a buffer or from a binary file into a variable.

Syntax:	`GET [#]filenum [, [recordnum] [, variable] ]`
Example:	`GET 3, MyRecord%`

GET   **Statement (graphics)**

Purpose:	Stores a graphics image from the screen into an array.
Syntax:	`GET [STEP] (upleftxy)- [STEP] (lowrightxy),` `arrayname[(indices)]`
Example:	`GET (10, 15)-(36, 45), MyArray%`

GOSUB   **Statement**

Purpose:	Branches to a subroutine.
Syntax:	`GOSUB {linenum¦label}`
Example:	`GOSUB ComputeSales`

GOTO   **Statement**

Purpose:	Branches to a specified statement.
Syntax:	`GOTO {linenum¦label}`
Example:	`GOTO 32100`

HEX$ **Conversion function**

Purpose:	Converts a numeric quantity into the equivalent hexadecimal string.
Syntax:	`HEX$(numexpr)`
Example:	`MyString$ = HEX$(32767)`

IF — Statement

Purpose: Conditionally executes specified statements depending on the evaluation of an expression.

Single-Line Form:

Syntax:
```
IF expr THEN thenpart [ELSE elsepart]
```

Example:
```
IF ValA% > ValB% THEN PRINT "Yes" ELSE PRINT "No"
```

Multiline Form:

Syntax:
```
IF expr THEN
    [instructions]
[ELSEIF expr THEN
    [instructions]] ...
[ELSE
    [instructions]]
END IF
```

Example:
```
IF Amount! > 100 THEN
    NumLargeChecks% = NumLargeChecks% + 1
    PRINT "Another large check"
ELSE
    NumSmallChecks% = NumSmallChecks% + 1
    PRINT "Just a small check"
END IF
```

IMP — Logical operator

Purpose: Creates the logical result of the implication operator on two quantities.

Syntax:
```
integerexpr1 IMP integerexpr2
```

Example:
```
IF (Angle! > 1.5) IMP (Diam! > 4.2) THEN PRINT "Circle"
```

INKEY$ — Device function

Purpose: Returns a character read from the keyboard.

Syntax:
```
INKEY$
```

Example:
```
MyKey$ = INKEY$
```

INP — Device function

Purpose: Returns a byte read from a specified I/O port.

Syntax: `INP(portnum)`

Example: `MyData% = INP(68)`

INPUT — Statement

Purpose: Reads input from the keyboard and prompts the user to provide the desired input.

Syntax: `INPUT [;] [promptstr {,¦;} ] varlist`

Example: `INPUT "What is your name and age"; FullName$, Age%`

INPUT — Embedded keyword

Purpose: Reads a line (ignoring delimiters) as part of the LINE INPUT or LINE INPUT # statement.

Keyboard Form:

Syntax: `LINE INPUT [;] [promptstr;] strvar`

Example: `LINE INPUT "What are your lucky numbers?"; LuckNm$`

Sequential File Form:

Syntax: `LINE INPUT #filenum, strvar`

Example: `LINE INPUT #12, NextLine$`

INPUT# — Statement

Purpose: Reads data from a sequential file or device into specified variables.

Syntax: `INPUT# filenum, varlist`

Example: `INPUT #6, Item$, Price!, Hue%, Supplier$`

INPUT$ — Device function

Purpose: Reads a string of a specified number of characters from the keyboard or from a file.

Syntax:
```
INPUT$(numchar [, [#] filenum])
```

Example:
```
Next8Bytes$ = INPUT$(8, #1)
```

INSTR — String function

Purpose: Searches a string for a specified substring and returns the position where the substring is found.

Syntax:
```
INSTR([startposition,] targetstr, substr)
```

Example:
```
Position% = INSTR(FullName$, "Phil")
```

INT — Numeric function

Purpose: Calculates the largest whole number less than or equal to a specified numeric expression.

Syntax:
```
INT(numexpr)
```

Example:
```
MyVal% = INT(3.1415 * Length#)
```

INTEGER — Embedded keyword

Purpose: Declares a variable's type as single-precision as part of the COMMON, DECLARE, DEF FN, DIM, FUNCTION, REDIM, SHARED, STATIC, SUB, and TYPE statements.

Syntax:
```
varname AS INTEGER
```

Example:
```
SHARED Diameter AS SINGLE, Area AS SINGLE
```

IOCTL — Statement

Purpose: Transmits string data to a device driver.

Syntax:	`IOCTL [#]`*`filenum`*`, `*`strexpr`*
Example:	`IOCTL #43, "PL44"`

IOCTL$ Device function

Purpose:	Reads a control data string from a device driver.
Syntax:	`IOCTL$([#]`*`filenum`*`)`
Example:	`ControlString$ = IOCTL$(#43)`

IS   Embedded keyword

Purpose:	Constructs relational expressions in a CASE clause as part of the SELECT CASE statement.
Syntax:	`CASE IS `*`relationaloperator expr`*
Example:	`CASE IS >= 15`

KEY   Statement (F-key display)

Purpose:	Assigns or displays strings associated with the function keys.

Assignment Form:

Syntax:	`KEY `*`funckeynum`*`, `*`strexpr`*
Example:	`KEY 1, "HELP"`

Display Form:

Syntax:	`KEY {ON¦OFF¦LIST}`
Example:	`KEY ON`

KEY   Statement (key trapping)

Purpose:	Assigns key trap values and enables or disables key trapping.

Assignment Form:

Syntax:	`KEY userkeynum, CHR$(shiftcode) + CHR$(scancode)`
Example:	`KEY 15, CHR$(&H12) + CHR$(&H22)`

Trapping Form:

Syntax:	`KEY(keynum) {ON¦OFF¦STOP}`
Example:	`KEY(8) OFF`

KILL   Statement

Purpose:	Deletes a file or files from a specified directory.
Syntax:	`KILL filespec`
Example:	`KILL "C:\SALARY\*.BAK"`

LBOUND   Memory function

Purpose:	Determines the minimum subscript value for the specified dimension of a previously defined array.
Syntax:	`LBOUND(arrayname[, dimension])`
Example:	`LowerBound% = LBOUND(MyArray, 3)`

LCASE$ String function

Purpose:	Returns the lowercase equivalent of a given string.
Syntax:	`LCASE$(strexpr)`
Example:	`LowerCaseName$ = LCASE$("Phillip S. Feldman")`

LEFT$ String function

Purpose:	Returns the specified number of leftmost characters from a given string.
Syntax:	`LEFT$(strexpr, strlength)`
Example:	`PRINT LEFT$("My dog has fleas", 6)`

LEN String function

Purpose: Returns the number of characters in a string or the number of bytes required by a variable or record.

Syntax: `LEN({strexpr¦variable})`

Example: `MyStringLength% = LEN(MyString$)`

LET Statement

Purpose: Assigns a value to a given variable.

Syntax: `[LET] varname = expr`

Example: `LET MyArray%(18) = 322`

LINE Statement

Purpose: Draws a line or rectangle on the screen.

Syntax: `LINE [(startpoint)]-(endpoint) [, [color] [, [B[F]]_`
     `[, pattern]]]`

Example: `LINE (5,12)-(75, 44), 6, B`

LINE INPUT Statement

Purpose: Reads a line typed at the keyboard (ignoring delimiters) into a string variable.

Syntax: `LINE INPUT [;] [promptstr;] strvar`

Example: `LINE INPUT "What are your lucky numbers?"; LuckyNums$`

LINE INPUT # Statement

Purpose: Reads a line from a sequential file (ignoring delimiters) into a string variable.

Syntax: `LINE INPUT #filenum, strvar`

Example: `LINE INPUT #12, NextLine$`

LIST   Embedded keyword

Purpose: Displays function-key assignments as part of the KEY statement.

Syntax: KEY LIST

Example: KEY LIST

LOC   File function

Purpose: Returns the current position within a specified file.

Syntax: LOC(*filenum*)

Example: PRINT "The file 3 pointer is at"; LOC(3)

LOCATE   Statement

Purpose: Moves the cursor to a specified position and/or changes the cursor's physical attributes.

Syntax: LOCATE [*row*] [, [*column*] [, [*cursorflag*] _
[, [*startline*] [,*stopline*]]]]

Example: LOCATE 10, 40, 1, 4, 7

LOCK   Statement

Purpose: Establishes the permissible access to an opened file in a network environment.

Syntax: LOCK [#]*filenum* [, {*recordnum*¦[*start*] TO *end*}]

Example: LOCK #5, 6 TO 18

LOF   File function

Purpose: Returns the number of bytes (length) of a specified file.

Syntax: LOF(*filenum*)

Example: FileLength% = LOF(8)

LOG   Numeric function

Purpose: Returns the natural logarithm (base *e*) of a given numeric expression.

Syntax: LOG(*numexpr*)

Example: PRINT "The natural log of 16 is"; LOG(16)

LONG   Embedded keyword

Purpose: Declares a variable's type as long integer as part of the COMMON, DECLARE, DEF FN, DIM, FUNCTION, REDIM, SHARED, STATIC, SUB, and TYPE statements.

Syntax: *varname* AS LONG

Example: FUNCTION GetState$(ZipCode AS LONG)

LOOP   Embedded keyword

Purpose: Terminates (physically and logically) loop structures as part of a DO statement.

Top-Test Form:

Syntax:
```
DO [{WHILE boolexpr¦UNTIL boolexpr}]
        [instructions]
LOOP
```

Example:
```
DO WHILE Index% <= NumEmployees%
        PRINT LastName$(Index%)
        Index% = Index% + 1
LOOP
```

Bottom-Test Form:

Syntax:
```
DO
        [instructions]
LOOP [{WHILE boolexpr¦UNTIL boolexpr}]
```

Example:
```
DO
        PRINT LastName$(Index%)
        Index% = Index% + 1
LOOP UNTIL Index% >= NumEmployees%
```

LPOS   **Device function**

Purpose: Returns the column position of the specified line printer's print head within the printer buffer.

Syntax: LPOS(*printernum*)

Example: PRINT "LPT1: is positioned at column"; LPOS(1)

LPRINT   **Statement**

Purpose: Prints data on the line printer (LPT1:).

Syntax: LPRINT [*exprlist*] [{;¦,}]

Example: LPRINT CompanyName$, Address$, Sales!

LPRINT USING   **Statement**

Purpose: Prints data on the line printer (LPT1:) under format control of a formatting string.

Syntax: LPRINT USING *formatstr*; *exprlist* [{;¦,}]

Example: LPRINT USING "$$###.##"; ItemCost!, TotalSale!, 442

LSET   **Statement**

Purpose: The LSET keyword has two purposes:

- Moves left-justified string data into a file buffer in preparation for writing to a random-access file
- Left-justifies a string expression within a string variable

Syntax: LSET *strvar* = *strexpr*

Example: LSET MyString$ = "Inventory List"

LTRIM$ **String function**

Purpose: Returns a copy of a specified string with leading spaces removed.

Syntax:　　　LTRIM$(*strexpr*)

Example:　　MyString$ = LTRIM$("　　No more leading blanks")

MID$　　　　Statement

Purpose:　Replaces a portion of a given string with another specified string.

Syntax:　MID$(*strvar, position* [,*length*]) = *strexpr*

Example:　MID$(MyString, 8) = "08/02/89"

MID$　　　　String function

Purpose:　Returns a length-specified substring from a given string expression.

Syntax:　MID$(*strexpr, startposition* [,*strlength*])

Example:　PRINT "Characters 10-15 are:"; MID$(MyString$, 10, 6)

MKDIR　　　　Statement

Purpose:　Creates a subdirectory.

Syntax:　MKDIR *pathname*

Example:　MKDIR "C:\ERRORLOG"

MKDMBF$　　　Conversion function

Purpose:　Converts a double-precision number in IEEE format to an eight-byte string in Microsoft-Binary-format.

Syntax:　MKDMBF$(*numexpr*)

Example:　DoublePrecisionString$ = MKDMBF$(MyDoubPrecNumber#)

MKD$ **Conversion function**

Purpose: Converts a double-precision quantity to the proper eight-byte string before writing to a random-access file.

Syntax: MKD$(*numexpr*)

Example: DoublePrecisionString$ = MKD$(MyDoubPrecNumber#)

MKI$ **Conversion function**

Purpose: Converts an integer quantity to the proper two-byte string before writing to a random-access file.

Syntax: MKI$(*integerexpr*)

Example: IntegerString$ = MKI$(MyInteger%)

MKL$ **Conversion function**

Purpose: Converts a long integer quantity to the proper four-byte string before writing to a random-access file.

Syntax: MKL$(*longintegerexpr*)

Example: LongIntegerString$ = MKL$(MyLongInteger&)

MKS$ **Conversion function**

Purpose: Converts a single-precision quantity to the proper four-byte string before writing to a random-access file.

Syntax: MKS$(*numexpr*)

Example: SinglePrecisionString$ = MKS$(MySingPrecNumber!)

MKSMBF$ **Conversion function**

Purpose: Converts a single-precision number in IEEE format to a four-byte string in Microsoft-Binary-format.

Syntax:	`MKSMBF$(numexpr)`
Example:	`SinglePrecisionString$ = MKSMBF$(MySingPrecNumber!)`

MOD   Arithmetic operator

Purpose: Calculates the modulo of one integer expression with respect to a second integer expression.

Syntax: `integerexpr1 MOD integerexpr2`

Example: `PRINT "Remainder of 89 divided by 7 is"; 89 MOD 7`

NAME   Statement

Purpose: Renames a specified disk file.

Syntax: `NAME oldfilespec AS newfilespec`

Example: `NAME "ROSTER88.DTA" AS "ROSTER89.DTA"`

NEXT   Statement

Purpose: Defines the end of loops created with the `FOR` statement.

Syntax: `NEXT [countervar [, countervar] ... ]`

Example: `NEXT Index%`

NOT   Logical operator

Purpose: Creates the logical (Boolean) negation of a quantity.

Syntax: `NOT integerexpr`

Example: `IF NOT (MyColor$ = "Red") THEN PRINT "It's not red"`

OCT$ Conversion function

Purpose: Converts a numeric quantity into the equivalent octal (base 8) string.

Syntax:	OCT$(*numexpr*)
Example:	MyString$ = OCT$(32767)

OFF   Embedded keyword

Purpose:	Disables event trapping of a particular device as part of the COM, KEY, PEN, PLAY, STRIG, or TIMER statement.
Syntax:	{COM(*port*)¦KEY¦KEY[(*keynum*)]¦PEN¦PLAY¦STRIG¦TIMER} OFF
Example:	PEN OFF

ON   Embedded keyword

Purpose:	Enables event trapping of a particular device as part of the COM, KEY, PEN, PLAY, STRIG, or TIMER statement.
Syntax:	{COM(*port*)¦KEY¦KEY[(*keynum*)]¦PEN¦PLAY¦STRIG¦TIMER} ON
Example:	PEN ON

ON COM GOSUB   Statement

Purpose:	Designates the subroutine to be invoked when a serial communication port event is trapped.
Syntax:	ON COM(*serialport*) GOSUB {*linenum*¦*label*}
Example:	ON COM(1) GOSUB TrapRoutine

ON ERROR GOTO   Statement

Purpose:	Enables run-time error trapping and designates the line to branch to when an error occurs.
Syntax:	ON ERROR {GOTO {*linenum*¦*label*} ¦ RESUME NEXT}
Example:	ON ERROR GOTO ErrorHandler

ON GOSUB   Statement

Purpose: Invokes one of a designated list of subroutines according to the value of a numeric expression.

Syntax: ON *numexpr* GOSUB {*linenumlist*¦*labellist*}

Example: ON Siblings% GOSUB OneSib, TwoSib, ThreeSib

ON GOTO   Statement

Purpose: Branches to one of a specified set of lines according to the value of a numeric expression.

Syntax: ON *numexpr* GOTO {*linenumlist*¦*labellist*}

Example: ON Strokes% GOTO HoleInOne, Eagle, Birdie, Par, Bogey

ON KEY GOSUB   Statement

Purpose: Specifies the first line of a trap subroutine to be invoked if a particular key is pressed.

Syntax: ON KEY (*keynum*) GOSUB {*linenum*¦*label*}

Example: ON KEY(6) GOSUB TrapRoutineForF6

ON PEN GOSUB   Statement

Purpose: Specifies the first line of a trap subroutine to be invoked if the light pen is activated.

Syntax: ON PEN GOSUB {*linenum*¦*label*}

Example: ON PEN GOSUB LightPenTrapRoutine

ON PLAY GOSUB   Statement

Purpose: Specifies the first line of a trap subroutine to be invoked when the music buffer has less than a certain number of notes.

Syntax: `ON PLAY (noteminimum) GOSUB {linenum¦label}`

Example: `ON PLAY(15) GOSUB MusicBufferTrapRoutine`

ON STRIG GOSUB   Statement

Purpose: Specifies the first line of a trap subroutine to be invoked when a certain joystick button is activated.

Syntax: `ON STRIG (button) GOSUB {linenum¦label}`

Example: `ON STRIG(2) GOSUB TrapRoutineForJoystick`

ON TIMER GOSUB   Statement

Purpose: Specifies the first line of a trap subroutine to be invoked at a given time interval.

Syntax: `ON TIMER (numseconds) GOSUB {linenum¦label}`

Example: `ON TIMER(60) GOSUB TrapRoutineForEachMinute`

OPEN   Statement

Purpose: Initializes a file or device for I/O activity.

Verbose Form:

Syntax: `OPEN filespec [FOR mode] [ACCESS accessmode] _`
                `[lockmode] AS [#]filenum [LEN=recordlength]`

Example: `OPEN "A:MYFILE.DTA" FOR INPUT AS #4`

Succinct Form:

Syntax: `OPEN modestr, [#]filenum, filespec [,recordlength]`

Example: `OPEN "I", #4, "A:MYFILE.DTA"`

OPEN COM   Statement

Purpose: Opens and initializes a serial communications port.

Syntax: OPEN "COM *portnum*: [*primaryoptions*] [*secondaryoptions*]"_
[FOR *mode*] AS [#]*filenum* [LEN = *numbytes*]

Example: OPEN "COM2: 1200, , 8, , LF" FOR RANDOM AS #2

OPTION BASE   Statement

Purpose: Declares, for subsequent DIM statements, the default minimum
value for array subscripts.

Syntax: OPTION BASE *integerexpr*

Example: OPTION BASE 1

OR   Logical operator

Purpose: Creates the logical (Boolean) result of ORing two quantities
together.

Syntax: *integerexpr1* OR *integerexpr2*

Example: IF (Debt! < 0) OR (NumOrders% > 9) THEN PRINT "Success"

OUT   Statement

Purpose: Transmits a data byte to an I/O port.

Syntax: OUT *portnum*, *databyte*

Example: OUT Port%, 127

OUTPUT   Embedded keyword

Purpose: Initializes a file or device to be written to as part of the OPEN
statement.

Syntax: OPEN *filespec* FOR OUTPUT [ACCESS *accessmode*] _
[*lockmode*] AS [#]*filenum* [LEN = *recordlength*]

Example: OPEN "A:MYFILE.DTA" FOR OUTPUT AS #4

PAINT Statement

Purpose: Fills a graphics region on the screen with a specified color or pattern.

Syntax: PAINT [STEP] (*startxy*) [, [,*paint*] [, [*bordercolor*] _
[,*background*]]]

Example: PAINT (60,35), ColorCode%, 1

PALETTE Statement

Purpose: Changes a color in the palette used for EGA, VGA, or MCGA graphics.

Syntax: PALETTE [*attribute, color*]

Example: PALETTE 1, 14

PALETTE USING Statement

Purpose: Redefines the 16 colors used in the palette for EGA, VGA, or MCGA graphics.

Syntax: PALETTE USING *arrayname* [(*arrayindex*)]

Example: PALETTE USING EGAColors%(4)

PCOPY Statement

Purpose: Copies a specified screen page to another screen page.

Syntax: PCOPY *sourcepage, targetpage*

Example: PCOPY 2, 3

PEEK Memory function

Purpose: Returns the value of the data byte stored at a specified memory location.

Syntax: `PEEK(offset)`

Example: `PRINT PEEK(&H4F)`

PEN   Statement

Purpose: Enables or disables the trapping of light-pen activity.

Syntax: `PEN {ON|OFF|STOP}`

Example: `PEN ON`

PEN   Device function

Purpose: Returns the status of light-pen activity.

Syntax: `PEN(penoption)`

Example: `IF PEN(0) THEN PRINT "Light pen is activated."`

PLAY   Statement

Purpose: Plays music specified with a special string definition language, or enables or disables music trapping.

Music-Playing Form:

Syntax: `PLAY strexpr`

Example: `PLAY "O2L4CC#DEFGAB-B"`

Trapping Form:

Syntax: `PLAY {ON|OFF|STOP}`

Example: `PLAY ON`

PLAY   Device function

Purpose: Returns the number of unplayed notes in the background music buffer.

Syntax: `PLAY(dummyargument)`

Example: `IF PLAY(1) < 10 THEN PRINT "Almost done"`

PMAP   **Screen function**

Purpose: Translates a physical coordinate into the proper world coordinate or vice versa.

Syntax: `PMAP(coordinate, mapoption)`

Example: `LINE -(PMAP(XValue%, 0), PMAP(YValue%, 1))`

POINT   **Screen function**

Purpose: Returns the color of a screen pixel or returns the *x* or *y* coordinate of a screen pixel.

Color Form:

Syntax: `POINT(xycoordinates)`

Example: `IF POINT(20,25) = 12 THEN PRINT "Light red"`

Coordinate Form:

Syntax: `POINT(pointoption)`

Example: `PRINT "Physical y coordinate is"; POINT(1)`

POKE   **Statement**

Purpose: Writes a specified byte into a given memory location.

Syntax: `POKE offset, databyte`

Example: `POKE &H1FFF, 255`

POS   **Device function**

Purpose: Returns the current horizontal position of the cursor.

Syntax: `POS(dummyargument)`

Example: `PRINT "The cursor is at column number"; POS(Dummy)`

PRESET   Statement

Purpose: Draws a point at a specified position on the graphics screen.

Syntax: `PRESET [STEP] (xypoint) [, color]`

Example: `PRESET (230, 55), 4`

PRINT   Statement

Purpose: Writes data on the video screen.

Syntax: `PRINT [exprlist] [ {,¦;} ]`

Example: `PRINT "The values of NumA% and StrB$ are", NumA%, StrB$`

PRINT #   Statement

Purpose: Writes data to a specified file.

Syntax: `PRINT #filenum, [exprlist] [ {,¦;} ]`

Example: `PRINT #7, "03/04/89", NumOrders%, Sales!`

PRINT USING   Statement

Purpose: Writes data on the video screen under formatting control.

Syntax: `PRINT USING formatstr; exprlist [ {,¦;} ]`

Example: `PRINT USING "$$####.##"; BankBalance!, CheckAmount!`

PRINT # USING   Statement

Purpose: Writes data to a specified file under formatting control.

Syntax: `PRINT #filenum, USING formatstr; [exprlist] [ {,¦;} ]`

Example: `PRINT #5, USING "$$####.##"; BankBalance!, CheckAmount!`

PSET   Statement

Purpose: Draws a point at a specified position on the graphics screen.

Syntax: PSET [STEP] (*xypoint*) [, *color*]

Example: PSET (230, 55), 4

PUT   Statement (files)

Purpose: Writes a record from a random-access buffer or a variable to a random-access file.

Syntax: PUT [#]*filenum* [[, *recordnum*] [, *variable*]]

Example: PUT #3, MyRecord%

PUT   Statement (graphics)

Purpose: Draws on the video screen a graphics image stored in a specified array.

Syntax: PUT [STEP] (*upleftxy*), *arrayname* [(*indices*)] [, *drawoption*]

Example: PUT (300, 106), MyImage%, AND

RANDOM   Embedded keyword

Purpose: Opens random-access files as part of the OPEN statement.

Syntax: OPEN *filespec* FOR RANDOM [ACCESS *accessmode*] _
              [*lockmode*] AS [#]*filenum* [LEN = *recordlength*]

Example: OPEN "MYFILE.DTA" FOR RANDOM AS #12

RANDOMIZE   Statement

Purpose: Reseeds the random-number generator.

Syntax: RANDOMIZE [*seed*]

Example: RANDOMIZE TIMER

READ   **Statement**

Purpose: Assigns to a variable or variables data values read from DATA
statement(s).

Syntax: `READ varname [, varname] ...`

Example: `READ ClubName$, NumMembers%, MeetingNight$`

REDIM   **Statement**

Purpose: Reallocates previously declared dynamic arrays.

Syntax: `REDIM [SHARED] varname(subscriptrange) [AS type] _`
`[, varname(subscriptrange) [AS type] ]...`

Example: `REDIM ArrayA$(10 TO 20), Grid!(20 TO 52, 250 TO 320)`

REM   **Statement**

Purpose: Declares the rest of a program line to be explanatory remarks
(and thus not source code for compilation).

Syntax: `REM remark`

Example: `REM This program computes your biorhythms.`

RESET   **Statement**

Purpose: Ceases I/O operations (close and flush) on all opened files and
devices.

Syntax: `RESET`

Example: `RESET`

RESTORE   **Statement**

Purpose: Resets the DATA statement pointer to a specified line for a
subsequent READ statement.

| Syntax: | RESTORE [{*linenum*¦*label*}] |
| Example: | RESTORE StudentData |

RESUME **Statement**

Purpose: Resumes program execution at a specified location after control is passed to an error-handling routine.

| Syntax: | RESUME [{0¦NEXT¦*linenum*¦*label*}] |
| Example: | RESUME NEXT |

RETURN **Statement**

Purpose: Terminates a subroutine and resumes execution at a specified location.

| Syntax: | RETURN [{*linenum*¦*label*}] |
| Example: | RETURN 3300 |

RIGHT$ **String function**

Purpose: Returns the specified number of rightmost characters from a given string.

| Syntax: | RIGHT$(*strexpr, strlength*) |
| Example: | PRINT RIGHT$("I don't think you are right", 13) |

RMDIR **Statement**

Purpose: Removes (deletes) an existing disk directory.

| Syntax: | RMDIR *pathname* |
| Example: | RMDIR "A:\OLDFILES" |

RND   Numeric function

Purpose: Returns a pseudo-random number between 0 and 1.

Syntax: `RND[(numexpr)]`

Example: `IF RND > .5 THEN PRINT "Coin toss is heads"`

RSET   Statement

Purpose: The RSET keyword has two purposes:

- Moves right-justified string data into a file buffer in preparation for writing to a random-access file.

- Right-justifies a string expression within a string variable.

Syntax: `RSET strvar = strexpr`

Example: `RSET MyString$ = "Inventory List"`

RTRIM$ String function

Purpose: Returns a copy of a specified string with trailing spaces removed.

Syntax: `RTRIM$(strexpr)`

Example: `MyString$ = RTRIM$("No more trailing blanks      ")`

RUN   Statement

Purpose: Restarts the current program or begins execution of another (specified) program.

Syntax: `RUN [{linenum¦filespec}]`

Example: `RUN "C:\DEMOS\BIRTHDAY.EXE"`

SCREEN   **Statement**

Purpose: Sets the screen display mode.

Syntax:
```
SCREEN [modecode] [, [colorswitch] [, [activepage] _
[, [visualpage]]]]
```

Example:
```
SCREEN 7, , 2
```

SCREEN   **Screen function**

Purpose: Returns the character or the character's color (attribute) at a specified row and column of the screen.

Syntax:
```
SCREEN(row, column [, optionflag])
```

Example:
```
PRINT "Upper left character is ASCII code"; SCREEN(1,1)
```

SEEK   **Statement**

Purpose: Sets the pointer in a file to a specified position.

Syntax:
```
SEEK [#]filenum, position
```

Example:
```
SEEK #10, &H100
```

SEEK   **File function**

Purpose: Returns the current file position.

Syntax:
```
SEEK(filenum)
```

Example:
```
IF SEEK(5) = 1 THEN PRINT "File #5 is ready to read"
```

SEG   **Embedded keyword**

Purpose: Assigns the default segment address as part of the DEF SEG statement.

Syntax:
```
DEF SEG [= segaddress ]
```

Example:
```
DEF SEG = &HB800
```

SELECT CASE   Statement

Purpose: Conditionally executes one of several series of statements depending on the value of a test expression.

Syntax:
```
SELECT CASE expr
      CASE testlist
         [instructions]
      [CASE testlist
         [instructions]] ...
      [CASE ELSE
         [instructions]]
END SELECT
```

Example:
```
SELECT CASE Age%
      CASE 1 TO 17
         PRINT "Minor"
      CASE IS > 17
         PRINT "Adult"
      CASE ELSE
         PRINT "Impossible"
END SELECT
```

SGN   Numeric function

Purpose: Returns the sign of a numeric expression.

Syntax: SGN(numexpr)

Example: IF SGN(MyScore% - YourScore%) = 1 THEN PRINT "I won!"

SHARED   Statement

Purpose: Declares one or more variables in a subprogram or function procedure global to the main program.

Syntax: SHARED varname [AS type] [, varname [AS type]] ...

Example: SHARED Index%, TempString$, MyArray()

SHELL   **Statement**

Purpose: Executes another program or DOS shell while retaining QBasic in memory.

Syntax: `SHELL [commandstr]`

Example: `SHELL "CHKDSK A:"`

SIN   **Numeric function**

Purpose: Returns the trigonometric sine of an angle.

Syntax: `SIN(angle)`

Example: `MyValue# = SIN(AngleInRadians#)`

SINGLE   **Embedded keyword**

Purpose: Declares a variable's type as single-precision as part of the `COMMON`, `DECLARE`, `DEF FN`, `DIM`, `FUNCTION`, `REDIM`, `SHARED`, `STATIC`, `SUB`, and `TYPE` statements.

Syntax: `varname AS SINGLE`

Example: `DIM Weight(100) AS SINGLE`

SLEEP   **Statement**

Purpose: Pauses program execution for a specified time period.

Syntax: `SLEEP [numseconds]`

Example: `SLEEP 15`

SOUND   **Statement**

Purpose: Sounds a tone from the internal speaker.

Syntax: `SOUND frequency, duration`

Example: `SOUND 4000, 100`

SPACE$ — String function

Purpose: Returns a string comprising a specified number of spaces (blank characters).

Syntax: SPACE$(*numspaces*)

Example: HeaderString$ = "1" + SPACE$(7) + "9"

SPC — Formatting function

Purpose: Generates a specified number of spaces within a PRINT or LPRINT statement.

Syntax: {PRINT¦LPRINT} [#*filenum*] SPC(*numspaces*)]

Example: PRINT FirstName$; SPC(25); SecondName$

SQR — Numeric function

Purpose: Returns the square root of a numeric expression.

Syntax: SQR(*numexpr*)

Example: Hypotenuse! = SQR(SideA! * SideA! + SideB! * SideB!)

STATIC — Statement

Purpose: Declares one or more variables in a user-defined function or subprogram to have static allocation.

Syntax: STATIC *varname*[()] [AS *type*] [,*varname*[()] [AS *type*]]...

Example: STATIC Index%, TempString$, MyArray()

STEP — Embedded keyword

Purpose: Specifies the increment to advance the counter variable as part of the FOR statement; also specifies relative (not absolute) coordinates as part of the CIRCLE, GET, LINE, PAINT, PRESET, PSET, and PUT statements.

Syntax:	`FOR` *countervar* `= ` *start* `TO` *end* `STEP` *increment*
Example:	`FOR Index% = 10 TO 200 STEP 5`

STICK   Device function

Purpose:	Returns the *x* or *y* coordinate of the specified joystick.
Syntax:	`STICK(`*stickoption*`)`
Example:	`PRINT "X value of Joystick B is"; STICK(2)`

STOP   Statement

Purpose:	Terminates program execution.
Syntax:	`STOP`
Example:	`STOP`

STOP   Embedded keyword

Purpose:	Suspends event trapping of a particular device as part of the `COM`, `KEY`, `PEN`, `STRIG`, or `TIMER` statement.
Syntax:	`{COM(`*port*`)¦¦KEY¦KEY(`*keynum*`)¦PEN¦PLAY¦STRIG¦TIMER} STOP`
Example:	`PEN STOP`

STR$ Conversion function

Purpose:	Converts the value of a numeric expression into the equivalent string representation.
Syntax:	`STR$(`*numexpr*`)`
Example:	`Equation$ = "Pi = " + STR$(4 * ATN(1))`

STRIG   **Statement**

Purpose: Enables or disables joystick-button trapping.

Syntax: STRIG (*button*) {ON¦OFF¦STOP}

Example: STRIG(2) OFF

STRIG   **Device function**

Purpose: Returns joystick-button activity.

Syntax: STRIG(*buttonoption*)

Example: IF STRIG(1) THEN PRINT "Joystick A button is down"

STRING   **Embedded keyword**

Purpose: Declares a variable's type as string as part of the COMMON, DECLARE, DEF FN, DIM, FUNCTION, REDIM, SHARED, STATIC, SUB, and TYPE statements.

Syntax: *varname* AS STRING

Example: DIM Members(500) AS STRING

STRING$ **String function**

Purpose: Returns a string consisting of a specified number of identical characters.

Syntax: STRING$(*strlength*, {*ASCIIcode*¦*strexpr*})

Example: DozenDash$ = STRING$(12, "-")

SUB   **Statement**

Purpose: Defines a subprogram.

Syntax:	```SUB subpgmname [(paramlist)] [STATIC]```
	``` [instructions]```
	``` [EXIT SUB]```
	``` [instructions]```
	```END SUB```

Example:	```SUB ShowSum (TermA!, TermB!, TermC!)```
	``` Sum! = TermA! + TermB! + TermC!```
	``` PRINT "The sum is"; Sum!```
	```END SUB```

SWAP   Statement

Purpose:	Exchanges the values of two variables or array elements.
Syntax:	```SWAP varname, varname```
Example:	```SWAP MyAge%, YourAge%```

SYSTEM   Statement

Purpose:	Terminates program execution.
Syntax:	```SYSTEM```
Example:	```SYSTEM```

TAB   Formatting function

Purpose:	Advances to a specified column position within a PRINT or LPRINT statement.
Syntax:	```{PRINT¦LPRINT} [#filenum] TAB(column)```
Example:	```PRINT TAB(5); Client$; TAB(25); City$; TAB(50); Phone$```

TAN   Numeric function

Purpose:	Returns the trigonometric tangent of an angle.
Syntax:	```TAN(angle)```
Example:	```MyValue# = TAN(AngleInRadians#)```

THEN   **Embedded keyword**

Purpose: Forms conditional tests as part of the IF statement.

Syntax: `IF expr THEN thenpart [ELSE elsepart]`

Example: `IF TermA% >= TermB% THEN PRINT "Yes" ELSE PRINT "No"`

TIME$ **Statement**

Purpose: Sets the current time.

Syntax: `TIME$ = timestr`

Example: `TIME$ = "14:08:35"`

TIME$ **String function**

Purpose: Returns the current time.

Syntax: `TIME$`

Example: `PRINT "The time is now"; TIME$`

TIMER   **Statement**

Purpose: Enables or disables the trapping of timer activity.

Syntax: `TIMER {ON¦OFF¦STOP}`

Example: `TIMER OFF`

TIMER   **Device function**

Purpose: Returns the elapsed time (in seconds) since midnight.

Syntax: `TIMER`

Example: `NumMinutes# = TIMER / 60`

TO   Embedded keyword

Purpose: Defines loops as part of the FOR statement, specifies a range in a CASE clause as part of the SELECT CASE statement, or specifies a range of records as part of the LOCK and UNLOCK statements.

TROFF   Statement

Purpose: Turns off the tracing of program statements.

Syntax:
```
TROFF
```

Example:
```
TROFF
```

TRON   Statement

Purpose: Turns on the tracing of program statements.

Syntax:
```
TRON
```

Example:
```
TRON
```

TYPE   Statement

Purpose: Declares and defines a record.

Syntax:
```
TYPE recordname
    elementname AS type
    [elementname AS type] ...
END TYPE
```

Example:
```
TYPE Employee
    FullName AS STRING * 30
    IDNumber AS INTEGER
    Salary AS SINGLE
END TYPE
```

UBOUND   Memory function

Purpose: Determines the maximum subscript value for the specified dimension of a previously defined array.

Syntax: UBOUND(*arrayname* [, *dimension*])

Example: UpperBound% = UBOUND(MyArray, 3)

UCASE$ String function

Purpose: Returns the uppercase equivalent of a given string.

Syntax: UCASE$(*strexpr*)

Example: UpperCaseName$ = UCASE$("Thomas H. Rugg")

UNLOCK   Statement

Purpose: Reestablishes full access to an access-restricted file in a network environment.

Syntax: UNLOCK [#]*filenum* [, {*recordnum*¦[*start*] TO *end*}]

Example: UNLOCK #5, 6 TO 18

UNTIL   Embedded keyword

Purpose: Creates a loop with testing expressions as part of the DO statement.

Top-Test Form:

Syntax:
```
DO UNTIL boolexpr
      [instructions]
LOOP
```

Example:
```
DO UNTIL Index% >= NumEmployees%
      PRINT LastName$(Index%)
      Index% = Index% + 1
LOOP
```

Bottom-Test Form:

Syntax:
```
DO
      [instructions]
LOOP UNTIL boolexpr
```

Example:
```
DO
    PRINT LastName$(Index%)
    Index% = Index% + 1
LOOP UNTIL Index% >= NumEmployees%
```

USING   **Embedded keyword**

Purpose: Prints data under formatting control as part of the PRINT (video screen) or LPRINT (line printer) statement, or changes palette colors as part of the PALETTE USING statement.

Syntax: `{PRINT¦LPRINT} USING formatstr; exprlist [ {;¦,} ]`

Example: `PRINT USING "$$####.##"; BankBalance!, CheckAmount!`

VAL   **Conversion function**

Purpose: Returns the numeric value of a string expression.

Syntax: `VAL(strexpr)`

Example: `ZipCode& = VAL(ZipCode$)`

VARPTR   **Memory function**

Purpose: Returns the offset address of a given variable.

Syntax: `VARPTR(varname)`

Example: `PRINT "The offset address of Index% is"; VARPTR(Index%)`

VARPTR$ **Memory function**

Purpose: Returns the address of a variable in string form.

Syntax: `VARPTR$(varname)`

Example: `PLAY "AB-CX" + VARPTR$(Refrain$)`

VARSEG   Memory function

Purpose: Returns the segment address of a given variable.

Syntax: VARSEG(*varname*)

Example: DEF SEG = VARSEG(MyVariable#)

VIEW   Statement

Purpose: Sets the rectangular area on-screen where future graphics can be displayed.

Syntax: VIEW [[SCREEN] (*upleftxy*)-(*lowrightxy*) _
[, [*viewcolor*] [, *bordercolor*]]]

Example: VIEW SCREEN (40,20)-(200,100), 4, 2

VIEW PRINT   Statement

Purpose: Sets the upper and lower row on-screen where text can be displayed.

Syntax: VIEW PRINT [*toprow* TO *bottomrow*]

Example: VIEW PRINT 10 TO 22

WAIT   Statement

Purpose: Pauses program execution until a specified input port presents a given byte pattern.

Syntax: WAIT *portnum*, *andbyte* [, *xorbyte*]

Example: WAIT &H20, 4

WEND   Statement

Purpose: Terminates loops created with the WHILE statement.

Syntax: WHILE *boolexpr*
    [*instructions*]
WEND

Example:
```
WHILE TermX% < 100
    Sum& = Sum& + TermX%
    PRINT TermX%, Sum&
WEND
```

WHILE   Statement

Purpose: Creates loops with a testing expression at the beginning.

Syntax:
```
WHILE boolexpr
    [instructions]
WEND
```

Example:
```
WHILE TermX% < 100
    Sum& = Sum& + TermX%
    PRINT TermX%, Sum&
WEND
```

WIDTH   Statement

Purpose: Sets the default line width on a given device or file, or changes the screen-display text mode.

Device and File Form:

Syntax:
```
WIDTH {devicename,¦#filenum} width
```

Example:
```
WIDTH "LPT1:", 255
```

Screen-Display Form:

Syntax:
```
WIDTH [numcolumns] [, numrows]
```

Example:
```
WIDTH , 43
```

WIDTH LPRINT   Statement

Purpose: Sets the line printer's default line width for use by subsequent LPRINT instructions.

Syntax:
```
WIDTH LPRINT width
```

Example:
```
WIDTH LPRINT 255
```

WINDOW   Statement

Purpose: Redefines the graphics coordinate system.

Syntax: `WINDOW [ [SCREEN] (leftxy)-(rightxy) ]`

Example: `WINDOW SCREEN (-100, -100)-(100, 100)`

WRITE   Statement

Purpose: Writes data on-screen with commas between items, quotes around strings, and no space before numbers.

Syntax: `WRITE [exprlist]`

Example: `WRITE YourName$,YourAge%`

WRITE #   Statement

Purpose: Writes data to a specified sequential file using the same formatting as the WRITE statement.

Syntax: `WRITE #filenum, exprlist`

Example: `WRITE #7, "03/04/89", NumOrders%, Sales!`

XOR   Logical operator

Purpose: Creates the logical (Boolean) result of exclusive ORing two quantities together.

Syntax: `integerexpr1 XOR integerexpr2`

Example: `IF (MyAge% > 21) XOR (YourAge% > 21) THEN PRINT "Same"`

$DYNAMIC   Metastatement

Purpose: Declares the default array allocation to be dynamic.

Syntax: `{REM¦'} $DYNAMIC`

Example: `REM $DYNAMIC`

$STATIC   **Metastatement**

Purpose: Declares the default array allocation to be static.

Syntax: `{REM¦'} $STATIC`

Example: `'$STATIC`

Reserved Words

The following list shows QBasic's reserved words (keywords). You cannot use any of these words as variable, label, or procedure names.

ABS	CDBL	CSRLIN	DIM
ABSOLUTE	CHAIN	CVD	DO
ACCESS	CHDIR	CVDMBF	DOUBLE
AND	CHR$	CVI	DRAW
ANY	CINT	CVL	ELSE
APPEND	CIRCLE	CVS	ELSEIF
AS	CLEAR	CVSMBF	END
ASC	CLNG	DATA	ENVIRON
ATN	CLOSE	DATE$	ENVIRON$
BASE	CLS	DECLARE	EOF
BEEP	COLOR	DEF	EQV
BINARY	COM	DEFDBL	ERASE
BLOAD	COMMON	DEFINT	ERDEV
BSAVE	CONST	DEFLNG	ERDEV$
CALL	COS	DEFSNG	ERL
CASE	CSNG	DEFSTR	ERR

ERROR	LBOUND	OCT$	RETURN
EXIT	LCASE$	OFF	RIGHT$
EXP	LEFT$	ON	RMDIR
FIELD	LEN	OPEN	RND
FILEATTR	LET	OPTION	RSET
FILES	LINE	OR	RTRIM$
FIX	LIST	OUT	RUN
FN	LOC	OUTPUT	SCREEN
FOR	LOCATE	PAINT	SEEK
FRE	LOCK	PALETTE	SEG
FREEFILE	LOF	PCOPY	SELECT
FUNCTION	LOG	PEEK	SGN
GET	LONG	PEN	SHARED
GOSUB	LOOP	PLAY	SHELL
GOTO	LPOS	PMAP	SIN
HEX$	LPRINT	POINT	SINGLE
IF	LSET	POKE	SLEEP
IMP	LTRIM$	POS	SOUND
INKEY$	MID$	PRESET	SPACE$
INP	MKD$	PRINT	SPC
INPUT	MKDIR	PSET	SQR
INPUT$	MKDMBF$	PUT	STATIC
INSTR	MKI$	RANDOM	STEP
INT	MKL$	RANDOMIZE	STICK
INTEGER	MKS$	READ	STOP
IOCTL	MKSMBF$	REDIM	STR$
IOCTL$	MOD	REM	STRIG
IS	NAME	RESET	STRING
KEY	NEXT	RESTORE	STRING$
KILL	NOT	RESUME	SUB

SWAP	TO	UNTIL	WAIT
SYSTEM	TROFF	USING	WEND
TAB	TRON	VAL	WHILE
TAN	TYPE	VARPTR	WIDTH
THEN	UBOUND	VARPTR$	WINDOW
TIME$	UCASE$	VARSEG	WRITE
TIMER	UNLOCK	VIEW	XOR

ASCII Character Set

Dec X_{10}	Hex X_{16}	Binary X_2	ASCII Character	Ctrl	Key
000	00	0000 0000	null	NUL	^@
001	01	0000 0001	☺	SOH	^A
002	02	0000 0010	●	STX	^B
003	03	0000 0011	♥	ETX	^C
004	04	0000 0100	♦	EOT	^D
005	05	0000 0101	♣	ENQ	^E
006	06	0000 0110	♠	ACK	^F
007	07	0000 0111	●	BEL	^G
008	08	0000 1000	■	BS	^H
009	09	0000 1001	○	HT	^I
010	0A	0000 1010	■	LF	^J
011	0B	0000 1011	♂	VT	^K
012	0C	0000 1100	♀	FF	^L
013	0D	0000 1101	♪	CR	^M
014	0E	0000 1110	♪♪	SO	^N

Dec X_{10}	Hex X_{16}	Binary X_2	ASCII Character	Ctrl	Key
015	0F	0000 1111	☼	SI	^O
016	10	0001 0000	►	DLE	^P
017	11	0001 0001	◄	DC1	^Q
018	12	0001 0010	↕	DC2	^R
019	13	0001 0011	‼	DC3	^S
020	14	0001 0100	¶	DC4	^T
021	15	0001 0101	§	NAK	^U
022	16	0001 0110	–	SYN	^V
023	17	0001 0111	↨	ETB	^W
024	18	0001 1000	↑	CAN	^X
025	19	0001 1001	↓	EM	^Y
026	1A	0001 1010	→	SUB	^Z
027	1B	0001 1011	←	ESC	^[
028	1C	0001 1100	FS	FS	^\
029	1D	0001 1101	GS	GS	^]
030	1E	0001 1110	RS	RS	^^
031	1F	0001 1111	US	US	^_
032	20	0010 0000	SP		
033	21	0010 0001	!		
034	22	0010 0010	"		
035	23	0010 0011	#		
036	24	0010 0100	$		
037	25	0010 0101	%		
038	26	0010 0110	&		
039	27	0010 0111	'		
040	28	0010 1000	(		
041	29	0010 1001	)		
042	2A	0010 1010	*		
043	2B	0010 1011	+		
044	2C	0010 1100	,		
045	2D	0010 1101	-		
046	2E	0010 1110	.		
047	2F	0010 1111	/		
048	30	0011 0000	0		
049	31	0011 0001	1		
050	32	0011 0010	2		

Dec X_{10}	Hex X_{16}	Binary X_2	ASCII Character
051	33	0011 0011	3
052	34	0011 0100	4
053	35	0011 0101	5
054	36	0011 0110	6
055	37	0011 0111	7
056	38	0011 1000	8
057	39	0011 1001	9
058	3A	0011 1010	:
059	3B	0011 1011	;
060	3C	0011 1100	<
061	3D	0011 1101	=
062	3E	0011 1110	>
063	3F	0011 1111	?
064	40	0100 0000	@
065	41	0100 0001	A
066	42	0100 0010	B
067	43	0100 0011	C
068	44	0100 0100	D
069	45	0100 0101	E
070	46	0100 0110	F
071	47	0100 0111	G
072	48	0100 1000	H
073	49	0100 1001	I
074	4A	0100 1010	J
075	4B	0100 1011	K
076	4C	0100 1100	L
077	4D	0100 1101	M
078	4E	0100 1110	N
079	4F	0100 1111	O
080	50	0101 0000	P
081	51	0101 0001	Q
082	52	0101 0010	R
083	53	0101 0011	S
084	54	0101 0100	T
085	55	0101 0101	U
086	56	0101 0110	V

Dec X_{10}	Hex X_{16}	Binary X_2	ASCII Character
087	57	0101 0111	W
088	58	0101 1000	X
089	59	0101 1001	Y
090	5A	0101 1010	Z
091	5B	0101 1011	[
092	5C	0101 1100	\
093	5D	0101 1101	]
094	5E	0101 1110	^
095	5F	0101 1111	–
096	60	0110 0000	`
097	61	0110 0001	a
098	62	0110 0010	b
099	63	0110 0011	c
100	64	0110 0100	d
101	65	0110 0101	e
102	66	0110 0110	f
103	67	0110 0111	g
104	68	0110 1000	h
105	69	0110 1001	i
106	6A	0110 1010	j
107	6B	0110 1011	k
108	6C	0110 1100	l
109	6D	0110 1101	m
110	6E	0110 1110	n
111	6F	0110 1111	o
112	70	0111 0000	p
113	71	0111 0001	q
114	72	0111 0010	r
115	73	0111 0011	s
116	74	0111 0100	t
117	75	0111 0101	u
118	76	0111 0110	v
119	77	0111 0111	w
120	78	0111 1000	x
121	79	0111 1001	y
122	7A	0111 1010	z

Dec X_{10}	Hex X_{16}	Binary X_2	ASCII Character
123	7B	0111 1011	{
124	7C	0111 1100	¦
125	7D	0111 1101	}
126	7E	0111 1110	~
127	7F	0111 1111	DEL
128	80	1000 0000	Ç
129	81	1000 0001	ü
130	82	1000 0010	é
131	83	1000 0011	â
132	84	1000 0100	ä
133	85	1000 0101	à
134	86	1000 0110	å
135	87	1000 0111	ç
136	88	1000 1000	ê
137	89	1000 1001	ë
138	8A	1000 1010	è
139	8B	1000 1011	ï
140	8C	1000 1100	î
141	8D	1000 1101	ì
142	8E	1000 1110	Ä
143	8F	1000 1111	Å
144	90	1001 0000	É
145	91	1001 0001	æ
146	92	1001 0010	Æ
147	93	1001 0011	ô
148	94	1001 0100	ö
149	95	1001 0101	ò
150	96	1001 0110	û
151	97	1001 0111	ù
152	98	1001 1000	ÿ
153	99	1001 1001	Ö
154	9A	1001 1010	Ü
155	9B	1001 1011	¢
156	9C	1001 1100	£
157	9D	1001 1101	¥
158	9E	1001 1110	Pt

Dec X_{10}	Hex X_{16}	Binary X_2	ASCII Character
159	9F	1001 1111	ƒ
160	A0	1010 0000	á
161	A1	1010 0001	í
162	A2	1010 0010	ó
163	A3	1010 0011	ú
164	A4	1010 0100	ñ
165	A5	1010 0101	Ñ
166	A6	1010 0110	a̲
167	A7	1010 0111	o̲
168	A8	1010 1000	¿
169	A9	1010 1001	⌐
170	AA	1010 1010	¬
171	AB	1010 1011	½
172	AC	1010 1100	¼
173	AD	1010 1101	¡
174	AE	1010 1110	«
175	AF	1010 1111	»
176	B0	1011 0000	
177	B1	1011 0001	
178	B2	1011 0010	
179	B3	1011 0011	│
180	B4	1011 0100	┤
181	B5	1011 0101	╡
182	B6	1011 0110	╢
183	B7	1011 0111	╖
184	B8	1011 1000	╕
185	B9	1011 1001	╣
186	BA	1011 1010	║
187	BB	1011 1011	╗
188	BC	1011 1100	╝
189	BD	1011 1101	╜
190	BE	1011 1110	╛
191	BF	1011 1111	┐
192	C0	1100 0000	└
193	C1	1100 0001	┴
194	C2	1100 0010	┬

Dec X_{10}	Hex X_{16}	Binary X_2	ASCII Character
195	C3	1100 0011	├
196	C4	1100 0100	─
197	C5	1100 0101	┼
198	C6	1100 0110	╞
199	C7	1100 0111	╟
200	C8	1100 1000	╚
201	C9	1100 1001	╔
202	CA	1100 1010	╩
203	CB	1100 1011	╦
204	CC	1100 1100	╠
205	CD	1100 1101	═
206	CE	1100 1110	╬
207	CF	1100 1111	╧
208	D0	1101 0000	╨
209	D1	1101 0001	╤
210	D2	1101 0010	╥
211	D3	1101 0011	╙
212	D4	1101 0100	╘
213	D5	1101 0101	╒
214	D6	1101 0110	╓
215	D7	1101 0111	╫
216	D8	1101 1000	╪
217	D9	1101 1001	┘
218	DA	1101 1010	┌
219	DB	1101 1011	█
220	DC	1101 1100	▄
221	DD	1101 1101	▌
222	DE	1101 1110	▐
223	DF	1101 1111	▀
224	E0	1110 0000	α
225	E1	1110 0001	β
226	E2	1110 0010	Γ
227	E3	1110 0011	π
228	E4	1110 0100	Σ
229	E5	1110 0101	σ
230	E6	1110 0110	μ

Dec X_{10}	Hex X_{16}	Binary X_2	ASCII Character
231	E7	1110 0111	τ
232	E8	1110 1000	Φ
233	E9	1110 1001	θ
234	EA	1110 1010	Ω
235	EB	1110 1011	δ
236	EC	1110 1100	∞
237	ED	1110 1101	ø
238	EE	1110 1110	∈
239	EF	1110 1111	∩
240	F0	1111 0000	≡
241	F1	1111 0001	±
242	F2	1111 0010	≥
243	F3	1111 0011	≤
244	F4	1111 0100	⌠
245	F5	1111 0101	⌡
246	F6	1111 0110	÷
247	F7	1111 0111	≈
248	F8	1111 1000	°
249	F9	1111 1001	•
250	FA	1111 1010	·
251	FB	1111 1011	√
252	FC	1111 1100	η
253	FD	1111 1101	²
254	FE	1111 1110	■
255	FF	1111 1111	

Keyboard Scan Codes

T he following table presents code values to use with the INKEY$ function and the KEY statement (*key trapping*).

The first column designates a physical key on the keyboard.

The second column is the scan code used when you key trap with the KEY statement.

The remaining columns represent ASCII values returned by the INKEY$ function for various keystrokes. The INKEY$ function returns a one- or two-character string for each recognized keystroke.

When INKEY$ returns a single character, that character's ASCII value is shown with a single number in the appropriate column. For example, pressing the Q key causes INKEY$ to return a one-character string whose ASCII value is 113. Pressing Shift-Q returns 81.

When INKEY$ returns a two-character string, the first character is always a null (ASCII value 0). The second character has an ASCII value greater than 0. For example, pressing Alt-Q causes INKEY$ to return a two-character string. The first character is NUL (ASCII value 0); the second character has the ASCII value 16.

Key	Scan Code	INKEY$ Key	INKEY$ Shift-Key	INKEY$ Ctrl-Key	INKEY$ Alt-Key
Esc	1	27	27	27	27
1 or !	2	49	33		NUL–120
2 or @	3	50	64	NUL–3	NUL–121
3 or #	4	51	35		NUL–122
4 or $	5	52	36		NUL–123
5 or %	6	53	37		NUL–124
6 or ^	7	54	94	30	NUL–125
7 or &	8	55	38		NUL–126
8 or *	9	56	42		NUL–127
9 or (	10	57	40		NUL–128
0 or)	11	48	41		NUL–129
- or _	12	45	95	31	NUL–130
= or +	13	61	43		NUL–131
BKSP	14	8	8	127	
Tab	15	9	NUL–15		
Q	16	113	81	17	NUL–16
W	17	119	87	23	NUL–17
E	18	101	69	5	NUL–18
R	19	114	82	18	NUL–19
T	20	116	84	20	NUL–20
Y	21	121	89	25	NUL–21
U	22	117	85	21	NUL–22
I	23	105	73	9	NUL–23
O	24	111	79	15	NUL–24
P	25	112	80	16	NUL–25
[or {	26	91	123	27	
] or }	27	93	125	29	
Enter	28	13	13	10	
Ctrl	29				
A	30	97	65	1	NUL–30
S	31	115	83	19	NUL–31
D	32	100	68	4	NUL–32
F	33	102	70	6	NUL–33
G	34	103	71	7	NUL–34
H	35	104	72	8	NUL–35
J	36	106	74	10	NUL–36
K	37	107	75	11	NUL–37
L	38	108	76	12	NUL–38

Key	Scan Code	INKEY$ Key	INKEY$ Shift-Key	INKEY$ Ctrl-Key	INKEY$ Alt-Key
; or :	39	59	58		
' or "	40	39	34		
` or ~	41	96	126		
LeftShift	42				
\ or |	43	92	124	28	
Z	44	122	90	26	NUL–44
X	45	120	88	24	NUL–45
C	46	99	67	3	NUL–46
V	47	118	86	22	NUL–47
B	48	98	66	2	NUL–48
N	49	110	78	14	NUL–49
M	50	109	77	13	NUL–50
, or <	51	44	60		
. or >	52	46	62		
/ or ?	53	47	63		
RightShift	54				
PrtSc•	55	42	(Print)	16	
Alt	56				
Space bar	57	32	32	32	32
CapsLock	58				
F1	59	NUL–59	NUL–84	NUL–94	NUL–104
F2	60	NUL–60	NUL–85	NUL–95	NUL–105
F3	61	NUL–61	NUL–86	NUL–96	NUL–106
F4	62	NUL–62	NUL–87	NUL–97	NUL–107
F5	63	NUL–63	NUL–88	NUL–98	NUL–108
F6	64	NUL–64	NUL–89	NUL–99	NUL–109
F7	65	NUL–65	NUL–90	NUL–100	NUL–110
F8	66	NUL–66	NUL–91	NUL–101	NUL–111
F9	67	NUL–67	NUL–92	NUL–102	NUL–112
F10	68	NUL–68	NUL–93	NUL–103	NUL–113
F11	133	NUL–133	NUL–135	NUL–137	NUL–139
F12	134	NUL–134	NUL–136	NUL–138	NUL–140
NumLock	69				
ScrollLock	70				
Home	71	NUL–71	55	119	
Up	72	NUL–72	56		
PgUp	73	NUL–73	57	NUL–132	
Grey–	74	45	45		
Left	75	NUL–75	52	NUL–115	

Key	Scan Code	INKEY$ Key	INKEY$ Shift-Key	INKEY$ Ctrl-Key	INKEY$ Alt-Key
Left	74	45	45		
Center	76		53		
Right	77	NUL–77	54	NUL–116	
Grey +	78	43	43		
End	79	NUL–79	49	NUL–117	
Down	80	NUL–80	50		
PgDn	81	NUL–81	51	NUL–118	
Ins	82	NUL–82	48		
Del	83	NUL–83	46		

Hotkeys and Mouse Commands

T his appendix presents tables that summarize QBasic's hotkeys and mouse commands. A *hotkey* is a keystroke or keystroke combination that instantly invokes a command available inside the QBasic environment. A *mouse command* is the mouse technique that invokes a particular command.

Menu and Window Commands

The following table lists the hotkeys and mouse techniques that invoke menu and window commands. A *menu command* invokes a command available within the QBasic menu system. A *window command* manipulates one of QBasic's four on-screen windows: the View window, Output window, Immediate window, and Help window.

Hotkey	Effect	Mouse
F1	Show help on keyword or topic	Click right button on keyword in program
Shift-F1	Show help on using help	Click on Using Help (Help menu)
Ctrl-F1	View next topic in help file	Click on <Next> (Reference bar)

continues

Hotkey	Effect	Mouse
Alt-F1	Review most recently viewed help screen	Click on <Back> (Reference bar)
Shift-Ctrl-F1	View previous topic in help file	None
F2	Display loaded procedures	Click on SUBs (View menu)
Shift-F2	Display next procedure	None
Ctrl-F2	Display previous procedure	None
F3	Repeat the last Find	Click on Repeat Last Find (Search menu)
F4	View the output screen	Click on Output Screen (View menu)
F5	Continue program execution	Click on Continue (Run menu)
Shift-F5	Start program execution	Click on Start (Run menu)
F6	Make next window active	Click inside desired window
Shift-F6	Make previous window active	Click inside desired window
F7	Execute program up to cursor position	None
F8	Execute next instruction (single step)	Click on Step (Debug menu)
F9	Toggle breakpoint on/off	Click on Toggle Breakpoint (Debug menu)
F10	Execute next instruction (procedure step)	Click on Procedure Step (Debug menu)
Ctrl-F10	Enlarge active window/ Restore split screen	Double-click Title bar/ Click maximize icon
Shift-Del	Cut selected text	Click on Cut (Edit menu)
Ctrl-Ins	Copy selected text	Click on Copy (Edit menu)
Shift-Ins	Paste text from clipboard	Click on Paste (Edit menu)
Del	Erase selected text	Click on Clear (Edit menu)
Ctrl-Q-A	Change text	Click on Change... (Search menu)
Ctrl-Q-F	Search for text string	Click on Find... (Search menu)
Esc	Terminate help system	Click on <Cancel> (Reference bar)
Alt	Enter menu-selection mode	None

Hotkey	Effect	Mouse
Alt-+	Enlarge active window	Drag Title bar up
Alt-–	Shrink active window	Drag Title bar down
Up	Scroll line up	Click on up arrow
Down	Scroll line down	Click on down arrow
PgUp	Scroll page up	None
PgDn	Scroll page down	None
Ctrl-Home	Scroll to top of window	None
Ctrl-End	Scroll to bottom of window	None

Editing Commands

The following tables list the hotkeys available while editing inside the QBasic environment. Hotkeys are shown both in the IBM keypad-style and the WordStar-style keystroke combinations. For detailed explanations of these editing commands, see Chapter 5, "Using the QBasic Editor."

Moving the Cursor

Effect	Keypad	WordStar Style
Character left	Left	Ctrl-S
Character right	Right	Ctrl-D
Word left	Ctrl-Left	Ctrl-A
Word right	Ctrl-Right	Ctrl-F
Line up	Up	Ctrl-E
Line down	Down	Ctrl-X
First indentation level	Home	None
Beginning of line	None	Ctrl-Q-S
End of line	End	Ctrl-Q-D
Beginning of next line	Ctrl-Enter	Ctrl-J
Top of window		Ctrl-Q-E

continues

Effect	Keypad	WordStar Style
Bottom of window		Ctrl-Q-X
Beginning of text	Ctrl-Home	Ctrl-Q-R
End of text	Ctrl-End	Ctrl-Q-C
Set marker		Ctrl-K-*n*
Move to marker		Ctrl-Q-*n*

Selecting Text

Effect	Keypad
Character left	Shift-Left
Character right	Shift-Right
To beginning of line	Shift-Home
To end of line	Shift-End
Current line	Shift-Down
Line above	Shift-Up
Word left	Shift-Ctrl-Left
Word right	Shift-Ctrl-Right
Screen up	Shift-PgUp
Screen down	Shift-PgDn
To beginning of text	Shift-Ctrl-Home
To end of text	Shift-Ctrl-End

Copying to the Clipboard

Effect	Keypad
Selected text	Ctrl-Ins

Inserting

Effect	Keypad	WordStar Style
Toggle insert/overstrike	Ins	Ctrl-V
Contents of clipboard	Shift-Ins	
Tab at cursor	Tab	Ctrl-I

Deleting

Effect	Keypad	WordStar Style
Character left	Backspace	Ctrl-H
Character at cursor	Del	Ctrl-G
Word	Ctrl-T	
Erase selected text	Del	
Current line to clipboard	Ctrl-Y	
To line end to clipboard	Ctrl-Q-Y	
Selected text to clipboard	Shift-Del	
Leading indentation spaces	Shift-Tab	

Scrolling

Effect	Keypad	WordStar Style
One line up	Ctrl-Up	Ctrl-W
One line down	Ctrl-Down	Ctrl-Z
Page up	PgUp	Ctrl-R
Page down	PgDn	Ctrl-C
One window left	Ctrl-PgUp	
One window right	Ctrl-PgDn	

Internal Data Formats

This appendix describes how QBasic stores simple variables.

Variable-Length Strings

QBasic stores a variable-length string variable as a four-byte string descriptor. As shown in Figure E.1, the string descriptor contains two fields: the length of the actual string text and the offset address at which that text is stored. Each field is two bytes long and therefore represents a number in the range from 0 to 65,535. (QBasic, however, limits the length of any individual variable-length string to 32,767 bytes.) The offset address points into the default data segment.

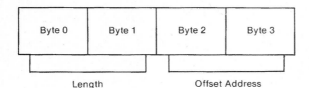

| Byte 0 | Byte 1 | Byte 2 | Byte 3 |

Length   Offset Address

The VARPTR function, when used with a string-variable argument, returns the first byte of the string descriptor. Table E.1 shows the values returned by combining PEEK and VARPTR for a string variable A$. Notice that for each two-byte value, the less significant byte is stored in the lower memory address.

Table E.1. Memory organization of a string descriptor.

Function	Value Returned
PEEK(VARPTR(A$))	Least-significant length byte
PEEK(VARPTR(A$) + 1)	Most-significant length byte
PEEK(VARPTR(A$) + 2)	Least-significant address byte
PEEK(VARPTR(A$) + 3)	Most-significant address byte

The following two instructions show how to calculate the length of A$ and the ASCII value of the first character in A$ by using the string descriptor for A$. The values of StrLength% and FirstASC% correspond to the values returned by the QBasic functions LEN(A$) and ASC(A$) respectively.

```
StrLength% = 256 * PEEK(VARPTR(A$) + 1) + PEEK(VARPTR(A$))

FirstASC% = PEEK(256 * PEEK(VARPTR(A$) + 3) + PEEK(VARPTR(A$) + 2))
```

Integers and Long Integers

QBasic stores an integer as a two-byte (16-bit) signed number. Positive numbers have a 0 in the highest order bit. Negative numbers are represented in two's complement form and have a 1 in the highest order bit.

In memory, the least significant byte is stored at the lower memory address. For example, the number 875 (decimal) equals &H036B (hex). This number is stored as the two-byte sequence of &H6B followed by &H03.

A long integer is a four-byte (32-bit) signed number. Negative numbers are represented in two's complement form. In memory, the bytes are stored from the least significant (at the lowest address) to the most significant (at the highest address).

For example, the number 1,234,567 (decimal) equals &H0012D687 (hex). This number is stored as the four-byte sequence of &H87, &HD6, &H12, &H00.

The following program fragment demonstrates the use of VARPTR to return the internal storage bytes for the integer 875 and the long integer 1,234,567:

```
A% = 875
FOR J% = 0 TO 1
   PRINT HEX$(PEEK(VARPTR(A%) + J%))
NEXT J%
PRINT
```

```
B& = 1234567
FOR J% = 0 TO 3
   PRINT HEX$(PEEK(VARPTR(B&) + J%))
NEXT J%
```

The output looks as follows:

```
6B
3

87
D6
12
0
```

Single- and Double-Precision Floating Point

QBasic uses the IEEE standard to represent single- and double-precision floating-point numbers (see Figure E.2). Single-precision numbers require four bytes (32 bits); double-precision numbers require eight bytes (64 bits). In memory, the bytes are stored with the least-significant byte in the lowest address up to the most-significant byte in the highest address.

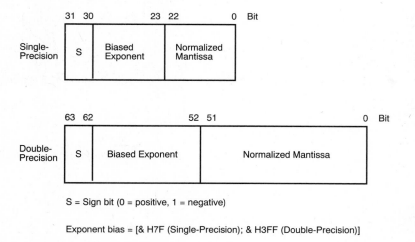

S = Sign bit (0 = positive, 1 = negative)

Exponent bias = [& H7F (Single-Precision); & H3FF (Double-Precision)]

Normalized Mantissa is preceded by an implicit 1 and binary point (1.)

Figure E.2.

Floating-point number representations.

Single-precision numbers consist of a 23-bit normalized mantissa, an eight-bit biased exponent, and a sign bit. The mantissa is normalized with a presumed bit of value 1 to the left of the binary point. The exponent is biased with a value of 127 (decimal).

Double-precision numbers consist of a 52-bit normalized mantissa, an 11-bit biased exponent, and a sign bit. The exponent bias is 1,023 (decimal).

The following program demonstrates single-precision representation:

```
REM Program: SINGPREC.BAS (Demonstrate single-precision format)
MyNum! = 421.75                    'Define sing. prec. number
VarAddress% = VARPTR(MyNum!)    'Offset location of byte 0
FOR Increment% = 0 TO 3
   ByteVal% = PEEK(VarAddress% + Increment%)
   PRINT HEX$(ByteVal%)
NEXT Increment%
END
```

The program displays the hexadecimal values of the four bytes that QBasic uses to represent the single-precision number 421.75. Here is the output:

```
0
E0
D2
43
```

To decode these values, first rearrange the bytes from the most significant to the least significant:

```
43 D2 E0 00
```

Next, consider these bytes to be a single value comprised of eight hexadecimal digits, and convert this value into binary:

```
   4    3    D    2    E    0    0    0      -- Hex
0100 0011 1101 0010 1110 0000 0000 0000      -- Binary
```

Break the binary number into the required fields: a one-bit sign, an eight-bit biased exponent, and a 23-bit normalized mantissa:

```
   0    10000111   10100101110000000000000
Sign    Exponent        Mantissa
```

The sign bit is zero, which indicates a positive number.

The exponent is biased by 127 (decimal), which equals 01111111 (binary). Therefore, subtract 01111111 from 10000111 to get the true binary exponent: 00001000, which equals 8 (decimal).

The mantissa has an assumed binary point at the left and an assumed 1 to the left of this binary point. Therefore, the following line shows the true mantissa:

`1.10100101110000000000000`

Because the exponent is 8, the mantissa must be shifted eight places to the right. The resulting binary number becomes

`110100101.110000000000000`

Converting this number to decimal yields 421.75, which is the original value.

Error Messages

This appendix lists QBasic's error messages. The error number is the value returned by the ERR function (see Chapter 21, "Trapping Errors and Events").

For each error, the comments indicate the most likely cause or causes. If your program generates an error message, this information should help you track down the problem.

Error number 1: NEXT without FOR

A NEXT instruction occurred when no FOR instruction was active. Look for unmatched variable names on the FOR and NEXT instructions, or two different NEXT instructions trying to match the same FOR instruction (each FOR instruction must correspond with a single NEXT instruction).

Error number 2: Syntax error

An instruction has a punctuation error, a misspelled keyword, unbalanced parentheses, or some similar violation of QBasic's syntax rules.

Error number 3: RETURN without GOSUB

No GOSUB instruction is active when a RETURN instruction executed. Look for "falling into" a subroutine or using a GOTO instead of a GOSUB to invoke the subroutine.

Error number 4: Out of DATA

No DATA values remain to be read by the READ instruction. Look for punctuation errors in the DATA instructions, such as using periods instead of commas, or for miscounting how many times the program executes the READ.

Error number 5: `Illegal function call`

The program attempts to call a function with an illegal argument. Examples: taking the `SQR` of a negative number; taking the `LOG` of zero or a negative number; using a negative subscript in an array reference; attempting to create a string longer than 32,767 bytes (characters); using an impossible number (usually negative or zero) in one of the string functions such as `LEFT$`, `MID$`, `RIGHT$`, and `STRING$`.

Error number 6: `Overflow`

A numeric variable or literal is larger than QBasic's maximum value for the given data type. The maximum value for each of the numeric data types is as follows: integer, 32,767; long integer, 2,147,483,647; single-precision, (approximately) 3.4E+38; double-precision, (approximately) 1.8D+308.

Error number 7: `Out of memory`

The program tries to use more memory than is available. Likely causes: the program is too big; arrays are `DIM`med too large; `GOSUB` instructions are repeatedly executed but never terminated by `RETURN`; `FOR-NEXT` loops or `GOSUB` instructions are nested too deeply. Try `PRINT FRE(0)` at various places (such as before and after `DIM` instructions) to monitor how much memory remains. Also, use `CLEAR` to reduce the stack size.

Error number 8: `Label not defined`

A program instruction references a line label or line number that doesn't exist. For example, `GOTO BlackHole` when the label `BlackHole:` does not appear anywhere in the program.

Error number 9: `Subscript out of range`

An array subscript is larger than the size of the array. If you have no `DIM` instruction for an array, the maximum allowable subscript is 10. Another possible cause is an array larger than the maximum size of 64 kilobytes. Also look for a misspelled function name: If you type `TAG(20)` when you mean `TAB(20)`, QBasic assumes you are referring to a `TAG` array, not the `TAB` function.

Error number 10: `Duplicate Definition`

An array is being defined for a second time, either because there are two `DIM` instructions (or one `DIM` instruction that is executed twice), or because an array is implicitly dimensioned by usage of an array variable name and then a subsequent `DIM` instruction tries to redimension the array. Other possible causes are a variable that has the same name as a procedure or a constant defined with `CONST` that has the same name as a variable.

Error number 11: `Division by zero`

The program attempts to divide a number by zero, which is mathematically impossible.

Error number 12: `Illegal in direct mode`

In the Immediate window, you tried an instruction that is only allowed as an executable program instruction. You cannot use the following statements in the Immediate window: `COMMON`, `CONST`, `DATA`, `DECLARE`, `DIM`, `REDIM`, `OPTION`, `SHARED`, `STATIC`; the metastatements `$DYNAMIC` and `$STATIC`; and block structure statements such as `FUNCTION-END FUNCTION`, `SUB-END SUB`, `DEF FN`, `ELSEIF`, and `END IF`.

Error number 13: `Type mismatch`

A conflict occurs between string and numeric data types. Either an assignment instruction tries to assign a string value to a numeric variable (or vice versa), or a function is asked to operate on the wrong type of data (such as trying to use `SQR` on a string).

Error number 14: `Out of string space`

The program tries to use more memory for string data than QBasic has available. Use `PRINT FRE("")` at a few points in the program to squeeze out fragmented string space.

Error number 16: `String formula too complex`

A string expression is too complex for QBasic to interpret. Break up the expression into two or more simpler expressions. This error also occurs if you try to read more than 15 string variables with an `INPUT` instruction.

Error number 17: `Cannot continue`

You cannot resume a suspended program (with F5) because you have significantly modified the program after the pause. Program changes that prohibit resuming an interrupted program include changing the dimensions of an array, editing the arguments of a procedure, or modifying certain declarative instructions.

Error number 18: `Function not defined`

You referenced a function with an `FN` name when no corresponding `DEF FN` instruction defined the function.

Error number 19: `No RESUME`

The program ran out of instructions in an error-handling routine. (You should place a `RESUME` instruction in every error handler.)

Error number 20: `RESUME without error`

A `RESUME` instruction occurs when no error is trapped. Either `RESUME` occurs outside of an error handler, or an error handler has control without trapping an active error.

Error number 24: `Device timeout`

An input/output device (such as a printer) has not responded within a set time period.

Error number 25: `Device fault`

An input/output device reports that a hardware error occurred, or an expected device reply does not occur within a prescribed time period.

Error number 26: `FOR without NEXT`

A `FOR` instruction has no matching `NEXT` instruction.

Error number 27: `Out of paper`

The printer is out of paper, or is not powered on, or is incorrectly cabled to the computer.

Error number 29: `WHILE without WEND`

A `WHILE` instruction has no matching `WEND` instruction.

Error number 30: `WEND without WHILE`

No `WHILE` instruction is active when a `WEND` instruction executes. This error also occurs when an improper control structure appears inside a `WHILE-WEND` loop—for example, when a multiline `IF` appears without a matching `END IF`.

Error number 33: `Duplicate label`

Two program lines have the same line number or same line label.

Error number 35: `Subprogram not defined`

A `CALL` instruction attempts to invoke a subprogram that does not exist.

Error number 37: `Argument-count mismatch`

A subprogram or user-defined function call specifies an incorrect number of arguments. Make sure the number of arguments in the calling instruction matches the `DECLARE` instruction and the `SUB` or `FUNCTION` definition.

Error number 38: `Array not defined`

The program attempts to use an array not yet defined with a `DIM` or `REDIM` instruction. (The error occurs only if subscript values are larger than 10. This condition ensures that the reference is not to an implicitly defined array.)

Error number 40: `Variable required`

An `INPUT`, `LET`, `READ`, or `SHARED` instruction does not contain a variable argument. This error also occurs with binary file processing if a `GET` or `PUT` instruction does not contain the required variable parameter.

Error number 50: `FIELD overflow`

A `FIELD` instruction specifies more data bytes than the record length given in the `OPEN` instruction.

Error number 51: Internal error

Something has gone wrong inside QBasic itself. Probable causes: a bug might exist in QBasic itself; your disk copy of QBasic might be damaged; an error in your program (especially if your program uses POKE or CALL ABSOLUTE) might result in the mistaken modification of a QBasic memory location.

Error number 52: Bad file name or number

An instruction uses the file number of an unopened file, or the file number is outside the legal range of file numbers.

Error number 53: File not found

The filename does not exist. Look for a misspelled filename, and make sure the entire filespec is correct, including the disk drive and subdirectory.

Error number 54: Bad file mode

The instruction attempts an operation that conflicts with the file specification. PUT and GET require files opened as random-access, not sequential. OPEN, when using a string expression for the file mode, requires that the mode be A, I, O, or R. FIELD must specify a file opened for random-access. INPUT# requires a sequential file opened for INPUT. PRINT# requires a sequential file opened for OUTPUT or APPEND.

Error number 55: File already open

The file is already open. Either this is an attempt to OPEN a file for the second time, or the program tries to KILL an open file.

Error number 56: FIELD statement active

GET or PUT specified a record variable on a file for which a FIELD instruction had already executed.

Error number 57: Device I/O error

An input/output error occurs from which DOS cannot recover.

Error number 58: File already exists

NAME tries to rename a file with a name that already exists in the same directory.

Error number 59: Bad record length

The length of a record variable in a PUT or GET instruction does not match the record length specified in the corresponding OPEN instruction.

Error number 61: Disk full

No more disk space exists on the referenced disk. This error occurs when CLOSE, PRINT#, PUT, or WRITE# try to write to a disk file.

Error number 62: `Input past end`

INPUT tries to read an empty file or past the end of the file. Use the EOF function to be sure the program doesn't attempt to read more data than the file contains. Also, be sure the file is open for INPUT, not OUTPUT or APPEND.

Error number 63: `Bad record number`

The record number is outside the legal range of 1 through 16,777,215. This error usually occurs when the record number is inadvertently set to zero.

Error number 64: `Bad file name`

The file name does not follow the rules for a legal filename. This error usually occurs with BLOAD, BSAVE, KILL, or OPEN.

Error number 67: `Too many files`

No disk space remains for more file directory entries, or a file's specifications are illegal.

Error number 68: `Device unavailable`

No such device exists for the file specified. The device has been disabled, or has not been installed.

Error number 69: `Communication-buffer overflow`

No more room exists in the communication buffer area. Either process the input characters faster, empty the buffer more often (using INPUT$), create a larger communication buffer (using the RB option with OPEN COM), slow down the speed of arriving characters, or change communications protocols so that your program can tell the other computer to stop sending data until your program can catch up. Try using LOC to check the buffer more frequently.

Error number 70: `Permission denied`

The program is not allowed to read or write to the file. Either the program attempts to write on a write-protected floppy disk (that is, one using tape to cover the notch), the UNLOCK range does not match the previous LOCK, or in a network environment another program already has exclusive control of the file.

Error number 71: `Disk not ready`

A floppy disk drive's door is open, or no floppy disk is in the drive. An ON ERROR GOTO routine can recover from this condition.

Error number 72: `Disk-media error`

An error occurs on a disk, probably due to a damaged floppy disk. Try recovering whatever data you can by copying to a new floppy disk. Then use the DOS FORMAT command to reformat the bad disk. If you cannot reformat, be sure to discard the bad disk.

Error number 73: Feature unavailable

The instruction uses a reserved word that is not implemented in QBasic. You might be using a feature found in some version of BASIC besides QBasic.

Error number 74: Rename across disks

A file being renamed must remain on the same disk. The new name cannot specify a different disk drive.

Error number 75: Path/file access error

A path or filename specifies an inaccessible file. Probable causes: the filename is really a directory name or volume label, or your program tries writing to a file marked with the read-only attribute. This error can occur with OPEN, MKDIR, CHDIR, or RMDIR.

Error number 76: Path not found

The path does not exist. Probable causes: you misspelled a directory name, you specified the wrong disk drive, or you have the wrong floppy disk in the disk drive. This error can occur with OPEN, MKDIR, CHDIR, or RMDIR.

Symbols

F

I

M

X-Z

Free Catalog!

Mail us this registration form today, and we'll send you a free catalog featuring Que's complete line of best-selling books.

Name of Book _____

Name _____

Title _____

Phone (____) _____

Company _____

Address _____

City _____

State _____ ZIP _____

Please check the appropriate answers:

1. Where did you buy your Que book?
   ☐ Bookstore (name: _____)
   ☐ Computer store (name: _____)
   ☐ Catalog (name: _____)
   ☐ Direct from Que
   ☐ Other: _____

2. How many computer books do you buy a year?
   ☐ 1 or less
   ☐ 2-5
   ☐ 6-10
   ☐ More than 10

3. How many Que books do you own?
   ☐ 1
   ☐ 2-5
   ☐ 6-10
   ☐ More than 10

4. How long have you been using this software?
   ☐ Less than 6 months
   ☐ 6 months to 1 year
   ☐ 1-3 years
   ☐ More than 3 years

5. What influenced your purchase of this Que book?
   ☐ Personal recommendation
   ☐ Advertisement
   ☐ In-store display
   ☐ Price
   ☐ Que catalog
   ☐ Que mailing
   ☐ Que's reputation
   ☐ Other: _____

6. How would you rate the overall content of the book?
   ☐ Very good
   ☐ Good
   ☐ Satisfactory
   ☐ Poor

7. What do you like *best* about this Que book?

   _____
   _____

8. What do you like *least* about this Que book?

   _____
   _____

9. Did you buy this book with your personal funds?
   ☐ Yes   ☐ No

10. Please feel free to list any other comments you may have about this Que book.

   _____
   _____

que

Order Your Que Books Today!

Name _____

Title _____

Company _____

City _____

State _____ ZIP _____

Phone No. (____) _____

Method of Payment:

Check ☐   (Please enclose in envelope.)

Charge My: VISA ☐   MasterCard ☐

American Express ☐

Charge # _____

Expiration Date _____

Order No.	Title	Qty.	Price	Total

You can **FAX** your order to **1-317-573-2583**. Or call **1-800-428-5331, ext. ORDR** to order direct.
Please add $2.50 per title for shipping and handling.

Subtotal	
Shipping & Handling	
Total	

BUSINESS REPLY MAIL
First Class Permit No. 9918   Indianapolis, IN

Postage will be paid by addressee

11711 N. College
Carmel, IN 46032

NO POSTAGE
NECESSARY
IF MAILED
IN THE
UNITED STATES

BUSINESS REPLY MAIL
First Class Permit No. 9918   Indianapolis, IN

Postage will be paid by addressee

11711 N. College
Carmel, IN 46032